Essays in International Litigation for Lord Collins

Essays in International Litigation for Lord Collins

Edited by

JONATHAN HARRIS QC (HON)
CAMPBELL McLACHLAN QC

Assistant Editor

PAUL DAVID MORA

OXFORD
UNIVERSITY PRESS

OXFORD
UNIVERSITY PRESS

Great Clarendon Street, Oxford, OX2 6DP,
United Kingdom

Oxford University Press is a department of the University of Oxford.
It furthers the University's objective of excellence in research, scholarship,
and education by publishing worldwide. Oxford is a registered trade mark of
Oxford University Press in the UK and in certain other countries

First Edition published in 2022

Impression: 1

Published in the United States of America by Oxford University Press
198 Madison Avenue, New York, NY 10016, United States of America

British Library Cataloguing in Publication Data

Data available

Library of Congress Control Number: 2022939115

ISBN 978–0–19–286798–8

DOI: 10.1093/oso/9780192867988.001.0001

Printed and bound by
CPI Group (UK) Ltd, Croydon, CR0 4YY

Contents

PART III ENGLISH PRIVATE INTERNATIONAL LAW

PART IV INTERNATIONAL ARBITRATION

PART V PUBLIC INTERNATIONAL LAW

Table of Cases

Table of Treaties

Note: Treaties and other international instruments are listed below alphabetically by reference to the short title by which they are referred in the text, with the full title given thereafter in brackets.

Table of Legislation

UNITED KINGDOM

Primary Legislation

Secondary Legislation

EUROPEAN UNION

Decisions

Directives

Regulations

COMMONWEALTH

BAHAMAS

BERMUDA

BRITISH VIRGIN ISLANDS

CANADA

List of Contributors

Richard Aikens studied history and law at St John's College, Cambridge, and started practice at the Bar in 1974. He was appointed QC in 1986, a judge of the High Court in 1999 (in charge of the Commercial Court, 2005–2006) and to the Court of Appeal in 2008, and retired in 2015. He was President of the British Insurance Law Association 2012–2014. He currently works as an arbitrator and is a Visiting Professor at King's College and Queen Mary, University of London. He is author of *Bills of Lading* (3rd edn, 2021) and one of the specialist editors of *Dicey, Morris & Collins, The Conflict of Laws.*

Andrew Dickinson is a Fellow of St Catherine's College, Professor of Law at the University of Oxford, and a Senior Honorary Fellow at the British Institute of International and Comparative Law. He is author of *The Rome II Regulation: The Law Applicable to Non-Contractual Obligations* and co-editor of *The Brussels I Regulation Recast.* He is a member of the Ministry of Justice's Private International Law Advisory Committee and one of the specialist editors of *Dicey, Morris & Collins, The Conflict of Laws.*

Elizabeth Gloster was educated at Girton College, Cambridge and practised at the Bar from 1971. She was appointed as a High Court judge in 2004—the first woman to be appointed a judge of the Commercial Court—and to the Court of Appeal in 2013, becoming Vice-President of the Civil Division of that Court in 2016. She was made a Dame in 2004 and a Privy Counsellor in 2013. Since retiring from the Bench, she practises as an international arbitrator at her former Chambers, One Essex Court. She was Treasurer of the Honourable Society of the Inner Temple for 2018 and is an Honorary Fellow of Girton College, Cambridge and Harris Manchester, Oxford. She sits as a Justice of the Court of Appeal of Bermuda and as a judge of the Abu Dhabi Global Markets Courts (both part-time).

Jonathan Harris is general editor with Lord Collins of *Dicey, Morris & Collins, The Conflict of Laws* (16th edn, 2022). He practises at Serle Court Chambers and is a Bencher of Lincoln's Inn. He is Professor of International Commercial Law at King's College, London and Senior Research Fellow at Jesus College, Oxford. He is co-editor of the *Journal of Private International Law* and a member of the Ministry of Justice's Private International Law Advisory Committee. He is co-author of *Underhill and Hayton, Law of Trusts and Trustees* (20th edn, 2022). He has drafted trusts legislation for a number of jurisdictions. In 2016, he was appointed Queen's Counsel (Honoris Causa).

Trevor Hartley was born in South Africa. He taught law in Canada (UWO) before being appointed at LSE in 1970, where he has remained ever since. He has been a Visiting Professor at the Universities of Michigan, California (Berkeley), and Texas, and given courses at the Hague Academy of International Law, the College of Europe and the European University Institute. He has published extensively on private international law and EU law. He is a member of the American Law Institute, European Group for Private International Law

(GEDIP), and the Ministry of Justice's Private International Law Advisory Committee. He was formerly one of the specialist editors of *Dicey, Morris & Collins, The Conflict of Laws.*

Frank Iacobucci was born and educated in Vancouver, graduating with BComm and LLB degrees from the University of British Columbia. Thereafter he attended Cambridge (LLM/Dip (Int'l Law)). After working in private practice in New York, in 1967, he joined the Faculty of Law, University of Toronto, where he was Professor and also served as Dean and as Vice-President and Provost of the University. In 1985, he was appointed Deputy Minister of Justice and Deputy Attorney General for Canada. In 1988, he was appointed Chief Justice, Federal Court of Canada; and from 1991 to 2004, he was a Justice of the Supreme Court of Canada. After retiring from the Supreme Court, he served as interim President of the University of Toronto (2004–2005). In 2005, he joined Torys LLP as counsel. He was appointed a Companion in the Order of Canada in July 2007 and has received numerous honours and awards in Canada. He has also been recognized with honours in the United States, the United Kingdom, and Italy.

David Lloyd Jones was a Justice of the UK Supreme Court from October 2017 to January 2022. A Welsh speaker, he was the first Justice of the Supreme Court to come from Wales. Lord Lloyd-Jones was born and brought up in Pontypridd, Glamorgan, and then went to Downing College, Cambridge. He was a Fellow of Downing College from 1975 to 1991. At the Bar his practice included international law, EU law, and public law. He was appointed to the High Court in 2005. From 2008 to 2011, he served as a Presiding Judge on the Wales Circuit and Chair of the Lord Chancellor's Standing Committee on the Welsh Language. In 2012 he was appointed a Lord Justice of Appeal, and from 2012 to 2015 he was Chairman of the Law Commission. In 2021, he was appointed inaugural President of the Welsh Law Council.

Jonathan Mance was a Justice of the UK Supreme Court from 2009 to 2018 (Deputy President 2017–2018). He read law at University College, Oxford, spent time with a Hamburg law firm and practised at the commercial bar, and sat as a Recorder until 1993. Until his appointment as a Lord of Appeal in Ordinary in October 2005, he was a judge of the High Court (QBD and Commercial Court) (1993–1999) and Lord Justice of Appeal (1999–2005). He represented the UK on the Council of Europe Consultative Council of European Judges from 2000 to 2011, being elected its first chair from 2000 to 2003, and was from 2010 to 2018 a member of the seven-person committee established under Article 255 of the TFEU to report on the suitability of candidates for appointment to the Court of Justice of the EU. He chaired the Executive Council of the International Law Association until 2021. He currently chairs the Ministry of Justice's Private International Law Advisory Committee, as well as sitting as an international arbitrator and part-time judge.

David McClean CBE represented the Commonwealth Secretariat for two decades at Sessions and Special Commissions of the Hague Conference on Private International Law. He sat as a judge in the consistory courts and served as Chair of the Ecclesiastical Judges Association. His publications include *Morris on The Conflict of Laws* (10th edn, 2021) and *International Cooperation in Civil and Criminal Matters* (3rd edn, 2012). Since 2000, he has been General Editor of *Shawcross and Beaumont on Air Law*. He is one of the specialist editors of *Dicey, Morris & Collins, The Conflict of Laws.* He is a Queen's Counsel (Honoris

Causa), a Fellow of the British Academy, a Bencher of Gray's Inn, and a member of the *Institut de Droit International.* He holds the DCL (Oxon) and HonLittD (Sheffield) degrees.

Campbell McLachlan is Professor of Law, Victoria University of Wellington and Arthur Goodhart Visiting Professor of Legal Science, University of Cambridge (2022–2023). He practised international litigation at Herbert Smith London with Lawrence Collins from 1988 until his return to New Zealand in 2003. He holds the Diploma *cum laude* of the Hague Academy of International Law. He is a member of the Permanent Court of Arbitration, the ICSID List of Arbitrators, and the *Institut de Droit International.* His publications include *International Investment Arbitration: Substantive Principles* and *Foreign Relations Law.* He is Joint Editor of *ICSID Review—Foreign Investment Law Journal.* He is one of the specialist editors of *Dicey, Morris & Collins, The Conflict of Laws.* In 2007, he was appointed Queen's Counsel.

Alex Mills is Professor of Public and Private International Law, Faculty of Laws, University College London. He has degrees in Philosophy and Law from the University of Sydney, and an LLM and PhD (awarded the Yorke Prize) from the University of Cambridge, where he also taught before joining UCL. His publications include *The Confluence of Public and Private International Law* (2009) and *Party Autonomy in Private International Law* (2018). He has contributed to *Cheshire North & Fawcett's Private International Law* (15th edn, 2017) and is one of the specialist editors of *Dicey, Morris & Collins, The Conflict of Laws.*

Horatia Muir Watt is Professor of Law at Sciences Po in Paris, where she is Co-Director of the Global Governance Studies programme. She received her PhD in private international law from the University of Panthéon-Assas Paris 2 in 1985 and taught at the University of Tours, at the University of Paris XI, and at the University of Paris I Panthéon-Sorbonne between 1996 and 2009. She was appointed to Sciences Po in 2009. She is Director of the *Revue Critique de Droit International Privé.* Her publications include Bureau & Muir Watt, *Droit International Privé* (5th edn, 2021), *Aspects économiques du droit international privé* (2005), and *Discours sur les méthodes du droit international privé* (2018). *Law's Last Frontier: For a Globalized Ecological Jurisprudence* (Hart Publishing) is forthcoming in 2022. She is a member of the *Institut de Droit International* and of the *Institut Universitaire de France.*

Peter North was educated at Oxford University. His first academic appointment was at Northwestern University, Chicago (1960), followed by University College of Wales, Aberystwyth and the University of Nottingham. In 1965, he returned to Oxford where he taught for a decade. In 1976, he was appointed a Law Commissioner for England and Wales. In 1984, he returned to Oxford as Principal of Jesus College, a position he held for over twenty years, also serving during this period as the Vice Chancellor of Oxford University. Whilst maintaining a continuing interest in private international law as well as chairing the Ministry of Justice's Private International Law Advisory Committee from 1998 to 2009, he also chaired a number of public inquiries. He edited (for forty years) what became *Cheshire, North & Fawcett's Private International Law.* He is a Fellow of the British Academy and a member of the *Institut de Droit International.* He is a Queen's Counsel (Honoris Causa) and was knighted in 1998.

Fausto Pocar is Professor Emeritus of International Law, Milan University and an *ad hoc* judge of the International Court of Justice. He was formerly member and President, ICCPR Human Rights Committee; judge and President, International Criminal Tribunal for the former Yugoslavia; and appeals judge, International Criminal Tribunal for Rwanda. He is a member of the *Institut de Droit International*; honorary President and former President, International Institute of Humanitarian Law; former President, Italian Society of International Law; founding member and former President, European Group for Private International Law (GEDIP); and Council Member, European Law Institute. He is Editor-in-chief of *Rivista di Diritto Internazionale Privato e Processuale* and served as Rapporteur for the revision of the Brussels Convention (1999) and Lugano Convention (2007). He holds honorary doctorates from the University of Antwerp and Kennedy University, Buenos Aires.

Linda Silberman is the Clarence D Ashley Professor of Law at New York University School of Law and Co-Director of the NYU Center for Transnational Litigation, Arbitration, and Commercial Law. She teaches and writes in the areas of conflict of laws, civil procedure, comparative civil procedure, transnational litigation, international commercial arbitration, and international child abduction. In 2018, she was the recipient of the American Bar Association's Leonard J Theberge Award for Private International Law for her distinguished contributions to the development of private international law. Her comparative law interests began in 1968–1969 as a Fulbright Scholar in London under the tutelage of the late Sir Jack Jacob. In recent years, she and Lord Collins have co-taught a course on international litigation and arbitration at NYU.

Hans van Loon was born in Utrecht, the Netherlands. After studies at the Universities of Utrecht and Leyden and the IHEID, Geneva, he practised law at the Supreme Court of the Netherlands before joining the secretariat of the Hague Conference on Private International law (1978). He was Executive Secretary of the Dutch Government Committee on Private International Law (1978–1996) and a deputy judge in the District Court of The Hague (1984–1996). As Secretary General of the Hague Conference on Private International Law (June 1996–June 2013), he contributed to the development of fifteen international instruments by the Hague Conference. He is a member of the *Institut de Droit International.*

Assistant Editor

Paul David Mora is an assistant editor of *Dicey, Morris & Collins, The Conflict of Laws* (16th edn, 2022), and an affiliate member of the Ghent Rolin-Jaequemyns International Law Institute. He holds a PhD in public international law from Ghent University, as well as LL.B and M.Jur degrees from University College, Durham. He has published extensively in the field of public international law.

Introductory Essay

Campbell McLachlan and Jonathan Harris

A. Introduction

Opening his 1994 *Essays in International Litigation and the Conflict of Laws*,[1] Lawrence Collins commented that:

> The differentiation between international litigation and the conflict of laws in the title of this collection is intended to convey the point that the majority (in size and number) of the pieces included deal with topics of great practical importance which have not traditionally been treated fully in the texts on the conflict of laws or private international law.[2]

The present collection is written by some of the many jurists who have been privileged to count Lawrence Collins as friend, mentor, and colleague over the course of a remarkable career of more than fifty years in practice and at the Bench,[3] in which throughout he also made a pre-eminent contribution as a scholar,[4] both as General Editor of *Dicey*[5] and through his monographs, articles, and reports. This book bears eloquent witness to the enduring influence that Lawrence's ideas about international litigation have had on the contemporary shape of private international law in England and across the world. It has been a half century in which the field has been dramatically shaped and reshaped: by the forces of globalization, but also—and more particularly—by the engagement of the UK with the EU and its subsequent disengagement. Lawrence's scholarship drew early attention to the

[1] OUP 1994.

[2] ibid vii.

[3] High Court judge 2000–07 (as Mr Justice Lawrence Collins); Court of Appeal 2007–09 (as Lord Justice Lawrence Collins); House of Lords, Supreme Court of the United Kingdom 2009–11 (as Lord Collins of Mapesbury); Privy Counsellor.

[4] LLD (Cantab), LLM (Columbia), FBA, Professor of Law, University College London; Honorary and Emeritus Fellow, Wolfson College Cambridge; Honorary Fellow, Downing College Cambridge; Member, Institut de Droit international (elected 1989 as associate, member since 1993); Hague Academy of International Law courses 1991 (Provisional and Protective Measures in International Litigation), 1998 (General Course), 2007 (Opening lecture: Revolution and Restitution: Foreign States in National Courts).

[5] General Editor, *Dicey & Morris* (now *Dicey, Morris & Collins*) *on the Conflict of Laws*, 11th–16th edns (16th edn with Jonathan Harris), since 1987.

Campbell McLachlan and Jonathan Harris, *Introductory Essay* In: *Essays in International Litigation for Lord Collins*.
Edited by: Jonathan Harris and Campbell McLachlan, Oxford University Press. © Oxford University Press 2022.
DOI: 10.1093/oso/9780192867988.003.0001

significance of European law[6] and its private international law rules[7] for English law, as well as commenting upon its proper limits.[8]

The contributors include those who (like the editors) have had the privilege of working with Lawrence on *Dicey*; distinguished past members of the judiciary, both in the UK and abroad; and scholars of global renown in private international law. The topics that they have chosen for their contributions speak both to the dynamic nature of international litigation as a field and to the breadth of Lawrence's own interests. Grouped into five Parts, the chapters consider cross-border litigation as it is developing globally (Part I); the role of the national judiciary in international cases (Part II); the reshaping of English private international law, in particular (but not only) following the withdrawal of the UK from the EU (Part III); the development of international arbitration (Part IV); and the impact of public international law (Part V).

This Introductory Essay takes Lawrence's own observation as its point of departure. It considers, by reference to his scholarship and judgments, three examples of the distinctive respects in which his approach to the practice of international litigation has led to the progressive and principled development of private international law. These examples are: (i) the scope of sovereign immunity as applied both to States and to heads of State; (ii) the assumption of judicial jurisdiction over foreign defendants and the determination of appropriate forum; and (iii) the grant of provisional measures and the international reach of enforcement jurisdiction. The choice of these three topics is not coincidental. Lawrence's own contribution is matched by the rising importance in practice of these issues in the conduct of international litigation.[9]

What these three topics have in common is that they are all concerned with the relation between the actual practice of international litigation and the wider context in which such litigation takes place—a world of independent sovereign States. Many of the most contentious issues in contemporary conflict of laws sit at the interface between private international law and public international law. In the language of common law judges, these issues are often addressed under the compendious label of 'comity'. As the Supreme Court of Canada put it, 'the realities that must be reflected and accommodated in private international law' include *both* 'the territorial limits of law under the international legal order' which 'other states as a matter of "comity" will ordinary respect' *and* the need 'to accommodate the movement of people, wealth and skills across state lines'.[10]

[6] Lawrence Collins, *European Community Law in the United Kingdom* (Butterworths 1st edn 1975, 2nd edn 1980, 3rd edn 1984, 4th edn 1990).

[7] Lawrence Collins, *The Civil Jurisdiction and Judgments Act 1982* (Butterworths 1983).

[8] Lawrence Collins, 'Forum Non Conveniens and the Brussels Convention' (1990) 106 LQR 535.

[9] Campbell McLachlan, 'International Litigation and the Reworking of the Conflict of Laws' (2004) 120 LQR 580, 593–600.

[10] *Tolofson v Jensen* [1993] 3 SCR 1022, 1047 (La Forest J).

In an important article written in 2002, Lawrence pointed out that: 'Comity may be a discredited concept in the eyes of the text-writers, but it thrives in the judicial decisions.'[11] He suggested that this concept had been unjustly overlooked and should not be 'dismissed as if it did not exist and had nothing to tell us about the function of private international law, the relations between legal systems, between courts and between public and private international law'.[12] Comity had been rejected because it did not provide a basis for the whole system of the conflict of laws, but it could nevertheless furnish 'a basis for the development of particular rules and attitudes in the resolution of international disputes'.[13] In the 15th edition of *Dicey, Morris & Collins* (2012), he rephrased the function of comity as 'a tool for applying or re-shaping the rules of the conflict of laws'.[14] The meaning and function of 'comity' as just such a tool for re-shaping the rules of the conflict of laws emerges from an examination of Lawrence Collins's work in the three facets of international litigation, to which we now turn our attention.

B. Sovereign Immunity

In his first published law review article, which appeared in 1965 as he was completing his LLM at Columbia University, Lawrence considered the restrictive theory of sovereign immunity.[15] He was concerned primarily with developments in the US, where the courts and the executive were still absorbing the implications of the Tate Letter, then published just thirteen years earlier, in which the US State Department had embraced the restrictive doctrine pursuant to which 'the immunity of the sovereign is recognized with regard to sovereign or public acts (*jure imperii*) of a state, but not with respect to private acts'.[16] At that stage, England remained firmly committed to the absolute doctrine of immunity.[17] Change was not to come to the English common law until the decision of Lord Denning in *Trendtex*

[11] Lawrence Collins, 'Comity in Modern Private International Law' in James Fawcett (ed), *Reform and Development of Private International Law: Essays in Honour of Sir Peter North* (OUP 2002) 95.

[12] ibid 110.

[13] ibid 91.

[14] Lord Collins (ed), *Dicey, Morris & Collins on the Conflict of Laws* (15th edn, Sweet & Maxwell 2012) para 1-009. For other views of the function of comity, see: Adrian Briggs, 'The Principle of Comity in Private International Law' (2012) 354 RdC 65; William Dodge, 'International Comity in Comparative Perspective' in Curtis Bradley (ed), *The Oxford Handbook of Comparative Foreign Relations Law* (OUP 2019) ch 39; Karen Knop, 'The Spectre of Comity' in Jacco Bomhoff, David Dyzenhaus, and Thomas Poole (eds), *The Double-Facing Constitution* (CUP 2020) ch 7.

[15] Lawrence Collins, 'The Effectiveness of the Restrictive Theory of Sovereign Immunity' (1965) 4 Colum J Transnatl L 119.

[16] Letter from Jack B Tate, Department of State Acting Legal Adviser, to Attorney-General Philip B Perlman (19 May 1952) in (1952) 26 Dept St Bull 984.

[17] *The Porto Alexandre* [1920] P 30 (CA).

in 1977[18] and in the legislative adoption of the restrictive theory the following year by the State Immunity Act 1978 ('the 1978 Act').

Lawrence considered the manner in which the US courts were developing a jurisprudence on the application of the restrictive doctrine in the absence of more specific indications from the executive (and prior to legislative enactment of the doctrine there, which was not to come until 1976[19]). His concerns were practical: 'is it possible to proceed *in personam* against a sovereign; is it possible to attach the sovereign's property in order to vest jurisdiction; and, if judgment can be rendered, is there any chance of execution?'[20] Criticizing the shift from reliance on international law to 'a new kind of executive "law"'[21] derived from the suggestions of the State Department, he argued that: 'Theories of immunity based on the dignity of states are now generally discredited. The prevalent theory of both sovereign and diplomatic immunity is that the immunity is a functional one.'[22] He proposed that: 'The solution must lie in a compromise between the reasonable expectations of the private parties and the proper functioning of governmental activities.'[23]

In practice, Lawrence came to have a significant engagement with the law of sovereign immunity—first as counsel and then as judge—in which the boundaries of immunity, both from jurisdiction and from execution, were tested.

In *Pinochet (No 3)*, he appeared for the Government of the Republic of Chile, which intervened in the rehearing of an appeal before the Judicial Committee of the House of Lords on the question of the proper interpretation and scope of the immunity enjoyed by a former head of State from arrest and extradition proceedings in the UK in respect of acts committed while he was head of State.[24] Lawrence Collins QC opened his submissions by stating that:

> Chile is intervening to defend its national sovereignty, to assert its interest in having the matters at issue dealt with in Chile, maintain the rule of law in Chile and to protect the national jurisdiction from outside interference contrary to international law, but not to defend the applicant's acts as head of state. The Government of Chile deplores the fact that the government at the time violated human rights and reaffirms its commitment to human rights. Chile's assertion of its own immunity is not intended as a personal shield for the applicant nor to grant him immunity from prosecution in Chile or impunity.[25]

[18] *Trendtex Trading Corp v Central Bank of Nigeria* [1977] QB 529 (CA). The Privy Council had reached the same conclusion in 1975: *The Philippine Admiral* [1977] AC 373 (PC).
[19] Foreign Sovereign Immunities Act of 1976, 90 Stat 2891.
[20] Collins (n 15) 125.
[21] ibid 150.
[22] ibid 149.
[23] ibid.
[24] *R v Bow Street Metropolitan Stipendiary Magistrate, ex p Pinochet Ugarte (No 3)* [2000] 1 AC 147. Campbell McLachlan assisted Lawrence Collins QC in the case.
[25] ibid 172.

Advancing the submission that the immunity of a former head of State 'is an aspect of state immunity', he argued that: 'The *rules of comity* require that the United Kingdom does not assert or assist in the assertion of jurisdiction over the internal acts of a foreign state'.[26] He cited Diplock LJ in *Buck v Attorney General*, who had described the doctrine of sovereign immunity as one of the commonest examples of rules of comity, which were:

> the accepted rules of mutual conduct as between state and state which each state adopts in relation to other states and expects other states to adopt in relation to itself. One of those rules is that it does not purport to exercise jurisdiction over the internal affairs of any other independent state, or to apply measures of coercion to it or to its property, except in accordance with the rules of public international law.[27]

As is well known, a majority of the House of Lords decided that 'Senator Pinochet as former head of state enjoys immunity ratione materiae in relation to acts done by him as head of state as part of his official functions'.[28] However (contrary to what had been the prior orthodox position at international law[29]), the ratification of the Convention against Torture by Chile and the United Kingdom constituted an implied waiver of immunity in respect of acts within the scope of the Convention.[30] Since, reasoned Lord Browne-Wilkinson, torture could only be committed by persons acting in an official capacity, any other conclusion 'produces bizarre results'.[31]

In a judicial capacity, Lawrence Collins LJ considered the scope of protections to be accorded to a serving head of State in *Aziz v Aziz*.[32] He opened his judgment for the Court of Appeal in the following terms:

> [1] This is an extraordinary case. The claimant, Mariam Aziz, met the tenth (and main) defendant, Mrs Aviva Amir, at a casino in 2003. Mrs Amir is a fortune teller born in Iraq, but now of Israeli nationality. The claimant came to regard Mrs Amir as a trusted friend and confidant. In early 2004 Mrs Amir purported to introduce the claimant over the telephone to a gentleman called Mr Aziz. The claimant and Mr Aziz never met, but over the following months

[26] ibid (emphasis added).

[27] [1965] Ch 745 (CA) 770.

[28] *Pinochet (No 3)* (n 24) 203 (Lord Browne-Wilkinson).

[29] See the dissent of Lord Goff at 215–23 (approving the arguments advanced on behalf of Chile by Dr Collins in this respect). Lord Goff concluded at 223: 'how extraordinary it would be, and indeed what a trap would be created for the unwary, if state immunity could be waived in a treaty sub silentio'.

[30] ibid 205 (Lord Browne-Wilkinson), 247 (Lord Hope), 267 (Lord Saville), and 290 (Lord Phillips). The House also endorsed the view of Lord Hope that it was only after the Convention against Torture was given statutory effect in the UK that the offence of torture committed outside the UK became an extradition crime.

[31] ibid 205.

[32] [2007] EWCA Civ 712, [2008] 2 All ER 501.

they developed what appeared to be a close relationship conducted by telephone and text message, and involving exchanges of gifts. Between May and November 2004, the claimant made bank transfers totalling over £1 million which were intended for Mr Aziz, as well as payments of more than £1 million in cash via Mrs Amir's driver. The claimant in the summer of 2004 recorded for Mr Aziz, and had delivered (as she believed) to him, two audio cassette tapes containing material of a confidential nature.

[2] Although Mr Aziz was originally named as first defendant it became the claimant's case that Mr Aziz never existed and that the other party to most, if not all, of her telephone and text message exchanges was in fact Mrs Amir who had the benefit of the £2 million and who had possession of the cassettes. Mr Aziz was named as first defendant but he has never been traced or served. After a trial in 2006, Underhill J found for the claimant against Mrs Amir, and ordered return of the payments and awarded damages in relation to the value of the gifts.

[3] The second unusual aspect of the case (and which gives rise to the present appeal) is that the claimant is the former wife of His Majesty the Sultan of Brunei (the Sultan), from whom she was divorced in February 2003.

The appellate judgment was entirely concerned with the Sultan's attempt to prevent publication of his name in connection with the proceedings on the alleged ground that, as a serving head of State, the UK was obliged to treat him with due respect and take all appropriate steps to prevent any attack on his dignity.[33]

Lawrence Collins LJ held that the obligation to take 'appropriate steps' is not absolute.[34] The privilege or immunity accorded to a serving head of State has the 'function in international relations to protect the ability of the head of state to carry out his functions and to promote international co-operation'.[35] As such, it is not limited to his or her official acts. The core of the issue in the case was the content of the obligation to take appropriate steps to protect the dignity of a foreign head of State in cases where the alleged offensive conduct was perpetrated by a private individual. After a review of State practice and the opinions of publicists, Lawrence Collins LJ concluded that in such a case, 'the state against which complaint is made regularly refers the complainant state to the remedies available in its courts, but subject to its constitutional guarantees of free speech'.[36] He considered that there was no doubt that the State was obliged to take steps to prevent a physical attack on a foreign head of State, but otherwise 'to the extent there is any uniform practice ... it amounts to no more than courtesy or comity'.[37]

[33] State Immunity Act 1978, s 20, applying Sch 1, art 29 of the Diplomatic Privileges Act 1964 to heads of State.

[34] *Aziz* (n 32) [54].

[35] ibid [61].

[36] ibid [73].

[37] ibid [89].

Here, Lawrence Collins LJ is using comity in a sense in which it is often used by publicists by way of contrast with a positive legal obligation. His essential point, consistent with international law, was that the immunities and privileges of a foreign head of State have their limits. He held: 'I find it extremely difficult, if not impossible, to envisage any situation in which speech, otherwise permitted under English law, could be prohibited on the ground that it was an attack on the dignity of a foreign head of state.'[38]

He considered the scope and limits of the restrictive doctrine of the immunity of the State itself in the context of the enforcement of foreign arbitral awards and judgments in two important cases: one in the Court of Appeal and the second in the Supreme Court. The first, *ETI v Bolivia*,[39] concerned the availability of interim relief by way of execution of an arbitral award rendered against a State before the International Centre for Settlement of Investment Disputes (ICSID). The case raised an aspect of one of the wider questions that he had considered in his 1965 article: the distinction between immunity of a State from suit and its immunities from execution.[40]

The first ground of objection raised by Bolivia, which the Court of Appeal upheld, was that whether considered as a matter of international law[41] or of English law,[42] an ICSID award creditor is not entitled to an English freezing order against the assets of a respondent State. The second ground was immunity from execution. It was no less fundamental. Indeed, as Lawrence Collins LJ observed, 'it is in fact a matter of the greatest importance ... and would normally fall to be considered first'.[43] The judge below had proceeded on the basis that the State, having given its consent in writing to submit the dispute to arbitration, was not immune from proceedings in the English court in connection with the arbitration.[44] However, that was to elide immunity from suit with the separate question of immunity from execution, including by way of injunctive relief. Under the express terms of section 13(1) of the 1978 Act, a foreign State is entitled to immunity from 'relief ... by way of injunction' and 'the property of a state shall not be subject to any process for the enforcement of ... [an] arbitration award'. The State's consent to arbitration does not amount to consent to such a process of execution.[45]

NML v Argentina[46] concerned proceedings for the enforcement of a New York judgment by a vulture fund that had purchased Argentine State bonds. Under the

[38] ibid [96].
[39] *ETI Euro Telecom International NV v Republic of Bolivia* [2008] EWCA Civ 880, [2009] 1 WLR 665.
[40] Collins (n 15) 136.
[41] ICSID Arbitration Rules 2006, r 39(6).
[42] No Order having been made under s 107(1) of the Arbitration Act 1996 extending s 44 to ICSID arbitrations.
[43] *ETI* (n 39) [110].
[44] State Immunity Act 1978, s 9.
[45] ibid s 13(3).
[46] *NML Capital Ltd v Republic of Argentina* [2011] UKSC 31, [2011] 2 AC 495.

terms of the bonds, Argentina had waived its immunity, submitted to the New York courts, and agreed that a final judgment obtained in New York would be enforceable against it in other courts in which it might be amenable to suit under the judgment. Lord Collins opened his judgment by pointing to the longstanding problem of defaults on sovereign bonds, especially in Latin America, and the tensions in international relations that had been caused as a result. He then observed:

> But law and practice was revolutionised in the second half of the 20th century by the widespread (but by no means uniform) adoption of the restrictive theory of sovereign immunity, and the modern law now depends on the application of the restrictive theory of immunity and on the almost invariable use in international loan agreements and bond issues since the 1970s of clauses providing for submission to national jurisdiction and waivers of immunity.[47]

Lord Collins held that Argentina was not immune from a suit to enforce the New York judgment. Section 2(2) of the 1978 Act had reversed the erroneous position that the English courts had reached, which had required consent in the face of the court. Henceforward, consent by prior written agreement would suffice. The provision in the bonds 'was the clearest possible waiver of immunity'.[48]

C. Judicial Jurisdiction and Appropriate Forum

Not long after his election to partnership in Herbert Smith in 1971, Lawrence Collins turned his scholarly attention to the important question of the scope and limits of the English court's personal jurisdiction over defendants abroad.[49] The neglect of this important topic in the early 1970s is almost impossible to imagine from the vantage point of the present day, in which litigation over the court's assumption of personal jurisdiction and the related question of whether it ought to decline jurisdiction on grounds of *forum non conveniens* loom so large (and will loom ever larger now that the EU and Lugano Convention rules of jurisdiction no longer apply in the UK). But fifty years ago, this topic had received scant attention. In part, this was because the English courts—in contrast to those in Scotland—had consistently refused to accept that mere balance of convenience was a sufficient ground on which they ought to decline jurisdiction where the defendant had been

[47] ibid [103]. The Supreme Court decided by majority (Lords Phillips and Clarke dissenting) that proceedings for the enforcement of a foreign judgment are not 'relating to a commercial transaction' so as to engage the restrictive doctrine under s 3 of the 1978 Act, even if the underlying claim in the foreign court concerned a commercial transaction.

[48] ibid [128].

[49] Lawrence Collins, 'Some Aspects of Service Out of the Jurisdiction in English Law' (1972) 21 ICLQ 656, reprinted in Collins (n 1) 226–52.

served in England.[50] The revolution that was to be wrought by the series of decisions of the House of Lords, which culminated in Lord Goff's embrace of the doctrine of *forum non conveniens* in all cases involving a significant foreign element in *The Spiliada*,[51] was all in the future.

What Lawrence Collins did in his 1972 article was to draw attention to the fact that the question of appropriate forum was *already* part of English law in cases where the defendant was to be served abroad. He had already had experience in practice of the potential significance of the point. In *Buttes Gas & Oil Co v Hammer*[52] (in which Herbert Smith acted for the defendants), Buttes Gas had brought defamation proceedings against Dr Armand Hammer, Chairman of Occidental Petroleum, arising out of remarks that he had made at a press conference in London concerning their rival claims to oil concessions in the Gulf. Buttes sought leave to serve Dr Hammer out of the jurisdiction. There was a plain ground for jurisdiction under the then long-arm provisions of the rules of court. Dr Hammer had made his allegedly slanderous remarks at a press conference in London. The claimant's action was 'founded on a tort committed within the jurisdiction'.[53] But, when the matter reached the Court of Appeal, that was not the end of things. The crucial question was whether England or California was 'the convenient forum'.[54] Lord Denning thought that England was as convenient as California for a dispute that involved witnesses from England, the Gulf, and California, and that the case ought therefore to be allowed to proceed in London.[55]

Lawrence showed that questions of appropriate forum had been part of the inquiry in cases where the defendant was to be served abroad since the enactment of the power to serve out in the mid-nineteenth century.[56] Both the establishment of such a power and the limits on its exercise were closely linked with international law and comity. In 1886, Lord Coleridge CJ had said that Order 11 was passed in order to bring the practice of the English courts 'into accordance with well-settled rules of international law, or, at all events, comity'.[57] It followed that, as Scott LJ put it in 1944: 'As a matter of international comity . . . no such service shall be allowed unless it is clearly within both the letter and the spirit of [Order 11].'[58] In exercising the court's discretion whether to allow service out of the jurisdiction, Lawrence showed that:

[50] *Maharanee of Baroda v Wildenstein* [1972] 2 QB 283 (CA).
[51] *Spiliada Maritime Corp v Cansulex Ltd (The Spiliada)* [1987] AC 460 (HL).
[52] *Buttes Gas & Oil Co v Hammer* [1971] 3 All ER 1025.
[53] Under the terms of the then applicable service out provision: RSC Ord 11, r 1(1)(h).
[54] *Buttes Gas* (n 52) 1027.
[55] The House of Lords subsequently dismissed the action on the ground that it raised non-justiciable questions concerning the relations between sovereign States in the Gulf: *Buttes Gas & Oil Co v Hammer (No 3)* [1982] AC 888.
[56] See further Chapter 11, this volume.
[57] *Field v Bennett* (1886) 3 TLR 239 (QB) 240.
[58] *George Monro Ltd v American Cyanimid and Chemical Corp* [1944] KB 432 (CA) 437.

> The notion of *forum non conveniens* is not frequently invoked in terms probably because English law does not know the doctrine as such. But the grounds of the decisions on Order 11 show clearly that the underlying principle is one of convenience.[59]

A decade after the adoption of the doctrine by the House of Lords in 1987 in *The Spiliada*, both in cases in which the defendant was to be served abroad and in cases in which the defendant had been served in England, Lawrence turned to consider the significance of the development in an international context, when appointed (with Georges Droz) Rapporteur of the Second Commission of the Institut de Droit international on the topic of the principles for determining when the use of the doctrine of *forum non conveniens* and anti-suit injunctions is appropriate. Their Preliminary Report recognized the importance of the development of the doctrine of *forum non conveniens* in common law countries and its potential broader impact on international litigation.[60] They referred to the recognition, both in the US and in England, of the impact of comity considerations on the grant of anti-suit injunctions. The Report cited Lord Goff in *Airbus Industrie GIE v Patel*, who held:

> As a general rule, before an anti-suit injunction can properly be granted by an English court to restrain a person from pursuing proceedings in a foreign jurisdiction in cases of the kind under consideration in the present case, *comity requires that the English forum should have a sufficient interest in, or connection with, the matter in question to justify the indirect interference with the foreign court which an anti-suit injunction entails.*[61]

The Institute recognized in its Resolution that the court seised might properly decide that the courts of another country were clearly more appropriate, taking into account the adequacy of the foreign forum, the residence of the parties, the location of the evidence, the law applicable to the issues, the effect of applicable limitation periods, and the enforceability of any resulting judgment.[62] It added: 'Courts which grant anti-suit injunctions should be sensitive to the demands of comity.'[63]

59 Collins (n 49) 660.
60 (2002–03) 70(1) Ann IDI 14.
61 *Airbus Industrie GIE v Patel* [1999] AC 119 (HL) 138 (emphasis added). Earlier in his judgment, Lord Goff had stated at 134: 'In alternative forum cases, in which the choice is between the English forum and some other forum overseas, an anti-suit injunction will normally only be applied for in an English court where England is the natural forum for the resolution of the dispute; and, if so, there will be no infringement of comity.' At 136, Lord Goff cites the 'valuable account' of Dr Lawrence Collins in 'International Jurisdiction and Forum-Shopping: An Overview' in National University of Singapore, *Current Legal Issues in International Commercial Litigation* (1997) 3.
62 IDI, Session de Bruges, Second Commission Resolution, 'The Principles for Determining When the Use of the Doctrine of *Forum Non Conveniens* and Anti-Suit Injunctions is Appropriate' (2004) 70(2) Ann IDI 251 [1].
63 ibid [6].

Comity here operates as a recognition of the limits imposed by public international law on the extent to which the national courts of a State may permissibly interfere with the legitimate sphere of jurisdiction of other States. Public international law is the applicable law of treaties,[64] including treaties on civil and commercial jurisdiction. Lawrence Collins drew attention to this fundamental point when writing about the impact of the jurisdictional rules of the Brussels Convention on the power of English courts to decline jurisdiction in favour of the courts of non-Contracting States on grounds of *forum non conveniens* or *lis alibi pendens*.[65] He wrote in 1990:

> When the European Court comes to consider the application of the Convention to non-Contracting States, it should seek the answer in treaty interpretation, and ultimately in public international law. The Convention was intended to regulate jurisdiction *as between* the Contracting States ... [T]he States which were parties to the Convention had no interest in requiring a Contracting State to exercise a jurisdiction where the competing jurisdiction was in a non-Contracting State. The Contracting States were setting up an intra-Convention mandatory system of jurisdiction. They were not regulating relations with non-Contracting States.[66]

The European Court did not take this view when, in 2005, it reached (on a reference from the English Court of Appeal) the question of the power of the English court to decline jurisdiction over a case against a defendant domiciled in England on grounds of *forum non conveniens* in favour of the courts of a third State.[67]

In his judicial capacity, Lord Collins considered the relation between appropriate forum and comity in two important final appellate judgments: *AK Investment*,[68] which concerned the application of the doctrine of *forum conveniens* in a service

[64] Vienna Convention on the Law of Treaties (signed 23 May 1969, entered into force 27 January 1980) 1155 UNTS 331, art 2(1)(a).

[65] Droz also took the view that the Convention's rules on *lis pendens* and on jurisdiction agreements must be given reflexive effect vis-à-vis the courts of third States: Georges Droz, *La compétence judiciare et l'effet des jugements dans la CEE* (1972) [164].

[66] Collins (n 8).

[67] Case C–281/02 *Owusu v Jackson* [2005] ECR I–1383, [2005] QB 801. The European Court also developed the 'mutual trust' doctrine, according to which the courts of each Contracting State were equally competent to apply the Convention: Case C–116/02 *Erich Gasser GmbH v MISAT srl* [2003] ECR I–14693, [2005] QB 1. This was used as a reason to allow no exception to the court first seised rule, even in respect of exclusive jurisdiction agreements (a position subsequently changed in Regulation (EU) 1215/2012, art 31(2)). It was also invoked to clip the wings of the common law by precluding the use by English courts of anti-suit injunctions to restrain the pursuit of proceedings in the courts of other Contracting States to the Convention (Case C–159/02 *Turner v Grovit* [2004] ECR I–3565, [2005] 1 AC 10), including in support of English arbitration agreements (Case C–185/07 *West Tankers Inc v Allianz SpA* [2009] ECR I–663, [2009] 1 AC 1138). The doctrine, while bearing some ostensible similarities to comity, was founded specifically on the nature of the Convention's common, compulsory rules of jurisdiction and regime to prevent irreconcilable judgments and promote the free movement of judgment between Contracting States.

[68] *AK Investment CJSC v Kyrgyz Mobile Tel Ltd* [2011] UKPC 7, [2012] 1 WLR 1804 (*sub nom Altimo Holdings and Investment v same*).

out context, and *Agbaje*,[69] a case on the principles applicable in the grant of English maintenance orders following the dissolution of a marriage by a foreign court.

AK Investment was a dispute between two Russian corporate groups concerning a telecommunications business in Kyrgyzstan. A Kyrgyz company applied in the Manx courts for enforcement at common law of a Kyrgyz judgment against the Respondents, three Isle of Man incorporated companies. The Respondents counterclaimed, one aspect of the counterclaim being that the Kyrgyz judgment was procured by fraud. Service of the counterclaim out of the jurisdiction was permitted by the Manx court. Several of the counterclaim defendants appealed to the Privy Council against that decision.

Lord Collins, giving the judgment of the Board, shortly characterized the legal and practical context of the case at hand:

5. This, like many such cases, is not really a dispute about forum. The connection which this case has with the Isle of Man is that BITEL seeks to enforce a Kyrgyz judgment by proceedings in the Isle of Man against the KFG companies, three companies incorporated in the Isle of Man, who seek to counterclaim against the appellants in relation to matters which occurred wholly outside the Isle of Man, and primarily in Kyrgyzstan. The KFG companies accept that Kyrgyzstan is the natural forum for the pursuit of their claims, in the sense of being the jurisdiction with which their claims have their most real and substantial connection: *Spiliada Maritime Corpn v Cansulex Ltd* [1987] AC 460, 478, per Lord Goff of Chieveley.
6. But the practical reality of the matter is that if the KFG companies are confined to their remedies against the appellants in Kyrgyzstan they will not in fact be able to pursue any of their claims there. Consequently, although this is in form a case about the appropriate forum, in reality it is a case in which, if the Isle of Man is not the appropriate forum, the KFG companies will have no practical remedy at all.

This consideration proved ultimately decisive in the Privy Council, which dismissed the appeal, allowing the case to proceed in the Isle of Man.

One of the issues that arose for decision was whether, in exercising its discretion, the court is entitled to rule that, as a result, for example, of endemic corruption, justice is not to be obtained in the foreign country in general. In addressing this issue, Lord Collins emphasized the importance of comity as a check on such a finding in the absence of compelling evidence. He held:

[69] *Agbaje v Agbaje* [2010] UKSC 13, [2010] 1 AC 628.

> The true position is that there is no rule that the English court (or Manx court) will not examine the question whether the foreign court or the foreign court system is corrupt or lacking in independence. *The rule is that considerations of international comity will militate against any such finding in the absence of cogent evidence.*[70]

Lord Collins elaborated further on the concept of comity in *Agbaje*. That case concerned the correct approach to Part III of the Matrimonial and Family Proceedings Act 1984 ('the 1984 Act'), which allows the court to make orders for financial relief after the dissolution of marriage by a foreign court. Section 16(1) of the 1984 Act requires the court, *before* making any such order, to consider whether 'it would be appropriate for such an order to be made by a court in England' and, if not, to dismiss the application. Section 16(2) enumerates a non-exhaustive set of connecting factors that the court is to take into account in determining the appropriateness of its intervention. As Lord Collins pointed out, section 16 is not to be treated as a statutory *forum non conveniens* test. In *forum non conveniens* cases, the court has to choose which of two jurisdictions is the most appropriate forum for the trial of the action, whereas in cases under the 1984 Act '[n]o choice between jurisdictions is involved. The whole basis of Part III is that it may be appropriate for two jurisdictions to be involved, one for the divorce and one for ancillary relief.'[71]

Lord Collins noted three ways in which comity may be relevant in approaching the 1984 Act. First, if comity is viewed as 'rules of public international law which establish the proper limits of national legislative jurisdiction in cases involving a foreign element', it would be contrary to that principle for an English court to make an order under Part III of the Act in a situation 'involving a foreign country when the United Kingdom has no reasonable relationship with the situation'.[72] That consideration did not arise in the instant case, since:

> There is nothing internationally objectionable in legislation which gives a court power to order financial provision notwithstanding a foreign decree of divorce, whether or not the foreign court has ordered financial provision, *provided that the forum has an appropriate connection with the parties or their property.*[73]

Second, comity informs the 'elementary principle' that 'a court in one country should not lightly characterise the law or judicial decisions of another country as unjust'.[74] Third, comity may serve as a doctrinal basis for the enforcement and

[70] *AK Investment* (n 68) [101] (emphasis added).
[71] *Agbaje* (n 69) [49]. Section 16 is now slightly amended by Jurisdiction and Judgments (Family) (Amendment etc) (EU Exit) Regulations 2019 SI 2019/519, Sch 1(1), para 13.
[72] ibid [52].
[73] ibid (emphasis added).
[74] ibid [53].

recognition of a foreign maintenance order. In the instant case, the Court of Appeal had wrongly applied the traditional *forum non conveniens* principles. The English connections were substantial and there was no basis for interference with the judge's determination that an award of maintenance to the wife, who was settled in England, was justified.[75]

In both of these cases, Lord Collins's analysis demonstrates that the determination of appropriate forum is not solely a question of the comparative convenience of the parties. It may also engage considerations of public international law as to the proper limits to the jurisdiction of the home State and its courts, and the respect due to foreign States and their courts, when acting within their own territory. In both cases, the court is ultimately guided by 'the ends of justice'.[76]

D. Provisional Measures and Enforcement Jurisdiction

A third issue of critical importance in the conduct of international litigation is the availability and scope of provisional measures. In practice, this gives rise to two sets of issues: (i) the reach of the court's interim enforcement jurisdiction in respect of persons or property abroad; and (ii) the availability of provisional measures in aid of proceedings on the substance in a foreign court.

Until the late 1970s, this would have been virtually a *non-sujet* in England. The most common context in which provisional measures are sought is to preserve the assets of the defendant over which an eventual judgment may be enforced. The traditional rule in England had been that '[y]ou cannot get an injunction to restrain a man who is alleged to be a debtor from parting with his property'.[77] But, in 1975, Lord Denning broke with the traditional position in recognition of the injustice that it caused in the efficacy of the litigation process, particularly in cases with an international element. He developed the remedy of the interim injunction (known as the *Mareva* injunction after one of his early decisions[78]) restraining a foreign defendant from removing its assets from the jurisdiction. The practice was given statutory authority in 1981.[79] Further development of the international dimension of the new remedy was checked early in its life by the decision of the House of Lords in *The Siskina* (1979), which decided that the English court 'has no power to grant an interlocutory injunction except in protection or assertion of some legal or equitable right which it has jurisdiction to enforce by final judgment'.[80] The new

[75] ibid [76].
[76] *Sim v Robinow* (1892) 19 R 665, 668 (Lord Kinnear).
[77] *Robinson v Pickering* (1881) 16 Ch D 660, 661 (James LJ).
[78] *Mareva Compania Naviera SA v International Bulkcarriers SA* [1975] 2 Lloyd's Rep 509 (CA).
[79] Senior Courts Act 1981, s 37(3).
[80] *Siskina (Owners of cargo lately laden on board) v Distos Compania Naviera SA* [1979] AC 210, 256 (Lord Diplock), citing *North London Railway Co v Great Northern Railway Co* (1883) 11 QBD 30 (CA).

remedy was to be available, but only in support of cases over which the English court had substantive jurisdiction.

In the meantime, negotiations had been proceeding to enable the UK to accede to the Brussels Convention 1968—the then applicable treaty between European Community Member States which dealt with jurisdiction and the enforcement of judgments in civil and commercial matters.[81] Article 24 of that Convention provides:

> **Provisional, including protective, measures**
> Application may be made to the courts of a Contracting State for such provisional, including protective, measures as may be available under the law of that State, even if, under this Convention, the courts of another Contracting State have jurisdiction as to the substance of the matter.

The accession negotiations were successfully concluded in 1978, but the Convention did not come into force in respect of the UK until 1987.[82] In order to give effect to Article 24, Parliament empowered the English court to grant interim relief in aid of proceedings in another Brussels Contracting State.[83]

Lawrence began exploring the implications of these developments in 1981, in the first year of publication of the *Yearbook of European Law*.[84] He returned to consider the territorial reach of *Mareva* injunctions in 1989 in the wake of a trio of Court of Appeal judgments, which had broadened the scope of such injunctions to cover the worldwide assets of the defendant.[85] He then turned to a wide-ranging synthesis of the principles underpinning the practice of provisional and protective measures in his 1991 Hague Lectures.[86]

An important and recurrent thread of Lawrence Collins's scholarship in this field was his criticism of the rule in *The Siskina*, which severely limited the ability of

[81] Convention on Jurisdiction and the Enforcement of Judgments in Civil and Commercial Matters (signed 27 September 1968, entered into force 1 February 1973) (1990) 29 ILM 1413 (hereafter 'Brussels Convention'). See now Regulation (EU) No 1215/2012 of the European Parliament and of the Council of 12 December 2012 on jurisdiction and the recognition and enforcement of judgments in civil and commercial matters (Brussels I Regulation Recast) [2012] OJ L351/1, art 35.

[82] Convention of Accession of 9 October 1978 of the Kingdom of Denmark, of Ireland and of the United Kingdom of Great Britain and Northern Ireland to the Convention on Jurisdiction and the Enforcement of Judgments in Civil and Commercial Matters and to the Protocol on its Interpretation by the Court of Justice [1978] OJ L304/1.

[83] Civil Jurisdiction and Judgments Act 1982, s 25(1).

[84] Lawrence Collins, 'Provisional Measures, the Conflict of Laws and the Brussels Convention' (1981) 1 YEL 249.

[85] Lawrence Collins, 'The Territorial Reach of *Mareva* Injunctions' (1989) 105 LQR 262, discussing *Babanaft International Co v Bassatne* [1990] Ch 13 (CA); *Republic of Haiti v Duvalier* [1990] 1 QB 202 (CA); *Derby & Co v Weldon* [1990] Ch 48 (CA); *Derby & Co v Weldon (Nos 3 & 4)* [1990] Ch 65 (CA).

[86] Lawrence Collins, 'Provisional and Protective Measures in International Litigation' (1992) 234 RdC 9, repr *Essays* (n 1) 3–188.

the English court to grant provisional measures in aid of proceedings on the merits in a foreign court save where the Brussels Convention applied. In his 1989 article, he situated the practical context against which the increasing use of *Mareva* injunctions in international litigation had occurred:

> the widespread abolition of exchange controls and the growth of offshore havens for cash and securities have made it easier for defaulters involved in international business to make themselves judgment proof, and for dishonest fiduciaries to enjoy the illegal fruits of breaches of trust.[87]

Turning to limitations on the courts' power to grant a *Mareva* injunction, Lawrence described the effect of *The Siskina* as 'unfortunate' and noted that its effect had been partially reversed by statutory incorporation of Article 24 of the Brussels Convention through section 25(1) of the Civil Jurisdiction and Judgments Act 1982 vis-à-vis litigation pending in other Contracting States.[88] In his Hague Lectures, he wrote:[89]

> It was regrettable that the English courts, having accepted in principle, a remedy of (indirect) attachment by means of the *Mareva* injunction, were constrained by history from developing the remedy to prevent an obvious injustice.

In a 1992 case note, Lawrence noted *The Siskina*'s continuing effect on cases in which a *Mareva* injunction was denied against a party with assets situate in England where the substantive dispute lay within the jurisdiction of a non-Brussels Convention State. He argued that this 'continuing legacy' of *The Siskina* ought to be overturned by an Order-in-Council under section 25(3) of the Civil Jurisdiction and Judgments Act 1982.[90] This step was finally taken in 1997.[91] Even so, *The Siskina* continues to cast a long shadow outside England. As recently as 2021, the Privy Council on appeal from the British Virgin Islands held that although the court has an inherent *power* to grant interim relief to restrain the disposition of the defendant's assets pending adjudication of the substance of the

[87] Collins (n 85) 262.
[88] ibid 289.
[89] Collins (n 1) 34.
[90] Lawrence Collins, 'The Legacy of *The Siskina*' (1992) 108 LQR 175, 180. See also Lawrence Collins, 'The End of *The Siskina*?' (1993) 109 LQR 342; and Lawrence Collins, '*The Siskina* Again: An Opportunity Missed' (1996) 112 LQR 8 (commenting on *Mercedes Benz AG v Leiduck* [1996] AC 284 (PC): 'Common sense would suggest that if proceedings are pending in one country, and the defendant's assets are situate in another country, the plaintiff ought to be able to obtain protective or interim relief by way of attachment in the latter country. That is indeed the law in most countries ... Yet ... a strong Privy Council has confirmed the result in *The Siskina*').
[91] The Civil Jurisdiction and Judgments Act 1982 (Interim Relief) Order, SI 1997/302. See: *ETI* (n 39) [63]–[69].

claim in a foreign court (rejecting the reasoning of Lord Diplock in *The Siskina* to that extent), the court's *jurisdiction* to permit proceedings for such relief against a defendant served abroad depends upon an express power by statute or rules of court. On that question, it was, in the view of the Board, simply too late to reverse prior precedent.[92]

Lawrence supported the development of a free-standing power to grant provisional measures in aid of proceedings on the merits in the foreign court on grounds that were both practical and principled. There was plainly a practical need to be able to preserve the position where the defendant or its property could be found pending a decision on the merits. In principle, such a power was justified, because the nature of the power that the court granting provisional measures was exercising was distinct from, and not dependent upon, its exercise of jurisdiction over the merits. It was an ancillary power, which had as its object to support, and make more effective, the foreign proceedings. As the Institut put it in its Resolution following Lord Collins's recommendations in his 2017 Report on Provisional Measures:

> A national court may make orders for provisional measures in relation to assets or acts within its territory even if a court in another country has jurisdiction over the merits. Such provisional measures may be ordered provided that they do not infringe upon the exclusive jurisdiction of foreign courts.[93]

The English court's development of worldwide injunctive relief raised more urgent questions of the relation between the exercise of the court's power and the potential for incursion upon the interests of foreign States. In his Hague Lectures, Lawrence suggested, under the heading 'Comity', that 'the exercise of civil jurisdiction by national courts is subject to the constraints of public international law'.[94] He cited in support Lord Donaldson MR, who had held that: 'Considerations of comity require the courts of this country to refrain from making orders which infringe the exclusive jurisdiction of the courts of other countries.'[95] Lawrence himself suggested that:

> the extension of the *Mareva* jurisdiction to assets abroad is justifiable in terms of international law and comity provided that the case has some appropriate connection with England, that the court does not affect title to property abroad, and that the court does not seek to control the activities abroad of foreigners who are not subject to the personal jurisdiction of the English court.[96]

[92] *Convoy Collateral Ltd v Broad Idea International Ltd* [2021] UKPC 24, [2022] 2 WLR 703.
[93] Lord Collins, 'Provisional Measures: Final Report' (2017) 77 Ann IDI 259, [53]–[59]; Resolution (2017) 78 Ann IDI 129 [8].
[94] Collins (n 1) 99.
[95] *Derby & Co v Weldon (Nos 3 & 4)* (n 85) 82.
[96] Collins (n 1) 99.

He developed the permissible scope of the exercise of the English court's provisional and protective measures jurisdiction in two important judgments in the long-running *Masri* litigation: one concerning the court's power to appoint a receiver by way of equitable execution of a judgment (*Masri (No 2)*[97]); and the second concerning the grant of an anti-suit injunction (*Masri (No 3)*[98]).

The Claimant, Mr Masri, had won a judgment in the Commercial Court against two companies incorporated in Lebanon. The litigation continued in multiple jurisdictions as Mr Masri sought enforcement of the English judgment. In *Masri (No 2)*, Lawrence Collins LJ held that it was within the court's power, in order to further the enforcement of the judgment, to appoint a receiver over foreign debts owed to the judgment debtor.[99] He emphasized that such an order operates *in personam* and does not have proprietary effect. The court had personal jurisdiction over the judgment debtors through their submission to jurisdiction in defending the claim on the merits. There was an important distinction between the power to appoint the receiver, which operates *in personam*, and the *execution* of a judgment by third-party debt order or garnishment of the debt, which, being a proprietary remedy, may not be granted over property abroad.[100]

Nevertheless, he held that the fact that the court is acting *in personam* is not dispositive. The court must still consider whether the things it may properly order a person within its personal jurisdiction to do abroad are within its subject matter jurisdiction, since:

> the mere fact that an order is in personam and is directed towards someone who is subject to the personal jurisdiction of the English court does not exclude the possibility that the making of the order would be contrary to international law or comity, and outside the subject matter jurisdiction of the English court.[101]

The court should be particularly concerned to ensure that its order does not produce adverse effects on third parties abroad. In the instant case, the order was not exorbitant, because third parties were protected by provisos in the order from being found in contempt.[102]

97 *Masri v Consolidated Contractors International (UK) Ltd (No 2)* [2008] EWCA Civ 303, [2009] QB 450.

98 *Masri v Consolidated Contractors International (UK) Ltd (No 3)* [2008] EWCA Civ 625, [2009] QB 503.

99 *Masri (No 2)* (n 97) [50]–[51].

100 *Société Eram Shipping Co Ltd v Cie Internationale de Navigation* [2003] UKHL 30, [2004] 1 AC 260.

101 *Masri (No 2)* (n 97) [35], citing *MacKinnon v Donaldson Lufkin & Jenrette Securities Corp* [1986] Ch 482 (Ch) (Hoffmann J).

102 ibid [61].

In *TMSF v Merrill Lynch*,[103] the Privy Council applied *Masri (No 2)*. Lord Collins delivered the opinion of the Board. The claimant, TMSF, had obtained a US$30 million *in personam* judgment against the defendant in Turkish proceedings, after which the defendant was made bankrupt in Turkey with the judgment debt unsatisfied. Upon discovering discretionary trusts in the Cayman Islands with significant assets of which the defendant and his wife were beneficiaries and over which the defendant had power of revocation, TMSF commenced proceedings in the Cayman Islands seeking appointment of a receiver over the power to revoke the trusts.

The Board noted that the Court in *Masri (No 2)* had held 'that the jurisdiction to appoint a receiver by way of equitable execution permitted of gradual and incremental development'.[104] Applying the principles in *Masri (No 2)* and considering that 'the demands of justice are the overriding consideration',[105] the Board determined that a receiver should be appointed over the defendant's power of revocation of the trusts, coupled with an order that the defendant delegate his powers of revocation to the receiver.[106] In 2017, the Supreme Court described the relevant principles for the making of a receivership order in international litigation as 'not in dispute', having been set out by Lawrence Collins LJ in *Masri (No 2)*.[107]

In *Masri (No 3)*, the claimant issued proceedings for an anti-suit injunction against the defendants, who had issued proceedings in Yemen for a declaration that they were not liable to the claimant. In agreeing with the first instance court that the injunction should be granted, Lawrence Collins LJ stated the principle in the following terms:

> [T]he English court has power over persons properly subject to its in personam jurisdiction to make ancillary orders in protection of its jurisdiction and its processes, including the integrity of its judgments. That power is of course a discretionary one, to be exercised in accordance with the requirements of international comity.[108]

As with the receivership order in *Masri (No 2)*, the anti-suit injunction was ancillary to extant proceedings in which the defendants had submitted to the English courts' jurisdiction. He rejected an argument based on *The Siskina* that it was necessary in such cases to establish a separate right not to be sued as an independent cause of action.[109] The consequence was that:

[103] *Tasarruf Mevduati Sigorta Fonu ('TMSF') v Merrill Lynch Bank and Trust Co (Cayman Ltd)* [2011] UKPC 17, [2012] 1 WLR 1721.
[104] ibid [6].
[105] ibid [56].
[106] ibid [64].
[107] *Taurus Petroleum Ltd v State Oil Marketing Co of the Ministry of Oil, Republic of Iraq* [2017] UKSC 64, [2018] AC 690 [48]ff.
[108] *Masri (No 3)* (n 98) [26].
[109] ibid [38]–[59].

> Where a party is properly before a court, an anti-suit injunction is not a separate claim requiring its own basis of jurisdiction. In alternative forum cases, such as the present, it is not necessary for the applicant to rely on a cause of action establishing a separate right not to be sued. The right to apply for an injunction is not of itself the cause of action but is ancillary and incidental to the existing proceedings. The judgment debtors' submission to the English jurisdiction in those proceedings is a sufficient basis for the imposition of the anti-suit injunction.[110]

The judgment debtors said that it was contrary to principle for an English court to grant an injunction solely on the ground that it is to restrain re-litigation elsewhere of a matter already decided by an English judgment. They submitted that the foreign court ought to be entitled to decide for itself, and according to its rules of the conflict of laws, what effect, if any, to give to the English judgment.

Lawrence Collins LJ said:

> This argument is an appeal to considerations of international comity. In modern times the courts have often emphasised the importance of comity in the exercise of the discretion to grant anti-suit injunctions. Although the injunction is directed to the parties it involves an indirect interference with the foreign court, and caution is required before the injunction is granted.[111]

He accepted that '[c]omity may be decisive where the English court is asked to grant an anti-suit injunction when the case has no relevant connection with England, since to grant an injunction in such a case may be a breach of international law'.[112] By contrast, he held that there could be no breach of comity in granting an anti-suit injunction to restrain the respondent from 'seeking to relitigate in a foreign jurisdiction matters which are already res judicata between himself and the applicant by reason of an English judgment'.[113] This was the classic case in which such an injunction would be granted, since it was protecting the jurisdiction of the English court, to whose processes the defendant had already submitted.[114]

E. Conclusion

These three examples, of course, can provide only a snap-shot of Lawrence's immense influence. They are characteristic of his intense interest in the *practice* of international civil and commercial litigation, a field that is a dynamic

110 ibid [99].
111 ibid [81].
112 ibid.
113 ibid [82].
114 ibid [95].

testing-ground for the ability of the courts to respond with effective remedies tailored to the contemporary realities of the way in which international business is conducted. Nor indeed is international civil and commercial litigation a dry contest of bloodless corporations. It is a hallmark of Lawrence Collins's writing style—academic and judicial—that he enlivens the discussions of principle with the personal stories of the human beings behind the cases and the infinitely various and colourful facts that give rise to international disputes.

Yet, the three sets of issues discussed above prompt a deeper reflection on the question that Lawrence himself raised in his 2002 article as to the contemporary meaning and function of comity in private international law, a concept which he pointed out 'thrives in the judicial decisions'.[115] He wrote that piece not long after he was appointed to the High Court Bench in 2000. Where suitable cases have arisen, he has not hesitated to deploy the concept of comity himself in his own judicial decisions.

His premise is that comity does not furnish the basis for the system of private international law as a whole, but rather serves as 'a tool for applying or re-shaping the rules of the conflict of laws'.[116] This nevertheless raises the question as to the content of the concept, by reference to which the field is to be developed, especially in the novel procedural contexts constantly presented for decision in international litigation.

In his 2002 article, Lawrence suggested a typology of different senses in which the courts have used comity: as denoting the binding rules of public international law on international jurisdiction, applicable to sovereign immunity, the reach of legislative jurisdiction and the exercise of civil jurisdiction over defendants served abroad; in informing respect for foreign public law; in limiting the grant of anti-suit injunctions; and in promoting cooperation between courts.

The examples reviewed above demonstrate the application of comity in each of these contexts.

1. *Sovereign immunity.* In the sovereign immunity cases, comity, seen as the binding rules of public international law, provides a rationale for the rules of immunity: *Pinochet (No 3)* (in argument). It is in this context to be distinguished from the sense in which the expression 'comity' is sometimes used to denote matters of courtesy and not binding rules: *Aziz.* The emergence of the restrictive doctrine nevertheless shows that what comity requires in international law may change over time to accommodate changing practice in the commercial context: *NML v Argentina.*
2. *Personal jurisdiction and appropriate forum.* In the assumption of personal jurisdiction over foreign defendants, the provisions permitting service

[115] Collins (n 11) 95.
[116] *Dicey, Morris & Collins* (n 5) para 1-009.

abroad were, as Lawrence had pointed out, a recognition of what comity *requires* in order to ensure that the English court could take jurisdiction over cases in which there is a substantial connection with the forum. These rules are not 'exorbitant', if by that it is meant that they are an unjustified incursion on the sovereign jurisdiction of foreign States.[117] 'In fact', as he has written, 'most of the heads of jurisdiction are found in other countries and are entirely unobjectionable'.[118] But an important check on the service of jurisdiction over foreign defendants is the requirement that the court must go on to consider whether, even if there is an applicable jurisdictional gateway, England is the appropriate forum.[119] In making that assessment, the court is not disabled by comity from considering whether the claimant can obtain justice in the foreign court, but comity does require that it will only reach a decision that justice cannot be obtained there on the basis of cogent evidence: *AK Investment*.

3. *Provisional measures and anti-suit injunctions.* There is an important distinction to be drawn between the jurisdiction of a court to order provisional measures and jurisdiction over the merits. A court is not limited in granting provisional measures to cases in which it has jurisdiction over the merits. As a result, it may properly grant such measures in aid of proceedings in foreign courts, where there is a sufficient connection between the measure sought and England: *Agbaje*. The starting point in considering the scope of the court's provisional measures power is the distinction between person and property, since the court has no power to issue an order that operates *in rem* over property abroad. That would be a breach of the permissible scope of enforcement jurisdiction in public international law. But this distinction does not end the inquiry. The court must go on to consider, even in respect of *in personam* orders over persons subject to its jurisdiction, whether it has subject matter jurisdiction to order such a person to carry out the relevant act abroad: *Masri (No 2)*. Comity also requires that there be an appropriate connection with the forum to justify the indirect interference with the foreign court necessarily involved in the grant of an anti-suit injunction, but such a connection will exist where the court acts to protect its own jurisdiction and judgments: *Masri (No 3)*.

What is striking about all of these cases is that they demonstrate the working out in a set of highly practical contexts of the extent and limits of the doctrine of jurisdiction in public international law and its relation with private international law.[120]

[117] *Abela v Baadarani* [2013] UKSC 44, [2013] 1 WLR 2043 [53] (Lord Sumption).
[118] Lawrence Collins, 'Sovereignty and Exorbitant Jurisdiction' (2014) 130 LQR 555, 556.
[119] *Brownlie v FS Cairo (Nile Plaza) LLC* [2021] UKSC 45, [2021] 3 WLR 1011 [77] (Lord Lloyd-Jones).
[120] See also: Alex Mills, *The Confluence of Public and Private International Law: Justice, Pluralism and Subsidiarity in the International Constitutional Ordering of Private Law* (CUP 2009).

It is now widely appreciated that the permissible extent of the international jurisdiction of States cannot be determined by fixed rules and categories. Rather, the overriding considerations in questions of jurisdiction in public international law are: (i) the existence of a sufficiently close connection between the subject matter and State claiming jurisdiction; and (ii) the extent of compatibility with the exercise of jurisdiction by other States.[121] The exercise of civil jurisdiction by courts is no less an exercise of the jurisdiction of the State, since, from the perspective of public international law, courts are an organ of the State.[122] The experience of international civil and commercial litigation demonstrates that these two interlinked questions—sufficiency of connection and avoidance of unjustified interference with the exercise of jurisdiction by other States—provide a sound basis for analysis in addressing novel problems.

It is rare indeed, in an era of increasing specialism, to find in a single person the ability to combine deep scholarly knowledge of both private and public international law with wide practical experience in international commercial litigation and arbitration. The authors of this volume offer it as a tribute to the contribution of Lawrence Collins in bringing together these fields and demonstrating their essential connection in the resolution of international disputes.

[121] Frederick A Mann, 'The Doctrine of Jurisdiction in International Law' (1964) 111 RdC 1, 43–51; Robert Jennings and Arthur Watts (eds), *Oppenheim's International Law* (9th edn, Longman 1992) vol 1, 456–58; and the further authorities cited in Campbell McLachlan, *Foreign Relations Law* (CUP 2014) paras 5.133–5.147.

[122] International Law Commission, 'Draft Articles on Responsibility of States for Internationally Wrongful Acts' [2001] 2(2) YB ILC 26, art 4.

PART I
CROSS-BORDER LITIGATION

1

Private International Law But Not as We Know It

'Firewall' Legislation in Offshore Jurisdictions

Jonathan Harris

A. Introduction

1987: a momentous year for private international law in England. The entry into force of the Brussels Convention[1] introduced a new way of thinking about jurisdiction and judgments. Meanwhile, the law on anti-suit injunctions was put on its modern footing by the Privy Council in *Société Nationale Industrielle Aérospatiale v Lee Kui Jak*.[2] Of course, 1987 also marked the publication of the 11th edition of *Dicey and Morris*, the first under the magisterial general editorship of Lawrence Collins. Almost thirty-five years on, his contribution to the development of the book and to private international law is unsurpassable.

Meanwhile, in a British Overseas Territory, 1987 also marked the beginnings of an important private international law development of a very different kind. The Trust (Foreign Element) Law 1987 introduced new provisions into the Cayman Islands Trusts Law.[3] Those rules, designed to promote and protect the lucrative local trusts industry, were, on any view, highly innovative and stood long-entrenched common law private international law orthodoxies on their head.

At around the same time,[4] the UK was placing its choice of law rules for trusts on a statutory footing by giving effect to the Hague Convention on the Law Applicable

[1] Given effect by the Civil Jurisdiction and Judgments Act 1982.

[2] [1987] AC 871 (PC). The law of *forum non conveniens* had recently been restated by the House of Lords in *Spiliada Maritime Corp v Cansulex Ltd* [1987] AC 460 (HL) in November 1986.

[3] Pt VII.

[4] The Convention entered into force in the UK on 1 August 1987. In the initial ratifying states of the UK, Australia, and Italy, the Convention came into force on 1 January 1992. The application of the Convention was extended by Recognition of Trusts Act 1987 (Overseas Territories) Order SI 1989/673 to jurisdictions including Bermuda and the British Virgin Islands. Other offshore jurisdictions bound by the Convention include: Gibraltar, Guernsey (the UK extended the operation of the Convention to Guernsey on 28 April 1993), the Isle of Man, and Jersey (the UK Recognition of Trusts Act 1987 was not extended to Jersey, but Jersey became a party to the Convention on 1 March 1992, having brought its Trusts (Jersey) Law 1984 into line with the Convention by the Trusts (Amendment No 2) (Jersey) Law 1991).

Jonathan Harris, *Private International Law But Not as We Know It* In: *Essays in International Litigation for Lord Collins*. Edited by: Jonathan Harris and Campbell McLachlan, Oxford University Press.
DOI: 10.1093/oso/9780192867988.003.0002

to Trusts and on their Recognition 1985 by the Recognition of Trusts Act 1987.[5] But the Convention was never adopted in the Cayman Islands; in part because, while it promoted the recognition of trusts in civil law countries, its choice of law rules were relatively conservative for common law countries (indeed, they were very similar in substance to the existing English common law rules in this field).[6] Also, to encourage civil law states to ratify it, the Convention contains numerous exceptions to application of the governing law of the trust, including for rules which cannot be derogated from the governing law designated by the forum's choice of law rules in related fields such as succession and matrimonial law.[7] These could, at least in principle, mean that a trust was affected by, for instance, foreign matrimonial property claims or compulsory heirship rules. The Convention also leaves significant gaps, since it applies only to a trust itself once validly constituted, and not to preliminary issues such as the validity of the transfer of assets from the settlor to the trustee.[8]

The Cayman Islands saw its future rather differently. It enacted choice of law rules, designed, in particular, to protect Cayman law trusts from testamentary and matrimonial claims arising under foreign laws. The template has since been widely adopted offshore and, over time, has been embellished with ever-more imaginative ways to protect local law trusts and local trust industries.[9]

This so-called 'firewall' legislation typically has two primary functions: (i) to lay down choice of law rules in favour of the application of the local law and restrict the application of foreign laws, particularly rules of forced heirship, matrimonial property, and ancillary relief; and (ii) to prevent the recognition or enforcement of foreign judgments that are 'inconsistent' with those rules.

This chapter considers the development of firewall legislation and certain issues to which it has given rise. It considers, first, the development of firewall legislation in the Cayman Islands and its courts and the subsequent experiences in Jersey. It then goes on to consider other particular questions, such as the use of firewall legislation within the EU, and whether any rapprochement between the approaches of offshore and onshore jurisdictions might be reached.

[5] And extended its ambit: see the 1987 Act, s 1(2).

[6] See *Chellaram v Chellaram (No 2)* [2002] EWHC 632 (Ch), [2002] 3 All ER 17 [166], where Lawrence Collins J (as he then was) doubted whether there was any significant difference between them.

[7] See art 15 of the Convention. Art 16 preserves the overriding mandatory rules of the forum. Art 18 states that the governing law may be disapplied if its application 'would be manifestly incompatible with public policy'.

[8] Art 4.

[9] Similar legislation can be found, eg, in: Bermuda's Trusts (Special Provisions) Act 1989, s 10 (as amended); Trusts (Jersey) Law 1984, art 9 (as amended); Gibraltar's Trusts (Private International Law) Act 2015; Isle of Man Trusts Act 1995 (as amended); Bahamas: Trusts (Choice of Governing Law) 1989 (as amended); BVI Trustee Act 1961, s 83A (as amended); Cyprus International Trusts Act 1992 (as amended); DIFC Trusts Law 2018, pt 2.

B. The Cayman Firewall

Firewall protection typically applies only to trusts governed by the local law. To this end, the Cayman Trusts Law contains a number of features which reinforce the applicability of Cayman law to a trust. Section 89(2) of the Trusts Law[10] provides that: 'A term of the trust expressly selecting the laws of the Islands to govern the trust is valid, effective and conclusive regardless of any other circumstances.' It is one thing, of course, to provide that a choice of law clause can survive the invalidity of the trust itself. But it is quite another seemingly to provide that it cannot be challenged *at all*. There is no provision as to what happens if the choice is the product, for instance, of a mistake, duress, fraud, or any other vitiating factor; and it remains unclear when, if ever, such a clause may be challenged.[11]

Moreover, section 89(3) states that if the trust contains a term to the effect that Cayman Islands law is to apply to a particular aspect of the trust, or that the Cayman Islands courts are the forum for the administration of the trust or any like provision, this is to be treated as conclusive evidence that Cayman Islands law is intended to govern the entire trust, subject to any express provision to the contrary in the trust. One might, however, think that if a settlor specifically chose Cayman law to govern one aspect of a trust only (such as its administration) that may (depending on the facts) tend to suggest that she did *not* intend it to govern the whole trust. As to the provision on forum for administration clauses, the Privy Council's decision in *Crociani v Crociani*[12] demonstrates such a clause may (depending on its context and construction) be concerned solely with non-contentious issues as to the management of the trust. Certainly, it is not invariably a comprehensive, exclusive jurisdiction clause in favour of the Cayman courts. Yet, the very existence of such a clause is, in and of itself, 'conclusive evidence' that Cayman law governs the whole trust, unless there is a term to the contrary in the trust. This, of course, departs from established common law principles as to implying a choice of law.[13] The undeniable effect is strongly to encourage the application of Cayman law and, in turn, to engage the firewall's choice of law rules.

[10] 2021 Revision.

[11] Moreover, in *Re Settlement made by deed dated 27 December 2017*, FSD Cause No 83 of 2020 (IKJ) [20], Kawaley J stated that s 89 (in tandem with s 90) was 'of general relevance to the question of whether the Trustee should be permitted to commence proceedings in the forum for administration and/or dispute the jurisdiction of the English Court over it in relation to the threatened claims'.

[12] [2014] UKPC 40, (2014) 17 ITELR 624. The 'homing' tendency to protect local law trusts itself and to ensure the application of local firewall legislation may have influenced the broad construction of forum for administration clauses in a number of cases prior to *Crociani*; although the Grand Court of the Cayman Islands considered *obiter* that such a clause did not apply to contentious breach of trust claims in *Helmsman Ltd and Hotham Trustee Co Ltd v Bank of New York Trust Co (Cayman) Ltd*, (2009) 13 ITELR 177. See also *EMM Capricorn Trustees Ltd v Compass Trustees Ltd* [2001] JLR 205; *Green v Jernigan*, 2003 BCSC 1097, (2003) 6 ITELR 330; *Koonmen v Bender* (2002) 6 ITELR 568 (Jersey CA); *Re Representation of AA* [2010] JRC 164; *Re A Trust* [2012] Bda LR 79.

[13] See Lord Collins (ed), *Dicey, Morris & Collins on the Conflict of Laws* (15th edn, Sweet & Maxwell 2012) paras 29-019 and 32-006.

Where the law of the Cayman Islands governs a trust, section 90 determines the scope of the governing law. It provides that:

> All questions arising in regard to a trust which is for the time being governed by the laws of the Islands or in regard to any disposition of property upon the trusts thereof including questions as to –
> (a) the capacity of any settlor;
> (b) any aspect of the validity of the trust or disposition or the interpretation or effect thereof . . .
> are to be determined according to the laws of the Islands without reference to the laws of any other jurisdictions with which the trust or disposition may be connected

Again, these provisions remove the shackles of previous private international law wisdom. A settlor's capacity is governed by the Cayman law where she chooses that law to govern the trust.[14] In effect, this enables a person to escape an incapacity, for example, under her personal law, so potentially rendering such restrictions nugatory. So too, subjecting transfers of assets to or from a Cayman trust, wherever located, and whatever their nature, to Cayman law represents a decisive break from the application of the law of the *situs* for *inter vivos* transfers. This approach has since almost become the new orthodoxy in the offshore trusts world.

Section 90 sets out certain restrictions to the scope of the applicable law. Three may be mentioned here.[15] First, the section does not validate any disposition of property not owned by the settlor or subject to a power vested in the settlor. This provision seems to be aimed at the disposition itself and the powers of the settlor. It is less clear that it reintroduces a role for foreign law in respect of the settlor's capacity. Second, as regards a corporation's capacity, it is provided that Cayman Islands law 'does not affect the recognition of the laws of its place of incorporation'. The word 'recognition' is open to different interpretations. It might suggest that the capacity to create a trust is governed *solely* by the law of the place of a company's incorporation; on another view, it means that a corporation must have capacity *both* by Cayman Islands law *and* the law of the place of incorporation; and on a third view, that Cayman Islands law still determines capacity, subject to a discretion to

[14] Cf *Dicey, Morris & Collins* (n 13) paras 29-014–29-015, which suggest that the question of whether a settlor has capacity to dispose of property *at all* should be governed by the choice of law rules for property transfers; with only the secondary question if that person has capacity to create a trust being governed by the law applicable to the trust. A similar approach has been adopted in the BVI firewall legislation: see Trustee Act 1961, s 83A (as amended).

[15] Section 90 also provides that it: (i) does not affect the recognition of formality rules of a foreign law applicable generally to dispositions of property (and not specific to trusts law); (ii) does not validate a testamentary trust or disposition which is invalid according to the law of the testator's domicile; and (iii) takes effect subject to any express contrary term of the trust.

apply the law of the place of incorporation where it is thought appropriate. Third, Cayman Islands law does not validate any trust or disposition of immovable property situated in a jurisdiction other than the Islands which is invalid according to the laws of such jurisdiction. This means that the vesting of property in the trustee will be determined by the *lex situs*; presumably it also refers capacity to the *lex situs*, since a disposition will not be valid according to the law of the place of the immovable property if the settlor lacked capacity to dispose of his property.[16] Nor does the statute state whether a transaction which is valid by the *lex situs* can be *invalidated* by Cayman Islands law. In principle, it seems that it should be, since, with the exception of the section 90 criteria, the scope of Cayman Islands law when applicable is almost unlimited. On the other hand, it would mean that the transfer would have to be valid by both the *lex situs* and Cayman Islands law in relation to immovable property, which would tend to mitigate against the validity of Cayman trusts of land.[17]

Section 91 contains a particular innovation:[18]

> **Exclusion of foreign law**
>
> 91. . . . it is expressly declared that no trust governed by the laws of the Islands and no disposition of property to be held upon the trusts thereof is void, voidable, liable to be set aside or defective in any fashion, nor is the capacity of any settlor to be questioned, nor is the trustee, any beneficiary or any other person to be subjected to any liability or deprived of any right, by reason that—
>
> (a) the laws of any foreign jurisdiction prohibit or do not recognise the concept of a trust; or
>
> (b) the trust or disposition avoids or defeats rights, claims or interests conferred by foreign law upon any person by reason of a personal relationship to the settlor or any beneficiary (whether discretionary or otherwise) or by way of heirship rights, or contravenes any rule of foreign law or any foreign judicial or administrative order or action intended to recognise, protect, enforce or give effect to any such rights, claims or interests.

In other words, the trust itself, and dispositions to that trust, are unimpeachable, and the trustees and beneficiaries (and *any* other person) shall not be subject to liability because a foreign law does not recognize the trust concept,[19] or, more significantly for present purposes, the trust might avoid rights or claims conferred

[16] See also the definition of 'disposition' in s 87.

[17] Another provision, in s 90(vi), that s 90 'does not validate any testamentary trust or disposition which is invalid according to the laws of the testator's domicile', seems overly broad, since that law only applies to succession to movable property: see *Dicey, Morris & Collins* (n 13) rr 149 and 154.

[18] Subject to the provisos in s 90 considered in the preceding paragraph.

[19] The fact that that property is located in a 'non-trust' State is not itself fatal to the existence of a trust: *Akers v Samba Financial Group* [2017] UKSC 6, [2017] AC 424.

by foreign law[20] upon parties by reason of a personal relationship to the settlor or beneficiary[21] (such as matrimonial property or ancillary relief claims) or by way of compulsory heirship rights. Some of the wording is perhaps imperfect: it is not clear, for instance, when a trust or disposition would 'defeat' such a rule; and if it matters whether the foreign heirship or matrimonial right pre-dates the trust or arises subsequently. Nonetheless, the intention[22] to prevent such foreign laws giving rise to any claims in Cayman, or in respect of Cayman trust assets, is evident. Some might question the appropriateness of a principle which allows a settlor, for example, to transfer assets to a Cayman trust in violation of the rules of community property of the matrimonial domicile[23] (or in circumstances which defeat any subsequent claims by a spouse). But the message to would-be settlors considering whether and where to establish a trust, and under which law, is loud and clear: if you place assets in a Cayman law trust, you can be safe in the knowledge that would-be claimants cannot claim them in Cayman[24] by relying on foreign succession and matrimonial laws.

Of course, choice of law rules can only provide so much protection. It is impossible to prevent other countries from exercising jurisdiction in respect of Cayman trusts trust assets. And it is almost unthinkable that any other jurisdiction would apply precisely the same choice of law rules as in the Cayman firewall.[25] The solution was to create a new rule on recognition and enforcement of foreign judgments in section 93: 'A foreign judgment shall not be recognised, enforced or give rise to any estoppel insofar as it is inconsistent with section 91 or 92.'[26] In other words, any foreign judgment giving effect to a foreign compulsory heirship or matrimonial rights would have no *res judicata* effect in Cayman. Again, the drafting may give rise to certain questions (to which we will return below). But the intention to prevent circumvention of the firewall's choice of law rules is clear.

Furthermore, section 88 of the Trusts Law states that the firewall provision applies 'to every trust and every disposition of property in trust made before, on or after the 31st May, 1987, whether such property is situate in the Islands or elsewhere'. The prospects of a transfer being retrospectively validated or invalidated by the advent of new legislation may be questionable in terms of legal principle and the security of property rights.[27] But the alternative was to apply the firewall only to trusts (or, at least, to transfers to trusts) made after its entry into force, which,

[20] Or contravenes a foreign judicial or administrative order intended to give effect to such rights.
[21] The reference to beneficiaries was subsequently added.
[22] Further reinforced in respect of heirship rights by s 92.
[23] See *Dicey, Morris & Collins* (n 13) r 165.
[24] Of course, this illustrates an obviously practical limitation of firewalls, if the assets are located elsewhere.
[25] Other jurisdictions are highly unlikely to apply another country's firewall choice of law rules (and, if they did, this would amount to the application of *renvoi*).
[26] Section 92 is also concerned with non-recognition of foreign law heirship rights.
[27] Cf *Wilson v First County Trust Ltd (No 2)* [2003] UKHL 40, [2004] 1 AC 816.

of course, would have rendered it less immediately attractive in the international marketplace. And that, ultimately, was a more important consideration.

Of course, the most effective way to ensure that Cayman law is applied to Cayman trusts is for the local courts to exercise jurisdiction over them. The Cayman firewall, however, lacks rules of jurisdiction.[28] This has led to some surprising jurisprudence. In *MLBTC v Demirel*,[29] Smellie CJ ruled that a claim for *Beddoe* relief[30] (in respect of a trust containing a Cayman governing law and forum for administration clause) could be served on defendants outside of the Cayman Islands without obtaining leave from the court to do so. The Grand Court Rules, Order 11(1)(2), then stated that:

> Service of a writ out of the jurisdiction is permissible without the leave of the Court if every claim made in the action begun by the writ is one which *by virtue of a Law the Court has power to hear and determine* notwithstanding that the person against whom the claim is made is not within the jurisdiction of the Court or that the wrongful act, neglect or default giving rise to the claim did not take place within the jurisdiction. [emphasis added]

Smellie CJ regarded section 90 of the Trusts Law as a 'Law' by which 'the Court has power to hear and determine' the application for *Beddoe* relief. He held:[31]

> It appears that the words 'without reference to the laws of any other jurisdictions with which the trust or disposition may be connected [in section 90]' are intended to abrogate the English common law rules of forum non conveniens and the exercise of judicial discretion which they imply insofar as those rules may otherwise apply to Cayman trusts. Thus, insofar as the application of the common law forum non conveniens rules would point to another jurisdiction as the appropriate forum for the resolution of disputes involving a Cayman trust by virtue of factors connecting the trust to that jurisdiction, then s.90 would operate to negate such factors.

Again, in *Re B*,[32] Henderson J stated:

> A trust in the Cayman Islands can only be varied in accordance with the law of the Cayman Islands and only by a court of the Cayman Islands. These overarching

[28] Other firewalls do have jurisdiction rules: see eg Trusts (Jersey) Law 1984, art 5; Trusts (Guernsey) Law 2007, s 4; BVI Trustee Act 1961, s 82.
[29] 2010 (2) CILR 75.
[30] Under the Trusts Law, s 48.
[31] *MLBTC* (n 29) [16].
[32] 2010 (2) CILR 348 [23].

> rules are provided for expressly in the Trusts Law (2009 Revision), in ss. 90, 91 and 93.

Certainly, this represented a robust interpretation of the firewall: but it was, with respect, one which could not withstand scrutiny. Section 90 contains choice of law rules, not jurisdiction provisions.

Some years later, Kawaley J in *HSBC International Trustee Ltd v Tan Poh Lee*[33] suggested that it was 'certainly arguable' that a foreign court could not under any circumstances, even when applying Cayman law, deal with issues relating to a Cayman trust containing an exclusive forum for administration clauses. Subsequently, in *Re Stingray Trust*,[34] however, he held that section 90 did not contain rules of jurisdiction at all (still less rules of exclusive jurisdiction). He concluded that the prior authorities were not incorrect: in particular, the decision in *MLBTC*[35] was not wrong on its facts as an application for *Beddoe* relief made in Cayman would normally have to be determined in Cayman. The difficulty, as we have seen, is that the reasoning *in that case* was broader and there is little doubt that the court in that case thought that section 90 had a wider effect than it did. But, belatedly, at least, some order has been restored. Even then, however, in granting a stay of proceedings in favour of Swiss courts, Kawaley J in *Stingray* imposed a condition that the foreign court applied Cayman law to a dispute as to the trust's validity. He held[36] that: 'In my judgment the policy imperatives of section 90 of the Law are sufficiently strong for such a condition to be imposed when granting the proposed stay'. That is itself, perhaps, a slightly surprising statement, given that, as he had earlier recognized, section 93 on foreign judgments 'only expressly renders unenforceable foreign judgments which are inconsistent with sections 91 or 92'.[37] In other words, it precludes enforcement of foreign forced heirship and matrimonial rights affecting Cayman trusts and not judgments applying foreign law to Cayman trusts more generally, as provided for in section 90.

Nevertheless, since its inception, the Cayman firewall has become an indispensable tool for promoting and protecting the local trusts industry; and one to be interpreted robustly, or perhaps even creatively, by the courts to protect the local industry. In *HSBC*, Kawaley J held[38] that the

33 FSD 175 of 2019 (IKJ), 16 October 2019.

34 FSD 248 of 2017 (IKJ), 21 December 2020 [84]. But if the Cayman proceedings were commenced prior to or shortly after foreign proceedings, this may lead the Cayman court to conclude that it is the most appropriate forum: [83]. See also *Re Settlement* (n 11) [22].

35 *MLBTC* (n 29). The court noted that s 90 was not relied on in *Re B*. But, again, there is little doubt that the court's reasoning in that case went too far.

36 *Stingray* (n 34) [84].

37 ibid [36].

38 *HSBC* (n 33) [36].

> [Cayman] decisions emphasise how important the statutory framework of the Trust Law is to Cayman Islands public policy relating to Cayman Islands trusts. That is entirely justified because the Cayman Islands is a jurisdiction which has a substantial number of highly valuable trusts, and it is not surprising that Parliament has sought to fortify that important industry by making it clear in the governing legislation that the fact that a settlor has chosen to apply Cayman Islands law to govern a trust is something that should be upheld by the Cayman Islands courts.

Subsequently, in *Re Settlement made by deed dated 27 December 2017*,[39] Kawaley J directed that a trustee be at liberty to issue an Originating Summons joining the claimants in English proceedings, to seek a declaration as to the validity of a Cayman law trust and to challenge the jurisdiction of the English court, if served in in those proceedings. He remarked that:

> Apart from the general consideration that this will ordinarily be the natural forum for claims against trustees who are resident and administering trusts here, it seems self-evident that this Court will normally be the appropriate court to develop Cayman Islands trusts law.
>
> Not only will there be no need for expert evidence to be adduced, but this Court can draw on its experience of similar distinctive trusts instruments and its well documented and longstanding appreciation of the public interest requirement to balance the 'local' interests of professional service providers with the 'international' interests of third party creditors contending that a trust has been improperly founded in violation of their rights.[40]

Hence, even though the Cayman firewall contains no rule of exclusive jurisdiction, the message remains that, prima facie, the Cayman courts will normally consider themselves to be the appropriate forum to hear matters that, in accordance with the firewall, are to be determined in accordance with Cayman law.

C. Developments in Jersey

The Cayman firewall proved a catalyst for similar legislation in other offshore jurisdictions, anxious to remove the straitjacket of conventional conflicts wisdom

[39] *Re Settlement* (n 11).

[40] ibid [24]–[25]. See also [29]: 'The validity issue raises par excellence, for the reasons already adumbrated above, the sort of Cayman Islands legislative and public policy issues which should naturally and normally be adjudicated in this forum.'

for the prospect of excluding foreign laws and attracting investment. But if the Cayman courts have occasionally pushed the boundaries of the firewall to protect local law trusts, the experience in Jersey has perhaps been the obverse: far-reaching legislation has been enacted to seek to outdo the protection offered elsewhere. But when Jersey trustees have been faced with an English ancillary relief award, and sought directions from the Jersey courts, those courts have often sought to find a balanced solution.

Trusts (Amendment No 4) (Jersey) Law 2006 ('Amendment No 4'), amended the Trusts (Jersey) Law 1984.[41] Article 9(1) stated that:

> 1. Subject to paragraph (3), any question concerning:
>   a. the validity or interpretation of a trust;
>   b. the validity or effect of any transfer or other disposition of property to a trust;
>   c. the capacity of a settlor;
>   d. the administration of the trust, whether the administration be conducted in Jersey or elsewhere, including questions as to the powers, obligations, liabilities and rights of trustees and their appointment or removal; or
>   e. the existence and extent of powers, conferred or retained, including powers of variation or revocation of the trust and powers of appointment and the validity of any exercise of such powers;
>
>   shall be determined in accordance with the law of Jersey and no rule of foreign law shall affect such question.

Article 9(3) provided that Jersey's choice of law rules in other areas of law should not affect these provisions. In other words (and in contrast to the position in Cayman), the Jersey legislation envisaged *no* role for foreign law at all.

Unlike Cayman, however, Jersey is one of many offshore states bound by the Hague Trusts Convention. As explained above, that Convention contains express provisions allowing a court to superimpose mandatory rules in related areas of law, including in matrimonial and succession law. This encouraged the leap of faith required of 'non-trust' States in ratifying the Convention and recognizing common law trusts *qua* trusts. Although the Convention is not reciprocal in nature, such would-be Contracting States might reasonably hope for a certain level of reciprocal protection for their rules of forced heirship or matrimonial laws in trusts jurisdictions. But any such aspiration has little place in a highly competitive offshore trusts industry.

Article 9(4) of Amendment No 4 then provided that:

[41] With effect from 27 October 2006.

> No foreign judgement with respect to a trust shall be enforceable to the extent that it is inconsistent with this Article irrespective of any applicable law relating to conflicts of law [sic].

It is not entirely easy to reconcile this provision with the terms of Judgments (Reciprocal Enforcement) (Jersey) Law 1960, which applies to certain money judgments of UK courts.[42] The 1960 Law may be extended to countries providing reciprocal treatment to Jersey judgments.[43] Article 6(2)(a)(i) of the 1960 Law provides that a foreign court shall be considered jurisdictionally competent in the eyes of Jersey law 'if the judgment debtor, being a defendant in the original court, submitted to the jurisdiction of that court by voluntarily appearing in the proceedings'. Although there is a public policy derogation in Article 6(1)(v) of the 1960 Law, the blanket exclusion in Article 9(4) of Amendment No 4[44] arguably does not fall within the purposes or intent of that provision, and leads to a lack of reciprocity with other countries.

Be that as it may, the ostensible effect of Article 9(4) of Amendment No 4 was that where, for example, an English court applied English law in varying a Jersey trust upon divorce pursuant to section 24(1)(c) of the Matrimonial Causes Act 1973,[45] the judgment was unenforceable. Notwithstanding this, in *Re the B Trust*,[46] the Jersey court considered that it could direct a trustee to comply with an English matrimonial order affecting a foreign trust on the grounds of comity.[47] One might think that the very purpose of the Jersey firewall was single-mindedly to protect the local trusts industry, rather than concern itself with questions of comity. Nor was it clear how 'comity' alone could have provided a substantive basis for directing a trustee to act in accordance with an English judgment.

Thereafter, the Royal Court in *Mubarak v Mubarik* [48] sought to reconcile the language of Article 9(4) with the decision in *Re the B Trust*. It did so by adopting a more balanced approach. It held that an English order could not be enforced, and the trustees could not be directed by the Jersey courts to comply with it, if

[42] Including judgments of the English High Court, Court of Appeal, and Supreme Court. The Act also applies to judgments from the Isle of Man and Guernsey. See also Maintenance Orders (Facilities for Enforcement) (Jersey) Law 2000 (as amended).

[43] 'Judgments' are defined in art 2(1) to include 'a judgment or order given or made by a court in any civil proceedings, or a judgment or order given or made by a court in any criminal proceedings for the payment of a sum of money in respect of compensation or damages to an injured party'. The scope of the 1960 Law would encompass an action against the trustee seeking compensation for breach of trust. Moreover, even if the 1960 Law were not applicable in a given case, one would expect the almost identical, rule-based general common law provisions on the recognition of foreign judgments to lead to the same result.

[44] And the replacement provision introduced in 2012 (described below).

[45] The approach of the English courts is considered further below.

[46] [2006] JRC 185, (2006) 9 ITELR 783.

[47] See Jonathan Harris, 'Jersey's New Private International Law Rules for Trusts—A Retrograde Step?' (2007) JGLR 184.

[48] [2008] JRC 136, [2009] 1 FLR 664.

the variation in question was not one which the trustees themselves could have made without the foreign court's intervention (albeit that, on the facts, the Jersey court found that the husband had given his consent to the Jersey courts themselves varying the trust on the terms of the English order). Otherwise, however, the court could direct the trustee[49] to comply with the English judgment. The Jersey Court of Appeal upheld the decision[50] on the basis that the approval of all relevant parties had been obtained,[51] so as to effect a variation of the trust.

In *Mubarak*, the court had endeavoured to give Article 9 a meaning which, in policy terms, provided an acceptable level of protection to Jersey law trusts, while not being seen to provide a sanctuary to escape the terms of English ancillary relief orders. Even so, if the existence of an English judgment remains the *reason* for the Jersey court to direct the trustee to act in a particular manner, regardless of whether it could, in principle, have done so anyway, then it may be argued that the rationale[52] of Article 9 has been at least partially negated.

The better course was rather to reform the language of Article 9 itself, to allow a more natural judicial interpretation of the wording of the law. Further reform duly arrived with the Trusts (Amendment No 5) (Jersey) Law ('Amendment No 5').[53] That amendment, however, while more measured in certain respects, went considerably further again in others.

For instance, Article 9(1)(e) had already made it plain that variation of a Jersey law trust is governed by Jersey law. But a new Article 9(1)(f) was added, which states that Jersey law applies to 'the exercise or purported exercise by a foreign court of any statutory or non-statutory power to vary the terms of a trust'. This represents a significant further step in seeking to instruct a *foreign* court directly as to *its* choice of law rules.

As against this, Article 9(2A) was introduced, which reintroduced some role for foreign law. This substantially resembles the derogations to foreign law permitted in section 90 of the Cayman Trusts Law described above. It properly recognized that transferring assets to a Jersey trust cannot simply be created as a mechanism to defeat pre-existing foreign rights and incapacities.

An interesting example of the interaction between different firewalls occurred in *Schroder Cayman Bank Trust Co Ltd v Schroder Trust AG*.[54] The case concerned the validity of certain appointments out of a trust governed by Cayman law to trusts governed by Jersey law in 2011. The Cayman court held that the appointments were excessive under Cayman law, alternatively that they should be

[49] Under Trusts (Jersey) Law 1984, art 51.
[50] [2008] JCA 196.
[51] Pursuant to Trusts (Jersey) Law 1984, art 47.
[52] Although, at the time, art 9(4) only prevented the 'enforcement' of foreign judgments and not their recognition.
[53] Which entered into force on 2 November 2012.
[54] [2015] JRC 125, (2015) 18 ITELR 616.

set aside on the grounds of mistake. It did so applying section 90 of the Cayman Trusts Law.[55] The trustees then applied to the Jersey courts seeking similar relief, so that they could properly rely on the Cayman court's decision and return the assets to the Cayman trusts. The Royal Court held that Article 9 of Amendment No 4 would have required the exclusive application of Jersey law to this issue, with the effect that 'the Court could not have acceded to the [trustees'] submission that the validity of the Appointments is to be determined by Cayman law'.[56] However, Article 9(2A)(c), introduced by Amendment No 5, made clear that the application of Jersey law to dispositions to a Jersey trust 'is subject to any express provision to the contrary in the terms of the trust or disposition'. The court held that if there was an express choice of law clause in the document which constitutes the disposition of property (here, in favour of Cayman law), that was a provision to the contrary which should be given effect in Jersey. Having determined that the firewall was not violated by the Cayman courts, it concluded that the matter was *res judicata* as a result of the Cayman judgments and that the trustees could safely return the assets to the Cayman trusts.

Whether the fact that the trusts from which the transfers were made had a choice of law clause really constituted an express provision that Jersey law should not apply to the transfers to Jersey trusts is debatable. It will seemingly lead to the law chosen to govern a trust from which a disposition is made applying to transfers to Jersey trusts, contrary to the apparent intention of Article 9(1)(b). But, at least a collision between two firewalls was avoided on this occasion. Even so, almost inevitably, such clashes will occur in the future, since no firewall is likely to be given effect in another jurisdiction and it will often only be a happy coincidence where the choice of law rules of the two offshore jurisdictions align.

Beyond this, Article 9(2A) is substantially negated by the fact that it is subject to Article 9(2). The latter provision contains rules precluding the application of foreign rules conferring rights by virtue of a personal relationship[57] to the settlor or beneficiary or heirship rights.[58] This means that, in relation to such issues, there is seemingly no permissible derogation to foreign law. So, if a settlor's assets are subject to a matrimonial property regime restricting the power of disposition, the disposition to a Jersey law trust may nonetheless be effective and unimpeachable.[59]

Pursuant to Amendment No 5, Article 9(4) of Jersey law was further strengthened to read:

[55] [2015] (1) CILR 23.

[56] *Schroder* (n 54) [17]. In *CC Ltd v Apex Trust Ltd* [2012] 1 JLR 314 [39], the Bailiff had said (in applying Amendment (No 4)) that: 'This seems to us clear and unambiguous in its terms. Article 9(1) provides that Jersey law is to apply to any question concerning the validity of a transfer of property to a trust and no rule of foreign law shall affect such question.'

[57] As defined in art 9(6).

[58] These rules, in turn, are stated to be subject to subs (1).

[59] This is further reinforced by the exclusion of any Jersey choice of law rules (other than art 9 itself) in related areas of law: see art 9(3A).

(4) No –

(a) judgment of a foreign court; or

(b) decision of any other foreign tribunal (whether in an arbitration or otherwise),

with respect to a trust shall be enforceable, or given effect, to the extent that it is inconsistent with this Article.

Hence Article 9(4) now precludes not just enforcement of inconsistent foreign judgments, but also the giving of any effect to them,[60] and extends to arbitral awards.

In contrast to the Cayman firewall, this provision applies to all foreign judgments and awards which are 'inconsistent' with the firewall's choice of law rules, not just those giving effect to foreign succession and matrimonial laws. The revised Article 9(4) sought to reinforce the protection against inconsistent foreign judgments, so they were *without any legal effect in Jersey*. They could not give rise to an estoppel and the intention, presumably, was that a Jersey court should not give its own remedies in support of such judgments.

Did this reinforcement of Article 9(4) affect how Jersey courts should direct Jersey trustees as to the effects of an English judgment? In *Re the R Trust*,[61] a Jersey discretionary trust was established in 2011 by Mr B. The only beneficiaries of the trust were the two minor children of Mr B and Mrs B. The trust instrument permitted the addition of beneficiaries. Mr and Mrs B were divorced in England. Mrs B had obtained an interim injunction in Jersey against the Representor preventing any dissipation of the assets of the trust. In 2015, the English court held that the family assets were not sufficient to maintain the house in England in which Mrs B and the two minor children resided and that access to the trust assets was necessary in order to enable Mrs B to retain the property. The Representor sought to rely upon the determinations of fact and assessment of the interests of the minor beneficiaries by the English court and proposed to act in accordance with them. It asked the Jersey court to approve the appointment of Mr B as a beneficiary and the distribution of the entirety of the trust fund to him for transmission to Mrs B.

Clearly, the English court order had sought to protect the interests of Mr B's family by virtue of their 'personal relationship' to him. To that extent, its judgment was apparently inconsistent with Article 9(2). But as the Jersey court noted, what was being asked of it 'would not be enforcement by this court or approval of the English Order but rather the approval of the decision of the Representor to take certain steps in the interests of the beneficiaries'.[62] The court held that the trustee

[60] An impetus for this reform was Trusts (Guernsey) Law 2007, s 14(4), which had extended the ambit of its firewall.

[61] [2015] JRC 267A. See also *Re Poon* [2015] JCA 109, affirming [2011] JRC 167, (2011) 18 ITELR 348.

[62] ibid [9].

could and should have regard to the conclusions of the English courts in exercising its discretion, and so granted its approval.[63] In many ways, the decision is unsurprising. Whatever local firewall legislation might say as to the *res judicata* effects of a foreign judgment affecting a Jersey law trust, the *fact* of its existence ought, just like any other relevant fact, to be taken into account by a trustee. Even so, it is difficult to determine the limits of the principle. In *Re the R Trust*, the English judgment was apparently 'inconsistent' with the Jersey choice of law rules in Article 9. As such, it was not to be 'given effect' under Article 9(4).

The Jersey courts are not alone in considering that the *existence* of a foreign judgment is something which a trustee cannot disregard, whatever the firewall legislation may say. The Grand Court of the Cayman Islands held in *Re B*[64] that although a foreign judgment may not be entitled to recognition and enforcement, its existence is a factor that a trustee might properly take into account:

> The Trustee cannot, of course, fetter its discretion now by suggesting how it may act in the future. In exercising its discretion, it must take into account all of the relevant circumstances existing at the time it is called upon to make a decision. One relevant circumstance, to which respectful and attentive consideration will be given is any judicious encouragement received in the form of a judgment or ruling from the Court in Hong Kong.

It might be argued that when a trustee asks for directions as to whether to comply with an English ancillary relief order: 'The Jersey Court would not be giving effect to the English judgment but to the decision of the trustees if it authorised their decision as within the parameters of the discretion afforded to them in the exercise of their own discretionary powers'.[65]

But if this appears both sensible and pragmatic, the elephant in the room is that *but for the existence of a foreign order of the kind that the firewall legislation typically seeks to discourage*, it is likely to be a rare case where a trustee would have proposed to act in precisely the same manner. Hence, the foreign judgment remains the *reason* for the trustee's proposed actions, whether or not he could have acted in the same way without that order.

Finally, Article 9(7) of the 1984 Law states that: 'this Article applies to trusts whenever constituted or created'. As with the Cayman statute, this reflects a desire, for evident commercial reasons, immediately to apply the latest firewall protection to Jersey trusts. The effect, however, is that every time Article 9 is amended, those amendments are themselves retrospective. Inevitably, this can have curious effects.

[63] Subject to certain refinements: see ibid [23].
[64] *Re B* (n 32) [35].
[65] David Hayton, 'Trusts (Amendment No. 5) (Jersey) Law 2012 (Legislative Comment)' (2012) PCB 102, 105.

It means that a trust, or a transfer into trust, that might have been invalid at its time of creation can (at least on the literal wording of Article 9) be validated retrospectively, and vice versa. The introduction of Amendment No 4 retrospectively meant that all issues relating to a Jersey trust were to be governed solely by Jersey law. So, for instance, the question of whether assets were validly transferred *inter vivos* into a Jersey law trust some thirty years beforehand was, retrospectively, to be determined by Jersey law, even if the disposition would have been invalid by the law of the *situs* at the time of the transfer. In turn, Amendment No 5 retrospectively changed the law again to reinstate some role for foreign law (leading to a different result in the *Schroder* case considered above, even though the transfers were made prior to the advent of Amendment No 5). The effect of Article 9(7) is that vested rights can be upset, and that since it is unlikely that the current law will be the very final word in Jersey, the position may change again, retrospectively, in the future.[66]

D. Firewall Legislation in the European Union

Of course, providing effective protection against the effects of foreign judgments affecting local law trusts presents a particular challenge for EU Member States. They are, after all, subject to EU rules on free movement of judgments, including those contained in the recast Brussels I Regulation.[67]

Gibraltar, which was, until the end of the EU transition period, bound by the relevant EU legislation, accepted this constraint. Section 4 of the Trusts (Private International Law) Act 2015 contains extensive protection for local law trusts. Section 4(5) provides that no inconsistent foreign judgment shall have *res judicata* effect. Section 7(b), however, states that the Act is subject to 'any EU Regulation, EU Directive or international convention by which Gibraltar is bound, or may become bound, which in relation to particular matters, contains rules as to jurisdiction or the recognition or enforcement of judgments'.

But not everyone has accepted this straitjacket. The Cypriot International Trusts Law, 1992, as amended, has very far-reaching protection for Cypriot international trusts.[68] Section 3(1A) provides that a wide range of matters, including 'any transfer or other disposition of property to a trust ... are to be determined according to the

66 Cf *Wilson* (n 27).

67 Regulation (EU) No 1215/2012 of the European Parliament and of the Council of 12 December 2012 on jurisdiction and the recognition and enforcement of judgments in civil and commercial matters [2012] OJ L351/1. See also Council Regulation (EC) No 4/2009 of 18 December 2008 on jurisdiction, applicable law, recognition and enforcement of decisions and cooperation in matters relating to maintenance obligations [2009] OJ L7/1.

68 As defined in s 2, which states, inter alia, that the settlor and beneficiaries (other than charities) must not be resident in Cyprus, whereas at least one trustee must be throughout the duration of the trust.

law of the Republic without reference to the law of any other jurisdiction'. There is protection in section 3(1A)(4) against any foreign rules of forced heirship or rights arising by 'reason of a personal relationship to a settlor or any beneficiary, or object of a discretionary trust or power of any nature'. Section 3(2) precludes any person from bringing any claim against a Cypriot international trust, including any action by creditors against the settlor, or where the trust was made for the benefit of the settlor or his family, unless they can prove an intent to defraud creditors at the time of transfer. Any such action must be brought within two years from the date of the transfer to or disposal of assets from the trust, regardless of knowledge.[69]

Enforcement, however, would seem to present a rather greater problem for Cyprus. Under the recast Brussels I Regulation, there is no *exequatur* procedure and only very limited defences to recognition and enforcement of judgments of other Member States are permitted. In particular, Article 45 states that:

> On the application of any interested party, the recognition of a judgment shall be refused:
> (a) if such recognition is manifestly contrary to public policy (ordre public) in the Member State addressed;

The Court of Justice of the European Union has stressed the need for this doctrine to be construed restrictively.[70] In *Krombach v Bamberski*,[71] it said that:

> In order for the prohibition of any review of the foreign judgment as to its substance to be observed, the infringement would have to constitute a manifest breach of a rule of law regarded as essential in the legal order of the State in which enforcement is sought or of a right recognised as being *fundamental within that legal order*.[72]

With this firmly in mind, section 12C of the International Trusts Law states:

> The provisions of this Law shall apply to international trusts containing a clause electing the law of the Republic as the governing law, irrespective of any other provisions relating to the rules on conflict of laws applicable in the Republic *and shall constitute a fundamental rule of law, whose observance is a matter of public order*.[73]

[69] See s 3(3).
[70] See *Dicey, Morris & Collins* (n 13) paras 14-225–14-228.
[71] Case C-7/98 *Krombach v Bamberski* [2000] ECR I-1935 [37].
[72] Emphasis added.
[73] Emphasis added.

In other words, the International Trusts Act: (i) takes the definition in *Krombach*; (ii) and treats *all* the provisions of the Act as rules of Cypriot public policy wherever there is an express choice of Cypriot law by the settlor, so that (iii) any judgment from another Member State that violates these choice of law rules will not be recognized and enforced in Cyprus. This is so notwithstanding Article 52 of the recast Brussels I Regulation, which provides that: 'Under no circumstances may a judgment given in a Member State be reviewed as to its substance in the Member State addressed.' Nonetheless, the perceived need for such a provision is clear: to keep up with non-EU offshore jurisdictions that have no such fetters on the scope of their firewall protection against foreign judgments.

E. 'Inconsistent' Foreign Judgments

As seen above, firewall legislation typically prevents the recognition and enforcement of foreign judgments that are '*inconsistent*' with the statute's choice of law rules. That word is, however, ambiguous. It could mean that: (i) the foreign court applied a different law to that prescribed in the local firewall legislation (which will very often be the case); or (ii) the substantive result was different from that which a local court would have reached (which might effectively require a retrial).

This issue was confronted in Gibraltar's Trusts (Private International Law) Act 2015. Section 4(5) seeks to steer a middle course, so that a judgment shall not be recognized:

> [I]f and to the extent that the foreign court or tribunal applied a foreign law or laws whose relevant provisions are substantively different to those which would be applicable by virtue of the choice of rules in this section. The burden of demonstrating that there is no such substantive difference shall lie on the party seeking recognition or enforcement of the foreign judgment or order.

In so doing, the firewall does not apply to foreign judgments applying a foreign substantive law that leads to the same result as Gibraltar's law; but seeks to maintain the strength of the firewall by placing the onus on the party seeking enforcement to show that there is no such inconsistency. This solution may not be entirely straightforward, but it is a balanced one, which, perhaps, only highlights the difficulty in defining exactly what it is about foreign judgments relating to local law trusts that is objectionable.

F. Submission to a Foreign Court

Firewalls almost eliminate the traditional common law understanding that a judgment of a foreign court that is jurisdictionally competent in the eyes of the forum is prima facie entitled to recognition.[74] But what if a trustee should choose to appear in foreign proceedings? Can the trustee then deny that it is bound by the foreign ruling?

The importance of submission in the eyes of Jersey law prior to Amendment No 4 was succinctly stated in *Re the H Trust*:[75]

> The significant factor from the point of view of whether the trustee should submit to the jurisdiction of the overseas court is that it will remain a matter of discretion for the Court as to the course it should take in the light of the overseas order if the trustee has not submitted, whereas if the trustee has submitted, the overseas order is likely to be enforced without reconsideration of the merits.

The firewall provision in Article 9(4) of the Trusts (Jersey) Law, however, in common with most other firewalls, appears not to depend upon submission to a foreign court. This was recognized by the Jersey Court of Appeal in *Mubarak*,[76] where it observed that: 'By reason of art. 9(4) of the 1984 Law, this court cannot enforce a judgment of the Family Division varying or altering a Jersey trust under the 1973 Act, even where the trustees have submitted to the jurisdiction of the Family Division.'

The Grand Court in the Cayman Islands also stated in *Re B* that its firewall legislation did not turn on the question of submission by the trustees to a foreign court:

> An order of the Hong Kong court purporting to effect a variation of the trust, whether in matrimonial proceedings or otherwise, cannot be recognized by the Trustee. That is so even if the Trustee were to attorn to the jurisdiction of the Hong Kong Court.[77]

Of course, a trustee must still have regard to all relevant considerations, including the existence of foreign proceedings and judgments. Above all, it must act in the best interest of the beneficiaries. So, for instance, in *Re Arpettaz Settlement*,[78] the Royal Court of Jersey approved the trustee's decision to participate in English

[74] See *Dicey, Morris & Collins* (n 13) r 43.

[75] [2006] JRC 57, (2006) 9 ITELR 133 [16]. See also *Minwalla v Minwalla* [2005] JRC 99; *Re Fountain Trust* [2005] JLR 359; *Re the B Trust* (n 46); *Re the H Trust* [2007] JRC 187, [2007] JLR 569; and *Re IMK Family Trust* [2008] JCA 196, [2008] JLR 430.

[76] *Mubarak* (n 50) [76]. But see *Barclays Private Bank and Trust Ltd v Hsu* [2010] JRC 003A [18].

[77] *Re B* (n 32) [23]. See also *Re A Trust* [2016] 2 CILR 416. Cf *Promyshlenniy Bank v Lenux Group Ltd* (BVIHC (COM) 2020/0188, 28 June 2021), in which the BVI court (applying *House of Spring Gardens Ltd v Waite (No 2)* [1991] 1 QB 241) held that a trustee who chose not to submit to English proceedings had privity of interest with minor beneficiaries (who did so) in resisting a claim that the trusts were invalid so that it was bound by the judgment. The BVI court recognized that the trustee accordingly held on bare trust and granted consequential relief. The case did not, however, engage the BVI firewall legislation as it did not concern BVI trusts.

[78] [2020] JRC 161. See also *M & L Trust* [2003] JRC 002A.

proceedings notwithstanding the Jersey firewall. It noted that, while 'in most circumstances it is unlikely to be in the interests of a Jersey trust for the trustee to submit to the jurisdiction of an overseas court',[79] the position may be different where, as in that case,[80] the trust assets are overseas and otherwise at risk.[81]

Even so, in some cases, firewall legislation may potentially offer a trustee the opportunity to defend the trust and its assets in foreign proceedings; only then to deny that it is bound by the resulting judgment in its local jurisdiction.[82]

G. English Courts and Offshore Trusts

Firewall legislation is broadly premised on the principle that local offshore courts should exercise jurisdiction over local law trusts; and if foreign courts must do so, they should apply the law applicable to the trust. At least in the Channel Islands, even before the advent of firewall legislation, the chief source of consternation was the approach of the English courts in ancillary relief proceedings. For example, in Jersey, in *Re Rabaiotti*, the Deputy Bailiff stated that:[83]

> The court regards it as unlikely that an English court would so exceed the normal bounds of comity as to purport to vary a settlement governed by Jersey ... law administered in Jersey by Jersey trustees, and which had no connection with England save that some of the beneficiaries resided there.

After the introduction of Amendment No 4, the Bailiff said in a postscript in *Re the B Trust*:[84]

> It would, in our view, avoid sterile argument, and expense to the parties, if the English courts were, in cases involving a Jersey trust, having calculated their award on the basis of the totality of the assets available to the parties, to exercise judicial restraint and to refrain from invoking their jurisdiction under the Matrimonial Causes Act to vary the trust.

It is not that the English courts are oblivious to the issue. In *Mubarak v Mubarik*,[85] Holman J varied a Jersey trust in ancillary relief proceedings to allow a wife to

[79] ibid [29].
[80] See also *Re Poon* (n 61).
[81] The trustee would normally take a neutral approach in the foreign proceedings, unless there is nobody else available to defend a claim: *Alsop v Wilkinson* [1996] 1 WLR 1220; *VV* [2012] JRC 207.
[82] The effectiveness of this approach may, of course, depend on the location of the trust assets.
[83] [2000] JLR 173 [65]. See also *Fountain Trust* (n 75); *Re the H Trust* (n 75).
[84] *Re the B Trust* (n 46) [32].
[85] [2007] EWHC 220 (Fam), [2007] 2 FLR 364.

recover assets where the husband had, over many years, failed to pay sums due to her. Nonetheless, he considered the remarks of the Bailiff in *Re the B Trust* and said:[86]

> I myself am very respectful indeed of the sovereignty of the foreign state and of the jurisdiction of the foreign court. I hope I do exercise considerable 'judicial restraint', but [this] does not preclude that the English court may yet, in some appropriate case, exercise its variation of settlement power, even in relation to a Jersey trust; and that in such a case, the Jersey court will not be 'insouciant of the reasoned decisions' of this court.[87]

He said that he did 'deeply appreciate' that 'as a general rule it will be an exorbitant exercise of jurisdiction for this court to purport to vary the terms of a Jersey settlement'.[88] He went on, however, to find that there were exceptional facts justifying intervention in the present case.[89]

A fundamental difficulty, however, is that an English court with divorce jurisdiction will normally go on to deal with matters of ancillary relief.[90] As *Dicey, Morris & Collins*, Rule 99(1) states: 'English courts have jurisdiction to make an ancillary order for financial provision on or after granting a decree of divorce, nullity of marriage or judicial separation whenever they have jurisdiction in the main suit'.

Rule 99(9) then states that: 'If a court has jurisdiction to make an order under this Rule, it will normally apply English domestic law'.

Later, the commentary is more explicit.[91] 'It has never been doubted that the court, when making an order for financial provision under the Matrimonial Causes Act 1973 or the Domestic Proceedings and Magistrates' Courts Act 1978 or their predecessors, always applies its own law, irrespective of the domicile of the parties'. That principle was affirmed by the Supreme Court in *Granatino v Radmacher*.[92]

As to the specific power to vary a trust upon divorce in section 24(1)(c) of the Matrimonial Causes Act 1973, in *C v C*,[93] the Court of Appeal considered a trust governed by Jersey law containing an exclusive jurisdiction clause for the

[86] ibid [146]. See also *Charman v Charman* [2007] EWCA Civ 503, [2007] 1 FLR 1246 [58].

[87] See also *A v A* [2007] EWHC 99 (Fam), [2007] 2 FLR 467, in which Munby J declined to rule that a trust governed by English law, but with substantial connections with Jersey, was a sham. See further *D v D* [2009] EWHC 3062 (Fam), [2011] 2 FLR 29.

[88] *Mubarak* (n 85) [159].

[89] Mostyn J held in *JB v DB* [2020] EWHC 2301 (Fam), [2020] 3 FCR 723 [12]–[13] that it would normally be appropriate to exercise jurisdiction to vary a foreign law trust in respect of property in England. He anticipated that a foreign court would be likely to recognize such an order, but ruled that, even if it did not, the order should still be made. He referred to his earlier decision in *BJ v MJ (Financial Order: Overseas Trust)* [2011] EWHC 2708 (Fam), [2012] 1 FLR 667, which, in turn, considered the first instance ruling by the Royal Court of Jersey in *Mubarak* (n 48).

[90] See *Dicey, Morris & Collins* (n 13) r 99(1).

[91] ibid para 18-230.

[92] [2010] UKSC 42, [2011] 1 AC 534.

[93] [2004] EWCA Civ 1030, [2005] Fam 250.

courts of Jersey. It ruled that it had jurisdiction to vary the trust. Thorpe LJ cited *Nunneley v Nunneley*[94] for the proposition that English law applies to the variation of the trust and not the law applicable to the trust. The *Nunneley* case referred to the competence of an English court to vary a settlement governed by a foreign law, not to the applicable law.[95] But in *Forsyth v Forsyth*,[96] this had been interpreted as meaning that the court had competence to vary such a settlement and that the substantive grounds for doing so were contained in the forum's statutory provisions. The court held that it could vary a Scottish settlement upon divorce pursuant to the Matrimonial Causes Act 1859. Thorpe LJ commented in *C v C* that these cases ' have stood unquestioned for a century'[97] and continue to be good law. In *Granatino*, the majority referred with apparent approval to the decision in *C v C*.[98]

One might, however, pause to consider why the *lex fori* should have priority over the law applicable to the trust, even though the starting point under Article 8(2)(h) of the Hague Trusts Convention is that the applicable law of the trust governs 'the variation or termination of the trust'. Nevertheless, the proposition that section 24(1)(c) of the Matrimonial Causes Act 1973 is an English mandatory rule that leaves no room for the law applicable to the trust[99] is entrenched.

A broader question is *why* foreign law should be substantially overlooked in ancillary relief proceedings. In her dissenting judgment in *Granatino*, Lady Hale observed that: 'English family lawyers seem to have a horror of having to apply foreign law which must appear strange to European lawyers who are quite used to doing so'.[100]

It might be questioned whether, in the twenty-first century, there is something so unique about ancillary relief claims as to require the exclusion of foreign law.[101] In any event, in respect of trusts, the result is a direct clash of approaches with firewall legislation.

H. 'Auxiliary' Jurisdiction

If offshore courts cannot prevent courts elsewhere from exercising jurisdiction over trusts governed by their local law, is there another way of bridging the divide?

[94] (1890) 15 PD 186.
[95] ibid [27].
[96] [1891] P 363.
[97] *C* (n 93) [31].
[98] Albeit without needing to address it in detail: see ibid [103].
[99] As permitted by arts 15 and 16 of the Convention.
[100] *Granatino* (n 92) [181]. In a number of cases, the courts have had regard to the connections of the parties to a foreign jurisdiction and foreign law in determining how to exercise its discretion as part of the *lex fori*. See, for instance, *Dicey, Morris & Collins*, 5th Supplement to the 15th edn, para 28-005.
[101] Even if this requires legislative reform.

In the postscript in *Re the B Trust*, the Bailiff suggested that rather than English courts determining questions relating to Jersey law trusts:[102]

> Instead they could request this court to be auxiliary to them. Such an approach is adopted by courts exercising jurisdiction in relation to insolvency and in other areas of law too. It is true that such jurisdiction to seek assistance from a foreign court may usually have its basis in statute. Nonetheless we can see no reason why the trustee or one or more of the parties before the English court as the case might be, should not be directed to make the appropriate application to this court for assistance in the implementation of the English court's order. It appears to us that this would be a more seemly and appropriate approach to matters where the courts of two civilised and friendly countries have concurrent interests. It would furthermore be more likely to avoid the risk of the delivery of inconsistent judgments.

More recently, the Cayman courts have similarly signalled their willingness to act as auxiliary courts. In *HSBC International Trustee Ltd v Tan Poh Lee*, Kawaley J had 'no difficulty' in approving a declaration[103] that the Cayman courts: 'are willing to act as a court auxiliary to the court in Singapore . . . so as to ensure that [the relevant issues] are determined by the courts of the Cayman Islands'.[104]

The principle is that if a foreign court refrains on ruling on issues appertaining to an offshore trust, then the local court can deliver a binding ruling, applying its own law. The foreign court can (and must) then apply that ruling.

Even so, this so-called 'auxiliary' role may appear to foreign courts to be less like assistance and more about ensuring that firewall provisions are upheld overseas. There is little evidence to date that onshore courts will welcome this role, or see it as genuinely supportive, rather than as encroaching on their own jurisdiction and their ability to apply foreign law, as appropriate, in accordance with their own choice of law rules.

I. Conclusion

The Cayman firewall fundamentally challenged established private international thinking, in order to protect Cayman trusts from foreign laws and judgments. In doing so, it also laid down the gauntlet to other offshore jurisdictions. Much of what seemed radical, and perhaps even heretical, in 1987, now commands widespread acceptance in the offshore world. Even so, foreign proceedings cannot, in

[102] *Re the B Trust* (n 46) [32].
[103] In the event that a jurisdiction challenge in Singapore failed.
[104] *HSBC* (n 33) [32].

practice, be wholly ignored by trustees; and trust assets overseas still have to be protected.

At the same time, the broad jurisdiction of English courts in ancillary relief proceedings, and long-established application of the *lex fori*, lead to an obvious clash of cultures. With little sign of onshore courts changing their approach in response to firewall legislation, and ever-greater competition in the offshore world to provide market-leading protection, there is little sign that the divide will be bridged any time soon.

2
The Conceptual Economy of Private International Law

Horatia Muir Watt

An uncharacteristically discursive observation is to be found among the 'Preliminary Matters' in the great *Dicey, Morris & Collins*:

> It has not been easy for the conflict of laws to adapt itself to the changes in social and commercial life which the 20th century has witnessed. Many of its rules were first laid down in the 19th century and seem better suited to 19th century conditions than to those of the 20th century.[1]

This serves to emphasize the significance of nineteenth-century legal thought in the shaping of modern private international law.[2] It further highlights the persistence of this same conceptual framework today, even when the obvious private dimensions of contemporary globalization might have provided an ideal opportunity for the evolution of this branch of the law. Together, these features invite an epistemological inquiry into the reasons for which the conflict of laws remains somehow suspended in the past. In looking for an answer within what will be termed the conceptual economy of the discipline (to be defined below), this contribution proceeds from the more general conviction that the intellectual fabric of modern legal thought affects our perceptions of the world that surrounds us. Hence our failure to 'face Gaia',[3] and other blind spots in our confrontation with contemporary forms of crisis.[4] A further underlying intuition is that private international law might serve as a heuristic for understanding the inherent limitations affecting the 'modes of existence' of modern legal thought.[5]

In this respect, it may be useful to start with a broader epistemological conundrum. The entry point here is the fundamental importance of Roman legal thought

[1] Lord Collins (ed), *Dicey, Morris & Collins on the Conflict of Laws* (15th edn, Sweet & Maxwell 2012) para 1-018 ('Late Development in England').

[2] The terms 'private international law' and 'the conflict of laws' will be taken as synonymous for the purpose of this text (see *Dicey, Morris & Collins* (n 1) paras 1-088 and 1-089).

[3] Bruno Latour, *Facing Gaia* (Polity Press 2017).

[4] These include issues related to digital governmentality, migration, economic inequalities ...

[5] After Bruno Latour, *An Inquiry into Modes of Existence* (Harvard UP 2013).

Horatia Muir Watt, *The Conceptual Economy of Private International Law* In: *Essays in International Litigation for Lord Collins.* Edited by: Jonathan Harris and Campbell McLachlan, Oxford University Press. © Oxford University Press 2022.
DOI: 10.1093/oso/9780192867988.003.0003

for the formation of Western law. Two different strands of legal scholarship draw attention to the persistence of Roman conceptual frames, pointing, however, in analogous terms to an apparent paradox in relation to the nature of modern legal knowledge. Thus, in his investigation into the origins of legal modernity, the historian Aldo Schiavone observes that the academic study of Roman law has been beleaguered by the difficulty of dissociating its history from the 'essence' of law itself.[6] Albeit on a different register, Geoffrey Samuel comes to a similar conclusion when laying the foundations of a comparative theory of legal epistemology; he points out that modes of legal knowledge are often indistinguishable from their object, that is, from the very methods to which they apply.[7]

This peculiar feature of legality, contrasted respectively by these two scholars with other objects of historical research on the one hand, or with the social sciences on the other, is particularly acute in the case of the conflict of laws. To have knowledge of the latter is to study its particular methods; such a study is indistinguishable in turn from a specific historical account, which can easily be mistaken for the very essence of the methods themselves. There is, of course, at least in so many words, a conventional or short explanation for this feature: the conflict of laws is quintessentially methodological, meaning that it is entirely composed of modes of reasoning that remain distinct from the register of substantive legality. In other words, to coin an aphorism borrowed from the field of law and digital coding, 'method is law'.[8]

However, a more attentive survey of textbook representations of our discipline[9] shows up a further epistemological singularity. Its distinctive structure, divisions, and schemes of intelligibility are deeply entangled with a peculiar, dualistic, foundational story, which serves as it were as a filter for legal knowledge in the field. Such entanglement of narrative and substance is the key to the idiosyncrasy of the latter. In short, a remarkably widespread tale of the genesis of the conflict of laws has given an enduring shape to its architecture and correlative content. In this respect, as suggested above, the conflict of laws might serve as a learning device in respect of other areas of legal knowledge.

Thus, according to a first narrative, the 'story of origin'[10] of the discipline tells of the advent of enlightenment through methodology. The invention of a whole new way of approaching colliding norms took place (as the story goes) more or

[6] See Aldo Schiavone, *The Invention of Law in the West* (Harvard UP 2012), showing the importance of Roman law, far more widely, for Western metaphysics.

[7] Geoffrey Samuel, 'Taking Methods Seriously (Part One)' (2007) 2(1) J Comp L 1.

[8] The reference is of course to Lawrence Lessig's, 'Code Is Law: On Liberty in Cyberspace', *Harvard Magazine*, 2000.

[9] On what is meant by a 'legal discipline', see Frédéric Audren and Ségolène Barbou des Places, *Qu'est-ce qu'une discipline juridique?* (LGDJ Lextenso 2018).

[10] This term borrows from the vocabulary of genealogical analysis, as will be seen below. For a brilliant critical study of this narrative, see Pierre Gothot, 'Simples réflexions à propos de la saga du conflit des lois' in *Le droit international privé: esprit et méthodes, Mélanges en l'honneur de Paul Lagarde* (Dalloz 2005).

less simultaneously across the (Western) legal world. During the second half of the nineteenth century, the three founding fathers[11] of the modern discipline, issuing from different legal traditions and in various political contexts, all broke clean with the legal consciousness of the past, turning their backs on the archaic doctrines associated with medieval scholarship. Modernity was to have dawned at that (somewhat late[12]) point, with the advent of a novel theoretical framework that contrasted with the previous confusion of the dark ages of unscientific pragmatism and disorder.[13] It was in this favourable context that the conceptual axes of the discipline took shape, in the principled form of 'multilateralist' rules, to which a 'general theory' or a set of 'fundamental problems' would soon be adjoined.

That this paradigmatic moment had occurred in a historical context of intense political and ideological turmoil is invisible in the retrospective account.[14] However, this troubled background, together with increasingly visible geographical variations in cultures of political theory and jurisprudence in the early twentieth century, may explain why a second narrative exists, whereby the current configuration of the discipline is the result of a long and reiterative confrontation between opposing methodological poles. Thus, according to this further and somewhat contradictory tale, the rationalist revolution is but one stage within a longer pendulum-like evolution, swinging endlessly from the threshold of modernity to the contemporary era, and between the common law and civilian traditions, in a constant dialectical exchange. This second narrative of reiterative contest

[11] Joseph Story in the US, Carl von Savigny in continental Europe, Albert Venn Dicey in England. The great Italian scholar and statesman Pasquale Stanislao Mancini (1817–88) was highly influential at the time in the promotion of a universalist-personalist doctrine embedded in a 'principle of nationality' drawn from public international law, but was eclipsed by the others within the retrospective account of the foundation of the modern discipline; his doctrine was not in phase with the separation of the public and the private characteristic of the legal consciousness of the early twentieth century (as will be seen below).

[12] On the late twentieth-century emergence of the fully fledged modern sovereign, see Poul Kjaer, 'Review of Hauke Brunkhorst: Critical Theory of Legal Revolutions: Evolutionary Perspectives, London: Bloomsbury, 2014)' (2015) 42(2) JLS 312–18.

[13] This widespread representation of past chaos may be due very largely to Savigny's rejection of previous strands of legal humanism as unscientific and the return to the textual (or mathematical? see Schiavone (n 6) 38) purity pursued by Justinian, who had forbidden interpretation of the *Digest*. On this point, see Alberto-Horst Neidhart, The Transformation of European Private International Law: A Genealogy, PhD Dissertation (European University Institute 2018). Whatever the political reasons for wishing to represent the move as a return to the past, the account of an enlightened renaissance was reinforced by later scholarship, as will be seen below. It is noteworthy that, at the same time, public international law was also replacing eighteenth-century humanism and the law of nations by the regulation of State sovereign equality.

[14] On this context, see Duncan Kennedy, 'Three Globalizations of Law and Legal Thought: 1850–2000' in David Trubek and Alvaro Santos (eds), *The New Law and Economic Development. A Critical Appraisal* (CUP 2006): the mid-nineteenth century saw the ravages of the industrial State in England, the rise of liberal economy according to Adam Smith, and the emergence of Marxist critique. In Germany, in reaction to British political economy, there also emerged a mixture of Hegelian thought and Catholic social doctrine, accompanying an intense interest in Germany's national past. Three decades on, the rise of Bismarck and the proclamation of the unified German State in 1871 led to war with France. Cf Jean Pascal Chazal, 'Le propriétaire-souverain: archéologie d'une idole doctrinale' (2020) 4 Rev trim dr civil 1.

and reciprocal conquest is similarly reflected in a moving, binary architecture: dichotomies and divisions, encounters and reactions, principles and exceptions, all surface and dissolve only to assemble anew in one of a limited number of shapes.

The conceptual economy of private international law refers, then, to these complex sets of linkages and loops, axes and categories, nuts and bolts, all operating in the light of a dual foundational story. Various sets of intellectual resources will be deployed below in order to explore this form of disciplinary exceptionalism.[15] In a first section, the insights of a genealogical analysis will be called upon in order to highlight the underlying disparities, contradictions, and dispersions underlying the dualistic 'story of origin'. Questioning the historical accuracy of this received account and the purported consensus regarding the received settings of the discipline, such insights suggest that the function of such a story is largely ideological (see the section A, below). In a second section, the potential of comparative legal epistemology and deconstruction will be mobilized in respect of the equally widespread representation of the subsequent evolution of the conflict of laws, as oscillating between the two prongs of a methodological dichotomy. This will show the ways in which the latter is structurally 'nested', or shaped by the constant assembling, disassembling, and reassembling of conceptual opposites, embedded, in turn, within wider, interchangeable, intellectual pairs (see section B, below).

A. Genealogy: A Dual Story of Origin

Applied to the emergence of this (as of any) modern discipline, the genealogical perspective proposed here differs from a strictly historical account.[16] The latter, and most usual, approach focuses on the chronological appearance of the various ideas and doctrines, including those that embody a radical break with a previous paradigm. In the case of the conflict of laws, the focus of conventional histories is first on the multiple successive strains of 'statutism' deployed from the late Middle Ages in the shadow of Roman law in order to reconcile diverging local customs;[17]

[15] On exceptionalism of the conflict of laws, see Joel Paul, 'The Isolation of Private International law' (1988) 7 Wis Intl LJ 149; in respect of family law, Albert-Horst Neidhardt, *The Transformation of European Private International Law: A Genealogy of the Family Anomaly* (European University Institute 2018).

[16] On this distinction, see Akbar Rasulov, 'New Approaches to International Law: Images of a Genealogy' in José Maria Beneyto and David Kennedy (eds), *New Approaches to International Law: The European and the American Experiences* (TMC Asser-Springer 2012) 151–91. A genealogy is essentially Foucauldian. It rejects any account of the birth of a discipline as the intellectual brainchild of a 'founding father', in favour of that of a myriad of smaller mutations across various areas of thought and practice. In this respect, it resembles the idea of a Kuhnian paradigm change.

[17] The origins of the modern discipline can be traced to the growing perception that local customary divergences from Roman law created a dilemma, at least if Roman law was to be considered as universally authoritative. The responses varied according to the status accorded to Roman law, as reason, science, custom, sovereign will, etc, and the ways in which universalism combined, say, with humanism or scientificity.

then, on the methodological resequencing by the triad of founding fathers, accompanying the entry on stage of the modern State. As recalled above, this historical representation of the genesis of the modern discipline is served by the narrative of a revolutionary dawn of enlightenment across various cultures and contexts in the nineteenth century.

A genealogical analysis, on the other hand, aims to uncover the disparities, contradictions, and dispersion hidden beneath such a retrospective construction. Thus, it will question the significance of purported moments of revelation in which structures and ideas took form. Beneath the 'grand narrative', it is far more likely that there are a multitude of smaller moves, which are not necessarily coherent as between themselves nor indeed the result of a univocal direction of history. In other words, significance may be conferred in retrospect on a particular selection of past events, to the exclusion of others, in support of a particular ideological vision of the present. With this distinction in mind, the first paragraph below will explore the connection between the conventional story of an enlightened dawn in the conflict of laws and a certain representation of the discipline as a rationalist governance project. A second paragraph will examine some of the knots or incoherences that muddle this apparently smooth reconstitution, in order better to underscore the vision of the functions and values of private international law that it is designed to support.

The Dawn of Shared Enlightenment

Progressively, by the turn of the twentieth century, at the time of the great universalist project of comparative law and the concomitant emergence of public international law as distinct from the venerable *ius gentium*,[18] a 'convergence thesis'[19] developed around the methodological discovery of the founding fathers, retrospectively described as 'revolutionary'.[20] Remarkably, despite very different political contexts and intellectual frameworks, the genesis of the discipline unfolds along similar lines in civil and common law traditions. Emerging some time

[18] A change in terminology had occurred (following Jeremy Bentham, 'Principles of International Law' in John Bowring (ed), *The Works of Jeremy Bentham* (Edinburgh 1838–43) vol II), from the 'law of nations', as directly descended from the *ius gentium* (both evocative of natural law) to positive 'international law' (whence private and domestic institutions were banished).

[19] Private international law provides an excellent example of the widespread epistemological bias in favour of similarity or convergence, highlighted and critiqued by comparative legal scholarship (see eg Pierre Legrand, 'The Same and the Different' in Pierre Legrand and Roderick Munday (eds), *Comparative Legal Studies: Traditions and Transitions* (CUP 2003) 240–311.

[20] The dubbing of this reversal as a 'copernician revolution' seems to be attributable to Paul Neuhaus, 'Savigny und die Rechtsfindung aus der Natur der Sache' (1949/50) IS RabelsZ 364, 366. Schiavone (n 6) 38 proposes a very different analysis of Savigny's contribution to the knowledge of Roman law more generally as a form of minor historicism that rapidly became a conservative apology within a wider Romanist myth of a classical law.

after the (scholarly[21]) events in question, the purported paradigm change is affected, however, by a paradox: at the foundational moment, and for clearly political reasons, neither tradition claimed to be doing more than reordering existing practice.

Thus, as is widely known, Savigny's account signalled the revival of Roman law in the form of a Christian-Germanic heritage, mirroring the doctrine of historical jurisprudence; as such, it was a political project of German unification and an antidote to the Napoleonic appropriation of the civil law. The methodological novelty consisted in reinterpreting existing local practices through the schemes of intelligibility derived from Roman law, itself supposedly part of the *volksgeist*. From this perspective, then, the new learning was located within the wider context of a celebration of the Roman heritage, while emphasizing the historical continuity between the latter and the intellectual and cultural community of the Germanic peoples. In terms of content, Savigny's was an emphatically holistic approach, appealing to the systematic structure of Roman law (as restated in the seven preceding volumes of his great *Treatise*). The latter led to the identification of the natural 'seat' of a legal relationship—a largely metaphysical concept that would in turn determine the governing law without the risk of overlap or hiatus. Nature and science converged in ensuring a rational, non-conflictual distribution of 'legal relationships' among legal systems.[22]

A parallel account of a foundational moment, where the chaos of ancient statutist doctrines was replaced by a principled approach, is shared in the common law world. Thus, Story's (earlier) systematization of the discipline in his *Commentaries* of 1834 was written in the context of imminent conflict among the States of the Union over the status of fugitive slaves. Its influence was immediate and widespread.[23] Methodologically, the central feature of his doctrine was the concept of a foreign territorially vested right, to which courts could give effect without violating the jurisdictional and prescriptive monopoly of the local sovereign. The inspiration for this territorialist conception lay in the writings of European medieval scholars, notably of the protestant Dutch School, made available in Latin. He took up Huber's reference to the (much misunderstood) *comitas* of nations as the ground for the application of foreign laws;[24] the enforcement of foreign rights was

[21] On the peculiar feature of private international law as 'droit savant', see Bruno Oppetit, 'Le droit international privé, droit savant' (1992) 234 RdC 331.

[22] Savigny famously asserted that his proposed methodology for the solution of the conflict of laws (beginning with the location of the 'seat' of the legal relationship within Roman categories) consisted in reframing the central question posed by the statutists ('what is the scope of a given statute?'), but that the new and the old methodologies remained otherwise strictly equivalent.

[23] On this resounding and immediate success of Story's account, see Paul (n 15) 159.

[24] Comity, diversely understood, offers an explanation as to if, why, and the extent to which sovereign States are compelled to apply foreign laws (see Paul (n 15); Hessel Yntema, 'The Comity Doctrine' (1966) 65 Mich L Rev 9). Story saw comity as 'the most appropriate phrase to express the true foundation and extent of the obligation of the laws of one nation within the territories of another', Joseph Story, *Commentaries on the Conflict of Laws* (8th edn, Little Brown 1883) §38.

mandated by deference to foreign sovereign within whose jurisdiction such rights had vested.

In 1896, Dicey's comprehensive *Digest* followed suit[25] with resounding (and perennial) success.[26] Embracing the territoriality of laws and its corollary, vested rights, in the wake of Joseph Story, the *Digest* nevertheless excluded the recourse to *comitas* as the foundation and justification of the conflict of laws. As the current edition of *Dicey, Morris & Collins* observes, Dicey qualified the latter as 'a singular specimen of confusion of thought produced by the laxity of language'.[27] Courts, it is said, give effect to foreign laws and judgments for reasons of justice, not by courtesy to foreign sovereigns.[28] Much could probably be said at this point about the role of the late emergence of the conflict of laws in England[29] and the concomitance between enlightened dawn and consolidation of empire. The parameters of jurisdiction and domicile would continue to ensure the prevalence of English law and *mores* in personal and family matters involving colonial territories and subjects, but the promising new opportunities of international commerce led to an opening (at least, discursively) in respect of foreign law and judgments.

By the early twentieth century, and whatever the variations in theoretical grounding or technical approach, a consensus emerged on each side of the Atlantic over the appearance of a novel, 'multilateralist' methodology. A form of new international common sense prevailed, so that forerunning, dissident, or alternative accounts were eclipsed and forgotten. English-speaking authors did not hesitate to cite Savigny's *Treatise* in translation (Savigny having in turn referred to Story's *Commentaries*[30]) reflecting a first Western globalization of legal consciousness, here as in other fields.[31] The scene was set for the flourishing of a form of methodological universalism at the turn of the century,[32] as if, like its public international counterpart, the understanding of the discipline was, subject to minor concrete adjustments, shared throughout the (civilized[33]) world. According to this

[25] On nineteenth-century English conceptions as imbued with continental legal consciousness, see Neidhart (n 13) 198ff.

[26] Albert Venn Dicey, *A Digest of the Law of England with Reference to the Conflict of Laws* (Stevens & Sons 1896).

[27] See *Dicey, Morris & Collins* (n 1) para 1-008.

[28] As seen in the latter observation, the key to the enduring misunderstanding over the latter concept lies in the shifting terrain of the question of the appropriate theoretical foundation for the conflict of laws, oscillating between the relations between sovereigns (deference, courtesy, reciprocity) and the duties or office of the local courts when asked to acknowledge foreign legal norms.

[29] Flagged by *Dicey, Morris & Collins* (n 1) para 1-018.

[30] On this intellectual relationship, see Gerhard Kegel, 'Story and Savigny' (1989) 37(1) Am J Comp L 39–66.

[31] Kennedy (n 14); Duncan Kennedy, 'Towards an Historical Understanding of Legal Consciousness: The Case of Classical Legal Thought in America, 1850–1940' (1980) 3 Res L & Soc 3–24.

[32] Of which a positivist variety, through the foundation of the Hague Conference of Private international law in 1893.

[33] References to 'civilization' were frequent and can be found within the works of the founding fathers themselves. Such references bear an obvious relationship to colonial capitalist expansion: Ntina Tzouvala, *Capitalism as Civilisation: A History of International Law* (CUP 2020).

convergence thesis, while the content of legal traditions varied, agreement could nevertheless be found on a common recipe for coordination between laws, for the benefit of an increasingly mobile citizenship and thereafter for international trade and investment more generally.

In this respect, the triumph of 'multilateralism' would progressively be flagged, in retrospect, as synonymous with that of modernist values. The brave new vision of the conflict of laws had induced an epistemological shift, away from a focus on the (near literal) thrust of sovereign power embodied in national statutes towards the systematic, or conceptual, architecture of a legal system.[34] Crafted in the throes of ultimate collapse of the Holy Roman Empire, this reversal of perspective, from sovereign power to the metaphysics of legality, paved the way for a representation of the discipline as essentially apolitical. In turn, such a reversal enabled a framing of the allocatory function of the conflict of laws[35] as proceeding from an Archimedean point, external to the laws to which it applied. The new perspective prevailing within the discipline, now conceived as distinct from the public international ordering of inter-State relationships, was that of a coordinated legal realm beyond the reach of State politics; under the aegis of the 'private', it was sheltered at the same time both from parochial struggles encased in domestic public or regulatory law and from colonial appetites that found support in its public international counterpart.[36]

Such a representation was certainly in phase with the legal consciousness that prevailed at the time of this reconstruction.[37] The era that saw the dawn of a golden age of (Roman or common law) private legal values and modes of reasoning within a new, scientific, apolitical learning was that of classical legal thought in national (Western) domestic settings.[38] Meanwhile, an important shift occurred in the

[34] As explained by Ralf Michaels in respect of Savigny's methodology, this reversal had a double component. On the one hand, Savigny was able to assert an argumentative primacy of the legal relation over the applicable law. It was not the lawmaker who decides what situations he wants to cover, it is the situation which determines the appropriate lawmaker. This emphasized the private, apolitical character of the choice-of-law process as opposed to statutism, that had a political, public overtone (Ralf Michaels, 'Globalization and Law: Law Beyond the State' in Reza Banakar and Max Travers (eds), *Law and Social Theory* (Hart 2013) 289).

[35] The dualism statutism/multilateralism persisted in a further difference between definitions framed in public or private law terms, as distribution of prescriptive jurisdiction, or of relationships between various national legal orders. On the reasons for the persistence of such dichotomies, see section C, below.

[36] On the colonial division of the 'pie of Africa' consummated in 1870, see Martti Koskenniemi, *The Gentle Civilizer of Nations: The Rise and Fall of International Law 1870–1960* (CUP 2001). The turn to positivism at this point seems to have lifted any natural law break on colonial appetites (international law was a 'thin' commitment: see Steven Ratner, *The Thin Justice of International Law: A Moral Reckoning of the Law of Nations* (OUP 2015). For an alternative, eminently humanistic, and feminist account of the (much earlier) foundational moments, see: Maria Teresa Guerra Medici, 'The Mother of International Law: Christine de Pisan' (1999) 19(1) Parliam Estates Represent 15–22.

[37] See again Kennedy (n 14) and Neidhardt (n 15).

[38] And of its nascent global reach. See Schiavone (n 6) 57, observing the correlation between the various morphologies of power and the models of legal thought.

prevailing vision of the international legal world.[39] By the turn of the twentieth century, the public and private spheres had become radically disjoined.[40]

A shared perception of the conflict of laws emerged, then, as a mode of legal governance of private relationships that transcended politics. After this point, rising above local struggles and aloof from the violent geopolitical sphere, the private international legal order was subject to a distinct, depoliticized, legal regime.[41] Pursuing a resolute quest for 'international harmony', in the light of the universalist aspirations of the time, it proved remarkably weatherproof in respect of the later geopolitical events that were to shake the Western world. Indeed, the return of sovereignty concerns (and the rise of national identity) between the two world wars in the first half of the twentieth century served, paradoxically, to strengthen and extend geographically the sway of a methodological model that had been expressly designed, in Savigny's highly political project for the unification of Germany, to ensure the articulation of difference in a culturally and politically homogeneous legal setting. And, again curiously, far from weakening this project, the (largely colonial) discovery of radical legal difference[42] gave rise to the (remarkably intense) doctrinal production of 'general theories' of the conflict of laws in a quest to reintroduce harmony against all the odds of evident disunity in a rapidly expanding world.[43]

In such a context, the story of origin of modern private international law served to consolidate a double legacy. On the domestic front, it provided the foundations for a mantra of neutrality that reflected at one and the same time the spirit of classical private law that prevailed in the formative moments of the modern discipline, and the Archimedean standpoint from which it allocated transnational, legal disputes.[44] On the international plane, it developed a deliberate strategy of insulation from the inroads of geopolitics, international relations, or the claims of foreign States. It came thereby to apportion and distribute jurisdiction in ways that proved increasingly irrelevant to the wider world of global governance.

[39] At this point, modern, positive, 'international law' banished private and domestic institutions from its scope. Modern private international law emerged, as it were, from public international law's move to positivism.

[40] Thereafter, public law was local law (see Neidhardt (n 15)).

[41] As seen above, the representation of the legal order beyond the State as 'depoliticized' does not mean, of course, that the whole Savignian project did not pursue a clearly political agenda in the context of the move towards the unification of Germany.

[42] This was also to lead to the demise of the 1900 comparative legal project as the 'Word Fair of legal thought' (see Mireille Fournier, *Comparative Law Gets Entitled*, Thesis (University of Victoria 2018) 15, ch 2).

[43] See more below on the various components of such a theory that emerged progressively to deal with the difficulties raised by non-universalizable legal concepts.

[44] This mantra made it vulnerable to the onslaughts of legal realism in the US, while in continental Europe it prepared the terrain for a renewed coordination function of private international law within the EU.

Frictions within the Consensual Tale

The conventional representation of a common genesis, epistemology, and methodology is in many ways problematic. Unsurprisingly, on closer scrutiny, accounts of the further evolution and contemporary status of private international law differ quite radically among legal traditions. Diverse geopolitical strategies or philosophical influences obviously contribute to such disparity; each culture spins a specific yarn of its own defining moments, adheres to an idiosyncratic perception of its essential schemes, and produces its own categories, conceptual grammar, and vocabulary. Such accounts come with contrasted ideas as to the function of the conflict of laws. Some narratives tend to focus on the just apportionment between laws or on the pursuit of justice in private cross-border relationships, while concurrent versions are harnessed to the protection of sovereignty or the effective enforcement of regulatory policies. Correlatively, various asperities appear underneath the consensual tale of a common origin. In particular, three significant difficulties reveal the artificial facture of the story of a common enlightenment.

The first problem is that the representation of a shared new start glosses over a reciprocal cultural misreading. Although Savigny's *Treatise* was reminiscent at first glance of Story's systematic exposition of the field, the resemblance was largely superficial. In Story's *Commentaries*, as indeed in Dicey's *Digest*, vested rights had indeed morphed into apparently multilateralist rules.[45] However, when compared with the continental version, it appears that the search for the metaphorical location of the legal relationship,[46] by means of an analysis—both axiological and teleological—of legal categories, was missing.[47] The intellectual focus of the discipline was different in each version. Indeed, on Savigny's side, as recalled above, the new method was rooted in a comprehensive, holistic inquiry into the conceptual and functional structure of (Roman) civil law, whereas the common lawyers were more concerned with providing descriptive accuracy and a comprehensive account of existing judicial practice.[48] In other words, there was an epistemological gap between the two accounts, mirroring differences in common law and civilian understandings of legality in general.[49]

[45] For example: 'Generally speaking, the validity of a contract is to be decided by the law of the place, where it is made.' Commentaries §242. Movables were subject to the law of the owner's domicile (indeed, 'mobilia sequuntur personam' 'has so general a sanction among all civilized nations, that it may be treated as a part of the jus gentium', §380); and so on.

[46] On the fact that 'place' in Savigny's conceptual scheme was metaphysical, not geographical location, see Michaels (n 34).

[47] Bernard Audit, 'Le caractère fonctionnel de la règle de conflit (Sur la crise des conflits de lois)' (1984) 186 RdC 219.

[48] Ernest G Lorenzen, 'Story's Commentaries on the Conflict of Laws—One Hundred Years After' (1934–35) 48 Harv L Rev 15, noting that at the time of the Commentaries, upwards of 500 decisions by Anglo-American courts relating to this subject existed and called for a 'comprehensive exposition'.

[49] On these aspects of comparative legal epistemology, see Geoffrey Samuel 'Epistemology and Comparative haw: Contributions from the Sciences and Social Sciences' in Mark Van Hoecke (ed), *Epistemology and Methodology of Comparative Law* (Hart 2004) 35–77. The common lawyers attempted

That despite apparent similarities, the common law tradition had followed a distinct trajectory became very clear a century later, at the time of the methodological controversy between 'Savignian' multilateralism and American policy-based interests analysis.[50] It was apparent then that the functionalist 'revolution' addressed the territorialist legacy of the Dutch School of vested rights, and left the core of continental doctrine untouched. What had migrated to the protestant Anglo-American world was both a vision of law as the expression of sovereign power and the conviction that the (purportedly) descriptive principle of territoriality sufficed to ensure the ensuing allocation of legal relations among the several laws of nation-States. By contrast, in a sense, the Savignian ideal of the naturality of legal order was more largely compatible with the new 'functional' or policy-based analysis vectored by legal realism.[51] The 'interests' that called for consideration in each case were those that structured the legal categories (for instance, the need for permanence of personal relationships) and mandated the distribution of 'legal relationships' according to their nature (the need for permanence leads to retain domicile as a connecting factor).

A second problem is what was rapidly omitted or forgotten from Savigny's *opus*—that is, its careful circumscribing of the new methodology to the culturally close communities comprised within the remit of what was to become the new German State—the heritage of the Holy Roman Empire common to the Germanic peoples—or 'community of laws'.[52] In this respect, the project underlying the *Treatise of Roman Law* was clearly to put an end to the confusion deriving from imperial disintegration and the correlative decline of the idea of a higher natural order that could govern interactions between the subjects of different local laws. But Savigny's intellectual authority survived its transplantation into the world beyond the Germanic 'legal community', for which it had not been designed.[53] The resulting strand of legal thought—claiming Savignian pedigree—has been eloquently dubbed 'Savignism',[54] in order to denote its distance from the actual

to organize (restate) a selection of solutions into a list (a commentary à la Blackstone, or a Digest of rules). Even as the European account accentuated historical continuities within a community of Roman legal consciousness, contemporaneous Anglo-American scholars had tended in turn to emphasize the role of indigenous ingenuity in the rise of a new legal discipline.

[50] Audit (n 47).

[51] See the 'rich vein of legal writing led by Currie', cited in *Dicey, Morris & Collins* (n 1), para 35.005, fn 17.

[52] Remarkably, the concert of European nations at the Vienna Congress of 1815 comprised over forty Germanic entities.

[53] As Ralf Michaels (n 34) points out, it was the use of natural law, or at least the naturality of Roman categories, that paradoxically led to 'universalizing Savigny', even when it was clear that the commonality that conditioned the possibility of this alternative methodology was limited to the Christian-Roman legal tradition.

[54] On this term, see Gothot (n 10) 343. It designates, in particular, the French strain of multilateralism incarnated in Bartin's scholarship at the turn of the twentieth century.

content of the great Romanist's doctrine and to emphasize the paradox of its cultural influence beyond the confines of the fallen Roman Empire.

Various aporia surfaced at the core of the method when it was confronted with divergent understandings of the nature of the legal relationships to be allocated. Thus, apparently similar legal categories proved to have diverging purviews or to signify dissimilar values; the contrasting virtues of nationality and domicile as connecting factors were at the heart of a battle for the soul of personal status; a decision on the applicable law did not prevent sub-conflicts from appearing in unexpected, nested, ways. A series of devices designed to restore the initial harmony was put into place. Redubbed 'general theory', a set of remedial contrivances—characterization, *renvoi*, preliminary questions, adaptation, and substitution, the exception of public policy—occupied several decades of academic controversy and judicial inventiveness. Each one developed its own variants and internal oppositions, appealing in turn to sovereignty or private law concerns, or to international, as opposed to material or substantive, justice. Most strikingly, all these devices represented a creeping return of statutist reasoning, initially repressed or banished from the multilateralist model.[55]

Indeed, a third problem with the conventional account is the hybridity of each tradition. As we have just seen, despite quite virulent methodological debates over issues such as characterization (*lege fori* or *lege causae*?), *renvoi* (single, double or not at all?), or preliminary questions (the conflict rules of the forum or those of the law applicable to the main question?), concessions to the alternative, competing visions were regularly made, nevertheless, in either camp. Now, such mixity is accounted for, on each side, by a further shared story of ceaseless, confrontational exchange between the two traditions. At an undetermined point in the narrative, the common moment of past enlightenment fades away in favour of a dialectical progression, through movement and countermovement towards an indeterminate, future synthesis. The history of the discipline, it is (re)told, is one of perpetual oscillation between two methodologies, each standing in for its own vision of the world, or governance project. Today, they are seen to be merging, in some unspecified way.[56]

Thus, since the end of the nineteenth century, three major occurrences of a symmetrical shift can be identified. First, protestant Dutch statutist theories of vested

[55] Nowhere was this clearer as on the French scene. For instance, after JP Niboyet's spectacular 'conversion' to unilateralism in his reflection on *renvoi* (which he believed to be mandated by deference to the foreign sovereign's own definition of the scope of its laws: see his note under the *Birchall* case: Req, 10 mai 1939 (*Birchall*), S.42.1.73.), he was seen as a traitor within his own field. This had also been the destiny of Pillet, a previously influential author who had wanted to return to a principled form of statutism. On the resurgence of statutism within the various devices comprised within the 'general theory' of the conflict of laws, see Didier Boden, *L'ordre public: limite et condition de la tolérance: recherches sur le pluralisme juridique*, Doctoral dissertation (Paris I 2002).

[56] Evidence of this lies in the remarkable spread of (similar) codes: see Symeon Symeonides, *Codifying Choice of Law around the World: An International Comparative Analysis* (OUP 2014).

rights crossed the Atlantic in the nineteenth century to infuse early accounts of the conflict of laws in the common law tradition, before crystallizing into a set of universalist rules based on territory. Thereafter, they gave rise to a neo-statutist, policy-driven backlash, propelled by the rediscovery of the virtues of a form of interest analysis. Paradoxically, this shift served only to separate the American tradition from its territorialist beginnings and bring it closer in substance to the previously disqualified Roman-continental model. Of course, the concept of 'policy' analysis was undoubtedly repugnant to a consciousness steeped in (Roman) private law. However, in no time the multilateralist model sought, conversely, to accommodate a greater spectrum of collective and categorical interests, with the beginnings of a social and consumer-focused orientation in private international law.[57]

How then can this peculiar, characteristic dualism be accounted for?

B. Architecture: Nested Dichotomies

This narrative of binary opposition and dialectical evolution[58] seems to echo that of the struggle between two models of governance that have coexisted in constant tension within Western legal consciousness. On the one hand, one of global imperial rule, on the other, the fragile equilibrium between fragmented territory-based sovereignties. Earlier and indeed subsequent fractures appear in this alternative story as discrete episodes within a timeless dialectical exchange. The pendulum of history swings from statutism to conflictualism to neo-statutism and back, setting in motion a further dynamic between opposing conceptual binaries such as the territoriality or personality of laws; the individual or society; public law or private law; universalism or particularism. Every so often, in various contexts of geopolitical, domestic or intellectual transformation, a shift occurs, within an endless sequence of influence and decline of these two opposing models.

Seen from a continental European perspective, the Anglo-American model itself came to be identified with an archaic past made of concerns—territoriality, particularism, statutism, public law, sovereignty—that the Savignian model had left behind. It sinned, therefore, through a highly political understanding of the thrust of statutes as expressions of sovereign will, propitious to the expression of protestant, independentist, and essentially localist claims or ideals. But from the reverse standpoint of the common law tradition, a continental Roman law model

[57] Going further back in history, the career of the *ius commune* and its authority in determining the thrust of local statutes in medieval Europe had, similarly, followed a pattern of successive transformations and revivals. The emergence, decline, and rebirths of Roman law in the legal history of Europe took place under various distinct guises—of natural law or canon law; of canon law or civil law; of logic or ethics; of natural reason or scientism; as part of local *geist* or as a form of universalism; as an organic whole or a pragmatic collection of rules.

[58] An example of this narrative can be found in Oppetit (n 21).

steeped in universalist ideals and naturalist thought came in turn to embody an unsustainably romantic, pre-realist vision of the law. Its weakness, both epistemological and functional, lay in its appeal to the purported 'essence' of legal relationships and their metaphorical correlation to geographical space. These opposing perspectives embody a wider mismatch that is at the heart of much debate (evoked above) within comparative legal studies over the extent of contemporary convergence or divergence as between common law and civilian traditions. Here, however, the point is that the early-twentieth-century disciplinary common sense may be far more chaotic than meets the eye, pervaded by 'irritants'[59] that cannot be captured by the idea of a simple dialectic.

Indeed, as we have seen, the binary methodological account coexists with an intense hybridization of each of the opposite poles. While changes in legal thought and practice are presented as a circular recurrence of antagonistic pairs, such a perception fails to capture further continuous internal mutations on lower or even microscopic scales. In other words, recurring sets of conceptual pairs move within, as much as between, each legal tradition, so that any attempt to tell the story of one leads into elements that turn, reverse, and borrow from the other. The received account of this complex struggle is therefore both diachronic, because it tracks the internal changes within each model (statutism evolves into neo-statutism), and synchronic, as it opposes at any given time two distinct but contemporaneous approaches (statutism versus conflictualism).

Thus, the 'swing of the methodological pendulum' narrative has to concede that there is also, beyond a dynamic of exchange, a movement of constant recomposition of each pole. Other dynamics are at work and new combinations occur. These may involve equally dualistic theories of the relationship between law and State, the distinction between the public and the private, the respective importance of the individual or society, the opposing attraction of territoriality or personality of law as a guiding principle; all these divides are underwritten furthermore by differences in legal traditions or belief systems, and historical and geographical contexts. Whatever the specific features attributed at a given time to either loadstone, each provides the frame for an endless assemblage, disassemblage, and reassemblage of recurrent ideational binaries. The latter are composed of nature and reason, policy thinking and science, organic and atomistic visions of society, cosmopolitan ideals and protectionist concerns, and all combine in various ways with the two available methodologies, justifying alternately their respective fortune and decline.

There are two possible keys for understanding this peculiarly circular narrative of change. The first paragraph below will envisage these poles in terms of paradigm dichotomies specific to Western legal thought. The second will envisage them under a deconstructive analysis as examples of 'nesting'.

[59] As in Gunter Teubner, 'Legal Irritants: Good Faith in British Law or How Unifying Law Ends Up in New Differences' (1998) 61 Modern L Rev 11–32.

Paradigm Dichotomies

Thus, a first explanation points broadly to the epistemological structure of Western legal thought, shaped in turn by the remarkable ubiquity and protean nature of the Roman legal legacy. Such a legacy is, as we know, peculiarly salient in the conflict of laws. As seen through the history of Dicey's *Digest*, this also applies to the common law tradition, where Roman frameworks were imported into the conflict of laws through the teachings of the Dutch statutists. Such an analysis leads to the idea that the binary structure through which the history of private international law is told is emblematic of a much broader model of legal thought. Periodically reborn or rediscovered over the centuries in an extraordinary variety of forms and contexts, influential in the fields of philosophy, ethics, and logic, alternately identified with religion or science, reason or naked power, natural law or local cultural genius, travelling beyond the geographical remit of the vestiges of the Roman Empire, Roman legal thought continues to shape our own intellectual paradigms and schemes of intelligibility.

Indeed, the Roman division of persons and things, *res/persona*, still structures our (modern, Western) consciousness in ways that are, in Alain Pottage's terms, 'profoundly juridical'.[60] Moreover, this divide is considered in philosophy and anthropology as foundational in the further bifurcation of mind and body, nature and culture. The Italian philosopher Roberto Esposito claims that the codification by Roman law of persons, things, and actions (categories and distinctions that had hitherto been widely accepted in Roman societies) became the presupposition of all types of thought, including philosophy, politics, and economics. The dichotomies run deep, however. What is of interest here, in particular, is the complex patterns of imbricated binaries that stemmed from this initial categorization. While persons were irreconcilably separated from things, the person came to be divided in turn, between body and soul. This further separation led to a continual rearticulation of the primary divide. Hence Esposito's thesis that the body is neither a person nor a thing, but an impersonal category capable of dissolving the binary dichotomy of persons and things.[61]

Such endless bifurcation evokes a further strand of specifically epistemological exploration. Thus, in respect of modern legal thought in general, Geoffrey Samuel observes that the whole career of modern legality is dominated by the continuity, under different guises, of 'paradigm dichotomies'.[62] Suggesting that (Western) law's

[60] Alain Pottage, 'Introduction: The Fabrication of Persons and Things' in Alain Pottage and Martha Mundy (eds), *Law, Anthropology and the Constitution of the Social* (CUP 2004) 4. Similarly, building on Latour's account of Law II as a mode of existence, Kyle McGee points out that the dichotomies of person/thing and body/soul are ingrained in legal reasoning and explains 'why chains of reasoning take the shape they do': Kyle McGee, 'On Devices and Logics of Legal Sense: Toward Socio-technical Legal Analysis' in Kyle McGee (ed), *Latour and the Passage of Law* (Edinburgh UP 2015) 61.

[61] Roberto Esposito, *Person and Things: From the Body's Point of View* (Polity Press 2015).

[62] Samuel (n 49).

epistemological development 'remains trapped in the seventeenth and eighteenth centuries', he looks for the cause of the arrested development of our categories of legal knowledge in the prevalence of the authority paradigm. This is the paradigm that, as opposed to inquiry, prevails in theology, or belief systems that appeal to a higher being (God or Nature). In Western legal thought, the history of law is so much entangled with that of theology that the survival of an analogous proximity in modes of knowledge production is hardly surprising. Such a paradigm explains, and results from, the extraordinary career of Roman law throughout the modern history of legal (and metaphysical) thought.[63]

In what we would now identify as political thought, throughout the long career of the Roman Empire, the *Dominus Mundi* embodied the divine order of the world.[64] At the time of the renewal of Roman law during the European Middle Ages, the belief continued in the authority of Roman law as text, supported by either divine or naked political power. Remarkably, such belief survived still further through the revolutionary ontological upheaval that took place in sixteenth-century Europe. In a radical intellectual shift, the humanists destroyed the medieval faith in the embodied authority of Roman law as text. The result, however, was still not to abandon the authority paradigm, but to propel the modern reconstruction of a wholly rational system of private law, of which the authority derived from that point in its internal (natural) coherence and the possibility of using it as a basis for deductive or syllogistic reasoning.

Savigny's systemic account of Roman law subscribes to this particular paradigm orientation. This does not exclude, however, a series of internal inconsistencies. We know that the great Romanist scholar was also the founder of the historical school, emphasizing (against the claims of codification, against the influence of Napoleonic institutions, against the competing arguments of Mancini's universalist-personalist doctrine drawn from public international law) the genius of local folk legal culture. Yet, he claimed all the while a Roman law pedigree for Germanic law and a striking coincidence between the latter and natural reason. Thus, his work also reflects an organic, holistic vision of legality with a belief in the normative force of national consciousness. Unsurprisingly, then, several of his own premisses were actually shared by his adversaries, notably in the context of the famous controversy over the codification of German law.[65]

[63] Aldo Schiavone (n 6) similarly observes that law resembles religion because it seeks to harmonize the world of belief with that of truth. The characteristic of the authority paradigm is that it leaves no room for falsification (following Karl Popper, such falsifiability is the parameter for scientific theory). Legal knowledge, like religion, cannot be proved empirically to be true or false.

[64] The reference is to Pier Giuseppe Monateri, *Dominus Mundi: Political Sublime and the World Order* (Bloomsbury 2020).

[65] On the codification debate opposing Savigny and Thibault, see Mathias Reimann, 'The Historical School against Codification: Savigny, Carter and the Defeat of the New York Civil Code' (1989) 37 Am J Comp Law 95, 97–98.

A closer look shows that within the authority paradigm, many possible schemes of intelligibility may combine in various, possibly contradictory, ways. Indeed, beyond the paradigms (or within each one), as Samuel explains, on a 'lower' epistemological register, schemes of intelligibility also appear as binaries (holism/atomism, universalism/particularism, naturalism/positivism) that are also constantly reassembling, but not necessarily in sync. In turn, in respect of the history of legal methods, 'at a very broad level, it is largely a history of what might be called dialectical tensions or movements between competing poles or approaches'. With particular relevance for private international law, these different epistemological registers all play out dialectically, in various combinations, with still further pairs of methods.[66] For instance, these multiple dialectical tensions explain why posterity retained from Savigny's doctrine, selectively, both the naturality of the seat of legal relationships and the scientificity of the proposed approach. Moreover, each of the guises of Roman law suggested above and their combinations with various epistemological schemes affected the representation of the conflict of laws: early Bartolist descriptions of local law as subordinated to Roman law; Savigny's account of divergence within a community of law; Huber's doctrine of territorial independence nevertheless regulated by the *ius gentium*. None of these models abandoned the authority paradigm and, in the context of successive apparently opposing doctrines, many subscribed to a preference for a holistic, or naturalistic, or scientific, or axiomatic model that had at least partly inspired their predecessor.

Nesting

At this point, a second, further lens for the reading of this long history of private international law can usefully be borrowed from deconstruction theory and its heritage of structural (Saussurian) linguistics.[67] If, as we have just seen, the combinations of these multiple epistemological levels seem paradoxical or contradictory, it is because the apparently opposite conceptual pairs, both initial and subsequent, are 'nested'. This means that each of the terms of a conceptual opposition contains the other, or shares something with the other. In his account of 'nested oppositions', Jack Balkin defines the deconstructive move that this analysis implies, in the following terms:

[66] The latter intervene at a still lower level, and in similarly binary form. Gaius' Institutes, we are reminded (by Samuel (n 49)), were not only a set of ordered rules, but above all a way of viewing social reality. With particular relevance for private international law, the series of oppositions on different epistemological registers described above all play out dialectically, in various combinations, with still further pairs of methods. Here again, on the level of methods, one finds the dichotomy between empiricism and rationality, casuistic and axiomatic reasoning, argumentation and reasoning, or the axiomatic and the axiological, functionalism and actionalism, literalism and teleology, etc.

[67] See Jack M Balkin, 'Nested Oppositions' (1990) 99 Yale LJ 1669.

> Deconstruction makes a basic claim about the logic of similarity and difference: All conceptual oppositions can be reinterpreted as some form of nested opposition. This follows from the contextual and relational nature of conceptual oppositions. Because opposition depends upon context and relation, recontextualization of a conceptual opposition may reveal similarities where before we saw only differences, or historical or conceptual dependence where before we saw only differentiation.[68]

Thus, first of all, 'nesting' also explains the propensity of legal argument to unfold in successive stages in which each borrows or reincarnates elements of the other. As Balkin shows, not only does each term of the dichotomy tend to produce the meaning assigned to the other, but in the process of their interpretation, sub-doctrines arise that borrow directly from the opposing intellectual cluster. In other words, in a strange reversal, such sub-doctrines rely on the same arguments initially used to justify the opposite concept. The argument used to legitimize an initial choice between two values or principles reappears whenever we consider sub-rules that flesh out their meaning. The debate between these principles is replicated within each subsequent debate over the content of the initial principle. The conflict of laws provides some very good examples. Thus, a clear instance of this embedded dialectic is the heated contest between partisans and opponents of *renvoi* in the early part of the twentieth century. All the protagonists belonged to the majoritarian, multilateralist methodological camp (by definition, since *renvoi* was conceived, as a corrective device or a complement, as an appendix to multilateralist or 'Savignian' choice of law rules). Both sides appealed to the exigencies of sovereignty, and particularly the respect due to foreign sovereigns in their legislative capacity, in support of their position. The *coup de théâtre* took place when, as we have seen earlier, the most prominent and staunchest supporter of the doctrine, the French scholar JP Niboyet, turned statutist on the strength of his own argument, redeploying the sovereignty arguments in support of the very opposite methodology to the one that he had initially harboured.

But applied more broadly to representations of the history of the conflict of laws, nesting shows each of the conceptual binaries encountered above—holism, individualism; territoriality, functionalism; statutism, multilateralism; etc—to be dialectically imbricated. Highlighting patterns of moving succession and recomposition of doctrines, such an approach implies that conceptual opposites share,

[68] Two ideas are key in deconstructive reading. These are 'différance' and 'trace', as proposed by the French theorist Jacques Derrida, to describe the mutual dependence and differentiation of concepts within a text. An example of the first is an attempt to invert hierarchies of concepts, so as to show that, within the opposition between a dominant and a subordinate term, the dominant term bears some form of conceptual dependence to the subordinated one. On the other hand, 'trace' is 'the retention of absent concepts in our understanding of other concepts'. As Balkin observes: 'Because claims of similarity and difference can be reinterpreted as conceptual oppositions, it follows that claims of similarity and difference can also be reinterpreted as forms of nested opposition.'

to a variable degree according to context, a common ground. For instance, to return to the example of the many historical lives of Roman law in European legal thought, the apparent antinomy between nature and reason, or custom and code, universalism and particularism, humanism and scientificism, can be seen more as a constantly shifting exchange between ideational clusters. Nesting explains the constant interweaving, reversals and reappearances of the authority paradigm combined with various schemes of intelligibility. Such shifts have imprinted in turn a similar dialectic, and a paradoxical imbrication, on the categories and modes of reasoning present in private international law. Hence the various 'odd' polarizations[69] within the conflict of laws. Among these, the paradoxical support of the historical school for the scientificity of Roman law; later traces of statutism within multilateralist doctrines; or the presence of balancing in the most dogmatic of concepts.

C. Conclusion

The analysis proposed above suggests that what is important for understanding the way in which the field has evolved is neither to identify some inherent dynamic of legal change, nor indeed to subscribe to any specific chronological account, but rather to reflect upon the ideological function of myth in this particular context. It is in this respect, too, that the study of the conflict of laws might serve, heuristically, to draw out the features of legal modernity.

As seen above, two contradictory narratives relating to the modern genesis and subsequent evolution of the discipline coexist within the conflict of laws, each federating at a given time a series of purposes or principles (justice or sovereignty), schemes (scope or seat), objects (laws or legal relationships), categories (*territoires*, persons), etc. The first is the tale of a rationalist revolution in the second half of the nineteenth century, when statutism was replaced by multilateralism. The second is the account of an ongoing evolutionary dialectic and a cultural opposition between these two opposing models. Both accounts are frequently repeated, even though most students or scholars of the discipline would readily accept the historical inaccuracy or approximation of either or both. This is precisely a characteristic feature of myth (legal or otherwise).

Thus, the first tale rests upon various implicit assumptions about the nature of law and legal change that hark back to the era of classical legal thought and ground a peculiarly widespread and resilient belief in the political neutrality, or

[69] The semiotics of contemporary legal argument provides an interesting twist or prolongation to this. Observing the (odd) polarization of contemporary legal thought today within a hermeneutic of suspicion, Kennedy (n 14) observes 'a situation in which the surface of supposedly non-ideological argument suggests the very thing that it firmly denies'.

non-instrumentality, of the discipline as a whole. The second, structuring the foundations of the conflict of laws in binary terms, suggests moreover that knowledge of the field can be captured through a series of determinate concepts and their antonyms (systematicity, sovereignty, territoriality, individualism, functionalism, rights, etc).

At the heart of the conceptual economy of the discipline, axiological neutrality, and dichotomic architecture emerge in combination as the essential features of a rationalist project of governance through law. The question is now whether such a project can or should withstand contemporary epistemological, and indeed possibly ontological, change in the world.[70] In other words, can legal modernity, in private international law and elsewhere, survive the shock?

[70] As explained by Monateri (n 64), radical change of this nature took place with the advent of modernity. A similar point is made by William Ewald 'Comparative Jurisprudence(I): What Was it Like to Try a Rat?' (1995) 143 U Pa L Rev 1889, taking us back to the beginning of this contribution and the question of whether we can 'face Gaia' within the frames of modern legal thought.

3

The 2019 Hague Judgments Convention

A Step into the Future or a Restatement of the Present?

Fausto Pocar

The adoption, on 2 June 2019, by the Hague Conference on Private International Law of a Convention on the recognition and enforcement of foreign judgments in civil or commercial matters[1] ('Judgments Convention' or 'Convention') was hailed as an important event within the domain of international judicial cooperation. There were indeed grounds for such an enthusiastic welcome, although it is not the first time that an international multilateral instrument aiming at the mutual recognition and enforcement of judicial decisions sees the light in States' practice. Most of the previous multilateral conventions, however, did not have a general approach and dealt with specific areas and kinds of decisions[2] or were restricted to the participation of a geographically limited number of States.[3] The most successful multilateral instrument so far was the Brussels Convention of 26 September 1968, which was later absorbed into the EU's legislation and lost its initial character of an international convention,[4] while the only existing multilateral convention

[1] English and French text in HCCH, *Statute—Conventions—Protocols—Principles* (9th edn, HCCH 2020) 468. See also Francisco Garcimartín and Geneviève Saumier, *Convention of 2 July 2019 on the Recognition and Enforcement of Foreign Judgments in Civil or Commercial Matters, Explanatory Report by F Garcimartín and G Saumier* (HCCH 2020) 41 ('*Explanatory Report*').

[2] Without going here into a detailed mention of all these conventions, which would take us back to the 1905 Hague Convention on civil procedure which contained a provision on the enforcement of foreign decisions for payment of costs and expenses of proceedings, it is worth recalling here the recent Hague Convention on Choice of Court Agreements 30 June 2005 which concerns, inter alia, the recognition and enforcement of foreign judgments given by a court designated in an exclusive choice of court agreement (text in HCCH (n 1) 360).

[3] See eg the Inter-American Convention on Jurisdiction in the International Sphere for the Extraterritorial Validity of Foreign Judgments (signed 24 May 1984) OAS Treaty Series No 64.

[4] While the 1968 Brussels Convention became a piece of EU legislation through the adoption of Council Regulation (EC) No 44/2001 of 22 December 2000 on jurisdiction and the recognition and enforcement of judgments in civil and commercial matters [2001] OJ L12/1 and its subsequent modifications (cf in particular Regulation (EU) No 1215/2012 of the European Parliament and of the Council of 12 December 2012 on jurisdiction and recognition and enforcement of judgments in civil and commercial matters [2012] OJ L351/1 (recast Brussels 1 Regulations)), the parallel 1988 Lugano Convention concluded by the European Community with the EFTA Member States was revised on 30 October 2007 (Convention on jurisdiction and the recognition and enforcement of judgments in civil and commercial matters [2009] OJ L147/5), is in force between the EU and Iceland, Norway, and Switzerland, and is still open to a wider participation. A demand of accession to the revised Lugano Convention was recently submitted by the UK when leaving the EU—which implied that the Brussels I Regulation ceased to be in force for the UK—but the demand has not been accepted so far by the EU as required under the

Fausto Pocar, *The 2019 Hague Judgments Convention* In: *Essays in International Litigation for Lord Collins*.
Edited by: Jonathan Harris and Campbell McLachlan, Oxford University Press. © Oxford University Press 2022.
DOI: 10.1093/oso/9780192867988.003.0004

open to a more general participation has been the Hague Convention of 1 February 1971, which collected the misery of five ratifications and was never regarded as an effective tool for international cooperation.[5]

The initial feeling of excitement for the event seems, however, attenuated in some of the reports and commentaries that have been published in legal journals on the new Convention, and their titles appear to refer to its value in doubtful form, by mentioning shortcomings arising out of the Convention or making use of interrogation marks which offer the opportunity to open a discussion about its actual role.[6] This chapter—dedicated to Lord Lawrence Collins, an eminent jurist who, as a professor, a practising lawyer, and a Supreme Court judge offered a prodigious contribution to private international law, including on matters related to recognition and enforcement of foreign judgments, and who honoured me with his friendship for several decades—is aimed at taking part in such a discussion with a view to contributing to clarification of the role of the Convention within the framework of the efforts towards the creation of a global system governing the circulation of judgments worldwide.

Now, is the Judgments Convention an instrument which will remedy the initial failure of the earlier efforts of the Hague Conference on private international law to achieve an international legal discipline of the recognition and enforcement of foreign judgments? Will it be a useful tool for the business community who are carrying out international activities? Will it change and develop the current legal framework governing international private litigation or is it rather constituting a mere restatement of the present state of affairs?

A full answer to these and similar questions will obviously be possible only in light of the application of the Convention after its entry into force, provided that it reaches that stage and a number of ratifications, including by major actors in international economic and commercial relations, which may allow for it taking on a significant role in international litigation. However, the prospects of reasonable

Convention: see the European Commission Doc COM(2021) 222 final of 4 May 2021, taking the view that the EU should not give its consent to the accession of the UK to the Lugano Convention.

[5] Text in <www.hcch.net>, under 'Instruments'. The Convention was only ratified by Cyprus, the Netherlands, and Portugal, which later became EU members, as well as by Albania and Kuwait.

[6] See eg Andrea Bonomi and Cristina Mariottini, 'A Game Changer in International Litigation? Roadmap to the 2019 Hague Judgments Convention' (2018/19) 20 YB Priv Intl L 537; Louise Ellen Teitz, 'Another Hague Judgments Convention? Bucking the Past to Provide for the Future' (2019) 29 Duke J Comp Intl L 491; Peter Amt Nielsen, 'The Hague 2019 Judgments Convention: From Failure to Success?' (2020) 22 J Priv Intl L 205; Catherine Kessedjian, 'Comment on the Hague Convention of 2 July 2019 on the Recognition and Enforcement of Foreign Judgments in Civil and Commercial Matters. Is the Hague Convention of 2 July 2019 a Useful Tool for Companies Who Are Conducting International Activities?' (2020) 38 Netherlands J Priv Intl L 19; Sandrine Clavel and Fabienne Jault-Seseke, 'La Convention de La Haye du 2 juillet 2019 sur la reconnaissance et l'exécution des jugements étrangers en matière civile ou commerciale: que peut-on en attendre?' (2021) Travaux du comité français de droit international privé, Années 2018–20 183; Alejandra Blanquet-Angulo, 'Les zones d'ombre de la Convention de La Haye du 2 juillet 2019' (2021) 73 Revue internationale droit comparé 53.

success of the Convention in terms of ratifications are favourable, even if its success will be measured on the pace of the ratifications and only three States have so far signed and not yet ratified it.[7] The main decisive factor appears again to be, as it was with the 2005 Hague Convention on Choice of Court Agreements ('Choice of Court Convention'),[8] the attitude of the EU, which represents around one-third of the membership of the Hague Conference, and is itself a member of the Conference.

Although the Judgments Convention does not offer any advantage with respect to the relations between the EU Member States—which have between them a much stronger bond ensured by the regulations in force that, unlike international conventions, may be easily updated if necessary—the EU appears to have an important interest in joining the Convention. This interest seems to lie in the opportunity to take a central position in this field suitable to attract the ratification of countries which may contribute to increasing its commercial relationships. This is an interest that does not appear necessarily linked to the ratification by other traditional commercial partners of the EU, especially like the US, but rather driven by the opportunity to strengthen its relations with other areas of the world.

There seems to be a change in the format of the negotiations that led to the Judgments Convention as compared with those that characterized the initial project of a worldwide convention towards the end of the last century. While that project mainly relied on the prospect of enhancing judicial cooperation between Europe and the US, the Judgments Convention aims at a global cooperation regardless of any special relationship between the two sides of the Atlantic. In other terms the action of the EU, strengthened by its internal position on judicial matters and by its significant role in the Hague Conference, appears to be focused on the promotion of a global judicial network that does not particularly privilege any third country, but may rather constitute a uniform pattern of States' behaviour for governing international private litigation between its Member States and the rest of the world.[9] In the light of this perspective, it is not without significance that the EU has taken leadership in favouring the entry into force of the 2005 Choice of Court Convention by ratifying it before and regardless of whether and when the US will ratify it.[10] It

[7] Uruguay, Ukraine, and Israel.

[8] English and French Text in HCCH (n 1) 360.

[9] See also Hans van Loon, 'Towards a Global Hague Convention on the Recognition and Enforcement of Foreign Judgments in Civil and Commercial Matters' (2020) 38 Netherlands J Priv Intl L 8.

[10] See the Council Decision 2014/887/EU of 4 December 2014 on the approval, on behalf of the European Union, of the Hague Convention of 30 June 2005 on Choice of Court Agreements [2014] OJ L353/5. Following the deposit of the EU ratification, the Convention entered into force on 1 October 2015 for the EU Member States (except for Denmark on 1 September 2018) and Mexico, which had earlier ratified it. Subsequently the Convention entered into force for Singapore (1 October 2016) and Montenegro (1 August 2018). The US has signed, but not ratified the Convention. The UK was a party to the Convention as an EU Member State and continues to be a party after Brexit following its accession to the Convention on 28 September 2020.

is therefore most likely that the Judgments Convention will soon receive the EU ratification.[11]

Thus, the questions posed above are of current relevance for tracing the development of the legal framework with respect to the international cooperation on the circulation of judicial decisions in civil and commercial matters.

Assuming that the Judgments Convention will come into force within a short time and gather a reasonable number of ratifications, its suitability to contribute to change and develop positively the current international legal framework governing international litigation needs of course to be checked against its scope of application and the conditions and procedures that it envisages for ensuring the recognition and enforcement of foreign judgments.

As far as its scope of application is concerned, a plain reading of the text shows that it does not cover entirely civil and commercial matters, not only because it reiterates—like other similar legal instruments, including the Brussels I Regulation—that it does not extend to revenue, customs, or administrative matters[12] or to activities of armed forces and to law enforcement activities, including the activities of the personnel assigned to them in the exercise of their official duties.[13] These matters do not belong, except marginally, to the civil and commercial field. Nor is it surprising that the Convention's scope of application does not encompass the status and legal capacity of natural persons, family matters, wills and succession, and maintenance obligations, which are frequently excluded from international general conventions and rather find an appropriate discipline in specific legal instruments, as it is in particular the case with several Hague conventions.[14]

The exclusions from the scope of application of the Convention are more problematic when they concern typical commercial matters like the carriage of passengers and goods, a significant number of maritime claims, defamation, privacy, intellectual property, and anti-trust matters. All these exclusions substantially restrict and impact negatively on the role of a convention on judicial cooperation in a global context characterized by an increasing movement of persons and goods through frontiers, by a need to ensure an international protection of intellectual property rights, and by the exigency to guarantee a fair competition between corporations that operate on different markets simultaneously. The consideration that some of these matters are subject to a number of other important conventions and

[11] The opposite view that the EU would have no reason to ratify the Convention unless the US has also ratified it, has been expressed by Haimo Schack, 'Das neue Haager Anerkennungs- und Vollstreckungsübereinkommen' (2020) 40 IPrax 6.

[12] Convention, art 1(1).

[13] Convention, art 2(1)(n), (o).

[14] Cf especially the successful Convention on the International Recovery of Child Support and Other Forms of Family Maintenance concluded on 23 November 2007, or the Convention on Jurisdiction, Applicable Law, Recognition, Enforcement and Co-operation in respect of Parental Responsibility and Measures for the Protection of Children concluded on 19 October 1996, in HCCH (n 1) 384, 282.

that their exclusion prevents conflicts arising with those instruments[15] does not necessarily justify their exclusion. Nor is it a persuasive argument to that effect that these matters are also excluded from the Choice of Court Convention and that the Judgments Convention's scope of application should be harmonized with that instrument. Indeed, although the initial idea was to keep the new convention complementary to the previous one,[16] a full parallelism of their scopes of application has been later abandoned even with respect to the definition of the matters which have been excluded therefrom, including the above-mentioned areas of intellectual property and anti-trust.

As to intellectual property, the Judgments Convention excludes it in a broad sense and the exclusion covers both matters that are internationally recognized as intellectual property and other matters which benefit from equivalent protection under certain national laws.[17] The approach followed in providing for this broad exclusion is different from the approach that guided the negotiations concerning the Choice of Court Convention, which limits the exclusion to 'the validity of intellectual property rights other that copyright and related rights',[18] as well as to the 'infringement of intellectual property rights, except where infringement proceedings are brought for breach of a contract between the parties relating to such rights, or could have been brought for breach of that contract'.[19] It may be arguable whether this last exception is applicable also under the Judgments Convention, when proceedings are brought for breach of contract rather than specifically for infringement of intellectual property rights.[20] However, a consideration that the exception made in the Choice of Court Convention has not been reproduced in the text of the Judgments Convention with a view to restricting a broad interpretation of the exclusion of intellectual property may also lead to answer negatively to the applicability of this exception to the most recent Convention.

By contrast, with respect to anti-trust matters, the Judgments Convention provides for a narrower exclusion than the one in the Choice of Court Convention, which excludes 'anti-trust (competition) matters' altogether. Under the Judgments Convention, on the contrary, a foreign judgment is not excluded from being eligible for recognition or enforcement where it is based on certain types of anti-trust conduct—such as an anti-competitive agreement or concerted practice among actual or potential competitors to fix prices, make rigged bids, establish output restrictions or quotas, or divide markets by allocating customers, suppliers,

[15] Cf *Explanatory Report* (n 1) para 44.
[16] Cf also the third recital of the preamble of the Convention.
[17] See *Explanatory Report* (n 1) para 64, mentioning the case of traditional knowledge or cultural expressions and genetic resources.
[18] Choice of Court Convention, art 2(2)(n).
[19] Choice of Court Convention, art 2(2)(o).
[20] As suggested by the *Explanatory Report* (n 1) para 65, which notes that the scope of the exclusion depends on the characterization of the dispute, ie on whether the judgment to be recognized or enforced 'was mainly based on general contract law or on intellectual property law'.

territories, or lines of commerce—and where such conduct and its effects both occurred in the State of origin.

It has to be further mentioned that the Judgments Convention, unlike the Choice of Court Convention,[21] does not exclude from its scope of application situations where a natural person acts primarily for personal, family, or household purposes (a consumer), and those relating to contracts of employment, including collective agreements. Similarly, the exclusion of claims for personal injury brought by or on behalf of natural persons, as well as of tort or delict claims for damage to tangible property that do not arise from a contractual relationship,[22] is not reproduced in the new Convention. The reason for not reproducing these exclusions lies in the different approach that guided the drafting of the two conventions: while the Choice of Court Convention was meant to encompass only 'business to business' relationships, the ambition of the Judgments Convention is to address more generally a wider users' community, including consumers and other persons acting for personal or family purposes.

In light of the above, any justification of the variations in the scope of application of the Judgments Convention based on the parallelism with the Choice of Court Convention bears little weight. The reasons have rather mostly to be found in a different approach adopted by the negotiating delegations on various issues. This remark can refer both to the wider and to the narrower exclusions. It remains, in any event, that the exclusions set forth in the Judgments Convention are numerous and significant.

Coming now to the conditions set forth in the Judgments Convention for the recognition and enforcement of foreign judgments, namely the jurisdiction of the court of the State of origin and the grounds for refusal, the Convention contains a detailed, sometimes even too detailed, description of the jurisdictional connections that make a judgment eligible for recognition or enforcement. The long list of criteria for indirect jurisdiction—that the Convention refers to using the generic expression 'bases for recognition and enforcement'—is the outcome of difficult negotiations whereby the delegations tried to identify specific and precise connections which would not allow for a flexible interpretation and would rather reflect actual agreement of the Contracting States, with a view to favouring their ratification of the Convention.[23]

Without going into an exhaustive consideration of these criteria, it has to be recognized that this inclination for a detailed description of the indirect heads of jurisdiction is to a large extent a matter of drafting and does not mean that the Convention does not retain most of the usual criteria for indirect jurisdiction contained in international instruments as well as in domestic legislations on

21 Choice of Court Convention, art 2(1).
22 Choice of Court Convention, art 2(1)(j), (k).
23 Bonomi and Mariottini (n 6) 548.

recognition and enforcement of foreign judgments. So, for example, a judgment is eligible for recognition and enforcement on the basis, inter alia, of: habitual residence in the State of origin of the person against whom recognition or enforcement is sought;[24] the existence of a place of business of that person in the State of origin if the claim on which the judgment is based arose out of the activities of that business;[25] or the existence of a defendant's branch, agency, or other establishment without separate legal personality in the State of origin, provided that the claim on which the judgment is based arose out of the activities of that branch, agency, or establishment.[26]

The same applies to the defendant's consent as a ground of jurisdiction of the court of the State of origin, which is normally accepted as a head of indirect jurisdiction. The Convention retains both an express and an implicit acceptance of the jurisdiction based on a defence on the merits without challenging the jurisdiction of the court, provided that a challenge to jurisdiction could have been successful under the law of the State of origin. With respect to express acceptance of jurisdiction, however, the Convention only retains it when the defendant consented in the course of the proceedings in which the judgment was given or, prior to the proceedings, when it is contained in a non-exclusive choice of court agreement, as the possibility for the plaintiff to avail himself of an exclusive choice of court agreement only exists under the specific 2005 Convention.[27]

A more detailed, but more restrictive, description of usual criteria for jurisdiction also concerns contractual and non-contractual obligations. As to the first ones, the jurisdiction of the State of origin is based on the place in which performance of the obligation in question took place or should have taken place in accordance with the agreement of the parties or, failing such an agreement, with the law applicable to the contract. In this case, however, the provision finds a restriction if the activities of the defendant in relation to the transaction did not constitute a purposeful and substantial connection to that State.[28] While this restriction is aimed at ensuring a stronger connection with the State of origin, it leaves to the court seised for the recognition and enforcement a margin of appreciation which

[24] Convention, art 5(1)(a).

[25] Convention, art 5(1)(b).

[26] Convention, art 5(1)(d). In passing, it may be noted that the description of these heads of jurisdiction shows that the more general principle of 'doing business' with the meaning it has in the US, which caused a lively debate during the negotiations at the end of last century, has not been retained by the Convention as an indirect ground for jurisdiction of the court of the State of origin.

[27] Convention, art 5(1)(m). As the scope of application of the Judgments Convention and the Choice of Court Convention do not entirely overlap, this provision implies that an exclusive choice of court agreement is not available to the parties as a ground of indirect jurisdiction with respect to matters which fall within the Convention, but are excluded from the scope of application of the 2005 Convention.

[28] Convention, art 5(1)(n).

will not contribute to legal certainty.[29] A restrictive approach also characterizes the provision on jurisdiction over non-contractual obligations. On one hand, it limits the scope of such jurisdiction to obligations arising from death, physical injury, damage to or loss of tangible property; on the other hand, it only recognizes a special head of jurisdiction when the act or omission directly causing such harm occurred in the State of origin, irrespective of where that harm occurred.[30] This solution has the undeniable advantage to concentrate the jurisdiction only at one place when the damage occurs in a plurality of States,[31] but also the equally undeniable disadvantage of putting in an unfavourable position the person suffering the damage far away from the act or omission directly causing the damage, who will be obliged to seise a court abroad in order to obtain a judgment eligible for circulation under the Convention. This approach clearly collides with, and constitutes a restriction of, the approach taken by the European case law which allows the person suffering the damage to choose whether to bring an action before the court for the place of the act or omission or before the court for the place of the damage.[32]

Without further indulging in the consideration of these jurisdictional requirements for the recognition and enforcement of a foreign judgment and moving on to the grounds for refusal thereof, it is worth mentioning that such grounds do not substantially diverge from the usual ones, with special attention to the respect for the principle of due process in the State of origin[33] and to the need to avoid conflicts of decisions in the requested State.[34] The only new addition concerns, like in the Choice of Court Convention, the situation where the foreign judgment has been obtained by fraud,[35] a ground for refusal, however, which tends to overlap with public policy.[36]

Likewise, no special attention deserves the provisions that allow, for purposes of recognition or enforcement, the severability of a foreign judgment[37] and the refusal to recognize damages, including exemplary or punitive damages, that do not compensate a party for actual loss or harm suffered.[38] Nor is it worth spending too many words in respect of the procedures to be followed for recognition,

[29] On the doctrine of 'purposeful and substantial connection', see especially Ronald A Brand and Cristina M Mariottini, 'Note on the Concept of "Purposeful and Substantial Connection" in Article 5(1)(n)(ii) of the February 2017 Draft Convention', Prel Doc No 6 (September 2017).

[30] Convention, art 5(1)(j).

[31] Cf *Explanatory Report* (n 1) para 197.

[32] As of the judgment of the European Court of Justice, Case 21/76 *Handelskwekerij GJ Bier BV v Mines de Potasse d'Alsace SA* [1976] ECR 1735, and its subsequent developments.

[33] Convention, art 7(1)(a), (d).

[34] Convention, art 7(1)(e), (f).

[35] Convention, art 7(1)(b).

[36] Especially because, while in the Choice of Court Convention this ground for refusal is limited to fraud in connection with matters of procedure (see art 9(d)), this limitation is not reproduced in the Judgments Convention, thus allowing also for fraud in connection with matters of substance (see *Explanatory Report* (n 1) paras 255–57).

[37] Convention, art 9.

[38] Convention, art 10.

declaration of enforceability, or registration for enforcement, as well as for the enforcement of a foreign judgment. Like many similar instruments, the Convention refers to the general rule according to which these procedures are governed by the law of the requested State, with the sole addition that the requested State shall act expeditiously.[39]

More noticeable is rather the last provision of the chapter concerning recognition and enforcement, according to which the Convention 'does not prevent the recognition or enforcement of judgments under national law'.[40] It is noticeable because it is unprecedented in international instruments of this kind and it was largely supported in the negotiations notwithstanding that it does not add anything to the obligations entered by States becoming parties to the Convention and is merely of a descriptive and pedagogical nature. It is indeed obvious that any convention on foreign judgments, whose aim is to facilitate their recognition or enforcement, only sets forth obligations for the Contracting States to recognize and enforce such judgments when the convention so provides, but does not prevent them from recognizing and enforcing foreign judgments otherwise. In other terms, States parties are obliged to set aside national law only if that law opposes recognition or enforcement, but remain free to apply it to the extent that it is more favourable to giving effect to the foreign judgments within the scope of the Convention. From the standpoint of the legal system of a Contracting State, the special rules of the Convention may only impact on the applicability of the national general rules only as far as it is required by the State's duty to implement its international obligations.[41]

Although unnecessary, the reference to the applicability of a more favourable national law may attract the attention and may constitute an incentive to apply national law instead of the Convention, taking also into account that national law is well known by a domestic court. It is therefore foreseeable that domestic case law will frequently be inclined to apply national law especially in those European countries, where the recognition of a foreign judgment does not depend on any procedure and is subject to requirements which are definitely less strict than those described in the Convention,[42] but also in other countries where a consistent practice exists on the recognition of foreign judgments.[43]

[39] Convention, art 13(1).

[40] Convention, art 15, which contains this general statement subject only to art 6, providing that a judgment that ruled on rights *in rem* in immovable property shall be recognized and enforced if and only if the property is situated in the State of origin.

[41] Cf Gaetano Morelli, *Diritto processuale civile internazionale* (2nd edn, CEDAM 1954) 379; Fausto Pocar, *L'assistenza giudiziaria internazionale in materia civile* (CEDAM 1967) 96.

[42] This will be in particular the case of Italy, where the jurisdictional bases for the recognition of a foreign judgment reflect the Brussels I Regulation even when the defendant is not domiciled in the EU: see art 3(2) of the Law No 218 of 31 May 1995 and Fausto Pocar, 'Criteri di giurisdizione nei confronti di convenuti domiciliati in Stati non membri dell'Unione europea e urgenza di una riforma' in Cristina Campiglio (ed), *Un nuovo diritto internazionale privato* (CEDAM 2019) 3.

[43] See eg for the US: Ronald A Brand, *Recognition and Enforcement of Foreign Judgments*, Federal Judicial Center International Litigation Guide (April 2012).

It has been earlier observed that the restrictions to the scope of application of the Judgments Convention are numerous and significant. Additional limitations are, however, contained in the general clauses of the Convention, which provide for the availability of some declarations that the Contracting States can make to this effect. In particular, a State may declare that its courts may refuse to recognize or enforce a foreign judgment if the parties were resident in the requested State, and the relationship of the parties and all other elements relevant to the dispute, other than the location of the court of origin, were connected only with the requested State.[44] Even if this clause also existed in the Choice of Court Convention,[45] its reproduction in the Judgments Convention may unduly restrict the latter's application and cause additional problems, as the requested court may be obliged to review the merits of the dispute for the purpose of verifying all its elements, including the applicable law, thus contravening the general prohibition to review the merits of the foreign judgment.[46]

A second declaration directly impacts on the scope of application of the Convention. Should a State have a strong interest in not applying the Convention to a specific matter, that State may declare that it will not apply it to that matter.[47] Although the State making such a declaration is under the obligation to ensure that the declaration is no broader than necessary and that the matter excluded is clearly and precisely defined, the unilateral and merely discretionary nature of the decision permits any Contracting State to restrict as it wishes the scope of the Convention with respect to all the other States parties. The consequence is indeed that on that matter the Convention is not applicable in the State that made the declaration as well as in the States where the recognition or the enforcement of a judgment rendered in that State is sought.

A third declaration may concern the non-applicability of the Convention to the judgments arising from proceedings to which the State making the declaration, or a natural person acting for that State, is a party or a government agency of that State, or a natural person acting for such a government agency is a party, either as a defendant or as a claimant.[48] This declaration too impacts on the relationship between the State that makes the declaration and all the other States parties.

It is worth noticing that all these declarations may be made not only at the time of the signature, ratification, acceptance, approval, or accession to the Convention, but also at any time thereafter and may be modified or withdrawn at any time.[49] Consequently, the scope of application of the Convention may vary at any time.

[44] Convention, art 17.
[45] Choice of Court Convention, art 20.
[46] Convention, art 4(2).
[47] Convention, art 18.
[48] Convention, art 19.
[49] Convention, art 30, which also establishes the moment when any declaration takes effect or ceases to have effect.

There is, however, another declaration of any State party that may affect the applicability of the Convention, which should in principle consist of a network whereby all States parties are bound by bilateral relations between themselves. A Contracting State may indeed notify the depositary that the ratification, acceptance, approval, or accession of another State shall not have the effect of establishing relations between the two States pursuant to the Convention. Likewise, a State may notify the depositary that its ratification, acceptance, approval, or accession shall not have the effect of establishing relations with a Contracting State pursuant to the Convention.[50] As a consequence of these notifications, bilateral relations will not be established between the two States concerned. Thus, the Convention applies between two States parties only if none of them has notified the intention of excluding its application towards the other. This provision finds its origin in the so-called 'bilateralization' that characterized the 1971 Hague Convention,[51] according to which a decision rendered in a State party would not be recognized or enforced in another State party under the Convention, unless the two States parties had concluded a supplementary agreement to this effect.[52] Unlike that convention, the new Convention requires the intention of a State party to exclude a bilateral relation with another State party rather than a positive determination to accept a bilateral relation with another State party.

This new formulation of the bilateralization of the relationships between contracting States may better favour the participation in the Convention, because of the greater political and diplomatic difficulties that a Contracting State may face in taking an initiative to exclude relationships with another contracting State than in simply abstaining to conclude an agreement with that State, and should make the taking of such initiative less likely.[53] However, if one looks at this instrument of fragmentation of the Convention together with the other tools represented by the above-mentioned unilateral declarations, one cannot exclude the risk that the Convention may become an instrument allowing for a participation *à la carte*, where the uniformity of the law that should characterize a multilateral agreement is set aside, and possibly also the promotion of its uniform interpretation, notwithstanding that its need has been expressly affirmed.[54]

In light of the positive and the more problematic aspects of the Convention, as briefly described in this chapter, what conclusion can be drawn about the role that this new legal instrument may play in contributing to enhance the international circulation of judgments in civil and commercial matters and to establish a global

[50] Convention, art 29(2), (3).
[51] Cf above, n 3.
[52] Cf 1971 Hague Convention, arts 21–23.
[53] David Stewart, 'The Hague Conference Adopts a New Convention on the Recognition and Enforcement of Foreign Judgments in Civil and Commercial Matters' (2019) 113 AJIL 772; Cristina Mariottini, 'Establishment of Treaty Relations under the 2019 Hague Judgments Convention' (2019–20) 21 YB Priv Intl L 217.
[54] Convention, art 20.

network for judicial cooperation in this field? Can the Judgments Convention be regarded as a tool that constitutes a progress and a step into the future, or is it rather a simple restatement of existing laws and practices that does not add much to the current international instruments and domestic laws already available for providing the recognition and enforcement of foreign judicial decisions? These questions may not require a single answer and both alternative views may hit the mark.

On one hand, from the observation point of a European lawyer, it may appear that the Judgments Convention is no more than a restatement of the present state of the art, and even a prudent and partial restatement. The material scope of application of the Convention has a range of restrictions that go far beyond those provided in other international instruments and in the domestic legislation of many countries governing the recognition and enforcement of foreign civil and commercial decisions. The same applies to the restrictions on the required bases of indirect jurisdiction, also due to their detailed description which does not allow for a broad interpretation, as well as to the grounds for refusal, where the inconsistency of judgments may play an exceedingly significant role because of the lack of coordination rules governing *lis pendens* and connection of claims.[55] The mere fact that the drafters of the Convention felt it appropriate to remind the reader that the Convention is without prejudice to the application of national law shows that States that have a developed legislation on recognition and enforcement wanted to avoid that such legislation might be derogated from in a negative sense under the Convention. It could even be argued that the Convention represents a poor common denominator of current national laws and practices that govern the recognition and enforcement of judgment in civil and commercial matters.

On the other hand, however, looking at the Convention from the standpoint of other countries between which no international conventional rules have been agreed upon so far or from the perspective of the efforts towards a global agreement on judicial cooperation in this field, the role of the Convention may be assessed in a different light, as a first step which may bring together the entire international community through an instrument providing for basic cooperation on an important issue of general relevance, with a view to raising at a later stage the common denominator that it currently expresses through further more progressive agreements.

It has already been mentioned that the Convention is likely to come into force soon because of an inclination of the EU towards its ratification, as it happened with respect to the Choice of Court Convention. It has also been mentioned that

[55] It is noticeable that even the mentioned 1971 Hague Convention provided for a prudent form of coordination in the case of concurrent actions concerning States that concluded a bilateral supplementary agreement, by allowing a court to dismiss an action or to stay proceedings when an action between the same parties, based on the same facts and having the same purpose, are pending in another State and may result in a decision that the judicial authorities of that court would be obliged to recognize under the terms of the convention (see art 20).

its purpose is to attract as many countries as possible worldwide, and not only traditional commercial partners, to join in order to enhance exchanges and investments, which require a solid and credible judicial framework as a guarantee. Although the pace of ratifications of the Choice of Court Convention may not appear too encouraging to this effect, it may increase in the near future because that Convention and the Judgments Convention are now available as a package, although their complementarity presents some insufficiencies and gaps, especially with respect to their scope of application. This package may constitute an incentive to ratify both conventions at the same time. The more so if the working group that has been recently established at the Hague Conference will be able to increase the substance of the package by adding a third prong to the existing ones, including some basic rules on direct jurisdiction and specific rules on *lis pendens* and the coordination of connected claims that may enhance the value of the Judgments Convention by reducing the resort to parallel proceedings as a means of preventing the international circulation of judgments.

4

Warming Up for Climate Litigation around the World

Recent Court Cases from the Netherlands, Germany, and the United Kingdom

Hans van Loon

A. Introduction

This chapter in honour of our jubilarian, who made such a splendid career in the judiciary and now continues unabated as an international arbitrator, discusses some recent court cases on climate change from three neighbouring jurisdictions: the Netherlands, Germany, and the UK. In all three countries the highest courts handed down judgments (the *Urgenda* judgment, the *Bundes-Klimaschutzgesetz* judgment, and the *Heathrow* judgment) relating to the duties of States regarding greenhouse gas[1] emissions. These judgments were delivered against the background of, but also interacted with, evolving domestic normative frameworks increasingly influenced by the 2015 Paris Agreement. Meanwhile, two ongoing cases, one in the Netherlands (*MD v RDS*), and one in Germany (*Lliuya v RWE*) are testing the courts regarding the responsibility, accountability, and liability of companies regarding their contributions to the warming up of the Earth.

We first briefly compare the normative frameworks for the three countries. Second, we shortly present the cases, grouped by countries. Third, we offer some comparative remarks, first on the judgments involving governments, then on the cases against companies. Finally, we draw some conclusions.

[1] 'A greenhouse gas is any gas in the atmosphere which absorbs and re-emits heat, and thereby keeps the planet's atmosphere warmer than it otherwise would be ... Carbon dioxide is the most common greenhouse gas emitted by human activities, in terms of the quantity released and the total impact on global warming', 'Greenhouse Gases, CO2, CO2e, and Carbon: What Do All These Terms Mean?' (<ecometrica.com>), with further details. In this contribution, both terms are used interchangeably.

Hans van Loon, *Warming Up for Climate Litigation around the World* In: *Essays in International Litigation for Lord Collins*. Edited by: Jonathan Harris and Campbell McLachlan, Oxford University Press. © Oxford University Press 2022.
DOI: 10.1093/oso/9780192867988.003.0005

B. The Normative Framework

The International and European Level

The UN Framework Convention on Climate Change (UNFCCC) (1992) laid the groundwork for a global legal system aimed at stabilizing greenhouse gas concentrations 'at a level that would prevent dangerous anthropogenic (human induced) interference with the climate system'. Next, the Kyoto Protocol (1997) sought to control the main greenhouse gas emissions, based on the principle of common but differentiated responsibilities. Industrialized countries, the so-called Annex I countries, being the source of most past and current emissions, were expected by the year 2000 to reduce their emissions to 1990 levels.[2] In addition, the Paris Agreement (2015)[3] acknowledges that climate change represents 'an urgent and potentially irreversible threat to human societies and the planet'. According to its Article 2:

> This Agreement ... aims to strengthen the global response to the threat of climate change, in the context of sustainable development and efforts to eradicate poverty, including by: (a) Holding the increase in the global average temperature to well below 2°C above pre-industrial levels and pursuing efforts to limit the temperature increase to 1.5°C above pre-industrial levels, recognizing that this would significantly reduce the risks and impacts of climate change; ...
>
> This Agreement will be implemented to reflect equity and the principle of common but differentiated responsibilities and respective capabilities, in the light of different national circumstances.

And Article 3:

> As nationally determined contributions [NDC] to the global response to climate change, all Parties are to undertake and communicate ambitious efforts as defined in Articles ... with the view to achieving the purpose of this Agreement as set out in Article 2.

Despite the common objectives it defines, the Agreement does not impose an obligation on any State to adopt a binding domestic target to ensure that those objectives are met. The specific legal obligation imposed in that regard is to meet any NDC applicable to the State in question.

[2] The Protocol establishes three 'flexibility mechanisms' that can be used by Annex I Parties in meeting their emission limitation commitments: the International Emissions Trading, the Clean Development Mechanism and Joint Implementation. International Emissions Trading allows Annex I Parties to 'trade' their emissions.

[3] Paris Agreement (adopted 12 December 2015, entered into force 4 November 2016) 3156 UNTS 1.

To implement the UNFCCC and the Kyoto Protocol, the EU in 2004 adopted measures aimed at monitoring, reporting, and offering regular assessments of Union and Member States' greenhouse gas emissions.[4] The EU and its Member States, acting jointly, committed to a binding target of a net domestic reduction of 40 per cent in greenhouse gas emissions by 2030 compared to 1990. The Commission has proposed to raise this target, as part of the European Green Deal,[5] to at least 55 per cent compared to 1990 and climate neutrality by 2050.[6]

Key input to the global climate negotiations has been supplied by the Intergovernmental Panel on Climate Change (IPCC). Established by the UN in 1988, the IPCC provides regular scientific assessments on climate change, its implications and future risks, and puts forward mitigation and adaptation options.[7]

The National Level

Well before the Paris Agreement, the UK was the first major country to adopt legislation on climate change targets, the Climate Change Act 2008. Also in 2008 the UK adopted the Planning Act concerning the authorization of projects for the development of nationally significant infrastructure, such as airports. In contrast, for example, to the US, climate change is a subject on which political parties in the UK are largely in agreement.

The Climate Change Act established a new system for setting domestic targets as well as tracking progress, comprising: (i) a legal requirement to ensure that the net UK carbon budget account for the year 2050 is at least 80 per cent lower than the 1990 baseline level; (ii) an independent Committee on Climate Change (CCC) to advise the UK on targets and the policies needed to meet them, and to monitor progress both on mitigation and adaptation; and (iii) a system of five-yearly carbon budgets to be set by government ten to fifteen years in advance, based on advice from the CCC.

In 2019, the CCC recommended to further reduce greenhouse gas emissions from 80 per cent to 'net zero' by 2050. This advice was accepted under the Climate Change Act, after a short debate in Parliament.

[4] Decision No 280/2004/EC of the European Parliament and of the Council of 11 February 2004 concerning a mechanism for monitoring Community greenhouse gas emissions and for implementing the Kyoto Protocol [2004] OJ L49/1; replaced by Regulation (EU) No 525/2013 of the European Parliament and of the Council of 21 May 2013 on a mechanism for monitoring and reporting greenhouse gas emissions and for reporting other information at national and Union level relevant to climate change and repealing Decision No 280/2004/EC [2013] OJ L165/13.

[5] 'EU Climate Action and the European Green Deal | Climate Action', available at <europa.eu>.

[6] The EU Emissions Trading System, the Effort Sharing Regulation with Member States' emissions reduction targets and the Land use, land use change and forestry Regulation will be updated with a view to implement the proposed at least 55 per cent net greenhouse gas reduction target by 2030.

[7] The IPCC does not conduct its own research, but identifies where there is agreement in the scientific community on topics related to climate change, and where further research is needed.

The Netherlands and Germany have been slower in adopting climate change legislation. The Dutch Climate Act (*Klimaatwet*) was adopted in July 2019 and entered into force on 1 September 2019. This was four years after the courts had first ordered the government to take measures to reduce greenhouse gas emissions at the end of 2020 by at least 25 per cent compared to 1990. The *Klimaatwet* establishes a framework for policy development aimed at reducing greenhouse gas emissions in 2050 by 95 per cent compared to 1990. Ministers should strive to reduce such emissions in 2030 by 49 per cent and ensure a 100 per cent carbon dioxide neutral electricity production by 2050. The government must adopt a Climate Plan, to be reviewed every five years. Every two years a report is made on the practical implementation of the Plan. The Council of State advises on the Plan and the progress report. In addition, an annual scientific report is submitted to Parliament by the national Planning Bureau for the Environment.

Germany adopted its Federal Climate Act (*Bundes-Klimaschutzgesetz*)[8] on 12 December 2019, and this entered into force on 19 December 2019. The basis of the Act is the 2°C to 1.5°C limit of the Paris Agreement, as well as Germany's commitment to pursue greenhouse gas neutrality by 2050. The Act sets an overall target for the reduction of greenhouse gas emissions by 2030 of at least 55 per cent, as well as annual allowable emission amounts per sector: energy, industry, transport, buildings, agriculture, waste, and others. The Federal Environment Agency (*Umweltbundesamt*) compiles the annual data on greenhouse gas emissions. A Council of Experts on Climate Change examines the emissions data of the Federal Environment Agency and presents the government and Parliament with an assessment of the published data.

Provisions applicable beyond 2030 were originally not contained in the Act. As we shall see, the German Constitutional Court ruled that this lack of provision for the reduction of greenhouse gas emissions from 2031 onwards was unconstitutional, and this has led the government to propose amendments to the Act.

C. The Judgments

Introduction

We start with the Dutch *Urgenda* case, a civil lawsuit, which began with a groundbreaking order of the Hague District Court in 2015, confirmed by the Hague Court of Appeal in 2018, and upheld by the Dutch Supreme Court on 20 December 2019. The courts ordered the Dutch Government to do more to reduce the greenhouse gas emissions from Dutch territory. *Urgenda* formed the inspiration for the civil

[8] 2019 Federal Climate Act (*Bundes-Klimaschutzgesetz*) (Germany).

lawsuit against a private company, *Milieudefensie and others v RDS*, again before the Hague District Court. This court handed down its judgment on 26 May 2021, ordering the company to further limit future carbon dioxide emissions into the atmosphere caused by the business of the Shell group.

Next, we move on to Germany, where on 24 March 2021 the German Constitutional Court gave a landmark order on the constitutionality of the Federal Climate Act. Earlier on, in 2015, in a civil lawsuit, a Peruvian farmer had sued the large German energy producer RWE before the German Regional Court in Essen. While that court rejected the claim, on appeal the Higher Regional Court in Hamm in 2017 declared the claim admissible, and issued an order for the hearing of evidence.

Finally, we turn to the UK for the *Heathrow* case, the outcome of which is no doubt of particular personal interest to the Collins family since it concerns the conditions for a possible future grant of development consent for the construction of a third runway at Heathrow Airport. In this administrative case, the Court of Appeal on 27 February 2020 ruled the expansion plans for Heathrow airport unlawful because the UK Government had failed to take into account its commitments under the Paris Agreement. While the government accepted the judgment, the owner company of Heathrow airport appealed, and on 16 December 2020 the judgment was overturned by the UK Supreme Court.

The Dutch Cases

Urgenda v the State of the Netherlands

This civil lawsuit started in 2013 when the NGO Urgenda, a Dutch foundation, asked the court to order the government to limit the volume of Dutch greenhouse gas emissions such that at the end of 2020 this volume would be reduced by 40 per cent, or at least 25 per cent, in comparison to 1990.[9] The case concerned the narrow question of whether Dutch emissions must be reduced by at least 25 per cent in 2020 compared to 1990, rather than by 14 to 17 per cent, which the government claimed was sufficient to ultimately reach the 2°C target.[10]

The Hague District Court's judgment of 24 June 2015[11] had the effect of a clarion call in the run up to the Paris Climate Change Treaty negotiations. It broke new

[9] For a more detailed discussion of the Dutch cases, see my 'Strategic Climate Litigation in the Dutch Courts: A Source of Inspiration for NGO's Elsewhere?' (2020) 4 *Acta Juridica Universitatis Carolinae* 69–84, <https://karolinum.cz/data/clanek/8615/Iurid_66_4_0069.pdf> accessed 18 May 2021. Note that the judgment was rendered before the Paris Agreement which set the target of 'pursuing efforts to limit the temperature increase to 1.5°C above pre-industrial levels'.

[10] In the appeal stage, due to a new calculation method more in line with IPCC methodology, the aimed percentage for the State's greenhouse gas reduction for 2020 was adjusted to 23 per cent with a margin of uncertainty of 19 to 27 per cent, still considered unacceptable by the Court of Appeal.

[11] *Urgenda v Netherlands (Ministry of Infrastructure and the Environment)* Rechtbank Den Haag, ECLI:NL:RBDHA:2015:7145; English tr ECLI:NL:RBDHA:2015:7196.

ground in several respects. First, the District Court held that the NGO Urgenda could act in the interest not only of the current Dutch population, but also of persons outside the Netherlands and of future generations. Second, the court found that the State was acting unlawfully towards Urgenda for its failure to observe its duty of care ensuing from the open norm of 'unwritten law pertaining to proper social conduct' of Dutch tort law.[12] Third, the court held that both the State's duty of care to avoid dangerous impairment of the living climate and its margin of discretion were informed by the global and European normative framework concerning climate change binding upon the Netherlands. Fourth, the court found that the causal link between emissions from Dutch territory and climate change, including its effects on the Dutch living climate, was sufficiently established. That the current Dutch greenhouse gas emissions were limited on a global scale did not alter the fact that they contribute to climate change. Therefore, the government had an obligation to take precautionary measures. The court concluded that the State's duty of care required immediate additional mitigation action to ensure that by 2020 the Dutch greenhouse gas emission level was reduced by 25 to 40 per cent. Given the State's margin of discretion, the reduction order was limited to 25 per cent only.

The Court of Appeal confirmed the District Court's judgment,[13] but took a different course both regarding the standing of Urgenda and the legal basis for the reduction order. The District Court had found that Urgenda was barred by Article 34 of the European Convention on Human Rights and Fundamental Freedoms (ECHR), and the case law of the European Court of Human Rights (ECtHR) to claim it was itself a victim of a violation of Articles 2 and 8. By contrast, the Court of Appeal held that, regarding access to the Dutch courts, Dutch law[14] was conclusive, and Urgenda's claim was admissible. This shift of focus regarding the *standing* of Urgenda paved the way for a shift in the *legal basis* for the order: the State was failing to fulfil its duty of care pursuant to the positive obligations flowing from Articles 2 and 8 of the ECHR.

The Supreme Court (the *Hoge Raad*)[15] followed the Court of Appeal. It held that Urgenda had the right to act before the Dutch courts on behalf of Dutch residents

[12] Art 162 of book 6 of the Dutch Civil Code defines a 'tortious act' as follows:

1. A person who commits an unlawful act toward another which can be imputed to him, must repair the damage which the other person suffers as a consequence thereof.
2. Except where there is a ground of justification, the following acts are deemed to be unlawful: the violation of a right, an act or omission violating a statutory duty or a rule of unwritten law pertaining to proper social conduct.
3. An unlawful act can be imputed to its author if it results from his fault or from a cause for which he is answerable according to law or common opinion.
   Translations from Peter Haanappel and Ejan Mackaay (eds), *Netherlands Civil Code*, Bk 6 (Kluwer 1990).

[13] *Netherlands (Ministry of Infrastructure and the Environment) v Urgenda* Gerechtshof Den Haag, ECLI:NL:GHDHA:2018:2591; English tr ECLI:NL:GHDHA:2018:2610.

[14] Dutch Civil Code, art 3:305a.

[15] *Netherlands (Ministry of Economic Affairs and Climate Policy) v Urgenda* Hoge Raad, ECLI:NL:HR:2019:2006; English tr ECLI:NL:HR:2019:2007. See Jaap Spier, 'The 'Strongest' Climate

who are in fact such victims, and, like the Court of Appeal, based the government's due care obligation not on Dutch tort law, but on the ECHR. The *Hoge Raad* decided that the 25 to 40 per cent target applied to each Annex I country individually, irrespective of EU arrangements.

Milieudefensie and others v RDS

The Hague District Court's judgment of 26 May 2021[16] in the dispute between the NGO Milieudefensie and others and the multinational Shell company (*MD v RDS*) has attracted wide interest and even caused commotion. The court found inspiration in, but went far beyond, *Urgenda*: first, because the defendant was a private company, operating in a global market, not a State with jurisdiction over a specific territory; second, because the issue was not about current unlawful behaviour as in *Urgenda*, but about possible future unlawful conduct; third, because RDS, as a private company, was not a party to the UNFCCC, the Kyoto Protocol, the Paris Agreement, the ECHR, or any of the other treaties the court referred to in its judgment; and, fourth, because the 45 per cent reduction target by 2030 defined by the IPCC formally applies to States, not to companies.

The court rejected RDS's standpoint that the energy transition required to achieve the goals of the Paris Agreement demands a concerted effort of society as whole, and that the solution should be provided not by a court, but by the legislator and executive. The court, similar to the District Court in *Urgenda*, based RDS's duty of care on the open norm pertaining to proper social conduct of Dutch tort law. It considered fourteen factors to give content to this open norm, concluded that RDS was not at present violating its due care obligations, but to avoid this happening in the future RDS should be ordered to further reduce its emissions. RDS has lodged an appeal against the judgment.

The German Cases

The constitutional challenge of the Bundes-Klimaschutzgesetz (Federal Climate Act)

In its judgment of 24 March 2021,[17] the Constitutional Court (*Bundesverfassungsgericht, BverfG*) ruled that in so far as the Federal Climate Act prescribed

Ruling Yet: The Dutch Supreme Court's Urgenda Judgment' (2020) 67 Netherlands Intl L Rev 319–91; and Chris W Backes and Gerrit A van der Veen, 'Urgenda: the Final Judgment of the Dutch Supreme Court' (2020) 17 J Eur Environ Plan L 307–21.

[16] *Milieudefensie v Royal Dutch Shell PLC* Rechtbank Den Haag, ECLI:NL:RBDHA:2021:5337; English tr ECLI:NL:RBDHA:2021:5339.

[17] *Bundes-Klimaschutzgesetz (Climate Protection Act Case)*, Order of the First Senate, Bundesverfassungsgericht, 24 March 2021, ECLI:DE:BverfG:2021, 1 BvR 2656/18, For an English summary see Federal Constitutional Court (*Bundesverfassungsgericht*), 'Constitutional complaints against the Federal Climate Change Act partially successful' (Press release No 31/2021, 29 April 2021) <www.

a reduction of greenhouse gas emissions by at least 55 per cent by 2030 relative to 1990 levels and sets out the reduction pathways applicable during this period by means of sectoral annual emission amounts, the legislator had not:

> violated its constitutional duty to protect the complainants from the risks of climate change or failed to satisfy the obligation arising from Article 20a of the Basic Law[18] ... to take climate action. However, the challenged provisions do violate the freedoms of the complainants, some of whom are still very young. The provisions irreversibly offload major emission reduction burdens onto periods after 2030.[19]

The court thus held back from criticising the 55 per cent reduction by 2030 target, but did censure the lack of sufficient specifications for further emission reductions after 2030. In order to safeguard the fundamental freedoms to future generations also, the legislator should take more detailed precautionary steps. The government reacted promptly, and on 12 May 2021 proposed a revised Act.[20] The revised Act defines for the years 2031 to 2040 cross-sector annual reduction targets and provides that the government must present in 2032 at the latest a legislative proposal in order to legally establish the further annual reduction targets up to net greenhouse gas neutrality by not 2050, but 2045, and in addition raises the reduction targets (65 per cent by 2030 and 100 per cent by 2045).

Saúl Lliuya v RWE

In 2015, the Peruvian farmer Saúl Luciano Lliuya, with the support of the NGO Germanwatch, filed a civil lawsuit, based on Article 1004 of the German Civil Code,[21] in the District Court of Essen against the German energy company RWE. Lliuya claimed compensation for the safety measures he had taken to reduce the risk of flooding of the lake above his village Huaraz in the Andes, fueled by the retreat of a glacier as a result of climate change. He based the amount claimed

bundesverfassungsgericht.de/SharedDocs/Pressemitteilungen/EN/2021/bvg21-031.html> accessed 16 May 2022.

[18] Basic Law, art 20a [Protection of the natural bases of life]:

(1) Every person shall have the right to free development of his personality insofar as he does not violate the rights of others or offend against the constitutional order or the moral law.
(2) Every person shall have the right to life and physical integrity. Freedom of the person shall be inviolable. These rights may be interfered with only pursuant to a law. Mindful also of its responsibility toward future generations, the state shall protect the natural bases of life by legislation and, in accordance with law and justice, by executive and judicial action, all within the framework of the constitutional order.

[19] See Summary (n 17) [2].

[20] Climate Change Act—climate neutrality by 2045, available at <bundesregierung.de> accessed 4 April 2022.

[21] 'Article 1004(1) [Claim for removal and injunction]: If the ownership is interfered with by means other than removal or retention of possession, the owner may require the disturber to remove the interference. If further interferences are to be feared, the owner may seek a prohibitory injunction.'

of €17,000 on the pro rata causal contribution of RWE's historical greenhouse gas emissions to global greenhouse gas emissions, approximately 0.5 per cent. Contrary to the Dutch cases, the plaintiff in this case did not seek injunctive relief, which requires a relatively low degree of proof of causality, but damages. Therefore, the causal link between RWE's greenhouse gas emissions and the risk for Lliuyas's property became the key question in this case.

The District Court ruled that it was not possible to prove a causal link between greenhouse gas emissions of single emitters and specific climate change impacts. In appeal, Lliuya successfully argued that there was a scientifically provable causal chain between RWE's emissions and the increasing danger to his property being exposed to a possible outburst flood caused by a glacial ice avalanche. The Higher Regional Court of Appeal of Hamm accepted that a private company is in principle responsible for its share in causing climate change. The court ordered the taking of evidence on three questions: (i) Is there indeed an acute threat to Lliuya's property by a glacier outburst flood? (ii) Do RWE's historical emissions amount to 0.5 per cent of global emissions since the beginning of industrialization? and (iii) Is there proof that these emissions contributed to accelerated glacier melting and the risk of flooding in Huaraz? The case is still in the evidentiary stage.[22]

The UK Heathrow Case

This administrative case concerned the much-debated plans of Heathrow Airport to develop a third runway. Under the Planning Act 2008 (see 'The National Level', above), these plans required the government's support. That support was given on 26 June 2018, when the UK Secretary of State for Transport designated the 'Airports National Policy Statement: new runway capacity and infrastructure at airports in the South East of England' (the ANPS). The ANPS gave the green light for a new Northwest runway. It set the fundamental *policy* framework within which further planning decisions, via a Development Consent Order, will be taken.

A court case against the Secretary of State's decision was first brought before the Divisional Court, which found that the UK Government's policy was produced lawfully. Local residents and councils, the Mayor of London, Greenpeace, Friends of the Earth, and Plan B Earth then brought the case before the Court of Appeal.

On 20 February 2020, the Court of Appeal granting the appeal in part, referring to the precautionary principle, held:

> The Paris Agreement ought to have been taken into account by the Secretary of State in the preparation of the ANPS, but was not … [T]his means … that the

[22] For the full texts of judgments and pleadings in English, see <https://germanwatch.org/en/14198> accessed 4 April 2022.

> Government when it published the ANPS had not taken into account its own firm policy commitments on climate change under the Paris Agreement. That ... is legally fatal to the ANPS in its present form.[23]

The government did not challenge the judgment (Prime Minister Johnson had famously declared after his election: 'I will lie down with you in front of those bulldozers and stop the construction of that third runway'), but Heathrow Airport Ltd appealed to the Supreme Court, and so the case became a 'Hamlet without the Prince'.[24] The Supreme Court reversed the judgment on 16 December 2020,[25] and ruled that the Secretary of State when he made his designation followed the advice of the CCC that the existing measures under the Climate Change Act 2008 were 'capable of being compatible' with the 2050 target set by the Paris Agreement. The words 'government policy' in the Planning Act should be given a 'relatively narrow meaning so that the relevant policies can readily be identified'.[26] As the domestic implementation of the Paris Agreement was still in development at the time of the Secretary's decision, its formal ratification did not mean that it constituted 'government policy'. The ANPS was structured in a manner to ensure that when Heathrow Airport actually applied for consent to construct the runway, it would have to show, at that stage, that the runway expansion would be compatible with the up-to-date requirements under the Paris Agreement and the Climate Change Act.

D. Comparative Remarks

Judicial Activism?

Did the courts in their judgments involving the Dutch, German, and UK Governments enter the political domain? The 2015 District Court's *Urgenda* judgment sparked enthusiasm, but also critique because, it was argued, the court overstepped the boundaries of its judicial powers. Many expected that the order would not stand in appeal. But it did. Yet, the confirmation of the order by the Court of Appeal upheld by the *Hoge Raad* met, once again, with considerable criticism. Likewise, in respect of the Court of Appeal's Heathrow judgment, former chancellor George Osborne, followed by others, complained of 'overreaching undemocratic judicial activism'.[27]

[23] *R (Plan B Earth) v Secretary of State for Transport* [2020] EWCA Civ 214, [2020] PTSR 1446.

[24] David Hart, 'When Is a Policy Not a Policy: Supreme Court on Heathrow Expansion', UK Human Rights Blog (21 December 2020) <https://ukhumanrightsblog.com/2020/12/21/when-is-a-policy-not-a-policy-supreme-court-on-heathrow-expansion/> accessed 4 April 2022.

[25] *R (Friends of the Earth Ltd) v Secretary of State for Transport* [2020] UKSC 52, [2021] 2 All ER 967.

[26] ibid [106].

[27] George Osborne on Twitter: 'Judges kill off Heathrow 3rd runway and Britain getting the modern air transport infrastructure we need, despite the elected Parliament voting for it overwhelmingly.

We do not share this view. The courts were right to provide legal protection by ensuring compliance by the executive of its duty of care regarding the greenhouse gas emissions from Dutch territory (*Urgenda*) and by ensuring that the correct procedures were followed for setting the government's policy with greenhouse gas emissions (*Heathrow*).

Part of the criticism about *Urgenda* (how can an NGO, acting without any check on whether it represents the interests it purports to promote, obtain an order from the courts requiring the State to reduce greenhouse gas emissions?) actually concerns the provision in Dutch law on collective actions upon which Urgenda relied, which is an unusually open-ended and hybrid procedural norm.[28] While certainly not beyond criticism, this norm did establish the legislative basis for the courts' taking up of the case. And, as the *Hoge Raad* pointed out, it is up to the courts to decide whether the government and parliament, notwithstanding their large degree of discretion, remained within the limits of the law, including those for the government arising from the ECHR. Although one may doubt whether the ECHR in fact supported the reasoning of the *Hoge Raad* (see 'Human Rights Aspects', below), the courts did not overstep their powers. This case was indeed, as the *Hoge Raad* noted, 'exceptional'.[29] The government, knowing it should do more to pursue an effective climate policy, nevertheless did not take the necessary action without a credible justification. Parliament let it happen. While pretending to lead, the government in fact stayed behind almost all other EU countries, thereby increasing the risk of irreversible harm to its own population and the rest of the world. Moreover, the government failed to demonstrate that the reduction of at least 25 per cent by 2020 was impossible or disproportionate, and also to provide any insight into which measures it intends to take in the coming years. The State of the Netherlands manifestly fell short of its duty of care.

In contrast to the *Hoge Raad*, the German *BVerfG* is a constitutional court, created to deal with constitutional matters only. Its members are elected by Parliament by a two-thirds majority. This gives the *BVerfG* the political clout to issue decisions on the constitutionality of legislation if challenged by citizens, political parties, or even parts of the government. In the case of the *Bundes-Klimaschutzgesetz* judgment, the judgment was criticized, but certainly not as broadly as *Urgenda* in the Netherlands. Indeed, the Constitutional Court deferred considerably more to the government than the *Hoge Raad*, in so far as it respected the greenhouse gas emission targets until 2030. Contrary also to *Urgenda*, those targets were defined by law, together with detailed reduction pathways. One may notice a tension between

Presumably this is the kind of overreaching undemocratic judicial activism Boris wants to curb … or perhaps not.'

[28] Art 3:305a. See van Loon (n 9) 71, 77.
[29] Judgment (n 15) [8.3.4].

the court's deferring attitude towards the 2030 targets and its criticism of the lack of post-2030 specifications. The government's proposed amendments to the law, however, resolve this tension, by not only providing clarity on the post-2030 policy, but also raising the targets themselves. Perhaps one might say that the court managed, in an elegant indirect manner, to make the government revise its policy beyond the strict limits of what the Constitution in the court's view required.

In comparison with both *Urgenda* and *Bundes-Klimaschutzgesetz*, the Court of Appeal's *Heathrow* judgment was a far more modest decision. It did not challenge the government's nationwide climate change mitigation targets, but reviewed the legality of the 2018 ANPS policy decision regarding one major infrastructure project. And while *Urgenda* and *Bundes-Klimaschutzgesetz* concerned the substance of the State's conduct and legislation, *Heathrow*, as the Court of Appeal stressed, dealt with a purely procedural issue. Also, there is nothing in the Supreme Court's reversal of the judgment suggesting that the Court of Appeal overstepped its powers.

The *MD v RDS* case was directed not against the government, but a private company. Yet, building on *Urgenda*, the Hague District Court ordered RDS 'to limit . . . the aggregate annual volume of all carbon dioxide emissions into the atmosphere . . . due to the business operations and sold energy-carrying products of the Shell group to such an extent that this volume will have reduced by at least net 45% at end 2030, relative to 2019 levels'.[30] One may agree with the court that '[a]ssessing whether or not RDS has the alleged legal obligation and deciding on the claims based thereon is pre-eminently a task of the court'. The question is, however, whether the legal foundation for this legal obligation by the court is sufficiently strong (see 'Human Rights Aspects', below). The case of *Lliuya v RWE* is different: there the issue is whether it is possible to attribute fractions of the *historical* accumulation of carbon dioxide in the atmosphere to a given company and to claim damages accordingly.

The Extraterritorial Aspect: Responsibility towards People Living Abroad

Urgenda initially brought the case both on its own behalf and on behalf of 886 individual persons, including people living outside the Netherlands. The District Court held that Urgenda, in so far as it was acting on its own behalf, could act in the interest not only of the current Dutch population, but also of persons outside the Netherlands, and of future generations, since 'all of them hav[e] an interest in a sustainable society which [Urgenda] seeks to protect'.[31] The court thus acknowledged that climate change affects people around the globe and, by implication,

[30] Judgment (n 16) decision 5.3.
[31] Judgment (n 11) [4.6]–[4.8].

that it affects them unevenly regarding time, space, and severity of and capability to cope with its impacts. As the individual plaintiffs lacked any additional personal interest, their claims were denied.[32] The Court of Appeal confirmed the District Court's order. However, contrary to the District Court's ruling that Urgenda was barred from relying on the ECHR, the Court of Appeal took the view that it could, and that its claim was 'already admissible insofar as Urgenda acts on behalf of the interests of the current generation of Dutch nationals'.[33] The *Hoge Raad* followed suit. Both higher courts—though without rejecting the District Court's view—thus focused on the vertical relation between the State of the Netherlands and persons 'within [its] jurisdiction' (Article 1 of the ECHR). They thereby narrowed the dispute to the interests of the current *Dutch* population (Court of Appeal) or residents (Supreme Court). The interests of people living outside the Netherlands, foremost inhabitants of developing countries, the 'Global South', who are particularly vulnerable to the adverse effects of climate change—as recognized in the Kyoto Protocol and the Paris Agreement—were thus out of sight.

By contrast, the *BVerfG* in *Bundes-Klimaschutzgesetz* declared the complaints by individuals admissible, but denied the standing of two environmental associations. As a result, this judgment was about individual people, not about Germany's population as a whole. Moreover, the court took account of the fact that the individual complainants included people living in Bangladesh and Nepal. The court admitted that under the German Constitution the government may have a duty to reduce German greenhouse gas emissions not only towards persons living in Germany, but also towards those living abroad:[34]

> In their home countries, the complainants are particularly exposed to the consequences of global warming caused by GHG emissions. Due to the global effects of greenhouse gases, further global warming can only be halted through climate protection efforts by all countries. To this end, GHG emissions must also be reduced to a climate-neutral level in Germany.

Further, a possible constitution-based legal obligation 'would be that the serious impairments to which the complainants could (further) be exposed due to climate change are caused, albeit to a small extent, by greenhouse gas emissions emanating from Germany'.[35]

[32] One would have expected the court to declare these claims inadmissible instead of denying them. The decision was not questioned in appeal, so that these individual claimants were no longer involved in the case, which reinforced the abstract nature of the claim and the case.

[33] Judgment (n 13) [37].

[34] 'Art. 1(3) of the Basic Law does not restrict the binding of the German state to fundamental rights on the national territory, but establishes a comprehensive binding of the German state authority to the fundamental rights of the Basic Law.'

[35] Judgment (n 17) [174], [175].

As the court implicitly recognizes the possibility of a causal link between exposure to the effects of climate change and greenhouse gas emissions from German territory, these passages will be read with interest by the parties in *Lliuya v RWE*. The content of this constitutional duty of care regarding persons abroad, however, according to the *BverfG*, is not necessarily the same as that towards persons living in Germany. Although Germany has a general obligation to reduce carbon dioxide emissions, its overall duty of care is a mix of measures of mitigation and of adaptation. Yet, Germany has no jurisdiction to take measures of adaptation in Bangladesh or Nepal. Ultimately, the court found no violation of fundamental rights towards these plaintiffs.

The *Heathrow* case was brought by, among others, two international NGOs, Greenpeace, and Friends of the Earth. But as pointed out already, contrary to both *Urgenda* and *Bundes-Klimaschutzgesetz*, this case did not deal with substantive issues, but with a specific procedural point, which did not affect its ultimate substantive outcome. The interests of persons outside the UK were not directly at stake.

In *MD v RDS*, the District Court went a step further than the Court of Appeal and the *Hoge Raad* in *Urgenda*. After declaring the claims of the 17,379 individuals inadmissible, it curiously decided that Milieudefensie's claim could not be admitted in so far as it extended to the interests of current and future generations of the world's population:

> Although the entire world population is served by curbing dangerous climate change, there are huge differences in the time and manner in which the global population at various locations will be affected by global warming caused by CO_2 emissions. Therefore, this principal interest does not meet the requirement of 'similar interest' as required [for the representation of interests by NGO's under Dutch law].[36]

That the global population's interests are diverse is, of course, correct. But that does not detract from the all-prevailing common, indeed 'principal' interest of the global population. Indeed, the court's heavy reliance on human rights in its assessment is difficult to reconcile with its decision not to consider the interests of individuals and local communities in developing countries. While the human rights of many of them are clearly at stake, this is doubtful with regard to *the* Dutch population.

[36] Judgment (n 17) [4.2.3], referring to art 3:305a of the Dutch Civil Code, cf n 15.

The Intertemporal Dimension: The Interests of Future Generations

While, as we saw, the Hague District Court had found that Urgenda could act in the interest not only of the current but also of future generations, the higher Courts restricted the scope of the dispute to the interests of the *current* Dutch generation, and found that their interests justified the greenhouse gas reduction order.

By contrast, in *Bundes-Klimaschutzgesetz*, the *BVerfG* placed full emphasis on

> the requirement arising from the principle of proportionality that the reduction in CO_2 emissions to the point of climate neutrality that is constitutionally necessary ... be distributed over time in a forward looking manner that respects fundamental rights ... [Therefore], one generation must not be allowed to consume large portions of the CO_2 budget while bearing a relatively minor share of the reduction effort if this would involve leaving subsequent generations with a drastic reduction burden and expose their lives to comprehensive losses of freedom ... [This requires] that precautionary steps are taken to manage the reduction efforts anticipated after 2030 in ways that respect fundamental rights ... Transparent guidelines for the further structuring of greenhouse gas reduction must be formulated at an early stage, providing orientation for the required development and implementation processes ... and planning certainty .... While it cannot be expected that the decreasing emission amounts already be precisely defined from the present time until the date envisaged for achieving climate neutrality in 2050, it is nonetheless insufficient that the Federal Government is only obliged to draw up a new plan once—in 2025—by means of an ordinance.[37]

Jointly with the *BVerfG*'s acceptance, in principle, of a constitutional duty towards persons living abroad, this ruling reinforces Germany's constitutionally based current and future responsibility worldwide regarding carbon dioxide emissions.[38]

Although in *Heathrow* the Court of Appeal did not raise any fundamental principles of fair distribution of the government's responsibilities over current and future generations, its decision breathes a similar 'forward-looking' spirit as the *Bundes-Klimaschutzgesetz* judgment, in so far as it found that the Secretary of State had not taken the Paris Agreement sufficiently into account. The Supreme Court's overturning judgment was watertight from a formal legal perspective. But the court, which dismissed the Court of Appeal's reliance on the precautionary principle,[39] might have conveyed, through its judgment, albeit *obiter*, more of

[37] Summary (n 17).

[38] Cf Frank Bierman, 'Germany's Climate Law Ruled Unconstitutional: First Reflections', <frankbiermann.org> accessed 4 April 2022; and Jaap Spier, 'Guest Commentary: A Ground-Breaking Judgment in Germany', <http://blogs.law.columbia.edu/climatechange/2021/05/10/guest-commentary-a-ground-breaking-judgment-in-germany> accessed 4 April 2022.

[39] [165].

the sense of urgency to reduce global warming that was also reflected in the CCC reports.[40]

In *MD v RDS*, the focus was again on the current residents of the Netherlands, which makes the question all the more pressing whether the court was right in its finding, based in part on human rights grounds, that those *current* interests justified the order against RDS.

The Role of the UNFCCC, the IPCC, and the Paris Agreement

The District Court in *Urgenda* based its finding that the government had failed to observe its duty of care on the rule of unwritten law pertaining to proper social conduct referred to in the Dutch Civil Code.[41] With this duty of care being an 'open norm', the court set itself the task of determining its content in the case at hand.

To this end, the court referred to international and European legal texts. Although those norms did not create rights that Urgenda could directly invoke, they did have a 'reflex effect' upon the State's duty of care, which should be interpreted so as to avoid a conflict with its international obligations. These obligations, moreover, had to be considered in the light of the reports of the IPCC. The IPCC had determined that developed countries listed in Annex I to the Kyoto Protocol, such as the Netherlands, should reduce their emissions in by 25 to 40 per cent by 2020 in comparison to 1990 levels. In essence, although via a different route, the Court of Appeal and the Supreme Court followed the same reasoning. Since the Paris Agreement had entered into force in the meantime, these courts could refer to this treaty in addition. The Supreme Court concluded that, although the 25 to 40 per cent target was not a binding rule or agreement itself, there was a high degree of international consensus on the urgent need for the Annex I countries to reach that target, in order to achieve at least the 2°C, the maximum target to be deemed responsible. This target applied to each Annex I country individually, irrespective of EU arrangements.

The *BVerfG* in *Bundes-Klimaschutzgesetz* based its ruling on the German Basic Act, but added that although it follows from Article 20a that greenhouse gas emissions must be reduced, this constitutional climate goal 'is more closely defined in accordance with the Paris target as being to limit the increase in the global average temperature to well below 2°C and preferably to 1.5°C above pre-industrial levels'. Contrary to the Dutch courts, the *BverfG* did not specify any detailed consequences or concrete policies, as the Paris Agreement 'left this to governments and parliaments'. However, as we saw (in 'Judicial activism?'), indirectly, the court's judgment caused the government to raise Germany's reduction targets.

[40] Including the CCC's *The Sixth Carbon Budget*, published on 9 December 2020.
[41] See n 13 above.

In *Heathrow*, the Court of Appeal ruled that the Secretary of State failed to take the Paris Agreement into consideration. The Supreme Court, while recognizing that the Paris Agreement was '[at] the heart' of the case, disagreed. Contrary to the *Hoge Raad* and the *BVerfG*, which looked to the Paris Agreement for guidance in the interpretation of the law, the Supreme Court was satisfied that the UK's obligations under the Paris Agreement were given sufficient consideration in the Secretary of State's decision. Further reference to the Paris Agreement was, at this stage, not required.

In *MD v RDS*, the Hague District Court, while admitting that the Paris Agreement is binding on the ratifying States only and not RDS, observed that the States parties:

> have sought out the help of non-state stakeholders … Since 2012 there has been broad international consensus about the need for non-state action, because states cannot tackle the climate issue on their own … the IPCC has found that the member states' national reduction pledges for 2030 added together are far from sufficient for reaching the goals of the Paris Agreement … it is generally accepted that global warming must be kept well below 2°C in 2100, and that a temperature rise of under 1.5°C should be strived for … in doing so [the court] does not formulate a legally binding standard for the prevention of dangerous climate change in the Netherlands … The court includes this broad consensus about what is needed to prevent dangerous climate change—viz. achieving the goals of the Paris Agreement—in its answer to the question whether or not RDS is obliged to reduce the Shell group's CO_2 emissions via its corporate policy. [Moreover] the court includes [the] broad consensus [about the reduction pathways of CO_2 emissions by net 45% in 2030, relative to 2010 levels, and by net 100% in 2050], in its interpretation of the unwritten standard of care. Again, the court does not formulate a legally binding standard for … a reduction pathway to be chosen.[42]

But can the insufficiency of the obligations established by the Paris Agreement for States be repaired via an obligation derived from the civil tort law of *one* State party in respect of *one* multinational company that happens to be based in that State?

The case of *Lliuya v RWE*, as we saw, is based on German tort law, Article 1004 of the German Civil Code. Although reference is made in the pleadings to foreign judgments, including *Urgenda*, they do not rely on the Paris Agreement.

[42] Judgment (n 16) [4.4.26]–[4.4.27].

Human Rights Aspects

The *Hoge Raad* in *Urgenda* based the due care obligation of the Dutch Government towards Urgenda on Articles 2 and 8 of the ECHR. The court stressed the serious risks of climate change for Dutch residents (sea level rising, heat stress, deteriorated air quality, increasing spread of infectious diseases, excessive rainfall, and disruption of food production and drinking water supply). The fact that these risks would only become apparent in a few decades did not mean that Articles 2 and 8 of the ECHR would not offer protection against this threat. Therefore, the risks caused by climate change were sufficiently 'real and immediate', as required by the ECtHR's case law to bring them within the scope of Articles 2 and 8.

One can agree with the *Hoge Raad* that Articles 2 and 8 of the ECHR may, in principle and under the appropriate circumstances, offer protection to individuals and local communities against harm caused by climate change, all the more because of its irreversible effects. Articles 2 and 8 indeed establish, largely overlapping, positive obligations for national authorities, and offer protection in the case of serious, specific, and immediate risk.[43] However:

> the Convention does not allow complaints in abstracto alleging a violation of the Convention. The Convention does not provide for the institution of an actio popularis, meaning that applicants may not complain against a provision of domestic law, a domestic practice or public acts simply because they appear to contravene the Convention. In order for applicants to be able to claim to be a victim, they must produce reasonable and convincing evidence of the likelihood that a violation affecting them personally will occur; mere suspicion or conjecture is insufficient in this respect.[44]

We do not think, in the light of the ECtHR's case law, that, in the circumstances of the *Urgenda* case, and certainly not given the narrow issue at hand, it is a tenable position to say that 'the *residents of the Netherlands*' are currently (potential) victims of a violation of their human rights under Articles 2 and 8 of the ECHR. The factual basis to which the *Hoge Raad* refers is weak. Moreover, the *Hoge Raad*—contrary to the *BVerfG* in *Bundes-Klimaschutzgesetz*—does not take into account the effect of adaptation measures which a rich Annex I country like the Netherlands can, must, and will take to prevent harm. The position of the *Hoge Raad* is also hardly defensible if one compares this case with cases of vulnerable people elsewhere on our planet—whose interests the *Hoge Raad* excludes from its

[43] Cf also Tim Eicke (Judge in the ECtHR), 'Human Rights and Climate Change: What Role for the European Court of Human Rights' (2 March 2021) paras 39ff <www.coe.int/en/web/portal/-/human-rights-and-climate-change-what-role-for-the-european-convention-on-human-rights->.

[44] *Centre for Legal Resources on behalf of Valentin Câmpeanu v Romania* ECHR 2014–V 1.

considerations. Such an overly broad interpretation of Articles 2 and 8 risks stripping these human right provisions of their effectiveness.[45] The court, having the choice to base the State's duty of care on civil tort law (following the District Court) or human rights (following the Court of Appeal),[46] chose the latter option. While agreeing with the outcome of the Supreme Court's judgment, we believe that the District's Court reasoning is more compelling than that of the Supreme Court.[47]

The legal context of *Bundes-Klimaschutzgesetz* was very different from *Urgenda*, because there it was not the ECHR, which lacks a provision on environmental damage, but the German constitution which does include such a provision.

Although the parties in *Heathrow* included human rights organisations, the arguments were based essentially on the Paris Agreement, which contains no substantive provision making the link between climate change and human rights.[48]

In *MD v RDS*, the District Court, as we have seen, based RDS's duty of care on the unwritten rule of Dutch tort law pertaining to proper social conduct. Although the court recognized that Articles 2 and 8 of the ECHR apply in the relations between citizens and the State only, so that Milieudefensie could not directly invoke them against RDS, the court 'factor[ed] the human rights and the values they embody in its interpretation of the unwritten standard of care'. The District Court in *Urgenda* had followed a similar reasoning, but there the defendant was the State, bound by the ECHR. Here, one would have expected the court to elaborate more on this 'horizontal effect' of human rights in the relation between two private parties. Still, referring to *Urgenda*, the court went on to hold that the 'serious and irreversible consequences of dangerous climate change in the Netherlands ... pose a threat to the human rights of Dutch residents'.[49] This argument suffers from the same weaknesses as that of the *Hoge Raad* in *Urgenda*. It *could* have been more compelling if invoked on behalf of individuals or local communities, in particular from parts of the Global South, exposed to serious, specific, and immediate risks. But, as we saw (in 'The Extraterritorial Aspect', above), they were excluded by the court's decision that the plaintiffs *could not* act on their behalf. Nonetheless, the least one can say is that this judgment animates the discussion on the role of (fossil fuel) companies' responsibility in dealing with the warming of the Earth.

In *Lliuya v RWE*, human rights arguments have not been raised so far.

[45] See, in more detail, van Loon (n 9).

[46] Cf *Netherlands (Ministry of Economic Affairs and Climate Policy) v Urgenda (Advisory Opinion of Procurator General)* Parket bij de Hoge Raad, ECLI:NL:PHR:2019:887; English tr ECLI:NL:PHR:2019:1026.

[47] See, on the human rights aspects, also Spier (n 15) 322–25 and Backes and Van der Veen (n 15) 312–15.

[48] WWF-UK, allowed to intervene, argued that when the Secretary of State exercises his functions under the Planning Act with the objective of achieving 'sustainable development' this must be interpreted in the light of the UK's obligations, in particular, under the 1989 UN Convention on the Rights of the Child.

[49] Judgment (n 16) [4.4.9], [4.4.10].

Private International Law Aspects

This brief comparison obviously has its limits. Even so, it would be incomplete, in the light of Lawrence Collins's interest in and major contributions to the conflict of laws, if it did not briefly touch on private international law aspects of some cases.

Before the District Court in *Urgenda*, which held that the NGO could act on behalf of worldwide interests, Dutch law was applied to the tortious negligent conduct of the Dutch State without further ado.[50] Since the higher courts only considered the interests of the Dutch population as being represented by the NGO, and so restricted the locus of the (threat of) damage to Dutch territory, they avoided applicable law issues.

By contrast, in *MD v RDS*, both parties raised issues concerning Article 7 of Rome II, invoked by Milieudefensie.[51] The court held, with the parties, that (dangerous) climate change due to carbon dioxide emissions constitutes 'environmental damage'. Regarding the question of what constitutes 'the event giving rise to the damage', the plaintiffs argued that this was the corporate policy as determined by RDS in the Netherlands, and that their choice of law for the country in which this event occurred led to the applicability of Dutch law. RDS did not contest that its corporate policy is or may be of influence on the group's carbon dioxide emissions. However, in its view, its corporate policy was a preparatory act that fell outside the scope of Article 7 because the mere adoption of a policy does not cause damage. The 'event giving rise to the damage' were the actual carbon dioxide emissions, which therefore led to the applicability of a plurality of legal systems.

The court, however, sided with the plaintiffs:

> Although Article 7 Rome II refers to an 'event giving rise to the damage', i.e. singular, it leaves room for situations in which multiple events giving rise to the damage in multiple countries can be identified, as is characteristic of environmental damage and imminent environmental damage … RDS' adoption of the corporate policy of the Shell group therefore constitutes an independent cause of

[50] Regulation (EC) No 864/2007 of the European Parliament and of the Council of 11 July 2007 on the law applicable to non-contractual obligations (Rome II) [2007] OJ L199/40, would probably not have been applicable because of its exclusion in art 1(1) of 'the liability of the State for … omissions in the exercise of State authority' (see Lord Collins (ed), *Dicey, Morris & Collins on the Conflict of Laws* (15th edn, Sweet & Maxwell 2012) para 34-015). Under art 10:159 of the Dutch Private International Law Act, Dutch law is applicable to obligations arising from the exercise of Dutch public authority.

[51] Rome II, art 7: Environmental damage:

> The law applicable to a non-contractual obligation arising out of environmental damage or damage sustained by persons or property as a result of such damage shall be [the law of the country in which the damage occurs], unless the person seeking compensation for damage chooses to base his or her claim on the law of the country in which the event giving rise to the damage occurred.

> the damage, which may contribute to environmental damage and imminent environmental damage with respect to Dutch residents.[52]

Presumably, the decision that climate change due to carbon dioxide emissions constitutes 'environmental damage' should be understood in the sense that *specific, concrete damage*, such as impairment of water, soil, air, ecosystems and species, personal injury, or material damages, *resulting from* climate change due to carbon dioxide emissions constitutes such damage. Also, the reasoning of the court regarding 'the event giving rise to the damage' is not entirely clear. Is (the adoption of) a policy an 'event giving rise to damage'? If so, one would presume that it is this single 'event' causing damage across the planet, so that persons around the world claiming damage as a result of this 'event' may also, under Article 7 of Rome II, choose Dutch law.

In the ongoing *Lliuya v RWE* case, the plaintiff is based in Peru and the defendant in Germany. The plaintiff's statement of claim sets out in detail the jurisdictional ground (Brussels I Recast) and designates, in respect of the applicable law, German law. Since 'there is no singular event giving rise to damages, but rather a chain of damaging events', this choice of German tort law is based on Article 7 of Rome II for the period after 11 January 2009 (the date from which it applied), and for the period before, on the pre-existing analogous rule of German private international law. The courts have not (yet) discussed these private international law aspects. But in contrast to *MD v RDS*, here the issue is not RWE's climate *policy*, but its concrete greenhouse gas *emissions* and their causal relationship to the damage in Peru. Therefore, and since the jurisdiction of the German courts is beyond doubt, no significant private international law questions are likely to arise in this case.

E. Concluding Remarks

1. One thing appears very clearly from the recent judgments here discussed: the courts in all three countries, the Netherlands, Germany, and the UK, now take climate change actions very seriously. But they deal with the claims in different ways, and their deference to the legislator and the executive varies according to the robustness of their domestic climate laws and the diligence of their executive branch in respect of greenhouse gas emission control.
2. The UK was first to adopt an ambitious Climate Act in 2008 with an effective monitoring system. In *Heathrow*, the UK Supreme Court refrained from correcting the executive regarding its plans for the airport's expansion, and even the Court of Appeal, though disapproving of the executive's conduct,

[52] Judgment (n 16) [4.3.1]–[4.3.7].

emphasized that its judgment was simply procedural. The *BVerfG* corrected the Climate Act 2019 on constitutional grounds, but only regarding its time frames for future reduction measures. Undoubtedly, the Dutch courts went furthest in directing the government to act on the warming up of the Earth. This can be understood, and justified, in the light of the flawed legal framework and the government's negligent conduct.

Most recently, the Hague District Court extended the responsibility for climate change damage to future emissions by a private company, RDS, holding it subject to a standard similar to that for States. It would seem unlikely that courts in Germany or the UK would follow this path and, indeed, it remains to be seen whether this judgment will be upheld on appeal, in particular in so far as it extends to the 'sold energy-carrying products of the Shell group'.

3. The courts differ in the way they take the interests of persons outside their own jurisdiction into account. In *Urgenda*, the District Court admitted that the plaintiff could act on behalf of current and future generations worldwide, yet the higher courts only considered the interests of the current Dutch population or residents. In *MD v RDS*, the court even ruled that only the interests of the current Dutch residents were admissible. In *Bundes-Klimaschutzgesetz*, the *BVerfG* accepted that the government's constitutional responsibility to control greenhouse gas emissions in principle also extends to the interests of persons outside Germany and recognized the particular vulnerability of those in the Global South. In *Heathrow*, the interests of persons outside the UK were not explicitly addressed. *Lliuya v RWE* illustrates how carbon dioxide emissions from Germany may lead to claims from persons living in other continents.
4. Climate change affects current and future generations. Again, in *Urgenda*, the District Court recognized the interests of future generations, yet those interests were not considered by the higher courts nor by the District Court in *MD v RDS*. In contrast, the interests of future generations were key to the German *Bundes-Klimaschutzgesetz* decision, which led the government to propose a new bill that also tightened the law's targets. The Court of Appeal's decision in *Heathrow* reflected a concern about insufficient consideration by the executive of future greenhouse gas emissions. However, the Supreme Court saw no legal fault in the government's conduct.
5. Through the Paris Agreement, States have embraced the aim of limiting the increase in the global average temperature to well below 2°C and preferably to 1.5°C above pre-industrial levels. The implementation, path, and pace of greenhouse gas reduction is left to the individual States 'in accordance with equity and the principle of common but differentiated responsibilities and respective capabilities'. 'Paris' does not create rights and obligations for individuals. Yet, *Urgenda*, *Bundes-Klimaschutzgesetz*, and *Heathrow* show different ways in which individuals may still invoke the Agreement. In *Urgenda*,

the Agreement informed the decisions of the higher courts. In *Bundes-Klimaschutzgesetz*, the *BVerfG* interpreted the German constitution in light of the Agreement, and in *Heathrow*, the Agreement was at the heart of the case, the Court of Appeal ruling that the government had failed to take it into account, but the Supreme Court deciding that it had sufficiently considered it.

The Hague District Court in *MD v RDS* based its decision on the standard of due care of Dutch tort law, which RDS must observe. In determining the obligations that follow from this standard for RDS, the court ruled that although RDS is not bound by the Paris Agreement, its obligations are nonetheless informed by the goals of the Agreement.

6. Climate change is ubiquitous. Yet, private international law is not (yet) prominent in these cases. It could have been raised in *Urgenda*, but it was not. On the other hand, *Lliuya v RWE* offers an archetypical example of a private international law case. The special article on environmental damage of Article 7 of Rome II supports the plaintiff's argument for the applicability of German law, as the law of the 'event giving rise to the damage', that is, the emissions from German territory. This article is also central to the most recent, but not evident, decision of the District Court of The Hague that RDS's global corporate policy constitutes itself such an 'event'.
7. It is estimated that over 1,800 climate lawsuits in thirty-five countries have already been brought against governments and corporations.[53] While more than 1,600 of these cases have been filed in the US, clearly the rest of the world is warming up to increase the volume of cases. In so far as States' legislative and executive branches fail to act upon the IPCC recommendations and the Paris Agreement, the climate crisis makes court action crucial. Civil climate litigation against companies is still in an early stage. The cases above demonstrate some of the challenges courts are already facing, but also some impressive, encouraging developments.

[53] See Climate Change Litigation Databases—Sabin Center for Climate Change Law, available at <climatecasechart.com> accessed 4 April 2022.

PART II

THE JUDICIAL ROLE IN INTERNATIONAL CASES

5

Soliciting Wise Counsel

Lord Collins's Contribution to the Judicial Approach in International Commercial Cases

Elizabeth Gloster[*]

A. Introduction

Even among the imposing ranks of those judges who have populated the UK Supreme Court, Lord Collins stands apart as a master of international commercial dispute resolution—those areas of law that regulate how the English legal system coordinates with the legal systems of other countries in facilitating the resolution of international disputes. In the Court of Appeal and Supreme Court, he was responsible for deciding the future development of this area of English law. As general editor of *Dicey, Morris & Collins on the Conflict of Laws*, he is responsible for guiding the views of lawyers, judges, and future generations of the English legal profession.

The importance of international commercial disputes to English law cannot be overstated: according to the most recent UK Legal Services Survey, three-quarters of the cases in the Commercial Court were international, increasing to 78 per cent in the year to the end of June 2019.[1] Not only does the influx of foreign cases lead to funds flowing into our legal system, but the multitude of factual and legal issues raised in these cases provides English law with more opportunities to develop in step with an ever-modernizing, ever-globalizing world.

Alongside litigation, international commercial disputes benefit London's arbitration community. The most recent Queen Mary Arbitration Survey reports that London is the world's most popular seat for arbitration, with 64 per cent of respondents placing it within their most preferred seats.[2] Not only is London the most popular seat at the global level, but London was the most popular seat in all regions examined.[3] The popularity of London as a seat of international arbitration

[*] I am grateful for the assistance given by my research assistant, Alfie Lewis, barrister, in completing this chapter.

[1] The CityUK, *Legal Excellence, Internationally Renowned: UK Legal Services 2019* (The CityUK 2019) 29.

[2] Queen Mary University of London, *2018 International Survey: The Evolution of International Arbitration* (Queen Mary University of London 2018) 9.

[3] ibid 10.

Elizabeth Gloster, *Soliciting Wise Counsel* In: *Essays in International Litigation for Lord Collins*. Edited by: Jonathan Harris and Campbell McLachlan, Oxford University Press. © Oxford University Press 2022.
DOI: 10.1093/oso/9780192867988.003.0006

not only provides English lawyers with a steady flow of work, but exposes them to the practices of other jurisdictions and expands their horizons.

On a more personal note, it is in the realm of international commercial litigation that the judicial careers of Lord Collins and myself overlap. Lord Collins sat on appeal from one of my judgments in *Masri v Consolidated Contractors International*—a sprawling saga of litigation that spent over five years before the English courts. Before me at first instance, the crux of the case was whether the claimant, Mr Masri, had any rights to a 10 per cent share of the defendants' interest in a concession for the exploration and exploitation of an oil field in Yemen. I found that Mr Masri did have rights to such a share, but the judgment went unsatisfied. I then went on to grant an affidavit of assets order to compel the judgment debtors to identify their assets, grant a limited freezing order in favour of Mr Masri with respect to the oil revenues from the relevant oil field, and appoint a receiver with respect to the oil revenues.

These three orders were subsequently appealed to the Court of Appeal before Lord Justice Collins, as he then was, Lord Neuberger, and Lord Justice Ward. Lord Collins, giving the lead judgment, upheld all three orders. However, this judgment is not only notable as an example of Lord Collins's wonderful eye for correct (!) lower court decisions, but also as an example of his prowess in comparative legal analysis. At [30]–[31] of his judgment, Lord Collins traces back the lineage of the concept of 'subject matter jurisdiction' to its American roots, using the knowledge of its international heritage to inform his development of the court's jurisdiction to appoint receivers over the equity to assets located abroad under English national law.

It is this aspect of Lord Collins's judicial approach to international commercial cases, his incorporation of comparative analysis, to which I devote this chapter. In the section that follows, I shall briefly outline the benefits of comparative analysis to judicial decision-making; I shall then go on to discuss the English comparative judicial tradition, in particular in English arbitration law. Finally, by reference to a case study, I will consider Lord Collins's place within, and contribution to, this tradition of English law.

B. Internationalism and the National Judge

In an article on foreign and comparative law, Lord Mance categorized the four situations in which an English court might be called upon to refer to foreign law. The first is where foreign law is directly in issue before the English court. The second is where the English court uses foreign law as an aide to the understanding of English law by means of comparative analysis. The third is where the English court turns to foreign law to interpret national legislation based on an international treaty; though this is properly characterized as a permutation of using foreign law as an aide to understanding national law, national law simply reflecting the UK's treaty obligations. Finally, the fourth is where the English court must apply principles of international law.[4] Of these situations, only the second and third, in which foreign law is used to assist the development of English law, involve comparative analysis.

Put at its most basic, comparative analysis entails the comparison of the laws of two jurisdictions. As simple as this may sound at first, the simplicity of this description belies its methodological complexity. The most prevalent methodology of comparative analysis is the functional approach.[5] This approach was raised to prominence by Zweigert and Kötz in their seminal *An Introduction to Comparative Law*.[6] The underlying principle of the functional approach is the assumption that all legal systems deal with similar problems. As stated by Lord Goff in extra-judicial writings, 'we can see the German judges struggling, as we have done, from case to case, with the same problems that have beset our courts'.[7] Once one accepts the idea that different legal systems address similar problems, it becomes possible to compare the different solutions that they reach. These different solutions are called functional equivalents.

A simple example of functional equivalents are the concepts involved in the formation of binding contracts. Under English law, a promise is only binding where there has been offer and acceptance, with consideration flowing from both sides.[8] Under §130 of the German Civil Code, parties may bind themselves to reciprocal promises through juristic acts. English offer and acceptance and German juristic acts are not identical as legal concepts: under German law parties can bind themselves by juristic acts to unilateral promises, which is not possible under English law. However, despite the differences in the nature of the relevant concepts, they perform identical functions in the formation of contracts.

More complex analysis requires the jurisprudential kenosis of the observer—in order fully to understand how another legal system solves a problem, the observer must abandon the legal terminology that she has inherited from her native legal system. Only by discarding any preconceived notions of how the law should be is it possible to understand how law could be in a foreign legal system. A famous example of this can be found in the overlap between English occupier's liability and German contract law.

Under English law, where a shopper is hurt due to the state of a shopkeeper's premises, he may be able to sue for damages under the shopkeeper's tortious occupier's liability. Under German law, such situations are caught by precontractual

[4] Lord Mance, 'Foreign and Comparative Law in the Courts' (2001) 36(3) Texas Intl LJ 415.

[5] Though functionalism is the predominant methodology in comparative legal analysis, it is not the only methodology and the hermeneutical and structural methods are also used. See further Geoffrey Samuel, *An Introduction to Comparative Law Theory and Methodology* (2nd edn, Hart 2014) chs 5, 6, 7.

[6] Konrad Zweigert and Hein Kötz, *Introduction to Comparative Law* (OUP 1998).

[7] Lord Goff, 'The Future of the Common Law' (1997) 46(4) ICLQ 745, 749.

[8] *Currie v Misa* (1875) LR 10 Ex 153, 162.

liability under §278 of the Civil Code, as the application of German tort law would make it too easy for a shopkeeper to avoid liability. By understanding the internal logic of the German legal system, it is possible to understand how English tort law and German contract law can perform the same function despite the taxonomical separation of tort and contract under English law.

By undertaking functional comparative analysis, one is able to see the road not taken by the development of one's own legal system. From the comparison of offer and acceptance and juristic acts, one can see that German law has divorced the concept of binding promises from the concept of reciprocity; whereas English law generally does not recognize a promise unilaterally made as binding upon its maker. An appreciation of how other legal systems address the same problem raises questions as to whether the road English law has taken is in fact the best, and provides alternatives for the future development of English law.[9]

Explained in these terms, comparative law becomes an exercise in identifying and understanding the solutions of other jurisdictions in solving specific legal problems. It should not come as a surprise that the common law judge, as someone entrusted with deciding how to solve legal problems, might benefit from the information to be gained from the solutions reached by foreign judges in solving the same problem under their own law.

Despite the rather unassuming role of comparative analysis as the provision of information, the reliance upon foreign law in developing one's own law is not uncontroversial. The late US Supreme Court Justice Scalia stated in *Roper v Simmons* that judges only 'invoke alien law when it agrees with [their] own thinking, and ignore it otherwise'.[10] His discomfort was with cutting corners in judicial decision-making where a judge has found a foreign rule that reflects their personal convictions. In such circumstances, there is a risk that a judge will treat the mere existence of a foreign rule as evidence that the rule is justified and might be adopted in the case before him, without going through the necessary consideration of his own national law to consider how it would most naturally develop in line with its legal, political, and social history.

Closer to home, Lord Mansfield was criticized in an anonymous letter published in the *London Evening Post* under the pseudonym 'Junius' for 'introduc[ing] into the court where you preside, maxims of jurisprudence unknown to Englishmen'.[11] According to the writer, 'by such treacherous arts, the noble simplicity and spirit of our Saxon laws were first corrupted'.[12] Unlike with Justice Scalia, Junius's problem

[9] Lord Sumption in fact recently called for a reassessment of the English doctrine of consideration at [18] of *MWB Business Exchange Centres Ltd v Rock Advertising Ltd* [2018] UKSC 24, [2019] AC 119. Were the English courts to ever look for a replacement for consideration under English law, comparative analysis would no doubt provide a number of options to choose from.

[10] *Roper v Simmons* 543 US 551, 627 (2005).

[11] Reprinted in Edmund Heward, *Lord Mansfield* (Barry Rose 1979) 129.

[12] ibid.

was not with judicial shortcuts, but rather with the incorporation into one's legal system of something foreign. If a foreign rule of law adequately solves a common problem, should we not trust our own judiciary to come to the same conclusion in a manner that conforms with our legal traditions? If our judiciary comes to a different conclusion from that of a foreign court, should we not trust our own judiciary over that of a foreign jurisdiction?

However, one cannot justify the rejection of comparative analysis on the basis of trust for one's own law or one's own judiciary. In fact, Scalia's and Junius's objections to invoking foreign laws in domestic courtrooms betray a mistrust of one's national judiciary and presume a degree of judicial laziness in consulting foreign laws. A conscientious judge, aware of the context of a particular foreign decision and how it fits within the broader context of its home jurisdiction, will be well-equipped to identify the information that is relevant to his decision-making and make good use of it to improve and not prevent the natural development of his national law.

The goal of comparative law is knowledge. Knowledge is useful. Comparative law does not supplant the judge's decision-making process, but rather supplements it to allow for a more informed decision. To refuse to learn from the successes and failures of other jurisdictions smacks of a kind of crude nationalism that has no place in the reasoned discourse of the courtroom. This sentiment was put rather more pithily by Elena Kagan during the hearings before her appointment to the US Supreme Court—asked whether judges should ever turn to foreign law in deciding domestic cases, she replied, 'I'm in favour of good ideas ... wherever you can get them'.[13]

Though comparative analysis is capable of rendering all sorts of information, the most relevant information for a judge is either path-finding or hazard-marking information. Path-finding information highlights how other jurisdictions have overcome a specific problem, and is able to guide judges in overcoming the same problem under their own law. Hazard-marking information illuminates the problems that other jurisdictions have encountered after adopting a particular solution, and is able to warn judges from leading their law into similar troubles. Path-finding information can weigh in favour of adopting a particular solution by illustrating that it has a track record in other jurisdictions; hazard-marking information can weigh against adopting a particular rule where it has proved itself to be ineffective or harmful in a foreign jurisdiction. Both forms of information may prove invaluable to a judge as he decides how to develop his own national law.

There are certain areas of law where insight into other jurisdictions is particularly important. One such area is international arbitration. One of the key benefits of international arbitration is its ability to focus jurisdiction over a case that

[13] Ruth Bader Ginsburg, *My Own Words* (Simon & Schuster 2016) 252.

might engage the jurisdiction of multiple legal systems into the single forum of arbitration. Where, for example, parties in England and France contract for the performance of a contract in Estonia, there are at least three jurisdictions in which the parties might sue each other. This plurality of fora may allow a recalcitrant defendant to delay a claim by disputing jurisdiction, wasting the parties' time and money. By including an arbitration clause in their contract, the parties bind themselves to a single forum—that of arbitration.

However, arbitration does not exist independently of national legal systems, but rather it relies upon their support. As per Lord Mustill, 'there is the plain fact, palatable or not, that it is only a court possessing coercive powers which can rescue the arbitration if it is in danger of foundering'.[14] In particular, an arbitration will rely on the legal system at its seat, which regulates the propriety of the arbitral proceedings, and the legal system of enforcement, which will be called upon to give effect to the resulting award.

As the legal system of enforcement will refuse enforcement of an award where it considers the arbitral proceedings to have been improper, how the seat regulates the arbitral proceeding will have an influence over whether an award is enforced. Where there is a significant divergence in the standards to which an arbitral award is held between two countries, there is the risk that the arbitral award from one country will not be enforced in the other. This not only undermines arbitration as an effective means of international dispute resolution, but puts arbitrators in the awkward position of having to navigate the different demands of those legal systems relevant to an arbitration.

Commentators have suggested sophisticated means of mitigating the harmful effects of such mismatched values in international arbitration. Of particular note is the late Emmanuel Gaillard's transnational legal order, which seeks to create autonomous values and standards for international arbitration which can guide both courts and arbitrators.[15] However, by far the most practical and effective means of resolving this problem is to encourage a greater dissemination of information about the arbitration laws of the world's legal systems and greater communication between these legal systems through comparative analysis. It should not be surprise that the English courts, renowned for their practicality and efficiency, have taken the latter approach.

Finally, international arbitration lends itself particularly well to comparative analysis. The modern international arbitration laws of many countries either replicate, or are influenced by, the UNCITRAL Model Law on International Commercial Arbitration:[16] there is therefore a significant degree of overlap in the way that different courts treat locally seated arbitrations. Furthermore, most

[14] *SA Coppée Lavalin NV v Ken-Ren Chemicals and Fertilizers Ltd* [1995] 1 AC 38 (HL) 53.

[15] Emmanuel Gaillard, *Legal Theory of International Arbitration* (Martinus Nijhoff 2010).

[16] The Model Law has been adopted in 118 jurisdictions as of March 2021.

countries in the world are party to the New York Convention,[17] which imposes certain rules on how courts may treat foreign arbitration clauses and arbitral awards: there is therefore also a large degree of overlap in how courts around the world treat foreign arbitration. With so much common ground, it becomes easier to embark upon a comparative functional analysis as different legal systems employ the same legal doctrines and concepts for the same problems. However, this does not mean that the arbitration laws of different countries are the same such as to make comparison pointless; rather comparative analysis becomes a matter of teasing out how different laws balance the competing policies relevant to any particular doctrine or concept of international arbitration law.

C. The English Tradition of Comparative Analysis

The value of internationalism is not new to English law; however, its status with the English judiciary has ebbed and flowed over time. Writing at a time when comparative analysis was enjoying a moment of popularity with English judges, Lord Bingham considered that '[i]n showing a new receptiveness to the experience and learning of others, the English courts are not, I think, establishing a new tradition but reverting to an old and preferable one'.[18] Lord Bingham pointed to historical examples of where English law has drawn on its continental sisters for inspiration, such as 'to the reception of continental commercial law in England in the eighteenth century [and] to the observation of Best J in 1822 that the authority of Pothier's *Treatise on the Law of Obligations* was "the highest that can be had, next to a decision of a court of justice in this country"'.[19]

English law is replete with decisions upon which one can see the imprint of comparative analysis. *Fairchild* is a good example of a case in which the English judiciary have recognized the path-finding potential of comparative analysis. The case turned on how to apply evidentiary rules on proof to an ex-employee's claim against numerous ex-employers for damages arising out of exposure to asbestos. Where the employee could not prove when he suffered damage from asbestos exposure, the standard rules on the balance of probability would preclude a successful claim against any one employer. In considering how to address this problem, Lord Rodger stated that material from European legal systems 'provides a check, from outside the common law world, that the problem identified in these appeals is a genuine one that requires to be remedied'.[20] Even where the case was decided in conformity with prior English case law, comparative analysis contributed to the

17 The New York Convention has 168 States Parties as of March 2021.

18 Thomas Bingham, 'There is a World Elsewhere: The Changing Perspectives of English Law' (1992) 41(3) ICLQ 513, 527.

19 ibid 527–28.

20 *Fairchild v Glenhaven Funeral Services Ltd* [2002] UKHL 22, [2003] 1 AC 32, [165].

identification of the relevant problem, thus marking the path along which English law would develop.

Comparative analysis has long been one of the driving forces in English international commercial arbitration. The UNCITRAL Model Law is itself a creation of comparative analysis.[21] Though England did not adopt the Model Law itself, Lord Steyn describes how it was used 'as a yardstick by which to judge the quality of our existing arbitration legislation and to improve it'.[22] Our current English legislation on arbitration, the Arbitration Act 1996, was drafted with the aim that it should, 'so far as possible, have the same structure and language as the Model Law'.[23] The Arbitration Act 1996 was itself created through the comparative analysis of the Model Law, and is in that sense the English legal system's contribution to the harmonization of international arbitration law.

Beyond the structure and language of the Arbitration Act 1996, the Model Law also inspired certain provisions of the Act. Section 7 of the Act explicitly provides for the separability of arbitration agreements from the contracts in which they are incorporated—as a result, where an arbitral tribunal rules on the invalidity of the contract, it does not simultaneously invalidate the arbitration agreement from which the tribunal derives its authority. Prior to the passing of the Act, this rule had already been established in English law by the Court of Appeal in *Harbour Assurance*.[24] However, in recognition that the English courts might be convinced to overturn *Harbour Assurance*, the Act contains a separability provision based on Article 16(1) of the Model Law.[25] Section 7 of the Arbitration Act 1996 is thus not only directly derived from the Model Law, but was so derived in recognition of the changeable nature of English common law precedent and the more stable nature of codified law.

Comparative analysis remains of the utmost importance in the area of English international arbitration law. Though London remains the most popular seat of arbitration according to the most recent Queen Mary International Arbitration Survey,[26] we must not allow ourselves to become complacent. International arbitration is a major legal industry, with the International Chamber of Commerce (ICC) alone responsible for $230 billion's worth of pending cases at the end of 2019.[27] It should come as little surprise that various legal systems around the world are vying to increase their market share of the international arbitration industry.

[21] Commonwealth Secretariat, *UNCITRAL Model Law on International Commercial Arbitration: Explanatory Documentation prepared for Commonwealth Jurisdictions* (Commonwealth Secretariat 1991) para 1.09.

[22] Johan Steyn, 'England's Response to the Model Law of Arbitration' (1994) 10(1) Arb Intl 1, 1.

[23] Report of the Departmental Advisory Committee on the UNCITRAL Model Law, Department of Trade and Industry, chaired by Lord Mustill (London, 1989) para 108.

[24] *Harbour Assurance Co (UK) Ltd v Kansa General International Assurance Co Ltd* [1993] QB 701 (CA).

[25] Steyn (n 22).

[26] Queen Mary University of London (n 2) 9–12.

[27] ICC, *2019 ICC Dispute Resolution Statistics* (ICC 2020) 14.

As stated by the late VV Veeder QC, 'significant changes to international arbitration are largely driven by users rather than States':[28] where users of arbitration become aware of a benefit of arbitrating in another country, they are likely to push for that same benefit to be incorporated into their own law. The recent reform of Russian arbitration law was initially sparked by just such a bottom-up initiative, with the local arbitration community pushing for Russian international arbitration law to be updated in line with the 2006 amendments to the UNCITRAL Model Law.[29] Within the competitive arena of international arbitration, legal systems are thus constant comparing notes with one another as they strive to maintain or increase their relevance to the world of international arbitration.[30]

Furthermore, it has become increasingly common for judges around the world to turn to soft law instruments that the arbitration community itself produces. These soft law instruments are the result of discussions between arbitration experts from around the globe, and provide rules that are themselves born of comparative analysis.[31] A good example of such reference by the English courts can be found in the recent Supreme Court decision of *Halliburton v Chubb*,[32] where the court had regard to the IBA Guidelines on Conflicts of Interest in considering how best to develop the English rules on disclosure and impartiality. The influence of these soft law instruments on national legal systems opens up a further avenue through which comparative analysis flows into English arbitration law to enrich it.

One final point to be made on the subject of the English tradition of comparative analysis is that Brexit poses no risk to this tradition. For all the nationalistic rhetoric surrounding Brexit, it will have little effect on how the judiciary approach the cases brought before them. Specifically within the area of international arbitration, the majority of the respondents to the 2018 Queen Mary survey did not see Brexit having any impact on London's popularity as a seat of arbitration as its formal legal infrastructure will remain unchanged.[33] Going forward, parties can expect the same level of professionalism, intellect, and practicality that the English courts

[28] VV Veeder QC, 'Arbitral Reform and Legal History: "The Blank Piece of Paper"' in AV Asoskov, RM Khodykin, and AN Zhiltsov (eds), *New Horizons of International Arbitration* (Russian Institute of Modern Arbitration 2019) 50, 52.

[29] Though note that the reform took a different path once the government got involved. See Gleb Vladimirovich Sevastyanov, 'Третейская реформа в России: хронология основных событий и специфика содержания', Zakon.ru (20 November 2015) <https://online.zakon.kz/Document/?doc_id=34232820> accessed 18 May 2021.

[30] A recent example of this process can be found in the Luxembourg 2020 arbitration reform bill, which is inspired by the rules on arbitration in the French Code of Civil Procedure.

[31] For example, the working group for the IBA Guidelines on Conflicts of Interest was comprised of nineteen pre-eminent arbitration experts from a mix of civil and common law jurisdictions (IBA, *IBA Guidelines on Conflicts of Interest in International Arbitration* (IBA 2015)); while the more recent Prague rules boasts a working group of forty-six representatives, though mostly from civil law jurisdictions ('Working Group', praguerules.com (2021) <www.praguerules.com/working_group/> accessed 4 April 2022).

[32] *Halliburton Company v Chubb Bermuda Insurance* [2020] UKSC 48, [2021] AC 1083.

[33] Queen Mary University of London (n 2) 9.

have always been known for, as well as the same sensitivity to the international legal landscape.

D. Lord Collins the Comparativist

Lord Collins stands as a prime example of the English judicial tradition of comparative analysis. It should come as no surprise that Lord Collins should feature alongside other members of the English judiciary who have navigated the waters that separate English law from the other laws of the world: Lord Collins is used to crossing frontiers, being the first solicitor directly appointed from private practice to the High Court. In the remainder of this chapter, I would like to focus on one case from Lord Collins's judicial career in particular, *Dallah*,[34] and Lord Collins's use of comparative legal analysis in it.

The case concerned a course of dealings between Dallah, the Government of Pakistan, and a trust established by the government. Dallah had made a proposal to the Government of Pakistan to provide housing for Pakistani pilgrims in Mecca. Dallah and the Government entered into a memorandum of understanding that Dallah would go on to provide this housing. Later, the Government established a trust for the purpose of investing in schemes such as that proposed by Dallah. Dallah and the trust entered into an agreement, which included a clause providing for ICC arbitration in Paris.

A few months after entering into the agreement, the Government collapsed the trust with which Dallah had contracted. The secretary of the board of trustees, who was also the Secretary of the Ministry of Religious Affairs of Pakistan, gave notice of termination of the agreement to Dallah. Dallah commenced ICC arbitration against the Government in Paris, eventually succeeding in receiving a number of awards against the government. The Government had refused to participate in the arbitration on the basis that it was not party to the agreement, and therefore was not bound by the clause providing for arbitration.

Dallah sought enforcement of the award before the English courts. The Government of Pakistan resisted enforcement on the basis that it was not bound by the arbitration clause. At first instance, Aikens J, as he then was, refused enforcement under section 103(2)(b) of the Arbitration Act 1996 on the basis that the arbitration agreement was not valid as between the parties under the law of France, as the country where the award was made.[35] Aikens J's decision was upheld by the

[34] *Dallah Real Estate and Tourism Holding Co v Ministry of Religious Affairs of the Government of Pakistan* [2010] UKSC 46, [2011] 1 AC 763.
[35] *Dallah Real Estate and Tourism Holding Co v Ministry of Religious Affairs, Government of Pakistan* [2008] EWHC 1901 (Comm), [2008] 2 Lloyd's Rep 535.

Court of Appeal, with Moore-Bick LJ giving lead judgment.[36] Finally, the case was appealed to the Supreme Court, where it was heard, inter alia, by Lord Collins.

The two key questions raised before the Supreme Court during the course of proceedings were: first, to what extent should a court of enforcement reconsider the issue of an arbitral tribunal's jurisdiction; and, second, was the Government of Pakistan bound by the arbitration clause under French law. The Supreme Court upheld the lower courts' decisions, finding that an English court of enforcement is entitled to redecide the question of a tribunal's jurisdiction *de novo*, and that the Government of Pakistan was not bound by the arbitration clause.

This chapter is concerned with Lord Collins's approach to the first question, and his use of comparative analysis in answering it. Though the second question also touched upon foreign law, it did not involve comparative analysis; rather it required the Supreme Court to answer the impossible question of how the French courts would decide a highly controversial point of law. The following section will describe how Lord Collins referred to German, French, and US law in considering the proper direction for English law to adopt in its development. I will then conclude by considering how the comparative tradition to which Lord Collins contributed has survived into recent Supreme Court decisions on international arbitration.

The issue of the court's power to review a tribunal's decision on jurisdiction is inseparably tied up with the competence-competence, or *kompetenz-kompetenz*, doctrine in international arbitration. The competence-competence doctrine holds that an arbitral tribunal has the power to rule on its own jurisdiction. Where one of the parties wishes to challenge the validity of the arbitration agreement, or to argue that the dispute does not fall within the scope of the arbitration clause, the very tribunal whose jurisdiction is in dispute is entitled to decide the issue. However, the fact that the tribunal is entitled to rule on its jurisdiction does not determine the consequences of such a ruling.

In particular, there is the question of the relationship between the tribunal's jurisdiction to rule on its own jurisdiction and the responsibility of the courts to ensure that a party is not forced to arbitration without having so consented. Courts fulfil this responsibility differently depending on their role in an arbitration: the courts of the seat will do so under their national law, while courts outside the seat will do so under the provisions of the New York Convention 1958.[37] Of particular relevance to the issue of the tribunal's jurisdiction are the exceptions to the recognition of an arbitration clause under Article II(3) where the clause is null and void, inoperative, or incapable of being performed; and the defences to an arbitral

[36] *Dallah Real Estate and Tourism Holding Co v Ministry of Religious Affairs of the Government of Pakistan* [2009] EWCA Civ 755, [2011] 1 AC 763.

[37] As under English law international treaties are not directly applicable without national legislation implementing them, the defences to a foreign arbitral award under English law are technically found in s 103 of the Arbitration Act 1996 as opposed to the Convention itself.

award under Articles V(1)(a) and V(1)(c), which provide defences where the parties are not bound by a valid arbitration clause and where the dispute falls outside the scope of the parties' submission to arbitration.

There is thus a tension between the doctrine of competence-competence and the role of the court in ensuring that defective arbitration clauses are not recognized and defective arbitral awards are not enforced. It is important in this regard to understand the conflicting policies at play in this tension. It is not difficult to understand the policy that supports court oversight in arbitration: it is important both for the integrity of national legal systems, and for the healthy development of arbitration, that arbitration should not become an instrument of abuse. Where tribunals are entitled to rule on their jurisdiction without any external check by the courts, parties may be unjustly forced into arbitration where a tribunal comes to the wrong conclusion as to their jurisdiction.

On the other hand, the competence-competence doctrine is underpinned by the policy of expediency. Without the competence-competence doctrine, the only forum in which the tribunal's jurisdiction could be determined would be the national courts. A recalcitrant defendant who regrets agreeing to arbitration or otherwise wishes to delay proceedings could initiate court proceedings to challenge the tribunal's jurisdiction: depending on the speed of the legal system in question, this could cause severe delay to the arbitration. The doctrine of competence-competence ensures expediency by allowing the arbitral tribunal to consider the question itself, and to continue with the arbitration should it conclude that it does have jurisdiction.

A further potential justification for the doctrine of competence-competence is party autonomy. Where the parties have agreed to arbitration, they have expressed a preference that their disputes be heard by their chosen arbitrators and not by a national judge. This preference might be construed in such a way that the parties intended that all issues relating to their dispute, including issues of the tribunal's jurisdiction, should be heard in arbitration and not before the courts of the seat. This vein of thought is closely tied up with the autonomist theory of arbitration which holds that arbitration does not depend on national legal systems for its authority but on party autonomy—in other words that arbitration can, and should, exist independently of national legal systems.

The specific question that was before the Supreme Court in *Dallah* was the related question as to how a court should approach a prior ruling by an arbitral tribunal that the arbitral tribunal had jurisdiction. On the one hand, Dallah argued that, as the tribunal had already addressed the question of jurisdiction, and thus the court should not conduct a full rehearing of the issue; the court should only conduct a limited inquiry into jurisdiction, giving weight to the arbitrators' decisions. On the other hand, the lower courts had decided that the English courts are entitled to hold a full inquiry into the arbitral tribunal's jurisdiction when the award was presented for enforcement. In other words, the Supreme Court had to decide how far the doctrine of competence-competence reached under English law, and whether a ruling by the tribunal was able to bind the court, or otherwise carry any weight, where the court comes to its own view on the arbitral tribunal's jurisdiction.

In his judgment at [86]–[92], Lord Collins considers how other jurisdictions have addressed this same question. By describing the position of other laws on the allocation of power between the courts and the arbitral tribunal in determining the tribunal's jurisdiction, Lord Collins is able to deploy both path-finding and hazard-marking information. This information supports the Supreme Court's decision to allow the English courts fully to review the tribunal's jurisdiction when enforcing an arbitral award.

The first jurisdiction that Lord Collins mentions is Germany. The competence-competence doctrine originated in German law, where it 'resolve[d] logical difficulties ... where the jurisdiction of state courts and the jurisdiction of arbitrators under a valid arbitration agreement are mutually exclusive'.[38] Historically, the German courts had allowed the parties to agree that the arbitral tribunal should be entitled to issue a final and binding decision as to their jurisdiction;[39] however, German law had abandoned this position by the time that *Dallah* was decided.[40]

At [87], Lord Collins refers to this historical development in German law. By doing so, he points out that even those jurisdictions which once allowed arbitral tribunals to come to final and binding decisions on their jurisdiction have subsequently abandoned this position to impose some form of court review. Where a foreign legal system has departed from a specific rule, this is a good indicator that the rule did not prove satisfactory. Lord Collins thus derived hazard-marking information from German law's departure from the rule by which courts had previously been prohibited from reviewing an arbitral tribunal's ruling on jurisdiction.

The second jurisdiction that Lord Collins considers in his judgment is that of France. French law has a reputation for pushing the boundaries of arbitration's autonomy from national legal systems. This is most notable in the French courts' treatment of foreign arbitral awards that have been annulled at the seat, which remain enforceable in France as long as they do not engage one of the defences to enforcement under Article 1520 of the French Code of Civil Procedure. As a jurisdiction that often prioritizes the autonomy of arbitration from national courts, French arbitration law provides valuable perspective when considering the range of available options when developing one's own law.

Prior to the issue of the award by an arbitral tribunal, French law takes a very light touch in its consideration of the arbitral tribunal's jurisdiction. At this stage,

[38] Department for Trade and Industry Departmental Advisory Committee, February 1994 Report on a Draft Arbitration Bill cited at [94] of *Dallah* (n 34).

[39] Klaus Peter Berger, 'Germany Adopts the UNCITRAL Model Law' (1998) 1(3) Intl Arb Rev 121, 122.

[40] Gary Born, *International Commercial Arbitration* (2nd edn, Kluwer Law International 2014) 1124.

the court may only intervene if the arbitration agreement is manifestly null or inapplicable.[41] Interim rulings on a tribunal's jurisdiction are thus limited to a prima facie examination of the issue, with a more substantive inquiry being left to the tribunal. The French position developed to prevent tactics by respondents seeking to slow down arbitral proceedings or otherwise escape their obligation to arbitrate.[42] Moreover, in the absence of an express choice of law for the arbitration clause itself, the French courts eschew a conflict of laws analysis to determine its governing law and instead apply mandatory rules of French law and international public policy.[43] The result is that prior to the issue of the arbitral award, the French courts not only restrict themselves to a prima facie analysis of an arbitration clause, but often do so under rules that favour the validity of the arbitration clause.

At [88]–[89], Lord Collins draws attention to the distinction under French law between the court's power to review an arbitral tribunal's jurisdiction prior to, and after, the issue of the award. Where an award is brought before the French courts either for enforcement if it is a foreign award, or annulment or enforcement if it is a French award, the French courts will conduct a full, *de novo* assessment of whether the arbitral tribunal had jurisdiction over the dispute.[44] By drawing attention to this distinction under French law, Lord Collins illustrates how even a jurisdiction that prioritizes the tribunal's autonomy from national courts acknowledges the necessity of providing for a full review on the matter of jurisdiction before giving effect to an award. In this sense, Lord Collins derives path-finding information from the development of French law. French law developed separate standards of review of an arbitral tribunal's jurisdiction at different points in the life cycle of an arbitration to ensure both that arbitration is not vulnerable to delaying tactics and that the courts may ensure that the tribunal wrongly assumed jurisdiction. Thus, the French courts, though they place great weight on the expediency and autonomy of arbitration, recognize the necessity of a full review of the tribunal's jurisdiction.

Finally, Lord Collins turns his attention to US arbitration law. US arbitration law is interesting in that it has adopted a position not dissimilar from the historic position under German law.[45] Where the parties have clearly and unmistakably agreed between themselves that the arbitral tribunal may give a final and binding ruling as to its jurisdiction, then the courts may not look behind the tribunal's decision; this has been recently reaffirmed by the US Supreme Court even in situations where the court considers that assumption of jurisdiction by the arbitral tribunal was wholly

[41] *Société LABM Caraïbes v Société Gaz transport et Tecnigaz* Cour de Cass 1re Ch civ, 18 May 2011, [2011](2) Rev arb 583.

[42] Born (n 40) 1111.

[43] *République de Guinée Équatoriale v société Fitzpatrick équatorial Guinea Ltd* Cour d'appel de Paris, Pôle 1 Ch 1, 7 April 2011, [2011] Rev arb 577; *Municipalité de Khoms El Mergeb v société Dalico* Cour de Cass 1re Ch civ, 20 December 1993, [1994] Rev arb 116.

[44] *Fondation Albert Abela Family Foundation (AAFF) v Fondation Joseph Abela Family Foundation (JAFF)*, Cour de cass 1re Ch civ, 6 October 2010 [2010] Rev arb 970.

[45] *Dallah* (n 34) 1123–24.

groundless.[46] The US position prioritizes party autonomy over the court review by allowing the parties to contract out-of-court review with respect to jurisdiction. On this point, US law resembles the laws of those countries that allow parties effectively to delocalize their arbitrations from the seat of arbitration by contracting out of the review mechanisms for arbitral awards found in local legislation.[47]

Having outlined the pro-party autonomy rule under US arbitration law, Lord Collins then turns to the application of the competence-competence doctrine in situations where a party resists arbitration on the basis that there was no arbitration agreement in the first place. Citing *China Minmetals*,[48] Lord Collins explains that US courts do conduct inquiries into the tribunal's jurisdiction in such circumstances as 'a contract cannot give an arbitral body any power, much less the power to determine its own jurisdiction, if the parties never entered into it'.[49] The underlying principle that the tribunal may not use its powers under the competence-competence doctrine to impose obligations upon the parties that they did not themselves agree is reflected in English case law, where it has previously been held that an 'arbitrator may not clothe himself with jurisdiction'.[50]

Lord Collins thus shows that even a jurisdiction which allows the parties to contract out of court review in arbitration does not oust the court's power to consider the issue of whether the parties have in fact so contracted. The US rules on competence-competence thus provides path-marking information by showing that, even where a national law allows parties to contract into an extreme form of competence-competence, the court must nevertheless retain the ability to rule on whether the parties have entered into such a contract. Without such a rule, the logical extreme of competence-competence would mean that as soon as a party claims to have entered into an arbitration clause, the court's jurisdiction would be ousted until an arbitral tribunal has been composed and ruled on the issue, regardless of whether there is any evidence whatsoever of the alleged arbitration clause's existence.

The information that Lord Collins derives from these three jurisdictions can thus be summarized as follows. German law has abandoned its previous position of allowing the parties to oust the court's power to review an arbitral tribunal's ruling on jurisdiction, suggesting that German law had found the previous position unsatisfactory. Despite its tendency to prioritize the expediency and autonomy of

[46] *Henry Schein, Inc v Archer & White Sales, Inc* 139 S Ct 524 (2019).

[47] These jurisdictions include Switzerland (Domitille Baizeau, 'Commentary on Chapter 12 PIL, Article 192 [Waiver of Annulment]' in Manuel Arroyo (ed), *Arbitration in Switzerland: The Practitioner's Guide* (2nd edn, Kluwer Law International 2018) 378–79), and Russia (Federal Law No. 382-FZ dated 29 December 2015 on Arbitration (Arbitral Proceedings) in the Russian Federation, arts 16(3), 34(1)). Though Russia only allows parties to do this where they arbitrate within one of the few government-licensed arbitral institutes.

[48] *China Minmetals Materials Import and Export Co Ltd v Chei Mei Corp* 334 F3d 274 (3d Cir 2003).

[49] ibid [288].

[50] *Heyman v Darwins* [1942] AC 356.

arbitration, French law only limits the court's powers of review prior to the issue of the award: French law thus recognizes the necessity of such review. Finally, even though US law goes as far as to allow the parties to contract out of the court's review of the arbitral tribunal's jurisdiction, it nevertheless insists that the courts have the power to determine if the parties have so contracted: US law thus emphasizes that, even where arbitration is given a great deal of autonomy, the courts must retain a minimum degree of supervision to protect against abuse.

Applied to the question of whether the English courts are entitled to decide *de novo* whether one of the parties to an arbitration was bound by the arbitration clause, Lord Collins's comparative analysis supported the Supreme Court's conclusion that the English courts should conduct a full review of the tribunal's jurisdiction. While this information did not change the substantive consideration of English law described in the judgments of both Lord Collins and Lord Mance, it nonetheless provided a sense-check to ensure that English law does not unduly deviate from international standards in arbitration.[51] Lord Bingham's comment that '[p]rocedural idiosyncrasy is not (like national costume or regional cuisine) to be nurtured for its own sake'[52] is particularly apt in an area like international arbitration, where parties have come to expect certain standards from the major arbitration centres, and unnecessary deviation from those standards may alarm parties and cause them to take their business elsewhere.

E. Concluding Remarks

The English judicial tradition of comparative analysis in international arbitration law, and Lord Collins's contributions to it, survives into the modern day. Since *Dallah* was decided in 2010, the Supreme Court has had occasion to rule on English arbitration law in six cases.[53] Of these cases, the Supreme Court gave consideration to the arbitration law of other jurisdictions in three of them: *Taurus*,[54] *Enka*,[55] and *Halliburton*.[56] The other three cases concerned matters which do not

[51] Comparative analysis has provided a similar 'sense-check' functions even in areas of law that are not as inherently international arbitration. See Lord Binghams's use of comparative analysis with respect to the risk (or lack thereof) of an opening of the floodgates with respect to the tortious liability of public authorities in *D v East Berkshire Community Health NHS Trust* [2005] UKHL 23, [2005] 2 AC 373.

[52] *Dresser UK Ltd v Falcongate Ltd* [1992] QB 502, 522.

[53] *AES Ust-Kamenogorsk Hydropower Plant LLP v Ust-Kamenogorsk Hydropower Plant JSC* [2013] UKHL 35, [2013] 1 WLR 1889; *IPCO (Nigeria) Ltd v Nigerian National Petroleum Corpn* [2017] UKSC 16, [2017] 1 WLR 970; *Fulton Shipping Inc of Panama v Globalia Business Travel SAU* [2017] UKSC 43, [2017] 1 WLR 2581; *Taurus Petroleum Ltd v State Oil Marketing Co of the Ministry of Oil, Republic of Iraq* [2017] UKSC 64, [2018] AC 690; *Enka Insaat ve Sanayi AS v OOO Insurance Company Chubb* [2020] UKSC 38, [2020] 1 WLR 4117; *Halliburton* (n 32).

[54] *Taurus* (n 53) [38]–[40].

[55] *Enka* (n 53) [55]–[58], [224]–[225].

[56] *Halliburton* (n 32) [112]–[114].

lend themselves to comparative analysis, as the issues involved were the grant of anti-suit injunctions,[57] security in enforcement proceedings,[58] and the English courts' power to review an arbitrator's application of English law under section 69 of the Arbitration Act 1996.[59] Of particular importance are the decisions in *Enka* and *Halliburton*: not only do these cases reflect the current predisposition of the Supreme Court, but they are also decisions on some of the most important aspects of English arbitration law.

Enka concerned the approach to be taken when considering the law applicable to an arbitration agreement. There were two conflicting paradigms that had been advanced in English case law: *XL Insurance*[60] held that in the absence of an explicit choice of law by the parties, the law of the seat should be the default choice due to the strong connection between the law of the seat and the arbitration clause; *Sulamérica*[61] held that in the absence of an explicit choice of law for the arbitration clause the most natural choice would be the law chosen to govern the rest of the contract. As arbitration clauses rarely have explicit choices of law, a Supreme Court decision in this area will necessarily have a long-lasting and major impact on English arbitration. Given the importance of this area, it is heartening to see at [55]–[58] and [224]–[225] that not only the majority (made up of Lord Hamblen, Lord Leggatt, and Lord Kerr) but also Lord Burrows, dissenting, reviewed the practice of other jurisdictions: particular stress was placed upon the arbitration law of Singapore, which is another major arbitration centre.

Halliburton concerned the rules on disclosure and the standards of impartiality applicable in situations of repeat appointment by an arbitrator by one of the parties. The case involved Chubb taking part in two arbitrations arising out of the same facts, involving two other parties, and where Chubb had appointed the chairman of the first arbitration as its arbitrator in the second. I recently had occasion to talk about *Halliburton* in the 2020 Chancery Bar Association Lecture, where I expressed concern that if the English courts took a more stringent approach to disclosure and impartiality than other jurisdictions, this would lead to a number of foreign arbitral awards being refused enforcement even though those awards would meet the requirements for enforcement in most other jurisdictions.[62] This in turn could hurt England's reputation as an arbitration-friendly jurisdiction. I am glad to say that these concerns were unwarranted, as the Supreme Court (Lord Hodge giving the lead judgment) at [112] to [115] reviewed both Scottish law and the common practice of those jurisdictions that have adopted the UNCITRAL Model Law. Where

[57] *Ust-Kamenogorsk* (n 53).

[58] *IPCO* (n 53).

[59] *Globalia* (n 53).

[60] *XL Insurance v Owens Corning* [2001] 1 All ER (Comm) 530.

[61] *Sulamérica Cia Nacional de Seguros SA v Enesa Engenharia SA* [2012] EWCA Civ 638, [2013] 1 WLR 102.

[62] Elizabeth Gloster, 'An Arbitration Perspective—Old Chestnuts and New Surprises?' (Chancery Bar Association Lecture, online, 2020).

the English judiciary is willing to learn from, and develop alongside, other jurisdictions, any possible fears of deviation from international standards and scaring parties from London arbitration may be put to rest.

That we can still celebrate this rich vein of English judicial practice today is thanks to those who have come before us. Judges like Lord Mansfield, Lord Bingham, and, of course, Lord Collins, have passed the torch from generation to generation within our judiciary, both maintaining, and highlighting the value of, comparative analysis in the development of English law. For that alone, we owe a great debt to Lord Collins and I am honoured to offer up this chapter in celebration of his achievements.

6

Foreign Affairs, Parliament, and the Judiciary

Campbell McLachlan

A. Introduction

Among the many areas of law illuminated by Lawrence Collins's scholarship has been his work in foreign relations law. It is a field that sits between the national and the international—between constitutional law, public international law and private international law—and often concerns matters of high political moment. In his influential 25th FA Mann lecture 'Foreign Relations and the Judiciary',[1] Collins suggested that, while the courts must show 'a sensitivity to foreign policy interests', and that matters of foreign policy may, 'at least in some respects', be non-justiciable,[2] this did not detract from their obligation to decide cases according to the law 'and certainly not deference to the views or objectives of the executive'.[3]

The relation between the three branches of government in the UK—executive, judiciary, and Parliament—was put to the test not once but twice in the course of the UK's most significant foreign policy decision of recent years: Brexit, its withdrawal from the EU. Much ink has been spilled on the judgment of the Supreme Court in the first case brought by Gina Miller against the government: *Miller (No 1)*.[4] However, despite the high drama occasioned by that case, the Court's decision turned in the end on an orthodox understanding of parliamentary sovereignty: Parliament's sovereign power to make the law applicable within the UK.

By contrast, *Miller (No 2)*[5] appears at first blush to be the more radical judgment. It does not turn on Parliament's sovereign power to legislate. Instead, the Court ruled that the government's exercise of its power to recommend to Her Majesty to

[1] Lawrence Collins, 'Foreign Relations and the Judiciary' (2002) 51 ICLQ 485.

[2] ibid 501–02, 510.

[3] ibid 510.

[4] *R (Miller) v Secretary of State for Exiting the European Union* [2017] UKSC 5, [2018] AC 61 (*Miller (No 1)*), as to which see: Mark Elliott, 'The Supreme Court's Judgment in *Miller*: In Search of Constitutional Principle' (2017) 76 Cambridge LJ 257; David Feldman, 'Pulling a Trigger or Starting a Journey? Brexit in the Supreme Court' (2017) 76 Cambridge LJ 217; Paul Craig, '*Miller*, Structural Constitutional Review and the Limits of Prerogative Power' [2017] PL 48; Campbell McLachlan, 'The Foreign Relations Power in the Supreme Court' (2018) 134 LQR 380.

[5] *R (Miller) v Prime Minister* [2019] UKSC 41, [2020] AC 373 (*Miller (No 2)*).

Campbell McLachlan, *Foreign Affairs, Parliament, and the Judiciary* In: *Essays in International Litigation for Lord Collins*. Edited by: Jonathan Harris and Campbell McLachlan, Oxford University Press. © Oxford University Press 2022.
DOI: 10.1093/oso/9780192867988.003.0007

prorogue Parliament was unlawful because it would interfere with 'a second constitutional principle, that of parliamentary accountability'.[6]

To its critics, this judgment is deprecated as an unwarranted and unprecedented interference by the judiciary in the exercise of an undoubted prerogative power in just that context of high political moment where the courts should not intervene.[7] The debate is cast in domestic terms, as a question of the separation of powers within the British Constitution. Among the criticisms levelled against the judgment is the proposition that the principle of parliamentary accountability may underpin various constitutional conventions, but is not a *legal* principle, capable of producing legal rather than merely political consequences if the executive fails to adhere to it.

It is the burden of this chapter to argue that this argument is fundamentally mistaken in the context in which the issue of accountability arose in that case. What was at issue in *Miller (No 2)* was not merely parliamentary accountability in general. It was the accountability of the executive for its exercise of the foreign relations power in its negotiations with the EU on the terms of Brexit. It is *this* context—parliamentary accountability in foreign affairs—that made a crucial difference in *Miller (No 2)*. Yet, it is precisely the scope of the constitutional principle of parliamentary accountability as it applies specifically to foreign affairs that has long been neglected.

The argument presented here is that parliamentary accountability for foreign affairs plays a role in the British Constitution that is both of great historical antiquity and of fundamental importance. It does not undermine the power of the executive as representative of the State on the international plane. Rather it acts as a check on the exercise of that power, confirming the indivisibility of Parliament's sovereignty within the constitutional structure. Foreign affairs are in this respect different: not because the constitution defers to the executive for their conduct, but because the *quid pro quo* for the allocation to the executive of the foreign affairs power is the equally legal power of Parliament to supervise its exercise.

In order to unpack this argument, it will be necessary to begin by examining the manner in which the issue arose in *Miller (No 2)* itself. Section B will then examine relevant British State practice, which may be traced to the earliest emergence of constitutional government. The origins of this practice are to be found in

[6] ibid [46].

[7] See eg Timothy Endicott, 'Making Constitutional Principles into Laws' (2020) 136 LQR 175; David Feldman, 'Prerogative Powers, Constitutional Principles and Legal Wrongs: Constitutional Implications of the Prorogation Judgment' (2020) 25 Judicial Rev 210; Martin Loughlin, 'A Note on Craig on *Miller; Cherry*' [2020] PL 278; John Finnis, *The Unconstitutionality of the Supreme Court's Prorogation Judgment* (Policy Exchange, 28 September 2019); and the written evidence of R Ekins to the UK House of Commons Public Administration and Constitutional Affairs Committee, 'Prorogation and the Constitutional Implications of the Supreme Court's Judgment Inquiry' (8 October 2019). For the contrary view: Mark Elliott, 'Constitutional Adjudication and Constitutional Politics in the United Kingdom: The *Miller II* Case in Legal and Political Context' (2020) 16 EuConst 625; Paul Craig, 'The Supreme Court, Prorogation and Constitutional Principle' [2020] PL 248.

the parliamentary power of impeachment. This power retains continuing salience outside the UK as a result of its adoption in the US Constitution, as witnessed in the impeachment proceedings against President Trump. While impeachment as a remedy may have fallen into desuetude in Britain, Parliament's legal power of supervision inherent in such a remedy has not. It has simply found other forms of expression. In section C, it will then be possible to consider the arguments in principle for the manner in which parliamentary accountability for foreign affairs may be exercised today. Section D will consider the contemporary implications for the legal powers of Parliament in this field.

B. *Miller (No 2)* and the Principle of Parliamentary Accountability

Applications for Judicial Review in London and in Edinburgh

Miller (No 2) was in fact a decision on two applications for judicial review: one commenced by a group of Scottish Members of Parliament before the Court of Session ('*Cherry*'); and one commenced by Mrs Gina Miller before the Divisional Court in England. In each case, the claims sought review of the same decision of the Prime Minister to advise the Queen to prorogue Parliament for up to five weeks until 14 October 2019. The significance of the date was that the government's then announced intention was to withdraw from the EU by 31 October 2019, whether or not terms for a Withdrawal Agreement had been agreed. The petitioners alleged that this decision would, if it were to remain in place, severely inhibit the sovereign powers of Parliament.

Prorogation is a prerogative power that brings a session of Parliament to an end. While Parliament is prorogued, neither House can meet, debate, or pass legislation. Neither House can debate government policy. Nor may members of either House ask questions of Ministers. The government, however, remains in office and can exercise all those powers that the law permits.[8]

There were material differences in the argument that was advanced before the courts in each case. In the Divisional Court, Lord Pannick QC, counsel for Mrs Miller, took as his starting point the principle of parliamentary sovereignty, which he characterized as:

> not confined to the principle that the Crown in Parliament is sovereign, and that primary legislation enacted by the Crown with the consent of both Houses of Parliament is supreme. It is a much broader legal principle than that. It entails

[8] *Miller (No 2)* (n 5) [2]; House of Commons Library, 'Prorogation of Parliament' (Briefing Paper No 8589, 11 June 2019) 3.

> the right of Parliament to make any law it sees fits and is therefore 'engaged' by a decision of the Executive to advise the Queen to exercise a prerogative power in order to 'prevent or impede' Parliament from sitting and making law as it thinks appropriate.[9]

In other words, the constitutional principle that Mrs Miller invoked in the English proceedings was the sovereignty of Parliament to *legislate*.

In the Court of Session, on the other hand, the petitioners argued that '[t]he Government was politically accountable to Parliament in the exercise of its powers. The Government would be acting unlawfully if it curtailed political accountability ... The power [of prorogation] was lawfully exercised only if it was consistent with constitutional principle. It had to be exercised for a proper purpose.'[10]

In London, a unanimous Divisional Court (Lord Burnett CJ, Sir Terence Etherton MR, and Dame Victoria Sharp P) rejected Mrs Miller's claim. It held that the Prime Minister's decision was non-justiciable as involving a 'political' issue, lacking measurable legal standards against which that decision could be judged by the courts.[11] The expanded conception of parliamentary sovereignty formulated by Lord Pannick QC would undermine the separation of powers by requiring the judicial arm to exercise 'hitherto unidentified power over the Executive branch of the state in its dealings with Parliament'.[12]

In Edinburgh, by contrast, the Inner House of the Court of Session (Lord Carloway, Lord Brodie, and Lord Drummond Young), reversing the Lord Ordinary, held unanimously that the petitioners must succeed. The Court's reasoning appears particularly clearly from the speech of Lord Drummond Young. He opens by distinguishing between parliamentary sovereignty as a legislative function on the one hand, and a separate principle, which his Lordship defined as follows:

> Parliament has a second equally important function, namely that of holding the Executive to account. The policies and actions of the government are subject to scrutiny in Parliament by Members of Parliament. The United Kingdom operates by a system of representative democracy, and it is Members of Parliament, representing the interests of their constituents and the wider interests of the country, who are responsible for ensuring that the executive operates in the national interest. In particular, Parliament is responsible for ensuring that the actions of the Executive are subject to critical scrutiny, with representatives of the government reporting on and explaining those actions. In this way Parliament performs the fundamental role of protecting the country from the arbitrary exercise or

[9] *R (Miller) v Prime Minister* [2019] EWHC 2381 (QB), [2019] 4 All ER 299 [25] (*Miller (No 2)*, Divisional Court Judgment).

[10] *Cherry v Advocate General* [2019] CSIH 49, 2020 SC 37 [29], [31].

[11] *Miller (No 2)*, Divisional Court Judgment (n 9) [47].

[12] ibid [63].

> abuse of Executive power. The importance of the latter function is obvious, both in the abstract and in the light of the events during the 17th century that gave rise to the principle of parliamentary sovereignty.[13]

It was, thought his Lordship, central to the rule of law that the courts retain the power to subject the act of the executive 'to judicial scrutiny to ensure that it is within the scope of the legal power under which it is exercised'.[14] This power must necessarily extend to the prorogation of Parliament.

Appeals in both cases were brought before the Supreme Court: in *Cherry*, the Advocate General appealed; in *Miller (No 2)*, Mrs Miller appealed. The Court heard both appeals together, as they both raised the same issue.

The course of argument largely followed the emphasis that counsel had adopted in the courts below. Lord Pannick QC for Mrs Miller opened with Parliament's sovereign ability to legislate as the prime ground upon which prorogation should be reviewed.[15] Sir James Eadie QC for the Prime Minister responded that 'prorogation is political in nature' and that, along with decisions of high policy in defence and foreign affairs, it was non-reviewable by the courts in view of the lack of manageable or judicial standards against which to test the exercise of the power.[16]

By contrast, Aidan O'Neill QC for the petitioners in *Cherry* submitted:

> Parliamentary accountability is the animating principle of the United Kingdom constitution. The executive is accountable to Parliament and Parliament is in turn accountable to the people. The UK Parliament represents the people and nations of the United Kingdom as its sovereign legislature to which the UK Government is on all matters politically answerable and accountable. To be accountable it has to come before, and speak under questioning to, the elected representatives of the people assembled in that Parliament. Unlike in other countries, the executive is not elected directly by the people and its accountability is not directly to the people. To claim otherwise is contrary to our principle of representative democracy and amounts to populism.[17]

Lord Keen of Elie QC in reply said: 'Here, we have reference to "Parliamentary accountability" but what legal content does that concept actually embrace as distinct from its practical and factual content?'[18]

[13] *Cherry* (n 10) [99].
[14] ibid [102].
[15] *Miller (No 2)* (n 5) 377.
[16] ibid 382.
[17] ibid 385.
[18] ibid 392–93.

Significantly, it was Sir John Major, a former Prime Minister, who particularly emphasized in his intervention that the issue was whether the use of the prorogation power materially impeded Parliament's ability to hold the government to account. He submitted:

> Parliament does not only exercise its sovereignty through legislation. It exercises it through summoning papers and people, through holding the Government to account on the floor of the Houses of Parliament, and if necessary by holding people in contempt of Parliament.[19]

The Supreme Court on Parliamentary Accountability

In its unanimous judgment, the Supreme Court accepted that parliamentary sovereignty—in the sense of Parliament's power to legislate—could be undermined if the executive was able, through the use of the prerogative, to prevent Parliament from legislating for an unlimited period.[20]

At the same time, it upheld 'a second constitutional principle, that of parliamentary accountability'. The Court explained this principle in the following terms:

> Ministers are accountable to Parliament through such mechanisms as their duty to answer Parliamentary questions and to appear before Parliamentary committees, and through Parliamentary scrutiny of the delegated legislation which ministers make. By these means, the policies of the executive are subjected to consideration by the representatives of the electorate, the executive is required to report, explain and defend its actions, and citizens are protected from the arbitrary exercise of executive power.[21]

The Court decided that the legal limit to the exercise of the prorogation power had to be set by reference to 'the extent to which the measure impedes or frustrates the operation of the relevant principle must have a reasonable justification'.[22] Here, it considered that there was no doubt that the decision to prorogue did impede the ability of Parliament to hold the government to account for its conduct of the Brexit negotiation in light of the 'fundamental change [that] was due to take place in the constitution of the United Kingdom on 31 October 2019'.[23] The remaining question was whether there was a reasonable justification for the measure. The

[19] ibid 390.
[20] ibid [42].
[21] ibid [46].
[22] ibid [49].
[23] ibid [57].

Court held that 'it is impossible for us to conclude, on the evidence which has been put before us, that there was any reason—let alone a good reason—to advise Her Majesty to prorogue Parliament for five weeks'.[24] As a result, it held that the decision was unlawful and that Parliament had not been prorogued.

Ultimately, then, it was the importance of the principle of parliamentary *accountability*, and not Parliament's sovereign power to legislate, that was held to justify the court's intervention to set aside the decision to prorogue. The decision prompts deeper reflection on the nature of this 'second constitutional principle'. It has long been regarded as axiomatic that 'the conduct of government by a Prime Minister and Cabinet collectively responsible and accountable to Parliament lies at the heart of Westminster democracy'.[25]

It is striking that it was invoked in *Miller (No 2)* in the context of the executive's exercise of its foreign affairs power to negotiate the terms of Brexit with the EU. This is the context that Lord Carnwath had anticipated in *Miller (No 1)*, when he observed:

> No less fundamental to our constitution is the principle of Parliamentary accountability. The executive is accountable to Parliament for its exercise of the prerogative, *including its actions in international law*. That account is made through ordinary Parliamentary procedures.[26]

Aside from citing these general statements of principle with approval, and noting that parliamentary accountability is often deployed 'as a justification for judicial restraint as part of a constitutional separation of powers',[27] the Supreme Court in *Miller (No 2)* did not elaborate on the origins and significance on the principle of parliamentary accountability in the specific context of the foreign affairs power, including the executive's power to negotiate and conclude treaties. Yet, the application of this principle in that context has had a centuries-long development. It is a development that has particular significance for the argument now raised by way of criticism of *Miller (No 2)*, in which it is claimed that the principle is a political convention and not law. It is to an understanding of the historical constitutional significance of the relationship between the executive and Parliament in the context of foreign affairs that we must now turn.

[24] ibid [61].

[25] *Bobb v Manning* [2006] UKPC 22, [2006] 4 LRC 735 [13] (Lord Bingham), cited in *Miller (No 2)* (n 5) [46].

[26] *Miller (No 1)* (n 4) [249] (emphasis added).

[27] *Miller (No 2)* (n 5) [47].

C. British Constitutional Theory and State Practice

Constitutional Theory

English constitutional theory has long accepted that the exercise of the foreign affairs power is allocated to the executive. But the correlative duty to that power is the obligation of Ministers to account to Parliament for the manner of its exercise. In his *Lectures on the Law of the Constitution*, Dicey wrote in 1885 that:

> the survival of the prerogative affects the position of the Cabinet. It leaves in the hands of the Premier and his colleagues, large powers which can be exercised and constantly are exercised free from Parliamentary control. *This is especially the case in all foreign affairs* ... [I]t is not Parliament, but the Ministry, who direct the diplomacy of the nation, and virtually decide all questions of peace or war.[28]

Yet, he distinguished between the exercise of the power on the one hand and accountability for its exercise on the other, holding that: 'Parliament may censure a Ministry for misconduct in regard to the foreign policy of the country.'[29] More generally, he took the view that the survival of the prerogative in its exercise by Cabinet, because it entails accountability to the House of Commons, increases the authority of the House and ultimately of electors. In this way, he thought, the 'prerogatives of the Crown have become the privileges of the people'.[30]

John Locke's *Second Treatise of Government*,[31] written two centuries earlier in 1690, constitutes in English political philosophy the foundational justification for leaving the foreign affairs power in the hands of the executive. Locke coined the term 'federative power' for 'the Power of War and Peace, Leagues and Alliances, and all the Transactions, with all Persons and Communities without the Commonwealth'.[32] He held that this power must be placed in the same hands as the executive power, since their separate exercise by different persons 'would be apt sometime or other to cause disorder and ruine'.[33]

Yet, he, too, accepted that just as the executive power is subordinate to the legislative, so is the federative. He explains:

> When the Legislative hath put the Execution of the Laws, they make, into other hands, they have a power still to resume it out of those hands, when they find

[28] Albert Venn Dicey, *Lectures Introductory to the Study of the Law of the Constitution* (MacMillan & Co 1885) 390–91 (emphasis added).
[29] ibid 391.
[30] ibid 392–93.
[31] John Locke, *Two Treatises of Government* (Peter Laslett ed, 2nd edn, CUP 1967).
[32] ibid II, para 146.
[33] ibid II, para 148.

> cause, and to punish for any maladministration against the Laws. *The same holds true also in regard to the Federative Power*, that and the Executive being both Ministerial and subordinate to the Legislative, which, as has been showed, in a Constituted Commonwealth is the Supreme.[34]

It is Blackstone, who, in his *Commentaries on the Laws of England* (first published in 1765), makes explicit the link between the prerogative power to conduct foreign affairs and Parliament's legal right to hold it in check through impeachment. Accepting that the King's prerogatives, including the prerogative power to make treaties, is 'irresistible and absolute', he adds:

> And yet, if the consequence of that exertion be manifestly to the grievance or dishonour of the kingdom, the parliament will call his advisers to a just and severe account. For prerogative consisting (as Mr Locke has well defined it) in the discretionary power of acting for the public good, where the positive laws are silent, if that discretionary power be abused to the public detriment, such prerogative is exerted in an unconstitutional manner. Thus the king may make a treaty with a foreign state, which shall irrevocably bind the nation; and yet, when such treaties have been judged pernicious, impeachments have pursued those ministers, by whose agency or advice they were concluded.[35]

Two points stand out about this passage. First, the unequivocal statement that, where the prerogative power—specifically the treaty-making power—is 'abused to the public detriment, such prerogative is *exerted in an unconstitutional manner*'. Second, the consequence of such unconstitutionality is a legal sanction exerted by Parliament, namely impeachment.

State Practice on Impeachment

There was nothing novel about Blackstone's proposition. The British Parliament had pursued impeachment proceedings against the King's advisers for alleged abuses of the foreign affairs power for some four centuries before Blackstone's *Commentaries* was written.[36] Indeed, one recent commentator argues that a persistent thread in impeachments has been the pursuit of a foreign policy against the national interest.[37]

[34] ibid II, para 153 (emphasis added).
[35] William Blackstone, *Commentaries on the Laws of England* (9th edn, London 1783) vol I, 251–52.
[36] Frank O Bowman III, 'British Impeachments (1376–1787) and the Preservation of the American Constitutional Order' (2019) 46 Hastings Const LQ 745, 754; and see also: Lori Fisler Damrosch, 'Impeachment as a Technique of Parliamentary Control over Foreign Affairs in a Presidential System?' (1999) 70 U Colo L Rev 1525.
[37] Bowman (n 36) 789–90.

Among the first true impeachments was that of Lord Latimer in 1376. In addition to allegations of self-enrichment and corruption, he was 'impeached in part for his failure as a military leader to hold the English-occupied French towns of Bécherel and St. Saveur'.[38]

Then, in 1450, the Commons sought to impeach William de la Pole, 1st Duke of Suffolk, for, inter alia, his role in arranging the marriage of Henry VI to Margaret of Anjou and for '[m]aking a convention of peace without the knowledge or assent of the other Lords of the Council'.[39] Rather than proceeding to trial in the Lords, Henry VI had de la Pole banished from England for five years.[40]

Impeachment was little used during the Tudor period, but experienced a revival in the seventeenth and eighteenth centuries. Prominent examples in this period of impeachments of civil officers for abuses related to war and external relations include the Earl of Strafford (1640), the Earl of Clarendon (1667), the Earl of Danby (1679), and the Earl of Oxford, Viscount Bolingbroke, and the Earl of Strafford (1715).[41]

Thomas Wentworth, Earl of Strafford, served as Charles I's Lord Deputy in Ireland. The Commons impeached him in 1640 on charges of high treason. The articles of impeachment include references to maladministration in foreign and military affairs, such as the allegation that 'he hath maliciously endeavoured to stir up enmity and hostility between his majesty's subjects of England and those of Scotland', and that 'he had traitorously broke the great trust reposed in him by his majesty, of lieutenant general of his army, by wilful betraying divers of his majesty's subjects to death, his army to a dishonourable defeat by the Scots at Newborne, and the town of Newcastle into their hands'.[42] Ultimately, the impeachment proceeding was dropped in favour of a bill of attainder containing the same arguments, which passed both Houses and to which Charles I reluctantly gave royal assent, leading to Strafford's beheading.[43]

Edward Hyde, Earl of Clarendon, was Lord Chancellor to Charles II. Clarendon had already been dismissed from office in the wake of a naval defeat and unpopular peace deal concluding the Second Anglo-Dutch War in 1667. The Commons impeached him that year. While the articles of impeachment centred on allegations that he advised the King to maintain a standing army and govern without Parliament, and violated habeas corpus during the war, a few articles are directly related to external relations. Article eleven charges that Clarendon 'advised and effected the Sale of Dunkirk to the French king, being part of his majesty's

[38] ibid 755; Theodore FT Plucknett, 'Presidential Address: The Impeachments of 1376' (1951) 1 Trans R Hist Soc 153, 158.

[39] John Hatsell, *Precedents of Proceedings in the House of Commons* (Hansard & Sons 1818) vol 4, 67.

[40] ibid 68–69. De la Pole was intercepted and killed before he could leave England for his banishment.

[41] Damrosch (n 36) 1529.

[42] *Trial of Thomas Earl of Stafford, Lord Lieutenant of Ireland, for High Treason* (1640) 3 St Tr 1381, 1386.

[43] Bowman (n 36) 772.

dominions; together with the ammunition, artillery, and all sorts of stores there; and for no greater value, than the said ammunition, artillery and stores, were worth'; Article sixteen that he 'hath deluded and betrayed his majesty and the nation in foreign treaties and negotiations, relating to the late war: and discovered and betrayed his secret counsels to his enemies'; and Article seventeen that 'he was a principal author of the fatal counsel of dividing the fleet [leading to the English defeat in the Four Days' Battle] about June 1666'.[44] Before the Lords could hold a trial and deliver a verdict, Clarendon fled to Calais, sending to the Lords a long letter arguing his innocence. His opponents took his flight to be an admission of guilt, and Parliament passed a Bill banishing him from England.[45]

Thomas Osborne, Earl of Danby (later Duke of Leeds) was Lord High Treasurer under Charles II. Amid disputes between the King and Parliament over finances, Danby, on the King's authorization, entered into correspondence sounding out the possibility of offering British neutrality in the Franco-Dutch Wars in exchange for annual payments to Charles II. When this correspondence was discovered, Danby was impeached by the Commons; the first article charged that Danby:

> hath traitorously encroached to himself Regal Power, by treating in matters of peace and war with foreign ministers and ambassadors, and giving instructions to his majesty's ambassadors abroad, without communicating the same to the secretaries of state, and the rest of his majesty's council, against the express declaration of his majesty and his parliament; thereby intending to defeat and overthrow the provision that has been deliberately made by his majesty and his parliament for the safety and the preservation of his majesty's kingdoms and dominions.[46]

Danby was imprisoned in the Tower of London for nearly five years. Prorogation of the Parliament and an attempt by the King to pardon Danby were considered ineffective to end the proceeding, though the matter was eventually abandoned.[47]

Nor was the parliamentary power of impeachment removed or amended in the Bill of Rights 1688[48] as a result of the Glorious Revolution. On the contrary, Parliament continued to use impeachment as a means of holding high State officials to account for their exercise of the foreign affairs power in the eighteenth century.

In 1715, the Earl of Oxford, Viscount Bolingbroke, and the Earl of Strafford faced impeachment for their role in advising Queen Anne to enter into the Treaty

[44] *Proceedings against the Earl of Clarendon, upon an Impeachment of High-Treason and High Misdemeanours* (1667) 6 St Tr 318, 333–34.
[45] ibid 322.
[46] *Proceedings in Parliament against Thomas Earl of Danby, Lord High Treasurer of England, upon an Impeachment of High Treason, and other High Crimes and Misdemeanours* (1678) 11 St Tr 599, 621–25.
[47] Bowman (n 36) 774–75. The rule that a pardon is not pleadable to an impeachment in the Commons was later put into statute: Blackstone (n 35) vol IV, 261.
[48] Bill of Rights 1688, 1 Will and Mar Sess 2 c 2.

of Utrecht, ending the War of the Spanish Succession.[49] The charges against Bolingbroke are characteristic of the allegations against all three. The first article of impeachment states that he did:

> maliciously and wickedly form a most treacherous and pernicious contrivance and confederacy, with other evil-disposed persons, then also of her majesty's privy council, to set on foot a private, separate, dishonourable and destructive negotiation of peace between Great Britain and France, without any communication thereof to her majesty's allies, according to their said several treaties: and was not only wanting in his duty and trust to her majesty, by not opposing, and, as far as was in his power, by not advising her majesty against going into any private separate negotiation with France.[50]

The most celebrated impeachment in the eighteenth century, and also one of the last ever, was the case against Warren Hastings, which lasted over nine years from 1786 to 1795.[51] The speech of Edmund Burke, who had been appointed by the House of Commons as lead counsel for the prosecution before the Lords, is one of the most celebrated pieces of advocacy in the English language.[52] The impeachment of Hastings was a general attack on the whole corrupt system of governance in India instituted under the aegis of the East India Company and continued under Hastings as Governor-General of Bengal. A particular focus of the charges were allegations of breaches of treaties entered into between the Company and the Rajah of Benares. The charges against Hastings could not be classed as offences against domestic English criminal law. Rather, Burke accused Hastings of 'crimes not against forms, but against those eternal laws of justice, which are our rule and our birthright. His offences are, not in formal language, but in reality, in substance and effect, *high* crimes and high misdemeanours.'[53]

Burke frankly recognized that what was at stake in the impeachment of Warren Hastings was not merely the reform of the governance of India and the control of the rapacious activities of the East India Company: it was also the remedy of impeachment itself, which had not then been used for sixty-three years. He spelled out the virtues of the remedy in a striking passage:

[49] Brian W Hill, 'Oxford, Bolingbroke, and the Peace of Utrecht' (1973) 16 Hist J 241, 241–42.

[50] *Proceedings on an Impeachment and Act of Attainder, for High Treason, against Henry Lord Viscount Bolingbroke* (1715) 15 St Tr 994, 996.

[51] The articles of impeachment are at (1787) 37 HLJ 678–96. For an account of the trial, see: William Dalrymple, *The Anarchy: The Relentless Rise of the East India Company* (Bloomsbury 2019) ch 8.

[52] Edmund Burke, 'Speech in Opening the Impeachment of Warren Hastings' (15 February 1788), reprinted in Edmund Burke, *Reflections on the Revolution in France and other Writings* (Jesse Norman ed, Knopf 2015) 403.

[53] ibid 409 (emphasis in the original).

> For this process is the cement which binds the whole together; this is the individuating principle, that makes England what England is. In this court it is, that no subject, in no part of the empire, can fail of competent and proportionable justice: here it is that we provide for that which is the substantial excellence of our constitution; I mean, *the great circulation of responsibility, by which (excepting the supreme power) no man, in no circumstance, can escape the account which he owes to the laws of his country. It is by this process that magistracy, which tries and controls all other things, is itself tried and controlled.*[54]

The issues provoked by the Hastings impeachment were well in the minds of the framers of the US Constitution, as the House of Commons approved the articles of impeachment less than a week before the Philadelphia Convention was due to begin in May 1787.[55] The incorporation in Article II section 4 of the US Constitution of a power of impeachment for 'Treason, Bribery, or other high Crimes and Misdemeanours' has continued to provide a basis for Congress to exert judicial control over the holders of high executive office in respect of their exercise of the foreign affairs power. The first attempt to impeach President Donald Trump for pressuring Ukraine into aiding his re-election is only the most recent example of its use in this context.[56]

For present purposes, it is more pertinent to trace the evolution of executive accountability to Parliament at Westminster.

Hastings was eventually acquitted by the House of Lords in 1795. His trial proved to be the high watermark for the use of impeachment in the British Constitution. The last impeachment by the Commons was that of Lord Melville in 1805, who was charged with mismanagement of public funds during the Napoleonic Wars. He was acquitted in 1806.[57] There was an attempt to move the Commons to impeach Lord Palmerston over a supposed secret treaty with Russia in 1848, which was defeated.[58] This marks the last time on which the impeachment process was invoked.[59]

54 ibid 405 (emphasis added).

55 Bowman (n 36) 777; Damrosch (n 36) 1532–38.

56 *In re Impeachment of President Donald J Trump*: Report of the Committee on the Judiciary House of Representatives (2019), 48–50; Trial Memorandum of the US House of Representatives (2019); Trial Memorandum of President Donald J Trump (20 January 2020); Tom Ginsburg, Aziz Huq, and David Landau, 'The Comparative Constitutional Law of Presidential Impeachment' (2021) U Chicago L Rev 81. For earlier examples in the foreign affairs context, see: Damrosch (n 36).

57 House of Commons Library, 'Impeachment' (Briefing Paper No 7612, 6 June 2016) 6.

58 ibid.

59 Rabinder Singh QC and Conor Gearty advised in a legal opinion dated 22 September 2004 that the power of impeachment remained extant and could potentially be used against Tony Blair in respect of the war in Iraq, but this did not result in parliamentary proceedings.

The Desuetude of Impeachment and the Rise of Ministerial Accountability

Even when Dicey gave his *Lectures* on the law of the Constitution in 1885, impeachment was regarded as an archaic remedy in the UK that had fallen into disuse.[60] Contemporary sources now regard it as obsolete.[61]

Dicey offered two parallel bases for the continuing accountability of Ministers. In the first place, he pointed to 'the underlying principle of all modern constitutionalism, which is nothing else than the principle of obedience to the will of the nation as expressed through Parliament [which] is so closely bound up with the law of the land that it can hardly be violated without a breach of the ordinary law'.[62] In modern terms, we would see this as the principle of legality, which accords Ministers only such powers as the law allows them, and for the breach of which they are criminally or civilly liable.[63] Yet, on Dicey's account, this would not apply to the exercise of the prerogative powers in foreign affairs. Here, as has been seen, Dicey regarded the remedy as accountability to Parliament.[64] He continued to emphasize the importance of the existence of impeachment (despite the evidence that it was then 'almost out of date'[65]) precisely because it demonstrated that, even in respect of those matters for which a Minister could not be made criminally or civilly responsible in the ordinary courts, be remained 'not only morally but legally responsible' for his acts.[66] He concluded: *Behind Parliamentary responsibility lies legal liability*, and the acts of Ministers no less than the acts of subordinate officials are made subject to the rule of law.[67]

Against this background, it is now possible to consider the criticisms ranged against the judgment of the Supreme Court in *Miller (No 2)* in order to see in which sense Ministerial accountability to Parliament for the exercise of the foreign affairs power may properly be said to be *legal* accountability.

60 Dicey (n 28) 380.

61 House of Commons, Report from the Select Committee on Parliamentary Privilege: Together with the Proceedings of the Committee, Minutes of Evidence Taken Before the Select Committee on Parliamentary Privilege in Session 1966–67, and Appendices (HMSO 1967) [115]; Joint Committee on Parliamentary Privilege, *Report: Volume I—Report and Proceedings of the Committee* (1998–99, HL 43-I, HC 214-I, 30 March 1999) 16; *Halsbury's Laws* (5th edn, 2014) vol 20, paras 12 fn 2, 229; David Natzler and Mark Hutton (eds), *Erskine May's Treatise on the Law, Privileges, Proceedings and Usage of Parliament* (LexisNexis, 25th edn, 2019) para 11.3.

62 Dicey (n 28) 380.

63 ibid 331.

64 ibid 391.

65 ibid 331.

66 ibid 332.

67 ibid (emphasis added).

D. Parliamentary Accountability: Political Convention or Legal Rule?

The Critique: Political Convention Converted into Legal Rule

The criticisms of the judgment of the Supreme Court in *Miller (No 2)* advanced by a prominent group of public law scholars did not take aim at the existence of the principle of parliamentary accountability per se. Rather, they have said, the judgment had the effect of turning a constitutional convention or principle into binding law, with the consequence that the Supreme Court found a justification to intervene in what should have been an essentially political matter. So, for instance, Timothy Endicott argues that the missing premise in the judgment is 'that the court can turn constitutional principles into legal rules as it sees fit . . . at least in respect of the role of the executive in Parliament'.[68]

David Feldman contrasts parliamentary accountability with parliamentary sovereignty for this purpose. He opines:

> Parliamentary sovereignty as a principle has long been accepted as imposing binding obligations on both the executive and judiciary and as being a basis for judicial control over the executive's use of statutory powers, and for limiting the scope of prerogative powers.... *By contrast, governmental accountability, or responsible government, had been regarded primarily as political; for the executive or courts to refuse to account to Parliament for their actions might give rise to conflict with Parliament but it would be for Parliament, not courts, to resolve it.*[69]

Opinions entered under the aegis of Policy Exchange's Judicial Power Project advance the argument more baldly. Richard Ekins, in written evidence to the House of Commons, writes of parliamentary accountability:

> The principle underpins a range of conventions and practices which make up our political constitution, in which the Government is formed by and accountable to the Houses of Parliament, especially the Commons. The principle is sometimes noted by courts *but it is not a legal principle and cannot justify novel judicial intervention*. On the contrary, the principle is a reason for courts to avoid intervention, precisely because the proper control on the abuse of some powers (like prorogation) is political rather than legal. The Supreme Court turns the principle on its head by invoking it as a ground for judicial intervention.[70]

68 Endicott (n 7) 180.

69 Feldman (n 7) 217 (emphasis added).

70 Richard Ekins written evidence to House of Commons, Public Administration and Constitutional Affairs Committee, 'Prorogation and Implications of the Supreme Court Judgment' (HC 2017–19, 2666) para 15 (emphasis added).

John Finnis alleges that the judgment 'was wholly unjustified by law' because it transferred the principle of parliamentary accountability from the domain of political convention into justiciable law.[71]

In part, this position is founded upon an argument about the scope of Article 9 of the Bill of Rights Act 1688, which provides that: 'Proceedings in Parliament ought not to be impeached or questioned in any Court or Place out of Parliament.' Finnis contends that this exclusion of judicial intervention applies as much to the Queen's prorogation of Parliament as it does to the making of legislation by the Queen in Parliament. As David Feldman pertinently observed, this is a flawed argument:

> It does not follow, however, that everything the Queen does in respect of Parliament is done by the Queen in Parliament. Legislation is only one of a number of functions exercised by each House independently (and occasionally in concert), and often, as in the case of scrutinising government, the Houses need no royal participation. *Prorogation ends all those activities, and in relation to them Her Majesty cannot be described as the Queen in Parliament.*[72]

This observation highlights a larger difficulty with the proposition advanced against *Miller (No 2)* that parliamentary accountability is a political, not a legal, principle in that it is for Parliament and not the courts to hold Ministers to account. Prorogation deprived Parliament of the opportunity to do just that. The Supreme Court intervened to preserve, not to supplant, Parliament's political role.

It is not the purpose of this chapter to engage with all of the arguments ranged against *Miller (No 2)* by its critics, a task that has so ably been undertaken by others.[73] Rather, the point that is developed here is one that neither the critics of the judgment nor its defenders have analysed. That is the *nature* of the executive power in respect of which the principle of parliamentary accountability was engaged. The fact that what was at stake was an exercise of the foreign affairs power—the negotiations with the EU concerning the basis of the UK's departure—has a set of major implications for the operation of parliamentary accountability as a *legal* principle.

What the constitutional practice over several centuries shows is that the essential correlative of placing the foreign affairs power in the hands of the executive within the British constitutional compact is the accountability of Ministers to Parliament for the exercise of that power. The fact that in earlier times this could lead to accountability by way of proceedings in Parliament for impeachment shows that the principle was no mere political convention. On the contrary, it carried with

[71] Finnis (n 7) 5.
[72] Feldman (n 7) 225 (emphasis added).
[73] Notably: Craig (n 7); Elliott (n 7).

it consequences for misuse that were binding in law upon the person of the responsible Minister.

Justiciability: The Limits of Judicial Accountability in Foreign Affairs

How, then, may we understand the legal significance of parliamentary accountability today? It is sometimes said that the need for impeachment died with the development of the judicial review of administrative action, which ensures the accountability of Ministers and officials to the courts for the exercise of their powers according to law.[74]

This point is good so far as it goes. But it has only limited purchase in the context of the exercise of the foreign affairs power. For reasons developed by the author more fully elsewhere,[75] the mere fact that the executive exercises a power derived from the prerogative does not preclude judicial review; nor does the fact that the subject matter of that exercise concerns foreign relations. What does matter is whether the exercise of the power directly engages the rights of the individual under municipal law or whether it involves instead the exercise of a general power on the plane of inter-State relations.

In the landmark *CCSU* case, in which the House of Lords held that prerogative powers were in principle amenable to judicial review, Lord Roskill still excluded treaty-making, commenting that:

> Prerogative powers such as those relating to the making of treaties [and] the defence of the realm ... are not, I think, susceptible to judicial review because their nature and subject matter are such as not to be amenable to the judicial process. The courts are not the place wherein to determine whether a treaty should be concluded or the armed forces disposed in a particular manner.[76]

This principle was applied in relation to attempts to challenge in the courts the executive decision to join the European Economic Community in 1972[77] and the Maastricht Treaty on the EU in 1992.[78]

Lord Sumption elaborated on the notion of non-justiciability in *Shergill v Khaira*, identifying a category of cases that:

[74] House of Commons Library (n 57) 7.
[75] Campbell McLachlan, *Foreign Relations Law* (CUP 2014) esp ch 6 and pt III.
[76] *Council of Civil Service Unions v Minister for the Civil Service* [1985] AC 374 (HL) 418.
[77] *Blackburn v Attorney General* [1971] 1 WLR 1037 (CA).
[78] *R v Secretary of State for Foreign & Commonwealth Affairs, ex p Rees-Mogg* [1994] QB 552 (DC).

> comprises claims or defences which are based neither on private legal rights or obligations, nor on reviewable matters of public law. Examples include ... issues of international law which engage no private right of the claimant or reviewable question of public law .... [W]hen the court declines ... to review the exercise of the Crown's prerogative in the conduct of foreign affairs, it normally refuses on the ground that no legal right of the citizen is engaged whether in public or private law .... But the court does adjudicate on these matters if a justiciable legitimate expectation or a [European] Convention right depends on it .... The same would apply if a private law liability was asserted which depended on such a matter.[79]

The courts have justified the non-justiciability of claims relating to the exercise of such powers not simply on the ground that they fall outside their own competence. They have added the concomitant explanation that the executive is accountable instead to Parliament. As Arden LJ explained:

> There is in effect a division of functions here between the court and the executive. The executive takes responsibility for issues of national security and the handling of international relations *and is democratically accountable for the merits of the decisions to Parliament*. The court reserves to itself the responsibility for seeing that the decision complies with the law, is not irrational and complies strictly with procedural requirements.[80]

But it should not be thought that this is a distinction between law, conceived as the province of the courts, and politics, regarded as the province of Parliament. Parliamentary accountability imports a legal duty on Ministers to account. Lord Mance drew out this point when discussing non-justiciability in *Serdar Mohammed* in terms that relate directly to the central theme of this chapter:

> The thinking behind all these concepts is linked in *Blackstone, Commentaries on the Laws of England* (1765), vol I, pp 251, 257–258. There, the non-justiciability of the royal prerogative of making war and peace or treaties is explained on the basis that the appropriate forum for its control is Parliament (including, in the last resort, as *Blackstone* notes, by impeachment).[81]

[79] *Shergill v Khaira* [2014] UKSC 33, [2015] AC 359 [43].

[80] *R (Lord Carlile of Berriew) v Secretary of State for the Home Department* [2013] EWCA Civ 199 [66] (emphasis added), upheld on appeal: [2014] UKSC 60, [2015] AC 945.

[81] *Mohammed (Serdar) v Ministry of Defence* [2017] UKSC 1, [2017] AC 649 [57]. The passage from *Blackstone* is cited above at n 35.

Parliamentary Accountability as a Legal Power

The existence of a *legal* power of Parliament to require executive accountability for exercise of the foreign relations power is important because it imposes a check on what would otherwise be an unfettered executive power. In a representative democracy, it is Parliament (and not the electorate directly) to whom the executive is accountable for its actions on the international plane. This is of the essence of a constitution founded upon a system of checks and balances.

Understanding the respects in which parliamentary accountability is a legal principle also helps to answer another misconception that may arise from the much-repeated proposition that '[t]he United Kingdom takes a dualist approach to international law'[82] such that what is done on the international plane operates in a separate sphere from domestic law.[83]

It is 'a well-established rule that the making of a treaty is an executive act'.[84] Such a 'power to make or unmake treaties is exercisable without legislative authority and that the exercise of that power is not reviewable by the courts'.[85] But the dualist system exists to protect parliamentary sovereignty: 'it exists to protect Parliament not ministers'.[86] It also exists to protect private citizens from the use of executive power to alter the law of the land.[87]

These twin functions of dualism operate to support and not to undermine the indivisibility of the sovereignty of Parliament. In his work on *Sovereignty*, the constitutional theorist Hermann Heller pointed out that:

> the existentiality of the decision-making unit prohibits splitting sovereignty into the sovereignty of a state law and a separate international law sovereignty .... The highest independent decision-making power is ... always the mark of one and not two facts.[88]

The consequence, he thought, was that, in a democratic State, while ultimate sovereignty rests with the people as the body politic, they could only govern through the appointment of representatives 'juristically dependant magistrates' that represent the common will.[89] The language is archaic, but the reference is unmistakably to Parliament.

[82] *R (Yam) v Central Criminal Court* [2015] UKSC 76, [2016] AC 771 [35].
[83] *Miller (No 1)* (n 4) [55].
[84] *Attorney-General for Canada v Attorney-General for Ontario* [1937] AC 326 (PC) 347.
[85] *Miller (No 1)* (n 4) [55].
[86] ibid [57].
[87] *Walker v Baird* [1892] AC 491 (PC); *Higgs v Minister of National Security* [2000] 2 AC 228 (PC) 241.
[88] Hermann Heller, *Sovereignty: A Contribution to the Theory of Public and International Law* (David Dyzenhaus ed, OUP 2019) 140.
[89] ibid 108.

The importance of this point here is that parliamentary accountability is the means by which a sovereign Parliament ensures that the executive is legally answerable to Parliament for the actions that the executive takes on behalf of the State on the international plane. This in turn ensures democratic accountability for those actions.

In some cases, the executive's international actions—especially where they result in the making or unmaking of treaties—may well require the legislative intervention of Parliament in order to take effect within the domestic sphere. That is the essential concomitant of dualism. But parliamentary accountability for the exercise of the foreign affairs power cannot be understood simply as a dress rehearsal, a form of advance vetting, for some subsequent moment in which Parliament's legislative powers will have to be engaged. A sovereign Parliament performs an independent function when it holds Ministers to account for the manner in which the foreign affairs power has been exercised, whether or not such exercise requires legislative action.

Was, then, *Miller (No 2)* nevertheless an arrogation of power by the judiciary because it made the enforcement of parliamentary accountability justiciable? The case arose on what was, on any view, a highly unusual set of circumstances within the Westminster system. The government of the day could not be certain of commanding a majority of the House of Commons. It faced external deadlines regarding the agreement of the terms of Brexit. The prorogation of Parliament would have had the effect of removing from Parliament its ability to ensure accountability of the executive at the very time at which the crucial decisions had to be made: decisions that would have far-reaching and irreversible consequences for the future direction of the UK. But the decision of the Supreme Court did not involve the judiciary substituting its decision for that of Parliament. It merely ensured that Parliament was placed in a position to exercise its sovereign power of supervision.

Lord Sumption succinctly explained the point in giving evidence to the House of Commons Public Administration and Constitutional Affairs Committee:

> It seems to me that parliamentary accountability is the whole basis on which the courts draw lines as to what decisions they may interfere with and which decisions they cannot. It is also an essential underpinning of the separation of powers because it enables the courts to distinguish between those matters in respect of which Ministers are responsible to the court and those matters in which they are responsible to Parliament. Parliamentary accountability is a very familiar concept in law and it is simply nonsense to say that it has no existence except as a political fact.
>
> ...
>
> *There is a world of difference between the courts arrogating to themselves a power that politically ought to belong to Ministers responsible to Parliament, on the one hand, and the courts simply saying, as they have done in their recent decision, that*

this is a matter on which Parliament must be enabled to make decisions. The difference is fundamental.[90]

E. Implications

In Constitutional Principle

In the result, then, the judgment of the Supreme Court in *Miller (No 2)* was a correct application of a fundamental legal principle of the British Constitution, namely parliamentary accountability. Contrary to the criticisms raised against it, this principle is no mere political convention. It is a binding principle of law, every bit as binding as Parliament's sovereign power to legislate. Both principles flow from the same fountainhead, namely that it is Parliament, and not the government, that is sovereign within the British polity.

The principle of parliamentary accountability has a role that is distinct from Parliament's legislative function. It is the means by which the executive is held to account for its actions by the elected representatives of the people. This role has a particular importance in the field of foreign relations, including in relation to the exercise of the treaty power. In this context, the source of the executive's power is the prerogative. Save where the exercise of this power invades private rights of the individual, the executive may not be answerable for its exercise before the courts. Its exercise may require no legislative action on the part of Parliament. As a result, it is the principle of parliamentary *accountability* that stands as a bulwark against misuse of the foreign affairs power to the detriment of the nation.

The practice presented above demonstrates that it was in particular recognition of the special context of foreign affairs that Parliament developed its legal powers of accountability through impeachment. The fact that it now exercises its powers through Ministerial responsibility rather than its own criminal process does not diminish the legal character of the principle.

The judgment of the Supreme Court does not represent an arrogation of judicial power from either the executive or Parliament. The Court exercised no decision of its own as to the issues of foreign policy then confronting the executive in its negotiations with the EU. Rather, it merely ensured that Parliament was placed in a position in which it was not, by reason of the executive's decision to prorogue its proceedings, deprived of the ability to exercise parliamentary accountability at a critical time.

[90] Lord Sumption, oral evidence before Public Administration and Constitutional Affairs Committee, *Prorogation and implications of the Supreme Court judgment* (HC 2017–19, 2666) questions 63, 64 (emphasis added).

It might be thought that, nevertheless, *Miller (No 2)* stands as a high water-mark judgment. It arose in a particular set of circumstances in which the government of the day had only a tenuous ability to command a majority of the House of Commons, and thereby to dictate parliamentary business, that are unlikely to arise again. Executive confidence in the value of the primacy of parliamentary sovereignty is much easier to maintain when it does have the ability to command such a majority. In those circumstances, it may be much more palatable for a government to affirm the primacy of the principle of parliamentary sovereignty. It may thereby seek to extend the principle to 'the role of the courts as "servants of Parliament", affirming the role of Parliament in creating law and holding the executive to account'.[91] It is important to recall that parliamentary sovereignty is not, after all, the only fundamental constitutional principle. The rule of law, and the role of the judiciary in maintaining the rule of law in part through the judicial review of administrative action, is an equally important and balancing principle.

Yet, the clear enunciation in *Miller (No 2)* of parliamentary accountability as a *legal* principle has important consequences for Parliament's ongoing exercise of this power in the context of foreign affairs.

In Parliamentary Practice

The departure of the UK from the EU has had the immediate consequence that treaties negotiated on an EU-wide basis with third States in the exercise of its external competence under the Treaty on the Functioning of the European Union[92] no longer apply to the UK. As a result, the UK Government has embarked on a major programme of treaty negotiation, both in order to provide continuity in respect of those States with which the Union had already concluded free trade agreements,[93] and in respect of new agreements.[94]

This exercise has in turn prompted fresh debate in Parliament about the practical exercise of parliamentary accountability in the field of treaty scrutiny. It is not the first time this century that this issue has arisen. Under Prime Minister Gordon Brown, the government sought to strengthen ministerial accountability to Parliament for the exercise of prerogative powers, notably in foreign affairs, including the treaty and defence powers.[95] One of the outcomes of this process was

[91] Ministry of Justice, 'Judicial Review Reform: The Government Response to the Independent Review of Administrative Law' (CP 408, 2021) 8–9.

[92] Consolidated Version of the Treaty on the Functioning of the European Union [2012] OJ C326/47, art 3.

[93] Trade Act 2021.

[94] Department for International Trade, 'Processes for Making Free Trade Agreements after the United Kingdom Has Left the European Union' (CP 63, 2019).

[95] The milestone reports are: Public Administration Select Committee, 'Taming the Prerogative: Strengthening Ministerial Accountability to Parliament' (HC 2003–04, 422); Ministry of Justice, 'The Governance of Britain' (CM 7170, 2007) ('2007 Green Paper'); Ministry of Justice, Ministry

Part 2 of the Constitutional Reform and Governance Act 2010 ('2010 Act'). This Act requires the government to lay a copy of any treaty that it proposes for ratification before Parliament for twenty-one sitting days and confers on the House of Commons a power of negative resolution.[96]

The form adopted for this reform is a curious one. No doubt Parliament may use its legislative power in this way to direct the conduct of Ministers. Yet, what is at issue in treaty scrutiny is really a question of parliamentary procedure. Parliament's procedures are properly to be provided for in its own standing orders.[97] Incorporation of the obligation to lay a proposed treaty before Parliament in an Act of Parliament carries with it a less durable consequence. That which one Parliament creates, the next may dispense. So it has been with the 2010 Act. By section 32 of the European Union (Withdrawal Agreement) Act 2020, Parliament simply agreed to disapply the 2010 Act, providing that section 20 of that Act 'does not apply in relation to the withdrawal agreement'. Section 20 was also disapplied in the case of the Trade and Cooperation Agreement, governing future relations with the EU.[98]

In practical terms, the critical missing elements necessary to ensure an effective exercise of parliamentary accountability for the exercise of the foreign affairs, including the treaty-making, power have been (i) the absence until very recently of a parliamentary select committee with the specific function of treaty scrutiny[99] that is (ii) armed with sufficient powers to ensure Ministerial accountability. As Jill Barrett concluded in March 2020: 'In practice Parliament's scrutiny of treaties is woefully inadequate. This is partly because its powers are limited but also because Parliament does not make effective use of the powers that it has.'[100]

The first of these gaps has now been filled by the establishment of an International Agreements Committee of the House of Lords,[101] which has begun its work. The

of Defence, and Foreign and Commonwealth Office, 'The Governance of Britain: War Powers and Treaties: Limiting Executive Powers' (CM 7239, 2007) ('2007 Consultation Paper'); Ministry of Justice, 'The Governance of Britain—Constitutional Renewal' (CM 7342-I, 2008) ('2008 White Paper'); Joint Committee on the Draft Constitutional Renewal Bill, 'Draft Constitutional Renewal Bill' (2007–08 HL 166-I, HC 551-I) ('Joint Committee Paper 2008'); Joint Committee on Human Rights, 'Legislative Scrutiny: Constitutional Reform and Governance Bill; Video Recordings Bill' (2009–10, HL 33, HC 249) ('Joint Committee on Human Rights Paper 2010'). For a general review, see House of Commons Library, 'Parliamentary Scrutiny of Treaties' (SN/IA/4693, 25 September 2009).

[96] Constitutional Reform and Governance Act 2010, s 20(4)(b); see generally McLachlan (n 75) paras 5.69–5.79.

[97] Natzler and Hutton (n 61) [20.96].

[98] European Union (Future Relationship) Act 2020, s 36.

[99] Ewan Smith, Eirik Bjorge, and Arabella Lang, 'Treaties, Parliament and the Constitution' [2020] PL 508.

[100] Jill Barrett, 'Treaties beyond the EU', *Parliament and Brexit* (UK in a Changing Europe, March 2020) 46.

[101] The key reports are: Select Committee on the Constitution, 'Parliamentary Scrutiny of Treaties' (HL 2017–19, 345); European Union Committee, 'Scrutiny of International Agreements: Lessons Learned' (HL 2017–19, 387); European Union Committee, 'Treaty Scrutiny: Working Practices' (HL 2019–21, 97); International Agreements Committee, 'Working Practices: One Year on' (HL 2021–22,

second constraint, however, is central to the theme of this chapter. The absence of adequate powers to ensure effective accountability is a constant theme of the Committee's review report after a year of its operation.[102]

The same constraints have also hindered the work of the House of Commons Foreign Affairs Committee. In the 'Iraq' inquiry,[103] that Committee sought the attendance of the Prime Minister and that of his press secretary Alastair Campbell, the Cabinet Office Intelligence Co-ordinator, the Chairman of the Joint Intelligence Committee, the Chief of Defence Intelligence, the Head of the Secret Intelligence Service and the Director of GCHQ. The Committee noted: 'None of them replied. It was the Foreign Secretary who informed us that they would not appear.'[104]

When it delivered its Report, the Committee made the following recommendations as to access to government information:[105]

> We conclude that continued refusal by Ministers to allow this committee access to intelligence papers and personnel, on this inquiry and more generally, is hampering it in the work which Parliament has asked it to carry out.
>
> We recommend that the Government accept the principle that it should be prepared to accede to requests from the Foreign Affairs Committee for access to intelligence, when the Committee can demonstrate that it is of key importance to a specific inquiry it is conducting and unless there are genuine concerns for national security. We further recommend that, in cases where access is refused, full reasons should be given.

There are in particular three powers that should be strengthened in Parliament's standing orders in light of the recent experience of parliamentary inquiries into foreign affairs.[106] First, it should not be left to the discretion of Ministers to decide whether to attend to give evidence to a select committee, when the committee requires his or her attendance.[107] Second, it should not be necessary for a select committee to seek an order or an address from the House in order to obtain documents from the government.[108] There is no plea of public interest immunity that may justify withholding documents from Parliament, including where those documents affect international relations or national security. It is for Parliament

75). The author submitted written evidence, at the Committee's request, to the Working Practices Report (TWP0003, 3 June 2020).

[102] International Agreements Committee (n 101).
[103] Foreign Affairs Committee, 'The Decision to Go to War in Iraq' (HC 2002–03, 813).
[104] ibid [6].
[105] ibid [167]–[169].
[106] See further McLachlan (n 75) paras 5.99–5.112; House of Commons Library, 'Select Committees: Evidence and Witnesses' (Briefing Paper No 6208, 2 June 2016); Smith, Bjorge, and Lang (n 99) 523–24.
[107] Natzler and Hutton (n 61) [38.34].
[108] ibid [38.32].

to find mechanisms to ensure that its committees can review sensitive material without imperilling those interests. Third, Ministerial advisers are employed by the government to support their exercise of executive powers. They should have no more immunity from appearance before a select committee than any other public servant.[109]

There is some contemporary practice evidencing a greater recognition on the part of the executive of the importance of enabling effective parliamentary scrutiny of treaties.[110] These fall some way short of a compact,[111] formalized in Standing Orders (and, on the part of the executive, in the Ministerial Code), that would govern Ministerial accountability in this context.

F. Conclusion

Miller (No 2) stands as a landmark judgment, because it upholds the legally binding character of the principle of parliamentary accountability, applied in the context of the foreign affairs and treaty power. As this chapter has demonstrated, the application of this principle as binding law has several centuries of parliamentary practice behind it and accords with the basic tenets of representative democracy.

Tony Judt, in one of his last essays in 2012, critiqued a tendency to talk generally about the need for more democracy. He argued that: 'the way to defend and advance large abstractions in the generations to come will be to defend and protect institutions and law and rules and practices that incarnate our best attempt at those large abstractions'.[112]

In an environment in which what is done in the name of the State in its international relations has ever-increasing impact at home, it is of some moment that the principle of parliamentary accountability upheld by the Supreme Court is applied in a living way in the practice of Parliament itself to the exercise of the foreign affairs power.

109 House of Commons Library (n 106) 14.

110 See notably 'the Grimstone rule' that the government will facilitate a debate in the House of Lords on a proposed treaty should the International Treaties Committee request one: HL Deb 23 February 2021, col 724; and the like undertaking to the House of Commons cited in 'Working Practices: One Year on' (n 101) para 32.

111 See eg the Draft Concordat proposed by the International Agreements Committee (n 101) app 2.

112 Tony Judt, *Thinking the Twentieth Century* (Heinemann 2012) 304.

7

The United Kingdom Supreme Court and References to the Court of Justice of the European Union

Past and Future

David Lloyd Jones[*]

As a student in the 1970s, I had the great good fortune to be taught private international law by Lawrence Collins. I shall always be grateful to Lawrence for those classes in which he inspired his pupils by drawing on his scholarship and his practical experience. Lawrence's immense distinction as a private international lawyer should not, however, be permitted to obscure the important contribution he has made in other fields. Following the accession of the UK to the European Economic Community, he was a pioneer among UK scholars and practitioners in what was to become EU law. His book *European Community Law in the United Kingdom*, first published in 1975, was a landmark in the process by which lawyers in this country sought to come to terms with this novel legal system. I am very grateful for this opportunity to thank Lawrence for his friendship over so many years and I hope that he will find this contribution of interest.

The withdrawal of the UK from the EU makes this an opportune moment at which to reflect on the past and future relationship between the UK Supreme Court and the Court of Justice of the European Union (CJEU) in Luxembourg, to take stock of the formal, procedural links which operated between the two courts from the inception of the Supreme Court in 2009, and to give some indication of the very different arrangements which have now replaced them.

Prior to the withdrawal of the UK, the formal dialogue between the two courts was conducted within the framework of the preliminary reference (or preliminary ruling) procedure[1] set out in Article 19(3)(b) of the Treaty on European Union

[*] I am extremely grateful to my judicial assistants Rebecca Fry, Isabella Buono, and Thomas Fairclough for their assistance in the writing of this chapter and to Anita Homji of the UK Supreme Court Registry for the provision of information relating to references.

[1] See generally David Anderson and Marie Demetriou, *References to the European Court* (2nd edn, Sweet & Maxwell 2002); Morten Broberg and Niels Fenger, *Preliminary References to the European Court of Justice* (OUP 2014); Anthony Arnull, 'The UK Supreme Court and References to the CJEU'

David Lloyd Jones, *The United Kingdom Supreme Court and References to the Court of Justice of the European Union* In: *Essays in International Litigation for Lord Collins*. Edited by: Jonathan Harris and Campbell McLachlan, Oxford University Press. © Oxford University Press 2022. DOI: 10.1093/oso/9780192867988.003.0008

(TEU) and Article 267 of the Treaty on the Functioning of the European Union (TFEU).[2] Under this procedure, the courts and tribunals of Member States are able, or in certain circumstances are required, to refer disputed issues of EU law to the CJEU for a ruling. The fact that EU law applies throughout the domestic legal systems of Member States means that national courts at all levels will encounter disputed issues of EU law which they are required to resolve and apply. The system of references therefore assists national courts, including those which may lack expertise in EU law. It also has the huge advantage of promoting consistency within the EU legal system.[3] It is easy to understand that, at the creation of the European Economic Community, such a system of preliminary references might have appeared more palatable to the original Member States than a more hierarchical appellate system. In most instances (to which the position of final courts of appeal is an important exception), a national court has a discretion as to whether to make a preliminary reference or to decide the issue itself. Nevertheless, when a reference is made, the resulting ruling by the CJEU is a definitive statement of the relevant EU law and is binding as such throughout the EU legal system.

While most national courts and tribunals can exercise a discretion in deciding whether or not to make a reference to the CJEU under Article 267(3) of the TFEU, if one of the matters listed in Article 267(1) 'is raised in a case pending before a court or tribunal of a Member State against whose decisions there is no judicial remedy under national law, that court or tribunal shall bring the matter before the Court'. As the Supreme Court is a court of last instance, it has therefore been obliged to refer relevant questions of EU law to the CJEU.

The withdrawal of the UK from the EU on 31 January 2020 was followed by a transition period which ran from 31 January 2020 to 31 December 2020 during which substantive EU law continued to apply directly in the UK.[4] Throughout that period, the preliminary reference procedure remained in force and the Supreme Court continued to be required to refer certain questions of EU law to the CJEU.[5] However, since the end of the transition period at 11pm on 31 December 2020, courts and tribunals in the UK have only been able (or, in the case of the Supreme Court, required) to make references to the CJEU in certain limited circumstances.

(2017) 36(1) YB Eur L 314; Sylvia de Mars, *EU Law in the UK* (OUP 2020) ch 7; Paul Craig and Gráinne de Búrca, *EU Law: Text, Cases and Materials* (7th edn, OUP 2020) ch 14.

[2] Consolidated Versions of the Treaty on European Union and the Treaty on the Functioning of the European Union [2016] OJ C202/1.

[3] For discussion on the importance of ensuring a uniform application of EU law, see Case 314/85 *Foto-Frost v Hauptzollamt Lübeck-Ost* [1987] ECR 4199 [13]–[15].

[4] Agreement on the Withdrawal of the United Kingdom of Great Britain and Northern Ireland from the European Union and the European Atomic Energy Community [2020] OJ L29/7 (Withdrawal Agreement), art 127; and European Union (Withdrawal) Act 2018 (2018 Act), s 1A.

[5] Withdrawal Agreement, art 131.

It is proposed to examine the functioning of the preliminary reference procedure between the Supreme Court and the CJEU during the UK's membership of the EU and the transition period, before turning to consider those situations in which a reference procedure now continues to apply and the status within the UK of past and future CJEU case law.

A. Past

The Appellate Committee of the House of Lords made forty references to the CJEU between the UK's accession to the European Communities in January 1973 and the Appellate Committee's demise on 30 September 2009.[6] Its successor, the Supreme Court, made twenty-three references between 1 October 2009 and 31 December 2020.[7] This indicates that the Supreme Court made roughly twice as many references to the CJEU per year as its predecessor did. However, this should not be taken to indicate any reluctance on the part of the Appellate Committee in complying with its obligations to make preliminary references, by comparison with the Supreme Court. It must be remembered that in the early years of the UK's membership of the European Economic Community, the scope of what was to develop into EU law was much more restricted. The vast expansion in the scope of EU law into many new areas is inevitably reflected in the number of cases coming before the courts raising issues of EU law and, therefore, the number of such cases arriving for decision in courts of final appeal. In the period immediately following the Brexit referendum in June 2016, the number of preliminary references made by UK courts and tribunals fell significantly, resulting in 22 per cent fewer references to the CJEU than previously.[8] This trend, however, is not reflected in the number of preliminary references made by the Supreme Court during the same period. As might be expected of a court of last resort subject to an obligation to refer, there was no significant variation. In fact, the number of references increased slightly: there were three in 2016, three in 2017, one in 2018, and three in 2019. It is also significant that, during the transition period, the Supreme Court made a reference in one further case.[9]

[6] Arnull (n 1) 327.

[7] Information supplied by Anita Homji, Supreme Court Registry. The cases in which the Supreme Court made a reference to the CJEU are listed in the Appendix.

[8] Arthur Dyevre, Monika Glavina, Nicolas Lampach, Michal Ovádek, and Wessel Wijtvliet, 'Uncertainty and Legal Disintegration: Evidence from Brexit' (31 October 2018) <https://papers.ssrn.com/sol3/papers.cfm?abstract_id=3276189> accessed 18 May 2021.

[9] *Zipvit Ltd v Commissioners for Her Majesty's Revenue and Customs* [2020] UKSC 15, [2020] 3 All ER 1017.

A Duty to Refer

In Case 283/81 *CILFIT Srl v Ministerio della Sanita*, the CJEU explained that the scope of the duty on a court of last instance to refer must be assessed in light of the overarching aim of the preliminary reference procedure, which is to ensure cooperation between national courts and the CJEU so that there can be uniform application of EU law in all of the Member States.[10] As a result, in appropriate cases the Supreme Court may conclude that a reference is not required because: (i) the question of EU law would not be relevant to the outcome of the appeal before the Court; (ii) the CJEU has already ruled on the question (ie it is *acte éclairé*); or (iii) the question is so clear that there is no need to ask the CJEU to rule on it (ie it is *acte clair*). In *PMS International Group plc v Magmatic Ltd*, Lord Neuberger explained that, if none of these exceptions applies in an appeal which raises issues of EU law, the Supreme Court will make a reference to the CJEU:

> There is no doubt that, if we are of the view that this appeal could only be resolved by determining a point of EU law which has not already been determined by the CJEU (ie is not *acte éclairé*) or whose determination nonetheless leaves room for reasonable doubt (ie is not *acte clair*), then, as the final court of appeal in the United Kingdom, we would be obliged to refer it to the CJEU pursuant to article 267 of the Treaty for the Functioning of the European Union[11]

Not Relevant to the Outcome of the Dispute

In *CILFIT*, the CJEU made clear that a final court of appeal has the same discretion as any other national court or tribunal to ascertain whether a decision on a question of EU law is necessary to enable it to give judgment.[12] Before making a reference, therefore, the Supreme Court was required to satisfy itself that a decision on the relevant question of EU law was needed to enable it to determine the dispute between the parties. In this regard, the CJEU has emphasized that it does not have jurisdiction under Article 267 of the TFEU to answer hypothetical questions, but only to contribute to the solution of actual disputes.[13] The Supreme Court has frequently relied on this ground in declining to make a preliminary reference. For example, in *The Trustees of the Olympic Airlines SA Pension and Life Assurance Scheme v Olympic Airlines SA*,[14] it decided that Olympic Airlines SA, a

[10] On the duty to refer, see generally Broberg and Fenger (n 1) ch 6. Case 283/81 *CILFIT Srl v Ministerio della Sanita* [1982] ECR 3415, [1983] 1 CMLR 472 [7].
[11] [2016] UKSC 12, [2016] 4 All ER 1027 [28].
[12] *CILFIT* (n 10) [10].
[13] Case 244/80 *Foglia v Novello* [1981] ECR 3045 [16]–[20].
[14] [2015] UKSC 27, [2015] 1 WLR 2399.

Greek company with its centre of main interests in Greece, did not have an establishment in the UK so as to permit it to be wound up in secondary insolvency proceedings under Council Regulation (EC) 1346/2000 of 29 May 2000 on insolvency proceedings.[15] Under the Regulation, Article 2(h), an establishment is a 'place of operations where the debtor carries out a non-transitory economic activity with human means and goods'. Giving the judgment, Lord Sumption considered that the necessity for showing at least some subsisting business with third parties before the definition of establishment could be satisfied was *acte clair*, even if the exact nature of that business and the degree to which it must be visible to outsiders might be open to argument. Since Olympic Airlines SA was not carrying on any business activity from its UK office at the relevant time, the court did not need to resolve the ambiguities around the definition of establishment and there was no point of principle calling for a reference.[16]

Similarly, in *Secretary of State for Health and others v Servier Laboratories Ltd*,[17] which concerned the EU principle of absolute *res judicata*, Servier contended that the circumstances in which, under EU law, a finding in a judicial decision by an EU court is binding in later judicial proceedings could not be characterized as *acte clair*. It therefore asked the Supreme Court to make a preliminary reference. The Supreme Court considered that, as the European Commission had appealed the judgment of the General Court upon which Servier sought to rely and the appeal was pending, the principle of absolute *res judicata* could not apply. In its view, the case law of the CJEU clearly establishes that the principle applies only to judicial decisions which have become definitive after all rights of appeal have been exhausted or after expiry of the time limits provided to exercise those appeal rights. The findings of the General Court on which Servier sought to rely might well be reversed or rendered redundant by the judgment of the CJEU on the appeal.[18] It was therefore unnecessary to resolve the issue to determine the dispute. The Supreme Court, nevertheless, went on to examine in detail the decisions of the CJEU on absolute *res judicata* before concluding, to the standard of *acte clair*, that in any event it had no application to the facts of that case.[19]

In *I (A Child)*,[20] the Supreme Court unanimously held that the courts of England and Wales had jurisdiction to determine the future level of contact between a child and his mother where the child does not habitually reside in an EU Member State. Under Article 12.3 of Council Regulation (EC) 2201/2003 of 27 November 2003,[21] parties are able to opt in to the jurisdiction of an EU court which would not

15 [2000] OJ L160/1.
16 ibid [16].
17 [2020] UKSC 44, [2020] 3 WLR 1207.
18 ibid [31]–[32].
19 ibid [62].
20 [2009] UKSC 10, [2010] 1 AC 319.
21 Council Regulation (EC) No 2201/2003 of 27 November 2003 concerning jurisdiction and the recognition and enforcement of judgments in matrimonial matters and the matters of parental responsibility, repealing Regulation (EC) No 1347/2000 [2003] OJ L338/1.

otherwise have jurisdiction to determine a child's future. There was a difference of opinion between the Justices on the precise meaning of Article 12.3(b), but it was clear on the facts of the case that the criteria of Article 12.3 were satisfied and that the parties had opted into this jurisdiction. It was not therefore necessary to make a reference to the CJEU to decide the case. However, Lady Hale noted that 'the diversity of views expressed by this court indicates that the interpretation [of Article 12.3(b)] is not *acte clair* and may have to be the subject of a reference to the [CJEU] in another case'.[22] Lord Collins referred to one possible interpretation which, while attractive, was by no means an inevitable or a clear one and considered that, if the appeal had depended on whether it was right, a reference would have been necessary.

Acte éclairé

Where a question of EU law arising in a dispute before the Supreme Court was the same as or 'materially identical to a question which has already been the subject of a preliminary ruling in a similar case',[23] the Supreme Court was not required to make a reference to the CJEU.[24] If a national court makes a preliminary ruling in these circumstances, the CJEU may well simply refer the national court to its previous rulings on the issue.[25] *Mirga v Secretary of State for Work and Pensions* and *Samin v Westminster City Council*[26] concerned benefits claims made in the UK by two EU citizens. The Court of Appeal had upheld determinations that under UK domestic law the appellants were not entitled to income support and housing assistance respectively. The essential issue before the Supreme Court was whether the provisions and the current implementation of the domestic law in question infringed the rights of residence in the UK of EU citizens. Shortly before the judgment was due to be handed down, counsel drew the court's attention to the opinion of the Advocate General in Case C-67/14 *Jobcenter Berlin Neukölln v Alimanovic*.[27] The Supreme Court decided to wait until the judgment of the CJEU in that case had been handed down before giving its own judgment. It went on to decline the appellants' request for a reference to the CJEU because it considered that, following

[22] ibid [35]. See also [62]–[63] (Lord Collins). See further *A v A (Children: Habitual Residence)* [2013] UKSC 60, [2014] AC 1.

[23] Joined Cases 28–30/62 *Da Costa en Schaake NV v Nederlandse Belastingadministratie* [1963] ECR 31, [1963] CMLR 224.

[24] ibid; see also *CILFIT* (n 10) [13]–[15].

[25] See eg Case 66/80 *International Chemical Corp v Amministrazione delle Finanze dello Stato* [1981] ECR 1191, [1983] 2 CMLR 593. See also Rules of Procedure of the Court of Justice [2012] OJ L265/1, art 99.

[26] [2016] UKSC 1, [2016] 1 WLR 481.

[27] EU:C:2015:597, [2016] 1 CMLR 29.

the judgment in *Alimanovic*, the questions of EU law raised had already been answered.[28]

Acte clair

The Supreme Court was not obliged to make a reference where it considered that the answer to the issue of EU law arising in the appeal was so clear that a reference was unnecessary.[29] In *CILFIT*, the CJEU set out the criteria for determining whether an issue is *acte clair*:

> Finally, the correct application of Community law may be so obvious as to leave no scope for any reasonable doubt as to the manner in which the question raised is to be resolved. Before it comes to the conclusion that such is the case, the national court or tribunal must be convinced that the matter is equally obvious to the courts of the other Member States and to the Court of Justice. Only if those conditions are satisfied, may the national court or tribunal refrain from submitting the question to the Court of Justice and take upon itself the responsibility for resolving it.[30]

In requiring that the correct application of EU law should be so obvious as to leave no scope for any reasonable doubt and that the application of EU law should be equally obvious both to courts of other Member States and the CJEU, the CJEU set a very high test indeed. It then went even further in requiring that an assessment of whether an issue is *acte clair* must be based by a national court on 'the characteristic features of Community law and the particular difficulties to which its interpretation gives rise'.[31] It identified three specific elements. First, there is a need to compare the different language versions of the relevant EU legislation, bearing in mind that it is drafted in several languages and that the different language versions are all equally authentic.[32] Second, EU law uses terminology peculiar to it and legal concepts do not necessarily have the same meaning in EU law and the law of the various Member States.[33] Third, every provision of EU law 'must be placed in its context and interpreted in the light of the provisions of Community law as a whole, regard being had to the objectives thereof and to its state of evolution at the date on which the provision in question is to be applied'.[34]

[28] *Mirga* (n 26) [3].
[29] As to *acte clair*, see generally Broberg and Fenger (n 1) 235–56.
[30] *CILFIT* (n 10) [16].
[31] ibid [17].
[32] ibid [18].
[33] ibid [19].
[34] ibid [20].

The obstacles to a holding of *acte clair* presented by these criteria have long been considered problematical.[35] Writing in 2002, Lord Slynn observed that, read literally, the *CILFIT* judgment imposes an impossible test for the national judge to satisfy. While acknowledging that an obligation to refer achieves uniformity in EU law, Lord Slynn argued that, in cases which it considers really clear, a national court of final appeal should be allowed a wider discretion and the tests set out in *CILFIT* should be relaxed. He drew attention to the work of a Reflection Group set up by the European Commission on the reform of court procedures which recommended that the predecessor of Article 267 be amended so as to require a final court to refer only where a question important to the development of EU law was involved and, otherwise, for the final court to exercise a discretion, but bearing in mind that there was no other national court to which an appeal could be brought. The recommendation was not adopted. He concluded that in a number of Member States the literal effect of the obligation was not strictly followed.[36]

In the years which followed, the problem was exacerbated by the substantial increase in the number of Member States. It is unrealistic to suppose that it may be possible for a national court of final appeal to be confident that its interpretation of a question of EU law would be equally obvious to the courts of all other Member States.[37] As Advocate General Stix-Hackl has observed, a national court can only rely on its own judgment.[38] Moreover, a proliferation of official languages within the EU, of which there are now twenty-four, has meant that it is a practical impossibility for a national court of final appeal to compare all the different language versions of EU legislation, in cases where this may be relevant. Few, if any, national courts have the resources to perform such an exercise. Indeed, as Advocate General Jacobs noted in his Opinion in Case C–338/95 *Wiener SI GmbH v Hauptzollamt Emmerich*, the CJEU itself rarely refers to all the language versions of the provisions of EU law in issue, 'although it is far better placed to do so than the national courts'.[39] In that Opinion, Advocate General Jacobs observed that if the *CILFIT* judgment were applied strictly, then every question of Community law would have to be referred by all courts of last instance.[40] In his view, the reference to different language versions of EU legislation was better regarded as an essential caution against taking too literal an approach to the interpretation of EU provisions, and for putting greater weight on the context and general scheme of the provisions and on their object and purpose rather than the text alone.[41] Subject to this point, however, he considered that the *CILFIT* criteria did not require reconsideration, but

[35] See eg Broberg and Fenger (n 1) 238.
[36] Anderson and Demetriou (n 1) Foreword, vi.
[37] Lord Mance, 'The Interface between National and European Law' (2013) 38(4) Eur L Rev 437, 444.
[38] Case C–495/03 *Intermodal Transports BV v Staatssecretaris van Financiën* [2005] ECR I–8151, [2006] 1 CMLR 32, Opinion of AG Stix-Hackl, [94].
[39] [1997] ECR I–6495, [1998] 1 CMLR 1110, Opinion of AG Jacobs, [65].
[40] ibid [58].
[41] ibid [65].

that they should apply only where there was a general question and where there was a genuine need for uniform interpretation of a provision of EU law across the Member States.[42]

Two more recent decisions of the CJEU might suggest a more relaxed approach to the issue.[43] In Joined Cases C–72/14 and C–197/14 *X v Inspecteur van Rijksbelastingdienst* and *Van Dijk v Staatssecretaris van Financiën*,[44] the CJEU repeated the general approach in *CILFIT* before stating that it is solely for the national court or tribunal to determine the need for a preliminary ruling in order to enable it to deliver judgment and whether the correct application of EU law is so obvious as to leave no scope for reasonable doubt.[45] In particular, the fact that a lower court has referred a similar question to the CJEU, while relevant, does not preclude a court of final appeal from deciding that the issue is *acte clair*.[46] Similarly, in Case C–160/14 *Ferreira da Silva e Brito and others v Estado português*, a judgment delivered on the same day as *X* and *Van Dijk*, the CJEU reiterated that the national court or tribunal has sole responsibility for determining whether the correct application of EU law is so obvious as to leave no scope for any reasonable doubt.[47] In its view, the fact that lower national courts or tribunals had given contrary decisions was not a conclusive factor requiring the making of a reference.[48] By contrast, Case C–416/17 *European Commission v French Republic* made clear that the *CILFIT* exceptions are to be strictly applied. In that case, the CJEU ruled that a failure by a national court of last instance to make a preliminary reference amounted to an infringement of Article 258 of the TFEU.[49] More recently still, however, in Case C–561/19 *Consorzio Italian Management v Rete Ferroviaria Italiana SpA*, Advocate General Bobek considered that 'the CILFIT criteria, if taken at face value one by one, are utterly unfeasible', with satisfaction of the objective criteria of the *acte clair* exception, in particular, being:

[42] ibid [64].

[43] Alexander Kornezov, 'The New Format of the *Acte Clair* Doctrine and its Consequences' (2016) 53 CMLR 1317, 1325.

[44] EU:C:2015:564, [2016] 1 CMLR 27.

[45] ibid [55]–[59].

[46] ibid para [60].

[47] EU:C:2015:565, [2016] 1 CMLR 26. See also *Intermodal Transports BV* (n 38) [37].

[48] ibid [40]–[42]. However, the CJEU ultimately held (at [45]) that there was an obligation on the court of last instance to make a reference because the rule of EU law in issue was the subject of conflicting decisions at the national level and frequently gave rise to problems of interpretation in other Member States.

[49] Case C–416/17 *European Commission v French Republic* EU:C:2018:811. See further Araceli Turmo, 'A Dialogue of Unequals—the European Court of Justice Reasserts National Courts' Obligations under Article 267(3) TFEU' (2019) 15(2) EuConst 340; and Daniel Sarmiento, 'Judicial Infringements at the Court of Justice—A Brief Comment on the Phenomenal Commission/France (C–416/17)' (9 October 2018) <https://despiteourdifferencesblog.wordpress.com/2018/10/09/judicial-infringements-at-the-court-of-justice-a-brief-comment-on-the-phenomenal-commission-france-c-416-17/> accessed 25 May 2021.

> unattainable … for mortal national judges not possessing the qualities, time, and resources of Dworkin's Judge Hercules (comparing (all) language version; interpreting each provision of EU law in the light of EU law as a whole, while having a perfect knowledge of its state of evolution at the date on which that provision is interpreted).

He also observed that the 'effective affirmation of "stricter CILFIT"' in C–416/17 *Commission v France* 'sits somewhat uneasily with the Court's latest case-law … in particular … the judgments in *X* and *van Dijk* and *Ferreira Da Silva e Brito*'. He concluded that the obligation under the third paragraph of Article 267 of the TFEU should arise where the case:

> raises (i) a general issue of interpretation of EU law (as opposed to its application); (ii) to which there is objectively more than one reasonably possible interpretation; (iii) for which the answer cannot be inferred from the existing case-law of the Court of Justice (or with regard to which the referring court wishes to depart from that case-law).[50]

The judgment of the Grand Chamber in *Consorzio Italian Management* has done little to resolve the tensions between these pronouncements. It held that a court of final appeal has an obligation to refer a question unless it finds that the question is irrelevant or that the provision of EU law in question has already been interpreted by the CJEU or that the correct application of EU law is so obvious as to leave no scope for any reasonable doubt. The existence of such a possibility, it held, must be assessed in the light of the characteristic features of EU law, the particular difficulties to which the interpretation of the latter gives rise and the risk of divergences in judicial decisions within the EU.[51]

Even where there is no definitive ruling by the CJEU on the precise point at issue, it is often possible for a national court to reason by analogy from decided cases and to conclude that it is not necessary to make a reference. The substantial body of CJEU jurisprudence enables national courts to extrapolate from established principles and to decide the point themselves.[52] The Supreme Court has shown itself willing to go to considerable lengths in examining decisions of the CJEU before declining to make a reference. An example is provided by *Routier v Commissioners for Her Majesty's Revenue and Customs*,[53] which concerned the applicability of EU rules on free movement of capital to transfers from the UK to Jersey. HMRC had

[50] Case C–561/19 *Consorzio Italian Management v Rete Ferroviaria Italiana SpA* EU:C:2021:291, Opinion of AG Bobek, 15 April 2021 [103], [104], [119], [134].

[51] ECLI:EU:C:2021:799, Judgment of the Court (Grand Chamber), 6 October 2021 [33], [51], [66].

[52] See further *Wiener SI GmbH* (n 39), Opinion of AG Jacobs [61].

[53] [2019] UKSC 43, [2021] AC 327. Another example is provided by the examination of the scope of the EU principle of absolute *res judicata* in *Servier Laboratories* (n 17).

determined that Mrs Coulter's gift to the Coulter Trust did not qualify for charitable gift relief from inheritance tax under section 23 of the Inheritance Tax Act 1984 which limited relief to trusts governed by the law of a part of the UK, because the Trust was governed by the law of Jersey at Mrs Coulter's death. The appellant executors appealed on the ground of incompatibility with what is now Article 63 of the TFEU,[54] which prohibits restrictions on the free movement of capital between EU Member States and between Member States and third countries. The issue turned on whether Jersey was to be regarded as a third country for this purpose. The Supreme Court considered that decisions of the CJEU, which it examined in detail, provided a systematic and consistent approach to the issue.[55] The question of whether a territory is to be regarded as a third country is context-specific and will depend on whether, under the relevant Treaty of Accession and supplementary measures, the relevant provisions of EU law apply to that territory. As EU rules on free movement of capital did not apply in Jersey, it was to be considered a third country for the purpose of a transfer from the UK.[56] The court therefore declined to make a reference.

In *Aspen Underwriting Ltd v Credit Europe Bank NV*,[57] one of the issues before the Supreme Court was whether Article 14 of section 3, chapter II of the Recast Brussels Regulation ((EU) 1215/2012),[58] which requires insurers to bring proceedings in the courts of the Member State in which the defendant is domiciled, only applies where the defendant to the proceedings is the weaker party. After a detailed examination of relevant EU authorities and many paragraphs of analysis as to what EU law required, Lord Hodge concluded that the relative economic strength of the parties did not determine the applicability of Article 14.[59] Applying the *CILFIT* criteria, he considered that it is *acte clair* that a person correctly categorized as a policyholder, insured, or beneficiary is entitled to the protection of section 3 of the Regulation, whatever its economic power relative to the insurer. It was, therefore, not necessary to refer a question on this issue to the CJEU.[60]

A similar approach can be seen in *AMT Futures Ltd v Marzillier, Dr Meier & Dr Guntner Rechtsanwaltsgesellschaft mbH*.[61] In that case, a German domiciled law firm was alleged to have procured a breach of contract by causing its clients to issue proceedings in Germany in breach of an exclusive jurisdiction clause in favour of England and Wales. The claimant, a UK-domiciled derivatives broker, wished to

[54] At the relevant time, art 56 of the Treaty Establishing the European Community.
[55] *Routier* (n 53) [19]–[29].
[56] ibid [35], [37].
[57] [2020] UKSC 11, [2021] AC 493.
[58] Regulation (EU) No 1215/2012 of the European Parliament and of the Council of 12 December 2012 on jurisdiction and the recognition and enforcement of judgments in civil and commercial matters [2012] OJ L351/1.
[59] *Aspen Underwriting* (n 57) [43].
[60] ibid [59].
[61] [2017] UKSC 13, [2018] AC 439.

bring proceedings in England and Wales against the law firm. The question was essentially whether the harm had occurred in England and Wales or in Germany. The claimant argued that because the cause of action was the tort of inducing breach of contract, and because the term that was alleged to be broken was an exclusive jurisdiction clause in favour of England and Wales, the harm should be considered to have taken place there because the rationale underlying Article 5(3) of the then Brussels regime would justify such an approach. The Supreme Court held that such a ruling would be contrary to clear CJEU jurisprudence which it cited. It held that the harm occurred in Germany, where the proceedings were issued, as this was the event which gave rise to damage for the purposes of Article 5(3). While there may have been consequential harm in England and Wales, CJEU case law established that the Brussels regime was not concerned with consequential losses when determining where harm occurred.

The Supreme Court has undoubtedly taken a broad view of when an issue may be considered *acte clair* within the *CILFIT* criteria. A number of writers have been critical of what they consider to be a reluctance on the part of the Supreme Court to refer.[62] Professor Arnull is particularly critical of the failure to refer in *Office of Fair Trading v Abbey National plc and others*,[63] where the majority of the Supreme Court declined to make a reference notwithstanding that it disagreed with the interpretation favoured by the lower courts.[64] The Supreme Court was asked whether the Office of Fair Trading could launch an investigation into whether the appellant banks' charges for unauthorized overdrafts were fair. The Office of Fair Trading had power to make an assessment for fairness, but this was subject to the limits laid down in the Unfair Contract Terms in Consumer Contracts Regulations 1999, which implemented European Council Directive 93/13/EEC.[65] Regulation 6(2)(b) (which implemented Article 4(2) of the Directive) stated that the assessment of the fairness of a term in a contract 'shall not relate ... to the adequacy of the price or remuneration, as against the goods or services supplied in exchange'. The Court of Appeal had held that this exclusion applied only to the 'core terms' of the contract and not to ancillary terms such as the charges for unauthorized overdrafts. However, the Supreme Court allowed the banks' appeal. It decided that, although the interpretation of Article 4(2) of the Directive was a question of European law, it was not necessary to refer the matter to the CJEU. Lord Walker said:

[62] See eg Arnull (n 1) 335ff. See also Marie Demetriou QC, 'Relations between the CJEU and National Courts: Have Our Courts Become Reluctant to Refer?', Bar European Group conference, Taormina (2016).

[63] [2009] UKSC 6, [2010] 1 AC 696.

[64] Arnull (n 1) 337–38, 356.

[65] Council Directive 93/13/EEC of 5 April 1993 on unfair terms in consumer contracts [1993] OJ L95/29.

> If … the Court is unanimous that the appeal should be allowed, then in my opinion we should treat the point as acte clair, and decide against making a reference. It may seem paradoxical for a court of last resort to conclude that a point is clear when it is differing from the carefully-considered judgments of the very experienced judges who have ruled on it in lower courts. But sometimes a court of last resort does conclude, without any disrespect, that the lower courts were clearly wrong, and in my respectful opinion this is such a case.[66]

He went on to observe that even if some or all of the court felt that the point was not *acte clair*, he would still not incur the delay involved in a reference since a decision on the correct construction of Article 4(2) of the Directive was not essential for the determination of the appeal.[67] Even if the Court of Appeal was not clearly wrong on the issue of construction, it was in his view clearly wrong in applying its construction to the facts. However, he also seems to have been influenced here by the consideration of the delay which would be caused by a reference to the CJEU observing that the court was 'entitled to take the likely delay into account, although not as an overriding consideration, in deciding whether to make a reference'.[68] Lord Walker acknowledged that:

> In other circumstances it might be regarded as rather unprincipled to take that means of avoiding an important issue of Community law, but in the special circumstances of this case I would regard it as the lesser of two evils. There is a strong public interest in resolving the matter without further delay.[69]

The likely delay to the litigation is strictly an irrelevant consideration when a court of final appeal is considering whether or not it is obliged make a reference. Nevertheless, it is understandable that national courts are, on occasion, concerned at the length of the delay which will inevitably be occasioned by a reference. This can be a particular cause for concern in jurisdictional disputes where the parties are sometimes compelled to follow a long road before they can identify the correct forum and address the substance of their cases.

The *Abbey National* case may, perhaps, be considered an extreme example of the willingness of the Supreme Court to conclude that a reference is unnecessary. However, it may be said in defence of Lord Walker's approach to deciding what is *acte clair* that it now finds a degree of support in the judgment of the CJEU in *Ferreira da Silva e Brito*. The fact that a lower court has taken a different view is not necessarily conclusive against a finding of *acte clair*, although it will be more

[66] *Abbey National* (n 63) [49]. See also Lord Mance at [115]. Contrast Lord Phillips at [91].
[67] ibid [50]. Lord Phillips [91] and Lord Neuberger [120] did not consider the issue *acte clair*, but agreed that its resolution was not essential to the determination of the appeal.
[68] ibid [48].
[69] ibid [50].

difficult for a court of last instance to reach this conclusion where there is evidence that a rule of EU law has also caused problems of interpretation in other Member States.[70]

By contrast, where the Supreme Court is itself divided in relation to an issue of EU law which is necessary to its decision, it seems that there is no alternative to making a reference.[71] Thus, in *Test Claimants in the Franked Investment Income Group Litigation v HMRC*,[72] Lord Hope observed:

> the one issue on which the court is divided ... raises a question of EU law and the division of opinion shows that the answer to it is not *acte clair*, it is plain that it will need to be the subject of a reference to the Court of Justice for a preliminary ruling under article 267 TFEU.[73]

A particularly striking example is provided by *O'Byrne v Aventis Pasteur MSD Ltd*,[74] which concerned limitation in proceedings pursuant to the Consumer Protection Act 1987. It was contended that the substitution of a defendant would be inconsistent with Article 11 of Council Directive 85/374/EEC.[75] The High Court made a preliminary reference. Following receipt of the judgment of the CJEU,[76] the High Court allowed the substitution[77] and the Court of Appeal dismissed an appeal.[78] On appeal to the House of Lords, a majority would have dismissed the appeal on the ground that it was clear that the CJEU was saying that, in some circumstances, proceedings which were obviously intended to be proceedings against the producer but which used the wrong name could properly be treated by national procedural law as having been proceedings against the producer. However, as this was not the unanimous view, the House of Lords referred the case to Luxembourg for a second time.[79] The answer provided by the CJEU in response to the second reference[80] was not in line with either of the interpretations of its judgment on the first reference which had been advanced before the Appellate Committee. The Supreme Court, which had replaced the Appellate Committee, allowed the appeal.[81]

[70] Lord Mance points out that *Abbey National* has also been criticized by Professor Hein Kötz for failure to address German and Dutch authority to which, however, the Supreme Court was not referred. See further Lord Mance (n 37) 444. See also *Ferreira da Silva e Brito* (n 47) [45].

[71] Broberg and Fenger (n 1) 241.

[72] [2012] UKSC 19, [2012] 2 AC 337.

[73] ibid [1].

[74] [2008] UKHL 34, [2008] 4 All ER 881.

[75] Council Directive 85/374/EEC of 25 July 1985 on the approximation of the laws, regulations and administrative provisions of the Member States concerning liability for defective products [1985] OJ L210/29.

[76] Case C-127/04 *O'Byrne v Sanofi Pasteur MSD Ltd (formerly Aventis Pasteur MSD Ltd)* [2006] ECR I-1313.

[77] [2006] EWHC 2562 (QB), [2007] 1 WLR 757.

[78] [2007] EWCA Civ 966, [2008] 1 WLR 1188.

[79] [2008] UKHL 34, [2008] 4 All ER 881.

[80] Case C-358/08 *Aventis Pasteur SA v OB* [2009] ECR I-11305.

[81] [2010] UKSC 23, [2010] 1 WLR 1412.

An effective dialogue

There is a particular responsibility on a referring court to ensure that the Luxembourg court is made fully aware of the precise issues which it is necessary for the referring court to decide and the precise context in which they arise. Full information must be provided as to the factual situation which has given rise to the dispute. Furthermore, it is essential that full details be provided as to the domestic legal context in which the dispute arises. In particular, the CJEU must be provided with a full picture of national substantive and procedural rules which have a bearing on the issue. It is only if a full picture is provided that an informed dialogue can take place between the national court and the CJEU. In general, while concerned not to over-burden a reference, the Supreme Court has sought to ensure that the CJEU is provided with all relevant material to enable it to perform its role.[82]

However, this has not invariably been the case, as *HMRC v Aimia Coalition Loyalty UK Ltd*[83] demonstrates. The case concerned a loyalty scheme and, in particular, whether the promoter was entitled to deduct the VAT element of the service charges it paid to redeemers for redeeming collectors' points and for providing it with other services. A panel of the House of Lords made a preliminary reference. Unfortunately, the panel did not identify the real issues in the case and, as a result, they were not addressed by the CJEU in its judgment.[84] As Lord Reed explained when the national proceedings were resumed:

> The House of Lords' reasons for concluding that it was necessary that a preliminary reference should be made are not recorded. Although the case was not straightforward, the view of the tribunal and of the Court of Appeal, that the issue in the case was as to how established principles should be applied to the particular facts, was one for which there was in my view much to be said. More importantly, it is apparent from what followed that the reference did not make sufficiently clear to the Court of Justice what the central issues were, as they emerged from the judgment of the Court of Appeal: issues which had appeared to the highest court in this country to be of such difficulty that a reference was required. Nor did the reference direct the attention of the Court of Justice to the facts found by the tribunal which bore most directly upon those issues.[85]

[82] See eg the Supreme Court's judgment in *SM (Algeria) v Entry Clearance Officer* [2018] UKSC 9, [2018] 1 WLR 1035, which sets out the applicable provisions of both EU and UK law and the facts and history of the litigation before turning to the three questions referred by the court to the CJEU.

[83] [2013] UKSC 15, [2013] 2 All ER 719.

[84] Joined Cases C-53/09 and C-55/09 *Commissioners for Her Majesty's Revenue and Customs v Loyalty Management UK Ltd and Baxi Group Ltd* [2010] ECR I-9187.

[85] *Aimia* (n 83) [30].

Lord Reed, with whom Lord Hope and Lord Walker agreed, explained that as a result, a situation was created in which the CJEU was not in a position to answer the questions referred, as it should have done, by reference to the entirety of the relationships between the participating parties and matters regarded as important in the national proceedings were left out of account.[86] The terms of the reference resulted in the CJEU approaching the facts on a different basis from that which the referring court was bound to adopt.[87] He drew attention to the distinct roles of national courts and the CJEU as expressed in Case C–30/93 *AC-Atel Electronics Vertriebs GmbH v Hauptzollamt München-Mitte*:[88] the evaluation of the facts of the case and the application of EU law to those facts are in general functions of the national courts.[89] In Lord Reed's view, the CJEU had recognized that the reference raised no new point of law, but had endeavoured to clarify how established principles applied in the circumstances of the case as they emerged from the reference. The Supreme Court could not treat the ruling of the CJEU as dispositive of its decision, in so far as it was based on an incomplete evaluation of the facts found by the tribunal or addressed questions which failed fully to reflect those arguments.[90]

In a dissenting judgment, Lord Carnwath, with whom Lord Wilson agreed, considered that the court could not go behind either the decision of the House of Lords to make the reference or the terms in which it was made. Nor was it appropriate or fair to decide that relevant facts had not been drawn to the attention of the CJEU or that the true issues were not issues of law at all.[91]

It is difficult to escape the conclusion that in *Aimia* the dialogue between the final court of appeal and the CJEU broke down.

In general, great care has been taken by the Supreme Court in drawing up the questions to be referred. While account is taken of the submissions of the parties as to the questions to be referred, this is clearly ultimately for the referring court which will have to decide the appeal on the basis of the answers given in due course by the CJEU. Unfortunately, the CJEU has a tendency, on occasion, to reformulate the questions referred, which can have an effect on the answers provided. In *R (ClientEarth) v Secretary of State for the Environment, Food and Rural Affairs*,[92] the Supreme Court referred to the CJEU four questions concerning the interpretation and relationship between Articles 13, 22, and 23 of Directive 2008/50/EC (the Air Quality Directive).[93] In its judgment,[94] the CJEU reformulated the first

[86] ibid [33]–[49].
[87] ibid [48].
[88] [1994] ECR I–2305 [16]–[18].
[89] *Aimia* (n 83) [54].
[90] ibid [55]–[56] (Lord Reed). See also [87]–[88], [103], [111] (Lord Hope), [118] (Lord Walker).
[91] ibid [120]–[124] (Lord Carnwath).
[92] [2013] UKSC 25, [2013] 2 All ER 928. See Arnull (n 1) 348–49.
[93] Directive 2008/50/EC of the European Parliament and of the Council of 21 May 2008 on ambient air quality and cleaner air for Europe [2008] OJ L152/1.
[94] Case C–404/13 *R (ClientEarth) v Secretary of State for the Environment, Food and Rural Affairs* EU:C:2014:2382, [2015] 1 CMLR 55.

two questions in a way which, as Lord Carnwath put it when the case returned to the Supreme Court, 'introduced a degree of ambiguity which it had been hoped to avoid in the original formulation' and which 'had the unfortunate effect of enabling each party to claim success on the issue'.[95] In the event, however, it was unnecessary to make a final ruling on this difference or to make a further reference in order to resolve it.[96]

In the great majority of cases, the dialogue has been effective and the CJEU has provided clear answers to the questions referred which have enabled the Supreme Court to resolve the issues on the pending appeal. However, this has not invariably been the case. Lord Mance draws attention to a number of cases in which, after a reference had been made and answered by the CJEU, the parties disagreed as to who had won.[97] Reference has been made above to *O'Byrne v Aventis Pasteur*, where this was the case even after a second reference. Similarly, in *British Airways plc v Williams*,[98] following a ruling by the CJEU, the parties were at odds as to its consequences for the dispute between them.

B. Future

The UK left the EU at 11pm on 31 January 2020 (exit day) and this was followed by a transition period which ended at 11pm on 31 December 2020. The terms of the UK's withdrawal from the Union are set out in the Agreement on the withdrawal of the United Kingdom of Great Britain and Northern Ireland from the European Union and the European Atomic Energy Community (2019/C 384 1/01) ('the Withdrawal Agreement').[99] The Withdrawal Agreement has been implemented domestically by the European Union (Withdrawal) Act 2018 ('the 2018 Act') and the European Union (Withdrawal Agreement) Act 2020 ('the 2020 Act').

References During the Transition Period

On exit day, the Withdrawal Agreement came into force and section 1 of the 2018 Act repealed the European Communities Act 1972 (the 1972 Act).[100]

[95] [2015] UKSC 28, [2015] 4 All ER 724 [6].
[96] ibid.
[97] Lord Mance (n 37) 443.
[98] [2012] UKSC 43, [2013] 1 All ER 443. See also *North Wales Training and Enterprise Council Ltd (trading as CELTEC Ltd) v Astley* [2006] UKHL 29, [2006] 1 WLR 2420.
[99] [2020] OJ L29/7.
[100] On references during the transition period generally, see Alexandra Littlewood, 'Preliminary References During the Transition Period: Business as Usual?', EU Relations Law (12 June 2020) <https://eurelationslaw.com/blog/preliminary-references-during-the-transition-period-business-as-usual> accessed 18 May 2021.

However, section 1A of the 2018 Act provided that the 1972 Act should continue to have modified effect in domestic law during the transition period. As a result, throughout the transition period, the Supreme Court remained under an obligation to make references for preliminary rulings in appropriate cases in accordance with Article 267 of the TFEU.[101] Furthermore, the Withdrawal Agreement provided that during the transition period the CJEU should have jurisdiction as provided for in the treaties.[102] In the event, the Supreme Court made only one reference to Luxembourg during the transition period: *Zipvit Ltd v Revenue and Customs Commissioners*.[103] The case concerned the implications for deduction of input VAT in circumstances where the tax authority, the supplier, and the trader had all misinterpreted the relevant EU legislation. It raised questions as to the correct interpretation of the words 'due or paid' in Article 168(a) and the relationship of Articles 168 and 226 of the Principal VAT Directive (2006/112/EC),[104] which the Supreme Court considered could not be regarded as *acte clair*. It therefore made a reference to the CJEU.[105]

The CJEU had not delivered its ruling in *Zipvit* by the end of the transition period. However, the Withdrawal Agreement provides that after the end of the transition period the CJEU will continue to have jurisdiction to consider requests for preliminary rulings from courts and tribunals in the UK, provided they were registered by the registry of the CJEU before the transition period expired.[106] The judgment of the CJEU in *Zipvit* was delivered on 13 January 2022[107] and is binding in its effect.[108]

References after the Transition Period

Since the end of the transition period on 31 December 2020, courts and tribunals in the UK are prohibited by section 6(1)(b) of the 2018 Act from making references to the CJEU.[109] However, this must be read subject to the provisions of sections 7A and 7C of the 2018 Act which give effect to the Withdrawal Agreement.

101 de Mars (n 1) 199.

102 Withdrawal Agreement, art 131.

103 [2020] UKSC 15, [2020] 3 All ER 1017.

104 Council Directive 2006/112/EC of 28 November 2006 on the common system of value added tax [2006] OJ L347/1.

105 See further Giles Salmond, 'Zipvit: An Interesting Referral to the CJEU', Tax Journal (26 May 2020) <www.taxjournal.com/articles/zipvit-an-interesting-referral-to-the-cjeu> accessed 21 December 2021.

106 Withdrawal Agreement, art 86.

107 Case C-156/20 *Zipvit Ltd v Revenue and Customs Commissioners* EU:C:2022:2, [2022] 1 WLR 2637.

108 Withdrawal Agreement, art 89; 2018 Act, s 7A. See further *Polakowski v Westminster Magistrate's Court* [2021] EWHC 53 (Admin), [2021] 1 WLR 2521 [32].

109 As to references after the transition period, see de Mars (n 1) s 7.6, 199–202; Alexandra Littlewood, 'Preliminary References after Transition: Out with the Old, in with the New', EU Relations Law (24 June

First, Article 158 of the Withdrawal Agreement makes provision for references from courts and tribunals in the UK concerning Part Two of the Withdrawal Agreement, which is concerned with citizens' rights, including rights of residence, rights of workers and self-employed persons, professional qualifications, and co-ordination of social security systems.[110] Article 158(1) provides that where, in a case commenced at first instance within eight years of the end of the transition period before a court or tribunal in the UK,[111] a question is raised concerning the interpretation of Part Two of the Withdrawal Agreement, and where that court or tribunal considers that a decision on that question is necessary to enable it to give judgment in that case, that court or tribunal may request the CJEU to give a preliminary ruling on that question. Article 158(2) provides that the CJEU shall have jurisdiction to give preliminary rulings on requests pursuant to Article 158(1) and that the legal effects in the UK of such preliminary rulings shall be the same as the legal effects of preliminary rulings given pursuant to Article 267 of the TFEU. These provisions are given effect in domestic law by sections 7A and 7C of the 2018 Act. It is possible therefore that the Supreme Court may be asked to make a reference to the CJEU on a point of law falling within these provisions. It should be noted, however, that in contrast to the position under Article 267 of the TFEU, there will be no obligation on the Supreme Court as the final court of appeal to make a reference in such circumstances.

Second, the Protocol on Ireland/Northern Ireland to the Withdrawal Agreement (the Protocol) makes special provision for future references to the CJEU. The Protocol sets out arrangements necessary to address the unique circumstances on the island of Ireland, to maintain the necessary conditions for continued North–South cooperation, to avoid a hard border and to protect the Good Friday or Belfast Agreement of 10 April 1998 in all its dimensions.[112] In particular, it makes special provision in respect of customs and movement of goods,[113] technical regulations,[114] VAT and excise duties,[115] the single electricity market,[116] and State aid.[117] Article 12(1) provides that the authorities of the UK shall be responsible for implementing and applying the provisions of EU law made applicable by

2020) <https://eurelationslaw.com/blog/preliminary-references-after-transition-out-with-the-old-in-with-the-new> accessed 18 May 2021.

Withdrawal Agreement, art 86.

110 Withdrawal Agreement, arts 9–39.

111 Where the subject matter of the case is a decision on an application made pursuant to art 18(1) or (4) or to art 19 of the Withdrawal Agreement, a request for a preliminary ruling may be made only where the case commenced at first instance within a period of eight years from the date at which art 19 applies. Withdrawal Agreement, arts 158(1), 185.

112 Protocol, art 1(3).

113 Protocol, art 5.

114 Protocol, art 7.

115 Protocol, art 8.

116 Protocol, art 9.

117 Protocol, art 10.

the Protocol to and in the UK in respect of Northern Ireland. Article 12(4) then provides:

> As regards the second subparagraph of paragraph 2 of this Article, Article 5 and Articles 7 to 10, the institutions, bodies, offices, and agencies of the Union shall in relation to the United Kingdom and natural and legal persons residing or established in the territory of the United Kingdom have the powers conferred upon them by Union law. In particular, the Court of Justice of the European Union shall have the jurisdiction provided for in the Treaties in this respect. The second and third paragraphs of Article 267 TFEU shall apply to and in the United Kingdom in this respect.

Sections 7A and 7C of the 2018 Act give effect to these provisions in domestic law. As a result, there may well be future references to the CJEU in respect of the effect of the relevant provisions of the Protocol. In this regard, two important differences from the provision in Article 158 of the Withdrawal Agreement should be noted. First, the provision for preliminary references in the Protocol is without any express limit of time. Second, the effect of Article 12(4) is to apply the second and third paragraphs of Article 267 of the TFEU in their full extent to references under the Protocol, with the result that in an appropriate case there will be an obligation on the Supreme Court, as a final court of appeal, to make a preliminary reference to the CJEU.[118]

The Status of CJEU Case Law after the Transition Period

Section 6(1) of the 2018 Act as amended provides that a UK court or tribunal is not bound by any principles laid down, or any decisions made, on or after the end of the transition period by the CJEU.[119] However, section 6(2) provides that, subject to this and subsections (3) to (6), a court or tribunal may have regard to anything done on or after the end of the transition period by the CJEU, another EU entity, or the EU so far as it is relevant to any matter before the court or tribunal. As a result, it is open to UK courts and tribunals to have regard to the way in which EU law has developed in the case law of the CJEU since the withdrawal of the UK. However,

[118] Littlewood (n 109) also draws attention in this regard to the Protocol to the Withdrawal Agreement relating to the Sovereign Base Areas of the United Kingdom in Cyprus. Art 2 of this Protocol provides that the Sovereign Base Areas will remain part of the customs territory of the EU. Art 12(1) provides that the CJEU shall have jurisdiction in relation to the Protocol as provided for in the treaties. Littlewood also notes that the Withdrawal Agreement envisages the possibility of a reference concerning the interpretation and application of EU law referred to in arts 136 and 138 of the Withdrawal Agreement relating to continuing budgetary obligations.

[119] This is subject to matters addressed in the Withdrawal Agreement, including judgments in references pending at the end of the transition period.

the section provides no guidance as to what authority or weight, if any, should be given to such developments and leaves this potentially contentious issue for decision by the judiciary.[120]

Interpretation of Retained EU Law: Departure from Pre-Brexit Decisions of the CJEU

Finally, it is necessary to say something about the status of pre-Brexit decisions of the CJEU within the body of retained EU law which has been transposed into domestic law by the withdrawal legislation. Put broadly, section 6(3) of the 2018 Act provides that any question as to the validity, meaning, or effect of any retained EU law is to be decided, so far as that law is unmodified and so far as they are relevant, in accordance with principles laid down by and any decisions of the CJEU as they have effect in EU law immediately before the end of the transition period. However, section 6(4) provides that the Supreme Court and, in certain circumstances, the High Court of Justiciary in Scotland are not bound by any retained EU case law. More recently, this provision has been modified by regulations made under sections 6(5A) and (5B), which provide that a relevant court is not bound by any retained EU case law except where there is post-transition case law which modifies or applies that retained EU case law and which is binding on the relevant court.[121] In essence, the power to depart from CJEU case law is extended to the Courts of Appeal in the three UK jurisdictions and certain equivalents.

These provisions apply only in relation to retained EU law. Thus, rights and obligations under the Withdrawal Agreement and the Northern Ireland Protocol must, where relevant, be given effect in accordance with CJEU case law. The intention here has been to balance legal certainty against a need for domestic law to evolve in the light of changed circumstances. Following a consultation, the government concluded that extending the power to depart from CJEU case law in this way would alleviate the pressures on the Supreme Court, while confining it to appellate courts would maintain legal certainty and reduce the risk of conflicting decisions and divergence between different jurisdictions. Furthermore, it should be noted that the courts and tribunals to which the power is extended are bound by the normal operation of domestic principles of precedent. They are not permitted

[120] The Bill which became the 2018 Act originally provided in clause 6(2): 'A court or tribunal need not have regard to anything done on or after exit day by the European Court, another EU entity or the EU but may do so if it considers it appropriate to do so.' European Union (Withdrawal) HC Bill (2017-19) 5. See further Lord Neuberger and Baroness Hale, 'Oral Evidence to the Select Committee on the Constitution' (29 March 2017) 2–3 <www.parliament.uk/globalassets/documents/lords-committees/constitution/Annual-evidence-2016-17/ucCC290317SupremeCourt.pdf> accessed 18 May 2021; David Lloyd Jones, 'Brexit and the Future of English Law' (2018) 49 Vic Univ Wellingt L Rev 1, 15–18.

[121] The European Union (Withdrawal) Act 2018 (Relevant Court) (Retained EU Case Law) Regulations 2020, SI 2020/1525 (the 2020 Regulations).

to depart from binding domestic case law relating to retained EU case law or from prior decisions of a more senior court on whether or not to depart from retained EU case law after the end of the transition period. The test to be applied by a court when considering whether to depart from a CJEU authority will be that applied by the Supreme Court when departing from its own earlier decisions.[122] This has the advantages that the test is well-established and there is considerable judicial guidance on its application. There are also clear advantages in all qualifying courts applying the same test.[123]

It is likely that appellate courts will have to consider these provisions in many appeals in the years ahead. However, no further guidance is provided in the legislation as to the authority or weight to be given to CJEU case law or the criteria to be applied when a court is asked to depart from CJEU case law. It appears, therefore, that the courts have been given very wide powers in what may prove to be a controversial area.

[122] 2018 Act, s 6(5); 2020 Regulations, reg 5.
[123] Ministry of Justice, 'Response to the Consultation on the Departure from Retained EU Case Law by UK Courts and Tribunals' (October 2020), CP 303 <www.gov.uk/government/consultations/departure-from-retained-eu-case-law-by-uk-courts-and-tribunals> accessed 18 May 2021.

Appendix Preliminary references from the Supreme Court to the CJEU 2009–2020[a]

Year	No of references	Supreme Court Case Details	CJEU Ruling
2009 (from 1 October)	0	n/a	n/a
2010	4	1. *Office of Communications v The Information Commissioner* [2010] UKSC 3, [2010] Env LR 20 2. *British Airways plc v Williams* [2010] UKSC 16, [2010] 2 All ER 1053 and [2012] UKSC 43, [2013] 1 All ER 443 3. *O'Brien v Ministry of Justice* [2010] UKSC 34, [2010] 4 All ER 62 and [2013] UKSC 6, [2013] 1 WLR 522 4. *(1) JP Morgan Chase Bank, NA (2) JP Morgan Securities Ltd v Berliner Verkehrsbetriebe (BVG) Anstalt des öffentlichen Rechts*	1. Case C–71/10 *Office of Communications v The Information Commissioner* EU:C:2011:525, [2012] 1 CMLR 7 2. Case C–155/10 *Williams v British Airways plc* EU:C:2011:588, [2012] 1 CMLR 23 3. Case C–393/10 *O'Brien v Ministry of Justice* EU:C:2012:110, [2012] 2 CMLR 25 4. Case C–54/11 *JP Morgan Chase Bank NA, JP Morgan Securities Ltd v Berliner Verkehrsbetriebe (BVG), Anstalt des öffentlichen Rechts* EU:C:2011:453*
2011	2	1. *Parkwood Leisure Ltd v Alemo-Herron and others* [2011] UKSC 26, [2011] 4 All ER 800 2. *R (on the application of Edwards and another) v Environment Agency and others* [2010] UKSC 57, [2011] 1 WLR 79 and [2013] UKSC 78, [2014] 1 WLR 55	1. Case C–426/11 *Alemo-Herron and others v Parkwood Leisure Ltd* EU:C:2013:521, [2014] 1 CMLR 21 2. Case C–260/11 *Edwards v Environment Agency* EU:C:2013:221, [2013] 3 CMLR 18

2012	2	1. *Test Claimants in the Franked Investment Income Group Litigation v Commissioners of Inland Revenue and another* [2012] UKSC 19, [2012] 2 AC 337 2. *Jessy Saint Prix v Secretary of State for Work and Pensions* [2012] UKSC 49, [2013] 1 All ER 752	1. Case C–362/12 *Test Claimants in the FII Group Litigation v Inland Revenue Commissioners* EU:C:2013:834, [2014] AC 1161, [2014] 2 CMLR 33 2. Case C–507/12 *Saint Prix v Secretary of State for Work and Pensions* EU:C:2014:2007, [2015] 1 CMLR 118
2013	2	1. *R (on the application of ClientEarth) v The Secretary of State for the Environment, Food and Rural Affairs* [2013] UKSC 25, [2013] 2 All ER 928 and [2015] UKSC 28, [2015] 4 All ER 724 2. *Public Relations Consultants Association Ltd v The Newspaper Licensing Agency Ltd and others* [2013] UKSC 18, [2013] 2 All ER 852	1. Case C–404/13 *R (on the application of ClientEarth) v Secretary of State for the Environment, Food and Rural Affairs* EU:C:2014:2382, [2015] 1 CMLR 55 2. Case C–360/13 *Public Relations Consultants Association Ltd v Newspaper Licensing Agency Ltd* EU:C:2014:1195, [2014] AC 1438
2014	0	n/a	n/a
2015	2	1. *Secretary of State for Work and Pensions v Tolley (Deceased acting by her personal representative)* [2015] UKSC 55, [2016] 1 All ER 40 2. *R (on the application of Hemming (t/a Simply Pleasure Ltd) and others) v Westminster City Council* [2015] UKSC 25, [2015] AC 1600 and [2017] UKSC 50, [2018] AC 676	1. Case C–430/15 *Secretary of State for Work and Pensions v Tolley* EU:C:2017:74, [2017] 1 WLR 1261 2. Case C–316/15 *R (on the application of Hemming (t/a Simply Pleasure Ltd)) v Westminster City Council* EU:C:2016:879, [2018] AC 650

Continued

Appendix *Continued*

Year	No of references	Supreme Court Case Details	CJEU Ruling
2016	3	1. *MP (Sri Lanka) v Secretary of State for the Home Department* [2016] UKSC 32, [2017] 2 All ER 155 2. *Secretary of State for the Home Department v Franco Vomero (Italy)* [2016] UKSC 49, [2017] 1 All ER 999 and [2019] UKSC 35, [2019] 1 WLR 4729 3. *MB v Secretary of State for Work and Pensions* [2016] UKSC 53, [2017] 1 All ER 338	1. Case C–353/16 *MP (Sri Lanka) v Secretary of State for the Home Department* EU:C:2018:276, [2018] 1 WLR 5585 2. Joined Cases C–316/16 and C–424/16 *B v Land Baden-Wurttemberg* and *Secretary of State for the Home Department v Vomero* EU:C:2018:256, [2019] QB 126 3. Case C–451/16 *MB v Secretary of State for Work and Pensions* EU:C:2018:492, [2019] 1 CMLR 4
2017	3	1. *Volkswagen Financial Services (UK) Ltd v HMRC* [2017] UKSC 26, [2017] STC 824 2. *Keefe (by his litigation friend Eyton) v Hoteles Pinero Canarias SL* 3. *Arcadia Petroleum Ltd and others v Bosworth and another*	1. Case C–153/17 *Volkswagen Financial Services (UK) Ltd v Revenue and Customs Commissioners* EU:C:2018:845, [2019] 4 WLR 32 2. Case C–491/17 *Hoteles Pinero Canarias SL v Keefe* EU:C:2018:422** 3. Case C–603/17 *Arcadia Petroleum Ltd v Bosworth* EU:C:2019:310, [2020] ICR 349
2018	1	1. *SM (Algeria) v Entry Clearance Officer, UK Visa Section* [2018] UKSC 9, [2018] 1 WLR 1035	1. Case C–129/18 *SM (Algeria) v Entry Clearance Officer* EU:C:2019:248, [2019] 1 WLR 5505

2019	3	1. *Computer Associates (UK) Ltd v The Software Incubator Ltd* 2. *R (on the application of Association of Independent Meat Suppliers and another) v Food Standards Agency* [2019] UKSC 36, [2020] 1 All ER 703 and [2021] UKSC 54 3. *X v Kuoni Travel Ltd* [2019] UKSC 37 and [2021] UKSC 34, [2021] 1 WLR 3910	1. Case C–410/19 *The Software Incubator Ltd v Computer Associates (UK) Ltd* ECLI:EU:C:2021:742 2. Case C–578/19 *R (Assn of Independent Meat Suppliers) v Food Standards Agency* EU:C:2021:665, [2022] PTSR 216 3. Case C–578/19 *X v Kuoni Travel Ltd* EU:C:2021:213, [2021] 1 WLR 3879
2020	1	1. *Zipvit Ltd v Revenue and Customs Commissioners* [2020] UKSC 15, [2020] 3 All ER 1017 and [2022] UKSC 12, [2022] 1 WLR 2670.	1. Case C-156/20 *Zipvit Ltd v Revenue and Customs Commissioners* EU:C:2022:2, [2022] 1 WLR 2637.
Total	**23**		

[a]Based on information supplied by Anita Homji, Supreme Court Registry.
[*]Case C–54/11 was removed from the Register of the CJEU after the Supreme Court confirmed that it did not wish to maintain the reference following the CJEU judgment in Case C–144/10 *Berliner Verkehrsbetriebe (BVG) v JPMorgan Chase Bank NA, Frankfurt Branch* EU:C:2011:300, [2011] ECR I-3961.
[**] Case C–491/17 was removed from the Register of the CJEU after the Supreme Court withdrew its request for a preliminary ruling by order of 16 May 2018.

PART III

ENGLISH PRIVATE INTERNATIONAL LAW

8

Rome I Repatriated

Post-Brexit, How Will the 'Retained' Rome I Determine the Applicable Law of Bill of Lading Contracts?

Richard Aikens

When Lawrence Collins first became an 'editor' of *Dicey & Morris*, for the tenth edition in 1980, the English common law determined the 'proper law' of a bill of lading contract. In 1990, when Lawrence had become the General Editor of the eleventh edition, the EEC Convention on the Law Applicable to Contractual Obligations (the 'Rome Convention 1980') had been incorporated into the law of the UK by the Contracts (Applicable Law) Act 1990. Then, in 2012, when Lord Collins of Mapesbury was the General Editor of the fifteenth edition of *Dicey, Morris & Collins*, Regulation (EC)593/2008 of the European Parliament and of the Council of 17 June 2008 on the law applicable to contractual obligations ('Rome I'), had come into force, replacing the Rome Convention.

Now, on the eve of the sixteenth edition of what Lord Goff of Chieveley called 'the prince of text books', again under the General Editorship of Lord Collins of Mapesbury,[1] Brexit has forced things to change again, although not quite full circle. The combined effect of section 3 of the European Union (Withdrawal) Act 2018 (as amended by the European Union (Withdrawal Agreement) Act 2020, hereafter together 'the 2018 Act') and the Law Applicable to Contractual Obligations and Non-Contractual Obligations (Amendment etc) (EU Exit) Regulations 2019 (2019 No 834), which I will give the ugly acronym 'LACONCOR', is that a modified Rome I Regulation continues to have effect in domestic UK law, as 'retained EU law'.[2] Remarkably, all the Recitals, with their reference to 'the Community', 'EU institutions', and 'Member States', have been retained as a part of UK domestic law, perhaps to show, in a whimsical manner, a historical continuity. It seems appropriate to call this domesticated law 'Rome I repatriated' or 'Rome I R'.

[1] Now jointly with Professor Harris.

[2] Rome I was given effect in domestic law by s 2(2) of the European Communities Act 1972 and, as EU-derived domestic legislation, continues to have effect in domestic law on and after 'exit day' under s 3(1) of the 2018 Act. But various amendments to the Rome I Regulation had to be made in order that it could be effective in UK domestic law. Those are set out in LACONCOR. It makes some modifications to Rome I, but none directly relevant to the matters discussed here.

Richard Aikens, *Rome I Repatriated* In: *Essays in International Litigation for Lord Collins.* Edited by: Jonathan Harris and Campbell McLachlan, Oxford University Press. © Oxford University Press 2022.
DOI: 10.1093/oso/9780192867988.003.0009

Article 1(1) of Rome I R states that the regulation shall apply in 'situations involving a conflict of laws, to contractual obligations in civil and commercial matters'. It is universal. Thus, subject to the threshold problem discussed below, in an English court Rome I R will determine the applicable law of bills of lading contracts, whatever the putative applicable law.

What are the particular issues for consideration? First, a threshold question: does Rome I R apply at all to bill of lading contracts? That raises a general preliminary issue of the interpretation of Rome I R. The particular issue concerns the scope of the exclusion of 'negotiable instruments' by Article 1(2)(d). Does this apply to bills of lading by virtue of the phrase in Recital (9) 'to the extent that the obligations under the bill of lading arise out of its negotiable character'? Second, the English court's approach where there is an express choice of law clause in a bill of lading, but there is said to be an 'overriding provision' of UK law so that the parties' choice must be rejected. Third, the question of an 'implied choice' of law, where (for example) there is an English exclusive jurisdiction clause or a London arbitration clause in the bill of lading. Both choice of court and arbitration agreements are outside the scope of Rome I R.[3] Fourth, determining the applicable law where a clause in a bill of lading purports to incorporate terms of a charterparty, such as an applicable law clause, a choice of court clause or an arbitration clause. Lastly, how is the applicable law determined when an entity becomes a subsequent holder of a bill of lading?[4] Will the subsequent holder simply 'step into the shoes' of the original party to the bill and be bound by the existing 'applicable law'?

A. What Is the Effect of Recital (9) and Article 1(2)(d) of Rome I R?

First, how is Rome I R to be interpreted in its new guise? Because Rome I is 'retained EU law', issues of interpretation are subject to the statutory rules in section 6 of the 2018 Act.[5] Any question as to the 'meaning or effect of any retained EU law is to be decided, so far as that law is unmodified' in accordance with any 'retained case law and retained general principles of EU law'.[6] The terms 'retained case law' and 'retained general principles of EU law' are defined in section 6(7) of the 2018 Act. The first covers both domestic case law and principles and decisions laid down

[3] Art 1(2)(e).

[4] In English law, this would be by s 2(1) of the Carriage of Goods by Sea Act 1992.

[5] For a detailed analysis of the effect of the new legislative structure relating to EU regulations and other EU laws retained in domestic law following the UK's withdrawal from the EU, see the judgment of Green LJ in *Lipton v BA City Flyer Ltd* [2021] EWCA Civ 454, [2021] 1 WLR 2545 [52]–[84], with which Coulson and Haddon-Cave LJJ agreed. That case concerned an EU regulation granting air passengers compensation for delayed or cancelled flights, save in 'extraordinary circumstances'.

[6] See s 6(3)(a) of the 2018 Act, but having regard (among other things) to the limits of EU competences before Brexit.

by the European Court ('CJEU'). The phrase 'General principles of EU law' means the 'general principles of EU law' as they had effect before 31 December 2020 and relate to retained EU law. The UK Supreme Court and other UK 'relevant courts' are not *bound* by any 'retained EU case law'.[7] However, section 6(5) of the 2018 Act imposes a test that must be applied before the Supreme Court (or any other designated UK court) can depart from 'retained EU law'. It is the same test 'as [the Supreme Court] would apply in deciding whether to depart from its own case law'. In *TuneIn Inc v Warner Music UK Ltd*, the Court of Appeal considered the criteria for exercising this new power to depart from 'retained EU law'. They are stringent. It must be shown that the CJEU's decision impedes or restricts the proper development of the law (ie UK law) or leads to results that are unjust or contrary to 'public policy'.[8] In the present context, the Supreme Court or Court of Appeal would probably have to conclude that a pre-Brexit CJEU decision on an issue of interpretation of Rome I was both 'wrong' and had wider adverse repercussions for UK conflict of law rules.

How will the English courts interpret Rome I R in general and Article 1(2)(d) and Recital (9) in particular? The Explanatory Notes to the 2018 Act on the effect of section 6(3) state that UK courts must take a 'purposive' approach to interpretation of retained EU law 'where the meaning of the measure is unclear'. This includes 'applying an interpretation that renders the provisions of EU law compatible with the treaties and general principles of EU law'.[9] In *Enka Insaat Ve Sanayi AS v OOO Insurance Co Chubb*,[10] the majority stated that in applying Article 3 of Rome I for determining whether parties have made a choice of law for a contract, the 'court should adopt a broad Regulation-based approach, not constrained by national rules of contractual interpretation'.[11] In practice, if any specific wording of

[7] Section 6(4)(a) of the 2018 Act applied only to the Supreme Court (SC). But s 6(4)(ba) and (5A) stipulate that regulations may be made designating other 'relevant courts or tribunals' apart from the SC that may not be bound by retained EU case law. By the European Union (Withdrawal) Act 2018 (Relevant Court) (Retained EU Case Law) Regulations 2020, SI 1525/2020, reg 3, several courts and tribunals, including the Court of Appeal in England and Wales and the Inner House of the Court of Session in Scotland, were designated 'relevant courts'. Regulation 4(2) states that if one UK court has modified or applied retained EU law and that UK decision is binding on another UK court, the latter is bound to follow it; so maintaining, broadly, the principle of *stare decisis*.

[8] [2021] EWCA Civ 441, [2022] 2 All ER 35 [73]–[89] per Arnold LJ, [184] per Rose LJ, [200]–[201] per Vos MR. See also the commentary of Professor David Feldman in 'Departing from Retained EU Case Law', UK Const L Blog (11 January 2021) <https://ukconstitutionallaw.org> accessed 4 April 2022.

[9] Explanatory notes, para 111. In *Lipton & another v BA City Flyer Ltd*, Green LJ stated that an EU Regulation that is 'retained EU law' 'should be given a purposive construction which takes account of its recital and other principles referred to in the body of the regulation and in the recitals': [83]. However, in 'Statutory Interpretation and the Role of the Courts after Brexit' (2019) 25(4) EPL 637–64, Martin Brenncke argues that it is unlikely that British judges will adopt wholesale the CJEU's 'teleological approach one-to-one' in interpreting 'retained EU law': 647ff.

[10] [2020] UKSC 38, [2020] 1 WLR 4117, 26, so decided before the 2018 Act and LACONCOR came into effect. The case concerned the vexed question of how to determine the applicable law of an arbitration agreement contained in a contract.

[11] Referring to Lord Collins (ed), *Dicey, Morris & Collins on the Conflict of Laws* (15th edn, Sweet & Maxwell 2012) para 32-048.

an Article or Recital in Rome I appears unclear, English judges will look for any guidance from the CJEU on the point. If there is none, then they will attempt an EU 'purposive' approach. But, as Martin Benncke has pointed out, national judges in domestic courts cannot simply 'turn off their deeply engrained and unconsciously functioning domestic legal culture when applying retained EU law'.[12]

The question arising on Article 1(2)(d) and Recital (9) is whether bills of lading are excluded altogether from the scope of Rome I R.[13] Article 1(2)(d) excludes 'obligations arising under … other negotiable instruments to the extent that the obligations under such negotiable instruments arise out of their negotiable character'.[14] Recital (9) stipulates that 'obligations under bills of exchange, cheques and promissory notes and other negotiable instruments should also cover bills of lading to the extent that the obligations under the bill of lading arise out its negotiable character'. Recital (9) thus confirms that bills of lading come within the scope of Article 1(2)(d). But do any of the obligations under a bill of lading 'arise out of its negotiable character'? It has been argued that they do, at least when a bill of lading is transferred to a lawful holder.[15]

It is respectfully suggested this view is wrong. In this context, 'obligations' must mean 'contractual obligations', because that is what Rome I R is about. In English law, those contractual obligations do not 'arise out of' the fact that, in certain circumstances, a bill of lading can be 'negotiated' or, more accurately, 'transferred' to a third party. The contractual rights and obligations between the original parties to a bill of lading do not arise out of the bill's 'negotiable character'. Notoriously, although the English common law permitted the transfer of property rights in the goods represented by the bill of lading, by the process of indorsement of the bill and delivery to another, it gave third parties to whom the bill of lading had been transferred no contractual rights under the bill of lading contract.[16] Hence the need for the Bills of Lading Act 1855 and its successor, the Carriage of Goods by Sea Act 1992, in order to give transferees of the bill such contractual rights and also (in certain circumstances) to transfer obligations. In English law, therefore, the existence of 'contractual obligations' as between a carrier and a transferee of a bill of lading depends not upon the negotiable character of the bill, but upon the fact that statute law transfers contractual rights and obligations to a subsequent holder of a bill in certain defined circumstances.[17]

[12] At 647.

[13] See Professor Yvonne Baatz, 'Should Third Parties Be Bound by Arbitration Clauses in Bills of Lading?' [2015] LMCLQ 85.

[14] Art 1(2)(c) of the Rome Convention contained identical wording, but there was no equivalent of Recital (9).

[15] Herman Boonk, 'Determining Jurisdiction and Choice of Law in Contractual Disputes Coupled with Property-Based Claims' [2011] LMCLQ 227, 231–32.

[16] *Lickbarrow v Mason* (1794) 5 TR 683, 685–686; 101 ER 380, 381–382; *Howard v Shepherd* (1850) 9 CB 297, 319; 137 ER 907, 916, where Maule J said: 'Now it is perfectly clear that a contract cannot be transferred so as to enable a transferee to sue upon it.'

[17] See ss 2(1) and (2) and 5(2) of the Carriage of Goods by Sea Act 1992.

Is that interpretation of Recital (9) and Article 1(2)(d) of Rome I R too anchored in English law notions? The question of whether 'obligations under the bill of lading' do or do not 'arise out of their negotiable character' could be determined either by rules of the putative applicable law of the bill or according to an 'autonomous' European rule. There is no CJEU decision on which approach should apply. But there are indications that the putative applicable law of the bill of lading should determine the issue. Thus, the Giuliano Lagarde Report on the Rome Convention, commenting on the equivalent Article 1(2)(c), states: 'whether a document is characterised as a negotiable instrument is not governed by this Convention and is a matter for the law of the forum (including its rules of private international law)'.[18] There was, of course, no equivalent report for Rome I, but this is a powerful indication that the issue of whether contractual obligations under a bill of lading arises 'out of its negotiable character' should be decided by the putative applicable law of the bill of lading. *Dicey, Morris & Collins* suggests the same approach in respect of Rome I.[19] English courts will therefore regard bills of lading as being subject to the Rome I Regulation, although that does not solve all problems.

B. Express Choice of Law in a Bill of Lading: 'Overriding Mandatory Provisions'

Article 3(1) of Rome I provides that 'a contract shall be governed by the law chosen by the parties'. This can be achieved either expressly or if 'clearly demonstrated by the terms of the contract or the circumstances of the case'. Thus, an English court will, subject to one major qualification, apply the law expressly chosen by the parties to the bill of lading contract.

The qualification concerns Article 9 of Rome I R. Article 9(2) states that 'nothing in this Regulation shall restrict the application of the overriding mandatory provisions of the law of the forum'. Thus, the rules for determining the applicable law set out in Rome I R will not apply if they would 'restrict' the application of 'overriding mandatory provisions' of the law of the forum. The definition of 'overriding mandatory provisions' is set out in Article 9(1). They are

> provisions the respect for which is regarded as crucial by a country for safeguarding its public interests, such as its political, social or economic organisation, to such an extent that they are applicable to any situation falling within their

[18] The Giuliano and Lagarde Report on the Convention on the law applicable to contractual obligations [1980] OJ C282/1, 11 (hereafter Giuliano Lagarde). It also confirms that it was contemplated that bills of lading would be included within 'other negotiable instruments'.

[19] Para 33-095 fn 427. See also Baatz (n 13) 105.

scope, irrespective of the law otherwise applicable to the contract under this Regulation.

When might this apply so that an English court would not give effect to the applicable law chosen by the parties to a bill of lading?

The classic example is when the Carriage of Goods by Sea Act 1971 ('COGSA 1971') applies to make a bill of lading contract compulsorily subject to the so-called Hague-Visby Rules.[20] By section 1(2) of COGSA 1971, 'the provisions of the [Hague-Visby] Rules as set out in the Schedule to this Act, shall have the force of law'. By section 1(3), the Hague-Visby Rules have effect 'and have the force of law in relation to and in connection with the carriage of goods by sea in ships where the port of shipment is a port in the United Kingdom'. The effect of those subsections was considered by the House of Lords before the UK had adopted the Rome Convention, in *The Hollandia*.[21] Goods were shipped in Scotland on board the *Morviken* under a bill of lading which provided expressly for Dutch law and Amsterdam jurisdiction. The cargo was damaged. An action *in rem* was brought by the shippers of the cargo in the English court against a sister ship, *Hollandia*. The carriers sought a stay of the English action on the basis of the Dutch law and jurisdiction clauses. It was common ground that if the action were tried in the Amsterdam court, it would follow Dutch law. Thus, the unamended Hague Rules and the limit of liability, as specified in the bill, would be applied, rather than the higher limits of liability set out in Article IV(5) of the Hague-Visby Rules as applied by the 1971 Act.

In the House of Lords, Lord Diplock[22] concluded that the effect of sections 1(2) and (3) of the 1971 Act was that the Hague-Visby Rules were 'to be treated as if they were part of the directly enacted statute law'.[23] Lord Diplock noted that Article X of the Hague-Visby Rules set out the circumstances in which those Rules would apply to bill of lading contracts and that Article X (with all the other articles) was given the force of law by sections 1(2) and (3) of the 1971 Act. That meant that all the provisions of those Rules had to be applied to the terms of the bill, including one term that the carrier's limit of liability would be governed by the old Hague Rules and so in a manner otherwise than under the Hague-Visby Rules. Because that limit of liability term would be contrary to the Hague-Visby Rules limits, Lord Diplock said

[20] Technically speaking, there is no such thing as 'the Hague-Visby Rules'. The International Convention for the unification of certain rules relating to bills of lading signed at Brussels on 25 August 1924 was amended by a Protocol signed at Brussels on 23 February 1968 and a further Protocol signed at Brussels on 21 December 1979. But the 1968 Protocol was the result of deliberations of the Comité Maritime International Conference in Stockholm in 1963 and thereafter in the ancient Hanseatic city of Visby, in Sweden, thereby giving the amended Hague Rules the commonly used sobriquet 'the Hague-Visby Rules'.

[21] [1983] 1 AC 565.

[22] The other four law lords agreed.

[23] See 575–76.

Article III(8) of the Hague-Visby Rules applied, so that the term was null and void and of no effect.[24]

In *United Antwerp Maritime Agencies NV (Unamar) v Navigation Maritime Bulgare*,[25] the CJEU considered Article 7(2) of the Rome Convention, which is in similar terms to Article 9(2) of Rome I R, although it refers to 'mandatory rules' rather than 'overriding mandatory provisions'. The CJEU held that the national court considering the relevant 'mandatory rule' must take account of the exact terms of the law, its general structure, and 'all the circumstances in which the law was adopted in order to determine whether it is mandatory in nature in so far as it appears that the legislature adopted it in order to protect an interest judged to be essential by the member state concerned'. In *Hellenic Republic v Nikiforidis*,[26] the CJEU emphasized that Article 9 of Rome I must be interpreted strictly, because it derogated from the general principle that the applicable law of a contract was to be freely chosen by the parties.[27]

If an English court were faced with a similar situation as *The Hollandia* now, that decision would not strictly be binding. A court now would have to decide whether the 1971 Act met the criteria set out in Article 9(1) of Rome I R. Only if it did could section 1(2) and (3) of the 1971 Act constitute 'overriding mandatory provision' of UK law, such that a court could disregard the express choice of law of parties to a bill of lading contract. It is clear, following the two CJEU cases, that a national court should assess the status of the relevant national law, viz COGSA 1971, in its national and international context. Would the powerful arguments of so distinguished a jurist as the late Dr Mann have renewed force? It is more likely a court would conclude that the international scope of the Rules, which were created to determine the rights and obligations of carriers and cargo interests and which have internal provisions for when they apply (Article X), would be fatally undermined if they were not given overriding effect.[28] Therefore, if the principal issue in *The Hollandia* arose again, it would be held that the 1971 Act was an 'overriding provision'.[29]

[24] Dr FA Mann described the decision as 'lacking principled explanation and analysis': (1983) 99 LQR 376, 494ff. In (1987) 103 LQR 526, Dr Mann returned to the charge, describing the decision as 'one of the most unfortunate decisions rendered by the House of Lords in recent years'. He urged its 'reconsideration by a reconstituted Appellate Committee willing to apply the Practice Statement of 1966': 527.

[25] Case C–184/12 *United Antwerp Maritime Agencies (UNAMAR) NV v Navigation Maritime Bulgare* EU:C:2013:663, [2014] 1 Lloyd's Rep 161. This was not a case concerning the Hague-Visby Rules.

[26] Case C–135/15 *Hellenic Republic v Nikiforidis* EU:C:2016:774, [2017] ICR 147.

[27] See [43].

[28] The view in *Dicey, Morris & Collins* (n 11) is that the 1971 Act does meet the criteria, because the statute gives effect in UK law to an international convention. See paras 33-110 and 33-111, and fn 502.

[29] The other issue in *The Hollandia* was whether the English proceedings should have been stayed in favour of the Amsterdam court. While Regulation (EU) 1215/2012 of the European Parliament and of the Council on jurisdiction and the enforcement of judgments in civil and commercial matters (Brussels I Regulation Recast) [2012] OJ L351/1 (Brussels I (recast)) was in force, the application of art 25(1) would have necessitated that the English court stayed the action to give effect to the parties' choice of jurisdiction. Since 1 January 2021, Brussels I (recast) no longer applies in the UK, so broadly the same

C. No Express Choice of Law

Can a choice of law be implied where there is no express choice, but there is an English exclusive jurisdiction clause or a London arbitration clause in the bill of lading? Article 3(1) of Rome I R states that there can be an implied choice of applicable law provided that the choice is 'clearly demonstrated by the terms of the contract or the circumstances of the case'. Recital (12) provides that 'an agreement between the parties to confer on one or more courts or tribunals of a Member State exclusive jurisdiction to determine disputes under the contract should be one of the factors to be taken into account in determining whether a choice of law has been clearly demonstrated'. How will these two linked provisions now be interpreted by an English court?

First, there is the reference to 'Member States' in the Recital's phrase 'courts or tribunals of a Member State'; which is now inapposite. In the body of Rome I R, the phrase 'Member States' has been amended to 'relevant state',[30] but that would make no sense in Recital (12). *Dicey, Morris & Collins* regarded the limitation to 'Member States' in Recital (12) as 'unprincipled' and submitted that the limitation could be 'safely ignored because the principle applied to other states'.[31] An English court must now interpret Recital (12) 'purposively'. It would probably disregard the limitation and interpret 'Member States' as a reference to 'any particular state'.

Second, what of the reference to 'one or more … tribunals'? Can that be interpreted to include 'one or more *arbitration* tribunals of a particular state'? That is more difficult, even adopting a 'purposive' construction. Arbitration tribunals are not tribunals 'of a particular state'. They all have a 'seat',[32] but that seat is 'in' a particular State, not 'of' it. So Recital (12) cannot be used directly in relation to arbitration agreements. Giuliano Lagarde stated that 'the choice of a place where disputes are to be settled by arbitration in circumstances indicating that the arbitrator should apply the law of that place' might 'impel' a court to the conclusion that a 'real choice' had been made by the parties.[33] That is not much help, as the argument is circular. If there is an indication that the arbitrator should apply the law of the place of the arbitration, that is tantamount to an express choice of law. Thus, recourse to finding an implied choice is not necessary.[34]

considerations as were applied by the House of Lords in *The Hollandia* (before the Brussels Convention) would apply once again to the issue of staying the English action.

[30] LACONCOR, art 10.
[31] Para 32-063.
[32] In English law, see the Arbitration Act 1996, s 3.
[33] 17.
[34] In English law under s 46 of the Arbitration Act 1996, if the parties have not chosen a law applicable to the substance of the dispute or come to some other agreement on applicable law, it is for the arbitral tribunal to 'apply the law determined by the conflict of laws rules which it considers applicable' (s 46(3)). For an arbitration with an English seat, those would be the conflicts rules of the forum, viz Rome I R: see *Enka* (n 10) [31]. In French law, the arbitrator's choice of law is wider: *Code de procédure civile*, art 1511.

When the 'proper law' of a bill of lading contract was determined by the common law, the existence of an English exclusive jurisdiction clause drew the inference that the parties had made an implied choice of English law as the applicable law of the bill, unless there were strong indications that they did not intend or may not have intended that result.[35] Given the terms of Giuliano Lagarde, that must equally have been the rule under the Rome Convention.[36] There is no example of a contrary conclusion (in the English courts) under Rome I. The inclusion of Recital (12) in Rome I R suggests strongly that this position will not change.

The existence of an English (or London) arbitration clause was traditionally regarded, under the common law, as a persuasive, but not conclusive, indication that the parties had impliedly chosen English law as the 'proper law' of the main contract.[37] While acknowledging that the 'test' was not precisely the same in the Rome Convention, Clarke J adopted a similar approach in *Egon Oldendorff v Libera Corporation (No 2)*. The judge concluded that even though the arbitration clause in that case (arbitrators appointed by the London Maritime Arbitrators' Association) did not indicate that the tribunal should apply English law, nonetheless, in the particular circumstances of the case the choice of a London arbitration clause established 'with reasonable certainty' that the parties had chosen English law to govern both the charterparty and the ship purchase contract.[38]

A similar bill of lading case has not arisen directly under Rome I.[39] However, the position has fundamentally changed following the reasoning of the majority of the Supreme Court in *Enka*. It concluded that times have moved on since *Tunisienne*. London has become more of an international arbitration centre; non-lawyers or lawyers qualified in other jurisdictions are as likely to be involved in arbitrations there as English qualified lawyers; other systems of substantive law may be involved in arbitrations whose seat is London. The majority concluded:

> There can in these circumstances be no general implication that a choice of London (or any other major arbitration centre) as the seat of arbitration demonstrates an intention that the parties' contractual obligations will be governed by

[35] *Hellenic Steel Co v Svolamar Shipping Co Ltd ('The Komninos S')* [1991] 1 Lloyd's Rep 370, 376 per Bingham LJ, with whom Nourse and Lloyd LJJ agreed. See also *Lupofresh Ltd v Sapporo Breweries* [2013] EWCA Civ 948, [2013] 2 Lloyd's Rep 444 [18] per Tomlinson LJ, although the case concerned the Rome Convention, not the common law, and is not a bill of lading case.

[36] 17, using similar wording to that of Bingham LJ in *The Komninos S*.

[37] *Compagnie Tunisienne de Navigation SA v Compagnie d'Armement Maritime SA* [1971] AC 572, 584, 588, 600, 605.

[38] [1996] 1 Lloyd's Rep 380, 389. That concerned a charter and option to purchase contract. This approach was approved by Mance LJ in *ISS Machinery Services Ltd v Aeolian Shipping SA ('The Aeolian')* [2001] EWCA Civ 1162, [2001] 2 Lloyd's Rep 641 [27]. *Egon Oldendorff* was approved, on its particular facts, in *Enka* (n 10) [114].

[39] In *Aquavita Inernational SA v Ashapura Minechem Ltd* [2015] EWHC 2807 (QB), a case under Rome I, Burton J accepted that an implied choice of English law in a guarantee was 'clearly demonstrated' by the terms of the contract or the circumstances of the case where the underlying contract of affreightment was expressly governed by English law: [96]–[105].

> the law of that place. This is equally so whether the question of implied choice is governed by Article 3 of the Rome I Regulation (in relation to the main body of the contract in that case) or the common law conflict rules (in relation to the arbitration agreement).[40]

In future, the mere existence of an English or London arbitration clause in a bill of lading contract would, on its own, be unlikely to lead to the conclusion under Rome I R that the parties had impliedly chosen English law.

D. Effect of Incorporation of Charterparty Clauses in a Bill of Lading Contract

When issues of the 'proper law' of a bill of lading contract were dealt with by the common law, matters were relatively straightforward. If the parties to a bill of lading contract had not expressly chosen a 'proper law' and there was nothing within the bill itself to assist in deciding whether there was an implied choice (such as a jurisdiction or arbitration clause), there might be help from terms that were incorporated into the bill from an associated charterparty. The first issue was whether any charterparty terms were incorporated into the bill of lading contract. An English court would use English law principles (including its conflict of laws principles[41]) to determine the question of whether a clause in the bill successfully incorporated particular terms of a charterparty. If the charterparty terms were incorporated, then English law principles would determine whether the incorporated terms assisted in ascertaining whether the parties had thereby made an implied choice of law in the bill of lading contract.[42]

The Rome Convention made things more complicated. The first issue remained: what are the terms of the bill of lading contract? In the language of the Rome Convention, that must mean whether the charterparty terms 'exist', or are 'valid' within the bill of lading contract? Before that can be determined, it is necessary to decide which law will be used to do so. A dispute as to whether a clause is incorporated in a bill of lading contract must be an issue as to 'the existence' or 'validity' of that 'term' within the bill of lading contract. Article 8(1) of the Rome Convention provided that 'the existence and validity of a contract, or of any term

40 *Enka* (n 10) confirmed, at [31], that the conflicts rules of the forum must be used.

41 Reaffirmed in *Enka* (n 10) [31]–[35].

42 See eg: *The Njegos* [1936] P 90; *Pacific Molasses Co and United Molasses Trading Co Ltd v Entre Rios Compania Naviera SA (The 'San Nicholas')* [1976] 1 Lloyd's Rep 8; *Compania Naviera Micro SA v Shipley International Inc ('The Parouth')* [1982] 2 Lloyd's Rep 351; *Partenreederei M/S 'Heidberg' v Grosvenor Grain and Feed Co Ltd (The 'Heidberg')* [1994] 2 Lloyd's Rep 287; *Siboti K/S v BP France SA* [2003] EWHC 1278 (Comm), [2003] 2 Lloyd's Rep 364. The leading case on 'incorporation' of charterparty terms in bills of lading is now *Caresse Navigation Ltd v Office National de l'Electricité ('The Channel Ranger')* [2014] EWCA Civ 1366, [2015] QB 366.

of a contract, shall be determined by the law which would govern it under this Convention if the contract or term were valid'.[43] Therefore, the question of whether a clause forms a part of a bill of lading contract will be governed by the law that would govern if it were valid and incorporated into the bill.

Article 10(1) of Rome I is in the same terms as Article 8(1), save for the reference to 'this Regulation' rather than 'this Convention'. Logically, the same process should be applied when there is a question concerning incorporation of a charterparty clause in a bill of lading. But there has been a difference of approach by judges at first instance in the English courts. In *Caresse Navigation Ltd v Office National de l'Electricité (The 'Channel Ranger')*,[44] the principal issue was whether a bill of lading contract incorporated an English exclusive jurisdiction clause in an identified charterparty when the bill provided that 'all terms, conditions, liberties and exemptions including the law and arbitration clause, are herewith incorporated'. Males J said the question of the governing law was to be determined by Article 3(1) of Rome I.[45] He did not refer to Article 10. However, in *Seniority Shipping Corp SA v City Seed Crushing Industries Ltd (The Joker)*,[46] where the issue of the applicable law of bills of lading arose, Andrew Baker J stated that the first question was whether the bills incorporated the express choice of English law clause from an associated voyage charter. He said this question was determined by Article 10(1), subject to arguments under Article 10(2). If the English law clause was incorporated, then the next question, viz whether the voyage charter arbitration clause was incorporated, was also governed by English law. But, he held, that issue must be determined through the 'putative proper law' rule of English common law, since Rome I did not apply to arbitration agreements. He concluded that both clauses were incorporated and that Article 10(2) did not apply to negative consent.[47] The same analysis was followed by Bryan J in *Ulusoy Denizilik SA v Cofco Global Harvest (Zhangjiagang) Trading Co Ltd*.[48]

On this point, the analysis of Andrew Baker and Bryan JJ is more precise. It acknowledges that the first stage of a two-stage process is the issue of which applicable law determines the question of incorporation, that is the 'existence' and 'validity', of the relevant clauses in the bill of lading contract. The incorporation of the express choice of law clause must be the first step. That is determined through Article 10. At the second stage, having determined that the express choice of law clause exists and

[43] Art 8(2) provided an 'escape clause' from that rule. It could be used to demonstrate that it did not consent to the contract or term. Art 8(2) and its successor, art 10(2) of Rome I, have not been successfully invoked in English courts. Moreover, the scope of art 10(2) is very limited. In *Lupofresh Ltd v Sapporo Breweries* [2013] EWCA Civ 948, [2013] 2 Lloyd's Rep 444, the CA held that art 10(2) only concerned the fact of consent, not whether consent was invalidated for some legal reason such as mistake.

[44] [2013] EWHC 3081 (Comm), [2014] 1 Lloyd's Rep 337.

[45] In the CA, the issue of how the applicable law of the bill of lading should be determined was not considered.

[46] [2019] EWHC 3541 (Comm), [2021] 1 Lloyd's Rep 169. See [12].

[47] See [12], [16]–[18].

[48] [2020] EWHC 3645 (Comm), [2021] 1 Lloyd's Rep 117 [26], [36].

is valid in the bill of lading, the question of incorporation of the arbitration clause has to be determined, again by reference to the putative applicable law. However, is it correct, as Andrew Baker J appeared to hold in *The Joker*, that this second exercise must be done 'by virtue of the "putative proper law" rule of the common law ... since Rome I does not apply to arbitration agreements' because arbitration agreements are excluded from the scope of Rome I by Article 1(2)(e)?[49]

With respect to Andrew Baker and Bryan JJ, that seems doubtful. Once the express choice of law clause is incorporated (according to the putative applicable law, viz English law in those cases), then the parties have expressly chosen English law. That law must then determine the existence and validity of all other putative terms of the bill of lading contract, including a possible jurisdiction or arbitration clause. There is no need to perform a separate exercise to rediscover the putative applicable law to see if the jurisdiction or arbitration clause is incorporated. The applicable law of the bill of lading contract is already fixed. As is well known, in English law if there are 'general words of incorporation' in a bill of lading they are sufficient to incorporate an express choice of law clause. However, more specific words are needed to incorporate an exclusive jurisdiction clause or an arbitration clause.[50]

What if there is no express choice of law clause in the charterparty? Instead, assume that the charterparty contains only an express choice of court or an arbitration clause and the bill of lading contains general words of incorporation such as 'all terms and conditions of the charterparty ... are incorporated herein'? That was the position in *The Njegos*.[51] The first issue is what applicable law will determine whether the choice of court/arbitration clause is incorporated as a term in the bill of lading. At this point, it may matter what the word 'it' refers to, in the phrase 'shall be determined by the law which would govern *it* under this Regulation if the contract or term were valid' in Article 10(1). The word 'it' could refer just to the term sought to be incorporated or to the contract (ie the bill of lading) as a whole? If it is the first, then it does not matter if the term in issue is a choice of law clause in a charterparty which is sought to be incorporated in a bill of lading contract. The law governing the choice of law clause will be express (as determined by Article 3) and that will decide whether that clause 'exists' or is 'valid' within the context of the bill

[49] As noted by Andrew Baker J at [12] in the same case. He referred to *Dicey, Morris & Collins* (n 11) paras 32-110–32-112. In *Ulusoy Denizilik SA v Cofco Global Harvest (Zhangjiagang) Trading Co Ltd* [2020] EWHC 3645 (Comm), [2021] 1 Lloyd's Rep 117 [26], [36], Bryan J followed the same route.

[50] See *Skips A/S Nordheim v Syrian Petroleum Co Ltd (The 'Varenna')* [1984] QB 599, which was not doubted in *Caresse Navigation Ltd v Office National de l'Electricité ('The Channel Ranger')* [2014] EWCA Civ 1366, [2015] QB 366.

[51] [1936] P 90. The issue in the case was the applicable law of the bill of lading. That purported to incorporate 'all the terms, conditions and exceptions' of the charterparty, 'including the negligence clause'. The charter included a 'Centrocon' arbitration clause which provided for arbitration in London, but it did not provide expressly for a choice of applicable law. In argument the distinguished commercial silk, HU Willink KC, conceded that the 'proper law of the charterparty, in view of the arbitration clause, is English' referring to *Hamlyn & Co v Talisker Distillery* [1894] AC 202. That would not be the position today, following *Enka* (n 10).

of lading contract. But if the 'it' refers only to the clause sought to be incorporated and that clause is either an 'arbitration agreement' or an 'agreement on the choice of court', then they are excluded from the ambit of the Rome I R under Article 1(2)(e). So, presumably, an English court would apply English common law principles of conflict of laws to decide which law governed the 'existence' or 'validity' of that arbitration agreement or jurisdiction agreement in the context of a bill of lading contract.[52] If, however, the 'it' in Article 10(1) refers to the bill of lading contract as a whole, then the issue of the existence or validity in the bill of lading of the term sought to be incorporated would be decided by the putative applicable law of the bill of lading as a whole, which would be determined by Articles 3 or 5(1) or (3) of Rome I R.

The more likely construction is that 'it' refers to the bill of lading contract as a whole. If so, the rule in Article 10(1) will be used to find the putative applicable law of *that contract*, but on the assumption that the choice of court/arbitration clause is incorporated.[53] The court would ask, first, whether there was any express choice of law or an implied choice that was 'clearly demonstrated by the terms of the contract or the circumstances of the case' pursuant to Article 3. In the case of a choice of court clause, if it is an *exclusive* jurisdiction clause, then Recital (12) dictates that this is a factor to 'take into account in determining whether a choice of law has been clearly demonstrated'. Given the context of Rome I R, it is likely that a court would hold that an English exclusive jurisdiction clause in a charterparty that was sought to be incorporated in a bill of lading contract would, for Article 10(1) purposes, indicate that the parties had clearly demonstrated that English law was their implied choice. That law would then be used to determine whether that jurisdiction clause was, in fact, incorporated into the bill. There is no need to go back to Article 10(1) and (2) to rediscover the applicable law of the jurisdiction clause.

What if there is an English arbitration clause in the charter that is sought to be incorporated in the bill of lading, but no express choice of law clause in the charter? If 'it' in Article 10(1) refers to the bill of lading contract as a whole, then Article 10(1) would still be used to determine the putative applicable law, on the assumption that the arbitration clause is incorporated. The question of how Recital (12) is to be interpreted could then be of importance. If (as concluded above) it is construed as not referring to arbitration tribunals, would a court, by analogy with the reasoning

[52] In *Welex AG v Rosa Maritime Ltd (The 'Epsilon Rosa') No 1 & No 2*, respectively [2002] EWHC 762 (Comm), [2002] 2 Lloyd's Rep 81, [2002] EWHC 2035 (Comm), [2002] 2 Lloyd's Rep 701, David Steel J was concerned with whether an arbitration clause in a charterparty was incorporated into a bill of lading. Although in the first judgment there is no mention of the Rome Convention, at [1] of the second judgment, David Steel J states his conclusion 'was premised on the assumption that English law was applicable to the issue by virtue of Article 8(1) of the Rome Convention as enacted in the Contracts (Applicable Law) Act 1990'. That seems doubtful, given the exclusion of arbitration agreements from the Convention by art 1(d). The point was not mentioned on appeal [2003] EWCA Civ 938, [2003] 2 Lloyd's Rep 509.

[53] Thus, at this point, any arguments under art 10(2) would have been rejected.

of the Supreme Court in *Enka*, hold that a London arbitration clause does not, for Article 3 purposes, indicate that the parties have 'clearly demonstrated' an implied choice of English law for the bill of lading? Logically, it should do so, unless there are other special additional factors.[54]

Continuing with the assumption that 'it' in Article 10(1) refers to the whole putative bill of lading contract overall, then if a court concluded that there was no implied choice of law in these circumstances, it would have to resort to Article 5(1) and (3) of Rome I R to discover the applicable law by which to decide whether or not the arbitration clause was incorporated. Article 5(1) and (3) contain the default rules for determining the law applicable in contracts for 'carriage of goods' when there has been no express or implied choice of law.[55] Often, where there is, potentially at least, an English arbitration clause in the bill of lading contract, Article 5(3) will be pressed. A court will be urged to conclude that it is 'clear from all the circumstances of the case that the contract, in the absence of a choice of law, is manifestly more closely connected with a country other than that indicated in paragraph 1', so that the law of that other country should apply. But this leads to a problem. In our example, if there is an arbitration clause in the charter, but only 'general words of incorporation' in the bill of lading, then, as already noted, in English law that is generally insufficient to incorporate the arbitration clause in the bill contract.[56] How can a putative arbitration clause in the bill be used as a factor to arrive at a conclusion that, in the absence of a choice of applicable law by the parties, in all the circumstances the bill of lading contract is more closely connected with the country of the seat of a putative arbitration which arbitration clause would ultimately not be incorporated in that contract? It surely could not, unless the wording at the end of Recitals (20) and (21) of Rome I R could be utilized. The question would be: does the bill of lading contract have a 'very close relationship' with the charterparty contract, which has the (English) arbitration clause in it, thus indicating a close connection with England, to the exclusion of all others and thus making English law the applicable law of the bill?[57] A court would be able to take account of Recital (16) of Rome I R, which says that while the conflict of law rules should be highly foreseeable, 'courts should, however, retain a degree of discretion to determine the law that is most closely connected to the situation'. However, such arguments might be regarded as inconsistent with the approach of the Supreme Court in *Enka*, which rejected the notion that the choice of a particular seat of an

[54] As the majority in *Enka* (n 10) concluded (at [114]) was the case in approving the decision of Clarke J in *Egon Oldendorff v Libera Corp (No 2)* [1996] 1 Lloyd's Rep 380.

[55] A bill of lading is the quintessential 'contract for the carriage of goods'. And for the reasons given above, an English court would hold that bills of lading are not excluded from Rome I R by the terms of art 1(2)(d) and Recital (9).

[56] See *Skips A/S Nordheim v Syrian Petroleum Co Ltd (The 'Varenna')* [1984] QB 599, which was not doubted in *Caresse Navigation Ltd v Office National de l'Electricité ('The Channel Ranger')* [2014] EWCA Civ 1366, [2015] QB 366.

[57] Cf *Dicey* (n 11) para 33-098.

arbitration demonstrated an *implied* intention that the parties' contractual obligations should be governed by the law of that place.[58]

If the word 'it' in Article 10(1) refers only to the specific putative clause in the contract (that is, here, the English arbitration clause), then Rome I R would become irrelevant at this stage, because choice of court and arbitration agreements are excluded from its scope by Article 1(2)(e).[59] In that case, an English court would have to apply the English common law conflict of laws rule that the putative applicable law will determine the existence or validity of a contract or a term of a contract.[60]

E. 'Lawful Holder' of a Bill of Lading

Is a person who becomes a 'lawful holder' of a bill of lading bound by the choice of applicable law agreed by the original parties of a bill of lading? In the trading world, a shipper of cargo is likely to sell the goods shipped and pass title to another. It could be a named consignee in a bill of lading or a receiver of the goods to whom the bill ultimately passes. The buyer may or may not become a party to the bill of lading contract. Whether it does may depend on the applicable law. Moreover, the issue of what terms might bind a successor party may depend upon the applicable law of the bill of lading contract as between the carrier and a successor party.[61] So it may be vital to ascertain the applicable law in order to determine the rights of possible successor parties to a bill of lading contract.

In English law, the original parties to a bill of lading contract will be the shipper of the goods on board and 'the carrier',[62] save in two particular circumstances. That is when, under a chartered ship, the voyage charterer is either the shipper of the goods or the consignee of the goods. In both of those cases, the contract of carriage will be in the voyage charter, not the bill of lading, which acts only as a receipt.[63]

[58] *Enka* (n 10) [113], [170] (vii).

[59] The analysis Andrew Baker J appeared to accept in *The 'Joker'*, (n 49), at [12].

[60] *The Parouth* [1982] 2 Lloyd's Rep 351; *Marc Rich & Co AG v Societa Italiana Imianti PA (The 'Atlantic Emperor')* [1989] 1 Lloyd's Rep 548; *Habas Sanai VE Tibbi Gazlar Istihsal Endustrisi AS v VSC Steel Co Ltd* [2013] EWHC 4071 (Comm), [2014] 1 Lloyd's Rep 479, approved in *Enka* (n 10) [31]–[35].

[61] As in the notorious case of *National Navigation Co v Endesa Genaracion SA (The 'Wadi Sudr')* which concerned rights and liabilities of receivers of cargo under a bill of lading contract that Gloster J concluded was governed by English law and incorporated a London arbitration clause: see [2009] EWHC 196 (Comm), [2009] 1 Lloyd's Rep 666 [109]–[112]; but a Spanish court had previously held that the applicable law was Spanish and that the arbitration clause did not bind the receiver. The CA held that as the Spanish decision had come first the English court was bound it, even if (in the view of English law) it was wrong: see [2009] EWCA Civ 1397, [2010] 1 Lloyd's Rep 193 [66] per Waller LJ, [125] per Moore-Bick LJ. In French law, a consignee is regarded as an *adhérent* to the bill of lading contract. CA d'Aix, 10 January 2013, observations Ph Delebecque in DMF 2010, Hors-série N° 14, n° 86, p 78. (I am grateful to Dr Aïda Ounissi of Sorbonne Université for assistance with some French law references.)

[62] In English law, the carrier could be either the shipowner or a time charterer. That is an issue of construction of the bill of lading contract: *Homberg Houtimport BV v Agarosin Private Ltd (The 'Starsin')* [2003] UKHL 12, [2004] 1 AC 715.

[63] *President of India v Metcalfe Shipping (The 'Dunelmia')* [1970] 1 QB 289.

However, once the bill of lading passes from a shipper/charterer to a lawful holder, a new contract, on the terms of the bill, 'appears to spring up' between the carrier and the lawful holder, to use Lord Atkin's words.[64] Once an entity has become the 'lawful holder' of a bill of lading, the rights given to the original party, the shipper, are transferred to the holder and, in certain circumstances, so are the liabilities.[65]

Take the classic case of a shipper who sells goods to a receiver, endorses the bill of lading 'in blank' and sends it to the receiver who presents it to the carrier at the discharge port. But the cargo is damaged. The receiver claims under the bill of lading contract, but the carrier disputes the receiver is a party to it; or there is a dispute as to whether a jurisdiction or arbitration clause in the bill binds the receiver. How do English conflict of laws rules determine the applicable law to decide whether a successor to the shipper has become a party to the bill of lading contract and which terms are binding on the successor?

Logically, the first issue is whether there is a contract at all between the carrier and the receiver. An English court must therefore apply Rome I R, Article 10(1) and (2) to establish which applicable law will determine that question. The court must examine the terms of the putative contract to see if the parties have expressly or impliedly agreed a putative applicable law (under Article 3) or, in default, determine the putative applicable law according to Article 5(1) or (3). In *Caresse Navigation Ltd v Office National de l'Electricité*,[66] the issue was whether the receiver of a coal cargo under a bill of lading was bound by an English law and exclusive jurisdiction clause in an identified voyage charterparty. Males J did not distinguish between the position of the shipper and the receiver under the bill of lading, nor did he refer to Article 10 of Rome I R. He stated simply that the governing law had to be determined in accordance with Rome I and went straight to Article 3. In *The Joker*,[67] the issue was whether the holder of the bills of lading and intended receiver of a cargo of soya bean meal was bound by an English law and London arbitration clause in an associated voyage charterparty, which clauses were said to be incorporated in the bill of lading. Andrew Baker J held that the issue of the putative applicable law was to be determined according to Article 10 of Rome I. Neither judge dealt specifically with the question of whether the search for an applicable law differed as between the original parties to the bill of lading and the receiver of the cargo.[68]

[64] *Tate & Lyle v Hain Steamship Co* [1936] 2 All ER 597, 603. There is some conceptual difficulty in how, using the standard English law doctrine of 'offer and acceptance', a contract is created, particularly when the document was a receipt as between the shipper and carrier.

[65] The current English law on the transfer of contractual rights and liabilities to 'lawful holders' of bills of lading is set out in the Carriage of Goods by Sea Act 1992, particularly ss 2, 3, and 5(2). It repealed the Bills of Lading Act 1855.

[66] [2013] EWHC 3081 (Comm), [2014] 1 Lloyd's Rep 337. The point here discussed was not considered on appeal.

[67] [2019] EWHC 3541 (Comm), [2021] 1 Lloyd's Rep 169.

[68] Neither did Gloster J in *The 'Wadi Sudr'* [2009] EWHC 196 (Comm), [2009] 1 Lloyd's Rep 666.

The approach of an English court appears to be, first, to examine the terms of the putative contract in the bill of lading as between the original parties and determine whether they have made an express or implied choice of law. Second, using that putative applicable law, to assume that unless there is any argument to the contrary, those same terms will bind the receiver.[69] This is, interestingly (if subconsciously), the same approach as that adopted by the CJEU in two cases when considering whether a receiver suing under a bill of lading is entitled to rely on or is bound by an exclusive jurisdiction clause for the purposes of determining jurisdiction under the Brussels Convention. The issue in those cases was whether there was sufficient consensus between the carrier and the successor party. The CJEU has held that 'consensus' between the original parties had to be established according to the 'autonomous' meaning of the provisions of Article 17 of the Convention. If there is consensus between the original parties, then any successor party will also be bound if, by the relevant national law, the conditions for its succession or assignment are fulfilled.[70]

The final question for consideration is how an English court should decide on the applicable law when a new contract 'springs up' when the bill which is a receipt in the hands of a shipper/charterer is transferred to a consignee or receiver who thereby becomes a holder of the bill. The relationship between a charter and a bill of lading may be a peculiarity of English law. The Law Commission Report that led to the Carriage of Goods by Sea Act 1992 stated blandly that the proposed clauses 2(1) and 5(1) of the Bill would give 'the holder rights as if he had been a party to the contract of carriage, which in the case of a bill of lading means the contract contained in or evidenced by the bill of lading'.[71] Except that before the bill was in the hands of the subsequent 'holder', it was not a contract of carriage; it was a receipt.

How does an English court determine the applicable law of a bill of lading in the hands of the consignee or receiver of cargo where the shipper was the charterer? No cases appear to have tackled this issue directly. It is submitted that a court should employ Article 10 of Rome I R, as at this stage it is not certain that there is a valid contract between the carrier and the holder of the bill. The court will examine the bill and all terms possibly incorporated by reference to the putative applicable

[69] In English law, the substitution of the Carriage of Goods by Sea Act 1992 for the 1855 Act has resolved many of the issues under the old Act about whether a receiver of goods and holder of the bill of lading became a party to the bill of lading contract.

[70] See Case 71/83 *Partenreederei ms Tilly Russ v NV Haven- & Vervoerbedrijf Nova* [1984] ECR 2417; and Case C–387/98 *Coreck Maritime GmbH v Handelsveem BV* [2000] ECR I-9337. These cases were referred to and applied, in the context of the Brussels I (recast) Regulation by the SC in relation to an insurance contract in *Aspen Underwriting Ltd v Credit Bank NV* [2020] UKSC 11, [2021] AC 493 [25]. Cf French law, where although the holder of a bill of lading succeeds to the rights and obligations of the shipper, it does not do so automatically in relation to a jurisdiction clause, which has to be specifically agreed by the holder: *Hapag Lloyd Container Line GmbH v La Réunionne Européene* Cour de Cass, 4 March 2003 [2003] I L Pr 779. Cf Cass. Civ 1re 11 juillet 2006 05–18.681.

[71] The Report of the Law Commission and the Scottish Law Commission (Law Com No 196, Scot Law Com No 130) on Rights of Suit in Respect of Carriage of Goods by Sea, March 1991 para 2.54.

law if the contract were valid. It will see if there was an express or implied choice (Article 3) or, if not, determine the choice by reference to Article 5(1) or (3). If, having done so, it concludes that the putative applicable law is English, it would take account of the 'rule' in the *Hain Steamship* case and the terms of sections 2, 3, and 5 of the 1992 Act. It could then determine whether the receiver was party to a contract that had 'sprung up' and also its contents.

F. Conclusion

There is scope for arguments on the interpretation of Rome I in its new, domesticated form. English courts will still need to have regard to European law in determining a number of questions on the applicable law of bills of lading. Professor Adrian Briggs once said that the EU had 'assumed responsibility for abolishing private international laws and setting up, in their place, a row of lifeless, grey statutes', which was a 'triumph of bureaucracy over individualism'.[72] One of those 'lifeless grey statutes' and the replacement of another[73] have now been adopted by the UK. The years to come will determine whether, in the hands of the English judges, they remain lifeless and monochrome or become more animate and colourful and whether, ultimately, bureaucracy or individualism triumphs. One thing is certain. *Dicey, Morris & Collins*, as shaped by Lawrence Collins, will both influence and record the process.

[72] Adrian Briggs, *The Conflict of Laws* (2nd edn, OUP 2008) preface. At that time these were: Brussels I, the Rome Convention and Rome II.

[73] Rome II and Rome I.

9
Abouloff v Oppenheimer Revisited

Andrew Dickinson

A. Introduction

During his tenure as a member of the Judicial Committee of the House of Lords and, subsequently, of the Supreme Court, Lord Collins was able to deploy his expertise in the conflict of laws most frequently with respect to the common law's treatment of foreign judgments. In *Rubin v Eurofinance SA*,[1] he examined the juridical basis for the recognition and enforcement of foreign judgments, with particular focus on judgments in insolvency proceedings and the significance of the defendant's active involvement in legal proceedings. In *Vizcaya Partners Ltd v Picard*,[2] he reviewed the common law's approach to recognition and enforcement based upon prior agreement.

This contribution to the collection of essays in Lord Collins's honour ventures elsewhere, in seeking to build upon observations that he made in delivering the opinion of the Judicial Committee of the Privy Council in *AK Investment CJSC v Kyrgyz Mobil Tel Ltd*,[3] a case concerned with questions of personal jurisdiction. These observations, concerning the effect of fraud upon the recognition and enforcement of foreign judgments *in personam*[4] under English common law, inspire a journey back in time to the decision of the Court of Appeal in *Abouloff v Oppenheimer & Co*.[5]

[1] [2012] UKSC 46, [2013] 1 AC 236.

[2] [2016] UKPC 5, [2016] 3 All ER 181. For analysis of Lord Collins's judgments in these two cases, see Andrew Dickinson, 'Schibsby v Westenholz and the Recognition and Enforcement of Judgments in England' (2018) 134 LQR 426, 439; and Andrew Dickinson, 'Foreign Submission' (2019) 135 LQR 294, 295–99.

[3] [2011] UKPC 7, [2012] 1 WLR 1804 (*sub nom Altimo Holdings and Investment v same*).

[4] As to judgments *in rem*, see Lord Collins (ed), *Dicey, Morris & Collins on the Conflict of Laws* (15th edn, Sweet & Maxwell 2012), para 14-148. As to decrees affecting matters of personal status, exemplified by decrees of divorce, see text to nn 71–81.

[5] (1882) 10 QBD 295.

Andrew Dickinson, Abouloff v Oppenheimer *Revisited* In: *Essays in International Litigation for Lord Collins.*
Edited by: Jonathan Harris and Campbell McLachlan, Oxford University Press. © Oxford University Press 2022.
DOI: 10.1093/oso/9780192867988.003.0010

B. *AK Investment CJSC v Kyrgyz Mobil Tel Ltd*

AK Investment involved proceedings to enforce a Kyrgyz judgment in the Isle of Man High Court. The Board (comprising Lords Collins, Phillips, Mance, Kerr, and Clarke) was asked to consider whether that court had jurisdiction to determine cross-claims brought by the judgment debtor against several foreign parties, alleging that they had wrongfully participated in a scheme to deprive the judgment debtor of its assets and had thereby been unjustly enriched. Lord Collins delivered the Board's unanimous opinion.

The specific issues before the court centred upon the requirements for service out of the jurisdiction, including as to the merits of the claims advanced,[6] the scope of the 'necessary or proper party' gateway for service out of the jurisdiction in the Manx High Court Rules,[7] and the approach that a court should take in determining whether it would be unjust to require the claimant to sue in a forum that had been identified as the natural forum for the dispute.[8] Having summarized the applicable legal principles, Lord Collins turned to consider their application to the case before him. One issue between the parties concerned the prospects of success of the defendant's plea in support of its cross-claim that judgments of the Kyrgyz courts (including the judgment sued upon) had been procured by fraud and could be impeached on that ground.

In their challenge to jurisdiction, the third parties disputed the correctness of the decision in *Abouloff* as well as its applicability under the law of the Isle of Man.[9] Lord Collins described the principle established in that case as follows:[10]

> [I]n the context of recognition and enforcement of foreign judgments at common law, a foreign judgment may be impeached for fraud even though no newly discovered evidence is produced and even though the fraud[11] might have been produced, or even was produced and rejected, in the foreign court.

It was not necessary for the Board to determine this point, as the defendant's cross-claim manifestly had sufficient prospects of success to justify service out of the jurisdiction. Although Lord Collins described the third parties' criticisms of the *Abouloff* principle as 'powerful', the matter was not—in the Board's view—suitable for resolution on an application to set aside service in view of the longstanding nature of the rule and the 'extremely important issues of policy' involved.[12] Moreover,

6 *AK Investment* (n 3) [71].

7 Ord 6, r 1(1)(g), corresponding to CPR PD6B, [3.1(3)] (see *AK Investment* (n 3) [64]–[66], [73]–[87]).

8 *AK Investment* (n 3) [88]–[102].

9 ibid [110], [115].

10 ibid [109].

11 Sic. One wonders whether his Lordship intended to refer to 'evidence of the fraud'.

12 *AK Investment* (n 3) [116].

even if *Abouloff* were overruled or held not to apply, it did not follow that the Kyrgyz judgments would be recognized and enforced in the Isle of Man[13] or that the judgment debtor's claims against the third parties were bound to fail.[14]

Two observations made by his Lordship regarding the possible future direction of the law nonetheless stand out. Both appear in the same paragraph of the opinion, as follows (numbering added):[15]

> [1] These are powerful arguments, but the present case shows that, even if the rule in *Abouloff v Oppenheimer & Co* were no longer to represent the law, simply to apply the English rules to foreign judgments might lead to real injustice.... [2] In particular the facts of this case shows that a nuanced approach might be required, depending on the reliability of the foreign legal system, the scope for challenge in the foreign court and the type of fraud alleged.

Lord Collins's reference to the 'English rules' ([1] above) refers to the rules for impeachment of English judgments on the ground of fraud, which his Lordship understood to require 'that the person seeking to impeach the judgment produces newly discovered evidence which could not have been produced at the trial with reasonable diligence'.[16] The law has since moved on. In *Takhar v Gracefield Developments Ltd*,[17] the Supreme Court held that the 'reasonable diligence' requirement did not apply to review of an English judgment on the ground of fraud, while emphasizing procedural limits upon pleas of fraud, principally via the abuse of process doctrine. It will be necessary to return to this important decision below (see sections G and I).

Lord Collins's two observations nonetheless raise the following questions:

- Would it indeed be unjust to apply the English rules (as restated in *Takhar*) to foreign judgments? If so, why?
- What adjustments (if any) to the English rules are required to remove that injustice? Might a 'nuanced approach', requiring attention to the circumstances of the particular case, meet that concern?

Our enquiry begins with the decision in *Abouloff*.

[13] ibid [117].
[14] ibid [118]–[119].
[15] ibid [116].
[16] ibid [109].
[17] [2019] UKSC 13, [2020] AC 450, noted Harry Stratton [2019] CJQ 311.

C. *Abouloff v Oppenheimer & Co*

The plaintiff, Sophia Abouloff, was the wife of Gregor Melcoevitch Abouloff, a trader at Tiflis (Tblisi, Georgia), then part of the Russian Empire.[18] The defendant, David Oppenheimer & Co, was a London-based partnership engaged in trading activities of various kinds.[19] In 1877, the plaintiff obtained a judgment against the defendant in the District Court of Tiflis that the defendant should return certain goods to the plaintiff or, failing which, pay the plaintiff their value totalling just over 10,000 roubles (around £1,000). The defendant, without admitting the judgment, asserted in its defence that the goods in question were or had been in the possession of the plaintiff or her husband, who had concealed that fact from the District Court.[20] The defence also denied the plaintiff's title to sue without joining her husband. The plaintiff demurred to both pleas.

The Divisional Court (Matthew and Cave JJ) upheld the plaintiff's title to sue without joining her husband. An application to stay the proceedings unless Mr Abouloff was joined as co-plaintiff was later rejected following an appeal in which the Divisional Court (Manisty and Stephen JJ) divided on the point.[21]

With respect to the fraud defence, the plaintiff's contention, in summary, was that the defendant had not pleaded any fact that released it from the obligation to comply with the judgment, as its allegations were entirely consistent with the proposition that the Russian court was mistaken without having been misled, given that the relevant facts had been put in evidence before it.[22] The plaintiff asserted that, as a matter of English law, the merits of the foreign judgment could not be re-investigated into when a claim was made to enforce it.[23]

The Court of Appeal rejected the defendant's demurrer to this part of the defence. The three judgments run to less than ten pages in the Law Report and can be briefly summarized. The reasoning of Lord Coleridge CJ is neatly captured in the final paragraph of his judgment, as follows:[24]

[18] *Abouloff v Oppenheimer and Co* The Times, 29 January 1883 (QB); (1882) 47 LT 702, 703.

[19] *The London Gazette*, 3 January 1871, 17 and 3 July 1888, 3651. The partnership had been founded by Charles Oppenheimer in 1860 and, at the time of this suit, was continued by his brother, David, and brother-in-law, Louis Adler. The firm's activities involved trading in commodities as diverse as French sardines and briar pipes, German porcelain dolls and Black Forest cuckoo clocks, as well as more exotic products from the Far East (David Kynaston, *The City of London*, vol 1: *A World of its Own* (Pimlico 1995) 307).

[20] ibid.

[21] (1882) 47 LT 702. Stephen J would have ordered a stay, but Manisty J sided with the Judge in chambers.

[22] *Abouloff* (n 5) 297–99 (argument of Sir Sydney Woolf for the plaintiff) and 299–300 (summary by Lord Coleridge CJ) of that argument.

[23] Relying upon *Bank of Australasia v Nias* (1851) 16 QB 717, 117 ER 1055 and *Godard v Gray* (1870) LR 6 QB 139.

[24] *Abouloff* (n 5) 302.

> I think, therefore, on the broad ground that no man can take advantage of his own wrong, and that it is a principle of law that no action can be maintained on the judgment of a court either in this country or in any other, which has been obtained by the fraud of the person seeking to enforce it, that the defence is good, that the demurrer must be overruled, and that the judgment of the Queen's Bench Division was right.

His Lordship here relies on two interlocking propositions, the first resting on the wrongful character of the plaintiff's conduct in procuring the judgment,[25] and the second resting upon a general legal principle denying the effectiveness of judgments procured by fraud.[26] Brett LJ adopted similar reasoning, treating the second proposition as a derivative of the first.[27] Baggallay LJ agreed that the appeal should be dismissed, and confined his judgment to a narrow and hypothetical point concerning the foreign court's complicity in the plaintiff's deceit.[28]

The court also concluded that the defence applied even if the defendant had advanced his case of fraud before the foreign court. In their Lordships' view, the foreign court could never have considered the question of whether it had been misled, and its judgment could not preclude an English court from undertaking that enquiry.[29] As Brett LJ put it:[30]

> [T]he issue in the Russian courts would be whether the defendants were wrongfully detaining the goods of the plaintiff. The question of fact[,] whether the plaintiff had the goods in her possession at the moment when the action was commenced, would be a circumstance very material to be considered in order to determine that issue: but in the present action, upon this paragraph of the defence the only issue is whether the judgment of the Russian courts was obtained by the fraud of the plaintiff successfully perpetrated on those courts. The issues in the two actions are not the same; and therefore the defendants are not estopped from setting up in this action the same evidence that was adduced at the trial of the action in the Russian courts.

Although it will be necessary to return to the point,[31] there are two matters of immediate significance. First, strictly speaking, the court did not need to decide this point in ruling upon the defendant's demurrer. This raised a question of law as to the viability of the defence, which fell to be considered on the assumption that the

[25] ibid 300.
[26] ibid 300–01.
[27] ibid 305–06.
[28] ibid 303–04 (see n 64).
[29] ibid 302–03 (Lord Coleridge CJ), 306–07 (Brett LJ).
[30] ibid 307.
[31] See section I, below.

facts pleaded in the Defence (ie the fraud perpetrated by the plaintiff and her husband) had been admitted by the plaintiff.[32] Secondly, the court treated the point as subsidiary to the question of whether a claim to enforce a foreign judgment in England could be defeated by a plea of fraud. Having given an affirmative answer to that question, the court had already rejected the submission that such a plea might be precluded by the *res judicata* effects of the foreign judgment. The Chief Justice and Brett LJ sought to reinforce their conclusion on this point by resorting to the technical rules governing issue estoppel.[33] Unfortunately, the prominence given to this element of the reasoning has served as a distraction from the logical force of the court's ruling on the demurrer: if (as their Lordships concluded) a foreign judgment shown to have been procured by fraud has no legal force under English law, any estoppel would have nothing to feed on.

With the benefit of hindsight, it would have been preferable if the two judges had eschewed the technical point in favour of a more detailed examination of the question of whether their apparently unqualified formulation of the primary rule was justified as a matter of precedent and principle.[34]

D. The Earlier Case Law

The most prominent authority in the judgments in *Abouloff* is the opinion of De Grey CJ in the State trial of the Duchess of Kingston for bigamy and, in particular, his *dictum* that 'fraud is an extrinsic, collateral act, which vitiates the most solemn proceedings of courts of justice'.[35] It is, however, of no great value for present purposes, being concerned with the binding force of a decision of an ecclesiastical court in later criminal proceedings in circumstances where the deception alleged was collusion between the parties to the original suit rather than misconduct by one party deceiving the other party and the court.[36]

In *Boswell v Coaks (No 2)*, Lord Selbourne LC described the *Duchess of Kingston's case* as:[37]

[32] Samuel Prentice, *Archbold's practice of the Queen's Bench, Common Pleas and Exchequer Divisions of the High Court of Justice* (13th edn, Stevens & Sons 1879) vol 2, 742; *Metropolitan Railway Co v Defries* (1877) 2 QBD 387; *Abouloff* (n 5) 298. See also Avigdor V Levontin, 'Two Paradoxes in the Recognition of Foreign Judgments' (1967) 2 Is L Rev 197, 199 fn 12.

[33] See, in particular, the judgment of Brett LJ (*Abouloff* (n 5) 307).

[34] Cf *Abouloff* (n 5) 300 (Lord Coleridge), describing the plaintiff's contention as 'unreasonable'; ibid 308 (Brett LJ), observing that 'if we were to accede to the argument for the plaintiff, the result would be that a plausible deceiver would succeed, whereas a deceiver who is not plausible would fail'.

[35] (1776) 20 St Tr 355, 544. See *Abouloff* (n 5) 301 (Lord Coleridge CJ), 305–06 (Brett LJ); also *White v Hall* (1806) 12 Ves J 321, 324; 33 ER 122, 123.

[36] Francis Taylor Piggott, *Foreign Judgments and Jurisdiction* (3rd edn, Butterworth & Co 1908) 395–96.

[37] (1894) 86 LT 365n, 366.

> [A]n example, in which by the collusion of the parties the process of the courts has been abused and the whole proceeding may be described as it was described in language used in that case as *fabula non judicium*[38].

He contrasted this with a case of the kind before him (alleging fraud by one of the parties), in which 'it is not sought to treat as a nullity what has passed, but to undo it judicially upon judicial grounds, treating it as in itself, and until judicially rescinded, valid and final'.[39] In *Baden v Société Générale*, Peter Gibson J quoted these passages with approval, observing that the generality of De Grey CJ's dictum and other similar statements 'has been qualified in subsequent cases and by the emergence of procedural rules', requiring impeachment of the judgment by the proper method.[40]

The two additional authorities cited by Lord Coleridge (*Bank of Australasia v Nias*[41] and *Ochsenbein v Papelier*[42]) are more obviously relevant. In the first, Lord Campbell CJ accepted that a foreign judgment may be impeached for fraud, among other grounds,[43] but no plea of this character was before him and he was principally concerned to establish the binding character of the foreign court's findings with respect to the substantive cause of action in fraud advanced in the original proceedings.[44] The following passage of the Chief Justice's judgment, emphasizing the recourse available to the judgment debtor in the foreign forum, and the risk of misconduct on his part, is however noteworthy:[45]

> [The defendant] may, from the loss of evidence by the plaintiffs, or from a temptation to bring forward false evidence himself, unconscientiously resist the payment of a just demand which had been solemnly adjudicated upon by a competent tribunal. No hardship whatsoever is cast upon him by requiring him to follow the course to obtain redress against an unjust or erroneous judgment which the law has provided for him.

[38] A fuller quotation, attributed only to 'a very sensible civilian', appears in the submissions of the Solicitor General, Alexander Wedderburn, in the *Duchess of Kingston's case*: *fabula non judicium, hoc est; in scena, non in foro; res agitur* (a play not a trial; the matter is acted out on the stage, not in the courtroom) ((1776) 20 St Tr 355, 479). For examples of such collusion involving foreign judgments, see eg *Dolphin v Robins* (1859) 7 HL Cas 390, 11 ER 156; *Shaw v Gould* (1868) LR 3 HL 55; *Bonaparte v Bonaparte* [1892] P 402.

[39] *Boswell* (n 37) 366.

[40] *Baden v Société Générale Pour Favoriser le, Developpement du Commerce et de L'industrie en France SA* [1993] 1 WLR 509n [308].

[41] n 23.

[42] (1873) LR 8 Ch App 695.

[43] (1851) 16 QB 717, 735;117 ER 1055, 1062.

[44] ibid 735–38 (1063). The distinction between pleas of these two kinds was blurred in submissions to, and in the reasoning of, the Court of Appeal in *Owens Bank Ltd v Bracco* [1992] 2 AC 443, 458–60, 465–66.

[45] ibid 737 (1063).

Ochsenbein deserves closer attention. The defendant in equity, Papelier (a French seed merchant), obtained a judgment in default against the plaintiff in equity, Ochsenbein (an English seed merchant), from the Tribunal de Commerce at Nancy. Ochsenbein claimed that the parties had agreed to refer their dispute to arbitration, and that he had been misled as to Papelier's intention to proceed to judgment in his French action upon the occasion that he was served. The alleged fraud was, therefore, perpetrated outside the courtroom.

Papelier sued upon the judgment in the Queen's Bench Division whereupon Ochsenbein filed a bill in Chancery seeking an injunction to restrain that action. The court upheld the Vice Chancellor's refusal to make that order, on the ground that Ochsenbein had a sufficient remedy in the common law court and 'perfect justice' could be done in that court.[46] Lord Selbourne LJ referred approvingly to the *dictum* in the *Duchess of Kingston's case*, describing it as 'sound law' which applied 'with at least as much force to foreign as to English judgments'.[47] He opined that there was 'no difference on this point between the doctrines of Courts of law and of equity'. In support of that proposition, he referred to *Bank of Australasia v Nias* and to the earlier decision of Shadwell VC in *Price v Dewhurst*,[48] as well as to the writing of Joseph Story.[49]

Mellish LJ also concluded that 'if the foreign judgment was obtained by fraud, that would be an answer to any proceedings founded on that judgment'.[50] He considered this to be a violation of the principles of natural justice, alongside the absence of notice of the action or a failure to summon or want of jurisdiction.[51]

The concept of natural justice is also central to the reasoning of Bramwell and Channell BB (the only judges to address the issue of fraud) in *Crawley v Isaacs*,[52] a decision of the Court of Exchequer cited in argument in *Abouloff*, but not referred to in the Court of Appeal's judgments.

In *Crawley*, the plaintiff obtained judgment against the defendant in the Court of Exchequer in Ireland and sought to enforce that judgment in England. In response, the defendant pleaded that he had not been notified of the proceedings. The plaintiff's reply to that plea relied on an order made by the Irish court authorizing substituted service upon an Irish attorney as the defendant's agent, but the defendant denied that relationship and asserted, by rejoinder, that the order had been procured by a fraudulent affidavit lodged by the plaintiff's legal representative. In argument, the defendant relied on 'the same principle as that on which a foreign judgment by fraud will not be enforced in this country'.[53]

[46] *Ochsenbein* (n 42) 697, 700 (Lord Selbourne LC).
[47] ibid 698.
[48] (1838) 8 Sim 279, 59 ER 111, a case in which the tribunal was not independent.
[49] Joseph Story, *Commentaries on the Conflict of Laws, Foreign and Domestic* (Isaac Redfield ed, 6th edn, Little, Brown & Co 1865) §§607–08.
[50] *Ochsenbein* (n 42) 701.
[51] ibid 700.
[52] (1867) 16 LT 529.
[53] ibid 530.

The principal ground for upholding the plaintiff's challenge to the defendant's plea and rejoinder was that, irrespective of the notice given to the attorney, he had actually received a copy of the pleadings at his London address. Kelly and Martin BB confined their judgments to that point. Bramwell B ventured further in disposing of the rejoinder alleging fraud, as follows:[54]

> I think the term 'natural justice' which has been used in reference to foreign judgments refers rather to the form of procedure than to the merits of the particular case. If this were the case of a judgment obtained by reason of untrue statements contained in an affidavit in a foreign court where the procedure is contrary to natural justice, then we might refuse to give effect to that judgment; but if the procedure be not contrary to natural justice, the defendant has a remedy by an application to the foreign court to get the proceedings set aside: so that in all cases there will be a remedy.

He continued:

> If the proceedings be in accordance with the practice of the foreign court, but that practice not in accordance with natural justice, this court will not allow itself to be concluded by them, but on the other hand, if the procedure be in accordance with natural justice, the foreign court itself will interfere to prevent the plaintiff taking advantage of the judgment irregularly and improperly obtained. Of course in the case of the procedure being contrary to natural justice, it would be useless to go to the foreign court and complain of its being so.

This approach, rooted in principles of natural justice, is much more nuanced than the apparently unqualified rule adopted in *Abouloff*. In particular, it accounts for the mechanisms available to the judgment debtor in the foreign forum to impeach the judgment debt for fraud.

Channell B, in turn, dealt with the point more briefly, stating that he would 'certainly hesitate very long' before re-trying the merits of the action or the truth of the evidence presented to the foreign court.[55]

In the earlier case of *Bowles v Orr*, the question had been treated as one of substance rather than procedure. There, the judgment debtor issued a bill in the Court of Exchequer to restrain a common law action upon a French judgment on the ground that it had been procured by the suppression of evidence. Disallowing a demurrer for want of equity, Abinger CB stated:[56]

[54] ibid 531.
[55] ibid.
[56] (1835) 1 Y & C Ex 464, 473; 160 ER 189, 193.

> A judgment obtained by a creditor abroad has been held to be conclusive in this country; therefore like any other security available in this country, it will be affected by fraud. Perhaps it might be said that shewing a strong case, the party might defeat the judgment even at law;[57] but was it ever doubted that a bill might be filed in equity to be relieved against a judgment, or any other security, obtained by fraud?

E. Evolution of the Rule

This survey of the case law up to and including *Abouloff* suggests three possible models to rationalize a plea that a foreign judgment had been procured by the fraud of another party. These may be briefly summarized as follows:

- A **substantive model**, in which proof that a judgment (English or foreign) was procured by a counterparty's fraud deprives that judgment of any force that it would otherwise have within the English legal system, as it would (for example) a contract.
- A **procedural (or natural justice) model**, in which the effect of fraud is accounted for in the same way as any other defect in the proceedings that led to the foreign judgment, by a plea that the foreign proceedings did not conform to the requirements of natural justice.
- A **public policy model**, by which considerations of the due administration of justice support the exclusion of a claim or defence founded on the wrongdoing of the pleading party (*ex turpi causa non oritur actio*).

In the following century, the substantive model came to the fore, as the other two withered on the vine, without being judicially pruned.

The first decisive step occurred in *Vadala v Lawes*, decided seven years after *Abouloff*.[58] The plaintiff, Giuseppe Vadala, a Sicilian stock broker, obtained a judgment from the Royal Tribunal of Commerce of Medina against the defendant, Sir Bennett Lawes, an eminent agriculturalist, upon certain bills of exchange accepted by one Luigi Reynolds as the defendant's agent. Lawes denied that Reynolds had any authority to bind him, and asserted that Vadala had originally relied on forged bills of exchange and then fraudulently concealed from the Sicilian court the fact that the bills of exchange were in settlement of Reynolds's gaming debts. Vadala, for his part, pleaded that the Sicilian court had already investigated and rejected the

[57] This proposition was accepted in *Ochsenbein* (n 42).
[58] (1890) 25 QBD 310.

defendant's allegations. Charles J gave a verdict for the claimant, but Denman and Wills JJ ordered a new trial.

The Court of Appeal, having heard full argument for the plaintiff, ruled in the defendant's favour without calling upon his counsel. Lindley LJ (with whom Bowen LJ agreed) noted a tension between two rules:[59]

> First of all, there is the rule which is perfectly well established and well known, that a party to an action can impeach the judgment in it for fraud. Whether it is the judgment of an English Court or of a foreign Court does not matter; using general language, that is a general proposition unconditional and undisputed. Another general proposition which, speaking in equally general language, is perfectly well settled, is, that when you bring an action on a foreign judgment, you cannot go into the merits which have been tried in the foreign Court. But you have to combine those two rules and apply them in the case where you cannot go into the alleged fraud without going into the merits.

In his view, *Abouloff* endorsed the proposition that 'if the fraud upon the foreign Court consists in the fact that the plaintiff has induced that Court by fraud to come to a wrong conclusion, you can reopen the whole case even although you will have in this Court to go into the very facts which were investigated, and which were in issue in the foreign Court'.[60] Putting to one side the technical point that had troubled the court in *Abouloff*, the thrust of his Lordship's analysis of the judgments in *Abouloff* was that re-opening the merits of the case was necessary to give effect to the fraud defence.[61] He was not prepared to depart from that view.[62]

In the first edition of his noted work on the *Conflict of Laws*, published in 1896, Professor Dicey supported the substantive model, relying principally on the judgment of Lindley LJ in *Vadala*. He formulated his Rule 90 in the following terms:[63]

> A foreign judgment is invalid which is obtained by fraud.
> Such fraud may be either:
> (1) fraud on the part of the party in whose favour judgment is given; or
> (2) fraud on the part of the Court pronouncing the judgment.

[59] ibid 316.
[60] ibid 317.
[61] ibid.
[62] ibid 320.
[63] Albert Venn Dicey, *A Digest of the Law of England with Reference to the Conflict of Laws* (Stevens & Co 1896) 404 (r 90). Dicey dealt with natural justice as a ground for opposing recognition and enforcement of a foreign judgment separately and narrowly in r 92 (409–10), treating it as an aspect of the foreign court's international competence. See now rr 50 and 52 within the fifteenth edition (n 4).

Although the nature of his work led to its formulation with reference to foreign judgments, Dicey saw the rule as equally applicable to judgments of courts in England.[64]

The substantive model was adopted in section 9(2)(d) of the Administration of Justice Act 1920 and section 4(1)(a)(iv) of the Foreign Judgments (Reciprocal Enforcement) Act 1933. The former prohibited registration of a foreign judgment under the 1920 Act if 'the judgment was obtained by fraud', whereas the latter made proven fraud a ground for the mandatory setting aside of registration of a judgment.

The latter provision fell to be considered by the Court of Appeal in *Syal v Heyward*,[65] upon the registration of judgment of the civil court at Saharanpur, India, in favour of Syal, an Indian moneylender, against Heyward and Davies, two senior British army officers. The defendants asserted that Syal had fraudulently concealed from the Indian court the fact that the sum claimed included amounts in respect of commission and interest, contrary to Indian moneylending legislation. In argument, the plaintiff relied on authorities relating to the effectiveness of English judgments[66] to support the submission that the evidence relied on to establish the fraud must have been discovered after the date of the judgment. Cohen LJ, delivering the court's judgment, cited *Vadala* in support of the proposition that the same tests applied to the setting aside of an English or foreign judgment, but he determined (incorrectly[67]) that the cases relied on by the plaintiff were concerned with re-trial of the question of whether the plaintiff had defrauded the defendant[68] rather than the question of fraud upon the court.[69] Relying on *Abouloff* and *Vadala*, he concluded that the defendants having established a prima facie case of fraud were entitled to have the matter tried.[70]

The procedural model resurfaced accidentally in the middle of the twentieth century in the context of proceedings for the recognition of foreign divorce decrees. In *Macalpine v Macalpine*, Sachs J suggested that 'where the foreign decree has been procured by fraudulent evidence at trial before a court of competent jurisdiction, the courts here will nonetheless treat the decree as valid as long as it subsists in that foreign country'.[71] However, the authority on which he relied[72] did not

[64] ibid. This chapter is concerned with the first limb. The second, echoing the point made by Baggallay LJ in *Abouloff* (text to n 28) is, today, best considered as an aspect of natural justice (*nemo iudex in re sua*) (see *Dicey, Morris & Collins* (n 4) para 14-144).

[65] [1948] 2 KB 443.

[66] *Boswell* (n 37); *Birch v Birch* (1894) 86 LT 364.

[67] Both *Boswell* and *Birch* were manifestly claims to set aside a prior judgment on the ground that it had been procured by perjured evidence (see *Boswell* (n 37) 366; *Birch* (n 66) 364–65); also text to nn 165–66).

[68] As in *Bank of Australasia v Nias* (text to n 44).

[69] [1948] 2 KB 443, 448.

[70] ibid 449.

[71] [1958] P 35, 42.

[72] *Bater v Bater* [1906] P 209.

support that general proposition, but only the more limited proposition that the decree (being in the nature of a judgment *in rem*) would continue to produce effects vis-à-vis a third party.[73] His Lordship nonetheless proceeded to identify two exceptions to the rule that he had erroneously adopted, allowing a decree procured by fraud to be treated as a nullity: first, in a case where the fraud establishes the basis for the foreign court's jurisdiction;[74] and, secondly, if the course of the foreign proceedings had run contrary to natural justice.[75] In *Macalpine*, the husband's fraud, stating that he was unaware of the whereabouts of his wife, had enabled him to obtain an undefended divorce without notification to her. That was sufficient to engage the natural justice exception.[76]

That reasoning was followed by Cairns J in *Middleton v Middleton*.[77] Having reviewed the case law concerning the impact of fraud and collusion upon divorce decrees, he referred to the, by then neglected, decision of the Court of Appeal in *Ochsenbein v Papelier*[78] and, in particular, to the judgment of Mellish LJ.[79] This prompted Cairns J to observe:[80]

> The interesting point is that Mellish LJ treated both want of jurisdiction and obtaining a judgment by fraud as instances of a judgment being contrary to the principles of natural justice.

He held that both of the grounds for impugning the decree given by Sachs J in *Macalpine* were applicable.[81]

In *Jet Holdings Inc v Patel*,[82] the judgment creditor sought to distinguish *Abouloff* and *Vadala* on the ground that the alleged fraud in those cases related to the cause of action, rather than some other aspect of the proceedings.[83] The judgment debtor alleged that the entry by a Californian court of a judgment in default against him was attributable to threats made against him by the judgment creditor. Staughton LJ (with whom Nicholls LJ agreed) rejected the judgment creditor's submission:[84]

[73] ibid 227–29 (Collins MR). In *Bater*, this had led to the conclusion that the divorcing wife's second husband could not invoke fraud to contest the validity of a New York divorce in his later English nullity suit.
[74] *Macalpine* (n 71) 42.
[75] ibid 43–44.
[76] ibid.
[77] [1967] P 62.
[78] Text to nn 46–52 above.
[79] *Middleton* (n 77) 75–76.
[80] ibid 76.
[81] ibid.
[82] [1990] 1 QB 335.
[83] Piggott (n 36) 393–98, suggesting that 'extrinsic' and 'intrinsic' fraud must be distinguished.
[84] ibid 345.

> I cannot accept that there is any such distinction to be drawn. If there is a difference, collateral fraud is a stronger case where the English court should be more ready to investigate anew matters which were considered by the foreign court than in the case of fraud going directly to the cause of action which was adjudicated upon by the foreign court. So I would conclude that the foreign court's views on fraud are neither conclusive nor relevant whether the fraud is said to be fraud going directly to the cause of action or collateral fraud, on the authorities as they have stood for 100 years.

Fraud for this purpose included 'every variety of mala fides and mala praxis whereby one of the parties misleads and deceives the judicial tribunal'.[85] There was, Staughton LJ held, a triable issue as to whether the Californian court had been misled.[86]

Hitherto, the entitlement of a judgment debtor to plead fraud in answer to a claim to enforce a foreign judgment at common law or under one of the statutory regimes had not been qualified in any way. In *House of Spring Gardens Ltd v Waite (No 2)*,[87] however, a novel fact pattern presented itself in that two of the three defendants in the original proceedings before the Irish High Court had unsuccessfully brought an action in Ireland to set aside the judgment for fraud. When the plaintiff brought an action to enforce the Irish judgment in England, the defendants pleaded fraud. Sir Peter Pain granted summary judgment against all three defendants. The third defendant, who had chosen not to participate in the Irish set-aside action, appealed that judgment, relying on *Abouloff*, *Vadala*, *Syal*, and *Jet Holdings* in support of the submission that the English court must decide for itself whether the original judgment had been procured by fraud.

In the course of his judgment in *House of Spring Gardens*, Stuart-Smith LJ noted academic criticism of *Abouloff* and the following cases, which he characterized as having been 'decided at a time when our courts paid scant regard to the jurisprudence of other countries'. Having expressed a reluctance to extend the scope of the rule,[88] he distinguished them, on the basis that the further judgment of the Irish High Court in the set-aside action (which had not itself been seriously impugned on the ground of fraud[89]) created an issue estoppel that prevented the first two defendants from re-litigating the fraud issue.[90] The third defendant was also treated as bound, although he had not participated, by reason of his privity of interest with

[85] ibid 347, with reference to *R v Humphreys* [1977] AC 1, 21 (Viscount Dilhorne).

[86] ibid.

[87] [1991] 1 QB 241.

[88] ibid 251.

[89] This may have been a tactical error on the part of those advising the judgment debtors, for it would have enabled the same technical answer to the estoppel point as given in *Abouloff*: that Egan J, the Irish judge considering the set-aside application, cannot have decided whether he (as opposed to the original trial judge) had been misled.

[90] *House of Spring Gardens* (n 87) 251.

the first two defendants as a joint tortfeasor[91] and his own reliance on the set-aside proceedings in his English pleading.[92] Aside from estoppel, Stuart-Smith LJ also held that it would be an abuse of process for the defendants to be able to re-litigate the question of fraud. The first two defendants had chosen the forum for their challenge, which was the natural forum, and had proceeded with that challenge when '[t]hey could, if they had wished, merely have waited for enforcement proceedings to be taken here and then attempt to set up fraud'.[93] It would equally be a 'travesty of justice' if the third defendant were allowed to re-open the fraud issue:[94]

> Not only would the plaintiffs be required to re-litigate matters which have twice been extensively investigated and decided in their favour in the natural forum, but it would run the risk of inconsistent verdicts being reached, not only as between the English and Irish courts, but as between the defendants themselves.

McCowan LJ reached the same conclusion principally on the ground that no triable issue of fraud had been raised, and alternatively on the basis that it would be an abuse of process for the third defendant to litigate this issue in England given that he had encouraged the set-aside action while not directly participating in it.[95]

In *Owens Bank Ltd v Bracco*, the authority of *Abouloff* and the cases following it was directly challenged before the Judicial Committee of the House of Lords in proceedings to register a judgment of the High Court of St Vincent and the Grenadines for enforcement pursuant to section 9 of the Administration of Justice Act 1920.[96]

Significantly, the plaintiffs' submissions rested on the proposition that '*Abouloff* … is held to have decided that at common law different rules apply to foreign judgments' than to English judgments.[97] That proposition is doubly remarkable. First, it seems to overlook the explicit statements to the contrary in earlier cases.[98] Secondly, although it no doubt reflected the predominant view of commentators when *Owens Bank* was decided (including the editors of *Dicey and Morris*, led by Lawrence Collins[99]), the explicit assumption[100] that an English

[91] ibid 253–54.
[92] ibid 254.
[93] ibid 251–52. As to whether such conduct might itself amount to an abuse of process, see text to nn 188–92 below.
[94] ibid 255.
[95] ibid 258–59. Fox LJ agreed with both judgments.
[96] *Bracco* (n 44). Additionally, the House of Lords referred to the European Court of Justice the question of whether these enforcement proceedings fell within the 1968 Brussels Convention. The European Court gave a negative answer (Case C–129/82 *Owens Bank v Bracco* [1994] ECR I–117).
[97] *Bracco* (n 44) 475.
[98] Most clearly by Lindley LJ in *Vadala* (text to n 59); also *Bowles* (n 56) 468 (191) (Abinger CB, in argument); *Ochsenbein* (n 42) 698 (Lord Selborne); *Abouloff* (n 5) 300–01 (Lord Coleridge CJ), 305–06 (Brett LJ); *Syal* (n 65) 447 (Cohen LJ).
[99] Lawrence Collins and others (eds), *Dicey and Morris on the Conflict of Laws* (11th edn, Sweet & Maxwell 1987) 467–68.
[100] In argument (*Bracco* (n 44) 475) and in the judgment of Lord Bridge (ibid 483).

judgment could be set aside only on the basis of evidence that was not available through reasonable diligence to the unsuccessful party at the trial of the action has since been refuted by the Supreme Court in *Takhar v Gracefield Developments*.[101] In *Takhar*, the majority of the Supreme Court declined to treat *dicta* in *Owens Bank v Bracco*[102] and in the later case of *Owens Bank Ltd v Etoile Commerciale SA*[103] as authority for the general application of a reasonable diligence requirement in actions to set aside English judgments.[104]

With these points in mind, there is little to be salvaged from the wreckage of *Owens Bank v Bracco*. Lord Bridge (with whom the other members of the committee agreed) treated the question as one of construction of section 9(2)(d) of the 1920 Act and declined to overrule *Abouloff* and *Vadala* on the ground that 'the whole field is effectively governed by statute and, if the law is now in need of reform, it is for the legislature, not the judiciary, to effect it'.[105]

It is, with respect to their Lordships, more fruitful to study the judgment of the Court of Appeal, delivered by Parker LJ. In particular, although considering themselves bound by *Abouloff* and the cases following it, the members of the court were critical of the technical, estoppel-based reasoning prominent in those cases:[106]

> Any court, in considering whether a claim is honest or fraudulent, having regard to the evidence of both sides, must, if it is acting in good faith, be considering and deciding whether the claimant is trying to mislead the court; and, in the absence of significant fresh evidence not before the foreign court, it seems to us that, in substance, the court in *Abouloff* was being asked to consider again the same question which the Russian court had decided. The decision in *Abouloff* was, no doubt, based at least in part upon the court's view of what was the better course, having regard to policy and expediency.

That passage was quoted, with approval, by Phillips J (as he then was) in *Interdesco SA v Nullifire Ltd*.[107] He suggested that the considerations of 'policy and expediency' underlying *Abouloff* had been identified by the Court of Appeal in *Bracco* in the following passage earlier in its judgment:[108]

101 See section G.
102 *Bracco* (n 44) 483 (Lord Bridge); also ibid 465 (CA).
103 [1995] 1 WLR 44, 48 (Lord Templeman); also *Baden* (n 40) [308]–[309] (Peter Gibson J).
104 *Takhar* (n 17) [40]–[41], [54] (Lord Kerr, with whom Lords Hodge, Jones, and Kitchin agreed), [65] (Lord Sumption). Cf [2018] Ch 1 [40]–[44] (Patten LJ, CA).
105 *Bracco* (n 44) 489. For criticism of this reasoning, see John Collier, 'Fraud Still Unravels Foreign Judgments' [1992] Cambridge LJ 441.
106 ibid 466. Cf text to nn 29–33.
107 [1992] 1 Lloyd's Rep 180, 187.
108 *Bracco* (n 44) 457–58.

> In short, the questions were whether the foreign court was to be trusted to have decided correctly, if raised before it, the issue whether the claim was fraudulently made, just as it was trusted to decide all other questions of law and fact; and whether a party to proceedings in a foreign court was to be required to bring forward for decision before that court all matters of defence, and evidence in support of them, available to him, as was a party to proceedings in this country.

Finally, in terms of the case law prior to *AK Investment*, the decision in the *Etoile Commerciale* case (an appeal to the Privy Council from the Court of Appeal of St Vincent and the Grenadines in proceedings to enforce a French judgment) was founded on the same error of law as *Bracco*.[109] The Board, declaring itself to be 'unenthusiastic' about the decision in *Abouloff*,[110] struck out the judgment debtor's fraud defence on the ground of abuse of process, based upon the lack of evidence to support the allegation.[111]

F. Contrast with the Brussels I Regime

In *Interdesco v Nullifire*,[112] Phillips J considered whether fraud in obtaining a judgment of a court of an EU Member State provided an answer to recognition and enforcement of that judgment under the Brussels I regime, at that time embodied in the 1968 Brussels Convention and given effect under section 2 of the Civil Jurisdiction and Judgments Act 1982.[113] The Convention, and its successors, do not specifically include fraud among the specific grounds for contesting recognition and enforcement. Instead, aggrieved parties must rely on the general public policy ground.[114]

In *Interdesco* (as in *House of Spring Gardens*), the English judgment debtor (Nullifire) had applied in France, by the procedure known as *recours en révision*, to set aside the original French judgment (itself upheld on appeal) on the basis of the fraud by the judgment creditor. At the same time, Nullifire sought to resist enforcement of that judgment in England on the ground of public policy. It relied, in

[109] *Etoile Commerciale* (n 103) 48.
[110] ibid 50.
[111] ibid 51.
[112] *Interdesco* (n 107).
[113] Later superseded by Council Regulation (EC) No 44/2001 of 22 December 2000 on jurisdiction and the recognition and enforcement of judgments in civil and commercial matters (Brussels I Regulation) [2001] OJ L12/1 Regulation (EU) No 1215/2012 of the European Parliament and of the Council of 12 December 2012 on jurisdiction and the recognition and enforcement of judgments in civil and commercial matters (Brussels I Regulation Recast) [2012] OJ L351/1. These instruments no longer apply to the UK after 1 January 2021. The identical question would arise if the UK were to succeed in its aim of rejoining the 2007 Lugano Convention ([2007] OJ L339/3).
[114] Brussels Convention, art 27(1); Brussels I Regulation, art 34(1); Brussels I Regulation Recast, art 45(1)(a); 2007 Lugano Convention, art 34(1).

particular, on the proposition that no one should be entitled to take advantage of his own wrong (ie the illegality model).[115]

Phillips J, having noted the explicit prohibition in the Convention on reviewing the substance of the judgment to be recognized or enforced,[116] refused to apply what he described as 'the rule in *Abouloff*' to the case before him. In his view:[117]

> [W]here registration of a Convention judgment is challenged on the ground that the foreign court has been fraudulently deceived, the English court should first consider whether a remedy lies in such a case in the foreign jurisdiction in question. If so it will normally be appropriate to leave the defendant to pursue his remedy in that jurisdiction. Such a course commends itself for two reasons. First it accords with the spirit of the Convention that all issues should, so far as possible, be dealt with by the State enjoying the original jurisdiction. Secondly, the courts of that State are likely to be better able to assess whether the original judgment was procured by fraud....
>
> [T]he proper course is to leave Nullifire to seek its remedy in the *recours en révision*. The French court is plainly best placed to decide whether there has been fraud and, if so, its implication on the French judgment.

That decision, echoing the judgment of Bramwell B in *Crawley* more than a century earlier[118] and conforming to the procedural (natural justice) model, was prescient. In its more recent jurisprudence on the public policy exception within the Brussels I regime, the European Court has emphasized that its application is conditional upon the complainant exhausting the remedies available to it in the Member State of origin, on the assumption that each Member State affords sufficient procedural guarantees:[119]

> [The Brussels I regime] is based on the fundamental idea that individuals are required, in principle, to use all the legal remedies made available by the law of the Member State of origin. Save where specific circumstances make it too difficult or impossible to make use of the legal remedies in the Member State of origin, the individuals concerned must avail themselves of all the legal remedies available in that Member State with a view to preventing a breach of public policy before it occurs.

[115] *Interdesco* (n 107) 184–85.
[116] Brussels Convention, art 34; also Brussels I Regulation, art 36; Brussels I Regulation Recast, art 52.
[117] *Interdesco* (n 107) 188–89.
[118] Text to n 54.
[119] Case C-559/14 *Meroni v Recoletos Ltd* EU:C2016:349, [2017] QB 85, [48].

The existence of an adequate remedy in the country of origin fulfils the complainant's right to a fair trial under Article 47 of the Charter, and excludes a public policy challenge on that ground.[120]

G. *Takhar*: Fraud and English Judgments

The story so far is a curious game of two halves: the first (up to the middle of the twentieth century) played on the assumption that the same rules and principles applied to English and foreign judgments; and the second played on the assumption that those principles had diverged. Before returning to Lord Collins's intervention in *AK Investment*, it is necessary to summarize the current state of the law concerning actions to set aside English judgments on the ground of fraud in obtaining them, as recently explained in *Takhar*.

For Lord Kerr (with whom Lords Hodge, Lloyd-Jones, and Kitchin concurred), an English judgment can be set aside for fraud if, after the trial, the claimant discovers fresh evidence[121] which, with other evidence including that presented to the court, 'demonstrates that the previous relevant evidence, action, statement, or concealment was an operative cause of the court's decision to give the judgment the way that it did' by reference to its impact on the evidence supporting the original decision.[122] It is not, in his Lordship's view, necessary for the claimant to show that the fresh evidence could not have been discovered with reasonable diligence prior to the trial and judgment.[123] Without expressing a final view, Lord Kerr suggested that the court has discretion to refuse the application if either (i) the issue of fraud has been raised at trial, or (ii) the claimant took a deliberate decision not to investigate the fraud in advance of the trial.[124]

Lord Sumption (with whom Lords Hodge, Lloyd-Jones, and Kitchin also concurred) expressed general agreement with Lord Kerr.[125] In his view, principles of estoppel *per rem judicatam* have no part to play when an action is brought to set aside a judgment for fraud—this is a cause of action in its own right, distinct from that underlying the original judgment, and any ruling upon a relevant issue in that judgment 'is vitiated by the fraud and cannot bind the parties'.[126] For Lord Sumption, the possibility of bringing such an action is, nevertheless, subject to

[120] ibid [49]–[54].

[121] *Takhar* (n 17) [49], referring to *Toubia v Schwenke* [2002] NSWCA 34, (2002) 54 NSWLR 46 [49] (Handley JA); *Elu v Floorweald Ltd* [2020] EWHC 1222 (QB), [2020] 1 WLR 4369. See also *Wentworth v Rogers (No 9)* (1987) 8 NSWLR 388 (CA), 396 (Kirby P), suggesting that it may suffice if the claimant has only put pre-existing evidence in context after the trial.

[122] *Takhar* (n 17) [57], approving the statement of Aikens LJ in *Royal Bank of Scotland plc v Highland Financial Partners LP* [2013] EWCA Civ 328, [2013] 1 CLC 596 [106].

[123] ibid [54].

[124] ibid [55]. His Lordship expressed no final view on these matters.

[125] ibid [59].

[126] ibid [61].

the flexible jurisdiction to restrain abusive litigation, but only in a case in which the claimant 'deliberately decided not to investigate a suspected fraud or rely on a known one', such that it could be said that he should have raised it at trial.[127] He was doubtful whether a different approach should be taken where the fraud had been raised in the earlier proceedings, but left the point open.[128]

Lord Briggs and Lady Arden delivered separate judgments, concurring in the result but not fully in the reasoning of the majority. Lord Briggs's proposal[129] for a more flexible abuse of process inquiry, reflecting the fact that '[t]he forensic pursuit and defence of the fraud allegation may well travel over, or at least overlap with, the ground travelled in the original proceedings',[130] was rejected by the majority, led by Lord Sumption.[131] Lady Arden was more hesitant, urging the Civil Procedure Rules Committee to consider the matter. In her view, the general rule, entitling the claimant to bring an action to set aside the judgment, rested upon the injustice of allowing a fraudster 'to obtain and retain the fruits of his fraud'[132] and any restriction on that rule had to be consistent with the claimant's 'core right of access to court'.[133]

H. A Wider Common Law Perspective

Elsewhere, the rules governing the effect of fraud upon foreign judgments have moved more closely into line with those for local judgments, although differences of detail remain. In Canada, the majority of the Supreme Court held in *Beals v Saldahna* that (subject to one exception, discussed below):[134]

> [T]he merits of a foreign judgment can be challenged for fraud only where the allegations are new and not the subject of prior adjudication. Where material facts not previously discoverable arise that potentially challenge the evidence that was before the foreign court, the domestic court can decline recognition of the judgment.

Consequently, in proceedings brought to enforce a foreign judgment, 'a defendant has the burden of demonstrating that the facts sought to be raised could not have

[127] ibid [63].
[128] ibid [66].
[129] ibid [85]–[87].
[130] ibid [84].
[131] ibid [63]–[64].
[132] ibid [92].
[133] ibid [94]–[95].
[134] [2003] 3 SCR 416 [51]; also Horace E Read, *Recognition and Enforcement of Foreign Judgments* (Harvard UP 1938) 277–81, considering earlier decisions of Canadian provincial courts declining to follow *Abouloff* and *Vadala*.

been discovered by the exercise of due diligence prior to the obtaining of the foreign judgment'.[135]

That approach has been followed by the appellate courts in Singapore[136] and in Jamaica,[137] while those in Ireland[138] and New Zealand[139] have kept faith with the *Abouloff* line.

In Australia, there is a division of authority as to whether fresh evidence is required to support a plea of fraud in answer to a recognition or enforcement of a foreign judgment.[140] The predominant view is that 'the party alleging fraud must establish that the allegation rests on evidence not previously available to be produced to the foreign court and that such evidence (whether alone or in combination with evidence given at the trial) would have probably altered the result in the foreign court'.[141] By contrast with the position in Canada and Singapore, this test focuses on the evidence actually available to the relevant party, rather than that discoverable by the exercise of due diligence.[142]

In *Beals*, the Canadian Supreme Court drew a distinction between fraud relating to the merits of the case, subject to the approach set out above, and 'fraud going to jurisdiction',[143] which it suggested 'can always be raised before a domestic court to challenge the judgment'.[144] Although this distinction has occasionally been drawn in English case law,[145] it is necessary to seek to reconcile it with the longstanding rule that a foreign judgment cannot be impeached on the ground that the court of origin lacked competence under its own law to give the judgment.[146] If, as Lindley LJ put it, 'the jurisdiction which alone is important in these matters is the competence of the Court in an international sense' (ie as recognized under the enforcing court's conflict of laws rules),[147] it appears illogical to distinguish fraud that leads a court to assume jurisdiction under its own laws from other frauds that cause it to give judgment in the wrongdoer's favour.

135 ibid.

136 *Hong Ping Tee v Les Placements Germain Gauthier* [2002] SGCA 17.

137 *Vasconcellos v Jamaica Steel Works Ltd* (2008) SCCA No 1 [45] (Harrison JA); *DYA Fishing v Perla del Caribe Inc* [2014] JMCA Civ 26.

138 *Bussoleno Ltd v Kelly* [2011] IEHC 220.

139 *Svriskis v Gibson* [1977] 2 NZLR 4 (CA); *Emajor v Emajor* [2016] NZHC 2022, (2016) 23 PRNZ 338.

140 The relevant case law is summarized by the Supreme Court of Victoria in *Doe v Howard* [2015] VSC 75 [105]–[122].

141 ibid [124], following the approach of Rogers CJ in *Keele v Findley* (1990) 21 NSWLR 444 (SC).

142 *Clone Pty Ltd v Players Pty Ltd* [2018] HCA 12, (2018) 264 CLR 165; also *Toubia* (n 121) (both cases involving local judgments); *Quarter Enterprises Pty Ltd v Allardyce Lumber Co Ltd* [2014] NSWCA 3, (2014) 85 NSWLR 404 [99]. Cf *Bao v Qu* [2020] NSWSC 588, (2020) 102 NSWLR 435 [35].

143 Including 'the kind of fraud that misleads the court, foreign or domestic, into believing that it has jurisdiction over the cause of action' (*Beals* (n 134) [45]; also *Powell v Cockburn* [1977] 2 SCR 218; *Lang v Lapp* 2010 BCCA 517, 328 DLR (4th) 372 [20]; *AK Investment* (n 3) [112]; Read (n 134) 274–75).

144 ibid [51].

145 Text to n 74.

146 *Pemberton v Hughes* [1899] 1 Ch 781; *Dicey, Morris & Collins* (n 4) paras 14R-128, 14-132–14-135. For criticism, see Dickinson, '*Schibsby*' (n 2) 437–39.

147 *Pemberton* (n 146) 791.

Two cases may, however, stand apart. First, if the true facts would, without further proceedings being necessary, render the judgment a nullity in its legal system of origin.[148] Secondly, if the fraud relates to a fact that establishes the 'international competence' of the foreign court under English conflicts principles, for example if the claimant fraudulently induces the defendant to travel to the country in which the foreign court sits and serves him with process there, or to enter into a choice of court agreement designating the foreign court, or to take a step in the foreign proceedings that is taken to amount to a 'voluntary submission' to the foreign court's jurisdiction.[149] In these instances, the fraud relates to a matter that is of such significance to the English court's decision to recognize or enforce a foreign judgment, that is, its essential force and the basis for recognizing the foreign court's competence in English law, that no qualifications should be placed upon the inquiry before the English court.

I. A Coherent Way Forward?

Takhar offers a prospect of a return to the orthodoxy that the same rules govern the effect of fraud upon the binding force of English and foreign judgments, with the qualification that due account must be taken of the very different substantive and procedural contexts in which those rules are being applied.

One apparent difference in approach between the two situations remains, in so far as passages in the judgments in *Abouloff*, cited with approval in later cases, suggest that it is not a requirement that the evidence relied on in opposition to the recognition and enforcement of a foreign judgment be 'fresh' in the sense described above.[150] All three judges in *Abouloff* were prepared to assume that the evidence raised in support of the fraud defence in England was the same as that presented to the court in Tiflis.[151] In their view, this fact was irrelevant to the availability of the fraud defence as the issues in the two sets of proceedings, Russian and English, were different. As Brett LJ put it:[152]

> [T]he mere fact of evidence having been brought forward to substantiate or defeat one issue, does not prevent a party from bringing forward the same evidence in a

[148] *Dicey, Morris & Collins* (n 4) para 14-135. Cf *Macalpine* (n 71) 44–45.

[149] Cf *Stein v Valkenhuysen* (1858) E, B & E 65, 120 ER 431; *Watkins v North American Land and Timber Co Ltd* (1904) 20 TLR 534 (both involving proceedings before an English court).

[150] *OJSC Bank of Moscow v Chernyakov* [2016] EWHC 2583 (Comm) [6] (Cranston J); *GFH Capital Ltd v Haigh* [2020] EWHC 1269 (Comm) [70] (Henshaw J); *Public Joint Stock Co ('Rosgosstrakh') v Starr Syndicate Ltd* [2020] EWHC 1557 (Comm) [96]; also Adrian Briggs, *The Conflict of Laws* (4th edn, OUP 2019) 144 and Adrian Briggs, *Private International Law in English Courts* (OUP 2014) para 6.194.

[151] *Abouloff* (n 5) 302–03 (Lord Coleridge CJ), 304 (Baggallay LJ), 306 (Brett LJ). See also: *Vadala* (text to n 60); *Syal* (text to n 70).

[152] ibid 307, relying on *Barrs v Jackson* (1842) 1 Y&C Ch 585, 62 ER 1028.

> subsequent action between the same parties, either to maintain or to defend other issues therein raised.

This is unsatisfactory for the following reasons.[153] First, it demonstrates an overly formal and general approach to defining the issues presented for decision at the original trial, a point forcefully made by the Court of Appeal in *Owens Bank v Bracco*.[154] As the judgments in *Takhar* affirm, it is perfectly possible for issues concerning the truth or genuineness of evidence presented to be raised and dealt with at the original trial.[155] For example, the authenticity of a document may be challenged,[156] or a previous inconsistent statement put to a witness to suggest perjury, or the means by which evidence has been gathered or suppressed may be relevant to a case management decision.[157]

Secondly, the analysis in terms of issue estoppel mischaracterizes the nature of the inquiry.[158] Fraud deprives the judgment of the legal force that is a prerequisite for any plea of estoppel *per rem judicatam*.[159] This point applies with the same force to foreign judgments as it applies to English judgments. Although the binding force of a judgment within its legal system of origin supports the recognition of the judgment in England,[160] and enforcement of the (monetary) obligation that it creates,[161] the judgment will be allowed no force within the English legal system[162] if it is shown to have been procured by fraud.

With respect to English judgments, the 'fresh evidence' requirement is a procedural restriction upon the application of the fraud rule, which is the rule that prevents an issue estoppel from arising.[163] In fairness to the courts sitting in *Abouloff* and in *Vadala*, that requirement, although now 'well established',[164] had not crystallized by the time that their decisions were handed down. Its provenance is usually traced to the judgment of Lord Selborne in *Boswell*[165] followed by the Court of Appeal in *Birch*.[166] Even these decisions, over a decade after *Abouloff*,

[153] Additionally, the observations on this point in *Abouloff* constitute *obiter dicta* in view of the fact that the point arose for decision upon the plaintiff's demurrer (text to n 32).

[154] Text to n 106; also Read (n 134) 276, describing the estoppel reasoning as 'a narrow "technical hocus-pocus" to enable [Brett LJ] to present that he was not violating the *res judicata* doctrine'.

[155] *Takhar* (n 17) [42], [55] (Lord Kerr), [66] (Lord Sumption).

[156] As in *Bracco* (n 44).

[157] As in *Jet Holdings* (n 82).

[158] Text to n 33.

[159] *Takhar* (n 17) [53] (Lord Kerr), [61] (Lord Sumption).

[160] *Carl Zeiss Stiftung v Rayner & Keeler Ltd* [1967] 1 AC 853, 919 (Lord Reid), 969 (Lord Wilberforce).

[161] *Nouvion v Freeman* (1889) 15 App Cas 1.

[162] The English court cannot speak for the effects of the judgment elsewhere (*Dicey, Morris & Collins* (n 4) para 14-121; *Yukos Capital Sarl v OJC Rosneft Oil Co (No 2)* [2012] EWCA Civ 855, [2014] QB 458; also *Mengiste v Endowment Fund for the Rehabilitation of Tigray* [2017] EWCA Civ 1326).

[163] *Takhar* (n 17) [61] (Lord Sumption).

[164] ibid [65].

[165] *Boswell* (n 37) 366 ('a new discovery of something material').

[166] *Birch* (n 66) 369 (Cozens-Hardy LJ). See also *Charles Bright & Co v Sellar* [1904] 1 KB 6, 12 (also Cozens-Hardy LJ); *McHarg v Woods Radio Pty Ltd* [1948] VLR 496; *Doe v Howard* (n 140) [101]

did not produce immediate clarity, as Cohen LJ's treatment of them in *Syal* demonstrates.[167]

To apply the dicta in *Abouloff* to foreign judgments only would acknowledge a distinction that the Court of Appeal in that case and in the later case of *Vadala* did not countenance.[168] Furthermore, there is no good reason to apply a different evidential threshold to the two situations. To conclude that a foreign court trying the action between the parties cannot be 'trusted'[169] to deal satisfactorily with a plea of fraud based on the evidence available to the aggrieved party at the date of the original trial would manifestly fall short of the degree of respect for the adjudicatory authority of the foreign court that comity demands from an English court.[170] It would also be inconsistent with the deference given to the decisions of foreign appellate and review courts in applying the abuse of process doctrine.[171]

Although the fraud defence can be seen as an aspect of English public policy (*ordre public*), it does not follow that the defendant has an absolute entitlement to reprise arguments presented at trial,[172] for it is necessary to take into account both the countervailing policy supporting the finality of litigation[173] and the need for public policy to be applied narrowly and flexibly taking due account of the international context and the facts of the particular case.[174] Consistently with the approach taken to the recognition and enforcement of judgments under the Brussels I regime in *Interdesco*,[175] the foreign forum's own procedural and remedial framework provides an essential part of that contextual framework.

At this point, it is desirable to return to Lord Collins's opinion in *AK Investment*. In the passage quoted above,[176] his Lordship suggests, first, that 'simply to apply the English rules to foreign judgments might lead to real injustice' and, secondly, that a 'nuanced approach might be required, depending on the reliability of the foreign legal system, the scope for challenge in the foreign court and the type of fraud alleged'. Although *AK Investment* preceded *Takhar*, his Lordship's reference to 'the English rules' must now be understood as a reference to the rules posited by the

(both Sup Ct Victoria). Cf DM Gordon, 'Fraud or New Evidence as Grounds for Actions to Set Aside Judgments' (1961) 77 LQR 358, 361, 376–78, although tending to conflate review for fraud with review on the ground of the discovery of material new evidence.

[167] Text to nn 66–69.

[168] Text to nn 24 and 59.

[169] Text to n 108; also Briggs, *Conflict of Laws* (n 150) 144–45.

[170] *Ecobank Transnational Inc v Tanoh* [2015] EWCA Civ 1309, [2016] 1 WLR 2231 [132] (Christopher Clarke LJ); Timothy Endicott, 'Comity among Authorities' (2015) 68 Curr Leg Probl 1.

[171] *House of Spring Gardens* (n 87); *Etoile Commerciale* (n 103).

[172] Cf Briggs, *Conflict of Laws* (n 150) 145; also Briggs, *Private International Law* (n 150) paras 6.192–6.193.

[173] *Etoile Commerciale* (n 103) 50 (Lord Templeman); *AK Investment* (n 3) [114]–[116] (Lord Collins).

[174] *Dicey, Morris & Collins* (n 4) para 5-006.

[175] See section F.

[176] Text to n 15.

majority of the Supreme Court in the latter case.[177] These rules place certain limits upon the proposition that a judgment shown to have been procured by fraud is to be set aside, in terms both of the evidential threshold (the 'fresh evidence' requirement) and of the defendant's conduct in the earlier proceedings (abuse of process or other case management powers).

The overall package in *Takhar* seeks to strike a fair balance between the principle that no person should be entitled to profit from wrongdoing and the principle of finality, as well as between the two participants' entitlements to a just determination of their civil rights.[178] Lord Collins was, very properly, concerned that this balance could be disturbed if the foreign court is demonstrably unreliable or if it does not offer the aggrieved party a realistic opportunity to prevent his opponent from securing or retaining a judgment by improper means.[179] Comity requires, nonetheless, that the English court acts on 'the normal assumption is that an English court has no superiority over a foreign court in deciding what justice between the parties requires'.[180] The burden of demonstrating the unsuitability of the foreign court, or the mechanisms that it offers, should lie with the party opposing recognition or enforcement, who should be required to produce cogent evidence that justice has not been done, or of a real risk that it will not be forthcoming, in the foreign forum.[181] Absent such evidence, a party to proceedings before a foreign court, and especially a party who has chosen to participate in those proceedings,[182] should take the foreign forum as he finds it, should raise the issue of fraud at trial using the evidence properly available at that time[183] and should not be entitled to relitigate that or substantially the same issue in later proceedings before an English court unless material new evidence is discovered in the meantime.

The demands of justice cut both ways: an unthinking equiperation of English and foreign judgments may cause injustice to the judgment creditor, as much as it may cause injustice to the judgment debtor. In a domestic context, the proper course for a party who discovers that an English judgment against him has been procured by fraud is to bring an action to set that judgment aside.[184]

[177] See section G.

[178] *Takhar* (n 17) [92], [94] (Lady Arden).

[179] It is less clear what his Lordship had in mind in his reference to 'the type of fraud alleged'. Most likely, he had in mind cases involving fraud relating to the court's jurisdiction (see *AK Investment* (n 3) [112], referring to the decision of the Supreme Court of Canada in *Beals* (n 134)). The merits of this suggested distinction have been addressed briefly in section H.

[180] *Barclays Bank plc v Homan* [1992] BCC 757, 762 (Hoffmann J); *Deutsche Bank AG v Highland Crusader Offshore Partners LP* [2009] EWCA Civ 725, [2010] 1 WLR 1023 [56] (Toulson LJ).

[181] *AK Investment* (n 3) [89]–[102].

[182] As Hoffmann J put it in *Mackinnon v Donaldson Lufkin & Jenrette Securities Corp* [1986] Ch 482, 492, '[i]f you join the game you must play according to the local rules'.

[183] Including, no doubt, evidence that would have been obtained upon further investigation that the party in question, being suspicious of fraud, has deliberately decided not to make (*Takhar* (n 17) [55] (Lord Kerr), [63] (Lord Sumption)).

[184] *Jonesco v Beard* [1930] AC 298, 300 (Lord Buckmaster); *Kuwait Airways Corp v Iraqi Airways Co (No 2)* [2001] 1 WLR 429; *Jaffray v Society of Lloyds* [2007] EWCA Civ 856, [2008] 1 WLR 75.

In cross-border litigation, a party in the same situation likely has both remedies in the local court (by way of appeal or review) and the possibility of opposing recognition or enforcement of the judgment in jurisdictions in which assets are located or follow-on litigation may take place. If the litigant chooses to exercise local remedies, or acquiesces in such action by others, that choice or acquiescence may preclude re-litigation of the fraud issue in later proceedings before an English court,[185] at least in the absence of material fresh evidence that could not have been presented in the foreign review proceedings[186] or cogent evidence that the foreign procedures were unjust.[187]

What if the litigant instead deliberately chooses not to exercise available local remedies and distances himself from others who do so? If (and only if) the English court considers that the aggrieved party's conduct in not seeking to challenge the judgment in its country of origin is unreasonable, the court should consider exercising its case management powers to strike out a subsequent fraud defence as an abuse of process or to stay the proceedings pending a determination of the fraud issue by the foreign court, although it should not do so if it has reason to believe that the local remedy is inadequate to protect the litigant's right to a fair trial. This solution accords, first, with the approach in particular of Lord Sumption to the abuse of process doctrine in *Takhar*, referring to 'something which the law would expect a reasonable person to do in his own interest and in that of the efficient conduct of a litigation';[188] secondly, with the *forum conveniens* doctrine, prominent in the reasoning of the Court of Appeal in *House of Spring Gardens*, in particular the guidance laid down by Lord Goff for cases in which the claimant had not brought proceedings in the natural forum within the limitation period;[189] thirdly, with the approach favoured by the Court of Appeal in *Adams v Cape Industries* with respect to alleged violations of the requirements of natural justice[190] (acknowledging here that the court in *Adams* felt constrained by the *Abouloff* line of cases to suggest that fraud was a case apart);[191] and, fourthly, with the approach within the Brussels I regime in *Interdesco*.[192]

There are evident benefits in evolving the law in the direction suggested here. By harmonizing the framework of rules governing the impact of fraud upon English and foreign judgments, the law in England would become more straightforward and coherent. At the same time, by encouraging the courts in taking case management decisions to adopt the 'nuanced approach' advocated by Lord Collins,

[185] *House of Spring Gardens* (n 87); *Etoile Commerciale* (n 103).
[186] *House of Spring Gardens* (n 87); *Etoile Commerciale* (n 103).
[187] Text to n 181.
[188] *Takhar* (n 17) [63] (Lord Sumption).
[189] *Spiliada Maritime Corp v Cansulex Ltd* [1987] AC 460, 483–84.
[190] *Adams v Cape Industries plc* [1990] Ch 433, 468–71.
[191] ibid 468–69.
[192] See section F.

the interests of justice in individual cases and the demands of comity would be better served. The contours of the law would fall into alignment with the procedural (natural justice) model suggested more than 150 years ago by Mellish LJ in *Ochsenbein*[193] and by Bramwell B in *Crawley*.[194] *Abouloff* could be laid to rest, and an unhappy episode in the English conflict of laws brought to a close.

193 Text to n 51.
194 Text to n 54.

10

Post-Brexit

The New Shape of English Private International Law

Trevor Hartley

A. Introduction

In order to understand the effect of Brexit on English private international law, we must consider what, in concrete terms, has changed with Brexit.[1] The first and most obvious thing is that EU measures—especially regulations—no longer automatically have the force of law in the UK. Being subject to EU law is, after all, one of the main consequences of membership of the Union. The most important EU regulations for commercial private international law (this chapter will not deal with family law and succession) are the two Rome Regulations (Rome I[2] and Rome II[3]) and the recast Brussels I Regulation.[4]

The effect of this as regards proceedings in the courts of EU Member States depends on whether or not the measure in question applies on the basis of reciprocity. The two Rome Regulations do not apply on the basis of reciprocity. They apply in exactly the same way if the law they designate is that of a non-Member State as they do if it is the law of a Member State. If, under Rome I, the law applicable to a contract is that of part of the UK, a court in an EU Member State will apply it in the same way after Brexit as before Brexit.[5] The same is true with respect to the habitual residence, domicile, or nationality of the parties. Regulations not based on reciprocity apply in the same way irrespective of whether or not the parties are habitually resident or domiciled in a Member State or nationals of a Member State.

[1] For convenience, the word 'Brexit' will be used to designate the moment when EU law ceased to apply in the UK (11pm UK time on 31 December 2020) even though the UK actually left the EU twelve months before this.

[2] Regulation (EC) No 593/2008 of the European Parliament and of the Council of 17 June 2008 on the law applicable to contractual obligations, [2008] OJ L177/6.

[3] Regulation (EC) No 864/2007 of the European Parliament and of the Council of 11 July 2007 on the law applicable to non-contractual obligations, [2007] OJ L199/40.

[4] Regulation (EU) No 1215/2012 of the European Parliament and of the Council of 12 December 2012 on jurisdiction and the recognition and enforcement of judgments in civil and commercial matters, [2012] OJ L351/1.

[5] Rome I, art 2.

Trevor Hartley, *Post-Brexit* In: *Essays in International Litigation for Lord Collins*. Edited by: Jonathan Harris and Campbell McLachlan, Oxford University Press. © Oxford University Press 2022.
DOI: 10.1093/oso/9780192867988.003.0011

So, in the case of such measures, Brexit had no effect as regards proceedings in the courts of a Member State.[6]

The position is different with regard to proceedings in the courts of the UK. However, the UK has come up with a simple solution: making the two Rome Regulations part of UK law. The phrase 'retained EU law' is used to refer to EU law that applies in the UK after Brexit as UK law. This will be considered in the section below.

Where an EU measure is based on reciprocity—the recast Brussels I Regulation is the prime example for our purposes—nothing would be gained by making it part of UK law. Whatever the position may be in the courts of the UK, this would have no effect on proceedings in the courts of EU Member States. The rules prohibiting exorbitant jurisdiction in the Regulation apply only if the defendant is domiciled in a Member State; the requirement not to hear a case if the courts of another country are seised first applies only if that other country is a Member State;[7] and the requirement to recognize judgments given by the courts of another country applies only if that other country is a Member State. The only way of securing these benefits after Brexit would be to obtain some sort of agreement with the EU. The possibilities will be considered in sections C to F, below.

The alternative would be to adopt a tough, strong-arm approach and try to maintain our position by means of antisuit injunctions and other measures regarded as illegitimate in the rest of Europe. This will be considered in section H, below.

Finally, it should be mentioned that there is one other effect of Brexit on private international law. Certain international conventions to which the EU is a party applied to the UK before Brexit because it was a Member State, even though it was not itself a party to the agreement. Leaving the Union brought this to an end. The most important example is the Hague Convention on Choice of Court Agreements of 2005. However, once the UK was no longer a Member State, it could become a party in its own right. In the case of the Hague Choice of Court Convention, it did that. This will be considered in section F, below.

B. Rome I and II: Choice of Law in Contract and Torts

Why make the two Rome Regulations part of UK law? Why not just go back to the rules of law applied before the UK joined the EU? It is suggested that there are two reasons. The first is that the two EU Regulations are a better product than the pre-EU common law and, in the case of torts, the Private International Law

[6] For small exceptions, see Rome I, arts 3(4), 7.

[7] For a quasi-exception, see recast Brussels I Regulation, arts 33, 34. These provisions permit, but do not require, the courts of a Member State to stay proceedings before them in certain circumstances if the courts of a non-Member State were seised first.

(Miscellaneous Provisions) Act 1995. They are better structured, clearer, easier to apply, and produce better results. The second reason is that foreign litigants may be more willing to bring their disputes to courts in the UK if they know that the familiar EU system will apply there as it does in the EU.

Since the two Rome Regulations are now UK law,[8] they can be amended. To a limited extent, this has already been done, as some technical changes have been necessary in order to transpose them from the EU legal system to the UK legal system. However, these changes do not change their basic nature. In substance, they apply as before. No attempt has been made to improve them. Whether such an attempt will be made in the future remains to be seen. To do so would detract from the objective of uniformity; so there would have to be a good reason. Minor tinkering would not be worthwhile.

Now the UK has left the EU, UK courts can no longer make references to the Court of Justice of the European Union (CJEU) in order to interpret the provisions of retained EU law.[9] To what extent will CJEU rulings on the interpretation of the two Rome Regulations be followed by UK courts? To answer this, we must draw a distinction between rulings given before Brexit and those given after Brexit.[10] Those given after Brexit[11] are not binding on any UK courts even if they relate to EU measures which have been retained as UK law.[12] However, UK courts can 'have regard' to such decisions.[13] It is suggested that, in order to maintain uniformity, they should follow these decisions unless there is a clear and definite reason why they should not.

CJEU rulings given before Brexit, on the other hand, constitute 'retained EU case law'[14] and as such will continue to apply in the UK. So the two Rome Regulations, as they apply in the UK, will continue to be interpreted according to pre-Brexit CJEU case law. However, the UK Supreme Court[15] (and, in Scotland, the High Court of Justiciary when sitting as a court of appeal)[16] are not bound by retained

[8] The UK provision making the two Rome Regulations part of UK law is The Law Applicable to Contractual Obligations and Non-Contractual Obligations (Amendment etc) (EU Exit) Regulations 2019, SI 2019/834.

[9] European Union (Withdrawal) Act 2018, s 6(1)(b), as amended.

[10] The legislation does not use the term 'Brexit', but talks of 'implementation period completion day', which is defined in the European Union (Withdrawal Agreement) Act 2020, s 39(1) as meaning 31 December 2020 at 11.00pm. One of the amendments made by the 2020 European Union (Withdrawal Agreement) Act to the 2018 Act is to substitute 'implementation period completion day' for 'exit day'.

[11] Technically 'implementation period completion day'—11pm on 31 December 2020.

[12] European Union (Withdrawal) Act 2018, s 6(1)(a), as amended.

[13] European Union (Withdrawal) Act 2018, s 6(2), as amended.

[14] 'Retained EU case law' is defined by the European Union (Withdrawal) Act 2018, s 6(7) (as amended) as the principles laid down by, and any decisions of, the CJEU, as they have effect in EU law immediately before Brexit, in so far as they relate to EU-derived UK legislation operative immediately before Brexit, direct EU legislation (eg regulations) operative immediately before Brexit, and rights under s 2(1) of the European Communities Act 1972. This is subject to various exceptions laid down in s 5 and Sch 1 of the Act.

[15] European Union (Withdrawal) Act 2018, s 6(4)(a).

[16] European Union (Withdrawal) Act 2018, s 6(4)(b). The High Court of Justiciary is the supreme criminal court in Scotland. It is both a trial court and a court of appeal. For certain exceptions and

EU case law.[17] In deciding whether to depart from any retained EU case law, the Supreme Court and the High Court of Justiciary must apply the same test as they would apply in deciding whether to depart from their own case law.[18]

One can conclude that, given the fact of Brexit, these rules provide the best that could be devised in the circumstances.

C. Jurisdiction and Judgments: The Consequences of Brexit

The key instrument in this area is the recast Brussels I Regulation. This ceased to apply to the UK on Brexit. In order to understand the consequences of this, we must see what the instrument does.

Protecting the Defendant

The recast Brussels I Regulation contains rules for jurisdiction over defendants. Where they apply, these take the place of national rules. The rules in the Regulation are intended to protect defendants from the exorbitant jurisdiction often found under Member State law. However, the rules in the Regulation apply only to defendants domiciled in another Member State. Since Brexit, the jurisdiction of courts in the EU over defendants domiciled in the UK is determined by Member State law, not by the Regulation.[19] The Member State rules are generally much more exorbitant and far-reaching than those in the recast Brussels I Regulation. For example, Article 14 of the French Civil Code permits a French court to take jurisdiction over a defendant whenever the *claimant* is a French citizen.[20] While the recast Brussels I Regulation applied to the UK, persons domiciled in the UK were protected from this rule; now, this is no longer the case. Moreover, judgments against a defendant not domiciled in a Member State must still be recognized and enforced

qualifications, see ibid s 6(4)(b)(i) and (ii). Since it is a criminal court, it is unlikely to be concerned with the two Rome Regulations.

[17] The High Court of Justiciary is included because there are no appeals from it to the UK Supreme Court (except in relation to devolution issues).

[18] European Union (Withdrawal) Act 2018, s 6(5).

[19] Recast Brussels I Regulation, art 6.

[20] There are similar rules in some other Member States. The actual text of art 14 appears to be limited to contracts. It reads: '*L'étranger, même non résident en France, pourra être cité devant les tribunaux français, pour l'exécution des obligations par lui contractées en France avec un Français; il pourra être traduit devant les tribunaux de France pour les obligations par lui contractées en pays étranger envers des Français.*' ('A foreigner, even if not resident in France, may be sued before the French courts for the performance of obligations contracted by him in France with a French citizen; he may be sued in the courts of France for obligations contracted by him in a foreign country with regard to French citizens.') However, it has been interpreted by the French courts to cover almost all claims. Actions concerning foreign land are one of the few exceptions.

in other Member States under the Regulation, even though the court which gave it took jurisdiction under Member State law.[21]

Exclusive Jurisdiction

The Regulation contains rules on exclusive jurisdiction.[22] Where these apply—for example, regarding proceedings concerning rights *in rem* over immovable property—no courts other than those on which exclusive jurisdiction is conferred are permitted to hear the case. However, they apply only if the courts having exclusive jurisdiction are the courts of a Member State. Post-Brexit, these rules no longer apply where the courts with exclusive jurisdiction are those of the UK.

Choice-of-Court Agreements

Under the Regulation, Member State courts are required to respect choice-of-court agreements only if the designated court is in a Member State;[23] post-Brexit, this provision no longer applies to choice-of-court agreements designating UK courts. This has two important consequences: first, courts in the EU are not required by the Regulation to decline jurisdiction if proceedings brought before them are covered by an exclusive choice-of-court agreement designating a court in the UK;[24] second, they are no longer required by the Regulation to recognize and enforce a judgment given by a court in the UK which had jurisdiction under a choice-of-court agreement. However, these problems have been largely solved because the UK has become a party to the Hague Convention on Choice-of-Court Agreements of 2005. Since the EU is also a party, this imposes similar—though slightly less extensive—obligations on the EU to respect choice-of-court agreements designating UK courts. These will be discussed further in section F, below.

Concurrent Proceedings

While the recast Brussels I Regulation applied to the UK, courts in other Member States were obliged under the *lis pendens* doctrine to stay (and subsequently dismiss) proceedings brought before them if a court in the UK was seised first of

[21] Recast Brussels I Regulation, Recital 27.
[22] Recast Brussels I Regulation, art 24.
[23] Recast Brussels I Regulation, art 25.
[24] It is a matter of controversy whether they are even *permitted* to decline jurisdiction if they have jurisdiction under the Regulation. For the details, see Trevor Hartley, *Civil Jurisdiction and Judgments in Europe* (OUP 2017) paras 13.17–13.32.

proceedings involving the same cause of action and between the same parties.[25] Since Brexit, this no longer applies to the UK; instead, courts in the EU are merely *permitted* to stay the proceedings provided certain conditions are satisfied.[26]

Recognition and Enforcement of Judgments

The Regulation provides a simple and effective way of enforcing judgments of one Member State in another Member State. This no longer applies between the EU and the UK. Now judgments from UK courts will be recognized and enforced in the EU, if at all, only under the provisions of Member State law.

These are the most important benefits that the UK has lost in this area from Brexit. In the next section, we will consider how they might be recovered through accession to the Lugano Convention. In sections E and F, we will discuss two Hague Conventions, and in section H, we will outline the powers that UK courts have regained through Brexit, and consider the possible advantages of going it alone.

D. The Lugano Convention of 2007

The original Lugano Convention was concluded in 1988.[27] All the Member States of the EU (then the European Communities) were parties in their own right; the EU (European Communities) was not a party. The other parties were members of EFTA, some of which subsequently became EU Member States. The original Lugano Convention of 1988 was replaced by the revised Lugano Convention of 2007.[28] This was largely based on the original Brussels I Regulation of 2000.[29] For this reason, it does not have anything equivalent to the new provisions introduced into the recast Brussels I Regulation of 2012.

At the time of writing, the parties to the Lugano Convention of 2007 are the EU, Denmark, Iceland, Norway, and Switzerland. It applies to all the EU Member States (except Denmark) by virtue of the fact that they are Member States. Denmark is in a special position because the provisions under which the recast Brussels I Regulation was adopted do not apply to Denmark.[30] The reason the EU is a party,

[25] Recast Brussels I Regulation, art 29.

[26] Recast Brussels I Regulation, arts 33, 34.

[27] Convention on jurisdiction and the enforcement of judgments in civil and commercial matters [1988] OJ L319/9.

[28] Convention on jurisdiction and the recognition and enforcement of judgments in civil and commercial matters [2009] OJ L147/5.

[29] Council Regulation (EC) No 44/2001 of 22 December 2000 on jurisdiction and the recognition and enforcement of judgments in civil and commercial matters (Brussels I Regulation) [2001] OJ L12/1.

[30] Treaty on the Functioning of the European Union, Protocol (No 22) on the Position of Denmark [2012] OJ C326/299. The recast Brussels I Regulation does not apply to Denmark as EU law; it applies by virtue of a special Agreement between Denmark and the EU. The Agreement was signed on behalf of

but not the Member States (except Denmark), is that in the *Lugano Convention* case[31] the CJEU held that the EU had exclusive competence to conclude the Lugano Convention of 2007 because of the impact that it would have on the original Brussels I Regulation of 2000.

On 8 April 2020, the UK applied to become a party to the Lugano Convention of 2007. To do this, it needed the consent of all the other parties, including the EU.[32] When this chapter was originally written, it was unclear whether or not the EU would give its consent. However, on 4 April 2021, the EU Commission issued a communication to the European Parliament and the Council recommending that the Union should *not* give its consent.[33] In view of this, it seems unlikely that the UK will become a party. However, it is still worthwhile considering some of the advantages and disadvantages of the Convention. If the UK had been allowed to join, the Convention would have solved many of the problems caused by the fact that the UK is no longer covered by the recast Brussels I Regulation. The Lugano Convention contains similar jurisdictional rules to Brussels; it has similar provisions regarding choice-of-court agreements and exclusive jurisdiction; it contains similar rules on *lis pendens*; and it has similar provisions on the recognition and enforcement of judgments.

However, since Lugano 2007 does not contain the new provisions introduced by the recast Brussels I Regulation, it does not contain any provisions to nullify the so-called 'Italian torpedo'.[34] This is the name given to the litigation tactic made possible by the decision of the CJEU in the *Gasser* case.[35] In this case, it was held that if there is an exclusive choice-of-court agreement designating the courts of Member State X and one of the parties sues the other first in a matter within the scope of the agreement in Member State Y, the courts of Member State X cannot hear the case until the courts of Member State Y have declined jurisdiction. Although the latter courts are obliged to decline jurisdiction if the choice-of-court agreement is valid, it could take many years for them to do so.[36] This defect was put right in the recast Brussels I Regulation;[37] however, these provisions do not apply under Lugano.

the Union (Community) on 19 October 2005; and concluded by the Union (Community) on 27 April 2006: Council Decision 2006/325/EC of 27 April 2006 concerning the conclusion of the Agreement between the European Community and the Kingdom of Denmark on jurisdiction and the recognition and enforcement of judgments in civil and commercial matters [2006] OJ L120/22.

[31] *Opinion 1/03 pursuant to Article 300(6) EC* EU:C:2006:81, [2006] ECR I-1145.

[32] Lugano Convention of 2007, art 70(1)(c) read with art 72.

[33] *Assessment on the application of the United Kingdom … to accede to the 2007 Lugano Convention*, COM(2021) 222 final, <https://ec.europa.eu/info/files/communication-assessment-application-united-kingdom-great-britain-and-northern-ireland-accede-2007-lugano-convention_nl> accessed 4 April 2022.

[34] This phrase was coined by an Italian *avvocato*, Mario Franzosi: see Mario Franzosi, 'Worldwide Patent Litigation and the Italian Torpedo' (1997) 7 EIPR 382.

[35] *Eric Gasser GmbH v MISAT Srl* (Case C-116/02) EU:C:2003:657, [2003] ECR I-14693.

[36] At the time of the case, the Italian courts were notoriously dilatory. This even gave rise to proceedings before the European Court of Human Rights: see *Ferrari v Italy* App no 33440/96 (ECtHR, 28 July 1999). It is possible that things may be better today.

[37] See recast Brussels I Regulation, arts 29(1), 31(2). See also Recital 22.

This means that the Lugano Convention of 2007 contains the same provisions as were held in the *Gasser* case to allow the 'Italian torpedo' to operate. The result could be that the 'torpedo' is still effective under the Lugano Convention. However, courts in parties to the Lugano Convention that are not EU Member States are not obliged to follow the judgments of the CJEU; they are merely obliged to 'pay due account' to them.[38] Moreover, the provisions of the original Brussels I Regulation of 2000 on which *Gasser* was based do not unequivocally lead to the result in that case—indeed, the UK argued vigorously before the CJEU for the contrary view—and since consistency between the Lugano Convention and the recast Brussels I Regulation is regarded as highly desirable, there is a good case for holding that *Gasser* should not be followed under the Lugano Convention. Nevertheless, the possibility that it might be followed is enough to make the Lugano Convention solution less attractive.

E. The Hague Convention on Recognition and Enforcement of Foreign Judgments of 2019

In 2019, the Hague Conference on Private International Law adopted the Convention of 2 July 2019 on the Recognition and Enforcement of Foreign Judgments in Civil or Commercial Matters.[39] This has a much narrower scope than the recast Brussels I Regulation or Lugano Convention. As its name suggests, it is concerned only with the recognition and enforcement of judgments, just one of the topics—though an important one—covered by the other two instruments. So far, neither the UK nor the EU has ratified it; however, in April 2021, the EU Commission said that it was planning to propose EU conclusion of the Convention in the near future.[40] If the Union does not become a party, it will be of no use as a substitute for the recast Brussels I Regulation.[41]

Like the recast Brussels I Regulation and Lugano Convention, the Hague Convention of 2019 is based on the idea that if the court of origin took jurisdiction on appropriate grounds, its judgment should be recognized and enforced unless there is a reason why it should not. However, this principle is applied in a very different way. The recast Brussels I Regulation and Lugano Convention are based on the principle of direct jurisdiction: the jurisdictional rules contained in them are applied when the court of origin assumes jurisdiction. Any disputes regarding jurisdiction are settled at this point. Once this is done, the jurisdiction of

[38] Lugano Convention of 2007, Protocol 2, art 1(1).

[39] The text is available at <www.hcch.net/en/instruments/conventions/specialised-sections/judgments> accessed 4 April 2022.

[40] COM(2021) 222 final (n 33) 4.

[41] Even if the EU decides to ratify, it could take many years before it is in force with regard to the EU: the Hague Choice of Court Convention took ten years to come into force.

the court of origin cannot normally be challenged in the course of the enforcement process.[42] The Hague Convention of 2019, on the other hand, is based on the theory of indirect jurisdiction: there is no restriction in the Convention on the grounds on which the court of origin may take jurisdiction, but its judgment will be recognized and enforced only if it took jurisdiction on the grounds specified in the Convention. This means that the issue of jurisdiction is contested at the enforcement stage, not when the judgment is originally given. For this reason, enforcement will be a much more complicated matter than under the recast Brussels I Regulation or Lugano Convention.

One can conclude that, though the Hague Convention of 2019 would be better than nothing, it is not a substitute for the Lugano Convention. However, if joining the Lugano Convention proves impossible, and if the EU joins the Hague Convention of 2019, the UK should join it too.

F. The Hague Convention on Choice-of-Court Agreements of 2005

The Hague Choice of Court Convention[43] is a very different proposition. The EU is already a party; so is the UK. It is already in force. It has similar provisions on choice-of-court agreements to those of the recast Brussels I Regulation: if the agreement is exclusive,[44] courts other than those designated must decline jurisdiction; and the judgment of the designated court must be recognized and enforced. Unlike the position under the Lugano Convention, the Italian torpedo does not work under it: see Article 5(2) and the relevant provisions of the Explanatory Report.[45]

The ratification process was subject to several problems. The first was that the decision of the CJEU in the *Lugano Convention* case[46] meant that the Hague Choice of Court Convention fell within the exclusive treaty-making competence of the EU. The Union could (and did) become a party, but the individual Member States (including the UK) could not. The only exception was Denmark, which ratified it in its own right.[47] Few other States ratified. Originally, the only other one

[42] Recast Brussels I Regulation, art 45(3); Lugano Convention of 2007, art 35(3). There are a small number of exceptions. For the recast Brussels I Regulation, see arts 45(1)(e)(i) (insurance, consumer contracts and employment contracts) and 45(1)(e)(ii) (exclusive jurisdiction). For the Lugano Convention of 2007, see art 35(1) (insurance, consumer contracts and exclusive jurisdiction, but not employment contracts).

[43] Available on the website of the Hague Conference: <www.hcch.net> accessed 4 April 2022.

[44] The Convention only applies if the agreement is exclusive: see below.

[45] Explanatory Report, paras 127, 133–34. The Report is available in English and French at: <https://assets.hcch.net/docs/0de60e2f-e002-408e-98a7-5638e1ebac65.pdf> accessed 4 April 2022.

[46] *Opinion 1/03 pursuant to Article 300(6) EC* EU:C:2006:81, [2006] ECR I-1145.

[47] For the reason, see text to n 30.

was Mexico; so it came into force between the EU (except Denmark) and Mexico on 1 October 2015,[48] some ten years after it was adopted. Denmark ratified separately, and it came into force for Denmark on 1 September 2018. Other States parties were Montenegro (in force on 1 August 2018) and Singapore (in force on 1 October 2016). It came into force in the EU Member States, other than Denmark, by virtue of their being Member States.[49] This occurred on 1 October 2015.

The Convention originally came into force in the UK (by virtue of it being an EU Member State) on 1 October 2015. It continued to be in force for the UK on that basis until the end of the transition period at 11pm (UK time) on 31 December 2020.[50] After this, it could no longer apply in the UK on that basis. However, Article 27(3) of the Convention provides that it is open to accession by all States. Instruments of accession must be deposited with the Ministry of Foreign Affairs of the Netherlands, the Netherlands being the depositary. Where a State accedes to the Convention, the Convention enters into force for that State on the first day of the month following the expiration of three months after the deposit of its instrument of accession.[51] The UK deposited its instrument of accession on 28 September 2020; so the Convention entered into force for the UK on the first day of January 2021. In the view of the UK, this meant 00.00 CET on 1 January 2021 (equivalent to 11pm UK time on 31 December 2020). This seems correct, since the Netherlands follows CET and, as the Netherlands is the depositary, this should apply for the purpose of the entry into force of the Convention. Since the Convention ceased to apply to the UK under EU law at this same moment, there seems to have been no gap in its application. One can conclude that it originally entered into force for the UK on 1 October 2015 and that it applied without interruption since that date.[52] The Status Table on the Hague Conference website is in accord with this: it states that the Convention entered into force for the UK on 1 October 2015 and gives the date of accession (the date when the UK deposited its instrument of accession) as 28 September 2020. This could be important with respect to the transitional problems discussed below.

[48] See the Status Table for the Convention on the Hague Conference website: <www.hcch.net/en/instruments/conventions/status-table/?cid=98> accessed 4 April 2022.

[49] See Hague Choice of Court Convention, art 30.

[50] Agreement on the Withdrawal of the United Kingdom of Great Britain and Northern Ireland from the European Union and the European Atomic Energy Community [2020] OJ L29/7, art 127(1). The Hague Choice of Court Convention falls within the definition of 'Union law' in art 2(a)(iv) of the Withdrawal Agreement.

[51] Convention, art 31(2)(a).

[52] This is the view of the UK Government: see the *Note Verbale* accompanying the UK Declaration of 28 September 2020, available on the Hague Conference website: <www.hcch.net/en/instruments/conventions/status-table/?cid=98> accessed 4 April 2022.

Transitional Problems

There is no doubt that choice-of-court agreements concluded after the beginning of 2021 which designate a court in the UK will be covered by the Convention. The problem lies with agreements concluded before that date (but after 1 October 2015) which come before the courts after the beginning of 2021. Will courts in EU Member States accept that the Convention applies to such agreements? According to Article 16 of the Convention, two conditions must be fulfilled. First, the agreement must have been concluded after the entry into force of the Convention for the State of the chosen court; second, the proceedings must have been instituted after its entry into force for the State of the court seised. In the situation we are considering, these conditions are clearly fulfilled.

A second problem concerns the effect of the recast Brussels I Regulation. A choice-of-court agreement designating a court in the UK which was concluded after 1 October 2015 but before the end of 2020 would almost certainly be covered by the recast Brussels I Regulation as well as the Hague Choice of Court Convention. It was originally thought that such an agreement would continue to be covered by the recast Brussels I Regulation, even if court proceedings in the UK did not begin until after the beginning of 2021. However, the EU–UK Withdrawal Agreement provides that the recast Brussels I Regulation will not apply unless the proceedings in the UK begin before the end of 2020.[53] So the recast Brussels I Regulation will not help in the situation we are considering.

But what about the Hague Choice of Court Convention? Originally, some people thought that if an agreement was covered by Brussels when it was made, this automatically meant that Hague could not apply. This view was based on Article 26(6) of Hague, which provides:

> (6) This Convention shall not affect the application of the rules of a Regional Economic Integration Organisation that is a party to this Convention, whether adopted before or after this Convention—
>
> a) where none of the parties is resident in a Contracting State that is not a Member State of the Regional Economic Integration Organisation;
>
> b) as concerns the recognition or enforcement of judgments as between Member States of the Regional Economic Integration Organisation.

The EU is a Regional Economic Integration Organization—the term was specially coined for this purpose—and the recast Brussels I Regulation is a 'rule' of the Union; so Hague does not 'affect' the application of the recast Brussels I Regulation where none of the parties is resident in a non-Member State. However, this does

[53] EU–UK Withdrawal Agreement, art 67(2)(a).

not mean that Hague does not apply to such an agreement: it simply means that Brussels prevails in the event of a conflict. This is made clear by the Explanatory Report to the Convention.[54] When the recast Brussels I Regulation ceased to apply in the UK (after the end of 2020), the Hague Choice of Court Convention could operate unencumbered by it: the requirements of Article 16 of Hague would be satisfied.

Exclusive Choice-of-Court Agreements

It is important to note that the Convention covers only *exclusive* choice-of-court agreements.[55] Article 22 provides for reciprocal declarations on non-exclusive choice-of-court agreements, but neither the EU nor the UK has made such a declaration. To be covered by the Convention, the agreement must designate, 'for the purpose of deciding disputes which have arisen or may arise in connection with a particular legal relationship, the courts of one Contracting State or one or more specific courts of one Contracting State to the exclusion of the jurisdiction of any other courts'.[56] However, agreements are deemed to be exclusive unless they expressly provide otherwise.[57] It was decided in the Conference that choice-of-court agreements must be exclusive irrespective of which party brings the proceedings: asymmetric choice-of-court agreements are *not* covered. This is made clear in the Minutes of the Proceedings[58] and in the Explanatory Report.[59]

Subject-Matter Scope

The subject-matter scope is distinctly narrower than that of either the recast Brussels I Regulation or the Lugano Convention. For example, the Convention does not apply to:

[54] Explanatory Report, paras 267, 291ff.

[55] Hague Choice of Court Convention, art 1(1). Art 22 provides for reciprocal declarations on non-exclusive choice-of-court agreements, but neither the EU nor the UK has made such a declaration.

[56] Hague Choice of Court Convention, art 3(a). This means, for example, that the parties can designate: 'the courts of the UK'; 'the courts of England'; or 'the courts of England or the courts of Scotland'. They cannot, however, designate 'the courts of England or the courts of Belgium'.

[57] Hague Choice of Court Convention, art 3(b).

[58] *Hague Conference on Private International Law, Proceedings of the Twentieth Session, Volume III, Choice of Court, Minutes No 3, Meeting of Wednesday 15 June 2005 (morning)*, 578. This states: 'The Chair concluded the debate noting that there was no support for the proposal to amend Article 3(a). He noted moreover that the view of the Commission was that asymmetric agreements were not covered by the Convention and that the Convention was not designed for clauses of this sort.' The word 'Commission' here refers to the Diplomatic Conference which drew up the text of the Convention.

[59] See paras 105, 106.

- the carriage of passengers and goods (which excludes choice-of-court agreements in bills of lading);[60]
- marine pollution, limitation of liability for maritime claims, general average, and emergency towage and salvage;[61]
- anti-trust (competition) matters;[62]
- the validity of intellectual property rights other than copyright and related rights;[63] and
- the infringement of intellectual property rights other than copyright and related rights, except where infringement proceedings are brought for breach of a contract between the parties relating to such rights, or could have been brought for breach of that contract.[64]

Greater Flexibility

Another feature of the Convention is that it is significantly more flexible than the recast Brussels I Regulation or Lugano Convention. The requirement that a non-designated court must give up jurisdiction is subject to several exceptions. For example, it is not required to suspend or dismiss the proceedings before it if a party lacked the capacity to conclude the choice-of-court agreement under the law of the State of the (non-designated) court seised;[65] or if giving effect to the agreement would lead to a manifest injustice or would be manifestly contrary to the public policy of the State of the court seised.[66] These features give a non-designated court more scope to hear the case despite the choice-of-court agreement. Moreover, judgments given by the designated court do not have to be recognized by courts in other States parties to the Convention in a wider range of circumstances than apply under the recast Brussels I Regulation or the Lugano Convention.[67]

If the UK Joins the Lugano Convention 2007

Since the Lugano Convention was concluded in 2007 and the Hague Choice of Court Convention was concluded in 2005, the Lugano Convention would prevail

[60] Art 2(1)(f).
[61] Art 2(1)(g).
[62] Art 2(1)(h).
[63] Art 2(1)(n).
[64] Art 2(1)(o).
[65] Hague Choice of Court Convention, art 6(b). This is in addition to the rule—also found in the recast Brussels I Regulation, art 25(1)—that the choice-of-court agreement will be invalid if it is null and void under the law of the *designated* court.
[66] Hague Choice of Court Convention, art 6(c).
[67] See Hague Choice of Court Convention, art 9.

over the Hague Choice of Court Convention, as between the UK and the EU Member States, to the extent of any incompatibility between the two treaties. This follows from Article 30(4)(a) of the Vienna Convention on the Law of Treaties 1969; it also follows from Article 26(2) of the Hague Convention. There would be an exception if one of the parties to the proceedings was resident in Mexico, Montenegro, or Singapore. Since this will rarely be the case, however, the Hague Convention would lose much of its importance if the UK joined the Lugano Convention. As far as choice-of-court agreements are concerned, the main drawback of joining the Lugano Convention would be that the 'Italian torpedo' might work under the Lugano Convention, while it does not work under Hague.[68] In addition, antisuit injunctions are probably prohibited under the Lugano Convention,[69] while they are not prohibited under the Hague Choice of Court Convention.[70]

G. Bilateral Arrangements?

Would it be possible for the UK to have bilateral arrangements in this field with individual States? In the case of non-Member States, there would seem to be no problem. The difficulty with entering into a bilateral arrangement with a Member State is that in the *Lugano Convention* case[71] the CJEU held that the EU had exclusive competence to conclude the Lugano Convention of 2007 because of the impact that it would have on the original Brussels I Regulation. It follows from this that EU Member States lack the competence to conclude any agreement with a non-Member State (such as the UK) if that agreement would impact on the recast Brussels I Regulation or any other EU measure.

This problem might be overcome by ensuring that the new convention did not in any way impact on the recast Brussels I Regulation or Lugano Convention. The convention could expressly provide that it would not affect the obligations of the Member State under EU law. Such a provision would not destroy the utility of the convention because it is only in limited areas that such a convention would impact on the recast Brussels I Regulation or Lugano Convention. In the *Lugano Convention* case, the CJEU came up with only two examples: choice-of-court agreements and exclusive jurisdiction.[72] However, it is possible that if a Member State were to conclude such a convention with the UK, the CJEU would produce some new ground for holding it contrary to EU law. In any event, Member States

[68] See text to n 45.
[69] See text to n 77.
[70] See text to n 78.
[71] *Opinion 1/03 pursuant to Article 300(6) EC* EU:C:2006:81, [2006] ECR I-1145.
[72] See para 153 of the judgment.

might be wary of entering into a bilateral convention for fear of the political consequences.[73] So this is a rather dubious proposition.

H. Going It Alone

Up until now, we have been considering what the UK has lost in the area of private international law as a result of Brexit. It should now be considered what advantages there are. In the area of civil jurisdiction and judgments, there are three areas in which limits on the powers of UK courts have been removed. The first is that they are no longer precluded from hearing cases which fall within the exclusive jurisdiction of the courts of an EU Member State—for example, concerning rights *in rem* in immovable property located in that Member State; second, they are no longer required to stay or dismiss proceedings if the courts of an EU Member State are seised first (*lis pendens* doctrine); third, they are no longer precluded from granting antisuit injunctions with respect to proceedings in the courts of a Member State.

The third of these is by far the most important. Even before the UK joined the EU, it was only in very rare cases that UK courts would not respect the exclusive jurisdiction of foreign courts. In the case of rights *in rem* in foreign land, for example, this was established as long ago as 1893 by the House of Lords in the well-known case of *British South Africa Co v Companhia de Moçambique*.[74] The *lis pendens* doctrine was not applied by English courts before the UK joined the EU; instead, the theory of *forum non conveniens* was applied. However, this is not fully viable unless it can be backed up by an antisuit injunction.

The prohibitions regarding exclusive jurisdiction and *lis pendens* follow from express provisions in the recast Brussels I Regulation[75] and Lugano Convention.[76] The rule outlawing antisuit injunctions, on the other hand, is judge-made. It was originally laid down by the CJEU in *Turner v Grovit*.[77] It was based on the principle of mutual trust and the idea—which the CJEU regarded as inherent in that principle—that the rules on jurisdiction in the Regulation (and earlier Convention) may be interpreted and applied with the same authority by all courts in the EU. So, any attempt by the courts of one Member State to impose their view on the courts of another Member State would be contrary to the principle of mutual trust. Since the Lugano Convention is based on the same principles as Brussels, the prohibition against antisuit injunctions probably applies under it as well.

[73] This might be the case even with respect to a purely informal arrangement in which the UK gave advantages to the Member State in the expectation that they would be reciprocated.
[74] [1893] AC 602.
[75] Arts 24 (exclusive jurisdiction), 29ff (*lis pendens*).
[76] Arts 22 (exclusive jurisdiction), 27ff (*lis pendens*).
[77] Case C-159/02 EU:C:2004:228, [2004] ECR I-3565 (Full Court).

There is no rule in the Hague Choice of Court Convention expressly dealing with antisuit injunctions. Article 7 of the Convention provides that interim measures of protection are neither required nor precluded by the Convention. If antisuit injunctions are regarded as 'interim measures of protection', this would establish that they are not precluded. Even if they are not regarded as interim measures, the result would be the same.[78] So antisuit injunctions are not precluded by the Hague Choice of Court Convention.

Antisuit injunctions are crucial to any policy of 'going it alone'. In the past, they proved extremely effective against the courts of continental European States. This was because European courts did not retaliate. With the US, it was a different story, as the *Laker Airways* litigation proved.[79] However, such injunctions are unlikely to be as effective in the future as they were in the past, since courts in EU countries will almost certainly grant counter-antisuit injunctions in response to them. A counter-antisuit injunction is an injunction requiring the party who obtained the antisuit injunction to have it rescinded. Such injunctions have recently been granted by leading continental courts with respect to antisuit injunctions granted by US courts.[80] They are enforced by a fine, possibly a penalty of a specified amount per day until the antisuit injunction is lifted.

Contrary to what might be thought, such a penalty would be enforceable in other EU Member States under the recast Brussels I Regulation, provided that the substantive claim to which the antisuit injunction applied came within the scope of the Regulation. This would be so even if the penalty was payable to, and enforceable by, the State or some other public authority. This follows from the rule of EU law that in deciding whether an ancillary order falls within the scope of the Regulation, one must consider not the nature of the order itself, but the nature of the rights it is intended to protect.[81]

The CJEU judgment in *Realchemie Nederland v Bayer CropScience*[82] is an example. This did not concern a counter-antisuit injunction, but an order given by a German court in a patent-infringement action under which the defendant, a Dutch company, was required to refrain from importing into, possessing, or marketing certain products in Germany. It was also ordered to provide details of its commercial transactions involving the product and to transfer its stock into the custody of the courts. The fine was imposed when it failed to obey the order. The

[78] Antisuit injunctions were not expressly mentioned in the discussions in the conference because they were regarded as too contentious.

[79] *British Airways Board v Laker Airways Ltd* [1985] AC 58. For a full description, see Trevor C Hartley, 'Comity and the Use of Antisuit Injunctions in International Litigation' (1987) 35 Am J Comp Law 487.

[80] *Continental v Nokia* Oberlandesgericht München [Munich Court of Appeal] 12 December 2019, case no 6 U 5042/19; *Lenovo (US) Inc v IPCom GmbH & Co Kg* Cour d'appel de Paris [Paris Court of Appeal] 3 March 2020, case no RG 19/21426.

[81] Case C–406/09 *Realchemie Nederland BV v Bayer CropScience AG* EU:C:2011:668, [2011] ECR I-9773, [40].

[82] ibid.

CJEU held, applying the principle set out above, that the fine had to be enforced in the Netherlands under the Regulation, even though it was payable to the German State, not to the claimant. The final ruling of the CJEU stated that the Regulation applies to 'the recognition and enforcement of a decision of a court or tribunal that contains an order to pay a fine in order to ensure compliance with a judgment given in a civil and commercial matter'. In view of this, a party who obtained an antisuit injunction in England might find that his assets throughout the EU were in jeopardy.

I. Conclusions

In the area of civil jurisdiction and judgments, joining the Lugano Convention would have had much to recommend it. If, as seems likely, this proves impossible, the Hague Choice of Court Convention would solve many of the problems in the limited, though important, area of choice-of-court agreements. If the EU joins it, the Hague Convention on Recognition and Enforcement of Foreign Judgments in Civil or Commercial Matters of 2019 would also be of help.

11
Exorbitant Jurisdiction and the Common Law

Alex Mills

A. Introduction

This chapter draws on two perennial themes in the uniquely distinguished career of Lord Collins in legal practice, the judiciary, and academia. The first is the topic of the common law rules on civil jurisdiction, including in particular the exercise of jurisdiction over defendants who are not present in England at the time of commencement of proceedings. The second is the relationship between public and private international law, two bodies of law which have sometimes been viewed by academics as unrelated (although it may tentatively be suggested that this is decreasing),[1] but which are frequently entangled in questions of legal practice.

In relation to these two themes, the chapter makes three points, in respect of which it happily acknowledges a debt to the work of Lord Collins. First, that the common law approach to civil jurisdiction has traditionally been based on an unfortunate conflation between adjudicative and enforcement jurisdiction as those concepts are now understood in public international law. Second, that this has led to some regrettable suggestions that the exercise of civil jurisdiction over non-present defendants necessarily raises significant concerns and may thus generally be labelled 'exorbitant'—although there have been at least partial moves away from this position in recent years. Third, that some of the grounds of jurisdiction under which the common law rules permit the exercise of jurisdiction over non-present defendants are, however, contentious as jurisdictional justifications, and their rationales deserve closer consideration. The usefulness of the term exorbitant to describe these grounds of jurisdiction is questionable, but their foundations in policy and principle, if accepted, suggest an important general shift in the perspective on the exercise of civil jurisdiction under the common law.

[1] See eg Duncan French, Kasey McCall-Smith, and Veronica Ruiz Abou-Nigm (eds), *Linkages and Boundaries in Private and Public International Law* (Hart 2018); Alex Mills, *The Confluence of Public and Private International Law* (CUP 2009).

Alex Mills, *Exorbitant Jurisdiction and the Common Law* In: *Essays in International Litigation for Lord Collins.*
Edited by: Jonathan Harris and Campbell McLachlan, Oxford University Press. © Oxford University Press 2022.
DOI: 10.1093/oso/9780192867988.003.0012

B. The Foundations of Common Law Jurisdiction

The modern English courts are undoubtedly a leading place, perhaps even *the* leading place, for the judicial resolution of international commercial disputes. The practice and perspective of the courts is intensely international. The courts are open and available to resolve the commercial disputes of the world—they are very likely, for example, to exercise jurisdiction over any dispute arising under a commercial contract which contains an English jurisdiction agreement, regardless of whether the parties or their dispute have any connection to England.[2]

The present international position and outlook of the English courts is all the more remarkable when it is considered that historically the jurisdiction of the English courts was deeply domestic and indeed somewhat parochial in its approach. Two features of the historical jurisdiction of the English courts may be illustrative here.

The first is that the jurisdiction of the courts was at one time limited to cases in which the subject matter of the dispute occurred in England.[3] This limitation arose because civil proceedings were traditionally subject to jury trial, and juries performed the role of both witnesses to and adjudicators of disputes. This meant that juries had to be empanelled from the local area in which a dispute arose—they were, in the words of the Magna Carta, 'reputable men of the neighbourhood'.[4] The English court had no power to order foreign parties to serve in juries, which initially rendered the courts powerless to deal with disputes concerning foreign property or events. Over time, however, the role of jurors as witnesses diminished, and the procedural difficulty of empanelling a local jury was overcome—initially through the adoption of legal fictions, which survived as late as the end of the eighteenth century. For example, in a case involving property in Brussels, a plaintiff might plead (and the defendant would accept) that Brussels was in London, in order that a 'local' jury could be empanelled.[5] The need for such fictions was itself ultimately eliminated, and it became possible for the English courts to hear disputes in which the relevant events occurred outside England.

A second and (for current purposes) more significant limitation on the jurisdiction of the English courts survived later, until the middle of the nineteenth century. The jurisdiction of the courts was historically limited to cases in which the defendant was 'present' in England at the time of commencement of the proceedings.

[2] This was traditionally the case under the common law rules, and continued to be the case under the EU rules on jurisdiction in the Brussels Convention and Brussels I Regulation during their time of application. Other international practice is more variable: see further eg Alex Mills, *Party Autonomy in Private International Law* (CUP 2018) ch 3.

[3] See eg Paul Torremans and others, *Cheshire, North & Fawcett: Private International Law* (15th edn, OUP 2017) 17ff; Alex Mills, 'The Private History of International Law' (2006) 55 ICLQ 1; JH Baker, 'The Law Merchant and the Common Law before 1700' (1979) 38 Cambridge LJ 295.

[4] Magna Carta (1215) [20].

[5] A typical example is *Mostyn v Fabrigas* (1774) 1 Cowp 161, 98 ER 1021.

For natural persons, this meant (and continues to mean) mere physical presence, however transitory, and for companies this has come to mean a fixed place of business.[6] This limitation arose because the initiation of civil proceedings was based on service of a writ on the defendant, a form of sovereign command which compelled the defendant to appear before court, and it was considered that such a sovereign command could only be issued within the territory of the State.[7] Up until the mid-nineteenth century, in order for civil proceedings to be commenced against a party in the English courts, it was *necessary*—indeed, it was also *sufficient*—for the courts to have physical authority over the person of the defendant.[8] Once the problem of empanelling juries was resolved, it was also unnecessary for the case to concern events which had taken place in England, as long as the defendant had been subject to service within English territory.

In modern international law terms, this was a conflation of what would now be considered adjudicative jurisdiction and enforcement jurisdiction (although it is not suggested that the law of jurisdiction was fully developed or understood in these terms in the nineteenth century).[9] In modern international law, enforcement jurisdiction, the power of a State to exercise physical control over a person or thing, remains strictly territorial in the absence of a special rule or permission. States generally may only seize a person or property within their territorial boundaries. Adjudicative jurisdiction, the exercise of judicial authority, is sometimes linked to enforcement jurisdiction in the criminal context. This is the case if, for example, a State does not permit a trial '*in absentia*', but requires the presence of the defendant (and thus their subjection to enforcement power) before a prosecution can take place. In the civil context, however, courts around the world readily hear cases brought against defendants who are not present in the territory in a range of circumstances, based on a connection between the dispute or the parties and the forum State. This is sometimes characterized as an exercise of prescriptive jurisdiction, and sometimes as a distinctive exercise of adjudicative jurisdiction—in the civil context, it is also complicated by the fact that courts may apply foreign law,

[6] See eg *Adams v Cape Industries* [1990] Ch 433 (CA); *HRH Maharanee of Baroda v Wildenstein* [1972] 2 QB 283.

[7] See further Lawrence Collins, 'Some Aspects of Service out of the Jurisdiction in English Law' (1972) 21 ICLQ 656, 658 (noting the enduring influence of this perspective in the statement of Scott LJ that service outside England constitutes an 'interference with the exclusive jurisdiction of the sovereignty of the foreign country where service is to be effected'—*George Monro v American Cyanamid* [1944] KB 432, 437).

[8] It has been persuasively argued that the early historical focus was not on presence, but rather the (voluntary or compelled) appearance of the defendant—though this does not affect the general point that enforcement power over the person was essential to the exercise of jurisdiction. See Andrew Dickinson, 'Keeping Up Appearances—The Development of Adjudicatory Jurisdiction in the English Courts' (2017) 86 Br YB Intl L 1.

[9] See generally eg Alex Mills, 'Rethinking Jurisdiction in International Law' (2014) 84 Br YB Intl L 187; Cedric Ryngaert, *Jurisdiction in International Law* (2nd edn, OUP 2015).

and thus effectively 'prescribe' the law of another State.[10] Whether the exercise of such jurisdiction will be practically enforceable is a further question, which in the civil context depends more on the location of the defendant's assets than the defendant themselves. Although the question of whether the defendant has assets in the territory may be taken into account in determining whether or not it would be appropriate for a court to exercise its jurisdiction, because this affects the potential appropriateness of the court hearing the case,[11] in the common law this does not affect the availability of jurisdiction per se.[12] The key point is that, from the perspective of international law, there is no reason why the commencement of civil proceedings should be understood to require the exercise or indeed even the possibility of enforcement jurisdiction over the defendant. The traditional common law position that enforcement jurisdiction was a *sine qua non* for adjudicative jurisdiction is anomalous.

The possibility for jurisdiction over non-present defendants was opened up in the mid-nineteenth century in England, through the adoption of rules permitting a defendant to be 'served' outside the territory where 'there is a Cause of Action, which arose within the Jurisdiction, or in respect of the Breach of a Contract made within the Jurisdiction'.[13] Power over the defendant was thus no longer *necessary* to the commencement of proceedings. To avoid the suggestion that this involved an impermissible sovereign command in a foreign territory, service in such cases was considered to be of *notice* of the writ, rather than the writ itself.[14] This subtle change reflected an important and fundamental shift in the perspective on the law of jurisdiction in the English courts, which was no longer considered to be founded only on *power* over the defendant, but also potentially based on a connection with the cause of action, combined with considerations of *fairness* in relation to the defendant. Notice of the proceedings is evidently not enough on its own to satisfy the requirements of fairness, but it is equally evidently an indispensable element. The requirements of fairness were further addressed by the narrowly defined circumstances in which proceedings could be commenced against a non-present defendant—these limited jurisdiction to cases in which the dispute had a connection with England which would justify the assertion of authority. The modern and enlarged version of this list of jurisdictional 'gateways' (as they are commonly known) is of course found in Practice Direction 6B of the Civil Procedure Rules,

[10] See eg Alex Mills, 'Private Interests and Private Law Regulation in Public International Law Jurisdiction' in Stephen Allen and others (eds), *Oxford Handbook of Jurisdiction in International Law* (OUP 2019).

[11] See eg *Colt Industries v Sarlie (No 1)* [1966] 1 WLR 440.

[12] It may, however, affect the orders which it is within the authority of the court to make, sometimes referred to as a question of subject-matter jurisdiction—see eg *SAS Institute Inc v World Programming Ltd* [2020] EWCA Civ 599; *Masri v Consolidated Contractors International (UK) Ltd (No 2)* [2008] EWCA Civ 303, [2009] QB 450 (Collins LJ).

[13] Common Law Procedure Act 1852, XVIII in conjunction with XVIX. See further Dickinson (n 8).

[14] Common Law Procedure Act 1852, XVIX and Sch A, No 3. See generally eg Collins (n 7) 656ff. This was not, however, the case for non-present British subjects: see Dickinson (n 8).

discussed further below. Finally, considerations of fairness to defendants and comity to foreign States have also long been taken into account in the fact that the commencement of proceedings against a non-present defendant requires the permission of the court—a feature of the English law of jurisdiction which remains prominent and significant today, under the doctrine of *forum conveniens*.[15] In 'service out' cases, the claimant is under a burden of proof to demonstrate that there is no other clearly more appropriate forum than the English courts which might deliver justice in the case. The exercise of this form of jurisdiction, although commonplace and largely normalized, retains residual markers of its historical origins as an exceptional and controversial expansion of jurisdiction based on power over the defendant, as discussed further below.

It remains the case that the jurisdiction of the English courts may be established based on the mere presence of the defendant in England at the time of commencement of proceedings.[16] However, this form of jurisdiction has also been modified by considerations of fairness and comity, through the adoption of the *forum non conveniens* discretion under which proceedings commenced on this basis may be stayed if there is another clearly more appropriate forum.[17] Power over the defendant is thus no longer considered *sufficient* to justify the exercise of jurisdiction—indeed, to the contrary, mere power over the defendant is likely to be insufficient to justify the exercise of jurisdiction, in the absence of other connecting factors justifying the involvement of the English courts.

For present purposes, the key conclusion is that the common law historically conflated enforcement and adjudicative jurisdiction, in a way which made the presence of the defendant at the time of commencement of the proceedings both necessary and sufficient for the exercise of jurisdiction. The law has significantly departed from that position, and the presence of the defendant is no longer either necessary or sufficient to the exercise of civil jurisdiction, but that historical perspective has continued to shape the jurisdiction of the English courts, as discussed above and as will be explored further in the next section.

C. Judicial Hesitancy in Service Out Cases

As noted above, it was not until the mid-nineteenth century that the English courts permitted proceedings to be commenced against defendants who were not able to be served with proceedings in English territory. The extension of jurisdiction beyond this restriction was initially somewhat hesitant, a hesitancy captured in

[15] An early and undoubtedly influential call for clarification of this doctrine may be found in Collins (n 7) at 660ff.

[16] See n 6.

[17] See generally *The Spiliada* [1987] AC 460, discussed further below.

the label 'exorbitant' which has frequently but not consistently been applied in this context. This has influenced approaches to the interpretation and application of the rules governing jurisdiction in cases in which the defendant must be served outside the territory, in two major ways: first, in relation to the exercise of the court's *forum conveniens* discretion; and, second, perhaps in a more limited way, in relation to the interpretation of the grounds of jurisdiction. More recent judicial pronouncements have, however, suggested a move away from characterizing the grounds or exercise of jurisdiction in this context as exorbitant, at least as a general matter. Each of these impacts is discussed in turn below, before consideration of what role is left for the term 'exorbitant' in this context.

The Exercise of Discretion in Service Out Cases

The traditional English hesitancy in exercising jurisdiction over a defendant who cannot be served within the territory has found expression through the *forum conveniens* discretion. Pursuant to this discretion, a claimant who seeks to commence proceedings against a defendant outside the territory is under a burden of proof to persuade the court that there is no other clearly more appropriate forum which would be able to deliver justice in the case. This may be contrasted with the doctrine of *forum non conveniens*, which applies where proceedings are commenced against a defendant present in England, and that defendant seeks to persuade the court to stay the proceedings in favour of an alternative foreign court. In this context, the defendant is under a burden of proof to persuade the court that there is another clearly more appropriate forum than the English courts, although if the defendant is successful in making this argument, the claimant has the further opportunity to persuade the court that the proceedings should not be stayed because they would be denied justice if denied access to the English courts (for which the burden falls on the claimant). The distinction between the *forum conveniens* and *forum non conveniens* tests may not always be practically decisive in particular cases, but it nevertheless reflects a basic assumption that the exercise of jurisdiction over a defendant who may be served in England is acceptable unless demonstrated otherwise, while the exercise of jurisdiction beyond those constraints is not acceptable unless demonstrated otherwise.

This assumption has further been reflected in judicial comment on the significance of the burden which must be overcome by the claimant in *forum conveniens* cases. An early indication of this influence was provided in *Société Générale de Paris v Dreyfus Brothers* (1885),[18] in which the court observed:

[18] 29 Ch D 239.

> It becomes a very serious question ... whether this court ought to put a foreigner, who owes no allegiance here, to the inconvenience and annoyance of being brought to contest his rights in this country, and I for one say, most distinctly, that I think this court ought to be exceedingly careful before it allows a writ to be served out of the jurisdiction.[19]

This statement was approved in *The Hagen* (1908)[20] and *Tyne Improvement Commissioners v Armement Anversois SA (The Brabo)* (1949).[21] Lord Collins, writing in 1972, observed that 'the trend of the authorities under Order 11 [the predecessor to Practice Direction 6B of the Civil Procedure Rules] is that extreme caution must be exercised before granting leave to serve out of the jurisdiction'.[22] He further submitted that 'the discretion *is* limited and should not be exercised against a foreigner in doubtful cases',[23] although it may be noted that this comment was made in the context of (rightly) criticizing a decision in which the court had exercised its discretion to hear a dispute in order to allow the claimant to avoid the application of foreign law.[24] In *Cherney v Deripaska* (2008),[25] Christopher Clarke J observed that '[i]n granting permission to serve out of the jurisdiction the court is exercising an exorbitant jurisdiction over those who are not within its ordinary reach',[26] and this was cited approvingly by the Court of Appeal in *Trust Risk Group SPA v Amtrust Europe Ltd* (2015).[27] Equivalent views were expressed strongly by the Court of Appeal in *Cecil v Bayat* (2011).[28] To similar effect, the distinguished authors of *Dicey, Morris & Collins* (15th edition, 2012) note that 'the court will refuse permission if the case is within the letter but outside the spirit of the Rule',[29] a proposition that goes at least as far back as *Johnson v Taylor Bros & Co, Ltd* (1920).[30] There is thus a clear line of authority[31] running from the nineteenth century almost to the present which indicates a continued reluctance to assert jurisdiction over defendants who are not present in the territory.

This line of cases has come, however, to something of a dramatic halt in recent years (a halt which, slightly awkwardly, pre-dates the most recent case cited above). In *Abela v Baadarani* (2013),[32] Lord Sumption (with whom the court agreed

19 At 242–43.
20 [1908] P 189, 201.
21 [1949] AC 326, 350.
22 Collins (n 7) 671.
23 ibid 672 (emphasis in the original).
24 *Coast Lines v Hudeg & Veder Chartering NV* [1972] 1 All ER 451.
25 [2008] EWHC 1530 (Comm).
26 At [41].
27 [2015] EWCA Civ 437, [2015] 2 Lloyd's Rep 154 [41].
28 [2011] EWCA Civ 135, [2011] 1 WLR 3086 [63].
29 Lord Collins (ed), *Dicey, Morris & Collins on the Conflict of Laws* (15th edn, Sweet & Maxwell 2012) para 11-142.
30 [1920] AC 144 (HL), 153 (Viscount Haldane).
31 For further cases, see citations in Lawrence Collins, 'Sovereignty and Exorbitant Jurisdiction' (2014) 130 LQR 555.
32 [2013] UKSC 44, [2013] 1 WLR 2043.

unanimously on this point)[33] expressly rejected the view that the permission to serve outside the jurisdiction should be approached from the perspective that such cases necessarily involved the exercise of an 'exorbitant' jurisdiction:

> in the overwhelming majority of cases where service out is authorised there will have been either a contractual submission to the jurisdiction of the English court or else a substantial connection between the dispute and this country ... Litigation between residents of different states is a routine incident of modern commercial life. A jurisdiction similar to that exercised by the English court is now exercised by the courts of many other countries.... It should no longer be necessary to resort to the kind of muscular presumptions against service out which are implicit in adjectives like 'exorbitant'. The decision is generally a pragmatic one in the interests of the efficient conduct of litigation in an appropriate forum.[34]

Taking up this approach, the Court of Appeal in *Kaefer Aislamientos SA De CV v AMS Drilling Mexico SA De CV* (2019)[35] has more recently held that:

> Historically, it has been said that the Courts should apply a high threshold before asserting jurisdiction because permitting parties from third countries to be made subject to the domestic courts through service of proceedings abroad was an '*exorbitant*' jurisdiction entitling the assertion of sovereign power over a defendant and a commensurate interference with the sovereignty of the state in which service is affected ... This logic was however doubted in *Abela* ... as unrealistic in the modern era: routinely where service out is authorised the defendant will have submitted contractually to the jurisdiction of the domestic courts (or there would be an argument to that effect) and in any event litigation between residents of different states is a normal incident of modern global business. As such the decision to permit service out is, today, more generally viewed as a pragmatic decision predicated upon the efficiency of the conduct of litigation.[36]

Issue should be taken with the suggestion that, in 2019, 'routinely where service out is authorized the defendant will have submitted contractually to the jurisdiction of the domestic courts' (which echoes directly Lord Sumption's judgment in *Abela*). Where the English courts are relying on a jurisdiction agreement in their favour, the basis of jurisdiction in a civil and commercial matter has, since 2015, been invariably provided by the Recast Brussels I Regulation 2012, in respect of which permission is not required to commence proceedings based on an English jurisdiction

[33] See also [45] (Lord Clarke).
[34] At [53]. See also discussion in *Tiger Yacht Management Ltd v Morris* [2019] FCAFC 8, (2019) 366 ALR 410.
[35] [2019] EWCA Civ 10, [2019] 1 WLR 3514.
[36] At [85].

agreement.[37] While the continued applicability of this Regulation in England has not survived Brexit, the Civil Procedure Rules have recently been amended to remove the requirement for permission to be obtained under the common law where the claim falls within an English jurisdiction agreement.[38] It is thus quite far from accurate to describe this as a 'routine' case in which the service out rules are applied. Nevertheless, setting this aside, the point remains that the Supreme Court has directed lower courts not to approach the exercise of service out jurisdiction from a cautious or hesitant standpoint.

Lord Sumption's remarks in *Abela* have prompted some lively academic debate. It was suggested, for example, that he had adopted a 'liberal approach to the exercise of the power to serve out in international cases' which might inappropriately prompt an expansion of the courts' jurisdiction.[39] Lord Collins responded to this charge (while noting that 'Lord Sumption needs no defenders') with the argument that:

> the notion that the exercise of the discretion to grant permission to serve proceedings outside the jurisdiction was the exercise of an exorbitant jurisdiction arose as a result of a misunderstanding.[40]

This argument has antecedents in Lord Collins's own work going back at least as far as 1991, in which he argued that the characterization of service out cases as necessarily involving an 'exorbitant' jurisdiction was mistaken.[41] In his response to criticisms of Lord Sumption's remarks in *Abela*, Lord Collins suggested further that this misunderstanding arose in part because of a confusion of public and private international law considerations in the exercise of jurisdiction, and that 'Lord Sumption was not asserting an expansive view of English jurisdiction. He was simply correcting [these] errors'.[42]

Lord Collins is at least equally in need of no defenders (let alone any defence of his defence), but the analysis in this chapter might be taken as a further explanation of these points—that the general caution with which the English courts have traditionally approached the exercise of jurisdiction in service out cases is largely

[37] Civil Procedure Rules, 6.33(2)(b)(v). Before 2015 it was necessary that at least one party be domiciled in an EU Member State for the equivalent rule to apply under the Brussels I Regulation or Brussels Convention, and so some cases remained governed by the common law.

[38] Civil Procedure Rules, 6.33(2B). This change may seem modest and offers continuity with the position under the Brussels I Regulation, but it breaks down the traditional distinction between 'service in' and 'service out' cases—where the English courts have jurisdiction based on an English choice of court agreement no permission is required to commence proceedings even where service outside the forum is required.

[39] Andrew Dickinson, 'Service Abroad—An Inconvenient Obstacle?' (2014) 130 LQR 197, 202.

[40] Collins (n 31) 556.

[41] Lawrence Collins, 'Temporary Presence, Exorbitant Jurisdiction and the US Supreme Court' (1991) 107 LQR 10.

[42] Collins (n 31) 556.

reflective of a historical conflation of adjudicative and enforcement jurisdiction in the context of private international law. It is difficult to see the justification for a 'muscular presumption' against the exercise of jurisdiction where, for example, proceedings are brought against a foreign party in relation to a car accident in England which has injured an English party, or in relation to a breach of a contractual obligation which was to be performed in England. Whether the same considerations ought to apply in relation to other jurisdictional gateways is a matter discussed further below.

A second academic response to Lord Sumption's arguments in *Abela* was to suggest that he had moved the law in the direction of abolishing the gateways altogether and leaving *forum conveniens* alone as the test of jurisdiction.[43] This suggestion was sharply repudiated by Lord Sumption himself in *Four Seasons Holdings Inc v Brownlie* (2017),[44] a case discussed further below, where (albeit *obiter* and in the minority, although the majority did not expressly reject this point) he reaffirmed what is an important point of principle:

> The jurisdictional gateways and the discretion as to forum conveniens serve completely different purposes. The gateways identify relevant connections with England, which define the maximum extent of the jurisdiction which the English court is permitted to exercise. Their ambit is a question of law. The discretion as to forum conveniens authorises the court to decline a jurisdiction which it possesses as a matter of law, because the dispute, although sufficiently connected with England to permit the exercise of jurisdiction, could be more appropriately resolved elsewhere. The main determining factor in the exercise of the discretion on forum conveniens grounds is not the relationship between the cause of action and England but the practicalities of litigation. The purpose of the discretion is to limit the exercise of the court's jurisdiction, not to enlarge it and certainly not to displace the criteria in the gateways. English law has never in the past and does not now accept jurisdiction simply on the basis that the English courts are a convenient or appropriate forum if the subject-matter has no relevant jurisdictional connection with England. In *Abela v Baaderani*, I protested against the importation of an artificial presumption against service out as being inherently 'exorbitant', into what ought to be a neutral question of construction or discretion. I had not proposed to substitute an alternative, and equally objectionable, presumption in favour of the widest possible interpretation of the gateways simply because jurisdiction thus conferred by law could be declined as a matter of discretion.[45]

[43] Adrian Briggs, 'Service Out in a Shrinking World' (2013) LMCLQ 415. See further discussion in Ardavan Arzandeh, '"Gateways" within the Civil Procedure Rules and the Future of Service-Out Jurisdiction in England' (2019) 15 J Priv Intl L 516.

[44] [2017] UKSC 80, [2018] 1 WLR 192.

[45] At [31].

The express rejection in this passage of the 'widest possible interpretation of the gateways' (let alone their mooted abolition) is clear in itself—but other than ruling out one extreme approach, leaves unaddressed the question of how the gateways should in fact be interpreted. This has also been a subject of contention, which is addressed in the next section.

The Interpretation of the Gateways

A second influence of the traditional view of jurisdiction over non-present defendants as 'exceptional' has often been suggested to arise in the context of the interpretation of the grounds of jurisdiction (the gateways) which a claimant must satisfy in order to obtain the court's permission to commence proceedings (previously in Order XI of the Rules of the Supreme Court, and now set out in Practice Direction 6B of the Civil Procedure Rules). This argument might appear to draw support from some of the authorities noted above which distinguish between the 'letter' and the 'spirit' of the rules. For example, in *George Monroe Ltd v American Cynamid and Chemical Corp* (1944),[46] the court held that '[a]s a matter of international comity it seems to me important to make sure that no such service shall be allowed unless it is clearly within both the letter and the spirit of Or. XI'.[47] Clearer authority for this argument may also be drawn from *The Siskina* (1979),[48] in which the House of Lords held that 'where there is any room for doubt as to their meaning the provisions of the sub-rules are to be strictly construed in favour of the foreigner',[49] citing with approval a passage from *The Hagen* (1908).[50] On the basis of these authorities, it has been argued—for example, by the defendants in *Sharab v Prince Al-Waleed Al-Saud* (2009)[51]—that the exorbitant nature of this jurisdiction requires the gateways to be interpreted narrowly and strictly. In *Sharab*, the Court of Appeal rejected that argument, however, Richards LJ finding that 'I do not accept ... that in order to get through the gateway a claimant has to bring himself within the "spirit" as well as the letter of the rule'.[52]

Examined closely, the authorities provide very clear support only for the proposition that the discretion to permit service outside the territory should be exercised circumspectly, and that in that discretion the manner in which a gateway is satisfied (in a narrow and technical way, or in a broad and substantial way) is an important relevant consideration. However, the authorities do not consistently and

[46] [1944] KB 432.
[47] At 437.
[48] [1979] AC 210 (HL).
[49] At 254–55.
[50] [1908] P 189, 210 ('if on the construction of any of the sub-heads of Order XI. there was any doubt, it ought to be resolved in favour of the foreigner').
[51] [2009] EWCA Civ 353, [2009] 2 Lloyd's Rep 160.
[52] At [35].

clearly suggest a particular approach to the interpretation of the gateways themselves. Perhaps for this reason, this issue has remained a contentious one in recent years. The same considerations that have in the past suggested a careful exercise of the *forum conveniens* discretion could be said to argue in favour of a narrow interpretation of the gateways themselves. On the other hand, the fact that the exercise of jurisdiction is subject to a limiting discretion is frequently relied on as a justification for a broad interpretation of the gateways. It is thus frequently argued that a narrow interpretation of the gateways is unnecessary, because the *forum conveniens* discretion acts as a safeguard that prevents them from having effect in cases in which the exercise of jurisdiction by the English courts would be inappropriate.[53]

One important gateway provides that the English courts may have jurisdiction over a claim in tort where the wrongful act was in England or damage was sustained in England.[54] The issue of how broadly or narrowly to interpret this gateway (in particular, whether it should be satisfied where only indirect or consequential damage has taken place in England) has been one of enduring controversy. It divided the Supreme Court in *Four Seasons Holdings Inc v Brownlie* (2017),[55] although it should be noted that the opinions expressed were *obiter dicta*. Lord Sumption argued that 'in different ways all the jurisdictional gateways in the Practice Direction are concerned to identify some substantial and not merely casual or adventitious link between the cause of action and England',[56] suggesting a need for the gateways to be interpreted relatively strictly to achieve this purpose. In suggesting that consequential loss in England should not be enough to satisfy the gateway, he was, however, in the minority. In a more recent decision of the Court of Appeal in the same litigation, Lord Justice Arnold followed this approach when, regarding the rule which sets out the gateways, he argued (in dissent) that 'the purpose of the rule is to identify situations in which there is a sufficient connecting factor with England and Wales to justify our courts asserting jurisdiction over foreign defendants ... It follows, in my opinion, that the courts should be cautious about interpreting the rule broadly'.[57]

[53] See eg *Booth v Phillips* [2004] EWHC 1437 (Admlty) ('it must be remembered that before jurisdiction is exercised the court must be satisfied that it is appropriate to exercise that jurisdiction, which involves considering whether England is the forum in which the case could most suitably be tried for the interest of all the parties and for the ends of justice. When regard is had to this requirement there does not appear to me to be anything objectionable about the Claimant's [broad] construction of the rule' (at [37])); *Cooley v Ramsey* [2008] EWHC 129 (QB) [35]; *Wink v Croatio Osiguranje DD* [2013] EWHC 1118 (QB) [41]; *FS Cairo (Nile Plaza) LLC v Brownlie* [2020] EWCA Civ 996, [2021] 2 All ER 605 ('it is important to recall that a vital part of the scheme under those provisions is precisely that residual discretion. In such circumstances, one need not be fearful of arguments raised *in terrorem* against supposedly exorbitant jurisdiction' (at [51])); see also *FS Cairo (Nile Plaza) LLC v Brownlie* [2021] UKSC 45, [2021] 3 WLR 1011 [64], [77].

[54] CPR Practice Direction 6B, 3.1(9).

[55] [2017] UKSC 80, [2018] 1 WLR 192. See generally Joseph Crampin, 'Fog in the Gateway: Brownlie v Four Seasons Holdings Inc' (2019) 82 Modern L Rev 376; Arzandeh Ardavan, 'The English Court's Service-Out Jurisdiction in International Tortious Disputes' (2017) 133 LQR 144.

[56] At [28].

[57] *FS Cairo (Nile Plaza) LLC v Brownlie* [2020] EWCA Civ 996, [2021] 2 All ER 605 [71].

Lord Justice Arnold also pointed out that a broad interpretation of the tort gateway, leaving the jurisdictional determination principally to the *forum conveniens* discretion, would mean that judicial intervention would be required in more cases in order for parties to know whether the court has jurisdiction—'a recipe for litigation'.[58] On appeal to the Supreme Court for a second time, however, the views of the majority of the Court of Appeal, and of the majority of the dicta in *Four Seasons Holdings Inc v Brownlie* (2017), were preferred by four out of the five justices. In *FS Cairo (Nile Plaza) LLC v Brownlie* (2021),[59] Lord Lloyd-Jones, writing for the majority, held that '[p]rovided that the discretionary test is correctly applied, there should … be no danger that the wider reading of "damage" would establish a jurisdiction simply on the basis of the English identity of the claimant or that it would permit foreign defendants to be brought before the English courts in cases where there is no substantial connection between the wrongdoing and the jurisdiction'.[60] While this was based on the (correct) observation that the existence of a substantial connection is a relevant consideration under the *forum conveniens* test, it perhaps overlooks the possibility that a substantial connection is not a *necessary* condition for the English courts to be the *forum conveniens*—for example, in a case where there is no alternative forum practically available in which the claimant may obtain justice. It may well be desirable that the English courts possess and exercise jurisdiction in such a case, to avoid a claimant being denied justice, but the justification for this is not the existence of a 'substantial connection' with England, nor do the courts require this in practice, beyond the demonstration that the gateway itself is satisfied.[61] In dissent, Lord Leggatt observed that the broad interpretation adopted by the majority meant that the jurisdictional basis for claims in tort 'is not so much a gateway … as an open territory with no fence',[62] arguing that '[t]he territorial nature of jurisdiction demands that there should be a substantial connection between the territory of the state from which the court's authority derives and either the proposed defendant or something which that person has done before the assertion of personal jurisdiction over the proposed defendant is justified'.[63] It should be acknowledged that the debate concerning the correct approach to interpretation of the tort gateway in these cases has generally not focused on principles guiding the interpretation of the gateways in general, but rather the specific wording and context of the tort gateway itself. Nevertheless, the key point

[58] ibid [75].
[59] [2021] UKSC 45, [2021] 3 WLR 1011.
[60] ibid [77].
[61] See discussion of Lord Leggatt at [203]–[208]. It is perhaps notable that the claimant could likely, in any event, have relied on paragraph (4A) of the gateways to support the claim in tort, since a basis of jurisdition in contract was established. The court (at [85]–[87] and [214]–[216]) held it unnecessary to address this point. This basis of jurisdiction at least arguably does not depend on a substantial connection—see further discussion in the next section below.
[62] ibid [171].
[63] ibid [193].

for present purposes is that there is at least some (contested) support for the proposition that the gateways themselves must be interpreted narrowly, because of the (perceived) 'exceptional' nature of the jurisdiction which they permit.

The Discretion and the Gateways in Combination

The two sections immediately above examined two influences of the traditional English hesitancy in exercising jurisdiction in service out cases. The first relates to the exercise of the *forum conveniens* discretion, in respect of which it was argued (consistently with the views of Lord Collins and Lord Sumption) that it is wrong to approach the discretion from the starting point that any exercise of jurisdiction over a non-present defendant is 'exorbitant'. This is a by-product of the historical conflation of enforcement and adjudicative jurisdiction in English law. The second influence of the hesitant approach towards the exercise of jurisdiction in service out cases arises in relation to the interpretation of the gateways themselves. Here, there remain competing views as to how narrowly or broadly the gateways should be approached, and the existence of the *forum conveniens* discretion has often been relied on as a justification for a broader interpretation.

This suggests an important interaction between the two points addressed above. If the courts prove more willing to give permission to serve outside the jurisdiction, following Lord Sumption's directive in *Abela*, that could equally provide a justification for a more cautious interpretation of the grounds of jurisdiction themselves, as Lord Sumption contended in *Brownlie*. This is because the constraint offered by *forum conveniens* is itself made weaker, through the (correct) rejection of the assumption that such jurisdiction is necessarily exorbitant. Although the criticism of Lord Sumption's position in *Abela* is (as Lord Collins has pointed out) misdirected, adopting those views without also adopting his views in *Brownlie* may thus be considered at risk of an inappropriate expansion of English jurisdiction.

D. Does the Term 'Exorbitant' Remain Relevant?

It has been argued above that the use of the term exorbitant as a general description of the exercise of jurisdiction over defendants who cannot be served within the territory is based on a historical conflation of enforcement and adjudicative jurisdiction. It may equally be argued that it is based on a misreading of some earlier authority, which suggests that the exercise of jurisdiction based on *particular* gateways may be considered exorbitant. For those gateways, a stronger argument may be made that a cautious approach to the exercise of jurisdiction should be adopted.

The idea that the gateways are themselves variable in terms of the foundations they offer for the exercise of jurisdiction is itself supported by significant authority.

In *The Siskina* (1979),[64] for example, Lord Diplock wrote (for a unanimous House of Lords) that:

> In several of the cases specified in the sub-rules (a) to (o) the jurisdiction exercisable over foreigners by the High Court is wider than that which is recognised in English law as being possessed by courts of foreign countries. These are 'exorbitant' jurisdictions which run counter to the normal rules of comity among civilised nations.[65]

In *The Spiliada* (1987),[66] the leading modern authority on the exercise of jurisdictional discretion under the common law, Lord Goff expressed similar sentiments (again on behalf of a unanimous House of Lords) in the following terms:

> the circumstances specified in Order 11, r. 1(1), as those in which the court may exercise its discretion to grant leave to serve proceedings on the defendant outside the jurisdiction, are of great variety, ranging from cases where, one would have thought, the discretion would normally be exercised in favour of granting leave (e.g., where the relief sought is an injunction ordering the defendant to do or refrain from doing something within the jurisdiction) to cases where the grant of leave is far more problematical.[67]

This, of course, raises the question of where particular gateways fall on this spectrum. The authorities identify several gateways as relatively weak foundations for jurisdiction, and three in particular may be highlighted here, without claiming that this is necessarily an exhaustive list.

Contract Governed by English Law

A first candidate for an 'exorbitant' basis of jurisdiction is the fact that proceedings may be commenced before the English courts on the mere basis that the claim relates to a contract governed by English law.[68] This basis of jurisdiction was particularly the focus on consideration in *Amin Rasheed Shipping Corp v Kuwait Insurance Co* (1984),[69] and in respect of this gateway Lord Diplock observed in the House of Lords that:

64 [1979] AC 210 (HL).
65 At 254.
66 [1987] AC 460.
67 At 481.
68 CPR, Practice Direction 6B, 3.1(6)(c).
69 [1984] AC 50.

> the jurisdiction exercised by an English court over a foreign corporation which has no place of business in this country, as a result of granting leave under R.S.C., Ord. 11, r. 1 (1) (f) for service out of the jurisdiction of a writ on that corporation, is an exorbitant jurisdiction, i.e., it is one which, under general English conflict rules, an English court would not recognise as possessed by any foreign court in the absence of some treaty providing for such recognition. Comity thus dictates that the judicial discretion to grant leave under this paragraph of R.S.C., Ord. 11, r. 1 (1) should be exercised with circumspection in cases where there exists an alternative forum[70]

It is worth highlighting that the context for this discussion in *Amin Rasheed* was the particular gateway based on the English governing law of the contract, a point in which this chapter once again echoes Lord Collins.[71] This passage has inaccurately been cited as authority for the proposition that *all* the gateways are 'exceptional' grounds of jurisdiction and thus the discretion should *always* be exercised with circumspection,[72] an argument rejected above. The basis for questioning this ground of jurisdiction is that the governing law of the contract does not necessarily establish a significant link between the English courts and the parties or their dispute. It may further be questioned whether this basis of jurisdiction offers another conflation of different concepts of jurisdiction in international law terms—this time allowing adjudicative jurisdiction to be established on the basis of the applicable law, which is a matter of prescriptive jurisdiction. This basis of jurisdiction is not widely available in other legal systems, which also raises questions about whether it may be characterized as consistent with international practice—it has, nevertheless, long been clearly established under the common law rules in England.

Necessary or Proper Party Jurisdiction

A second gateway which might be viewed as establishing an 'exorbitant' ground of jurisdiction is the exercise of jurisdiction over a party on the basis that they are a 'necessary or property party' to proceedings brought against another party, over whom the court has jurisdiction.[73] As noted above, Lord Sumption argued in *Four Seasons Holdings Inc v Brownlie* (2017)[74] that 'in different ways all the jurisdictional gateways in the Practice Direction are concerned to identify some substantial and not merely casual or adventitious link between the cause of action and England'.[75]

[70] At 65.
[71] Collins (n 31) 556.
[72] See eg *Deripaska v Cherney (No 2)* [2009] EWCA Civ 849, [2010] 2 All ER (Comm) 456 [15].
[73] CPR, Practice Direction 6B, 3.1(3).
[74] [2017] UKSC 80, [2018] 1 WLR 192. See generally Crampin (n 55).
[75] At [28]. See also *FS Cairo (Nile Plaza) LLC v Brownlie* [2021] UKSC 45, [2021] 3 WLR 1011 [192] (Lord Leggatt, in dissent on this point).

It may be questioned whether this basis of jurisdiction in fact establishes a link between the cause of action and England—at most, it establishes a link between the cause of action and another cause of action, brought against another party, which is connected with England.

In *AK Investment CJSC v Kyrgyz Mobil Tel Ltd (Isle of Man)* (2011),[76] Lord Collins wrote for the Privy Council that:

> The necessary or proper party head of jurisdiction is anomalous, in that, by contrast with the other heads, it is not founded upon any territorial connection between the claim, the subject matter of the relevant action and the jurisdiction of the English courts

Lord Collins also cited with approval the conclusions of Lloyd LJ in *The Goldean Mariner* (1990)[77] that:

> caution must always be exercised in bringing foreign defendants within our jurisdiction under O.11 r.1(1)(c). It must never become the practice to bring foreign defendants here as a matter of course, on the ground that the only alternative requires more than one suit in more than one different jurisdiction.[78]

Further support for this proposition may arguably be found in the recent Supreme Court decision in *Vedanta Resources plc v Lungowe* (2019),[79] in which the court considered that the risk of split proceedings should not be viewed as a 'trump card'[80] in favour of allowing proceedings against 'necessary or proper party' defendants to be brought in the English courts. This was particularly the case because, in those proceedings, the English 'anchor' defendant had undertaken to submit to the Zambian courts, which would then be available as an alternative forum to hear the claims against all defendants. It is unclear whether the case provides authority for a more circumspect approach towards necessary and proper party jurisdiction in other contexts, but at least in this situation it suggests a greater reluctance to consolidate the proceedings in England, because the inefficiencies in split proceedings may be attributable to the claimant's own choice to litigate in England rather than in an available alternative foreign court.

76 [2011] UKPC 7, [2012] 1 WLR 1804 (*sub nom Altimo Holdings and Investment v same*).
77 [1990] 2 Lloyd's Rep 215.
78 At 222.
79 [2019] UKSC 20, [2020] AC 1045.
80 At [84].

Related Claim Jurisdiction

A third gateway which may be vulnerable to the label 'exorbitant' is a more recent addition to Practice Direction 6B of the Civil Procedure Rules, which permits the addition of further claims against a defendant against whom proceedings have been brought in reliance on one of a number of other enumerated grounds of jurisdiction under the Practice Direction. In full, paragraph 4A provides that proceedings may be commenced where: 'A claim is made against the defendant in reliance on one or more of paragraphs (2), (6) to (16), (19) or (21) and a further claim is made against the same defendant which arises out of the same or closely connected facts'.

Before this basis of jurisdiction existed, each cause of action brought against a single defendant required separate jurisdictional justification under Practice Direction 6B—the gateways supported only a particular claim against the defendant, rather than establishing general jurisdiction.[81] The addition of this paragraph expands the jurisdiction of the court to cover not only claims falling under one of the enumerated gateways, but also other claims arising out of the same or closely connected facts.[82] The reason why this basis of jurisdiction may be questioned is, once again, that it does not establish a link between the cause of action and England, but rather a link between the cause of action and another cause of action, which itself has a connection with England (through one of the other gateways).

The effect of this gateway is arguably magnified because it may be used in conjunction with necessary or proper party jurisdiction, discussed above. In *Eurasia Sports Ltd v Aguad* (2018),[83] the Court of Appeal held that a party (D2) could be subject to the jurisdiction of the English courts where they were a necessary or proper party to a claim brought against another defendant (D1) which was brought in reliance on paragraph 4A—that is, a claim which was itself permitted only because it arose out of the same or closely connected facts as another claim against D1 over which the court had a basis of jurisdiction. The jurisdiction over D2 is here doubly indirect—the cause of action is not itself directly connected with England, but rather connected with a cause of action against D1, which is itself connected with a different cause of action against D1, which establishes a connection with England.

[81] General jurisdiction might be established under paragraph 1, where 'A claim is made for a remedy against a person domiciled within the jurisdiction' (but who is not present at the time of service), but in practice this paragraph has long been dormant as jurisdiction over UK-domiciled parties was governed by the Brussels Convention and Brussels I Regulation.

[82] An equivalent effect is provided under some jurisdictional rules in Australia, in which jurisdiction over one claim may establish jurisdiction over the whole proceedings: see eg *Tiger Yacht Management Ltd v Morris* [2019] FCAFC 8, (2019) 366 ALR 410.

[83] [2018] EWCA Civ 1742, [2018] 1 WLR 6089.

E. Efficiency Justifications for Jurisdiction

The three gateways discussed above are at least arguably controversial because they do not seem to be readily justifiable on the basis that they establish a connection between the cause of action and England. This raises the question of whether the term 'exorbitant' might retain some relevance in these particular contexts, or whether an alternative justification may be offered to support these grounds of jurisdiction. The strongest candidate for this justification is that each may promote the efficient resolution of the dispute—understood broadly to encompass related actions against a single defendant or multiple defendants.

The exercise of the *forum conveniens* (and indeed *forum non conveniens*) discretion in English law has long required careful attention to the question of which court is best placed to resolve the dispute between the parties most efficiently, as well as other factors such as ensuring that claimants are able to obtain justice.[84] In relation to the three gateways identified above, this creates some overlap between the gateways themselves and the factors relevant to the exercise of the discretion to permit service out. For example, the courts have long considered the applicable law to be a relevant consideration in *forum conveniens* and *forum non conveniens*—if a dispute is governed by English law, in particular if it raises controversial questions of English law, this will make it more appropriate for the English courts to exercise jurisdiction.[85] This is considered to promote the efficient resolution of the dispute, because all other things being equal, a court applying its own law will resolve the dispute more efficiently than a court applying foreign law, due to the additional expense and complexity of establishing the content of foreign law. The existence of closely related proceedings in the English courts is also, similarly, a significant factor in favour of the exercise of jurisdiction by the English courts, in order to consolidate if possible complex proceedings in a single forum, and avoid the inefficiency of split litigation.[86]

The three gateways examined above arguably demonstrate that the concern for efficiency in dispute resolution is not only a factor in the discretion whether or not to *exercise* jurisdiction, but also at least arguably an additional foundation for jurisdiction itself. Jurisdiction is being founded over a party not because there is a connection, or at least a direct connection, between the party or the cause of action and England, but because it would be in the interests of the efficient resolution of the dispute as a whole for that party or the issues concerned to be brought before the English courts. This is a highly significant feature of the common law approach to jurisdiction. It is also contentious, because it represents a departure of the rules

[84] See eg Torremans and others (n 3) 351ff, 392ff.
[85] See eg *EI Du Pont de Nemours v Agnew* [1987] 2 Lloyd's Rep 585 (CA).
[86] See eg *Petroleo Brasiliero SA v Mellitus Shipping Inc* [2001] EWCA Civ 418, [2001] 1 All ER (Comm) 993.

of civil jurisdiction from their traditional foundations in public international law. The exercise of civil jurisdiction involves the assertion of regulatory, adjudicative, and potentially enforcement power, and although doubts have sometimes been raised about whether international law regulates civil as well as criminal assertions of jurisdiction, there is little in principle to justify this distinction, although the application of the public international law principles in the civil context clearly has some particular features.[87] Aside from those situations exceptionally covered by universal jurisdiction, public international law jurisdictional rules require a justificatory link for the exercise of jurisdiction, which may be found on the basis of territorial connection, active or passive personality, or exceptional national interest.[88] In public international law, efficiency might affect the propriety of a State's exercise of these jurisdictional grounds, but it cannot provide a foundation for their exercise in its own right. In the criminal context, in the absence of universal jurisdiction or some other special justification, it is clear that a State cannot prosecute a foreign national for acts without a relevant connection to the forum, even if it would be efficient to do so—including where there are related proceedings brought against that defendant or against other defendants. (The question of applicable law as a basis for criminal jurisdiction does not similarly arise, because each national court always applies its own criminal law—the potential application of foreign private law rules is a unique feature of the context of civil jurisdiction which necessarily complicates the analysis, as it means that States are sometimes applying the prescriptive rules of other States,[89] but are always applying their own procedural[90] and mandatory[91] rules.)

These developments might invite one of two responses. A first response would be to say that the gateways examined above are indeed inconsistent with traditional public international law jurisdictional justifications for adjudicative jurisdiction, and are rightly labelled exorbitant. The consequence of this approach would be that these gateways should be approached cautiously by the English courts, and indeed should be viewed critically by foreign parties and States. A second response would be to say that these grounds of jurisdiction have not provoked widespread protest, and similar grounds of jurisdiction (although not often as broadly cast) are exercised under other jurisdictional regimes. For example, the Recast Brussels I Regulation permits proceedings to be brought against a defendant under Article 8(1):

[87] See further eg Mills (n 10).
[88] See further eg Mills (n 9); Ryngaert (n 9).
[89] See further Mills (n 10).
[90] See further Richard Garnett, *Substance and Procedure in Private International Law* (OUP 2012).
[91] See generally eg Alex Mills, *Party Autonomy in Private International Law* (CUP 2018) ch 9; Torremans and others (n 3) 143ff.

> where he is one of a number of defendants, in the courts for the place where any one of them is domiciled, provided the claims are so closely connected that it is expedient to hear and determine them together to avoid the risk of irreconcilable judgments resulting from separate proceedings

The Regulation also permits, in Article 8(2), the addition of third parties in defined circumstances, including where they are implicated in a warranty or guarantee of the defendant. These rules allow for proceedings to be brought against a defendant in courts which do not have a direct connection with that party or the cause of action being brought against that party, but only an indirect link. Further, in Article 8(4), there is a limited possibility to add a contractual claim to a claim brought against a defendant in matters relating to rights *in rem* in immovable property, where the actions can be combined, even if that court would not normally have jurisdiction over the contractual claim. Although these rules are much narrower than their common law equivalents (and there is no direct equivalent under the Recast Brussels I Regulation for the exercise of jurisdiction based on the law applicable to the contract), they nevertheless provide some support for the idea that efficiency may provide the basis for an assertion of jurisdiction, or at least for the expansion of jurisdiction grounds to indirect justificatory links. This suggests a broader shift in the international law of jurisdiction—one which suggests that in this context the rules are less focused on the rights and interests of States seeking to regulate parties, and more focused on the interests of the parties themselves,[92] balancing claimants' rights of access to justice with the inconvenience imposed on defendants, mindful of the general desirability of promoting efficient resolution of international disputes in the interests of the functioning of globalized economic relations.

As already observed above, Lord Sumption argued in *Four Seasons Holdings Inc v Brownlie* (2017)[93] that the gateways play a fundamentally distinct role from the *forum conveniens* discretion and it was important to maintain their particular function as a constraint on jurisdiction. In making this argument, he observed that 'English law has never in the past and does not now accept jurisdiction simply on the basis that the English courts are a convenient or appropriate forum if the subject-matter has no relevant jurisdictional connection with England'.[94]

The analysis above raises questions about whether this is strictly speaking the case. It is, of course, true that the gateways discussed are limited, and require some connection with England—the applicable law of the contract, or a related claim or related party subject to the jurisdiction of the court. But it is at least arguable that these grounds of jurisdiction are not themselves premised on a subject-matter

[92] See further generally Mills (n 9).
[93] [2017] UKSC 80, [2018] 1 WLR 192.
[94] At [31].

connection with England, but rather on the basis that the English courts will be 'a convenient or appropriate forum' for the litigation.

F. Conclusions

In the context of the jurisdiction of the English courts over non-present defendants, it is time to set the label 'exorbitant' to one side.[95] This is not to say that the establishment and exercise of jurisdiction should be carried out without consideration of their appropriate limits, but rather that the label serves only to obscure deeper questions regarding the foundational principles of the common law rules on jurisdiction, including particularly the question of how fairness to individual defendants and respect for the authority of foreign courts and sovereigns should be balanced against the general interests of efficient dispute resolution. As the landscape of English jurisdictional rules shifts in the aftermath of Brexit, it is undoubtedly timely to reflect on these issues, and in doing so, it will be invaluable to continue to draw on the wealth of Lord Collins's judicial and academic contribution.

[95] For another context in which it undoubtedly remains relevant, see *SAS Institute Inc v World Programming Ltd* [2020] EWCA Civ 599.

PART IV
INTERNATIONAL ARBITRATION

12

Jurisdiction under Article 25 of the International Centre for Settlement of Investment Disputes Convention

Jonathan Mance

A. Lawrence Collins

Lawrence Collins's remarkable contributions to the law need little elaboration: brilliant academic; editor of the leading textbook whose title joins him with two previous giants, AV Dicey and JHC Morris; solicitor practitioner at Herbert Smith; Judge of the Commercial Court and Court of Appeal Judge; and finally Justice of the Supreme Court (and a stimulating colleague) for an all-too-brief two years, until reaching the statutory retirement age. In the subsequent ten years, Lawrence has shown how arbitrary that retirement age was, maintaining a packed agenda which has included university teaching, lecturing, sitting in the Hong Kong Final Court of Appeal, and a busy arbitral practice.

The writer has chosen an arbitral theme. Both the writer's first memorable collaboration with Lawrence and his most recent encounter with Lawrence's work have been in that field. The memorable encounter involved an arbitration in an overseas jurisdiction to which Lawrence and the writer repaired with our principal witness, expecting a hearing with evidence and submissions extending over two days. However, our local lawyer-arbitrator's opening remark was a proposal to start by reading his draft award. We inferred that his (evidently diligent) assistant had prepared this, and (correctly, as it proved) that it might prove more favourable to our client than would be easy to justify. We were able to restrain the arbitrator throughout the morning, but after lunch he proved irresistible. As we feared, the award was (to say the least) generous. It was no surprise when the loser mounted a strong, though I believe narrowly unsuccessful, challenge on procedural grounds all the way to the highest local court. I have never ascertained whether our experience was typical of local arbitration, though it was in one sense very welcome, freeing me for two days' holiday in agreeable local surroundings. At the recent end of our long mutual engagement, Lawrence has been an invaluable guide to the practice of arbitration, as well as the author of an award (including an important

Jonathan Mance, *Jurisdiction under Article 25 of the International Centre for Settlement of Investment Disputes Convention* In: *Essays in International Litigation for Lord Collins*. Edited by: Jonathan Harris and Campbell McLachlan, Oxford University Press. © Oxford University Press 2022. DOI: 10.1093/oso/9780192867988.003.0013

examination of the operation of *res judicata* in arbitration) requiring close attention during my own engagement in the field.

B. Article 25 of the ICSID Convention

My subject is the effect and operation of Article 25 of the Convention on the Settlement of Investment Disputes between States and Nationals of Other States (the 'ICSID Convention').[1] The ICSID Convention was submitted to the Executive Directors of the World Bank on 18 March 1965 and entered into force on 14 October 1966 after ratification by twenty countries. Article 25 provides, inter alia:

> Jurisdiction of the Centre
> Article 25
> (1) The jurisdiction of the Centre shall extend to any legal dispute arising directly out of an investment, between a Contracting State (or any constituent subdivision or agency of a Contracting State designated to the Centre by that State) and a national of another Contracting State, which the parties to the dispute consent in writing to submit to the Centre. When the parties have given their consent, no party may withdraw its consent unilaterally.
> (2) …
> (3) Consent by a constituent subdivision or agency of a Contracting State shall require the approval of that State unless that State notifies the Centre that no such approval is required.

This provision falls to be interpreted in accordance with the general rule of interpretation stated in Article 31 assisted, where relevant, by the supplementary means of interpretation stated in Article 32 of the Vienna Convention on the Law of Treaties (the 'Vienna Convention').[2] Article 31 of the Vienna Convention states:

> 1. A treaty shall be interpreted in good faith in accordance with the ordinary meaning to be given to the terms of the treaty in their context and in the light of its object and purpose.
> 2. The context for the purpose of the interpretation of a treaty shall comprise, in addition to the text, including its preamble and annexes:
>   (a) any agreement relating to the treaty which was made between all the parties in connection with the conclusion of the treaty;

[1] Convention on the Settlement of Investment Disputes between States and Nationals of Other States (signed 18 March 1965, entered into force 14 October 1966) 575 UNTS 159.

[2] Vienna Convention on the Law of Treaties (signed 23 May 1969, entered into force 27 January 1980) 1155 UNTS 331.

(b) any instrument which was made by one or more parties in connection with the conclusion of the treaty and accepted by the other parties as an instrument related to the treaty …

Article 32 states:

> Recourse may be had to supplementary means of interpretation, including the preparatory work of the treaty and the circumstances of its conclusion, in order to confirm the meaning resulting from the application of article 31, or to determine the meaning when the interpretation according to article 31:
> (a) leaves the meaning ambiguous or obscure; or
> (b) leads to a result which is manifestly absurd or unreasonable.

Article 6(1)(b) of the ICSID Convention provides that the Administrative Council, composed of one representative of each Contracting State, 'shall … adopt the rules of procedure for the institution of conciliation and arbitration proceedings'. Rule 1(1), headed *The Request*, of the current Rules of Procedure for the Institution of Conciliation and Arbitration Proceedings so adopted ('the ICSID Rules')[3] provides, inter alia:

> (1) Any Contracting State or any national of a Contracting State wishing to institute conciliation or arbitration proceedings shall address a request to that effect in writing to the Secretary-General at the seat of the Centre.

Rule 2, headed *Contents of the Request*, continues:

> 1) The request shall:
> (a) designate precisely each party to the dispute and state the address of each;
> (b) state, if one of the parties is a constituent subdivision or agency of a Contracting State, that it has been designated to the Centre by that State pursuant to Article 25(1) of the Convention;
> (c) indicate the date of consent and the instruments in which it is recorded, including, if one party is a constituent subdivision or agency of a Contracting State, similar data on the approval of such consent by that State unless it had notified the Centre that no such approval is required;
> (d) …

[3] ICSID Rules of Procedure for Arbitration Proceedings (April 2006).

Constituent Subdivision or Agency

What is meant by 'any constituent subdivision or agency of a Contracting State designated to the Centre by that State'? On one view, that could depend entirely upon what a Contracting State decides to 'designate to the Centre' as its 'constituent subdivision or agency'. Why should a Contracting State not decide for itself what bodies or entities can agree with a foreign investor to expose themselves to investment claims using the ICSID facilities? The more natural and plausible meaning is, however, that there is an objective boundary around the concept of a 'constituent subdivision or agency'.

It follows that an ICSID tribunal may, as a matter of jurisdiction, have to consider whether a body against which a claim is made satisfies the test of being a 'constituent subdivision or agency'. The existence of a designation would in practice deserve considerable respect, but it would not be conclusive.[4]

Jurisdiction under Article 25 would depend on satisfying this test, just as it depends on there being a 'legal dispute arising directly out of an investment'. The existence of an 'investment' is a matter of objective and sometimes detailed analysis, based on a proper understanding of the concept.

The existence of a dispute ought, in the writer's view, to be a much simpler matter. A claim which is denied should suffice. A tribunal should not be led into elaborate arguments about whether the defence or indeed the claim is good or even prima facie good. Tribunals dealing with a BIT claim against a State arising out of a transaction with a separate legal entity for which, or in relation to which, the State is said to have incurred responsibility have sometimes undertaken at the jurisdictional stage elaborate examination of the merits or prima facie merits of the claim against the State.[5] That can only confuse the jurisdictional and merits stage.[6]

The natural meaning is also that the adjective 'constituent' qualifies only 'subdivision' and not 'agency' in Article 25(1). The word underlines the closeness of the connection with the State of the sort of 'subdivision' contemplated by Article 25(1). A 'constituent agency' would, in contrast, be on its face an unnatural conjunction.[7]

[4] This view is supported by the weighty authority of Professor Schreuer's 'Article 25' in Christoph H Schreuer and others (eds), *The ICSID Convention: A Commentary* (2nd edn, CUP 2009) 154, para 244.

[5] See eg *Toto Construzioni Generali SpA v Lebanon*, ICSID Case No ARB/07/12, Decision on Jurisdiction, 11 September 2009.

[6] The writer is reminded of the former English domestic law practice under the old Arbitration Acts 1950 and 1975, where courts used to refuse to recognize that there was a dispute which should be remitted to arbitration, if it appeared to them that the denial of the claim was clearly unfounded: see Sir Michael J Mustill and Stewart C Boyd, *The Law and Practice of Commercial Arbitration in England* (2nd edn, Butterworths 1989) 123–24 for the former law. Under the Arbitration Act 1996, this practice is no longer possible.

[7] This view is also consistent with the phrasing of the two other official languages of the ICSID Convention additional to English, that is French and Spanish. In the French version, the phrase used

Indeed, there would seem, otherwise, little point in the contrast with a subdivision of the State.

These conclusions about the meaning of 'any constituent subdivision or agency of a Contracting State designated to the Centre by that State' receive clear support from the attention paid during the drafting process to the phraseology which finally became 'constituent subdivision or agency'. That process appears from the *ICSID, History of the ICSID Convention: Documents Concerning the Origin and Formulation of the Convention on the Settlement of Investment Disputes Between States and Nationals of Other States* (1968) ('*History of the ICSID Convention*'), vol II-2. The position is summarized by Professor Schreuer in 'Article 25' in *The ICSID Convention: A Commentary*:[8]

> During the Convention's drafting, there were lengthy discussions concerning the general description of the entities to be included and the precise meaning of the terms chosen. Two main groups of entities were debated. One group consisted of constituent or component parts of States, such as states, provinces, cantons and municipalities. The other group consisted of public agencies performing governmental functions, such as development corporations or investment boards (History, Vol. II, pp. 288/9, 321, 366, 393, 396/7, 446/7). The wording suggested initially was 'political subdivision or instrumentality' (at pp. 288, 396, 492). Both parts of the phrase came under criticism. It was suggested that the first part did not adequately express the idea of a State's component part (at pp. 502, 507) and that the second might include mere government-owned companies (at p. 507). Mr. Broches explained that the word 'instrumentality' was only intended to include governmental agencies (at p. 507).

The word 'instrumentality' was then replaced by the word 'agency'. In another article, 'The Jurisdiction of the International Centre for the Settlement of Investment Disputes', published in 1979,[9] Professor CF Amerasinghe, senior counsel in the legal department of the International Bank for Reconstruction and Development, summarizes the intention as being that: '[W]hat were covered were only governmental agencies which were normally legally part of and indistinguishable from the government but could sometimes have separate legal personalities and be

is 'telle collectivité publique ou tel organisme dépendant de lui' (or, in art 25(3) 'dépendant d'un Etat'). In Spanish, it is 'cualquiera subdivisión política u organismo público de un Estado'. Neither phrase appears to the writer to confine the latter organism to one which 'forms a component part of the State'. An organism can be dependent on, or a public organism of, a State without being an integral element or component part of it.

[8] Schreuer and others (n 4) 152–53, para 240.

[9] Chittharanja F Amerasinghe, 'The Jurisdiction of the International Centre for the Settlement of Investment Disputes' (1979) 19 IJIL 166.

entrusted with governmental functions, as distinguished from government-owned companies'.[10]

Professor Amerasinghe thought that the concept of an agency related 'normally' to bodies 'legally part of and indistinguishable from the government', but could sometimes also extend to bodies with 'separate legal personality'.[11] The *History of the ICSID Convention* indicates, as Professor Schreuer's and Professor Amerasinghe's accounts confirm, that the concerns expressed during the negotiations of the ICSID Convention were that 'mere' government ownership (or control) might be regarded as sufficient to constitute an entity as a government agency. Such concerns were understandable. There are many government-owned or (in corporate law terms) controlled companies which carry on their own separate business as independent entities and would not normally be described as government 'agencies'. It is, however, equally clear in practice that entities with legal personality may constitute 'agencies' of the State under Article 25(1).[12]

The question is what test, or criteria, to use to determine whether an entity qualifies as an 'agency' for the purposes of Article 25. It is clear that the entity need not be acting for and on behalf of the State in a strict agency sense. If it were so acting, then the State itself would become a primary target of any ICSID arbitration claim. Mr Broches, chair of the Legal Committee responsible for considering the ICSID Convention in draft, put the correct position clearly during the Committee's discussion in this area on 4 January 1965:[13]

> If an agency was acting on behalf of the State, then there was no distinction any more between the agency and the State. If it was a case where it was not acting on behalf of the State in a legal sense, where a State was not really a party, then the consent requirement would apply. If a State did not want to run the risk of consent by a political subdivision, it had always the possibility of not designating that political subdivision at all.

The concept of agency must nonetheless connote a close link between the relevant entity's role and the State's interests. It has been argued that the Articles on State Responsibility adopted in 2001 by the International Law Commission[14] as a codification of customary international law may assist in the application of Article 25(1)

[10] ibid 185.
[11] ibid.
[12] See Scheuer (n 4) 154, para 246.
[13] ICSID, *Convention on the Settlement of Investment Disputes between States and Nationals of Other States: Documents Concerning the Origin and Formulation of the Convention* (ICSID 1968) vol II-2, 859 (hereafter *History of the ICSID Convention*).
[14] International Law Commission, 'Draft Articles on Responsibility of States for Internationally Wrongful Acts' [2001] 2(2) YB ILC 26; commended to the attention of Governments by the UN General Assembly in Resolution 56/83 of 12 December 2001.

in various contexts, for example: firstly, to determine when a separate legal entity is to be regarded not as a 'national of another Contracting State', but as the State itself, so as to be disqualified from bringing an ICSID claim; secondly, to determine when a State may be made liable by a BIT claim as a result of a transaction involving a separate entity linked to the State; and, thirdly, to determine when a claim may be made against a separate entity on the basis that it is an 'agency' within the meaning of Article 25(1).

The Articles, although formulated as a codification of customary international law, were not in existence when the ICSID Convention was agreed. They deal also with a different subject matter from Article 25, as their full title shows: 'The Responsibility of States for internationally wrongful acts'. The elements of such an act are defined in Article 2:

> There is an internationally wrongful act of a State when conduct consisting of an action or omission:
> (a) is attributable to the State under international law; and
> (b) constitutes a breach of an international obligation of the State.

Like Article 25, the Articles do, however, address situations in which the link between a State and a separate legal entity may, for international law purposes, be so close as to justify a certain assimilation. In the ILC's valuable Commentary, Chapter II reads:[15]

> (2) ... the general rule is that the only conduct attributed to the State at the international level is that of its organs of government, or of others who have acted under the direction, instigation or control of those organs, i.e. as agents of the State.
> (3) As a corollary, the conduct of private persons is not as such attributable to the State....
> (7) The purpose of this chapter is to specify the conditions under which conduct is attributed to the State as a subject of international law for the purposes of determining its international responsibility. Conduct is thereby attributed to the State as a subject of international law and not as a subject of internal law. In internal law, it is common for the 'State' to be subdivided into a series of distinct legal entities. For example, ministries, departments, component units of all kinds, State commissions or corporations may have separate legal personality under internal law, with separate accounts and separate liabilities.

[15] International Law Commission, 'Responsibility of States for Internationally Wrongful Acts: General Commentary' [2001] 2(2) YB ILC 31, 38–39.

> But international law does not permit a State to escape its international responsibilities by a mere process of internal subdivision. The State as a subject of international law is held responsible for the conduct of all the organs, instrumentalities and officials which form part of its organization and act in that capacity, whether or not they have separate legal personality under its internal law.

More particularly, Articles 4, 5, and 8 also state:

> Article 4. Conduct of organs of a State
>
> 1. The conduct of any State organ shall be considered an act of that State under international law, whether the organ exercises legislative, executive, judicial or any other functions, whatever position it holds in the organization of the State, and whatever its character as an organ of the central Government or of a territorial unit of the State.
> 2. An organ includes any person or entity which has that status in accordance with the internal law of the State.
>
> Article 5. Conduct of persons or entities exercising elements of governmental authority
>
> The conduct of a person or entity which is not an organ of the State under article 4 but which is empowered by the law of that State to exercise elements of the governmental authority shall be considered an act of the State under international law, provided the person or entity is acting in that capacity in the particular instance.
>
> Article 8. Conduct directed or controlled by a State
>
> The conduct of a person or group of persons shall be considered an act of a State under international law if the person or group of persons is in fact acting on the instructions of, or under the direction or control of, that State in carrying out the conduct.

It is understandable that the Articles and Commentary should have been found useful as a guide when deciding whether a State's responsibility is engaged under a BIT by virtue of the conduct of a separate legal entity with a close link to the State: see, for example, *Gustav FW Hamester GmbH & Co KG v Republic of Ghana*,[16] which concerned a claim to hold Ghana answerable for a liability allegedly incurred by the Ghanaian Cocao Board. The tribunal said:[17]

[16] *Gustav FW Hamester GmbH & Co KG v Ghana*, ICSID Case No ARB/07/24, Award, 18 June 2010.
[17] ibid [171]–[172].

> The Tribunal must decide the issue of attribution under international law, and is guided by the Articles on State Responsibility adopted on second reading in 2001 by the International Law Commission and commended to the attention of Governments by the UN General Assembly in Resolution 56/83 of 12 December 2001 (the 'ILC Articles') as a codification of customary international law.
>
> In order for an act to be attributed to a State, it must have a close link to the State. This close link can result from the fact that the person performing the act is part of the State's organic structure (Article 4); or is utilising the State's specific governmental powers to perform such act, even if it is a separate entity (Article 5); or is acting under the effective control (on the instructions, or under the direction or control) of the State, even if it is a private or public party (Article 8).

An article by Mr Aron Broches, chair of the legal committee which produced the text of the ICSID Convention written in 1972 some years after the Convention, suggested that a government-owned corporation should not be disqualified from being regarded as a 'national of another Contracting State' under Article 25(1), 'unless it is acting as an agent for the government or is discharging an essentially governmental function'.[18] That language comes close to the thinking behind Articles 5 and 8 of the later ILC Articles. But it is not axiomatic that the test for the right to claim under Article 25(1) should depend upon whether an entity might in different circumstances engage the responsibility of the State with which it is linked.

This is even less obviously axiomatic, when the question is whether a State is entitled to designate an entity as an agency for the purposes of enabling it to agree with a national of another Contracting State party to submit to ICSID arbitration under Article 25(1), with the State's specific agreement (where required) under Article 25(3). Nothing in Article 25(1) links the concept of agency directly to a hypothetical situation, in which the State is not seeking to confer status on a linked entity which will only be relevant if the entity and another State's national agree to submit to ICSID, but is rather in receipt of a claim by a third party resulting from that entity's conduct. There seems no reason to tie the concept of agency in Article 25(1) strictly to a definition conceived solely for the latter purpose.

That said, the occasions when an entity is an agency for the purposes of Article 25(1) but not under the ILC Articles seem unlikely to be many. The one area where there may perhaps be a difference derives from the limitation of ILC Article 5 to situations in which an entity is exercising specific governmental powers. Bearing in mind the frequency with which State-linked entities engage in commercial activity, the writer wonders whether the drafters of the ICSID Convention would have intended that limitation. However, they clearly did not intend to embrace every State-owned corporation's activity. So it may be that agency in terms of Article 25(1) will

[18] Aron Broches, 'The Convention on the Settlement of Investment Disputes between States and Nationals of Other States' (1972) 136 RdC 331, 355.

only exist in the case of an entity conducting commercial activity, in circumstances falling within, or at least coming close to falling within, ILC Article 4 and/or 8. The writer's basic caveat about subscribing wholeheartedly to the treatment of the ILC Articles as 'the' test is that they were conceived later and for a quite different purpose from the one currently under discussion.[19]

Designation and Approval

Assuming that a body or entity is a 'constituent subdivision or agency' of the State, the application of Article 25(1) depends on the following:

(i) its designation as a constituent subdivision or agency to the Centre by the State;
(ii) a legal dispute arising directly out of an investment between it and the national of another Contracting State;
(iii) the consent in writing of the parties to the dispute to submit the dispute to the Centre;
(iv) under Article 25(3), the approval of the subdivision or agency's State to such consent, unless such State notifies the Centre that no such approval is necessary.

No particular order is stated in Article 25 in which these events need occur. It is clear that designation and approval are concurrent but conceptually different requirements. During the drafting of the ICSID Convention, the former was seen as a prerequisite to capacity to engage in ICSID proceedings. Professor Schreuer explains that the 'idea of a designation arose from a British proposal to create some machinery for enabling investors to identify political subdivisions or agencies'.[20] More particularly, at the Legal Committee's drafting session on 4 January 1965, when a requirement of designation was discussed in detail and accepted, the UK delegate, Mr Burrows, saw designation as intended to enable investors to know 'the ... subdivisions or agencies which may appear before the Centre'.[21] But, as already indicated, that does not leave it open to a State to designate as such any body or entity it wishes. Distinguishing designation and approval near the end of the critical drafting session of the Legal Committee on 4 January 1965, Mr Broches

[19] The writer would therefore reject the conclusion that the principles governing attribution to the State of alleged wrongdoing are necessarily transposable to the question whether an entity constitutes an 'agency' for the purpose of designation under art 25(1) reached by Giulio Alvaro Cortesi, PhD Candidate at the Sorbonne, in 'ICSID Jurisdiction with regard to State-Owned Enterprises—Moving Toward an Approach Based on General International Law' (2017) 16 LPICT 108, 137.

[20] Schreuer and others (n 4) 154, para 247.

[21] *History of the ICSID Convention* (n 13) 857.

spoke of 'designation, without which the body concerned was completely outside the scope of this Convention'.[22] Summarizing the position immediately before the delegates voted in favour of both requirements, he then stated that 'several problems had been presented. In the first place, the proposition that none of these bodies should have the capacity to be a party to proceedings before the Centre unless they have been designated. Second, there was the question of approval'.[23]

The conceptual distinction is evident from the fact that designation must be 'to the Centre by the State', while approval, if required, can on its face be a private matter, between the State and the subdivision or agency; approval need not on its face even be communicated to the subdivision or agency, although the claimant national of another Contracting State will in practice have to know or get to know of it or be unable to satisfy Rule 2(1)(c) of the ICSID Rules. Rule 2(1)(c) also indicates an expectation that any approval will be recorded in some 'instrument(s)', though that cannot be a condition.

The focus, when the Convention was agreed, appears to have been, understandably, on the making by States of general designations to the Centre of subdivisions and agencies. After a general designation, any subdivision or agency proposing to consent to ICSID jurisdiction in respect of a particular investment need do no more than obtain its State's approval domestically, without the Centre being involved. The Centre would merely be informed of the State's approval when either the subdivision/agency or the investor made a request for arbitration, as contemplated in Rule 2(1)(c).

Specific (ad hoc) designations were, however, expressly contemplated from the outset; thus, during the meeting on 4 January 1965, when the UK delegate asked whether the designations should be made for a particular purpose or in general, Mr Broches as chairman replied that 'this should be left entirely to the Contracting States'.[24] The list of 'Designations by Contracting States regarding Constituent Subdivisions or Agencies' maintained by ICSID carries the Note: 'ad hoc designations and notifications made by Contracting States pursuant to Articles 25(1) and 25(3) are excluded from this listing'. The tribunal in *Niko Resources* pointed out that ad hoc designations do not receive general publicity, although they are accessible by contacting the Secretariat.[25]

Judging by the limited number recorded by ICSID, any expectation that general designations would be the normal rule has not been realized. Instead, it is common ground that ad hoc designations not only can be, but are in practice, made in the context of particular investments. The concepts of designation and approval may well as a result become blurred. A designation by a State of a particular constituent

[22] ibid 859.
[23] ibid.
[24] ibid 858.
[25] *Niko Resources (Bangladesh) Ltd v Bangladesh Petroleum Exploration & Production Co Ltd*, ICSID Case No ARB/10/11, Decision on Jurisdiction, 19 August 2013 [291] n 184.

subdivision or agency to the Centre in the specific context of a particular investment may constitute, at one and the same time, approval of the subdivision or agency's consent to ICSID jurisdiction.

The ordinary contemplation would be that both designation and approval would occur by the time the ICSID facilities are invoked. This is confirmed by Rule 2 of the ICSID Rules, requiring the Request to ICSID to:

> (b) state, if one of the parties is a constituent subdivision or agency of a Contracting State, that it has been designated to the Centre by that State pursuant to Article 25(1) of the Convention; and
> (c) indicate the date of consent and the instruments in which it is recorded, including, if one party is a constituent subdivision or agency of a Contracting State, similar data on the approval of such consent by that State unless it had notified the Centre that no such approval is required.

That does not mean that, if one of the requirements is not fulfilled by the time of any Request, the shortfall may not be made good, and the ICSID proceedings validated, by subsequent State act.

Approval to parties consenting to submit to ICSID any dispute arising out of an investment between them is a relatively straightforward concept. The difficulties which have arisen have tended to focus on the requirement of designation 'to the Centre by that State' and how it may be fulfilled. Different views have been taken by both academic commentators and ICSID tribunals.

Designation: The Views of Commentators

Professor Schreuer draws the contrast between designation and approval as follows:[26]

> Therefore, it is clear that designation and approval are two distinct acts with different functions. The existence of an approval cannot be inferred from the existence of a designation, although it is arguable that the approval of consent that is notified to the Centre may be interpreted as ad hoc designation of the constituent subdivision or agency.
>
> . . .
>
> The Convention does not require any particular form for the approval of consent. In particular, unlike designation of the constituent subdivision or agency and unlike waiver of approval, the approval need not be communicated to the

[26] Schreuer and others (n 4) 338, para 905 and 339, paras 909–10 (internal citations omitted) (original emphasis).

Centre. In principle, approval is a unilateral act of the host State that need not be formally communicated to anyone. For practical reasons, it is desirable that the foreign investor and the constituent subdivision or agency are informed of the approval so that they may rely on the validity of consent. An investor will be well-advised to insist on approval by the State prior to or simultaneously with the consent agreement.

Approval may be contained in a separate agreement between the host State and the investor. Or the approval may be contained in an instrument of designation communicated to the Centre. It may be practical to obtain approval by way of making the host State a party to the consent agreement. Alternatively, written approval by the host State may be affixed directly to the agreement between the constituent subdivision or agency and the investor. In addition, the consent clause may confirm that the investor's partner is indeed a designated subdivision or agency. The Model Clauses of 1993 offer the following choices in regard to a constituent subdivision or agency:

The name of constituent subdivision or agency is [a constituent subdivision]/[an agency] of the Host State, which has been designated to the Centre by the Government of that State in accordance with Article 25(1) of the Convention. In accordance with Article 25(3) of the Convention, the Host State [hereby gives its approval to this consent agreement]/[has given its approval to this consent agreement in citation of instrument in which approval is expressed]/[has notified the Centre that no approval of [of this type of consent agreement]/[of consent agreements by the name of constituent subdivision or agency] is required.

Professor Amerasinghe writes to like effect:[27]

> What is necessary for a valid approval? A clause in an agreement with the host State in which the host State approves the consent to submit disputes to the Centre given by the subdivision or agency is an adequate form of approval. It is also a valid and effective approval where a designating instrument contains an approval of the consent to arbitration given by the subdivisions or agencies. It is not necessary for a valid approval under Article 25(3) of the Convention of a consent given by a subdivision or agency that such approval be communicated to the subdivision or agency or that such subdivision or agency accept it as a party to the agreement in which it may be contained or otherwise. Technically, it is not necessary that even the investor be party to the approval or be aware of it. All the same, it is useful from the point of view of the functioning of the disputes settlement mechanism of the Convention that such approval be communicated both to the subdivision or agency and to the investor so that they may rely on it more easily.

[27] Amerasinghe (n 9) 189.

A surprisingly minimalist view was taken by Mr Broches himself nearly thirty years after the Convention. He wrote:[28]

> The limited purpose of the requirement of designation is to avoid doubt whether an entity is a constituent subdivision or agency and thus qualified to be a party to a dispute before the Centre. Failure of a formal designation should therefore not itself defeat jurisdiction if the entity concerned is proved or conceded to be a constituent subdivision or agency of a contracting state.

It appears from Professor Schreuer's Commentary that Mr Broches relied in this connection on the unpublished ICSID tribunal decision in *Manufacturers Hanover Trust Co v Arab Republic of Egypt and General Authority for Investment and Free Zones*.[29] This is described by another ICSID tribunal in *Cambodia Power Co v Kingdom of Cambodia and Electricité du Cambodge* as a case where 'there was no indication that the Arab Republic of Egypt, the Contracting State, had ever notified the Centre that it had designated [the General Authority for Investment and Free Zone] as its agency',[30] and in which the tribunal had held that: 'no particular form [wa]s required for such designation and approval. Whereas it may be assumed that a writing is needed, such writing can be contained in an Investment Law'.[31]

A view more consistent with the terminology and the course of the original drafting negotiations is given by Professor Amerasinghe, who writes:[32]

> A relevant question is whether the designation of a subdivision or agency must be officially and formally notified to the Centre by the Contracting State concerned. What the Convention states is that the subdivision or agency must be 'designated to the Centre'. Normally, this would mean that there should be some kind of formal communication of the designation to the Centre. Thus, a mere designation of a subdivision or agency in an investment agreement to which both the Contracting State and the subdivision or agency are parties would *per se* be inadequate. Likewise an undertaking in a similar agreement or in an agreement between the Contacting State and an investor to file the designation with the Centre or to take the necessary steps under the Convention coupled with a designation in the agreement clearly does not *per se* fulfil the requirements of the Convention.

[28] Aron Broches, 'Convention on the Settlement of Investment Disputes between States and Nationals of Other States 1965: Explanatory Notes and Survey of its Application' (1993) 18 YB Com Arb 627, 642.

[29] *Manufacturers Hanover Trust Co v Egypt*, ICSID Case No ARB/89/1, Decision on the Jurisdiction and the Constitution of the Arbitral Tribunal and on Recommendation of Provisional Measures, 6 June 1991.

[30] *Cambodia Power Co v Cambodia and Electricité du Cambodge*, ICSID Case No 09/18, Decision on Jurisdiction, 22 March 2011 [175].

[31] *Manufacturers Hanover* (n 29), as quoted in *Cambodia Power* (n 30) [175].

[32] Amerasinghe (n 9) 188.

Significantly, Professor Amerasinghe continues:[33]

> On the other hand, it is a moot question whether there must always be an official communication of the designation to the Centre. *It is arguable that where there was a clear intention on the part of the Contracting State to file the designation with the Centre at the time the designation was made but the actual communication is not made by that State to the Centre, it is adequate if instead of there being a formal communication of the designation to the Centre by the State it is brought to the attention of the Centre in some way whether by the State concerned or by one of the parties to the consent agreement provided this is done before the initial intention is changed.* Equally, it is clear that, if an agreement to which the Contracting State is a party and in which it designates a subdivision or agency is communicated by that State to the Centre, this would be an adequate designation to the Centre for the purposes of the Convention.
>
> There is no specific time at which the designation to the Centre should be made. Technically, the 'notification' of the designation to the Centre can be executed even after the dispute has arisen. Clearly, however, it must be made before a request involving the subdivision or agency concerned has been filed with the Centre or at the time such request is filed, for in the absence of a designation to the Centre, the Secretary-General will under Article 28(3) or Article 36(3) be forced to refuse registration of the request on the ground that there is manifest lack of jurisdiction in the Centre. However, this defect may be cured for a subsequent request, if the designation is filed with the Centre before such request is filed. [emphasis added]

Citing Professor Amerasinghe, Ms C Lamm subsequently wrote: 'Arguably, a clear intention on the part of the Contracting State to file a designation may be sufficient to satisfy the designation requirement so long as that intention is somehow brought to the Centre's attention'.[34]

Finally, Professor Schreuer analyses the requirement of designation in cautious terms, while declining to go as far as Mr Broches, and saying, with reference to Professor Amerasinghe:[35]

> The designation must be made to the Centre. Therefore, designation in an agreement with the investor is not enough. It is clear that the entity concerned cannot designate itself. But even an agreement of the Contracting State with the investor or a promise to make the designation to the Centre will not suffice. *There must be*

[33] ibid.

[34] Carolyn B Lamm, 'Jurisdiction of the International Centre for Settlement of Investment Disputes' (1991) 6 ICSID Rev 462, 469.

[35] Schreuer and others (n 4) 156, para 252.

> *some communication by the host State to the Centre. The designation is not subject to any formal requirements. It need not be made in a separate document. The notification to the Centre of an agreement with the investor containing the designation is enough. It has been argued that where there is a clear intention to designate, it does not matter how and through whom the communication reaches the Centre. Broches has said that failure of a formal designation should not defeat jurisdiction if the entity concerned is proved or conceded to be a constituent subdivision or agency of a Contracting State. It seems that this goes too far. Designation cannot be dispensed with altogether. But it is submitted that designation by a Contracting State can take any form that gives it general notoriety and comes to the Centre's attention. Legislation by the Contracting State that clearly includes a designation in the sense of Art. 25 should suffice. This would also apply to a designation contained in a bilateral investment treaty.* Despite all this, it is advisable that the Contracting State sends a clear and separate notification of the designation to the Centre in order to avoid any misunderstandings and jurisdictional difficulties. [emphasis added]

Designation: ICSID Tribunal Decisions

East Kalimantan

ICSID tribunals have also expressed differing views. In *Government of the Province of East Kalimantan v PT Kaltim Prima Coal and others*,[36] the claim to ICSID arbitration was made by the Government of East Kalimantan. East Kalimantan was a province of the Republic of Indonesia. The tribunal had no hesitation about treating it as a subdivision of a Contracting State, and the question was whether it was a 'designated' subdivision as required by Article 25 of the ICSID Convention. The claim failed because, on an analysis of various minutes, agreements, and a judgment lodged with the request for arbitration, the tribunal could not identify any designation by the Government of Indonesia of East Kalimantan as a constituent subdivision or agency.

The tribunal in *East Kalimantan*, agreeing with Professor Schreuer and citing the decision in *Cable Television*,[37] held that Mr Broches went 'too far'. But it took nonetheless a broad view of the way in which a designation may be communicated, stating:

> 192. ICSID's public list of designations made by Contracting States, specifically the footnote appearing at the end, show that designations can be made ad hoc

[36] *Government of the Province of East Kalimantan v PT Kaltim Prima Coal and others*, ICSID Case No ARB/07/3, Award on Jurisdiction, 28 December 2009.

[37] *Cable Television of Nevis Ltd v St Kitts and Nevis*, ICSID Case No ARB/95/2, Award, 16 December 1996, 13 ICSID Rev—FILJ 328.

> and need not appear on the list ('[a]d hoc designations and notifications made by Contracting States pursuant to Articles 25(1) and 25(3) are excluded from this listing.') In fact, commentators generally consider that designations are not subject to any formal requirement as long as they are made to the Centre. Christoph Schreuer stresses that '[i]t has been argued that where there is a clear intention to designate, it does not matter how and through whom the communication reaches the Centre.' In other words, the form and channel of communication do not matter, provided that the intention to designate is clearly established.
>
> 193. The designation requirement in Article 25(1) must be read in conjunction with ICSID Institution Rule 2(1)(b), which provides that '[t]he request [for arbitration] shall state if one of the parties is a constituent subdivision or agency of a Contracting State, that it has been designated to the Centre by that State pursuant to Article 25(1) of the Convention.' *Consequently, the designation requirement may in particular be deemed fulfilled when a document that emanates from the State is filed with the request for arbitration and shows the State's intent to name a specific entity as a constituent subdivision or agency for the purposes of Article 25(1).* [emphasis added]

If the last proposition is correct, it draws no distinction between cases where the claimant filing the document emanating from the State is the subdivision or agency or is the national of another Contracting State. It can be said that it would be incongruous if an alleged subdivision or agency (like the Government of East Kalimantan) could file such a designation, but a claimant national of another Contracting State could not.

Cambodia Power

In *Cambodia Power*, the Kingdom of Cambodia, the Ministry of Industry, Mines and Energy ('MIME'), and a State-owned company ('EDC') were all parties to a power purchase agreement with an investor, Cambodia Power Company (a Cambodian company wholly owned by a Delaware corporation). The agreement provided that, if and when Cambodia 'implemented' the ICSID Convention, any dispute would be submitted to ICSID arbitration; and that MIME would procure that Cambodia notified ICSID that it had designated each of MIME and EDC as a subdivision or agency of Cambodia. It further provided for ICC arbitration unless and until Cambodia implemented the ICSID Convention or if for any other reason the dispute could not be settled under the ICSID Convention. Cambodia later ratified the ICSID Convention, but communicated no designation of EDC or MIME to ICSID.

Cambodia Power Company argued that there had been sufficient designation. The tribunal started by agreeing with the *East Kalimantan* tribunal and with Professor Schreuer that Mr Broches's view—that designation could be dispensed with when the existence of a subdivision or agency could otherwise be shown—went too far. It held that communication was inherent in the very notion of 'designation' in Article 25(1). It saw the designation requirement as providing 'both clarity and a guarantee of protection to investors (or at least some certainty in this regard', and, citing Professor Schreuer, also as a 'gate-keeping' function for Contracting States, embodying their desire 'to preserve control over semi-autonomous entities in their dealings with foreign investors'.[38] The present writer notes in passing that Professor Schreuer put this aspect slightly differently in his 2009 Commentary on Article 25, writing: 'A secondary purpose of designation may be a desire on the part of the State to preserve control over semi-autonomous entities in their dealings with foreign investors. But this purpose is more readily achieved by withholding approval of consent to jurisdiction under Art. 25(3)'.[39]

The tribunal in *Cambodia Power* also noted in support of its view a possible argument that an ICSID award against a subdivision or agency designated by a State may 'at least arguably' be binding on the State.[40]

However, the *Cambodia Power* tribunal gave a limited latitude to the requirement of communication which it held to be inherent in designation, saying:[41]

> As a matter of convenience, and with the objective of communicating the designation to all potential investors, as well as clarifying each Contracting State's potential exposure, it is logical that Article 25(1) requires designation of an agency or subdivision to be brought to the Centre's attention.
>
> This is not to say, however, that a formal notification to the Centre is the only means by which a designation might be brought to the Centre's attention. So long as the designation of an entity as an agency or subdivision of a Contracting State is given public notoriety by the Contracting State such as to come to the Centre's attention, the use of other channels of communication can attain the objective of Article 25(1) of the Convention and thus comply with its designation requirement.
>
> ...
>
> [I]t is not Professor Schreuer's position [as quoted in paragraph 76 above] that anybody through any type of channel or form can communicate the designation of an agency of a Contracting State. Quite the contrary, as the Tribunal concludes in the present case, Professor Schreuer favours a serious threshold in that the form of designation must give 'general notoriety' to the designation, such as to come to the Centre's attention.

[38] *Cambodia Power* (n 30) [226]–[227].
[39] Schreuer and others (n 4) 155, para 248.
[40] *Cambodia Power* (n 30) [230].
[41] ibid [239]–[240] and [244].

Commenting on the *East Kalimantan* case, the tribunal in *Cambodia Power* considered that the tribunal in *East Kalimantan* appeared to misquote Professor Schreuer's view and that this had led it to conclude mistakenly that: 'the form and channel of communication do not matter provided that the intention to designation [sic] is clearly established'.[42]

The *Cambodia Power* tribunal distinguished the decision in *Manufacturers Hanover*, on the basis that the tribunal there had been concerned with the publication of a designation in an investment law which had achieved public notoriety, and that, whether or not it was correctly decided, the circumstances in *Cambodia Power* were far removed. It said:[43]

> Publication by a Contracting State in national legislation is quite a different act to the insertion of a reference to a designation in a private contract. The former reflects an intention to notify the world. The latter is a private act, without any public notoriety. In circumstances where the Contracting State has taken no step to bring the private contract to the attention of the Centre, the Tribunal considers that the requirements of Article 25(1) have not been met.

As to the mode of any communication, the *Cambodia Power* tribunal held that the designation requirement plays 'a critical role in delimiting the scope of the Convention regime'.[44] A 'structured and standardised system of notification' consisting in Article 25(1) of 'communication to the Centre' is necessary.[45] In these circumstances, there has to be 'a written designation which is communicated to the Centre'; and that, while:[46]

> [i]t may be possible for this to be done other than in a direct communication from the Contracting State to the Centre, such as in a Treaty or Legislation that would inevitably have public notoriety[,] . . . in most cases, it would be by direct communication and thus cannot be complied with by the investor itself providing a document to the Centre which contains, or is said to contain, a designation.

Addressing specifically the reference to designation words 'by that State', the tribunal added that: 'for Article 25(1) to serve a "gate-keeping" function . . . it is obviously essential that communication be the sole preserve of the State itself—and not a function which investors can discharge'.[47]

[42] ibid [243].
[43] ibid [245].
[44] ibid [226].
[45] ibid [227].
[46] ibid [246].
[47] ibid [250].

Finally, on the facts of the case before it, the tribunal was 'not convinced' that, even if the arbitration provisions had been properly communicated to ICSID, their wording demonstrated ICSID's unequivocal consent.

Niko Resources

A quite different analysis was adopted by the tribunal in *Niko Resources*. The claimants there were party to a general sale and purchase agreement (and in one case also a joint venture) with agencies of the State of Bangladesh. The agreement and joint venture provided for ICSID arbitration by clauses which the tribunal found had been approved or intended, if not initiated or instructed by the State. The agencies denied that they had been designated. The tribunal held the contrary.

The tribunal in *Niko Resources* reasoned as follows:

(i) Under Article 25(1) a distinction can be drawn between a designation and its communication and the requirement of 'designation "by the State" does not necessarily apply to the manner in which designation is made known 'to the Centre'.[48] In support, it noted the references, in other Articles of the Convention, to designation to, or to serve on, the panels of ICSID conciliators or arbitrators (see ICSID Convention Articles 13 and 14), and to notification and notice (see Articles 16(3), 25(4), 28(3), 49, 66(1), 70, 71, 72 and 75), counterpoised expressly in some instances by reference to designation (see Articles 16(3) and 54(2).

(ii) The principal purpose of designation is to confer on subdivisions and agencies competence to become party to ICSID proceedings. Any 'gate-keeping' function can be discounted, on the basis that any such function is or can be fulfilled by the separate requirement of approval under ICSID Convention Article 25(3) (as Professor Schreuer himself has indicated).[49]

(iii) Designation can be general or ad hoc, i.e. limited to a specific investment, and the possibility of ad hoc designations means that 'the publicity objective may be useful, but is not a necessary feature of designation'.[50]

(iv) Neither ICSID Convention Article 25(1) nor Rules 2(1)(b) and (c) of the ICSID Rules prescribes any form of designation (a point also made by Schreuer),[51] and implicit designation must be possible 'when the intention to designate clearly appears under the circumstances and is not contradicted by other indications'.[52]

Applying this reasoning, the tribunal in *Niko Resources* said that in its view:[53]

48 *Niko Resources* (n 25) [327].
49 See n 39 above.
50 ibid [291].
51 See n 35 above.
52 ibid [299].
53 ibid [301]–[302].

> a particularly strong case of implicit designation occurs when the State expressly and formally approves in writing that one of its agencies enters into an investment agreement containing an ICSID clause. Since designation has as its purpose and objective to confer on the agency the competence or capacity to become party to an ICSID arbitration, the approval by the State of an ICSID arbitration commitment by one of its agencies presupposes that this agency has the capacity to conclude such a commitment, which means that it must be capable to be a party to an ICSID arbitration.
>
> If the State has not already conferred this capacity on the agency by an earlier (general) designation, the approval necessarily must include the intention to confer this capacity on the agency by an ad hoc designation. Assuming the contrary would mean that the State, when granting its approval of the agency's consent, intended to leave this approval without effect. It would require very strong evidence to establish that a State intended to act in such contradictory fashion. Even then, it is doubtful that such a contrary intention should be given effect in view of the overriding principle requiring good faith conduct.

With regard to communication, the tribunal left open whether 'public notoriety' was, as held in *Manufacturers Hanover*, an adequate or admissible form of 'communication'. What it saw as critical was that, while the communication could take any form, it must come 'to the Centre's attention'. The tribunal drew in the passages highlighted in the citations above from Professors Amerasinghe's and Schreuer's writings and on the tribunal's reasoning in *East Kalimantan*. It disagreed with the contrary reasoning of the tribunal in *Cambodia Power*.

In the circumstances before it, the *Niko Resources* tribunal held: first, that the State of Bangladesh had, by authorizing the agencies to conclude the agreements containing ICSID arbitration clauses, designated, implicitly but necessarily, the two agencies in the sense of Article 25(1) of the ICSID Convention; and, second, that such designation could be and had been communicated validly to ICSID by the requests for arbitration.

Designation: Analysis

In the above light, what is meant by or involved in the phrase 'designated to the Centre by that State' remains very open to argument. The phrase appears in an article defining the extent of the Centre's jurisdiction and, more particularly, in the context of an extension of the Centre's jurisdiction beyond investor claims against a State to claims against a constituent subdivision or agency of a State. Its satisfaction is key to the conferral on such a subdivision or agency of capacity or competence to use the ICSID facility. While a requirement of designation was originally justified as intended to enable investors to know 'the … subdivisions or agencies which may appear before the Centre', it has necessarily a de facto 'gate-keeping' effect which is, at least potentially, in the interests of States. Either way, designation should therefore consist in conduct or words which are, viewed objectively, clear. But, apart from that, the writer does not see any basis for any particularly restrictive understanding of the concept. The 'gate' which the parties to the ICSID Convention have established is whatever gate appears, on a true construction of the Convention having regard to the principles established by the Vienna Convention. The Tribunal also notes and sees force in this connection in Professor Schreuer's comment to the effect that any gate-keeping purpose is, generally at least, more readily covered by the presence of ICSID Convention Article 25(3).

The number of leading commentators taking a generous view of the nature of permissible designation under Article 25(1) is notable. In common with Professor Schreuer and with the tribunals in *East Kalimantan* and *Cambodia Power*, the writer agrees that Mr Broches, the founding figure of the Convention, must have gone 'too far' in suggesting that no form of designation at all is required if it is otherwise shown that a constituent subdivision or agency is involved. It is still interesting that Mr Broches, with his intense understanding of the background and objectives of the Convention, did not feel it important to take a restrictive approach to the requirement of designation to the Centre by the State. Nor did Professor Amerasinghe and Ms Lamm (see above).

The limited support by distinguished commentators for any very restrictive reading of the requirement of designation to the Centre by the State may be because such a reading could give rise to obvious risks of impracticality or absurdity. The tribunal in *Manufacturers Hanover* evidently felt so, when it considered that a publicly promulgated investment law enacted domestically by the State sufficed. Professor Schreuer expressly endorses this view; he submits that designation can take any form that gives it general notoriety and comes to the Centre's attention and contemplates designation in this way through either domestically enacted legislation or a bilateral investment treaty.

It is not particularly fruitful to consider whether the distinguished tribunal in *East Kalimantan* misquoted or misunderstood Professor Schreuer in paragraph 192 of its award (quoted above). The view expressed by the *East Kalimantan* tribunal in paragraph 193 of its award must, on any analysis, be seen as the independent view of an experienced tribunal. It was also supported by a positive reason, derived from ICSID Institution Rule 2(1)(b) and independent of anything said by Professor Schreuer or other commentators.[54]

[54] However, so far as it is appropriate to consider the (admittedly rather compressed) reasoning of paragraphs 192 and 193 of the *East Kalimantan* award, the writer wonders whether the tribunal in *Cambodia Power* itself read paragraph 193 of the *East Kalimantan* award correctly. The statement in *East Kalimantan* that 'In other words, the form and channel of communication do not matter', was building on the three previous sentences of paragraph 192 of the *East Kalimantan* award, which had noted, first, that designations could be ad hoc; second, that commentators generally considered that designations were not subject to any formal requirement; and, third, that Professor Schreuer had stressed that '[it]

In the light of the above differences of view and approach, it is necessary to go back to first principles, construing the key phrase in Article 25 of the ICSID Convention in its context and in the light of its object and purpose as identified above, and with the benefit of the supplementary principles stated in the Vienna Convention.

The key difference between approval and designation is, as stated, that the former can take place at a simple domestic level, whereas the latter has under Article 25(1) of the ICSID Convention to be 'to the Centre by that State'. To meet the difficulty which this presents where approval is clear at the domestic level but designation at the international level is not, the tribunal in *Niko Resources* detected a distinction between designation, which could take place domestically, and its communication, which could follow subsequently and separately by any route. The writer has difficulty with this reasoning. He recognizes that the ICSID Convention speaks in other connections of designation to, or to serve on, a panel and of notices or notification (see above). But even in Articles 16(2) and (3) of the ICSID Convention, where notification and designation both appear as concepts, he is not persuaded that notification is referred to in distinction from, rather than as an element of, designation. Be that as it may, the present problem concerns words in Article 25(1) of the ICSID Convention which on their face appear to import that some form of communication is an aspect of designation to the Centre by the State. The word 'to' can have either a directional or a connectional connotation—examples of the latter being 'true to type', 'a room to herself', 'dedicated to charitable causes', or, in Article 13 of the ICSID Convention, 'may designate to each Panel' or 'designated to a Panel'. But the phrase 'designated to the Centre by that State' seems naturally to import some form of communication. The opposite view taken by the tribunal in *Niko Resources* appears either to delete the words 'by the State' or to convert the words 'to the Centre' into something like 'for the purposes of the Centre'.

What satisfies the requirement of designation 'to the Centre by that State' of an entity as a subdivision or agency for the purposes of Article 25(1) of the ICSID Convention must, in the present writer's view, be considered objectively in the light of all relevant words and conduct of those concerned and all relevant circumstances within their knowledge. Such circumstances can, in the writer's view,

has been argued' that it does not matter how and through whom the communication of a clear designation reaches the Centre. In support of the last point, paragraph 192 of the *East Kalimantan* award expressly footnoted paragraph 252 of Professor Schreuer's Commentary on art 25, which in turn footnoted, in relation to what had been 'argued', the passages from Professor Amerasinghe's and Ms Lamm's works (quoted above). It is difficult to believe that the tribunal in *East Kalimantan*, having expressly quoted what Professor Schreuer recited as 'argued', then treated it as his opinion, rather than the opinions of the authors whom Professor Schreuer was actually citing. The tribunal in *East Kalimantan* was, in the final sentence of paragraph 192, certainly summarizing the views of commentators and of those advancing the argument recited by Professor Schreuer and it did so with implicit approval. But it did not misquote Professor Schreuer and it does not follow or seem very likely that it was misled by any misunderstanding that Professor Schreuer had endorsed, rather than referred to, the arguments of Professor Amerasinghe and Ms Lamm.

include not merely the ICSID Convention, but also the ICSID Rules in so far as those involved must be taken to have been aware of them.

Take a case where a State has clearly approved the entry into by a constituent subdivision or agency of an investment agreement containing consent to submit to arbitration by the Centre any dispute arising directly out of the investment. In such a case, all concerned must know or be taken to be aware that the investor will in the event of any dispute invoke the use of the ICSID facilities, by a request for arbitration or conciliation. The State's approval of the commitment to ICSID arbitration carries with it objectively awareness and acceptance that its endorsement of the commitment to ICSID arbitration by its subdivision or agency will be communicated to the Centre at the latest whenever any occasion arose for such arbitration to take place.

There is considerable and in the writer's view understandable support for the view that direct communication to the Centre by the State is not a necessary component of designation. The tribunal in *Manufacturers Hanover* accepted an investment law as capable of constituting sufficient designation. Professor Schreuer accepts both a domestic law and an investment treaty as capable of doing so, and the tribunal in *Cambodia Power* likewise. The rationale given by Professor Schreuer and taken up in *Cambodia Power* is that 'designation can take any form that gives it public notoriety and comes to the Centre's attention'.[55] This conclusion has, in the present writer's respectful view, obvious good sense, it ties in with the Vienna Convention's caution against results which would be 'manifestly absurd or unreasonable', and it accords with principle.[56] A public manifestation of a designation can be seen objectively as a communication *ergo omnes*, that is, to the world at large, including ICSID.

At the same time, it can hardly be inevitable that a domestic law (or even a bilateral investment treaty) will come to the Centre's attention—at least, prior to a dispute arising and ICSID jurisdiction being invoked. Not even ICSID presumably maintains a complete overview of all potentially relevant domestic legislation in every Contracting State. And, even if it is likely that ICSID will get to know of such a law at some point prior to a dispute arising, it may do so through channels or media which have nothing to do with the State. The one real certainty is that, if and when ICSID jurisdiction is invoked by either party, the relevant law or treaty will be relied upon and brought to the Centre's attention.

Public notoriety is significant, because it points to at least the high probability, or perhaps even inevitability, as a matter of reasonable expectation, that the designation will be communicated—at least at the point when it becomes material. There

[55] See Schreuer and others (n 4) 156, para 252; *Cambodia Power* (n 30) [241].
[56] Vienna Convention on the Law of Treaties (n 2) art 32(b).

does not appear to the writer to be any other inherent value in public notoriety. What matters is communication to the Centre by the State. If a State makes clear that it accepts an agency as such, when approving a commitment to ICSID arbitration under a particular investment and for the express purpose of Article 25(1) of the ICSID Convention, then the State must be taken, viewing the position objectively, to be aware and accept that this will necessarily be communicated to the Centre, by whichever party institutes ICSID arbitration.

The present writer suggests that that is what matters, and that it satisfies the requirement in Article 25(1) of the ICSID Convention that the agency be 'designated [as such] to the Centre by that State' for the purposes of the agency's commitment to ICSID arbitration to which the State was giving its approval. In these particular circumstances, the approval and the designation do run hand in hand. This is in accordance with the view of the tribunal in *East Kalimantan* and that of Professor Amerasinghe. It also fits with Professor Shreuer's general statement that 'it is arguable that the approval of consent that is notified to the Centre may be interpreted as an ad hoc designation of the constituent subdivision or agency'.[57] It builds on the reasonable expectations of all concerned to explain why the concept of notification may extend beyond situations where the State itself directly notifies the Centre of the approval or does some act giving 'public notoriety' to the designation.

C. Conclusions

In the light of the above, the writer summarizes his conclusions as follows:

1. Designation of a subdivision or agency to the Centre by the State cannot axiomatically be assimilated with approval by the State of a subdivision or agency's consent to ICSID arbitration in respect of an investment; but the separate requirements of designation and approval may in a particular case be satisfied by virtue of the same conduct and/or communication.
2. A designation may take any form, and may be implicit, so long as it is clear.
3. An essential element of designation is communication to the Centre by the State.
4. If a State makes clear that it accepts an agency as such, in the context of a commitment to ICSID arbitration under a particular investment and for the express purpose of satisfying Article 25(1) of the ICSID Convention, then the State must, objectively and in the light of Institution Rule 2, be taken to be aware and to accept that this will be communicated to the Centre by the

[57] Schreuer and others (n 4) 338, para 905.

investor at latest when it becomes material for the investor to institute ICSID arbitration.

5. In such a case, the reasonable expectations of all concerned that such communication will take place in this way are, when it does happen, sufficient to satisfy the requirement in Article 25(1) of the ICSID Convention that the agency be 'designated to the Centre by that State'.

13

Discovery, Arbitration, and 28 USC §1782

Rules or Standards?

*Linda Silberman**

A. Introduction

I am honoured to participate in this Festschrift for my close friend and colleague, Lawrence Collins. I am indebted to my late colleague Andy Lowenfeld, who first connected me with Lawrence when Andy and I worked together with Lawrence on a US judgment recognition matter that Lawrence was handling when he was a partner in Herbert Smith. Because Lawrence and I shared common interests in so many aspects of private international law, our initial professional relationship deepened and grew. Even more importantly, we developed a close and rewarding friendship over the years, which came to include our entire families. Together we have enjoyed dinners, theatre, jazz, movies, and conversations on both sides of the Atlantic. Additionally, NYU Law School and I were able to persuade Lawrence to become an NYU Global Professor, and for a number of years Lawrence and I co-taught the International Litigation/Arbitration course that Andy had first developed at the Law School many years before.

In choosing a topic for this Festschrift, I have selected one that builds on Lawrence's extensive experience and interest in international arbitration. It also draws on my own present preoccupation with the tension between 'rules' and 'standards', which was the theme of my General Course on Private International Law at the Hague Academy given remotely this past summer. Also, the precise issue—whether 28 USC §1782, which provides for US judicial assistance to obtain evidence for use in foreign or international proceedings, extends to investor-State and/or private commercial arbitral tribunals—is awaiting decision by the Supreme Court. In writing about this issue for this Festschrift in honour of Lawrence, I will also draw some comparisons with practice in the UK, an aspect of my teaching and scholarship that has been greatly enriched by my work and teaching with Lawrence.

* I am grateful to and thank my research assistants, Jeremy Jacobson, JD New York University School of Law (May 2021) and Kateryna Shokalo, LLM New York University School of Law (January 2022) for their valuable help on this chapter.

Linda Silberman, *Discovery, Arbitration, and 28 USC §1782* In: *Essays in International Litigation for Lord Collins.* Edited by: Jonathan Harris and Campbell McLachlan, Oxford University Press. © Oxford University Press 2022.
DOI: 10.1093/oso/9780192867988.003.0014

B. Access to US Information in Foreign Proceedings under 28 USC §1782 and the Supreme Court Decision in *Intel*

The need to obtain evidence for use in a foreign proceeding, whether for trial or pre-trial, was traditionally viewed as a matter of international cooperation. Such cross-border cooperation began with letters rogatory[1] and was greatly improved by the adoption of a multilateral international treaty, the Hague Convention on the Taking of Evidence Abroad in Civil or Commercial Matters (the 'Hague Evidence Convention').[2] However, when information is sought from a person subject to jurisdiction in the US, a more direct route is available on the basis of a US statute, 28 USC §1782. Section 1782 provides that a district court of the district in which a person resides or can be found may order testimony or the production of documents for use in a proceeding in a foreign or international tribunal. The Senate Report on the statute explained its purpose as follows: to provide 'equitable and efficacious procedures for the benefit of tribunals and litigants involved in litigation with international aspects … [and to] invite foreign countries similarly to adjust their procedures'.[3] Applications under §1782 can be made pursuant to a letter rogatory or by a foreign or international tribunal, or by any interested person. Once the statute is held to apply, the traditional balancing of factors to resolve discovery disputes comes into play, including concerns relating to comity.[4]

The origins of 28 USC §1782 can be traced back to 1855, with many of its present elements appearing in several different statutes over the years.[5] The modern evolution came as the result of a Congressional Commission on International Rules of Judicial Procedure, created in 1958 to study and recommend improvements to the existing framework for judicial cooperation with foreign countries and to draft legislation to streamline the procedures necessary for rendering assistance to foreign tribunals.[6] Specifically, Congress expanded the scope of judicial assistance to reach a 'proceeding in a foreign or international tribunal' instead of 'any judicial proceeding pending in any court in a foreign country'.[7] As the Commission Report explained:

[1] See generally Harry Leroy Jones, 'International Judicial Assistance: Procedural Chaos and a Program for Reform' (1953) 62 Yale LJ 515, 529–34.

[2] Hague Convention on the Taking of Evidence Abroad in Civil or Commercial Matters (opened for signature 18 March 1970, entered into force 7 October 1972) 847 UNTS 231 (hereafter 'Hague Evidence Convention').

[3] S Rep No 88-1580 (1964), reprinted in 1964 USCCAN 3782, 3793 (hereafter 'Senate Report').

[4] See *Intel Corp v Adv Micro Devices, Inc* 542 US 241 (2004), which is discussed in the text accompanying nn 10–23.

[5] For a detailed account, see Report of the New York City Bar Committee on International Commercial Disputes, 28 USC §1782 As a Means of Obtaining Discovery in Aid of International Commercial Arbitration—Applicability and Best Practices (February 2008), <www.nycbar.org/pdf/report/1782_Report.pdf> accessed 4 April 2022 (hereafter 'Bar Committee Report').

[6] See Act of 2 September 1958, Pub L No 85-906, §2, 72 Stat 995, 997, 1743.

[7] ibid 11.

> The word 'tribunal' is used to make it clear that assistance is not confined to proceedings before conventional courts. In view of the constant growth of administrative and quasi-judicial proceedings all over the world, the necessity for obtaining evidence in the United States may be as impelling in proceedings before a foreign administrative tribunal or quasi-judicial agency as in proceedings before a conventional foreign court.[8]

In both the 1963 Commission Report and the final revision of §1782 in 1964, it was clear that district courts would be given substantial discretion in its application. On that point, the Senate Report stated: 'In exercising its discretionary power, the court may take into account . . . the character of the proceedings in that country, or in the case of proceedings before an international tribunal, the nature of the tribunal and the character of the proceedings before it.'[9]

The first (and only) Supreme Court interpretation of §1782 came in 2004 in *Intel Corp v Advanced Micro Devices, Inc.*[10] *Intel* involved an application by AMD, a US company, seeking discovery from Intel, another US company, in connection with a complaint that AMD had filed against Intel in the European Commission, alleging a violation of European competition law. An initial question before the district court was whether the Directorate General for Competition that was undertaking the initial investigation was a 'tribunal' at all so as to fall within §1782. A second question, which had divided the appeals courts in the US, was whether a 'foreign-discoverability or admissibility' rule should be imposed as a prerequisite to issuing an order to obtain information. The argument in favour of such a requirement was that to the extent that the foreign jurisdiction would not allow for such discovery or the admissibility of such evidence, a court in the US should not interfere with the procedures and laws that the foreign jurisdiction has chosen for litigation in its own proceedings.[11]

On the first question—the definition of 'tribunal'—the Supreme Court rejected the views of the European Commission set forth in an amicus brief, contending that the DG-Competition was itself not a 'tribunal'.[12] The Court described the structure and operation of DG-Competition, which it characterized as the investigatory arm of the European Commission to which it makes a recommendation.[13] The European Commission issues a final, binding decision that is enforceable

[8] Historical and Explanatory Notes to the Proposed Bill 'To Improve Judicial Procedures for Servicing Documents, Obtaining Evidence and Proving Documents in Litigation with International Aspects' (note to subs (a)), 45.

[9] Senate Report (n 3) 3788.

[10] *Intel* (n 4).

[11] Two other questions were raised in the case: whether the foreign proceeding had to be currently 'pending' and whether 'interested persons' must be litigants in the foreign proceeding. The answers to both questions were 'no'. See ibid 247, 256, 259.

[12] See Brief for Commission of the European Communities as Amicus Curiae at 2, *Intel Corp v Advanced Micro Devices, Inc* 542 US 241 (2004) (No 02-572).

[13] *Intel* (n 4) 254.

through fines and penalties, and its action is subject to review in the Court of First Instance and the European Court of Justice. The Supreme Court explained that the Court of First Instance and the European Court of Justice would clearly qualify as 'tribunals', and that the Commission should also be regarded as a §1782 tribunal because it 'acts as a first-instance decisionmaker' for those tribunals.[14]

With respect to the second question as to whether the information must be discoverable or admissible under the rules of the foreign jurisdiction where the case was proceeding, the Supreme Court refused to impose any such categorical restriction, reasoning that neither the text of the statute nor the legislative history indicated that such limitations were intended. The Court noted: 'If Congress had intended to impose such a sweeping restriction on the district court's discretion, at a time when it was enacting liberalizing amendments to the statute, it would have included statutory language to that effect.'[15] The Court also referred to the Senate Report, which had observed that §1782(a) 'leaves the issuance of an appropriate order to the discretion of the court, which in proper cases, may refuse to issue an order or may impose conditions it deems desirable'.[16]

Notwithstanding its reluctance to impose categorical limitations with respect to the interpretation of §1782, including the meaning of 'tribunal' or 'foreign discoverability', the Supreme Court did not dismiss concerns about interference with foreign proceedings or the need to maintain parity between the litigants. Rather, it emphasized that such concerns may be relevant in determining whether an application should be granted and an order issued in a particular case. Accordingly, the Court identified four specific factors that 'bear consideration' when a court rules on a §1782 request: (i) whether the person from whom the information is sought is a party in the foreign proceeding; (ii) the nature of the foreign tribunal, the character of the proceeding abroad, and the receptivity of the foreign court or agency to federal-court judicial assistance; (iii) whether the request is an attempt to circumvent foreign proof-gathering restrictions or other policies of the foreign country; and (iv) whether the request is unduly intrusive or burdensome.[17] But the Court specifically declined to exercise its supervisory authority to adopt presumptive 'rules' that would provide further guidance.[18]

Justice Breyer, in dissent, explained his objections to this case-by-case approach. He pointed out that discovery matters 'take time, they are expensive, and cost and delay, or threats of cost and delay, can themselves force parties to settle underlying disputes'.[19] He also observed that expensive and time-consuming battles

[14] ibid 258.
[15] ibid 260.
[16] ibid 260–61 (citing S Rep No 1580 at 7, US Code Cong & Admin News 1964, pp 3782, 3788).
[17] ibid 264–65.
[18] ibid 265 ('We decline, at this juncture, to adopt supervisory rules. Any such endeavor at least should await further experience with § 1782(a) applications in the lower courts.').
[19] ibid 268 (Breyer J, dissenting).

about discovery take up domestic judicial resources, crowd dockets, and potentially interfere with foreign proceedings.[20] Accordingly, he urged that the Supreme Court impose categorical limits on the use of §1782, particularly with respect to discovery. First, he advised that when the entity had few tribunal-like characteristics that left its status in doubt, a US court should pay close attention to the foreign country's view of whether or not it should be considered a 'tribunal'.[21] Second, he indicated that a court should not permit discovery where the foreign law would not permit discovery and where US law would not authorize discovery in similar circumstances.[22]

The actual holding in *Intel* did not involve the issue of whether an arbitral panel is a 'tribunal' within the meaning of 28 USC §1782. However, in discussing the meaning of 'tribunal' in *Intel*, Justice Ginsburg, writing for the majority, referenced the Senate Report indicating the congressional purpose of §1782 to provide the possibility of US judicial assistance in connection with administrative and quasi-judicial proceedings abroad. She cited to an article by Professor Hans Smit, which itself contained a footnote with a parenthetical stating that the 'term "tribunal" ... includes investigating magistrates, administrative and arbitral tribunals, and quasi-judicial agencies, as well as conventional civil, commercial criminal, and administrative courts'.[23] Because the Smit article explicitly mentioned 'arbitral tribunals' (even though the Senate Report did not) and the parenthetical in a footnote in the Smit article was quoted in the reference by Justice Ginsburg, a number of courts have held that the Court implicitly endorsed the Smit view that 'arbitral tribunals' are included within the scope of §1782.[24]

The more difficult question, however, is whether the term was meant to encompass anything other than governmental or intergovernmental arbitral tribunals. It had been generally accepted that some types of arbitral tribunals were within the ambit of §1782. Indeed, when the language of the 1964 version of the statute was changed from 'courts' to 'tribunals', the clear intention was to extend judicial assistance to reach 'governmental or intergovernmental arbitral tribunals ... and other state-sponsored adjudicatory bodies'.[25] Indeed, prior statutes (now subsumed

[20] ibid 269.

[21] ibid 269–70.

[22] ibid 270.

[23] ibid 258 (citing S Rep No 1580, 7–8, US Code Cong & Admin News 1964, pp 3782, 3788, and Hans Smit, 'International Litigation under the United States Code' (1965) 65 Colum L Rev 115, 1026–27, nn 71, 73).

[24] *In re Application of Babcock Borsig AG*, 583 F Supp 2d 233, 238–39 (D Mass 2008) (acknowledging that *Intel*'s reference to arbitral tribunals was dicta, but noting that it provided 'meaningful insight' nonetheless); *In re Roz Trading Ltd*, 469 F Supp 2d 1221, 1225 (ND Ga 2006) (relying on *Intel*'s quotation as one of the reasons for its finding that the arbitral tribunal was within the §1782 scope and consistent with *Intel*); *In re Hallmark Capital Corp*, 534 F Supp 2d 951, 955 (D Minn 2007) (concluding that the Supreme Court in *Intel* cited Smit's article approvingly). But see Stacie I Strong, 'Discovery under 28 USC § 1782: Distinguishing International Commercial Arbitration and International Investment Arbitration' (2013) 1 Stan J Complex Litig 295, 11–12.

[25] *Abdul Latif Jameel Transp Co v FedEx Corp* 939 F3d 710, 726 (6th Cir 2019) (quoting *NBC v Bear Sterns & Co* 165 F3d 184, 190 (2d Cir 1999)).

within §1782) used the term 'international tribunal' expressly to be able to include governmental and intergovernmental arbitral tribunals.[26] The Commission itself cited to an earlier article by Professor Smit, where he explained that an international tribunal is one created by an international agreement.[27]

Because the legislative history gave no indication of extending judicial assistance to international arbitral panels created exclusively by private parties, two Courts of Appeals, prior to *Intel*, held that private arbitral panels were not a 'foreign or international tribunal' within the meaning of §1782.[28] In *National Broadcasting Co v Bear Stearns*,[29] the Second Circuit traced the legislative history of §1782 and concluded that such an expansion of US judicial assistance to international arbitral panels created exclusively by private parties 'would not have been lightly undertaken by Congress without at least a mention of this legislative intention'.[30] The Court of Appeals also observed that private arbitration did not generally include the broad discovery characteristic of US litigation and that discovery under the US Federal Arbitration Act, whether domestic or international, was substantially more limited than pursuant to §1782.[31] The Court of Appeals pointed out that under §7 of the Federal Arbitration Act, only the arbitrators have authority to summon a witness to appear before the arbitrators and to produce materials.[32] In addition, although §7 gives district courts authority to enforce the summons or cite a person in contempt for failure to appear,[33] an order directed to a non-party is generally for attendance or production at the arbitral hearing and not for pre-trial discovery.[34]

[26] See 22 USC §§270–270g (repealed) (providing for judicial assistance in a proceeding 'before an international tribunal or commission, established pursuant to an agreement between the United States and any foreign government or governments'). Originally, 22 USC §§270–270c was confined to assistance to a tribunal established by a treaty to which the US was a party and then only in proceeding involving a claim in which the US or one of its nationals was interested. Later provisions, contained in §§270d–270g extended that assistance to international tribunals even if the US was not a party. Section 1782 eliminated the restriction that the evidence should relate to a matter in which the US or one of its nationals was involved. See Senate Report (n 3) 3784–89. See also *NBC* (n 25) (recounting the history of §§270–270g and the various amendments and purposes behind those amendments).

[27] See Commission Report (n 8) (citing Hans Smit, 'Assistance Rendered by the United States in Proceedings before International Tribunals' (1962) 62 Colum L Rev 1264, 1267 ('Since an international tribunal owes both its existence and its powers to an international agreement, its powers can be extended only by such an agreement and not by a unilateral act.')).

[28] See *NBC* (n 25); *Republic of Kazakhstan v Biedermann International* 168 F3d 880, 881–83 (5th Cir 1999).

[29] *NBC* (n 25).

[30] ibid 190.

[31] ibid 187–88. The application in *NBC* (n 25) was clearly an attempt to obtain information for discovery purposes since it was made in anticipation of an ICC arbitration in Mexico but prior to the appointment of the panel.

[32] See 9 USC §7.

[33] Section 7 provides that if any person refuses or neglects to obey such summons, upon petition, the district court can enforce the summons or punish said person for contempt.

[34] Courts in the US are divided on whether an arbitral tribunal may order a non-party to produce documents other than at an evidentiary hearing, but courts consistently refuse to enforce arbitral subpoenas for pre-trial deposition testimony. See eg *Life Receivables Trust v Syndicate 102 at Lloyd's of London* 549 F3d 210 (2d Cir 2008) (holding arbitrators may not compel pre-hearing discovery from non-parties); *Hay Group, Inc v EBS Acquisition Corp* 360 F3d 404, 410 (3d Cir 2004) (same). But see *Sec Life Ins Co of Am v Duncanson & Holt, Inc* 228 F3d 865, 870 (8th Cir 2000) (ruling that §7 may apply to

The Court of Appeals concluded that Congress would not have conferred broader evidence-gathering mechanisms that could create a conflict between the two statutes.

The Fifth Circuit in *Republic of Kazakhstan v Biedermann International* reached the same conclusion.[35] Echoing themes similar to those of the Second Circuit in *NBC* and citing its reasoning, the Fifth Circuit viewed the statutory language as ambiguous, thus requiring an examination of the legislative history. It found that §1782 was drafted to incorporate the predecessor statute which 'facilitated discovery for international government-sanctioned "tribunals"' and that Congress gave no indication of 'extending § 1782 to the then novel-arena of international commercial arbitration'.[36] The Fifth Circuit also expressed concern that permitting discovery in this context would frustrate the 'speedy, economical and effective means' of dispute resolution that are private arbitration's greatest benefits.[37]

C. Post-*Intel* Case Law

In the aftermath of the Supreme Court's decision in *Intel*, numerous commentators read the Court's opinion to suggest that private arbitral tribunals are indeed within the scope of §1782.[38] That same position is taken by the American

pre-hearings). See generally: Report of the International Disputes Committee of the Association of the Bar of the City of New York, Obtaining Evidence from Non-Parties in International Arbitration in the United States (2009) 20 Am Rev Intl Arb 421, 422, 426–28; Alan Scott Rau, 'Evidence and Discovery in American Arbitration: The Problem of "Third Parties"' (2008) 19 Am Rev Intl Arb 1, 9. See Restatement of the US Law of International Commercial and Investor-State Arbitration, §3.4 cmt b(i) and Reporters' Note b(i) (Am Law Inst, Proposed Final Draft, 24 April 2019) (hereafter 'Arbitration Restatement').

[35] *Biedermann* (n 28).

[36] ibid 882. Notwithstanding the language used by the court, *Biedermann* appears to be an investor-State arbitration based on the US–Kazakhstan bilateral investment treaty. See Jarrod Hepburn, 'Looking Back: In First Treaty Claim under SCC Rules, Arbitrators in the Long-Opaque Biedermann Case Held Kazakhstan Liable for Breaching US–Kazak BIT, and Rejected Counterclaim on Merits', IAReporter (1 November 2017), <www.iareporter.com/articles/looking-back-in-first-treaty-claim-under-scc-rules-arbitrators-in-the-long-opaque-biedermann-case-held-kazakhstan-liable-for-breaching-us-kazak-bit-and-rejected-counterclaim-on-merits/> accessed 4 April 2022.

[37] ibid 883.

[38] See eg Arthur Rovine, 'Section 1782 and International Arbitral Tribunals: Some Key Considerations in Key Cases' (2012) 23 Am Rev Intl Arb 461, 466–67 (reading the *Intel* decision to support Professor Smit's stated intent that §1782 apply to private arbitral tribunals); Kenneth Beale, Justin Lugar, and Franz Schwarz, 'Solving the § 1782 Puzzle: Bringing Certainty to the Debate over 28 USC § 1782's Application to International Arbitration' (2011) 47 Stan J Intl L 51; Pedro Martinez-Fraga, 'The Future of 28 USC § 1782: The Continued Advance of American-Style Discovery in International Commercial Arbitration' (2009) 64 U Miami L Rev 89, 90 (stating that post-*Intel*, international commercial arbitrations constitute a 'foreign or international tribunal' under §1782 as a matter of law); Okezie Chukwumerije, 'International Judicial Assistance: Revitalizing Section 1782' (2005) 37 Geo Wash Intl L Rev 647, 676–80 . However, not all commentators were in agreement that §1782, as it was written, encompassed private arbitral tribunals. See eg Daniel Rothstein, 'A Proposal to Clarify US Law on Judicial Assistance in Taking Evidence for International Arbitration' (2008) 19 Am Rev Intl Arb 61; Martin Davies, 'Court-Ordered Interim Measures in Aid of International Commercial Arbitration' (2006) 17 Am Rev Intl Arb 299, 313–14.

Law Institute in the Proposed Final Draft of its new Restatement of the US Law of International Commercial and Investor-State Arbitration.[39] Several appellate courts also reached that conclusion. In *Abdul Latif Jameel Transportation Co Ltd v FedEx Corp*, the Court of Appeals for the Sixth Circuit reversed a district court's refusal to order discovery pursuant to a §1782 application for use in a dispute to be arbitrated in Dubai under the rules of the Dubai International Financial Centre–London Court of International Arbitration.[40] The district court had held that the arbitration panel did not constitute a 'foreign or international' tribunal within the meaning of §1782(a). On appeal, the Sixth Circuit reversed. It first explored the 'dictionary definition' of 'tribunal', but failed to find any consensus as to whether private arbitrations were included.[41] The appellate court then examined the term 'tribunal' in legal writing, concluding that 'American lawyers and judges understood and use the word "tribunal" to encompass privately contracted-for arbitral bodies with the power to bind the contracting parties'.[42] Nor did the Sixth Circuit find any indication that Congress intended to give the term 'tribunal' in §1782 a narrower understanding than its linguistic meaning in legal writing. In addition, the Court of Appeals relied on the Supreme Court's decision in *Intel* as support for its conclusion that arbitrations qualified as 'tribunals' in that they act as 'first-instance decisionmakers'.[43]

As to the argument that only State-sponsored and international governmental tribunals were included within §1782—as the Second Circuit (prior to *Intel*) held in *NBC*, and as the Fifth Circuit (prior to *Intel*) concluded in *Biedermann* to which it cited (post-*Intel*) in *ElPaso Corp v La Comisión Ejecutiva Hidroeléctrica Del Rio Lempa*[44]—the Sixth Circuit rejected the reasoning in those decisions. The Sixth Circuit found the resort to legislative history by those courts unwarranted, and in any event, read the legislative history differently. It noted that the 1964 amendment broadened the scope of §1782 and that the repeal of §§270–270g removed the requirement that the US be a party to an international agreement under which a proceeding takes place.[45] In considering the policy objections to an interpretation that brought private commercial arbitration within §1782, the Sixth Circuit pointed

[39] See Arbitration Restatement (n 34) §3.5(a), cmt b ('The Restatement takes the position that the plain language of §1782 should prevail and that the statute should be interpreted as applying to international arbitral tribunals.'). Although the Restatement provision acknowledged that the lower courts were divided with respect to the issue, the Proposed Draft was approved in April 2019, prior to later appellate decisions, discussed below, creating the post-*Intel* circuit split.

[40] *Latif* (n 25).

[41] ibid 719–20.

[42] ibid 722. As one example, the Court of Appeals observed that the US Supreme Court, in *Mitsubishi Motors Corp v Soler Chrysler-Plymouth* 473 US 614, 636 (1985), used the phrase 'international arbitral tribunal' to describe a private arbitration.

[43] *Latif* (n 25) 724.

[44] 341 F Appx 31 (5th Cir 2009). The Fifth Circuit concluded that *Intel* did not unequivocally overrule its holding in *Biedermann* and thus it was bound by the earlier precedent.

[45] *Latif* (n 25) 729.

again to the Supreme Court's decision in *Intel*. It noted first that the Supreme Court in *Intel* itself rejected the imposition of categorical limitations on the statute. The Sixth Circuit emphasized the Supreme Court's focus in *Intel* on the broad discretion courts have to shape discovery under §1782 and the specific factors that a district court should take into account in considering a discovery request pursuant to the statute. Specifically, the Court of Appeals indicated that this discretion 'presumably extends to consideration of any agreements between the availability and scope of discovery in arbitration'.[46]

A subsequent decision of the Court of Appeals for the Fourth Circuit, *Servotronics, Inc v The Boeing Co*,[47] also reversed a district court decision that had relied on *NBC* and *Biedermann* to hold that a UK arbitration panel was not a 'foreign or international tribunal' within the meaning of §1782.[48] Citing the post-*Intel* Sixth Circuit decision in the *Latif* case, the Fourth Circuit observed that there was now a split of authority among the circuits and noted that the Fourth Circuit had never addressed the issue, either before or after *Intel*.[49] Assuming that certain types of arbitral tribunals were intended to fall within the §1782 definition of 'tribunal', the Court of Appeals in *Servotronics* focused its attention on whether the tribunal must be one that exercised 'government-conferred authority'.[50] Referencing the position taken by the appellate courts in *NBC* and *Biedermann* that the term 'foreign or international tribunal' referred only to 'entities acting with the authority of the State', the Fourth Circuit concluded that even under that definition, the UK arbitral panel satisfied the criteria.[51] The Court pointed to the English Arbitration Act, which it characterized as providing governmental regulation of arbitration, referencing various provisions of the Act that address, among other matters, stays of legal proceedings, schedules, summoning witnesses, the composition of the tribunals, the power to appoint experts, the review of awards, and the enforcement of awards.[52] As to arguments that the application of §1782 to private arbitration proceedings would undermine the parties' bargained-for method of dispute resolution by introducing US discovery into foreign proceedings, the Fourth Circuit underscored the point that §1782 is not only about discovery—indeed that statute does not use the term 'discovery'—but about judicial assistance by a US court to obtain information 'for use' in the proceeding before the foreign tribunal.[53] In addition, unlike discovery in a US litigation which initially is in the control of the parties, the ability to obtain any information under §1782 is within the discretion of the district court.[54]

[46] ibid 730.
[47] 954 F3d 209 (4th Cir 2020).
[48] ibid 214.
[49] ibid 212.
[50] ibid 214.
[51] ibid 214–15.
[52] ibid.
[53] ibid 215.
[54] ibid.

Other appellate courts took a different view. Notwithstanding the decisions of the Fourth and Sixth Circuit Courts of Appeals, the Second Circuit, in *Hanwei Guo v Deutsche Bank Securities Inc*,[55] reaffirmed its pre-*Intel* precedent in *NBC* excluding private commercial arbitration from §1782 judicial assistance. Guo was seeking discovery of documents from four investment banks for use in an arbitration in China in which he claimed that an individual and several companies had defrauded him in an investment. In rejecting the §1782 application, the Court of Appeals adhered to its decision in *NBC*, holding that a private commercial arbitral tribunal was not a 'foreign or international tribunal' within the meaning of §1782.[56] The Court of Appeals acknowledged that the Sixth and Fourth Circuits had reached a different conclusion on that point after the Supreme Court's decision in *Intel*, but concluded that *Intel* itself did not cast 'sufficient doubt' on its earlier precedent to justify departing from it.[57] The Second Circuit pointed out that these recent appellate cases did not suggest that *Intel* had overruled *NBC*, but rather read *Intel* to contain 'no limiting principle' that the word 'tribunal' excluded arbitration.[58] In reaffirming *NBC* in *Hanwei Guo*, the Court of Appeals for the Second Circuit emphasized that its prior *NBC* decision found that private commercial arbitration was excluded because §1782 only had in mind 'State-sponsored' arbitrations, and nothing the Supreme Court said in *Intel* was inconsistent with such a finding. The Second Circuit observed that even if the Supreme Court's indirect reference in *Intel* to 'arbitral tribunals' in the parenthetical quotation in Professor Smit's article is given weight, it would have no bearing on whether non-governmental private commercial arbitrations were included in §1782.[59]

In *Hanwei Gou*, the Second Circuit then turned its attention to the particular tribunal that was at issue—a tribunal established under the auspices of the Chinese International Economic and Trade Arbitration Commission (CIETAC). Guo contended that even if private arbitrations are not within §1782, a CIETAC arbitration is in fact a State-sponsored adjudicatory body because it was originally founded by the Chinese Government. Even if so, the Court reasoned that CIETAC had evolved to the point that it presently functions independently of the Chinese Government and maintains a high degree of independence and autonomy.[60] Moreover, the Court viewed the provisions of Chinese arbitration law that cover the enforcement of agreements and awards as no different from the provisions of the Federal Arbitration Law and 'do not convert CIETAC arbitrations into state-sponsored endeavors'.[61]

[55] 965 F3d 96 (2d Cir 2020).
[56] ibid 105–07.
[57] ibid 103–04.
[58] ibid 104 (referencing *Latif* (n 25) 725–26). In addition, the Second Circuit viewed the Fourth Circuit's decision in *Servotronics* as resting on its finding that the English Arbitration Act was the 'product of government-conferred authority'. Ibid.
[59] ibid 105.
[60] ibid 107.
[61] ibid 108.

A subsequent Court of Appeals decision in the Seventh Circuit, *Servotronics, Inc v Rolls-Royce plc*,[62] involved a different discovery application by the same party in the same arbitration that generated the decision in the earlier Fourth Circuit *Servotronics* decision.[63] The Seventh Circuit, unlike the Fourth Circuit, held that private foreign arbitrations were not included within §1782. The Court of Appeals considered the split of authority in the other Circuits, siding with the decisions of the Fifth and Second Circuits excluding private arbitrations from §1782.[64] In reaching its decision, the Court reviewed dictionary definitions of 'tribunal', but found them inconclusive.[65] It then examined the 1964 overall statutory revisions that had adopted recommendations by the earlier Rules Commission to related statutes. The Court found that the term 'foreign and international tribunal' appeared in these other provisions and referred to 'state-sponsored, public, or quasi-governmental' tribunals and not private arbitration tribunals, noting that '[i]dentical words or phrases' used in related statutes 'are presumed to have the same meaning'.[66] The Court also emphasized that this 'narrow understanding' of the word 'tribunal' avoided a 'serious conflict with the Federal Arbitration Act',[67] which authorizes the arbitrators but not the parties to order testimony or the production of documents.[68] Also, the language of §7 of the FAA—to attend before [the arbitrators] or any of them as a witness and to bring any 'book, record, document, or paper'—has been interpreted by most US courts not to extend to discovery.[69] Finally, the Court rejected the argument that the Supreme Court in *Intel* had signalled its view that §1782 authorized district courts to provide discovery assistance in private foreign arbitrations. As it explained, a 'law-review article in a passing parenthetical' which itself did not reference *private* arbitral tribunals could not tip the scales.[70] The well-established Circuit split resulted in an initial grant of certiorari by *Servotronics*, but the Supreme Court subsequently dismissed the case pursuant to the joint stipulation of the parties.

Nonetheless, the Supreme Court may have an opportunity to address the question of the availability of 28 USC §1782 discovery in arbitration, this time in *Application of the Fund for Protection of Investor Rights v AlixPartners*,[71] in the

[62] 975 F3d 689 (7th Cir 2020), *dismissed* 142 S Ct 54 (2021).

[63] In the Fourth Circuit case, Servotronics sought discovery of documents from three Boeing employees in South Carolina. In the Seventh Circuit case, Servotronics sought documents from the Boeing Corporation itself.

[64] *Servotronics* (n 62) 692–93.

[65] ibid 693.

[66] ibid 694–95. In a footnote, the Seventh Circuit characterized the Fourth Circuit's position that the UK arbitral panel was the 'product of government-conferred authority' as 'mistaken'. Ibid 693, n 2.

[67] ibid 695.

[68] See nn 32–34 and accompanying text, discussing Federal Arbitration Act, §7.

[69] See Practical Law Arbitration, Compelling Evidence from Non-Parties in Arbitration in the US 6–8 (2021). See also n 34 and accompanying text.

[70] *Servotronics* (n 62) 696.

[71] 5 F4th 216 (2d Cir 2021).

context of investor-State arbitration. Notwithstanding its prior decision in *Hanwei Guo*, the Court of Appeals for the Second Circuit in *Fund* held that an investment treaty arbitration, unlike a private commercial arbitration, may constitute a 'foreign international tribunal' for purposes of the statute. *Fund* involved an arbitration proceeding brought by a Russian investment entity (as the assignee of claims of a shareholder of a failed Lithuanian Bank) against Lithuania pursuant to a Russia–Lithuania bilateral investment treaty. A New York federal district court granted the Fund's §1782 discovery application seeking documentary materials and testimony from two non-parties relating to their role in the alleged expropriation of the bank. In affirming the district court order, the Second Circuit engaged in what it characterized as a 'functional approach' to determine whether this arbitral proceeding between an investor and a foreign State pursuant to a bilateral investment treaty constituted a 'proceeding in a foreign or international tribunal'.[72] Although the Court of Appeals acknowledged that this arbitral panel, made up of private parties, functioned independently from any government, it nonetheless concluded that because the panel was convened pursuant to a bilateral investment treaty that is considered important to international relations, it constitutes a foreign or international tribunal 'consistent with § 1782's modern expansion to include intergovernmental tribunals'.[73] The Second Circuit maintained that it was not creating a 'bright-line rule' that all arbitrations conducted pursuant to a bilateral investment treaty would qualify as a 'foreign or international tribunal',[74] but it is difficult to fathom from this opinion as to when they would not. A petition for certiorari was filed by the non-parties in *Fund*,[75] presenting the question of whether an 'ad hoc arbitration to resolve a commercial dispute between two parties is a foreign or international tribunal under 28 USC § 1782(a) where the arbitral panel does not exercise any governmental or quasi-governmental authority'. The petition pointed out that the US Government, in a Supreme Court amicus brief filed in the now-dismissed *Servotronics* case, had argued that neither private commercial arbitration nor investor-State arbitration qualified as a 'foreign or international tribunal' within the meaning of §1782. Along with another petition involving commercial arbitration, the Supreme Court granted certiorari to both petitions to consider whether private commercial and/or investor-State tribunals come within §1782.[76]

[72] ibid 225–26.
[73] ibid 229.
[74] ibid 233.
[75] See Petition for a writ of certiorari, *AlixPartners, LLP v The Fund for Protection of Investor Rights in Foreign States* 2021 WL 4705742 (2021) (No 21–518).
[76] See *ZF Automotive US Inc v Luxshare Ltd,* Petition for certiorari filed 10 September 2021, 142 S Ct 637 (2021). That petition came after a district court had ordered discovery, presumably on the authority of the earlier Sixth Circuit decision in *Latif,* discussed at nn 40–43, 45–46. Petitioners in *Fund* argue that its petition is a better vehicle to clarify the entire landscape. Both cases were argued in the Supreme Court on 23 March 2022.

D. Wherefore of Rules and Standards

In one sense, the issue of whether private commercial arbitration and investor-State arbitration fit within the definition of 'foreign or international tribunals' for purposes of §1782 is a straightforward question of statutory interpretation. Resolution of such questions employs the traditional tools of statutory interpretation—plain text, legislative history, legal commentary, purpose, and policy. How the circuit split is resolved will also have implications for the ongoing tension in private international law about the desirability of rules over standards.

The Supreme Court has various options for resolving the statutory issue. The Court could exclude both private commercial and investor-State arbitration from the scope of the statute, thereby adopting a clear rule. Alternatively, it might find that all such tribunals come within §1782 and then offer only an 'approach' to address concerns about the use of discovery in these different contexts.[77] Or the Court could draw a distinction between investor-State arbitration and private commercial arbitration and include investor-State tribunals[78] and exclude private arbitral tribunals from the scope of the statute. Even then, investor-State arbitration may present its own complication since it can take different forms.[79] Finally, the Court could adopt the 'functional approach' used by the Second Circuit in

[77] In *Intel*, the Court adopted such an 'approach' and declined to provide 'supervisory rules' to guide the process.

[78] Lower courts appear to permit §1782 assistance in arbitrations conducted pursuant to a bilateral investment treaty. See eg *Fund* (n 71); *In re Chevron* 633 F3d 153 (3d Cir 2011); *In re Veiga* 746 F Supp 2d 8 (DDC 2010); *In re Application of Oxus Gold PLC*, No Misc 06–82, 2006 WL 2927615 (DNJ 11 October 2006). See generally Strong (n 24) 322; see also Roger Alford, 'Ancillary Discovery to Prove Denial of Justice' (2012) 53 Va J Intl L 127, 136–37, n 56 (asserting that after *Intel* lower courts unanimously apply §1782 to arbitrations brought under BITs, and compiling such cases).

[79] Investor-State arbitration may be treaty-based via bilateral or multilateral investment treaties, contract-based, or statute-based. For a further explanation, see Chapter 5, Investor-State Arbitration, Introductory Note, Arbitration Restatement (n 34). Critically, however, a tribunal in an investor-State arbitration derives its authority from the consent of both parties, ie a host State and an investor, and in that sense can be said to be 'private'. Another distinction might be drawn between investment arbitration conducted pursuant to the self-contained regime established by the ICSID Convention and other rules. Specifically, art 26 of the ICSID Convention which excludes remedies outside of ICSID could be read to preclude a party's access to a national court for assistance in evidence taking. See Christoph Schreuer, *The ICSID Convention: A Commentary* (2nd edn, CUP 2009) art 26, 162–78; Gabrielle Kaufmann-Kohler and Michele Potestà, *Investor-State Dispute Settlement and National Courts: Current Framework and Reform Options* (Springer 2020) 118–21, 137–40. In *In re Application of Caratube International Oil Co, LLP* 730 F Supp 2d 101 (DDC 2010), the Court declined to order discretionary discovery in ICSID arbitration based on the US–Kazakhstan bilateral investment treaty, but refused to decide conclusively whether that tribunal was 'a foreign or international tribunal' for the purpose of §1782. Subsequently, lower courts have tended to include treaty-based ICSID tribunals within §1782. See eg *In re ex parte Eni SpA*, No 20-mc-334-MN, 2021 WL 1063390 (D Del 19 March 2021) (granting §1782 discovery in support of ICSID arbitration pursuant to the Netherlands–Nigeria BIT); *Islamic Republic of Pak v Arnold & Porter Kaye Scholer LLP* 2019 WL 1559433 (DDC 10 April 2019) (denying discovery in support of ICSID annulment proceedings, but agreeing that ICSID tribunals conducted pursuant to bilateral investment treaties 'regularly' qualify as international tribunals under §1782); *In re Republic of Turkey* Civil Action No 19-20107 (ES) (SCM), 2020 WL 4035499 (DNJ 17 July 2020) (holding that an ICSID tribunal in arbitration pursuant to a multilateral treaty falls within §1782, but denying discovery on a discretionary basis).

Fund and *Hanwei Gou* and attempt to identify those characteristics that define a 'State-sponsored' or 'governmental' tribunal that would bring a tribunal within §1782. However, that choice inevitably involves the application of 'standards' and is likely to produce inconsistency in the lower courts, as the case law already indicates. The Fifth Circuit in the pre-*Intel Biedermann* case concluded that arbitration under the rules of the Arbitration Institute of the Stockholm Chamber of Commerce, apparently based on a claim pursuant to the US–Kazakhstan bilateral investment treaty, was private arbitration outside §1782,[80] although the opinion in *Biedermann* did not identify the investment-treaty nature of the claim. The Fourth Circuit in *Servotronics* held that the UK private commercial arbitration panel in question was a 'State-sponsored' or 'governmental' tribunal because it had 'government-conferred authority' pursuant to the English Arbitration Act.[81] The Seventh Circuit in its *Servotronics* opinion rejected that characterization of the same arbitral tribunal out of hand.[82] The Second Circuit in *Hanwei Guo* had reached a similar conclusion as regards CIETAC, but a different Second Circuit panel viewed *Fund*'s UNCITRAL tribunal in a dispute under the Russia–Lithuania bilateral investment treaty as an intergovernmental tribunal.[83] Should the Supreme Court endorse such a 'functional approach', lower courts will be tasked with determining when a particular tribunal can be characterized as 'private' or some type of governmental tribunal.

And even if the Supreme Court interprets §1782 to encompass both commercial and investor-State arbitration, lower courts will still need to exercise their discretion in deciding whether or not to order judicial assistance. In such a regime, is the only option a 'fuzzy multi-factor' test of *Intel* to guide their decision-making?[84] Perhaps not. The Supreme Court itself could offer a set of guidelines, such as those suggested by a New York City Bar Association Report,[85] as to when an order of judicial assistance is appropriate for use in support of arbitration.[86] One possible presumptive rule would be to authorize discovery only if the arbitrator(s) made or approved the request. Although such a rule may be in tension with the §1782 statutory language of 'any interested person', it would provide greater guidance than the mere recitation of the *Intel* factors. It is also consistent with two of the *Intel* discretionary factors: receptivity of the foreign tribunal to US assistance and

[80] *Biedermann* (n 28) 883. However, the investment-treaty nature of the case is not referenced in the opinion. See n 36.

[81] *Servotronics* (n 47) 214.

[82] See *Servotronics* (n 62) 693, n 2.

[83] See *Hanwei Guo* (n 55) 107.

[84] That characterization of the *Intel* factors comes from Gary Born and Peter Rutledge, *International Civil Litigation in US Courts* (Wolters Kluwer 2018) 1062.

[85] Bar Committee Report (n 5).

[86] See David Zaslowsky, '3 Ways to Let Arbitrations Control International Discovery', Law360.com (21 May 2020), <www.law360.com/articles/1275559/3-ways-to-let-arbitrators-control-int-l-arbitration-discovery> accessed 4 April 2022.

concern about circumventing truth-gathering restrictions.[87] Indeed, courts have themselves indicated that they first want to hear from the arbitrators as to whether the arbitrators desire the information being sought under §1782.[88] However, the Supreme Court has been reluctant to impose such prophylactic rules when the text of a statute does not include restrictions, as evidenced by the *Intel* decision itself.

E. A Comparison with UK Practice under the 1996 Arbitration Act

As noted above, a ruling by the US Supreme Court that §1782 extends to private commercial and/or investor-State arbitration would leave numerous other details about the statute still unanswered.[89] Even a negative decision with respect to both types of arbitral tribunals would not necessarily mean a conclusive end to the broader debate. If the availability of US judicial assistance for use in arbitration were to be strongly favoured by the international arbitration community, legislative action by Congress to broaden §1782 is always possible. Indeed, the legislative option might be the preferable one. Specific limitations appropriate to the unique setting of private commercial and investor-State arbitration could be included in such legislation. Recall that judicial assistance under §1782 generally enables a party to obtain evidence from non-parties for use at a trial or hearing and thus is not only about pre-trial discovery.[90] A request for judicial assistance by a party to an arbitration to obtain information from a non-party might be more palatable if its use were confined to the presentation of evidence in a hearing before the arbitrators rather than for pre-trial discovery that is disfavoured by many arbitration regimes. Such a distinction is drawn to some extent in §7 of the Federal Arbitration Act, as well as in the 1996 English Arbitration Act.

[87] *Intel* (n 4) 264–65.

[88] See eg *InterGlobe Enters Private Ltd v Khanna*, 19-mc-595-PWG (D Md 3 February 2020); *Jankovska v PKB Privatbank SA*, No 19-mc-80208-VKD, 2019 WL 4040552 (ND Cal 26 August 2019) (weighing the fact the tribunal requested the discovery itself in favour of issuing a subpoena under §1782); *In re Finserve Group Ltd*, CA No 4:11-mc-2044-RBH, 2011 WL 5024264 (DSC 20 October 2011) (raising concerns over §1782 discovery when there was no indication the arbitrators would be receptive of it); *Babcock Borsig* (n 24) 241 (requiring proof the tribunal would make use of the discovery prior to issuing an order under §1782); *Hallmark* (n 24) 957 (finding the arbitrator's stated 'receptivity' to the discovery weighed in favour of applying §1782 to arbitration). As noted in *Hallmark*, the Supreme Court's opinion in *Intel* listed as one of its factors the 'reciprocity of the foreign government or the court or agency abroad to US federal-court judicial assistance' (*Intel* (n 4) 264). Professor Smit, in arguing that §1782 does extend to private international tribunals, also asserted 'that judicial assistance should not be rendered until and unless the arbitral tribunal had authorized or made the request for such assistance'. See Hans Smit, 'American Judicial Assistance to International Arbitral Tribunals' (1997) 8 Am Rev Int'l Arb 153, 153.

[89] See nn 77–89 and accompanying text.

[90] See nn 33–34 and accompanying text.

That English Arbitration Act includes detailed provisions directed to 'evidence gathering' by English courts for use in arbitration. Section 44 of the Act lists 'court powers exercisable in support of arbitral proceedings'[91] and states that, unless otherwise agreed by the parties, with respect to a list of specific matters, the court has the same power to make orders in relation to arbitral proceedings as it has for legal proceedings.[92] Two express limitations are operative. First, the opening words in section 44(1) are 'unless otherwise agreed by the parties'. Second, section 44(4) states that, except in a case of urgency, the court shall act only on the application of a party made with the permission of the tribunal or the agreement in writing of the parties. Notice of the application must be given to the parties and to the tribunal.

The specific powers that a court can order with respect to an arbitration are listed in section 44(2)(a) through (e); one of those matters is 'the taking of the evidence of witnesses'.[93] It should be noted that this judicial power is limited to obtaining evidence or documents for *use at trial* and does not include pre-trial discovery. That said, there is not always a clear line between the two in arbitration, but the distinction is important in understanding what assistance an English court is willing to provide. Notwithstanding such circumscribed use, the reach of section 44 to obtain information from a non-party located in England for use in a foreign-seated arbitration was not always clear. However, in a recent case, *A and B v C, D, and E (taking evidence for a foreign seated arbitration)*,[94] the English Court of Appeal held that section 44 applied in that situation.[95] The first instance judge had determined that the powers identified in section 44 did not extend to orders against non-parties, and therefore the judge did not reach the issue of the propriety of issuing an order in aid of a foreign arbitration. The Court of Appeal reversed and held that at least with respect to the matter of 'taking of evidence', the court's authority extended to non-party witnesses.[96] The Court of Appeal went on to consider whether such evidence-gathering pursuant to section 44 was permitted if the statement was for use in aid of a foreign-seated arbitration. In answering that question in the affirmative, the Court relied on section 2(3) of the Arbitration Act,[97] which provides that the powers conferred under sections 43 and 44 apply 'even if the seat of the arbitration is outside England and Wales or northern Ireland'.[98]

[91] English Arbitration Act, 1996, ch 23, s 44.
[92] ibid §44(1).
[93] ibid §44(2)(a).
[94] [2020] EWCA Civ 409, [2020] 1 WLR 3504.
[95] The purpose of obtaining the information was for use in the foreign-seated arbitration because the witness was not amenable to service in the New York arbitration. The court permitted the 'deposition' of the non-party, but bear in mind that under English law a deposition is only aimed at securing evidence for trial and is not appropriate as the kind of 'discovery' device used in US law. CPR 34.8 authorizes a court to order evidence to be given by deposition.
[96] *A* (n 94) [49]. The Court of Appeal did not express a view as to whether a court can make orders against third parties with respect to the other powers listed in s 44(2).
[97] ibid [36]–[39].
[98] English Arbitration Act, 1996, ch 23, s 2(3).

That section also states that a court may refuse to exercise any such power if, when the seat is outside of the UK, it would be inappropriate to do so.[99] The Court of Appeal rejected the argument that because an English court could not, at the request of the parties, order a witness statement in aid of foreign proceedings, it also could not issue such an order in aid of foreign arbitral proceedings.[100] The Court of Appeal explained that with respect to foreign court proceedings, the 1975 Act implementing the Hague Evidence Convention authorizes only a court or tribunal (and not the parties) to make a request for information via a letter of request.[101] But an arbitral tribunal cannot make such a request because it is not considered a 'tribunal' within the meaning of the English Act,[102] which states that an application for a letter of request must be made 'by or on behalf of a court or tribunal'.[103] The Court viewed section 44(2) of the English Arbitration Act as the only available mechanism through which a witness statement of a non-party located in England could be obtained for use in the foreign arbitral proceeding and accordingly held it to apply.

Other countries have similar legislation that authorizes judicial assistance in foreign arbitrations.[104] The German Arbitration Law provides that an arbitral tribunal, or a party, with the consent of the arbitral tribunal, may request a court to provide assistance in taking evidence where the arbitral tribunal is not authorized to act.[105] Such an application is authorized even if the seat of the arbitration in located outside of Germany.[106] However, as in England, the 'taking of evidence' is for use in the main proceeding and not for discovery purposes. Thus, any analogy to present 28 USC §1782 is imperfect, but perhaps offers insights for developing an alternative regime.

F. A US Legislative Solution?

Addressing Arbitration Specifically

This comparative look at modern arbitration statutes offers a possible model for the US to follow by enacting comprehensive federal legislation for international

[99] ibid.
[100] *A* (n 94) [39].
[101] ibid [38].
[102] *Commerce and Industry Insurance Co of Canada v Certain Underwriters of Lloyd's of London* [2002] 1 WLR 1323. The Act provides that an application for a letter of request must be made 'by or on behalf of a court or tribunal'.
[103] Evidence (Proceedings in Other Jurisdictions) Act of 1975, s 1(a).
[104] See generally Oliver Knöfel, 'Judicial Assistance in the Taking of Evidence Abroad in Aid of Arbitration: A German Perspective' (2009) 5 J Priv Intl L 281.
[105] Code of Civil Procedure (*Zivilprozessordnung*) 2005 (Germany), §1050, translation at <www.gesetze-im-internet.de/englisch_zpo/englisch_zpo.html> accessed 4 April 2022.
[106] Ibid §1025(2).

arbitration. The 1925 Federal Arbitration Act (Chapter 1) is severely outdated and its interface with both Chapters 2 and 3, implementing the New York and Panama Conventions, is complex and unclear. A legislative revision and overhaul of Chapters 1, 2, and 3 of the Federal Arbitration Act could address not only the very limited issue of US discovery for use in international arbitrations, but a variety of other complex issues in US international arbitration law. Many of those questions are discussed in the recent ALI Project to restate US international arbitration law in the Restatement of the Law, The US Law of International Commercial and Investor-State Arbitration.[107] Although it is possible that the US Supreme Court could resolve some of those questions within the present statutory scheme,[108] a comprehensive Federal International Arbitration law—in the model of the 1996 English Arbitration Act—would be a better option. A more modest suggestion would be to amend 28 USC §1782 to legislatively answer the question of whether US judicial assistance, and specifically pre-hearing discovery, should be made available to international arbitral tribunals, and if so, at whose request. In addition, several other controversial issues in the application of §1782, discussed below, as well as other management techniques,[109] could be addressed in this more limited legislation.

Additional Issues under 28 USC §1782

An amendment to 28 USC §1782 could clarify other points of statutory interpretation of §1782 in its application to foreign proceedings of any type, whether that proceeding is a court, administrative agency, or arbitral tribunal. Two important issues have arisen with respect to the application of §1782 in aid of both judicial and arbitral proceedings: (i) whether the document(s) that a §1782 petitioner seeks must be physically located inside the US; and (ii) whether a person subject to a §1782 application 'resides' or is 'found' within the district. In some cases, but not all, these issues may overlap. For example, if the person asked to produce the information is a US corporation with its principal place of business in the district, such corporation would definitely be said to 'reside' in the district.[110] Nonetheless, if the information sought were not located in the US but abroad, the question would

[107] See Arbitration Restatement (n 34).

[108] Among the more significant unresolved issues involving international arbitration are: (i) whether the grounds for annulment of a Convention award *made in the US* are those in Chapter 1 of the FAA or the grounds listed in the Convention; (ii) whether an arbitrator or a court decides whether an arbitration clause authorizes class arbitration; (iii) what country or State's law is law applicable to the validity of an arbitration agreement; (iv) what bases of jurisdiction are necessary to bring an action to recognize and enforce a foreign arbitral award; (v) whether *forum non conveniens* can be invoked to dismiss an action for recognition and enforcement of an award.

[109] See Yanbai Andrea Wang, 'Exporting American Discovery' (2020) 87 Chi L Rev 2089, 2146–54.

[110] Cf *Daimler AG v Bauman* 571 US 117, 137 (2014).

still arise as to whether the statute extended to reach such information. On the other hand, if a foreign party possesses information located abroad but has only an office or limited contacts in the district, a determination that the corporation is not subject to jurisdiction in the district would eliminate the need to answer the question of whether information located abroad is within the scope of the statute.[111] However, neither of these issues—the extraterritorial scope of §1782 or the requirements for obtaining jurisdiction over a person to obtain an order under §1782—has found a conclusive answer in the courts.

Recently, two Courts of Appeals have held that documents, even if located abroad, are within the scope of §1782. The Eleventh Circuit in *Sergeeva v Tripleton Intern, Ltd*[112] rejected the argument that a request for documents located in the Bahamas was impermissibly extraterritorial. The Court emphasized that the statutory text of §1782 authorizes production of documents 'in accordance with the Federal Rules of Civil Procedure' and that Federal Rule 45 requires subpoenaed parties to produce documents and electronically stored information in the parties' possession, custody, or control.[113] Because the target of the subpoena, Trident Atlanta, was one of a group of companies that offered clients international financial planning through 'production and client liaison companies' around the world, the Court held that Trident had control of documents even though they were in the physical possession or custody of a related liaison Bahamian company.[114] The Court of Appeals for the Second Circuit, in *In re del Valle Ruiz*,[115] citing *Sergeeva*, also held that documents located abroad were within the scope of §1782. *Ruiz* involved an application for discovery directed to both the Spanish bank, Santander and its New York-based affiliate, Santander Investment Securities Inc; the documents sought were located abroad. Although the Court of Appeals determined that it could not exercise jurisdiction over the Spanish Bank Santander itself, the New York-based Santander Investment Securities Inc was clearly 'found' within the district.[116] The Court of Appeals then proceeded to analyse the question of whether information located abroad is within the scope of §1782. In holding that it is, the Court of Appeals first responded to Santander Investment Securities Inc's argument that the presumption of extraterritoriality operates as a per se bar against §1782 discovery. Citing the recent Restatement (Fourth) of Foreign Relations,[117] the Court of Appeals viewed the presumption as pertaining primarily to the

[111] See eg *In re Petrobras Securities Litigation* 393 F Supp 3d 376 (SDNY 2019) ('it may be the case that in the post-*Daimler* context, personal jurisdiction provides the simpler doctrinal tool' to address the concern as to whether §1782 authorizes courts to order the production of evidence located outside US territory).

[112] 834 F3d 1194 (11th Cir 2016).

[113] Ibid 1200.

[114] Ibid 1201.

[115] 939 F3d 520 (2d Cir 2019).

[116] Ibid 531.

[117] Restatement (Fourth) of the Foreign Relations Law of the United States, §404 cmt a and n 3 (Am Law Inst 2019).

regulation of conduct or providing a cause of action, and thus not applicable in this context.[118] Even if the presumption did apply, the Court noted that it would view the presumption as having been rebutted by the provision in the statute that the order should issue 'in accordance with the Federal Rules of Civil Procedure',[119] thereby reaching documents abroad if in the 'possession, custody or control' of the person to whom a discovery order is directed.[120] The Court of Appeals in *Ruiz* acknowledged that lower courts in the Circuit were divided on whether §1782 can be used to reach documents stored overseas.[121] Indeed, a pre-*Intel* decision of the Second Circuit, *In re Sarrio*,[122] had indicated in dicta that §1782 did not reach documents located abroad.[123] However, the Court of Appeals in *Ruiz* rejected that dicta and discounted language in the Senate Report that referred to 'oral and documentary evidence *in the United States*'[124] on which *Sarrio* had relied. Nor was the Court of Appeals persuaded by a 1998 article by Professor Hans Smit who wrote that §1782 was not intended to become a clearing house for information from courts and litigants all over the world.[125] The Court of Appeals explained that 'given the plain meaning of the statute ... these considerations were insufficient to win the day'.[126]

A final limiting factor for obtaining a discovery order pursuant to §1782 is the requirement that the person against whom the order is sought 'resides' or is 'found' within the district. Like so many other issues of interpretation involving this statute, there is no clear answer as to the meaning of those terms. The best understanding of the requirement is that the object of the discovery request must be amenable to jurisdiction in the district. The language of 'resides' or 'found' traditionally referred to the grounds for general jurisdiction.[127] An individual would be subject to jurisdiction if he resided in the district or was served with process while physically there.[128] A corporation pre-*Daimler* would 'reside' or be 'found' in the district if it

[118] *Ruiz* (n 115) 532.

[119] Ibid 532, n 14.

[120] See *Société Internationale pour Participations Industrielles et Commerciales, SA v Rogers* 357 US 197, 199–200 (1958); *Shcherbakovskiy v Da Capo Al Fine, Ltd* 490 F3d 130, 138 (2d Cir 2007). See also *In re Plygon Global Partners*, No 21-mc-007 WES, 2021 WL 1894733 (DRI 11 May 2021); *In the Matter of Application of De Leon*, No 1:19-mc-15, 2020 WL 1180729 (SD Ohio 12 March 2020); *Illumina Cambridge Ltd v Complete Gnomics, Inc*, No 19-mc-80215-WHO(TSH), 2020 WL 820327 (ND Cal 19 February 2020); *In re Hulley Enters*, 358 F Supp 3d 331, 344 (SDNY 2019); *In re Ferrer*, No 18-20226-CIV-O'SULLIVAN, 2018 WL 3240010 (SD Fla 3 July 2018).

[121] Cf *In re Godfrey* 526 F Supp 2d 417, 423 (SDNY 2007) and *In re Microsoft Corp* 428 F Supp 2d 188, 194 n 5 (SDNY 2006) (no extraterritorial application) with *In re Accent Delight International Ltd*, No 16-MC-125 (JMF), 2018 WL 2849724 (SDNY 11 June 2018) (location of documents abroad does not establish a per se bar to discovery).

[122] 119 F3d 143 (2d Cir 1997).

[123] ibid 147 ('there is reason to think that Congress intended [the statute] to reach only evidence located within the United States').

[124] Sen Rep No 88-1580 (1964), reprinted in 1964 USCCAN 3782, 3788 (emphasis added).

[125] See Hans Smit, 'American Assistance to Litigation in Foreign and International Tribunals: Section 1782 of Title 28 of the USC Revisited' (1998) 25 Syracuse L & Com 1, 11.

[126] *In re del Valle Ruiz* 939 F3d 520, 532-33 n 16 (2d Cir 2019).

[127] See *Daimler* (n 110) 137.

[128] See *Burnham v Superior Court of Cal* 495 US 604, 611–12 (1990).

were incorporated there, had its principal place of business there, or had systematic and continuous activities there.[129] As Professor Hans Smit explained in a 1998 article, the statutory purpose of the requirement was to create adjudicatory authority to issue an order under §1782. He explained that in so far as the term applied to legal rather than natural persons, 'it may safely be regarded as referring to judicial precedents that equate systematic and continuous local activities with presence'.[130] However, following the Supreme Court's decision in *Daimler*, the assertion of general jurisdiction over a corporation on the basis of its systematic and continuous activities does not satisfy the constitutional standard for due process—at least with respect to a plenary action.[131] Whether the same constitutional test for general jurisdiction applies in a §1782 application to obtain information from a corporation is unclear. As I have argued in earlier writing,[132] the *Daimler* standard should not be a one-size-fits-all constitutional limitation. Because the target of a §1782 application is merely called upon to offer up information or documents rather than to litigate a plenary claim, the burden on that person is significantly less than the burden of litigation would be with respect to a plenary claim.[133] Given the lesser burden, perhaps the pre-*Daimler* 'systematic and continuous activities' standard ought to satisfy the constitutional threshold for adjudicatory authority for a court to make an order to produce information. On the other hand, where foreign parties, in particular, are the object of the request and the information is located abroad, those parties may be subject to the competing laws of another sovereign and subject to prosecution if not relieved of the US order to produce under the doctrine of sovereign compulsion, discussed earlier. But perhaps that issue ought to be separated from the question of jurisdiction and resolved through specific analysis of the propriety of a discovery order issuing.[134]

Most lower courts have reflexively held that the *Daimler* constitutional standard limits the assertion of general jurisdiction when applying the 'resides' or 'is found' requirement in §1782.[135] The Court of Appeals for the Second Circuit addressed

[129] See eg *Godfrey* (n 121) ('Insofar as the word "found" is applied to corporations, "it may safely be regarded as referring to judicial precedents that equate systematic and continuous local activities with presence"'); *In re Inversiones y Gasolinera Petroleos Valenzuela S de RL*, No 08-20378-MC, 2011 WL 181311, at *8 (SD Fla 19 January 2011).

[130] See Smit (n 125) 294–96.

[131] *Daimler* (n 110) 137.

[132] See Linda Silberman and Aaron Simowitz, 'Recognition and Enforcement of Foreign Judgments and Awards: What Hath Daimler Wrought?' (2016) 91 NYU L Rev 344. The primary emphasis in that article was that the *Daimler* constitutional standard should not apply to actions for recognition and enforcement of foreign arbitral awards and foreign judgments.

[133] See eg *First Am Corp v Price Waterhouse LLP* 154 F3d 16, 20 (2d Cir 1998) ('a person who is subjected to liability by service of process far from home may have better cause to complain of an outrage to fair plan than one similarly situation who is merely called upon to supply documents or testimony').

[134] See eg *Shcherbakovskiy* (n 120) 139 (finding foreign law relevant to compliance with a discovery order).

[135] See eg *Petrobras* (n 111); *In re Fornaciari*, No 17-mc-521, 2018 WL 679884, at *2 (SDNY 29 January 2018) ('Although § 1782 does not define what it means to reside or be found in a district, court in this District—including this one—have held that at minimum, compelling an entity to provide discovery under § 1782 must comport with constitutional due process'). See also *In re Sargeant* 278 F Supp

the issue in the same *Ruiz* case,[136] concluding that the 'resides or is found' language was not limited to acquiring general jurisdiction over the target of the request and that specific jurisdiction could suffice if its requirements were met. However, the Court agreed with the district court that the constitutional due process limits on personal jurisdiction required for both general and specific jurisdiction also applied in the context of §1782.[137] The Court relied on a prior Circuit precedent, *Gucci America, Inc v Weixing Li*,[138] which held that a court must have personal jurisdiction over a non-party in order to compel it to comply with a valid discovery request pursuant to Rule 45 of the Federal Rules.

In the context of ascertaining specific jurisdiction in *Ruiz*, the Court of Appeals rejected the argument that a categorically lower showing of due process could justify jurisdiction to obtain discovery from a non-party, such as the foreign bank in this case.[139] However, it did accept that when applying specific jurisdiction, it was sufficient for purposes of due process that 'the nonparty's contacts with the forum go the actual discovery sought rather than the underlying cause of action'.[140] In the context of a §1782 request for discovery from a non-party, the Court of Appeals stated that 'where the discovery material sought proximately resulted from the respondent's forum contacts, that would be sufficient to establish specific jurisdiction for ordering discovery'.[141] The Court recognized that the terminology of causation was an awkward fit for discovery, but argued that 'the focus on the relationship between a § 1782 respondent's forum contacts and the resulting availability of the evidence is a workable translation of the normal personal-jurisdiction framework'.[142] Applying that analysis, the Court of Appeals found that the in-forum conduct of Bank Santander in finding a buyer did not relate to the bulk of discovery sought that pertained to the forced sale of Banco Popular.[143]

A district court case, *In re Petrobras Securities Litigation*,[144] decided prior to the Second Circuit decision in *Ruiz*, used a similar test to determine whether specific

3d 814, 820 (SDNY 2017); *Australia & New Zealand Banking Grp Ltd v APR Energy Holding Ltd*, No 17-MC-00216 (VEC), 2017 WL 3841874, at *2 (SDNY 1 September 2017). A few district courts post-*Daimler* appear to have issued a discovery order against entities who carried on substantial activities in New York, stating that those entities were 'found' in New York. See eg *Ayyash v Crowe Horwath LLP*, No 17-mc-482(AJN), 2018 WL 1871087, at *2 (SDNY 17 April 2018); *In re Kleimar NV* 220 F Supp 3d 517 (SDNY 2016) (relying on various activities of the company to satisfy the requirement that it is 'found' in the district).

136 *Ruiz* (n 115).
137 ibid 528.
138 768 F3d 122 (2d Cir 2014).
139 The Court of Appeal did not consider whether the standard for general jurisdiction over the bank for purposes of discovery was different because the plaintiffs did not make that argument on appeal. See *Ruiz* (n 115) 528, n 9.
140 ibid 530.
141 ibid.
142 ibid 530, n 12.
143 ibid 531.
144 *Petrobras* (n 111).

jurisdiction was satisfied with respect to a §1782 request for documents from a Brazilian defendant for use in an arbitration in Brazil. Noting that the Circuit in *Gucci* had embraced specific jurisdiction in the context of subpoenas, the court looked to the purposeful conduct of the party in the forum and whether the discovery requested related to that conduct. The district court ruled that the argument for specific jurisdiction fell short in two ways. The conduct by Petrobras that was the subject of the Brazilian arbitration occurred entirely in Brazil and it was the Brazilian conduct from which the discovery order arises.

G. Conclusion

It is difficult to predict how the Supreme Court will eventually decide the issue of whether judicial assistance pursuant to §1782 extends to investor-State and/or commercial arbitration. The Court's approach is likely to be a purely textual one, or perhaps if the Justices find the statutory language ambiguous, they will engage with the legislative history. But the possibility for nuance, such as drawing a distinction between the use of information for 'discovery' and for a 'hearing' or requiring permission of the arbitral tribunal to make an application, is unlikely. An amendment to §1782 could provide answers to many of the questions that have been raised about §1782 judicial assistance more generally, including the specific issue as to whether and how judicial assistance might be used in arbitration. My thinking on this subject has been influenced by my co-teaching with Lawrence and my many discussions with him about these issues. Whether or not he will agree with my overall observations and conclusions only he can say, and so I look forward to those conversations in the coming years.

H. Postscript

On 13 June 2022, as this chapter went to print, the United States Supreme Court decided the two §1782 cases before it, *ZF Automotive US, Inc v Luxshare* and *AlixPartners, LLP v Fund for Protection of Investors' Rights in Foreign States*. In a unanimous opinion written by Justice Barrett, the Supreme Court held that neither the private commercial tribunal nor the investor-State tribunal involved in the cases came within the meaning of a 'foreign or international tribunal' pursuant to §1782. The Supreme Court found that §1782 was intended to reach only governmental or intergovernmental bodies. The private commercial arbitration panel (DIS) seated in Germany could not be said to be 'governmental' merely because it was subject to German Arbitration Law. The ad hoc arbitration panel established pursuant to a bilateral investment treaty did not possess governmental authority merely because nations have agreed in such a treaty to offer investors the option of bringing the dispute to a private arbitration panel; the relevant question was whether the nations intended that the ad hoc panel exercise governmental authority, and the Supreme Court found that they did not. The Supreme Court viewed the question with respect to investor-State arbitration as a harder question but nevertheless opted for a clear rule that excludes all arbitral tribunals without governmental authority from the scope of §1782. As I have suggested in my discussion of the developments leading up to this case, the Supreme Court's decision has the benefit of leaving further action on this issue to Congress.

PART V
PUBLIC INTERNATIONAL LAW

14

The United Nations Declaration on the Rights of Indigenous Peoples and Canadian Law

*Frank Iacobucci**

A. Introduction

This Festschrift for Lord Collins of Mapesbury is both an honour and celebration that are richly deserved. The glittering career of Lawrence is marked by professional excellence and accomplishment that are not only breathtaking, but also part of English legal history. My wife, Nancy, and I met Lawrence at Cambridge in 1963 while the three of us were graduate students in international law. Lawrence was at the start of his passion for the law and the attainment of academic distinction that was a foundation on which he built his brilliant professional and judicial career. Two of his mentors come to mind, Professor Clive Parry of Downing College and Francis Mann of the law firm Lawrence entered. They were part of the launch of Lawrence into a legal journey that has been unique. In fact, to elaborate on that voyage could fill this volume. Suffice it to say on my behalf that having him as a close friend for going on to sixty years has been one of the cherished blessings of both my personal and my professional life. Gifted intellectually, his insightful judgment, empathy, loyalty, humour, and humanity are impeccable. Warmest congratulations on joining the Fourscore Club!

This chapter proceeds in four sections. In section B, I provide a brief history of the Canadian Government's mistreatment of Indigenous people and an overview of the legal frameworks governing Indigenous rights in Canada. Section C contains an overview of the United Nations Declaration on the Rights of Indigenous Peoples (UNDRIP),[1] focusing on its core principles of free, prior, and informed consent and the corresponding duty to consult. In section D, I examine potential issues and tensions that may arise in adopting UNDRIP as domestic law in

* I wish to thank Jon Silver and Julie Lowenstein, two colleagues at Torys LLP, for their invaluable assistance in the research and preparation of this chapter.

[1] United Nations Declaration on the Rights of Indigenous Peoples, UNGA Res 61/295 (13 September 2007) UN Doc A/RES/61/295.

Frank Iacobucci, *The United Nations Declaration on the Rights of Indigenous Peoples and Canadian Law* In: *Essays in International Litigation for Lord Collins.* Edited by: Jonathan Harris and Campbell McLachlan, Oxford University Press.
 DOI: 10.1093/oso/9780192867988.003.0015

Canada. Finally, section E looks ahead and discusses strategies to build partnerships between Indigenous groups and the Canadian Government as a path forward to achieving reconciliation.

B. A Brief History of the Indigenous Experience and Aboriginal Legal Rights in Canada

The Historical Relationship between Canada and Indigenous People

Indigenous[2] peoples have lived in what is now called Canada since 'time immemorial'.[3] In this chapter, I cannot possibly do justice to the history of Indigenous peoples in Canada and the historic relationship (and mistreatment) of Indigenous peoples by European settlers and Canadian governments. Many other sources provide rich accounts.[4] To set the stage for the sections that follow, I endeavour to provide a brief summary of that history.

Long before European settlers arrived in North America, Indigenous peoples established distinct societies, cultures, economies, and forms of government. These societies and traditions continued, to some extent, after European contact.

[2] 'Indigenous' is a collective term that refers to people native to colonized lands. It is also the legal term used to describe the people onto whom UNDRIP confers rights. This chapter uses 'Indigenous' to refer to all people native to what is now called Canada. The term 'Aboriginal' also refers to the first inhabitants of Turtle Island, now known as North America. In Canada, 'Aboriginal' describes Inuit, Métis, and First Nations people. 'Inuit' (formerly 'Eskimo') refers to Indigenous people whose traditional lands are in northern regions of what is now Canada; 'Métis' refers to members of the Métis Nation, a distinct Aboriginal group consisting of people with mixed Aboriginal and European heritage; and 'First Nation' refers to all Aboriginal people of Canada who are neither Inuit nor Métis (see 'Terminology', Indigenous Foundations, University of British Columbia (2009), <https://indigenousfoundations.arts.ubc.ca/terminology/> accessed 4 April 2022; 'Definition of Métis', Métis Nation of Alberta (2021), <http://albertametis.com/registry/application-guidelines/definition-of-metis/> accessed 4 April 2022). Some legal texts, including the Canadian Constitution, use the term 'Indians'. This term has dubious origins: Christopher Columbus mistakenly thought he had discovered India when he traversed the Atlantic Ocean. The umbrella term 'Indians' also wrongly groups various diverse Aboriginal peoples into one category. For these reasons, many eschew the term. However, given its use in Canadian legal texts such as the Indian Act and Constitution Acts, 1867 to 1982, 'Indian' is sometimes used in legal contexts (see Peter Hogg, *Constitutional Law of Canada* (5th edn, Thomson Reuters 2007) (loose-leaf updated 2019), ch 28.1(b)).

[3] *Calder v British Columbia (Attorney General)* [1973] SCR 313 [2].

[4] See eg 'The Final Report of the Truth and Reconciliation Commission of Canada, Volume 1: Canada's Residential Schools: The History, Part 1, Origins to 1939', Truth and Reconciliation Commission of Canada (2015), <www.trc.ca/assets/pdf/Volume_1_History_Part_1_English_Web.pdf> accessed 4 April 2022; 'The Final Report of the Truth and Reconciliation Commission of Canada, Volume 1: Canada's Residential Schools: The History, Part 2, 1939 to 2000', Truth and Reconciliation Commission of Canada (2015), <www.trc.ca/assets/pdf/Volume_1_History_Part_2_English_Web.pdf> accessed 4 April 2022; Thomas King, *The Inconvenient Indian: A Curious Account of Native People in North America* (Penguin Random House Canada 2012); Bob Joseph, *21 Things You May Not Know about the Indian Act* (Indigenous Relations Press 2018); James V Right, *A History of the Native People of Canada* (University of Ottawa Press 1995); Marianne Ignace and Ronald E Ignace, *Secwépemc People, Land, and Laws* (McGill-Queen's UP 2017).

But the arrival of European settlers began to destabilize and destroy Indigenous ways of life.

In the earliest stages of European settlement, the British Crown entered into 'peace and friendship' treaties with Indigenous peoples to define their mutual rights and obligations. These treaties often followed violent confrontations or were signed under coercive pressures. Settlers would threaten to take Aboriginal peoples' land by force if they did not agree to sell it. Settlers were also known to deliberately mislead Indigenous peoples to make them think they could use their lands, particularly for hunting or fishing, after selling them. Land purchasers would misrepresent the amount of land being transferred or, in some cases, forge documents of sale.[5] These practices led the British Government to recognize the 'Great Frauds and Abuses [that] have been committed in purchasing Lands of the Indians' in the Royal Proclamation, 1763.[6]

The first Prime Minister of the Dominion of Canada, Sir John A Macdonald, described the government's responsibility to Indigenous people as one of 'guardianship as of persons underage, incapable of managing their own affairs'.[7] This official condescending attitude largely defined the Canadian Government's approach to Indigenous people in the decades that followed. In 1876, following Confederation, the Canadian Parliament implemented the Indian Act,[8] which effectively made 'Indians' wards of the State, unable to vote, seek professional employment, or freely engage in spiritual or cultural practices.[9] The government also established a system of reserves, consisting of tracts of land set aside for the exclusive use of an 'Indian' band with the Crown holding title to the land. Indigenous communities, both on and off reserves, have been subject to unacceptably low standards of living and an insufficient welfare system. The gap between Indigenous people and non-Indigenous Canadians in well-being and access to basic services and human rights, such as clean water, health care, and education, persists to this day.[10]

Since before Confederation, the Canadian Government also established a system of Indian Residential Schools. The government's goal was to 'assimilate' Indigenous children into Canadian society by forcibly removing them from their families and placing them into residential schools run by Christian religious

[5] Truth and Reconciliation Commission Final Report, vol 1, pt 1 (n 4) 51, citing Stuart Banner, *How the Indians Lost Their Land: Law and Power on the Frontier* (Belknap Press 2007) 82, 87.

[6] Truth and Reconciliation Commission Final Report, vol 1, pt 1 (n 4) 51, citing The Royal Proclamation of 7 October 1763, reproduced in Ian Getty and Antoine Lussier, *As Long as the Sun Shines and Water Flows: A Reader in Canadian Native Studies* (UBC Press 1983) 35.

[7] ibid 106, citing Getty and Lussier (n 6) 56.

[8] Indian Act, RSC, 1985, c I-5.

[9] Truth and Reconciliation Commission Final Report, vol 1, pt 1 (n 4) 110, citing Colin G Galloway, *The Scratch of a Pen: 1763 and the Transformation of North America* (OUP 2007) 70.

[10] The Honourable Frank Iacobucci, John A Terry, Valerie Helbronner, and others, 'Free, Prior and Informed Consent in Canada: Towards a New Relationship with Indigenous Peoples' (2016) 4 Torys LLP, <www.torys.com/-/media/files/insights/publications/2016/07/free-prior-and-informed-consent-in-canada-towards-a-new-relationship-with-indigenous-peoples.pdf> accessed 4 April 2022.

denominations. Abuse was rampant: at least 3,200 children died (burial records are scant and the death toll is likely higher) and countless more were subject to physical and sexual abuse and malnutrition.[11] The residential schools have been described as 'one of the gravest injustices in Canadian history',[12] 'the most disgraceful, harmful, racist experiment ever conducted in our history',[13] and 'cultural genocide'.[14] Unfortunately, these Residential Schools are not ancient history: the last residential school in Canada closed in 1996.

During the latter half of the twentieth century, the Canadian Government also forcibly removed thousands of Indigenous children from their families and placed them into the child welfare system, as part of what is known as the 'sixties scoop'. Similar to children in Residential Schools, these children lost their names, languages, cultures, and connections with their heritage. Many were abused and made to feel ashamed of their roots.[15] Collectively, government efforts aimed at 'assimilating' Indigenous children tore families apart and harmed and killed many children, causing intergenerational trauma among Indigenous peoples.

As part of the settlement of class action litigation, as well as thousands of individual actions, arising from the Indian Residential Schools, the Canadian Government established the Truth and Reconciliation Commission. The Commission set out to document the atrocities committed within the residential school system, provide victims with an opportunity to tell their stories, and educate the public about the legacy of the schools. In 2015, as part of its final report relating to recommendations, the Commission released ninety-four 'Calls to Action'. Calls to Action numbers 43 and 44 called upon Canadian governments to 'fully adopt and implement [UNDRIP] as a framework for reconciliation' and to 'develop a national action plan, strategies, and other concrete measures' to achieve UNDRIP's goals.[16] These Calls to Action, in part, have motivated Canada to implement UNDRIP as domestic law.

[11] ibid.

[12] Mayo Moran and Kent Roach, 'Introduction: The Residential Schools Litigation and Settlement' (2014) 64(4) UTLJ 479, 480.

[13] Liberal Justice Minister Irwin Cotler, cited in George Jonas, 'Residential Schools Were a Savage Solution to a Lingering Problem', *National Post* (16 January 2013), <http://news.nationalpost.com/full-comment/george-jonas-residential-schools-were-a-savage-solution-to-a-lingering-problem> accessed 4 April 2022.

[14] Truth and Reconciliation Commission Final Report, vol 1, pt 1 (n 4) 3; The Right Honourable Beverley McLachlin, PC, 'Reconciling Unity and Diversity in the Modern Era: Tolerance and Intolerance' (Global Centre for Pluralism Annual Pluralism Lecture 2015, delivered at the Aga Khan Museum, 28 May 2015), *Globe and Mail*, <www.theglobeandmail.com/news/national/unity-diversity-and-cultural-genocide-chief-justice-mclachlins-complete-text/article24698710/> accessed 4 April 2022.

[15] Christopher Dart, 'The Sixties Scoop Explained', *CBCDocsPOV* (2021), <www.cbc.ca/cbcdocspov/features/the-sixties-scoop-explained> accessed 4 April 2022.

[16] 'Truth and Reconciliation Commission of Canada: Calls to Action', Truth and Reconciliation Commission of Canada (2015) 4, <www.trc.ca/assets/pdf/Calls_to_Action_English2.pdf> accessed 4 April 2022.

Aboriginal and Treaty Rights in Canada

Broadly speaking, Aboriginal rights are *sui generis*, or unique, rights held by Aboriginal peoples 'by reason of the fact that aboriginal peoples were once independent, self-governing entities in possession of most of the lands now making up Canada'.[17] Aboriginal rights protect traditional activities, such as hunting or fishing. In order to be an Aboriginal right, an activity 'must be an element of a practice, custom or tradition integral to the distinctive culture of the aboriginal group asserting the right'.[18] Treaty rights arise from treaties or land agreements between Indigenous groups and the Canadian Government. They typically include the rights to own and use land, sometimes exclusively, and to access natural resources contained on the land.

As mentioned above, in the seventeenth and eighteenth centuries, the Crown entered into 'treaties of peace and friendship' with the Indigenous peoples of what is now Canada. These agreements conferred rights, such as hunting and fishing rights, onto Indigenous peoples in exchange for peace, and typically did not involve the cession by Indigenous peoples of their lands.[19] In the Royal Proclamation, 1763, the British Government recognized the prior entitlements of Indigenous peoples to the lands of North America, requiring the Crown to 'treat with [Indigenous peoples] and obtain their consent before their lands could be occupied'.[20] Accordingly, the Crown had to establish treaties with Indigenous peoples in order to allow for the purchase of their lands for settlement or development. These historical treaties and their modern equivalents confer title to Indigenous lands onto the Crown, in exchange for certain Aboriginal rights over the lands and the creation of reserves.

In the 1973 case *Calder v British Columbia*, despite there being no explicit constitutional recognition of Aboriginal rights at the time, six of the seven justices of the Supreme Court of Canada held that the Nishga people possessed Aboriginal rights to their land.[21] These rights pre-dated and survived the European settlement of what is now the province of British Columbia. Recognizing that Indigenous peoples occupied organized societies with distinctive social and political structures long before European settlement, the court held that the sovereignty of the Crown did not automatically extinguish pre-existing Indigenous laws and interests. Rather, these laws and interests were absorbed into the common law as Aboriginal rights and could be extinguished only by explicit acts of the Crown.[22]

[17] Brian Slattery, 'The Constitutional Guarantee of Aboriginal and Treaty Rights' (1983) 8 Queen's LJ 232, 242.

[18] *R v Van der Peet* [1996] 2 SCR 507 [45].

[19] Hogg (n 2) ch 28.6(b). In *Simon v The Queen* [1985] 2 SCR 387, the Supreme Court of Canada recognized a treaty of peace and friendship made in 1752.

[20] Right Honourable Beverly McLachlin, PC, 'Aboriginal Peoples and Reconciliation' (2003) 9 Canterbury L Rev 240; see also *Calder* (n 3) [2]; *Van der Peet* (n 18) [110]–[112]; *Delgamuukw v British Columbia* [1997] 3 SCR 1010 [200].

[21] *Calder* (n 3).

[22] ibid.

Canada's Constitution Act, 1982 now protects these 'existing rights'. In 1982, when the Canadian Constitution was repatriated from Britain, several sections were added, including an amending formula and the Canadian Charter of Rights and Freedoms (hereafter 'the Charter'). Importantly, the new constitution also gave constitutional recognition to Indigenous rights: providing in section 35 of the Constitution Act, 1982: 'The existing aboriginal and treaty rights of the aboriginal peoples of Canada are hereby recognized and affirmed.'[23]

The honour of the Crown

Section 35 of the Constitution Act, 1982 invokes the 'honour of the Crown' in all dealings between the Canadian Government and Indigenous peoples. The term 'Crown' is commonly understood to symbolize executive power in Canada.[24] It refers to the personification of Her Majesty the Queen, as well as to the sovereign exercise of Her Majesty's formal legislative role in assenting to, refusing to assent to, or reserving legislative or parliamentary bills.

The Supreme Court of Canada has explained that the honour of the Crown 'recognizes that the tension between the Crown's assertion of sovereignty and the pre-existing sovereignty, rights and occupation of Aboriginal peoples creates a special relationship that requires that the Crown act honourably in its dealings with Aboriginal peoples'.[25] The underlying purpose of the honour of the Crown is to facilitate the reconciliation of these interests by promoting negotiation and the just settlement of Aboriginal land claims as alternatives to litigation or judicially imposed outcomes.[26] To achieve these objectives, the honour of the Crown imposes certain obligations when it is engaged, including the duty to negotiate Aboriginal land and rights claims with First Nations.[27] While these claims are being resolved, the Crown is under a duty to consult and, if necessary, accommodate First Nations before authorizing action that could impact land or resources subject to an ongoing claim. Because Aboriginal land and rights claims take many years to resolve, Canadian jurisprudence under section 35 has focused on the 'duty to consult', to which I now turn.

The Canadian duty to consult

The honour of the Crown gives rise to a justiciable duty to consult when the Crown contemplates executive action that may adversely affect rights protected by section

[23] Constitution Act, 1982, Schedule B to the Canada Act 1982 (UK), s 35.

[24] *Clyde River (Hamlet) v Petroleum Geo-Services Inc*, 2017 SCC 40, [2017] 1 SCR 1069 [28].

[25] *Mikisew Cree First Nation v Canada (Governor General in Council)*, 2018 SCC 40, [2018] 2 SCR 765 [21], citing *Manitoba Metis Federation Inc v Canada (Attorney General)*, 2013 SCC 14, [2013] 1 SCR 623 [67]; Brian Slattery, 'Aboriginal Rights and the Honour of the Crown' (2005) 29 SCLR (2d) 433, 436.

[26] *Mikisew Cree* (n 25) [22], citing *Manitoba Metis* (n 25) [66]–[67]; *Taku River Tlingit First Nation v British Columbia (Project Assessment Director)*, 2004 SCC 74, [2004] 3 SCR 550 [24].

[27] *Haida Nation v British Columbia (Minister of Forests)* 2004 SCC 73, [2004] 3 SCR 511 [20]; Slattery (n 25).

35 of the Canadian Constitution.[28] This duty can also apply to statutory actors that, while not part of the executive, act on behalf of the Crown.[29] Underlying the duty to consult is the principle that 'acting unilaterally in a way that may adversely affect [section 35] rights does not reflect well on the honour of the Crown and may thus warrant intervention on judicial review'.[30]

The Supreme Court of Canada first recognized the duty to consult and accommodate in the 2004 case *Haida Nation v British Columbia*. The British Columbia Government had authorized a logging company to cut trees on the Queen Charlotte Islands, which form part of the traditional homeland of the Haida people. The Haida people had asserted a claim over the Islands, which had been accepted for negotiation but was not yet resolved. The Supreme Court held that, in those circumstances, section 35 obliged the Crown to consult and, if necessary, accommodate the Haida people, given that the impugned logging could impact their section 35 rights.[31]

The content of the duty to consult varies with context. The extent of the consultation and accommodation required is proportionate to the strength of the claim to the Aboriginal right or title and the seriousness of the potential adverse effect on the claimed right or title.[32] For instance, the Supreme Court of Canada has held that when there is a strong prima facie case for an Aboriginal claim, the potential infringement is significant, and the risk of non-compensable damage is high, 'deep consultation' is required.[33] 'Deep consultation' may require specific procedural rights, such as the opportunity to make submissions for consideration; formal participation in the decision-making process; the provision of written reasons for the decision; and alternate dispute resolution proceedings before impartial decision-makers.[34] Canadian courts have compared the duty to consult to the duty of procedural fairness in administrative law, as both require the State to afford contextual participatory rights to those affected by government decisions.[35]

The goal of reconciliation animates the Canadian duty to consult.[36] When assessing whether the Crown has discharged its duty to consult, the controlling question is: 'What is required to maintain the honour of the Crown and to effect

[28] *Mikisew Cree* (n 25) [25]. See, for instance, *Haida Nation* (n 27); *Taku River* (n 26); *Mikisew Cree First Nation v Canada (Minister of Canadian Heritage)*, 2005 SCC 69, [2005] 3 SCR 588; *Beckman v Little Salmon/Carmacks First Nation*, 2010 SCC 53, [2010] 3 SCR 103.

[29] *Clyde River* (n 24) [29].

[30] *Mikisew Cree* (n 25) [25].

[31] *Haida Nation* (n 27) [38], [67].

[32] ibid [29].

[33] ibid [44].

[34] *Chippewas of the Thames First Nation v Enbridge Pipelines Inc* 2017 SCC 41, [2017] 1 SCR 1099 [47]; *Haida Nation* (n 27) [44]; *Squamish First Nation v Canada (Fisheries and Oceans)*, 2019 FCA 216, 436 DLR (4th) 596 [36]. See also *Yellowknives Dene First Nation v Canada (Minister of Aboriginal Affairs and Northern Development)*, 2015 FCA 148, 93 CELR (3d) 39 [66].

[35] *Coldwater First Nation v Canada (Attorney General)*, 2020 FCA 34, [2020] 3 FCR 3 [38], citing *Haida Nation* (n 27) [41]; *Little Salmon* (n 28) [46].

[36] See *Little Salmon* (n 28) [10].

reconciliation between the Crown and the Aboriginal peoples with respect to the interests at stake?'[37] As the Supreme Court of Canada has explained, reconciliation is the 'grand purpose' of section 35:

> The reconciliation of Aboriginal and non-Aboriginal Canadians in a mutually respectful long-term relationship is the grand purpose of s. 35 of the Constitution Act, 1982. The modern treaties, including those at issue here, attempt to further the objective of reconciliation not only by addressing grievances over the land claims but by creating the legal basis to foster a positive long-term relationship between Aboriginal and non-Aboriginal communities. Thoughtful administration of the treaty will help manage, even if it fails to eliminate, some of the misunderstandings and grievances that have characterized the past. Still, as the facts of this case show, the treaty will not accomplish its purpose if it is interpreted by territorial officials in an ungenerous manner or as if it were an everyday commercial contract. The treaty is as much about building relationships as it is about the settlement of ancient grievances. The future is more important than the past. A canoeist who hopes to make progress faces forwards, not backwards.[38]

Ultimately, reconciliation is about relationship building. It involves 'sincere acts of mutual respect, tolerance, and goodwill that serve to heal rifts' and includes 'facing past evil openly, acknowledging its hurtful legacies, and affirming the common humanity of everyone involved'.[39] Meaningful and genuine consultation advances reconciliation.

While consultation need not be perfect,[40] it must be meaningful. Canadian appellate jurisprudence following *Haida Nation* indicates that this means consultation must be more than 'blowing off steam';[41] there must be two-way dialogue;[42] and the Crown must act in good faith,[43] be open-minded to accommodation,[44] and grapple with the concerns of the affected First Nation.[45] However, consultation does not mean the Crown must obtain consent from affected Indigenous groups or

[37] *Haida Nation* (n 27) [45].

[38] *Little Salmon* (n 28) [10].

[39] Mark Walters, 'The Jurisprudence of Reconciliation: Aboriginal Rights in Canada' in Will Kymlicka and Bashir (eds), *The Politics of Reconciliation in Multicultural Societies* (OUP 2008) 168.

[40] *Coldwater* (n 35) 38, citing *Haida Nation* (n 27) [62]; *Tsleil-Waututh Nation v Canada (Attorney General)*, 2018 FCA 153, [2019] 2 FCR 3 [226], [508]. See also *Gitxaala Nation v Canada*, 2016 FCA 187, [2016] 4 FCR 418 [182]. For instance, courts have held that, to satisfy the duty to consult, consultation must be 'reasonable', meaning that Canada has considered and addressed the Aboriginal rights claimed in a meaningful way (*Coldwater* (n 35) [40], citing *Haida Nation* (n 27) [62]–[63], [68], [42]; *Gitxaala* [8], [179], [182]–[185]; *Tsleil-Waututh* [226], [508]–[509]; *Squamish* (n 34) [31], [37]; *Clyde River* (n 24) [41]).

[41] *Mikisew Cree First Nation* (n 28) [54].

[42] *Gitxaala* (n 40) [279].

[43] ibid [233].

[44] *Haida Nation* (n 27) [41]; *Clyde River* (n 24) [23]–[24]; *Chippewas* (n 34) [44].

[45] *Tsleil-Waututh* (n 40) [6].

that a lack of consent undermines reconciliation. As the Canadian Federal Court of Appeal has recently explained, 'reconciliation does not dictate any particular substantive outcome. Were it otherwise, Indigenous peoples would effectively have a veto over projects such as this one. The law is clear that no such veto exists.'[46] The process of engaging in genuine consultation based on a relationship of mutual respect advances reconciliation regardless of the outcome.[47]

Established Indigenous title provides First Nations groups with the highest degree of protection and control over land. But while Indigenous title confers on a First Nation the right to exclusively use and occupy the land, reap benefits from the land, and proactively manage the land,[48] it does not give First Nations an unqualified veto power. The Crown retains the power to infringe Indigenous title if it can establish that infringement is necessary 'on the basis of the broader public good'.[49] To meet this stringent test, the government must show that: it discharged its duty to consult and accommodate; the infringement serves a compelling and substantial objective; and the governmental action is consistent with the Crown's fiduciary obligation to the First Nation group.[50] The test, which the Supreme Court of Canada articulated in *Tsilhqot'in Nation v British Columbia*, is strict but leaves open the possibility of infringement where it is necessary and serves a compelling purpose. Interestingly, the *Tsilhqot'in* test mirrors the test for justifying infringements of the Canadian Charter: any infringement of a Canadian Charter right must be rationally connected to its objective, minimally impairing, and proportional, in that its salutary effects must outweigh its deleterious effects.[51] As the following sections explain, it is unclear whether UNDRIP rights are subject to similar limitations.

C. The UN Declaration on the Rights of Indigenous People

In 2007, after twenty-five years of negotiation among States, Indigenous groups, human rights organizations, and other stakeholders, the UN General Assembly adopted UNDRIP. There was overwhelming support for adopting the declaration, with 143 Member States voting in favour of its adoption. Notably, Canada, Australia, New Zealand, and the US were the only four countries that voted against it. These nations were generally concerned about the scope of some of UNDRIP's

[46] *Coldwater* (n 35) [53], citing *Haida Nation* (n 27) [62]–[63].
[47] ibid [52].
[48] *Tsilhqot'in Nation v British Columbia*, 2014 SCC 44, [2014] 2 SCR 257 [2], [67], [73]; *Delgamuukw* (n 20) [117].
[49] *Tsilhqot'in* (n 48) [77].
[50] ibid, citing *R v Sparrow* [1990] 1 SCR 1075. An infringement of Indigenous title will not be consistent with the Crown's fiduciary duty owed to First Nations if it would: substantially deprive future generations of the benefit of the affected land; disproportionately infringe in a manner not rationally connected to the objective of the infringement; infringe more than necessary to achieve the objective; or cause adverse effects that outweigh its benefits (see *Tsilhqot'in* (n 48) [86]–[87]).
[51] *R v Oakes* [1986] 1 SCR 103.

rights and how they might interact with domestic legal systems.[52] However, these countries have since endorsed the declaration to some extent.

Canada initially expressed concern that UNDRIP would conflict with existing guarantees and rights under section 35 of the Canadian Constitution or call into question the finality of Canada's Indigenous treaties and land claims. In 2010, however, Canada changed its position and endorsed UNDRIP by stating its view of the Declaration as a 'non-legally binding aspirational document'.[53] Indeed, since UNDRIP is neither a convention nor a treaty, it does not impose legally binding obligations on any Member State unless its guarantees are adopted in domestic legislation.[54] In May 2016, Canada announced it would remove its 'permanent objector' status and work towards fully implementing UNDRIP as a matter of domestic law.[55] Canada's attempts to implement UNDRIP are canvassed later in this chapter, but first I wish to deal specifically with UNDRIP.

The Principles of Free, Prior, and Informed Consent

The principles of free, prior, and informed consent are pillars of UNDRIP. The principles have their origins in the Indigenous and Tribal Peoples' Convention, 1989, negotiated through the International Labour Organization (ILO).[56] Article 16 of the 1989 ILO Convention guarantees Indigenous people the right to not be unnecessarily removed from their lands without 'free and informed consent'. If consent for removal cannot be obtained, the Convention requires a public

[52] Iacobucci and others (n 10) 9, note 20, citing Report of the Special Rapporteur on the situation of human rights and fundamental freedoms of indigenous people, UNGAOR, 64th Sess, UN Doc A/64/338 (2009) [40].

[53] Iacobucci and others (n 10) 16–17; 'Canada Endorses Indigenous Rights Declaration', *CBC News* (12 November 2010), <www.cbc.ca/news/canada/canada-endorses-indigenous-rights-declaration-1.964779> accessed 4 April 2022; Indigenous and Northern Affairs Canada, 'United Nations Declaration on the Rights of Indigenous Peoples' (9 May 2016), Government of Canada, <www.aadnc-aandc.gc.ca/eng/1309374407406/1309374458958> accessed 4 April 2022; Tom Flanagan, 'Squaring the Circle: Adopting UNDRIP in Canada' (10 March 2020), Fraser Institute, <www.fraserinstitute.org/studies/squaring-the-circle-adopting-undrip-in-canada#:~:text=Because%20UNDRIP%20is%20neither%20a,consistent%20with%20Canadian%20constitutional%20law> accessed 4 April 2022.

[54] Canadian courts have held that UNDRIP is not binding in Canada: see *Snuneymuxw First Nation v Board of Education—School District #68*, 2014 BCSC 1173, 67 BCLR (5th) 388; *Mississaugas of Scugog Island First Nation v National Automobile, Aerospace, Transportation and General Workers Union of Canada* 2007 ONCA 814, 287 DLR (4th) 452; *Hupacasath First Nation v Canada (Foreign Affairs)*, 2013 FC 900, [2014] 4 FCR 836.

[55] 'Canada Removing Objector Status to UN Declaration on the Rights of Indigenous Peoples' (8 May 2016), *CBC News*, <www.cbc.ca/news/Aboriginal/canada-position-un-declaration-indigenous-peoples-1.3572777> accessed 4 April 2022; Indigenous and Northern Affairs Canada, News Release, 'Canada Becomes a Full Supporter of the United Nations Declaration on the Rights of Indigenous Peoples', Government of Canada (10 May 2016), <https://www.canada.ca/en/indigenous-northern-affairs/news/2016/05/canada-becomes-a-full-supporter-of-the-united-nations-declaration-on-the-rights-of-indigenous-peoples.html> accessed 4 April 2022.

[56] The ILO is a UN agency. Its mandate is to advance social and economic justice through setting international labour standards.

consultation process. It also establishes Indigenous peoples' right to return to their lands and guarantees full compensation where return is impossible.[57] Article 15 protects Indigenous peoples' right to the natural resources on their lands.[58]

Only twenty-two countries ratified the 1989 ILO Convention (Canada did not).[59] Since the 1989 Convention, the human rights bodies of the Organization of American States have developed complementary jurisprudence recognizing Indigenous peoples' rights to land, resources, and, ultimately, free, prior, and informed consent with respect to large-scale development projects impacting them.[60] These rights are grounded in the rights to the protection of property, culture, and due process in the American Declaration on the Rights and Duties of Man and the American Convention on Human Rights,[61] which are also the building blocks of free, prior, and informed consent.

The principles of free, prior, and informed consent are reflected in several of UNDRIP's articles. For instance, Article 10 protects Indigenous peoples from being 'forcibly removed from their lands or territories. No relocation shall take place without the free, prior and informed consent of the indigenous peoples concerned and after agreement on just and fair compensation and, where possible, with the option of return.'[62] The declaration also requires States to obtain Indigenous peoples' 'free, prior and informed consent' before implementing legislative or administrative measures that may affect them,[63] approving projects that may impact their lands or resources,[64] and storing or disposing of hazardous materials on their

57 Convention (No 169) concerning indigenous and tribal peoples in independent countries (adopted 27 June 1989, entered into force 5 September 1991) 1650 UNTS 383 art 16.

58 ibid art 15.

59 'Ratifications of C169—Indigenous and Tribal Peoples Convention, 1989 (No. 169)', International Labour Organization (2017), <www.ilo.org/dyn/normlex/en/f?p=1000:11300:0::NO:11300:P11300_INSTRUMENT_ID:312314> accessed 4 April 2022.

60 Iacobucci and others (n 10) 7–8, citing Tara Ward, 'The Right to Free, Prior, and Informed Consent: Indigenous Peoples' Participation Rights within International Law' (2011) 10(2) Nw J Intl Hum Rts 54, 61; *Mayagna (Sumo) Awas Tingni Community v Nicaragua*, Merits, Reparations, and Costs, Inter-American Court of Human Rights Series C No 79 (31 August 2001); *Mary and Carrie Dann v United States* (2002), Inter-Am Comm'n HR, Case 11.140, Report No 75/02, OEA/Ser.L/V/II.118, doc 5 Rev [1]; *Maya Communities of the Toledo District v Belize* (2004), Inter-Am Comm'n HR, Case 12.053, Report No 40/04, OEA/Ser.L/V/II.122 doc 5, Rev 1 [194]; *Saramaka People v Suriname*, Judgment, Inter-American Court of Human Rights Series C No 174 (28 November 2007) [131], [136]; *Kichwa People of Sarayaku v Ecuador*, Judgment, Inter-American Court of Human Rights Series C No 245 (27 June 2012).

61 American Declaration of the Rights and Duties of Man, Organization of American States Res XXX (1948) reprinted in Basic Documents Pertaining to Human Rights in the InterAmerican System OEA/Ser L V/II.82.Doc 6. Rev 1 at 17 (1992) arts 13, 23, 26; American Convention on Human Rights (signed 22 November 1969, entered into force 18 July 1978) 1144 UNTS 123 arts 21, 26; Ward (n 60) 61; Alex Page, 'Indigenous Peoples' Free Prior and Informed Consent in the Inter-American Human Rights System' (2004) 4(2) SDLP 16.

62 UNDRIP (n 1) art 10.

63 ibid art 19.

64 ibid art 32.

lands.[65] Article 28 establishes a right to redress for Indigenous peoples whose lands, territories, or resources have been 'confiscated, taken, occupied, used or damaged without their free, prior and informed consent'.[66]

The Duty to Consult under United Nations Declaration on the Rights of Indigenous Peoples

As part of the requirement of obtaining free, prior, and informed consent for activities that may impact Indigenous peoples, UNDRIP establishes a duty to consult. Like the duty to consult under section 35 of the Canadian Constitution, the duty to consult under UNDRIP varies with context. The nature of the Indigenous right or interest at stake and the anticipated impact of the proposed activity inform the duty's content.[67]

The Special Rapporteur on the Rights of Indigenous Peoples has explained that the duty to consult arises whenever a State decision may impact Indigenous peoples 'in ways not felt by others in society', or when an activity implicates rights or interests specific to Indigenous peoples.[68] The aim of consultation is obtaining consent. The Special Rapporteur identified elements that should be part of most consultation processes, including: paying attention to the existence of power imbalances; making information about the proposed project accessible; engaging in consultation before any project activity begins; and facilitating consultation through Indigenous peoples' own institutions, leadership, and decision-making structures.[69]

While the Special Rapporteur's comments help to clarify the nature and content of the duty to consult under UNDRIP, critics have noted that the requirements of consultation under UNDRIP remain unclear in certain situations. For instance, as one commentator has observed:

> [T]here is not adequate clarity on how to undertake a consultation process. The quality of the information provided, how the information is to be provided, the role of the project developers in the consultation process, and how to proceed in situations where women and adolescents are formally sidelined

[65] ibid art 29.

[66] ibid art 28.

[67] Report of the Special Rapporteur on the situation of human rights and fundamental freedoms of indigenous people, HRC, 12th Sess, UN Doc A/HRC/12/34 (2009) [47].

[68] Special Rapporteur Report 2009 I (n 52) [43]; Report of the Special Rapporteur on the rights of indigenous people, GA 66th Sess, UN Doc A/66/288 (2011) [81]–[83].

[69] Report of the Special Rapporteur on the rights of indigenous people, HRC, 24th Sess, UN Doc A/HRC/24/41 (2013) [70]–[71].

from the decision-making process are among the issues that require further clarification.[70]

Given that UNDRIP is not a legally binding document and is not subject to frequent judicial interpretation, it is unsurprising that there remains some uncertainty about the contents of its protections. In comparison, domestic Indigenous rights-granting provisions, such as section 35 of the Canadian Constitution, have been defined with considerable precision through decades of judicial analysis. As the following section explains, one particular aspect of UNDRIP that remains uncertain is whether the declaration gives Indigenous groups a 'veto' to block activities that may impact their land or resources.

Does United Nations Declaration on the Rights of Indigenous Peoples Give Indigenous Groups a 'Veto Power'?

UNDRIP's emphasis on free, prior, and informed consent opens the door to an interpretation that it confers a 'veto power' onto Indigenous groups. In other words, if an affected Indigenous group does not give free, prior, and informed consent to a project, the project would not be able to proceed. Such a veto power would effectively grant Indigenous peoples the power to control whether development projects and other activities that may impact them are permitted to proceed.

UNDRIP can be interpreted in a way that stops short of granting Indigenous groups a veto power. Indeed, many commentators take this view. The Special Rapporteur has stressed that, while UNDRIP imposes an obligation to engage in good faith dialogue aimed at obtaining free, prior, and informed consent, it should not be regarded as giving Indigenous groups a veto power. According to the Special Rapporteur, the Declaration establishes 'consent as the objective of consultations with indigenous peoples', rather than as a free-standing right in all circumstances.[71] During the 2015 Canadian federal election, the National Chief of the Canadian Assembly of First Nations, Perry Bellegarde, also expressed the view that UNDRIP does not give Indigenous groups a veto power, observing that 'the term veto is not used in the UN Declaration. Veto implies an absolute right or power to reject a law or development that concerns Indigenous peoples, regardless of the facts and law in any given situation.'[72]

[70] Hans Morten Haugen, 'The Right to Veto or Emphasising Adequate Decision-Making Processes: Clarifying the Scope of the Free, Prior and Informed Consent (FPIC) Requirement' (2016) 34(3) Netherlands QHR 273.

[71] Special Rapporteur Report 2009 II (n 67) [46].

[72] Gloria Galloway, 'Trudeau's Promises to Aboriginal People Feared to Be Unachievable', *The Globe and Mail* (22 October 2015), <www.theglobeandmail.com/news/politics/trudeaus-promises-to-aboriginal-people-feared-to-be-unachievable/article26946111/> accessed 8 April 2022.

Scholars and practitioners have also argued that the declaration does not give Indigenous groups a veto power because it recognizes the sovereignty of independent States and contemplates limitations to its rights. Article 46 confirms that nothing in the Declaration is to be 'construed as authorizing or encouraging any action which would dismember or impair, totally or in part, the territorial integrity or political unity of sovereign and independent States' and that the rights set out in the Declaration 'shall be subject only to such limitations as are determined by law and in accordance with international human rights obligations'.[73] These limitations shall be 'non-discriminatory and strictly necessary solely for the purpose of securing due recognition and respect for the rights and freedoms of others and for meeting the just and most compelling requirements of a democratic society'.[74] According to one scholar, Article 46 permits infringements of Indigenous rights in limited circumstances, but it creates a higher threshold for justifying an infringement than the Canadian standard:

> Article 46 would seem to impose a slightly higher standard than the *Tsilqoth'in-Oakes* test [the Canadian test to justify infringement of established Indigenous title, discussed above]. In a very limited number of cases FPIC might amount to a veto, but these would only be cases in which good faith negotiations fail to reach a reconciliation of interests and where no justification meets the specifications of Article 46.[75]

The reference to the limitation of UNDRIP rights for 'the just and most compelling requirements of a democratic society' suggests that the declaration does account for scenarios where an activity that affects an Indigenous group can proceed without consent. As a group of Canadian legal practitioners has observed: 'the application of free, prior, and informed consent should not be interpreted to mean Indigenous groups are conferred a veto right. Like section 35 of the Constitution Act, 1982, the rights articulated in UNDRIP are not absolute and must be balanced against other important societal priorities, including the rights of others'.[76]

The notion that UNDRIP rights would be subject to certain limitations is not unusual. Indeed, fundamental rights are rarely—if ever—absolute. In Canada, our most fundamental civil and human rights are subject to section 1 of the Charter, which allows the government to impose 'reasonable limits' upon constitutional rights and freedoms, so long as they can be 'demonstrably justified in a free and

[73] UNDRIP (n 1) art 46.

[74] ibid.

[75] Sasha Boutilier, 'Free, Prior, and Informed Consent and Reconciliation in Canada' (2017) 7(1) Western J of Leg Stud 1.

[76] Sam Adkins, Lisa Jamieson, Terri-Lee Oleniuk, and others, 'UNDRIP as a Framework for Reconciliation in Canada: Challenges and Opportunities for Major Energy and Natural Resources Projects' (2020) 58(2) Alta L Rev 339, 348.

democratic society'.[77] Section 1 of the Canadian Charter reflects the influence of international human rights instruments, particularly the European Convention on Human Rights and the International Covenant on Civil and Political Rights, which contain limitation clauses with similar language to section 1 of the Canadian Charter.[78] While the US Bill of Rights contains no limitation clause, US courts have had to infer qualifications on many rights—such as freedom of speech and equal protection—since these rights 'cannot be absolute'.[79]

Even though the principles of free, prior, and informed consent can be interpreted as subject to certain narrow limitations, it can be argued that, in practice, there remain activities that could not proceed without consent under UNDRIP. In situations where Indigenous consent cannot be obtained, the Special Rapporteur recommends that the State suspend the project in question unless the State demonstrates that the rights of affected Indigenous peoples will be adequately protected and that the impacts of the project will be mitigated as much as possible. This may involve compensating the affected Indigenous group.[80] If the State cannot fulfil these requirements, it must justify the infringement by balancing the Indigenous rights at issue with the need to respect other human rights and the public interest in 'meeting the just and most compelling requirements of a democratic society'.[81]

The Special Rapporteur has expressed doubt that, without consent, a 'purely commercial' venture would satisfy the requirements for proceeding.[82] If the Special Rapporteur is correct, this would effectively mean that Indigenous groups retain the right to veto purely commercial projects. The Canadian doctrine of consultation and accommodation strikes a different balance, as it does not grant Indigenous groups veto powers over any type of project. As Adjunct Professor Kerry Wilkins has observed, 'the several mentions in UNDRIP of "free, prior and informed consent" would, if given domestic effect, almost certainly impose more stringent obligations on mainstream governments than does the current domestic law requiring Crown consultation'.[83] The potential discrepancies and tensions between UNDRIP and Canadian law are canvassed in more detail below.

This brings us to the Canadian Government's recent announcement regarding its desire to incorporate UNDRIP into Canadian law and the legal challenges that thereby arise.

[77] Constitution Act 1982 (n 23) s 1.

[78] Hogg (n 2) ch 38.1.

[79] ibid. See eg *Central Hudson Gas & Electric Corp v Public Service Commn of NY* 447 US 557, 566 (1980), where the Court set out a four-part test as the standard for the validity of restrictions on commercial speech. This test is similar to the test for limiting rights under s 1 of the Canadian Charter.

[80] Special Rapporteur Report 2011 (n 68) [86], [98].

[81] UNDRIP (n 1) art 46.

[82] Special Rapporteur Report 2013 (n 69) [35].

[83] Kerry Wilkins, 'So You Want to Implement UNDRIP' (2021) UBC L Rev (forthcoming) 4–5.

D. Implementing United Nations Declaration on the Rights of Indigenous Peoples in Canada

Bill C-15: An Act Respecting the United Nations Declaration on the Rights of Indigenous People

After Canada's Truth and Reconciliation Commission released its final report with its Calls to Action, the federal government committed to adopting UNDRIP through domestic legislation. There have been two attempts to do so thus far. First, in April 2016, a Member of Parliament and member of the Cree First Nation, Romeo Saganash, introduced Bill C-262, the United Nations Declaration of the Rights of Indigenous Peoples Act. This bill was passed by the Canadian House of Commons, but failed to pass in the Senate before Parliament dissolved in advance of the 2019 Canadian federal election.

Recently, on 3 December 2020, the Canadian Parliament released a draft of Bill C-15: An Act respecting the United Nations Declaration on the Rights of Indigenous People. The Bill, which is currently before the Canadian House of Commons, aims to ensure that all of Canada's laws are consistent with UNDRIP. The Act's preamble grounds the need for adopting UNDRIP as domestic law in the historic injustices suffered by Indigenous peoples in Canada, including the dispossession of their lands, territories, and resources.[84] The preamble also states that the protection of Aboriginal and treaty rights enshrined in section 35 of the Canadian Constitution is 'an underlying principle and value of the Constitution of Canada'.[85] Section 2 confirms that the Act 'is to be construed as upholding the rights of Indigenous peoples recognized and affirmed by section 35 of the Constitution Act, 1982, and not as abrogating or derogating from them'.[86]

Sections 5 and 6 of the Bill impose substantive obligations on the Canadian Government. Respectively, these sections would require the federal government to 'take all measures necessary to ensure that the laws of Canada are consistent with' UNDRIP[87] and, in consultation and cooperation with Indigenous peoples, prepare and implement national action plans to achieve the objects of the Declaration.[88] Section 7 imposes a reporting requirement on the Minister of Crown-Indigenous Relations with respect to the national action plans.

Canada's UNDRIP Bill is a well-intended response to the real and grave injustices suffered by Indigenous people since European contact. The Bill's goals are laudable and important. However, aspects of UNDRIP may be at odds with the

[84] Bill C-15: An Act respecting the United Nations Declaration on the Rights of Indigenous People, 2nd Sess, 43rd Parl, 2020, Preamble.
[85] ibid.
[86] ibid s 2.
[87] ibid s 5.
[88] ibid s 6(1).

Canadian doctrine of consultation and accommodation and broader administrative law principles. Consequently, Parliament must be careful to ensure that any legislation implementing UNDRIP works in harmony with established Canadian consultation and accommodation jurisprudence.

Potential Tensions between United Nations Declaration on the Rights of Indigenous Peoples and Canadian Law

As discussed above, it is possible to interpret UNDRIP in a way that stops short of giving Indigenous groups the power to veto projects to which they do not consent. Such an interpretation would more closely align with the Canadian doctrine of consultation and accommodation, which leaves the final power to approve natural resource and other development projects to delegated administrative bodies. In 2008, Canadian constitutional law scholars and experts signed an open letter stating that UNDRIP is consistent with the Canadian Constitution and Charter.[89] But given UNDRIP's emphasis on obtaining free, prior, and informed consent, contradictory interpretations are possible.[90]

Commentators have cautioned against watering down UNDRIP rights in order to fit the declaration into existing domestic legal frameworks. Professor Wilkins has warned that implementing UNDRIP in Canada might mean 'that in the long run, UNDRIP rights would be read down as necessary, sized to fit more or less unobtrusively within the mainstream Canadian legal framework'.[91] Wilkins expands on his concerns about implementing UNDRIP:

> Unless the only real purpose of UNDRIP implementation is cosmetic, such an outcome ought to give the enacting government, and the rest of us, pause. No less troubling is the prospect that answers to any of the threshold questions whose resolution UNDRIP presupposes will have to await potentially highly contentious litigation: litigation likely to strain the resources of many Indigenous collectives worthy of consideration as bearers of UNDRIP rights.[92]

[89] Open Letter—UN Declaration on the Rights of Indigenous Peoples Canada Needs to Implement This New Human Rights Instrument, NationTalk (3 May 2008), <https://nationtalk.ca/story/open-letter-un-declaration-on-the-rights-of-indigenous-peoples-canada-needs-to-implement-this-new-human-rights-instrument>.

[90] Arguably, UNDRIP goes beyond the rights set out in s 35 of the Canadian Constitution by giving Indigenous groups more power to prevent the approval of development projects that may impact their rights. Does this interfere with the Constitution's position as the supreme law of Canada? While beyond the scope of this chapter, the question of whether legislation that upsets the balance struck under s 35 by providing stronger protections for Indigenous rights, subject to fewer limitations, is an interesting one.

[91] Wilkins (n 83) 7–8.

[92] ibid.

Wilkins raises important considerations. And yet, implementing UNDRIP without including some measured and appropriate limits risks upsetting the balance between Indigenous groups and other stakeholders carefully struck by decades of section 35 jurisprudence.

Requiring Indigenous consent could also amount to an improper fettering of administrative discretion. In other words, if Indigenous groups have the power to veto certain initiatives, this may effectively sub-delegate the power to approve the initiative to the affected Indigenous group, rather than to the administrative body vested with regulatory authority. In a democracy, administrative action must be statutorily grounded. While Indigenous groups are important stakeholders and have constitutionally protected rights, they have no statutory authority to approve development projects. Without such authority, a veto power (and the consequent sub-delegation of the decision) might warrant relief on judicial review in some cases. Professor Wilkins acknowledges these concerns.[93]

While Parliament could theoretically grant Indigenous groups the requisite statutory authority to have the final say in approving development projects, this sub-delegation of legislative power may not be feasible in practice. For instance, would Parliament be able to grant Indigenous groups a veto power before their land or rights claims have been resolved? Would this effectively by-pass the legal procedure for establishing Indigenous title and Aboriginal rights? What would happen when there is disagreement within an Indigenous group as to whether a project should proceed? Would every member of an Indigenous community need to consent to the project or what majority is required for consent? While Indigenous groups are certainly key stakeholders whom the Crown must consult according to its duty to consult and accommodate, these questions highlight issues that could arise if Parliament were to extend statutory power to Indigenous groups to approve projects.

In Canada, the regulators who do have the statutory authority to approve natural resource and development projects, such as the Canada Energy Regulator, are specialized experts in their fields. Canadian courts are highly deferential to their decisions. As a group of Canadian legal practitioners has explained, these regulators perform important adjudicatory functions that are inconsistent with a veto:

> Although the regulatory process in an administrative context is less formalized than a court room setting, energy and natural resource regulators do perform an adjudicative function. The regulator must weigh the evidence and work to resolve those issues as between the parties that can be resolved. Concerns and issues that arise between the proponent and stakeholders must be considered by the regulator, and may be addressed by imposing project approval conditions that limit

[93] ibid 64–65.

> certain activities or that obligate the proponent to accommodate the issues raised by parties that have an interest in the outcome of the regulatory proceedings and the development of a proposed project.[94]

Indeed, in deciding whether to approve a given development project, regulators engage in a careful balancing exercise informed by decades of jurisprudence from Canadian courts. Implementing UNDRIP principles in domestic law should not create any instant, sweeping changes to the current system of project consultation and regulatory review. Procedural fairness and natural justice can be reconciled with the implementation of UNDRIP into our regulatory processes, but will require frank discussions about both the importance and limits of UNDRIP in a diverse and democratic country like Canada.[95]

Adopting UNDRIP principles through domestic legislation would also change the status of the Declaration's provisions from 'constraints' on administrative action to binding obligations. As a declaration, UNDRIP is not legally binding on individual States. In Canada, the principles underpinning the relationship between non-binding international declarations and domestic State action have been developed by the courts. In the recent case *Canada (Minister of Citizenship and Immigration) v Vavilov*, the Supreme Court of Canada discussed the effect of non-binding international law on administrative action:

> We would also note that in some administrative decision-making contexts, international law will operate as an important constraint on an administrative decision maker. It is well established that legislation is presumed to operate in conformity with Canada's international obligations, and the legislature is 'presumed to comply with ... the values and principles of customary and conventional international law': *R. v. Hape*, 2007 SCC 26, [2007] 2 S.C.R. 292, at para. 53; *R. v. Appulonappa*, 2015 SCC 59, [2015] 3 S.C.R. 754, at para. 40. Since *Baker*, it has also been clear that international treaties and conventions, even where they have not been implemented domestically by statute, can help to inform whether a decision was a reasonable exercise of administrative power: *Baker*, at paras. 69–71.[96]

The Supreme Court also recently confirmed that international law should be used to support and confirm interpretation of Charter rights, but not to define the scope of Charter rights.[97] If Parliament implements UNDRIP through domestic

[94] Adkins and others (n 76) 359.

[95] ibid 369.

[96] *Canada (Minister of Citizenship and Immigration) v Vavilov*, 2019 SCC 65, 441 DLR (4th) 1 [114].

[97] *Quebec (Attorney General) v 9147-0732 Québec inc.*, 2020 SCC 32, 451 DLR (4th) 367 [28]. There remains a question of whether the Aboriginal and treaty rights protected by s 35 of the Canadian Constitution are part of the Canadian Charter. While s 35 falls outside the Charter, s 25 of the Constitution—which is within the Charter—protects Aboriginal and treaty rights from Charter

legislation, the declaration will bind State action in Canada and become another factor that decision-makers will need to consider and comply with.

Given the potential for UNDRIP to conflict with established Canadian legal doctrines, any legislation implementing UNDRIP must carefully define its rights and principles. Adopting UNDRIP without clear guidance on if or when Indigenous consent is required could disrupt decades of jurisprudence that provides a degree of certainty as to what kinds of consultation and accommodation are required in various circumstances. This certainty is crucial for Indigenous groups and natural resource and development industry stakeholders alike. Any legislation implementing UNDRIP should ideally acknowledge and work in harmony with existing Canadian legal frameworks.

Consultation can and should proceed with the aim of obtaining consent. It may even be feasible to prescribe certain specific and limited circumstances in which Indigenous consent is required. For instance, if a proposed activity would take place on an Indigenous reserve, or directly impact an Indigenous community by causing flooding or waste impacting the community's resources, the governing legal framework could require Indigenous consent. Any requirement for consent should be closely tied to the circumstances surrounding the project, such as where the activity would occur, whether the relevant Indigenous claim has been proven (and if not, the strength of the claim), the extent to which it would impact the Indigenous community, and the benefits that would flow from the activity. In short, any legislation implementing UNDRIP should complement and reinforce, rather than subvert, the principles developed under section 35 of the Canadian Constitution.

E. Conclusion: Towards Reconciliation and Partnership

Implementing UNDRIP may serve as a means of building respect and trust between the Canadian Government and Indigenous peoples.[98] But failing to clearly define UNDRIP's rights and protections in ways that accord with other areas of Canadian law could hinder efforts to build a partnership between Canada and Indigenous peoples which I believe should be the aim of the relationship. In my view, UNDRIP must advance, rather than undermine, reconciliation.

Reconciliation must animate every aspect of the relationship between the Canadian Government and Indigenous people. Canada's treatment of Indigenous

challenges. Whether this brings s 35 rights within the Charter is an interesting question beyond the scope of this chapter.

[98] It is important to note that respect for each other is necessary for trust between the parties to be achieved.

people has caused immeasurable harm. Reconciliation requires the government to acknowledge and take responsibility for this harm. Empty promises will not suffice—the Canadian Government must earn Indigenous peoples' respect and trust through action. Part of reconciliation must mean action to remedy problems impacting Indigenous communities in other contexts, such as the well-being gap between Indigenous people and other Canadians, the over-representation and mistreatment of Indigenous people in the criminal justice system, and systemic racism against Indigenous people in Canadian society.

The Canadian Government and Indigenous groups must strive to build a long-term partnership, aimed at mutually and continuously satisfying both parties' needs and interests, rather than implementing piecemeal consultation processes for individual transactions. Partnership requires good faith, transparency, collaboration, and recognition of the capacities and constraints of the other parties. Indigenous groups must also have meaningful opportunities to participate in all procedural and substantive elements of the partnership. The partnership must support Indigenous people as they heal from the destruction of colonization. While not parties to the partnership, corporations carrying out activities that impact Indigenous communities must also align their policies and actions with the goals of reconciliation and partnership.

As the Truth and Reconciliation Commission concluded, UNDRIP can serve as a framework for reconciliation.[99] Any attempt to implement UNDRIP must not distract or detract from the goal of building a mutually trusting and beneficial partnership between the Canadian Government and Indigenous peoples. The Canadian Federal Court of Appeal recently offered valuable guidance:

> Reconciliation must nonetheless begin by looking back and developing a deep understanding of the centuries of neglect and disrespect toward Indigenous peoples, well-summarized in a number of reports and studies (see, *e.g.*, Royal Commission on Aboriginal Peoples, *Report of the Royal Commission on Aboriginal Peoples* (Ottawa: The Commission, 1996); Truth and Reconciliation Commission, *Honouring the truth, reconciling for the future: summary of the final report of the Truth and Reconciliation Commission of Canada* (Winnipeg: The Commission, 2015)). Too often decisions affecting Indigenous peoples have been made without regard for their interests, dignity, membership and belonging in Canadian society, with terrible neglect and damage to their lives, communities, cultures and ways of life. Worse, almost always no effort was made to receive their views and try to accommodate them—quite the opposite. The duty to consult is aimed at helping to reverse that historical wrong.

[99] 'What We Have Learned: Principles of Truth and Reconciliation', Truth and Reconciliation Commission of Canada (2015) 3, 125, <www.trc.ca/assets/pdf/Principles%20of%20Truth%20and%20Reconciliation.pdf> accessed 4 April 2022.

> Reconciliation also looks forward. It is meant to be transformative, to create conditions going forward that will prevent recurrence of harm and dysfunctionality but also to promote a constructive relationship, to create a new attitude where Indigenous peoples and all others work together to advance our joint welfare with mutual respect and understanding, always recognizing that while majorities will sometimes prevail and sometimes not, concerns must always be taken on board, considered and rejected only after informed reflection and for good reason. This is a recognition that in the end, we all must live together and get along in a free and democratic society of mutual respect.[100]

Partnership and reconciliation are the way forward.

[100] *Coldwater* (n 35) [48]–[49].

15
National Obstinacy and International Conventions

David McClean

One of the pleasures of teaching in a Law School is seeing your students, or at least the better ones, beginning to 'think like a lawyer'. I imagine that pupil-masters and those mentoring trainee solicitors will have similar experiences. So will teachers of other disciplines. Mathematicians reach the stage at which they begin to appreciate what they describe as the qualities of elegance or beauty in mathematics, qualities that remain forever hidden to the rest of us.

The analogy I have drawn between law and mathematics is flawed. The truths of mathematics, if we lay aside the General Theory of Relativity, are the same everywhere; they are universal. The very existence of private international law reminds us that law is emphatically not the same everywhere. Learning to think like a lawyer actually means learning to think like a particular type of lawyer. The successful practitioner in private international law has to become familiar with that phenomenon.

Many aspects of private international law address the divide between the common law and the Roman-Napoleonic traditions of the civil law. We could essay a more detailed differentiation. US litigation lawyers certainly behave and so presumably think in rather different ways from those who practise in the City of London.[1] Psychologists debate the extent to which the particular language we speak influences the way we think, so it may be that, for example, a Mandarin-speaking lawyer will approach complex issues by using categories that would not suggest themselves to an English speaker. For present purposes, we need not press the point that far. This chapter has a much more limited aim. It seeks to show how the ingrained ideas of the common law can affect, and I think distort, the interpretation of what is essentially a civil law text.

[1] Some even argue that practice in the fields proper to the Chancery Division produces minds more acute and refined than those of practitioners who toil in tort or crime. There is some empirical evidence for this, but it is inconclusive of the general proposition.

David McClean, *National Obstinacy and International Conventions* In: *Essays in International Litigation for Lord Collins.* Edited by: Jonathan Harris and Campbell McLachlan, Oxford University Press. © Oxford University Press 2022.
DOI: 10.1093/oso/9780192867988.003.0016

A. Warsaw and Montreal

The text is Article 17 of the two international conventions that have since 1929 governed the liability of carriers by air, the Warsaw Convention of 1929 and the Montreal Convention of 1999. The original text of the Warsaw Convention is in French, and Article 17 provides:

> Le transporteur est responsable du dommage survenu en cas de mort, de blessure ou de toute autre lésion corporelle subie par un voyageur lorsque l'accident qui a causé le dommage s'est produit à bord de l'aéronef ou au cours de toutes opérations d'embarquement et de débarquement.

The official English translation in UK legislation is:

> The carrier is liable for damage sustained in the event of the death or wounding of a passenger or any other bodily injury suffered by a passenger, if the accident which caused the damage so sustained took place on board the aircraft or in the course of any of the operations of embarking or disembarking.[2]

The equivalent article in the Montreal Convention avoids some of the problems caused by the description of the non-fatal injuries in the earlier text and has a small drafting change, but is substantially unchanged:

> The carrier is liable for damage sustained in case of death or bodily injury of a passenger upon condition only that the accident which caused the death or injury took place on board the aircraft or in the course of any of the operations of embarking or disembarking.

The whole point of Article 17 is that the claimants (the injured passenger or the dependants of a deceased passenger) do not have to prove fault on the part of the pilot or the owner or operator of the aircraft. So far as Article 17 is concerned, the presence of absence of fault is quite immaterial. A part of that is that the claimants do not have to produce the highly technical evidence needed to prove, for example, that the aircraft was defective or that its operation was in some way negligent.

Judges in common law jurisdictions are accustomed to the flexible and open-textured nature of negligence analysis. An interesting social science exercise would involve asking judges whether they thought the outcome of the cases they had decided was fair and just. Perhaps self-criticism is not a prominent characteristic of the judiciary, but the nature of the tort of negligence may justify a fairly high

[2] Carriage by Air Acts (Application of Provisions) Order 2004, SI 2004/1899, Sch 2.

satisfaction rating. Where there is liability even in the absence of fault, those same judges may feel that the outcome is unjust; there must be a, probably subconscious, wish to avoid 'unjust' decisions by defining terms in ways that reduce the risk of that outcome. The convention texts nowhere speak of the 'negligence' of the carrier.[3] That is quite unsurprising as in the 1920s the notion of a tort of negligence was still unknown to English law. If fault is irrelevant, so is negligence, or indeed any state of mind of the defendant. Nonetheless, judges in common law jurisdictions sometimes allow notions proper to the tort of negligence to affect their analysis.

Almost certainly common lawyers looking at the Warsaw Convention in 1929 would see the carrier's liability as primarily contractual. The issue of the proper categorization of a claim under the Convention was not really of any importance to English lawyers, but it was much more troublesome in the US. Federal jurisdiction depended in many cases on there being a cause of action arising under a treaty and until 1978 the prevailing view was that the Convention did not itself create a cause of action at all: a would-be plaintiff had first to find an appropriate cause of action in domestic law. That view was abandoned in a majority decision of the Court of Appeals for the Second Circuit,[4] essentially because it was inconsistent with the aim of the drafters of the Convention to agree a set of liability rules applying in all Contracting States, whatever the nature of their domestic law.

That, of course, did not settle any question about the nature of liability under the Convention. Another decision of the Second Circuit Court of Appeals[5] held that Warsaw Convention claims sounded in tort; they were types of claims the common law normally associated with the law of tort. One can doubt if that was the case in 1929. Other courts have preferred the view that, although founded on a contract of carriage, an action under the Convention is simply 'a cause of action created by statute';[6] or have decided to duck the issue, holding that it is a bit of both contract and tort.[7] Perhaps the Montreal Convention has laid the issue to rest by speaking of actions 'whether under this Convention or in contract or in tort or otherwise';[8] the Convention action is there presented as *sui generis*.

None of this justifies applying principles derived from the tort of negligence to determine the liability of the carrier. A negligence analysis will use the notion of a duty of care and look to see if there has been a breach of that duty. Any examination of the scope of the carrier's duty of care will potentially limit the carrier's liability for what occurs on the aircraft. We may, for example, decide that the carrier's duty

[3] But see art 21, which does refer to the contributory negligence of the passenger. This is not considered in detail here; it is not thought to affect the main argument.

[4] *Benjamins v British European Airways* 572 F2d 913 (2d Cir 1978), cert den 439 US 1114 (1979).

[5] *Re Air Disaster at Lockerbie, Scotland on December 21, 1988; Rein v Pan American World Airways Inc* 928 F2d 1267 (2d Cir 1991), cert den sub nom *Rein v Pan American World Airways* 502 US 920 (1991). Cf P Barlow in (1992) 17 Annals ASL (II) 97–101.

[6] *Proctor v Jetway Aviation Pty Ltd* [1982] 2 NSWLR 264 (SC).

[7] *Ltd Stores v Pan American World Airways Inc* 600 NE 2d 1027 (Ohio 1992).

[8] Montreal Convention 1999, art 29.

of care extends only to aviation-related matters. The notion of 'aviation-related risk' has in fact been used in French and German cases[9] to define an area of risk and so to address that element in Article 17 that speaks of the 'operations of embarking or disembarking'; one element in determining when the process of disembarkation is complete is whether the passenger is now removed from the area of aviation-related risk.

It is, of course, possible that in some cases liability based on negligence or some other principle of tort law might give a passenger a remedy when the Convention does not. As was pointed out in a dissenting judgement in the US Supreme Court:[10] 'It is a mistake to assume that the Convention must provide relief whenever traditional tort law would do so. To the contrary, a principal object of the Convention was to promote the growth of the fledgling airline industry by limiting the circumstances under which passengers could sue'.

The Convention texts are agreed internationally and courts in many countries have stressed the desirability of a uniform interpretation of the conventions. In one of the earliest English cases, *Grein v Imperial Airways Ltd*,[11] Greene LJ emphasized that the aim had been to produce a uniform code. Lord Hobhouse of Woodborough spelt this out in *King v Bristow Helicopters Ltd*:[12]

> Considerations of national or local law should not be allowed to intrude upon, let alone govern, any question of construction that may arise on the provisions for division of risk.... It is not right to attempt to construe the words of the Convention by reference to the rules of any domestic law, English, American, German or even French. We know that those rules were and are not all identical. The purpose of uniformity means that it is the duty of the national court to put to one side its views about its own law and other countries' laws. Quite apart from defeating uniformity, such a course can only lead to the complication of simple issues, the inadequately informed investigation of other legal systems and, most importantly, to uncertainty.

Much the same has been said by the highest courts in Australia[13] and Canada.[14] The US courts have a more chequered record, but many have stressed the need for uniformity.[15] This does not, of course, mean that the decisions of foreign courts must be followed slavishly;[16] the primary focus must be the text of the Convention

[9] See Shawcross and Beaumont, *Air Law* (Butterworths, loose-leaf), para VII[721].

[10] Scalia J in *Olympic Airways v Husain* 540 US 644, 664 (2004), cited with approval by Lord Scott in *Re Deep Vein Thrombosis and Air Travel Group Litigation* [2005] UKHL 72, [2006] 1 AC 495 [11].

[11] [1937] 1 KB 50 (CA) 74–75.

[12] [2002] UKHL 7, [2002] 2 AC 628 [147] (Lord Hobhouse).

[13] *Povey v Qantas Airways Ltd* [2005] HCA 33, (2005) 223 CLR 189 esp per Kirby J at [130]–[135].

[14] *Thibodeau v Air Canada* 2014 SCC 67, [2014] 3 SCR 340.

[15] See eg *Block v Compagnie Nationale Air France* 386 F2d 323 (5th Cir 1967), 10 Avi 17, 518.

[16] On the weight to be given to decisions of foreign courts in this context, see *Abnett v British Airways plc* [1997] AC 430.

itself. The language of Article 17 does not at first sight seem to offer many problems, but experience has proved otherwise, not least as regards the word 'accident'.

B. Accidents

At one time, the word 'accident' meant simply something that happened, an event. It has come to mean (in the words of the *Oxford English Dictionary*) an 'unexpected or unforeseen circumstance; chance, fortune'. There is no evidence that those who drafted the Warsaw Convention pondered long over the word 'accident'. In the 1920s, aviation was a much riskier activity than it has since become; we need to think ourselves into a world with no radar and certainly no GPS. It would have been as natural to speak of an aircraft accident as it is of a road accident; one would think of a 'prang', a crash, or an emergency landing after some technical failure. In some aviation contexts, 'accident' is defined in ways that are close to that understanding: Annex 13 to the Chicago Convention of 1944, dealing with accident investigation, defines 'accident' simply as 'an occurrence associated with the operation of an aircraft'. Section 75(4) of the Civil Aviation Act 1982, also for the purposes of accident investigation, defines 'accident' as including 'any fortuitous or unexpected event by which the safety of an aircraft or any person is threatened'.

It is difficult to imagine the delegates to the Warsaw Conference contemplating such modern candidates for inclusion in the 'accident' category as the experiences of passengers having hot coffee poured into their laps by the cabin crew, suffering from acute food poisoning after eating an airline meal, having a suitcase fall on them from an overhead locker, or being indecently assaulted in their sleep by the passenger in the adjacent seat.[17] Making that point is not to adopt what Lord Mance described[18] as 'an originalist approach to the application of art 17 . . . a limitation of the term "accident" by reference to the type of aviation disaster affecting a whole airplane that was probably all too familiar in 1929'. He cited with approval a dictum of Lord Hobhouse:

> Words have a meaning which does not change but the application of those words to the decision of any question depends on the facts and circumstances of the case in which that question arises. It is the facts and circumstances of the cases that change, not the meaning of the contractual words.[19]

There has in recent decades been a great deal of litigation, especially in the US, on the meaning of 'accident'. It has been encouraged by a remarkable re-alignment of

[17] All actual cases, some of which are discussed below. The reported cases identify hazards so numerous and varied that it is a wonder students of aviation law ever board an aircraft.
[18] In *Re Deep Vein Thrombosis and Air Travel Group Litigation VT* (n 10) [63].
[19] *Morris v KLM Royal Dutch Airlines* [2002] UKHL 7, [2002] 2 AC 628 [149].

legal forces in 1999. Until that year, carriers were quite often happy to accept that there has been an 'accident' as that meant that the case could be dealt with under the Warsaw Convention, with its tight cap on the level of damages, rather than on some other legal basis that might be available on the facts and allow full compensatory and possibly also exemplary damages. When the US Supreme Court held in *El Al Israel Airlines v Tseng*[20] that where the matter fell within the scope of the Convention no other remedies were available, carriers immediately began to argue that there was no accident, and so seek to escape liability.

The meaning of 'accident' in the context of Article 17 has been considered by the highest courts in the US, England, and Australia. All deserve close examination.

C. The United States

The decision of the US Supreme Court in *Air France v Saks*[21] has been cited countless times in courts around the world. The facts were that in November 1980, Valerie Saks travelled on an Air France aircraft from Paris to Los Angeles, a flight of some 12 hours. As the aircraft descended to Los Angeles, she felt severe pressure and pain in her left ear. The pain continued after the plane landed, and five days later she consulted a doctor who found that she had become permanently deaf in her left ear. She brought a claim under the Warsaw Convention.

As often happens, the terms of the question the Supreme Court eventually examined were set by what had happened in the courts below. The plaintiff's original claim, unwisely, alleged negligent maintenance and operation of the aircraft's pressurization system. Air France successfully moved for summary judgment on the ground that the claimant could not prove that her injury was caused by an 'accident' within the meaning of the Warsaw Convention, which Air France argued meant 'an abnormal, unusual or unexpected occurrence aboard the aircraft'; it relied on evidence that the pressurization system had operated normally. The claimant then accepted that the only issue was 'whether a loss of hearing proximately caused by normal operation of the aircraft's pressurisation system is an "accident" within the meaning of Article 17'. The Court of Appeals for the Ninth Circuit reversed, and after a detailed examination of the Convention held that 'an occurrence associated with the operation of an aircraft which takes place between the time any person boards the aircraft with the intention of flight and all such persons have disembarked' could be an accident. A unanimous Supreme Court found in favour of Air France.

The lower court had used the word 'occurrence'. The Supreme Court noted that the word 'occurrence' was used in Article 18 of the Convention which deals with

[20] 525 US 155 (1999).
[21] 470 US 392 (1985).

loss of or damage to checked baggage and cargo, but Article 17 used 'accident'. As O'Connor J saw it: 'This difference in the parallel language of Articles 17 and 18 implies that the drafters of the Convention understood the word "accident" to mean something different than the word "occurrence," for they otherwise logically would have used the same word in each article.'[22] One could argue that the difference in language does not have that significance: it is more natural to speak of a passenger 'meeting with an accident' than to say that of cargo; but the highest courts in several countries have committed themselves to the *Saks* view.

The Supreme Court examined the, quite limited, *travaux préparatoires*. One reason for the different treatment of passengers and goods was that delegates thought that liability for baggage should commence upon delivery to the carrier, whereas liability for passengers should commence when the passengers later embarked on the aircraft. O'Connor J notes[23] the comment of the president of the drafting committee that passenger and goods were treated in separate articles because they were *entirely different* liability cases. This, said O'Connor J, at least implies that 'the addition of language of causation to Articles 17 and 18 had a broader purpose than specification of the time at which liability commenced'. It is certainly true that liability is on a different basis: damages in the case of goods depend on the weight of the lost or damaged goods; the weight of a passenger is immaterial,[24] but it is far from clear what else the president had in mind.

The Court's conclusion[25] was that

> liability under Article 17 of the Warsaw Convention arises only if a passenger's injury is caused by an unexpected or unusual event or happening that is external to the passenger.... When the injury indisputably results from the passenger's own internal reaction to the usual, normal, and expected operation of the aircraft, it has not been caused by an accident.

It added that '[t]his definition should be flexibly applied after assessment of all the circumstances surrounding a passenger's injuries', and that it recognized that any standard requiring courts to distinguish causes that are 'accidents' from causes that are 'occurrences' required drawing a line, and that 'reasonable people might differ widely as to the place where the line should fall', statements seldom relied on in later cases, probably because of the difficulty of seeing how, if at all, they qualify the definition announced by the Court.

[22] ibid 398.
[23] ibid 403.
[24] The obesity of some passengers is becoming an issue for the airlines, but not primarily in the context of liability.
[25] ibid 405.

D. The *Saks* Definition

Looking more closely at that definition, there is no doubt that the unexpectedness of what has happened is central to the idea of an accident. It seems important that unexpectedness be viewed from the standpoint of the passenger; to see it from that of the carrier would attract ideas of foreseeability that belong to a negligence analysis. But 'unusual' is a more difficult adjective. There are many instances of slips and falls where ice has accumulated on the aircraft steps or the surface of the apron across which a passenger must walk from aircraft to terminal or vice versa. Ice frequently forms at some locations at some times of the year. Is it 'usual'? Is turbulence usual? Or turbulence severe enough to cause injury?

The element in the *Saks* definition that the accident must be external to the passenger has proved especially significant. We may suppose a case of a passenger with a history of serious heart attacks who is sitting in the aircraft shortly after boarding, the aircraft still being stationary at the gate, and who sustains a further and fatal attack. Clearly that was not caused by anything external to the passenger; his or her location on board the aircraft may have not have affected the condition at all. But one has to ask, what does this requirement of 'externality' add to the need for causation? If there is nothing that can be identified as causing the attack, can there be any liability?[26]

It is clear that the 'externality' element was inspired by the facts of the *Saks* case itself. There is no doubt at all that the hearing loss was caused by the workings of the pressurization system. Many aircraft passengers, including no doubt many on the Air France flight that day, experience much discomfort and some temporary effect on their hearing from that cause. The reaction of Valerie Saks's body was more extreme, and the Supreme Court spoke of lower court decisions that refused to extend the term 'accident' to cover routine travel procedures that produce an injury due to the peculiar internal condition of a particular passenger. This comes very close to saying that some discomfort to passengers may have been entirely foreseeable, but not the lasting injury to that particular passenger. Where in the Convention text is there anything that absolves the carrier from liability in such a case?

It is in this type of context that judges seem most tempted to use concepts appropriate to a negligence analysis. A particularly interesting case, and one that reached the US Supreme Court, is *Olympic Airways v Husain*.[27] A passenger allergic to cigarette smoke had been allocated a seat close to the smoking section of the aircraft. He repeatedly asked to be given an alternative seat, but the cabin crew refused. He

[26] See *Barclay v British Airways plc* [2008] EWCA Civ 1419, [2010] QB 187, where Laws LJ considered this as a hypothetical example and said it was clearly not within the 'accident' category. Even were the attack to be triggered by excitement or fear, that would still be internal to the passenger.

[27] 540 US 644 (2004).

died. The trial court held that there was an accident because of the crew's blatant disregard of industry standards.[28] A similar view was taken by the Ninth Circuit Court of Appeals, which in effect endorsed the plaintiff's argument 'that a flight attendant who does nothing to deal with a known risk to a passenger's health-related travel problems is negligent'.[29] Liability under the Convention is not based on negligence, so this approach is inappropriate. In the Supreme Court, the carrier argued in effect that this was a *Saks* case, with a peculiar reaction of an individual passenger to ambient smoke which was, in those days, a normal feature of conditions on board an aircraft. The Court held, by a majority, that many causes contributed to the passenger's death, one of which was the admittedly unexpected and unusual behaviour of the cabin crew. Both the majority and minority addressed what was then a hypothetical case in which the crew of an aircraft refused to divert to a nearby airport in circumstances in which that action could save a seriously ill passenger from imminent death. The majority regarded the crew's failure to divert as an unusual event within the *Saks* definition; the dissenting justices took the opposite view. That does expose the problems with the definition; in practice, the assessment of an event as unusual is difficult to isolate from the reasonableness of the conduct, which has no place in the Convention text.

E. England

The ability of an aircraft to fly longer and longer distances has given rise to concerns about deep vein thrombosis. Although the medical evidence is not wholly consistent, the courts have been prepared to assume that sitting in cramped seating (hence the references to 'economy class syndrome') for a prolonged period of time can cause this, potentially serious and sometimes fatal, condition. That assumption was made in the leading English case, *Re Deep Vein Thrombosis and Air Travel Group Litigation*.

In the Court of Appeal, counsel for the passengers who had suffered deep vein thrombosis argued that: (i) the manner of operating an aircraft will be 'unexpected or unusual' in so far as it departs from the manner in which the airline could 'reasonably be expected' to operate its aircraft, applying an objective test and having regard to all the material circumstances; and (ii) 'event or happening' covers both acts and omissions of those operating the aircraft. Thus, if those operating the aircraft act in a way which one would not reasonably expect, this will constitute an 'accident'. Equally, if they fail to take some action which one would reasonably expect them to take, this also will constitute an 'accident'. A further element in the argument was that, as operators of the aircraft were aware of the risk of deep vein

[28] 116 F Supp 2d 1121 (ND Cal 2000).
[29] 316 F3d 829 (9th Cir 2002).

thrombosis, they could, without difficulty or expense, have warned passengers of that risk and given them advice as to how to reduce it. In these circumstances, they could reasonably have been expected to give the warning and advice in question, and their omissions constituted 'accidents'.

Those arguments refer repeatedly to what is reasonable, a key question in assessing negligence. So did the arguments put forward for the carriers. It was argued that in deciding whether an event was 'unexpected or unusual', the touchstone of what is expected or usual is the practice generally adopted by airlines. An act which complies with such practice could not properly be described as an 'accident'.

Lord Phillips focused rather on the word 'event'. He identified as a critical issue whether a failure to act, or an omission, can constitute an accident for the purposes of Article 17. A failure to act might form part of a series of acts and omissions which together constitute an accident; in such circumstances, it may not be easy to distinguish between acts and omissions. Lord Phillips insisted, however, that inaction itself could never properly be described as an accident. It was not an event; it was a non-event. 'Inaction is the antithesis of an accident.'

He went on to consider the timescale of an 'event'. Article 17 speaks of an accident which 'takes place on board the aircraft or in the course of any of the operations of embarking or disembarking'. That suggests that an accident will be an ephemeral event. Lord Phillips conceded that the requirement of flexibility and a purposive approach meant that he could not preclude the possibility that an activity that continues for a period, such as circulating contaminated air, could amount to an accident for the purposes of Article 17. However, the cramped seating and other cabin conditions relevant on the facts were integral and permanent features of the aircraft and carriage throughout the flight, and were not capable of amounting to an 'event'.

A claim based on the failure to warn of the risk of deep vein thrombosis, or to advise on precautions which would avoid or minimize that risk, was also to be rejected. It had become common practice for airlines to include advice on exercises to be used on long flights in the announcements given or videos shown to passengers before take-off.[30] Such a failure could not be an accident: it was simply something that did not happen, a non-event. For that reason alone, a failure to warn of or to advise about the dangers of deep vein thrombosis was not capable of amounting to an accident under Article 17.

Lord Phillips had to consider a US District Court decision, *Fulop v Malev Hungarian Airlines*.[31] The passenger had a heart attack during a flight and claimed

[30] And commonly ignored by passengers more interested in seeing what in-flight movies might be available. A failure to take action in response to more specific warnings, for example, about anticipated turbulence, may be relevant to a claim under art 21 of the Warsaw Convention that the carrier may be exonerated on proving that the damage was caused or contributed to by the negligence of the passenger: see *Goldman v Thai Airways International Ltd* [1983] 1 WLR 1186 (CA) (turbulence; failure to wear a seatbelt).

[31] 175 F Supp 2d 651 (SDNY 2001).

that the consequences were aggravated because the airline refused to deviate so that he could receive urgent attention. The matter was considered on an application by the airline for summary judgment, which was refused. What was interesting was the judge's approach. He relied on what an ordinary traveller would reasonably expect: that, as the normal, usual, and expected response to such urgencies, and as a fair balancing of interests and risks characteristic of air travel, in handling life-threatening exigencies, airlines rendering services as common carriers would be particularly scrupulous and exacting in complying with their own industry norms, internal policies and procedures, and general standards of care. On the facts, the carrier had departed not merely from general standards, but from its own internal rules and procedures and a finding of an accident was well possible. Lord Phillips seemed to regard this as not a case of an omission; the failure to deviate was the corollary of the decision to fly on to the plane's destination notwithstanding the fact that a passenger had had a heart attack. If this was contrary to standard practice, or even the airline's internal practice, then it was perhaps arguable that there occurred an unusual or unexpected 'event'.

Much closer to the facts in the case before the English Court of Appeal was a decision by a federal District Court in Texas, *Blansett v Continental Airlines Inc*,[32] where the passenger suffered an episode of deep vein thrombosis during a flight, resulting in a stroke that left him with permanent disabilities. The trial judge held that an airline's violation of an industry standard of care, alone, can be 'an unusual or unexpected event or happening that is external to the passenger' in the terms of the *Saks* definition. Lord Phillips, while appreciating the policy considerations that influenced this decision, rejected it. As indeed did the Fifth Circuit Court of Appeals, which refused to lay down a per se rule that any departure from industry practice must be an accident.[33]

The House of Lords affirmed the Court of Appeal's decision. Lord Scott of Foscote followed the *Saks* court in pointing to the contrast between Articles 17 and 18 of the Convention:[34]

> '[O]ccurrence' is entirely general in its natural meaning. It permits no distinction to be drawn between different types of happening. 'Accident' on the other hand must have been intended to denote an occurrence of a particular quality, an occurrence having particular characteristics.... It is evident that it was never, or should never have been, enough for there to have been an occurrence that caused the damage. For article 17 liability the occurrence had to have the characteristics of an 'accident'.

[32] 246 F Supp 2d 596 (SD Tex 2002).
[33] 379 F3d 177 (5th Cir 2004).
[34] *Re DVT* (n 10) [7].

The House followed *Saks* again in holding, in Lord Steyn's words, that if

> it can be shown that an event affecting a passenger adversely on an aircraft was unexpected and unusual, [that] is generally ... not enough to make it an accident. It is an integral part of the test of what amounts to an accident that it must have a cause external to the passenger. In the case of DVT this factor is absent.[35]

The speeches speak in quite emphatic language of the danger of treating a judicial formulation of the characteristics of an Article 17 accident as a substitute for the language used in the Convention. Although they tactfully do not make the point in quite this way, Lord Phillips's judgment in the Court of Appeal concentrated on the word 'event', which is found in the *Saks* definition, but not in the text of the Convention. It is often said, with justification, that the style of judgments is a great strength of the common law tradition, building up a sound structure in a way that the terse and formal judgments in some (not all) civil law countries cannot do. Over-reliance of the language used by judges, often giving us a striking and memorable phrase, may be a weakness if it distracts attention from the statute or international convention that governs the case.

F. Australia

The absence of liability for deep vein thrombosis has been asserted by many courts in different jurisdictions; indeed, the *Saks* court cited one such case from 1976.[36] Claimants soon began to base themselves on the carrier's failure to warn passengers of the danger. A decision of the High Court of Australia, *Povey v Qantas Airways Ltd*,[37] held that such a failure did not constitute an accident. The judgments refer in different ways to the use that can be made of common law negligence concepts.

So the majority judgment firmly rejected any use of such concepts:[38]

> References to 'failure' to warn in this context are irrelevant and unhelpful. They are irrelevant because they must proceed from unstated premises about the content or origin of some duty to warn. There is no basis for introducing, for example, concepts of the common law of negligence to the construction or application of an international treaty ... And unless there is resort to some standard of legal behaviour to determine whether what happened was a 'failure', the description of what happened as a failure is, in truth, no more than an assertion that there was no warning.

35 At [33].
36 *Scherer v Pan American* 387 NYS 2d 580 (1976).
37 [2005] HCA 33, (2005) 223 CLR 189.
38 At [41].

The sole dissentient, McHugh J,[39] actually drew upon common law experience in a notably original judgment. He pointed out that the US Supreme Court in *Olympic Airways v Husain* had identified two plausible definitions of 'accident'. One was 'a happening that is not intended'; the other 'an unusual, fortuitous, unexpected, unforeseen, or unlooked for event, happening or occurrence'. It then concluded that *Saks* had authoritatively 'discerned the meaning of "accident" under Article 17 of the Convention as an "unexpected or unusual event or happening that is external to the passenger"'.

McHugh J argued that common law cases group a wide array of untoward events and happenings under the umbrella concept of 'accident', and the experience of those cases could throw light on the meaning in Article 17. The concept of 'accident' could be categorized in terms of events involving human actions and in terms of happenings that do not involve human action, for example, mechanical, or technological operations and 'acts of nature'. In the case of human actions, such as the behaviour of the cabin crew, it made sense to describe some things as 'not intended'. In *Saks*, where no human action was involved, it would have made no sense for the court to have described the operation of the pressurization system as 'a happening that is not ... intended'; the system operated independently of any actor who could have formed an intention to do an act that had consequences that were not intended or expected. The *Saks* formula should be applied only to its own category of cases. It was wrong to apply one of the two 'plausible' definitions to all cases. One of the objects of the Convention is to provide compensation for injured passengers without the need to prove fault on the part of the air carrier. The Convention's object of compensating passengers without proof of fault, however, would be undermined by a refusal to give the term 'accident' one of the ordinary meanings of which it is capable.

Lord Mance in the *Deep Vein Thrombosis* case[40] favoured the majority view in *Povey*. He observed that references to fault (eg in failing to warn) could be attractive to the domestic lawyer, familiar with contractual or tortious claims for failure to exercise due skill and care. But it is the nature of the event, rather than the care taken to avoid injury, which is the focus of the term 'accident' in Article 17.

G. Man or Machine

McHugh J's interesting distinction has not been picked up in later cases, and indeed His Honour did not set out the possible implications of the distinction. It does serve to point to a group of cases in which the 'accident' complained of involves the harmful activities of other passengers on the same flight. The cases are many

[39] At [45]ff.
[40] *Re Deep Vein Thrombosis and Air Travel Group Litigation e VT* (n 10) [78].

and varied, but few are as alarming as *Li v Quraishi*,[41] where the allegation was that a fellow passenger on a flight from Tokyo to New York had exposed himself and urinated over the claimant and her two-year old daughter.

A key decision in this area is another case before the Second Circuit Court of Appeals, *Wallace v Korean Air*.[42] Ms Wallace was a passenger on a flight from Seoul to Los Angeles. During the night she awoke to find that the male passenger in the next seat, with whom she had had no conversation, had unzipped her shorts and was fondling her private parts. She claimed under the Warsaw Convention against the carrier. The law as set out in the *Saks* judgment seems clear enough; this was surely an event external to the passenger that was unexpected and (one trusts) unusual. The Court of Appeals agreed that that was the case, but only Judge Pooler, one of the three hearing the appeal, would decide the case on this ground. The majority, despite making reference to the 'virtual strict liability' imposed on carriers by the Convention, found it unnecessary to address the issue of whether tortious behaviour by other passengers could make the carrier liable. Instead the majority examined whether what had happened was 'a risk inherent in air travel', asserting that in all the lower court cases cited with approval in *Saks* the passenger injuries seemed to have arisen out of risks that were inherent to air travel, or out of the operation of the aircraft itself. So, the majority held that the characteristics of air travel increased Ms Wallace's vulnerability. Their view of the facts was that she was seated in economy class, cramped into a confined space beside two men she did not know, one of whom turned out to be a sexual predator;[43] the lights were turned down and the sexual predator was left unsupervised in the dark; for the entire duration of Mr Park's attack, not a single flight attendant noticed a problem; and when Ms Wallace woke up, she could not get away immediately, but had to endure another of her neighbour's advances before clambering out to the aisle.

This approach comes very close to an examination of whether the carrier was at fault. Were the cabin crew negligent in failing to notice what was going on in a darkened cabin? Was the carrier at fault in allowing a 'sexual predator' on board? The judgment is really quite extraordinary, but noteworthy in picking up an idea mentioned earlier in this chapter: that of 'aviation-related risks'.

Unfortunately, Lord Phillips in *Morris v KLM Royal Dutch Airlines*, also involving an indecent of assault by a fellow passenger, followed *Wallace*. The Court of Appeal's approach is illustrated by the following passage:[44]

[41] 780 F Supp 117 (EDNY 1992). The claim failed for reasons not here relevant.

[42] 214 F3d 293 (2d Cir, 2000).

[43] The assailant was convicted of an offence in respect of the incident, but there is no suggestion that he had a history of sexual offences. It is not industry practice for airlines routinely (or at all) to inquire of passengers seeking to book flights as to their sexual proclivities.

[44] [2001] EWCA Civ 790, [2002] QB 100 [29].

> All that the authorities relied upon by the defendant require is that the accident should be brought about or facilitated by some special feature of air travel, not that that feature should be unique. Judges do not travel exclusively in first class seats and can take judicial notice of the fact that those who travel economy have to accept relatively cramped conditions which bring them into close proximity with their neighbours. Circumstances are rare that result in a 15-year-old girl settling down to sleep in close proximity to an unknown man. Indeed, as [counsel] pointed out, the youth of the claimant was an additional special feature that was absent in *Wallace v Korean Air*.

The case went to the House of Lords, but on a different point. However, the Court of Justice of the EU (CJEU), where its rulings apply, seems to have barred the form of argument favoured in *Wallace* and *Morris*. The facts can be seen in the question posed by the highest court in Austria:

> Where a cup of hot coffee, which is placed on the tray table of the seat in front of a person in an aircraft in flight, for unknown reasons slides and tips over, causing a passenger to suffer scalding, does this constitute an 'accident' triggering a carrier's liability within the meaning of Article 17(1) of the [Montreal Convention]?

The CJEU held that it did:

> making the carrier's liability subject to the condition that the damage is due to the materialization of a hazard typically associated with aviation or to there being a connection between the 'accident' and the operation or movement of the aircraft is not consistent with the ordinary meaning of the concept of 'accident' referred to in Article 17(1) of the Montreal Convention or the objectives pursued by that convention.[45]

That is clear on the 'aviation-related risk' issue. The CJEU's reference to there being no need for a connection between the 'accident' and the operation or movement of the aircraft may have wider implications that have yet to be explored.

H. Industry Standards and Practice

Aviation is a highly regulated activity, the regulations being based on internationally agreed recommended standards and practices. All that is very important to the

[45] Case C-532/18 *GN v ZU (administrator in insolvency of Niki Luftfahrt GmbH)* EU:C:2019:1127, [2020] 1 WLR 3059 [41].

safety of air travel, but that does not mean that is relevant to the interpretation of the governing conventions.

Reference has already been made to *Blansett v Continental Airlines Inc*, where the Court of Appeals for the Fifth Circuit reasserted that the test was always whether there was an 'unexpected or unusual event', but went on to say that some departures from an industry standard might be qualifying accidents under Article 17, and some might not. In fact, any talk of departure from industry practice is only appropriate for liability based on negligence. The confusion of ideas can be found in the earlier case of *Fishman v Delta Air Lines Inc.*[46] The court there held that an injury resulting from routine procedures in the operation of an aircraft or airline could be an 'accident' 'if those procedures or operations are carried out in an *unreasonable* manner' (emphasis added). In a Ninth Circuit decision, *Caman v Continental Airlines Inc*,[47] the court referred to the question of whether an air carrier's departure from either industry standard or its own company policy was the appropriate benchmark for determining whether an event was 'unexpected', but found it unnecessary to answer it.

There have been other cases in which the issue has surfaced and it has never been satisfactorily cleared away. It is to be hoped that this particular incursion of negligence ideas will one day be effectively halted.

I. Usual and Normal

Courts across the common law world repeat, mantra-like, the *Saks* definition:

> liability under Article 17 of the Warsaw Convention arises only if a passenger's injury is caused by an unexpected or unusual event or happening that is external to the passenger.... When the injury indisputably results from the passenger's own internal reaction to the usual, normal, and expected operation of the aircraft, it has not been caused by an accident.

There seems to be a growing tendency to run elements of that definition together, quite improperly, so that what is 'unexpected or unusual' is made to turn upon whether the operation of the aircraft was normal. We can take three recent, and in a sense quite unremarkable, cases by way of illustration.

In the English case of *Labbadia v Alitalia (Societa Aerea Italiana SpA)*,[48] the carrier was held liable for the fall of a passenger from the disembarkation stairs of an aircraft which had landed at Milan airport. There was snow and the stairs were not

[46] 132 F3d 138 (2d Cir 1998).
[47] 455 F3d 1087 (9th Cir 2006).
[48] [2019] EWHC 2103 (Admin), [2019] 2 Lloyd's Rep 273.

covered by a canopy. The judge devoted a section of her judgment to the question of whether there was an 'unusual' event. She held that there was nothing unexpected or unusual about adverse weather in Milan during the month of February. The use of aircraft stairs without a canopy was 'a different matter':

> There was no dispute that aircraft stairs were always used at Milan airport for the disembarkation of passengers. These stairs conformed to the technical specifications for safety required by the aeronautical regulations and by the national and community regulations for the protection of health and safety of passengers and airport personnel. There was no evidence that the stairs were defective in any way. As the passengers prepared to disembark, they may or may not have been forewarned that it was snowing. The Claimant could not recall any such warning, but in any event, inaction could not, in and of itself, be properly characterised as an event and [counsel] did not suggest that the failure to warn of a potential risk could constitute a relevant event. However, the use of the stairs without a canopy was not a non-event. It required a positive decision on the part of the airport personnel to use stairs either with or without a canopy. This decision involved a series of actions and omissions culminating in the aircraft stairs being aligned to the aircraft and the authority being given for the passengers to disembark. This was an event. According to the evidence ... in bad weather stairs with a canopy should be used 'where possible'. On occasions when canopied stairs are not available, for whatever reason, in accordance with the airport's operating manual policy, prior to authorising passengers to disembark, the stairs should be free from the accumulation of snow or ice.... The use of the uncovered stairs at the point of disembarkation did not comply with the airport's operating manual and was therefore not the 'normal operation of the aircraft'.

One may ask whether a judgment in a claim based on an allegation of negligence would have been any different. What seems to be happening is that while negligence is irrelevant as a basis for liability under the Convention, it gets in by the back door in analysing what is 'unusual'. The judge could simply have held that the Convention, which requires no proof of fault, makes the carrier liable whenever there is an accident, and that is what Mr Labbadia suffered.

A US case, *Bintz v Continental Airlines*,[49] provides our second example. A passenger had what appeared to be a heart attack (itself a purely 'internal' event). A nurse on board volunteered help, and the cabin crew alerted the pilot who got in touch with Medlink, which provides advice in such circumstances; in the event the flight was *not* diverted to a nearby airport. The case was heard simply on a motion for summary judgment, but the court held that there had to be an assessment of all

[49] *Bintz v Continental Airlines Inc*, Civil Action No 4:13-0566, 2016 WL 6906901 (SD Tex 3 March 2016).

the circumstances surrounding a passenger's injuries, and listed as relevant facts to be ascertained: what was communicated to or known by the flight attendant assisting the volunteer nurse during the flight; what the flight attendant communicated to the captain; what the captain communicated to Medlink; whether the proper protocol was followed; and, under the totality of these circumstances, whether Mr Bintz's symptoms *should* have required a diversion. Those are plainly negligence-related questions.

Finally, I turn to a case from New South Wales with very simple facts. In *Salih v Emirates (No 2)*,[50] the plaintiff claimed for an injury caused when the door of an overhead luggage compartment fell on her hand. Judgment was given for the carrier and leave to appeal was refused.[51] The trial judge referred to the *Saks* definition and held, quite correctly, that:

> Where the injury to a passenger results from the passenger's own internal reaction to the usual, normal and expected operation of the aircraft as opposed to an unexpected or unusual event or happening that is external to the passenger on board the aircraft, there is no accident within the meaning of the Convention.

In the next paragraph, this became: 'If the cause is solely due to the usual, normal and expected operation of the aircraft, then it will not be considered to be an accident within the meaning of Article 17 of the Convention.' Although what happened may have been unusual and unexpected from the plaintiff's point of view, the judge accepted the evidence that the door was not defective or faulty, held that the thumb was injured by the door dropping in the usual, normal, and expected way, and dismissed the claim.

J. The European Union

The CJEU's occasional rulings on the Montreal Convention have not been very helpful. In the case usually referred to as *Niki Luftfahrt*,[52] the Advocate General, after a long examination of various approaches, found that the meaning of 'accident' was an event 'of a sudden or unusual nature [which] has an origin outside the person of the passenger concerned'. The court itself observed shortly that the ordinary meaning of the concept of 'accident' was that of 'an unforeseen, harmful and involuntary event'.[53] The use of 'unforeseen', which is, of course, not in the

[50] [2019] NSWDC 715.
[51] [2020] NSWCA 215.
[52] Case C-532/18 *GN v ZU (administrator in insolvency of Niki Luftfahrt GmbH)* EU:C:2019:1127, [2020] 1 WLR 3059.
[53] At [35].

Saks definition, is not explained and was not something proposed by the Advocate General.

More recently, in *YL v Altenrhein Luftfahrt GmbH*,[54] the Court has again looked at 'accident' in terms of foreseeability. Should it be judged from the perspective of the passenger concerned or that of the normal operating range of the aircraft on board which that event occurred (the latter possibility being dictated by the facts, of a hard landing that injured a passenger)? The Court rejected the first approach: 'expectations may vary from one passenger to another, such an interpretation could lead to a paradoxical result if the same event were classified as "unforeseen" and, therefore, as an "accident" for certain passengers, but not for others'.[55] This ignores the possibility that reference could be made to the expectations of passengers generally; but it demonstrates that 'foreseeability' is a tricky concept in this context.

Even more surprisingly, the Court examines provisions in Annex IV to Regulation 216/2008[56] that a flight must be performed in such a way that the operating procedures specified in the Flight Manual or, where required the Operations Manual, for the preparation and execution of the flight are followed, and that an aircraft must be operated in accordance with its airworthiness documentation and the aircraft's scheduled performance. It held that a landing which does not exceed the limits laid down by the procedures applicable to the aircraft in question, and which takes place in accordance with those procedures and taking into account the rules of the trade and best practice in aircraft operation, cannot be regarded as 'unforeseen'.[57]

These cases need a fuller examination than is possible here, but some observations must be made. The CJEU seems determined to devise a new set of relevant terms, ignoring the well-established case law in other jurisdictions. So, it uses a test of 'foreseeability' and throws in that obscure reference to 'the rules of the trade' as well as best practice; all this seems to be language pointing to negligence. It is difficult to see how the approach in *YL v Altenrhein Luftfahrt GmbH* can be used outside the special facts of the case. It is certainly to be hoped that plaintiffs will not be required to demonstrate in every case that there was some deviation from the (very extensive) aviation safety regulations or the terms of the flight or operations manual.[58]

[54] Case C-70/20 *YL v Altenrhein Luftfahrt GmbH* EU:C:2021:379, [2021] 4 WLR 111.
[55] At [35].
[56] Regulation (EC) No 216/2008 of the European Parliament and of the Council of 20 February 2008 on common rules in the field of civil aviation and establishing a European Aviation Safety Agency, and repealing Council Directive 91/670/EEC, Regulation (EC) No 1592/2002 and Directive 2004/36/EC [2008] OJ L79/1.
[57] At [40].
[58] Or indeed that any such deviation would be treated as negligence per se.

K. Conclusion

The *Saks* definition has been welcomed by judges, spared the task of producing an apt definition of 'accident' in the case before them. Experience has shown that it is a definition that is not fit for purpose. Or, a more moderate proposition, it is not for universal application to cases of every type. And the way in which some courts use the definition makes matters worse.

In the days of the Warsaw Convention, courts were often persuaded that its purpose was to protect an infant industry. That was certainly true of the limit on the level of damages, but it was never the whole story. By the time of the Montreal Convention, aviation had long passed infancy. That Convention sought to ensure that claimants had access to a range of courts and could recover compensation without facing onerous legal obstacles. Much earlier in this chapter, I wrote that the whole point of Article 17 is that the claimants (the injured passenger or the dependants of a deceased passenger) do not have to prove fault on the part of the pilot or the owner or operator of the aircraft. So far as Article 17 is concerned, the presence of absence of fault is quite immaterial. A part of that is that the claimants do not have to produce the highly technical evidence needed to prove, for example, that the aircraft was defective or that its operation was in some way negligent. But the cases so often seem to require the claimant to prove just that, that there was some abnormality in the aircraft, its operation, or the behaviour of the crew; otherwise the claim fails.

To a common lawyer, that accords with an understanding of fault based on a breach of a duty owed to passengers. Negligence is entering by the back door. It is a familiar and comfortable notion for courts in common law jurisdictions. My argument is that it does not accord with the plain meaning of the Conventions.

16

British Members of the Institut de Droit International

Peter North[*]

A. Introduction

The early 1870s was hardly a peaceful time in the world. France and Prussia were at war; there was civil war in Spain; the US was still recovering from the trauma of the American Civil War; and conflict between Austria and Prussia and between Prussia and Denmark, as well as military conflict in South America, were all problems of the recent past. It was also a period when there was little, if anything, in the way of global or regional organizations which might play a significant role in the peaceful resolution of international disputes. This was a world some thirty years before the creation of the Permanent Court of Arbitration and long before the establishment of the League of Nations or the Permanent Court of International Justice at The Hague—and the better part of a century before the establishment of the UN, the International Court of Justice, and the International Law Commission.

It was against this background that eleven international law experts met in 1873 in Ghent to establish the Institut de droit international. Under the presidency of the great Italian political and legal figure, Pasquale Mancini, the members of this group were widely drawn, not only from Western Europe, but also from Russia, the US, and Argentina, the British founder member being Professor James Lorimer from the University of Edinburgh. The significance of the establishment of the Institut can be seen from the fact that within some thirty years it was awarded the Nobel Peace Prize.

Ever since the founding of the Institut, British international lawyers, both public and private, including Lawrence Collins, have been strongly represented among what is now a maximum of 132 Members and Associates worldwide. There follows some reflections on the makeup of the British membership of the Institut de

[*] The year 2023 will be the 150th anniversary of the establishment of the Institut de droit international and, to mark that occasion, the Institut has established a nine-person Commission on the History of the institute, of which the author is one of the members. This contribution to the volume of essays honouring Lawrence Collins is based on work done for the Commission and is published with the consent of the Institut de droit international.

Peter North, *British Members of the Institut de Droit International* In: *Essays in International Litigation for Lord Collins*. Edited by: Jonathan Harris, Campbell McLachlan and Paul David Mora, Oxford University Press. © Oxford University Press 2022. DOI: 10.1093/oso/9780192867988.003.0017

droit international and then short biographical accounts of all sixty-seven of our members.

B. Some Reflections on the British Membership

There have been sixty-seven British citizens elected to the Institut in the 147 years of its existence—only three of whom are women! Of the sixty-seven, all but seven have been British subjects at birth. Some two-thirds have been graduates of either or both of Oxford University and Cambridge University (twenty-two from each university). In this regard, there may be some link with the fact that all British holders of the Chichele Chair of Public International Law at Oxford have been members; and, in the case of the Whewell Chair of Public International Law at Cambridge, all but two British holders of the Chair have been elected to the Institut. The two Cambridge exceptions were the first holder of the Chair, Sir Vernon Harcourt, who was too busy being an MP, Home Secretary, and Chancellor of the Exchequer to make much of an impression as an international lawyer—and whose Deputy, Reverend Thomas Lawrence, was elected—and Sir Henry Maine, the distinguished legal historian, who died within a year of taking up the Chair.

If one looks to the judicial experience of the British members, all but one of the British judges on the Permanent Court of International Justice and of its successor, the International Court of Justice, have been members. The one not elected was Viscount Finlay, though he turned out to be more of an international lawyer, and became a British member of the Permanent Court of Arbitration, than his successor as Lord Chancellor, Viscount Birkenhead, who was elected! Considering other judicial experience, nearly a third of those elected up until the end of the First World War had been judges, ranging from the county court to the House of Lords and other courts within the British Empire and beyond. However, in the next 100 years, there have been only three members who have held British judicial office. Turning to other career patterns, a noticeable change in membership after the First World War was the election of public servants, most noticeably six holders of the position of Legal Advisor to the Foreign Office, along with three members whose careers have been those of overseas/international public servants.

By far the greater number of British members have been predominantly interested in public international law, with only thirteen or so out of sixty-seven being members whose main interest has been private international law. Of these, only three were elected in the first sixty years of the Institut, but more than half in the last sixty years. This is not wholly surprising because, for many decades, consideration of private international law in Britain was essentially limited to the study of the subject within the common law world—and two of our most distinguished twentieth-century private international lawyers in fact resigned from the Institut. However, in more recent times, the work in this field of the Hague Conference on

Private International Law and of the EU has had a profound impact on the international study of this area of law and appears to have led to an increase in the number of British private international lawyers elected to the Institut. The British private international lawyers have, in relation to their work in this area of scholarship, almost without exception been generalists addressing the whole range of issues arising in their field. This may be illustrated by the fact that, of the thirteen of them, all but three have been the authors or editors of major textbooks covering the whole subject; though most have also published works on specific topics.

Turning to those British members who have been predominantly public international lawyers, their careers and interests have covered a much wider spectrum. A considerable number have been judges and public servants and their work has often revolved around the major international issues of the day—wars and their aftermaths, the creation of and work in new international bodies, not least international courts and bodies such as the UN. Among the public international lawyers with a predominantly academic background, at least in the earlier parts of their careers, quite a number have written or edited wide-ranging books, often for students, covering the whole field. Other writings have focused on particular areas, often influenced by the particular issues of the day. Examples might be: 'Neutrality of Great Britain during the American Civil War'; 'The Law of Nations'; 'Law and Usage of War'; 'War and Neutrality in the Far East'; 'The Hague Peace Conferences'; 'A Guide to Diplomatic Practice'; 'The Law of the Air'; 'Space Law'; International Law and Human Rights"; 'The Law of the Sea'; 'Self Defence in International Law'; 'Human Rights in the World'; 'International Law and the Antarctic Treaty System'; and 'Whaling and International Law'.

It might be noted that among the first half of those elected to the Institut, that is, those elected up until the end of the First World War, a third never progressed to full membership.[1] This may say something about the extent of their real interest in international law and, also, reflect the complexities of international travel in those days. Of the British members elected since then, all but five have become Members. One final comment on the British membership of the Institut concerns career patterns within or outside the academic world. While there is no doubt that many of those with a predominantly academic career also appeared as practising lawyers or for a period undertook judicial responsibilities, it is fair to say that just over half the British members held, or hold, significant academic appointments.

[1] The statutes of the Institut provide that all those newly elected are 'Associates'. Full Membership is not conferred until the Associate has 'participated effectively' in three biennial Sessions of the Institut, which are held in a different country each time.

C. The British Members

James Lorimer FRSE (b 1818; d 1890); one of the eleven Founders of the Institut; 1873 (Founder Member)

Educated at Edinburgh University, he was admitted to the Faculty of Advocates in Scotland in 1845, but his practice at the Bar was not particularly successful. However, in the 1850s, he was very active in promoting reform of the Scottish universities; and in 1862 he was appointed Regius Professor of Public Law at the University of Edinburgh. In 1884, he published his major work *The Institutes of the Law of Nations*; and he was primarily concerned with the application of natural law to international issues, not least the question of inter-State recognition.

Mountague Bernard (b 1820; d 1882); elected 1873 (original Member); 1880–82 (President); presided over the meeting in Oxford in 1880

Educated at Oxford University, he was Called to the Bar in 1846, and in 1859 he was appointed the first Chichele Professor of International Law in Oxford. In 1870, he published *An Historical Account of the Neutrality of Great Britain during the American Civil War*. He was a government advisor on international law issues, not least in the negotiation of the Treaty of Washington in 1871, defining the duties of neutral States in times of war. The same year, he was appointed a member of the Judicial Committee of the Privy Council. He resigned his Chair in 1874 and two years later was appointed a member of the Royal Commission on the duties of naval commanders in relation to foreign slaves. In 1880, he became Chairman of the Commission on the University of Oxford, under the Universities of Oxford and Cambridge Act 1877.

He was committed to promoting the exchange of ideas between international jurists from different countries, in order to help stimulate the study of comparative law and to harmonize the principles of international law, both public and private; and he was one of the original members of the Institut de droit international, founded in 1873. *The Dictionary of National Biography*, 1885–1900, Volume 04 1880, records that he presided over the Oxford meeting in 1880 with much tact and dignity.

John Westlake KC (b 1828; d 1913); elected 1873 (original Member); 1898 (Honorary Member); 1895 (President); 1911 (Honorary President); presided over the meeting in Cambridge in 1895

Educated at Cambridge University and Called to the Bar in 1854, he practised as a barrister for some thirty years, though was described as a better drafter of opinions than an advocate. It was only four years after he started at the Bar that he published his hugely well-received work, *Treatise on Private International Law* (1858). Much of his practice as a barrister involved cases with an international flavour, a considerable number involving appeals to the Judicial Committee of the Privy

Council. In 1885, he was elected an MP, but lost his seat a year later. In 1888, he was appointed as the third Whewell Professor of International Law at Cambridge; and for the next two decades made substantial contributions to the field of international law, not least through his major books on the subject, especially his two-volume *International Law* (1904–07). He also served as a British member of the International Court of Arbitration from 1900 to 1906.

Sir Travers Twiss QC FRS (b 1809; d 1897); elected 1874 (Member); 1891 (Honorary Member)

Educated at Oxford University, the early part of his career was in the academic world, as a Fellow of his Oxford College, University College. Although Called to the Bar in 1840, the following year he was elected Drummond Professor of Political Economy in Oxford. In 1849, he then became the first Professor of International Law at King's College, London, returning to Oxford in 1855 as Regius Professor of Civil Law. Over the next fifteen years, he was very active as an author, publishing *The Law of Nations Considered as Independent Political Communities* (1861–63), as an arbitrator determining the boundaries of New Brunswick and Canada, serving on Royal Commissions on, for example, neutrality laws (1867–68) and naturalization (1868–69), and as a practitioner in the Ecclesiastical and Admiralty Courts. All this came to a shuddering halt in 1872 when a court case revealed that the woman whom he had married in Dresden a decade earlier was not, as claimed, the daughter of a Polish Count, but rather a French prostitute. Although Twiss generally withdrew from public life, his interest in international law continued and he was three times the Vice President of the Institut, and was the English Vice President of the Association for the Reform and Codification of the Laws of Nations.

William Edward Hall (b 1835; d 1894); elected 1875 (Associate); 1882 (Member)

Although Called to the Bar in 1861, as a young man he was more interested in art and mountaineering (becoming a long-standing member of the Alpine Club in London), as well as in military matters, than in law. It was said that he 'took no great interest in law as a profession, lacking the patience necessary for the steady pursuit of a career as a lawyer'. He found himself under fire on the Danish side in the Second Schleswig War of 1864; and later he was an advocate of national service for all young men. Though very much a country gentleman, later in life he provided advice to government on a variety of matters; but his legal reputation rests on his highly regarded major work *International Law*, published by Oxford University Press in 1880. He also published books on *Rights and Duties of Neutrals* (1874) and *Foreign Jurisdictions of the British Crown* (1894).

Sir Thomas Erskine Holland KC FBA (one of the Founding Fellows of the British Academy) (b 1835; d 1926); elected 1875 (Associate); 1878 (Member); President (1913); presided over the meeting in Oxford in 1913

Educated at Oxford University, he was Called to the Bar in 1863 and practised as a barrister for about a decade. However, in 1874, he returned to Oxford when he was elected Chichele Professor of International Law, a position he held until his retirement in 1910. Perhaps his most significant work was *The Elements of Jurisprudence* (1880), thirteen editions of which were published in his lifetime. It has been said that his 'contributions to the field of international law were less fundamental', and that his *Studies in International Law* (1898) 'did not place him among the modern founders of this legal discipline'. However, on the more practical side, in 1906, he represented Britain at the conference to revise the Geneva Convention of 1864 dealing with the sick and wounded in warfare. More widely in the academic world he was said to have provided the intellectual leadership which led to the founding of the *Law Quarterly Review*, Britain's pre-eminent legal journal.

Sir Donald Mackenzie Wallace KCIE, KCVO (b 1841; d 1919); elected 1878 (Associate); 1895 (Member)

In his youth, he studied at both Scottish and German universities, receiving a doctorate in law from the University of Heidelberg. He then spent five years in Russia, the outcome of which was *Russia*, a very substantial and highly regarded work on that country, still described as 'a very important source for the history of late-tsarist Russia'. In 1877, he was appointed a foreign correspondent of *The Times* newspaper and covered the Congress of Berlin the following year (also the year of his election to the Institut). In later life, he served as Private Secretary to the Viceroy of India and then Private Secretary to the future King George V. He does not appear to have been actively involved in international law.

Sir George Sherston Baker Bt (b 1846; d 1923); elected 1879 (Associate); 1921 (Member)

Not a great deal seems now to be known about him. He was Called to the Bar in 1871. He became the Recorder of Barnstaple and then a County Court judge in Lincolnshire. His connection with international law seems to have come substantially from the fact that in 1878 he took over the editorship of Halleck's *International Law: Rules Regulating the Intercourse of States in Peace and War*, first published in America in 1861; he also wrote *First Steps in International Law* (1899), as well as *The Laws Relating to Quarantine* (1879). An obituarist said that 'his contributions to international law were not many but he was greatly interested in the subject'.

Albert Venn Dicey KC FBA (one of the Founding Fellows of the British Academy) (b 1835; d 1922); elected 1880 (Associate)

Educated at Oxford University, he was Called to the Bar in 1863 and practised as a barrister for some twenty years with no more than moderate success, taking on a number of journalism projects as well, probably to supplement his income. He did, however, also engage in scholarly writing, for example, publishing his work on *The*

Law of Domicil in 1879. This scholarly writing led to his election in Oxford to the Vinerian Professorship of English Law in 1882. There is no doubt that his lengthy period in the Chair transformed its reputation which had sunk to a low ebb since the days of Blackstone 100 years earlier. It was as Vinerian Professor that he produced the greatest of his books, *Law of the Constitution* (1885) and *Conflict of Laws* (1896), works whose influence is still great (albeit edited by other hands, two of the General Editors of the latter also being elected to the Institut). His clear commitment to the study of law can be seen from the fact that he also did some part-time teaching for the London School of Economics in its earliest days. Dicey had wider concerns than just the study of the law, particularly over the future of Ireland on which he was publicly very outspoken in favour of the preservation of the Union.

Donald James Mackay, Lord Reay KT, GCSI, GCIE, PBA (b 1839; d 1921); elected 1882 (Associate); 1886 (Member); President (1904–06); presided over the meeting in Edinburgh in 1904

Born in the Netherlands, his father being a Scottish peer though Dutch by nationality, he became a British citizen in 1877 and, in 1891, he was created a UK peer as Baron Reay. In 1885, he had been appointed as Governor of Bengal and, on his return from India, he served as a government minister from 1894 to 1895. He was the Founding President of the British Academy, serving from 1902 to 1907, as well as serving as President of the Council of University College London. He campaigned vigorously and successfully for the establishment of the School of Oriental Studies in London University. Though it appears that he never published anything in the field of international law, his interest was evidenced by his support for the Institut, serving as Vice President in 1896 and 1902, as well as President in 1904. In 1915, he became the first President of the newly established Grotius Society. Furthermore, he was a British delegate in 1907 to the Peace Conference at The Hague on the laws and customs of war on land.

James, Lord Hannen FRS (b 1821; d 1894); elected 1883 (Associate); 1885 (Member)

After attending St Paul's School, he studied at the University of Heidelberg. Called to the Bar in 1848, his reputation was enhanced by his role as an adjudicator on the Anglo-American mixed arbitral tribunal in the 1850s. Appointed as a judge in 1868, with the reorganization of the court system in 1875, he became the first President of the Probate, Divorce and Admiralty Division. In 1891, he was promoted to the House of Lords as a Law Lord. It is not clear that his judicial experience at the time of his election to the Institut in 1883 involved much consideration of international law issues; though in 1892, the year after his appointment as a Law Lord, he was chosen as the British arbitrator in the Paris arbitration on the Anglo-American dispute over fishing in the Bering Sea.

Sir Robert Joseph Phillimore Bt (b 1810; d 1885); elected 1883 (Associate)

Educated at Oxford University, his distinguished career as a lawyer started with practice in the ecclesiastical courts, culminating with his appointment in 1867 as Dean of Arches, combined with extensive Admiralty work, becoming as well a Judge of the Cinque Ports. During this period, he also served briefly as an MP. With the total reorganization of the court system in 1875, he became a judge of the Probate, Divorce and Admiralty Division. It has been said that his interest in international law stemmed from his experience as a law officer during the American Civil War. This interest led, among other things, to his Presidency of the Association for the Reformation and Codification of the Law of Nations, and the publication of his four-volume work *Commentaries upon International Law* (1879).

Sir Thomas Barclay (b 1853; d 1941); elected 1885 (Associate); 1891 (Member); Honorary Member (1927); President (1919); presided over the meeting in Paris in 1919

Born in Scotland, he was educated at University College London and various European universities. His career started as a journalist, but he was Called to the Bar in 1881 and practised law in Paris, becoming President of the British Chamber of Commerce in Paris in 1899. He served briefly as an MP in 1910. He wrote quite extensively on international law; his books included *Problems of International Practice and Diplomacy* (1907) and *Law and Usage of War* (1914). He was nominated, unsuccessfully, for the Nobel Peace Prize no fewer than ten times!

Reverend Thomas Joseph Lawrence (b 1849; d 1920); elected 1885 (Associate); 1908 (Member)

Educated at Cambridge University, he became a Fellow of Downing College where he taught international law in the 1870s and 1880s. He was appointed by Sir Vernon Harcourt, the Whewell Professor of International Law, as his deputy from 1883 to 1887. It might be noted that Harcourt was the only British Whewell Professor not to be elected to the Institut. Lawrence then taught at the Royal Naval College Greenwich and the Royal Naval College Portsmouth from 1884 to 1909. In the 1890s, he also taught for two years at the University of Chicago as Professor of International Law. Later he became Reader in International Law at the University of Bristol. He combined his academic life with that of being an active Church of England vicar in a number of rural parishes, as well as being Assistant Chaplain at the Chapel Royal, Savoy from 1884 to 1909. He wrote quite widely on international law; his works included *A Handbook of Public International Law* (1885) and *The Principles of International Law* (1895), both of which went into a number of editions. It was said of the former that a copy of it 'was to be found on every British, American and Japanese man-of-war'! Other works were *Disputed Questions in Modern International Law* (1884), *War and Neutrality in the Far East* (1902),

International Problems and Hague Conferences (1908), and *The Society of Nations* (1918).

Sir Frederick Pollock Bt, FBA (one of the Founding Fellows of the British Academy) (b 1845; d 1937); elected 1885 (Associate)

Educated at Cambridge University, he was Called to the Bar in 1871. However, his life was devoted more to the study of the law than to practice. The breadth of his knowledge and the range of his scholarship were quite remarkable, with works such as *Principles of Contract at Law and in Equity* (1876), *Essays in Jurisprudence and Ethics* (1882), *The Law of Torts* (1887), the two-volume Pollock and Maitland, *History of the English Law before the Time of Edward I* (1895), and *The Genius of the Common Law* (1912), a number of these being written when he was Corpus Professor of Jurisprudence in Oxford from 1883 to 1903. Not satisfied with such scholarly activity which also included serving as the founding editor of the *Law Quarterly Review* from 1885 until 1919, he also served as Chief Editor of the Law Reports from 1895 to 1935 (when he was 90!). Although in later life he also served on a number of public bodies, including the Royal Commissions on Labour and on Public Records, there is little evidence that he had a particular interest in international law, public or private, such as to explain his Membership of the Institut.

Sir John Scott KCMG (b 1841; d 1904); elected 1891 (Associate)

Educated at Oxford University, for whom he played cricket against Cambridge in 1863, he was Called to the Bar in 1865, but his career as a barrister was cut short by ill health and, in 1872, he went to live in Egypt. In 1874, he was appointed a judge of the international court of appeal there and then vice president of the court in 1881. A year later, he moved to India as a judge of the High Court of Bombay. In 1890, he was invited back to Egypt and successfully proposed wholesale reform of the Egyptian legal system—and acted as Inspector of the whole new system until his retirement in 1898. Though appointed a vice president of the International Law Association, the origin of his interest in international law is not clear; and he appears to have attended few Institut meetings.

Sir Robert Hart Bt, GCMG (b 1835; d 1911); Honorary Member (1892)

Born in Northern Ireland, he was educated at what became Queen's University, Belfast. From there, he joined the British Consular Service in China in 1854 and lived in China for all but the last three years of his life. In 1859, with British agreement, he transferred to the Chinese Customs Service and over the next fifty years became the most significant public administrator in the country and was described as the most influential Westerner in the Qing dynasty. Towards the end of his career, he survived the very real dangers of the Boxer uprising in 1900. He was not a lawyer, but, not long after his arrival in China, he had translated into Chinese large sections of *Elements of International Law* by the distinguished American lawyer, Henry Wheaton. He would appear to have been elected directly as an Honorary Member; and, given the nature of his career, it seems unlikely that he ever managed to attend meetings of the Institut.

John Alderson Foote KC (b 1848; d 1922); elected 1895 (Associate)

Educated at Cambridge University where he was a Senior Whewell Scholar in International Law, he was Called to the Bar in 1875. His career appears to have been substantially that of a barrister on the Western Circuit, becoming Recorder of Exeter in 1899; and he was Chairman of the Bar Council from 1918 to 1920. He stood for election to Parliament in Bristol in 1910, as a Liberal Unionist, but without success. He found time in his practice at the Bar to write two very different books. His election to the Institut must have depended on his *Foreign and Domestic Law: A Concise Treatise in Private International Law*, first published in 1878 and running into a number of editions. He also wrote *Pie-Powder, Being Dust from the Law Courts, Collected and Recollected on the Western Circuit by a Circuit Tramp*; not a heavyweight work!

Henry Goudy (b 1849; d 1921); elected 1895 (Associate)

Born in Ireland, he studied in Scotland at Edinburgh and Glasgow Universities, and then at the University of Konigsberg. He qualified to practise law in Scotland and later published a book on the *Law of Bankruptcy* (1886). He returned to university life in 1889 on his appointment as Professor of Civil Law at Edinburgh University—a role which required the teaching of Roman Law. In 1893, he moved to Oxford to the Regius Chair of Civil Law—again teaching Roman Law, a subject on which he published a little, but of no great distinction. There is no doubt that he had an interest in international law; though it was not a subject on which he wrote. However, he was one of the founders of the Grotius Society in 1915 and its first vice president. He may also be remembered in the British academic world as the first president of the Society of Public Teachers of Law in 1908.

Richard Everard Webster, Viscount Alverstone GCMG, FRS (b 1842; d 1915); elected 1902 (Associate); 1904 (Member)

Educated at Cambridge University where he was a keen sportsman, he was Called to the Bar in 1868, where he combined a successful career as a barrister with that of an MP. He served as Attorney General for most of the period from 1885 to 1900. During that time (in 1893), he represented Great Britain in the Bering Sea and the Venezuela arbitrations. In 1900, he was appointed directly to the Bench as Master of the Rolls and, within six months, had been promoted to Lord Chief Justice. In 1903, while in office, he served as one of the arbitrators in the Alaska boundary dispute. He retired in 1913. His only publication appears to have been *Recollections of Bar and Bench* (1914).

Major General Sir John Charles Ardagh KCMG, KCIE, CB (b 1840; d 1907); elected 1904 (Associate)

Educated at Trinity College, Dublin and at the Royal Military Academy, Woolwich, for almost the whole of his adult life he was a serving army officer. Commissioned into the Royal Engineers, he served in Canada, the Balkans, Italy, and Egypt; and in India as the Private Secretary to the Viceroy and then, ultimately, as Director of Military Intelligence. He served in 1901 as a member of the tribunal dealing with the Chile–Argentina boundary dispute. However, it was when he retired from the army in 1902 that he became more significantly involved in international law matters, becoming a member of the Permanent Court of Arbitration at The Hague and in 1906 serving as a British delegate at the Swiss Conference which successfully revised the 1864 Geneva Convention.

Lassa Francis Lawrence Oppenheim (b 1858; d 1919); elected 1908 (Associate); 1911 (Member)

Born in Germany near Frankfurt, he was educated at the Universities of Berlin, Gottingen, Heidelberg, and Leipzig. His academic career, teaching at the Universities of Freiburg and Basle, was primarily in the field of criminal law, on which he wrote a number of books. In 1895, he decided to move to England, not as a refugee, but simply out of choice, aided by the fact that he was financially independent, and he became a British citizen in 1900. Not only did he change countries, but he also changed academic disciplines—moving from criminal law to international law, a subject which did not require a basic training in English law. He taught first at the London School of Economics and was then, in 1908, appointed Whewell Professor of International law in Cambridge, a post he held until his death. His Cambridge appointment was no doubt due to the great success of his two-volume *International Law: A Treatise*, published in 1905–06, which has now run into ten editions. In his last years, he was a strong advocate of the foundation of a League of Nations and, at home, of the establishment of the *British Yearbook of International Law*, his obituary appearing in the first volume.

Sir William Rann Kennedy FBA (b 1846; d 1915); elected 1910 (Associate); 1913 (Member)

Educated at Cambridge University (President of the Union), he was Called to the Bar in 1871. His first practice was mainly in commercial and shipping matters; and he published *The Law of Civil Salvage* in 1891. Having failed on a number of occasions to get elected to Parliament, he was appointed a High Court judge in 1892, and promoted to the Court of Appeal in 1907. He was said to have been 'deeply interested in international law', being active in the International Law Association of which he was President from 1908 to 1910; although he does not appear to have published on the subject.

Sir John Macdonell KCB, FBA (b 1846; d 1921); elected 1900 (Associate); 1912 (Member)

He was a Scot, educated at the Universities of Aberdeen and Edinburgh, but Called to the Bar in England in 1873. In 1889, he was appointed a Master of the Supreme Court, later promoted as the King's Remembrancer, offices he held while also Quain Professor of Comparative Law at University College London and, in 1908, he was appointed the first Dean of the Faculty of Law of the University of London. He was particularly interested in the reform of the judicial system and was at the forefront of ensuring that there were comprehensive judicial statistics. His interest in international law is evidenced by his being a founder member of the Grotius Society, of which he was President from 1919 to 1921. He chaired a committee of experts advising the government on breaches of international law committed by German forces during the First World War.

Sir Henry Erle Richards KCSI KC (b 1861; d 1922); elected 1913 (Associate)

Educated at Oxford University, he was Called to the Bar in 1887. His practice is said to have involved 'government work'; and he was one of the lawyers representing Britain in the Samoa (1902) and Venezuela (1904) arbitrations at The Hague. He then spent five years in India as Legal Member of the Government in India. He returned to practice mainly before the Judicial Committee of the Privy Council; and in 1910 he acted for Newfoundland and Canada in the North Atlantic Fisheries Arbitration at The Hague. He was appointed Chichele Professor of International Law at Oxford in 1911; but he appears to have published little.

Frederick Edwin Smith, Earl of Birkenhead GCSI (b 1872; d 1930); elected 1921 (Associate)

Educated at Oxford University (President of the Union), reading law, he taught there from 1896 to 1899. Called to the Bar that year, he practised so successfully that, within nine years, he was made a KC at the age of 36. He had already been elected as a Conservative MP in 1906. At the beginning of the First World War, he served in France as an officer, but was appointed Solicitor General in 1915 and then, within six months, appointed Attorney General. After the war was over, in 1919, he was appointed Lord Chancellor by the Prime Minister, Lloyd George, serving until 1922, and was thus the only example of a serving Lord Chancellor elected to the Institut. Out of office for two years, he was then appointed Secretary of State for India, an office which he held from 1924 to 1928, dying two years later. He had been a powerful, influential—and controversial—political figure; but his election to the Institut will have depended on his reputation as an international lawyer which, presumably, stemmed from two books written during his time as a practising lawyer, namely *International Law in the Far East* (2nd edn, 1908) and *International Law* (4th edn, 1911); and from his experience in dealing with international law matters while Attorney General, as well as having to consider whether there should be war crimes trials at the end of the First World War. It might be worth noting that his immediate predecessor as Lord Chancellor, Viscount Finlay, who was an experienced international lawyer and the first UK judge of the Permanent Court of International Justice, did not become a member of the Institut.

Walter George Frank, Lord Phillimore GBE Hon FBA (b 1845; d 1929); elected 1921 (Associate); 1922 (Member)

He provides the first example of a son following his father (Sir Robert Phillimore) as a member of the Institut. Educated at Oxford University, he was Called to the Bar in 1868 and, in the early part of his career, specialized predominantly in the ecclesiastical and admiralty courts. He was appointed a High Court judge in 1897 and promoted to the Court of Appeal in 1913, where he served for only three years. However, it is said that during that period the court benefitted greatly from his expertise in international law. Two years after his retirement, he was granted a peerage and, for a decade or so, heard cases both in the House of Lords and the Judicial Committee of the Privy Council. His interest in international law is evidenced by his enthusiastic support of the International Law Association of which he was President from 1919 to 1920, his chairing a Committee to consider proposals for a League of Nations, and his serving on a committee in 1920 which drew up the statute establishing the Permanent Court of International Justice at The Hague. In 1917, he published *Three Centuries of Treaties of Peace and their Teaching*.

Thomas Baty (b 1869; d 1954); elected 1922 (Associate)

He is the most unusual of all the British Members of the Institut. Educated at both Oxford and Cambridge Universities, later with doctorates in law from both, he concluded that, though Called to the Bar, his career lay in academia, first teaching international law at the University of Nottingham during which period he published *International Law in South Africa* (1900) and *International Law* (1909), and acted as joint honorary secretary of the International Law Association. In 1910, he was encouraged to apply, albeit unsuccessfully, for the Chichele Chair in International Law at Oxford; but he continued to publish books and articles on international law, including *Britain and Sea Law* (1911); *Polarized Law (Private International Law)* (1914) and *Canons of International Law* (1930); and he was one of the original members of the Grotius Society when it was established in 1915. That year, he was encouraged to apply, successfully as it turned out, for the position of Foreign Legal Advisor to the Government of Japan, based in Tokyo. From 1916 until his death in 1954, he lived in Japan with the consequence that he never became a full Member of the Institut. In effect, he continued in a Japanese Government advisory role until 1945. Not surprisingly, there was concern in London over a British subject being a senior advisor to the Japanese Government when the Second World War broke out and even more so after Japan entered the war. After the war, consideration was given to charging Baty with treason. While forming the view that he was indeed guilty, the Foreign Office decided that it was not worth prosecuting someone who was 'old and senile'. However, his British passport 'and all other forms of protection as a British subject' were withdrawn and he never returned to Britain despite a clear wish to do so. In his private life, he wrote two novels under the female nom de plume of 'Irene Clyde'; and he has been described as 'transgender'.

Hugh Hale Leigh Bellot (b 1861; d 1928); elected 1922 (Associate); 1927 (Member)
Educated at Oxford University, he was later Called to the Bar. He became Professor of Constitutional Law at University College London in the early part of the twentieth century, but his interests ranged quite widely. He wrote a *History of the Inner and Middle Temple* in 1902 and much later produced an edition of Thomas and Bellot's *Leading Cases on Constitutional Law* in 1927. However, he had long had an interest in aspects of international law with, for example, his *Commerce in War* (1907) and the fourth edition of Cobbett's *Leading Cases on International Law* (1922). Having resigned from his Chair, he became the first secretary of the Grotius Society when it was established in 1915. He was also a very active member of the International Law Association, being an ardent advocate of the establishment of an international criminal court, writing widely on the issues of war crimes. He was clearly frustrated when his draft statute for such a court was rejected by the ILA in 1924. His son was Vice Chancellor of London University in the 1950s.

Alexander Pearce Higgins CBE KC FBA (b 1865; d 1935) elected 1922 (Associate); 1923 (Member); President (1929–31); presided over the Meeting in Cambridge in 1931
Educated at Cambridge University, he was admitted as a solicitor in 1899, but then Called to the Bar in 1908. He taught international law in Cambridge and then at the London School of Economics. During the First World War, he acted as an advisor to the Treasury Solicitor on international law and prize law matters. After the war he was a professor at the University of London before returning to Cambridge as Whewell Professor of International Law from 1920 to 1935. He was appointed a member of the Permanent Court of Arbitration at The Hague from 1930 until his death. His publications were extensive, including: *Employers' Liability on the Continent* (1898); *The Hague Peace Conferences* (1909); *The Binding Force of International Law* (1910); *The Law of Nations and the War* (1914); *Defensively Armed Merchant Ships and Submarine Warfare* (1917); Hall's *International Law*, 7th and 8th editions (1917, 1924); and *Studies in International Law and Relations* (1928).

Sir Ernest Mason Satow GCMG (b 1843; d 1929) elected 1922 (Associate)
Educated at University College, London, he was a man of many parts—a mountaineer, botanist, writer of guide books—but the major part of his life was his

link with the Far East, especially Japan. On leaving university at the precocious age of 19, he joined the Foreign Office Consular Service and was sent as an interpreter to Japan in 1862. There he had an 'unofficial' Japanese wife and two sons, one of whom became a very distinguished Japanese botanist. After serving in Japan for twenty years, he was promoted to being a member of the Diplomatic Service, moving to Siam (Thailand) as consul general, and serving afterwards in Uruguay and Morocco. He returned to Japan in 1895 as Minister Plenipotentiary, followed in 1900 by appointment to China as Minister. There he played a major role in the Boxer conference, negotiating agreement between China and the Western powers after the Boxer Uprising. Retiring to England in 1906 at the age of just over 60, he put his wide diplomatic experience to full use. He was one of the British Representatives (along with Lord Reay, a fellow Member of the Institut) in 1907 at the Second Hague Conference; but most particularly he wrote *A Guide to Diplomatic Practice*, published in 1917, a book which has been widely relied on by the British Diplomatic Service ever since, the 6th edition of which was published in 2017, exactly 100 years after the first.

Sir Cecil James Barrington Hurst GCMG KCB QC (b 1870; d 1963) elected 1922 (Associate); 1925 (Member); President (1936–37); Honorary Member (1950); presided over the meeting in Luxembourg in 1937

Educated at Cambridge University, he was Called to the Bar in 1893, but, in 1902, he was appointed as an assistant legal advisor in the Foreign Office; and he served in the Foreign Office for twenty-seven years, ultimately as Legal Advisor. He played a major role on behalf of the British Government in the development of the League of Nations and of a Permanent Court of International Justice. Active in examination of the laws of war, he was a prominent figure in the negotiation of the 1925 Treaty of Locarno. He was particularly concerned with the development of the literature on international law, and was the founding father of the *British Yearbook of International Law*, of which he served as editor until 1928, and was President of the Grotius Society. In 1929, he was elected a judge of the Permanent Court of International Justice, and served as President from 1934 to 1936, remaining as a judge until its replacement in 1946 by the International Court of Justice. He served as a British Member of the Permanent Court of Arbitration from 1929 to 1950, and as Chairman of the UN War Crimes Commission from 1943 to 1945.

James Leslie Brierly CBE (b 1881; d 1955); elected 1929 (Associate); 1937 (Member)

Educated at Oxford University, he was Called to the Bar in 1907; but the start of an academic career in Oxford in 1913 was disrupted by the outbreak of the First World War in which he served in the Adjutant General's Department. Appointed to a professorship in Manchester in 1920, he stayed only two years before his return to Oxford as Chichele Professor of International Law, a post he held for twenty-five years until retirement. He then spent two years in Edinburgh as Professor of International Relations. He was for nine years, from 1929 to 1938, the Editor of the *British Yearbook of International Law*; and, though he published quite widely on international law, his best-known work was his short masterpiece *The Law of Nations*, first published in 1928 and which has run so far to seven editions. Outside the academic world, he served on League of Nations committees, acted as legal advisor to the Emperor of Abyssinia, and, in 1948, became one of the original members of the International Law Commission which he chaired in 1951.

Sir John Fischer Williams CBE KC (b 1870; d 1947); elected 1929 (Associate); 1936 (Member)

Educated at Oxford University, he was Called to the Bar in 1894 and successfully practised as a Chancery barrister for the next twenty years. His interest in international law developed out of his wartime service in the aliens branch of the Home Office. For ten years, from 1920 to 1930, he was legal advisor to the British delegation on the reparations commission established by the Treaty of Versailles; and he also represented the delegation in arbitrations with Germany. In later years, he appeared as counsel or acted as an arbitrator in a variety of arbitrations; and in 1934 he published *Some Aspects of the Covenant of the League of Nations*. In 1936, he became a member of the British panel on the Permanent Court of Arbitration.

Arnold Duncan, Lord McNair CBE QC FBA (b 1885; d 1975); elected 1931(Associate); 1947 (Member); 1961 (Honorary Member); 1948–50 (President); presided over the meeting in Bath in 1950

He was educated at Cambridge University (President of the Union), having already qualified as a solicitor. After a few years in practice, he returned to Cambridge to an academic post, and then worked as a civil servant during the First World War, also being Called to the Bar in 1917. He resumed an academic career after the war, first in London and then returning to Cambridge in 1927. He was appointed Whewell Professor of International Law in Cambridge in 1935, but left after two years to become Vice Chancellor of the University of Liverpool. In 1945, at the end of the war, he returned to Cambridge as a professor of comparative law. Within a year he had been elected as a judge of the International Court of Justice, serving as President from 1952 to 1955. On retirement from the court, he served as the first president of the European Court of Human Rights from 1959 to 1965. His legal interests were wide ranging, including Roman law and the common law, particularly the law of contract. However, international law became his predominant interest, publishing, for example, *The Legal Effects of War* (1920), *The Law of the Air* (1931), *The Law of Treaties* (1938), and three volumes of *International Law Opinions* (1956).

Harold Cooke Gutteridge QC (b 1876; d 1953); elected 1936 (Associate); 1948 (Member)

Born in Italy, he was educated at Cambridge University and Called to the Bar in 1900, where he had a commercial law practice until the First World War. During the war, he served in the Army Ordnance Corps. In 1919, he was appointed Professor of International and Commercial Law at the University of London, but his interests developed in the fields of comparative law and private international law. This led to his moving to Cambridge, ultimately to a professorship of comparative law and the publication of *Comparative Law* in 1946—a landmark work in the modern development of comparative law as a subject of study. In the years between the wars, he served on a number of government commissions and similar bodies.

Sir William Eric Beckett KCMG QC (b 1896; d 1966); elected 1937 (Associate); 1950 (Member)

Educated at Oxford University, having served in the Cheshire Regiment during the First World War, he was Called to the Bar in 1922. In 1925, he joined the Foreign Office as an assistant legal advisor, eventually being appointed Legal Advisor from 1945 to 1953, a period during which he is said to have put 'the legal service of the Foreign Office on a modern footing'. In his earlier days, he had provided 'behind the scenes' advice on a number of international conferences, but he was particularly active in the later part of his career, for example, advising the British Government on the negotiation of the Bretton Woods Agreement in 1944, in early UN sessions, and appearing on behalf of the British Government in significant litigation before the International Court of Justice, including the *Corfu Channel Case* (1947–49), the *Anglo-Norwegian Fisheries Case* (1951), and the *Anglo-Iranian Oil Co Case* (1952). It might be noted that Beckett was the son-in-law of another British Member of the Institut, Sir Henry Erle Richards.

Sir Hersch Lauterpacht QC FBA (b 1897; d 1960); elected 1947 (Associate); 1952 (Member)

Born in part of the Austro-Hungarian Empire in what is now an area of Ukraine, he was educated first at the University of Lvov and then at the University of Vienna. In 1923, he moved to London where, in 1925, he obtained a PhD in international law from the London School of Economics. Two years later, he joined the law faculty there and, in 1931, he became a British subject. In 1935, he was promoted to a readership, and three years later he moved to Cambridge as Whewell Professor of International Law, a chair he held for twenty years. Alongside his academic responsibilities, he had a flourishing career as a barrister, having been Called to the Bar in 1936. He appeared in many major arbitrations and acted for the UK in litigation before the International Court of Justice, such as the Corfu Channel and Anglo-Iranian Oil Co litigation. He combined this work not only with his teaching responsibilities, but also with publishing a number of books, not least *Recognition in International Law* (1947) and *International Law and Human Rights* (1950), editing the *British Yearbook of International Law* for a decade from 1944 to 1954, and for nearly thirty years was responsible for what is now known as the International Law Reports. For four years, he served on the International Law Commission and, in 1955, was elected as a Judge of the International Court of Justice, serving until his death in 1960.

Sir Gerald Gray Fitzmaurice GCMG QC (b 1901; d 1982); elected 1948 (Associate); 1954 (Member); 1969–71 (President); presided over the meeting in Edinburgh in 1969

Educated at Cambridge University, he was Called to the Bar in 1925. He practised as a barrister for a few years before joining the Foreign Office in 1929 as a legal advisor, a role which he performed for the next thirty years, being appointed Legal Advisor from 1953 until 1960, appearing on behalf of the UK in cases before the International Court of Justice. He also served on the International Law Commission from 1955 to 1960 until his appointment as a Judge of the International Court of Justice. When he retired from the court in 1973, he was appointed a Judge of the European Court of Human Rights, serving until 1980. Described as 'one of the greatest international lawyers of his generation', his experience ranged from participation in the conference which considered the drafting of the UN Charter and consideration of the Italian and Japanese peace treaties to presiding over the Beagle Chanel court of arbitration, all this in addition to his contribution to international law in his judicial capacity. He also served as President of the Grotius Society from 1956 to 1960.

Geoffrey Chevalier Cheshire FBA (b 1886; d 1978); elected 1950 (Associate); 1956 (Member); he had resigned by 1965

Educated at Oxford University, he first taught law at the University College of Wales, Aberystwyth; but in 1911 he returned to Oxford to join the law faculty there. In the First World War, he was twice wounded serving in the Cheshire Regiment and then in the Royal Flying Corps (a remarkable link to his son, Leonard, who was awarded the VC serving in the Royal Airforce in the Second World War). Although he was Called to the Bar in 1922, he continued in Oxford with an academic career, ultimately being appointed Vinerian Professor of English Law in 1944, from which he took early retirement in 1949. He has been described as 'without doubt, the most eminent English academic lawyer of his generation', a judgment based not only on his skill as a teacher, but also on the fact that he produced major books on three very different areas of the law. The first, *The Modern Law of Real Property*, was published in time for examination of the new legislation making fundamental changes to that area of law in 1925; the second was *Private International Law* (1935), and, finally, *The Law of Contract* (1945), jointly with Cecil Fifoot. These books on which generations of law students have relied have, between them so far, gone into forty-nine editions.

Sir Claud Humphrey Meredith Waldock CMG OBE QC (b 1904; d 1981); elected 1950 (Associate); 1961 (Member)

Born in what is now Sri Lanka, he was educated at Oxford University and was Called to the Bar in 1928, but returned to Oxford in 1930 to start on a career as an academic lawyer. During the Second World War, he was employed by the government in a military branch of the Admiralty, which sparked his interest in international law, as he was engaged in considering the Royal Navy's foreign relations with neutral States and legal issues arising from the war at sea. His first peacetime international role was as a member of the commission of experts examining the Italian/Yugoslav border—the Trieste question. Appointed as Chichele Professor of International Law in Oxford in 1947, he combined those responsibilities with a specialist practice as a barrister, appearing in leading cases before the International Court of Justice and providing expert advice to a number of governments. He served as a member of the International Law Commission from 1961 to 1972, of the European Committee on Human Rights from 1954 to 1961 (including six years as President), as a Judge of the European Court of Human Rights from 1966 to 1971, and then in 1971 as a Judge of the International Court of Justice, becoming President of the Court in 1979 and sadly dying in office. In 1963, he edited one of the editions of Brierly's *Law of Nations*.

Clarence Wilfred Jenks (b 1909; d 1973); elected 1952 (Associate); 1963 (Member)

He was educated at Cambridge University (President of the Union), after which he joined the International Labour Organization (the ILO) as a legal advisor. Although Called to the Bar in 1936, he worked his way up the ILO until he became the principal legal advisor, with overall responsibility for the postwar revision of the ILO Constitution, as well as advising on the many legal conventions and reports which were, in a way, the lifeblood of the ILO. He represented the ILO on such significant occasions as the Bretton Woods Conference of 1944, the San Francisco Conference of 1945 (establishing the UN), and the 1966 UN Conference on the Law of Treaties. His general ability was recognized when he moved across from the role of legal advisor to that of the general running of the ILO as Assistant Director General, eventually taking full responsibility as the Director General. Alongside his lifetime's work with the ILO, he was a prolific writer on international law—as exemplified by books such as *The Proper Law of International Organisations* (1962), *The Prospects of International Adjudication* (1964), and *Space Law* (1965). Sadly, he died of a heart attack during the meeting of the Institut in Rome in 1973.

John Humphrey Carlile Morris QC FBA (b 1910; d 1984); elected 1954 (Associate); he had resigned by 1959

Educated at Oxford University, he was Called to the Bar in 1934, but returned to academic life two years later as a Fellow of Magdalen College, Oxford, where he spent the rest of his academic life, never, out of choice, becoming a professor. During the Second World War, he served as a Lt Commander in the Royal Navy Volunteer Reserve, being a very keen sailor. His central, but not his only, academic interest was private international law, or the conflict of laws as he preferred to describe it. His influence on the subject in England during the second half of the twentieth century was profound, as a teacher of graduate students, advising judges, and through his editorship of what became known as Dicey and Morris, *The Conflict of Laws*, of which he was the General Editor of five editions over thirty years. He was very much an English lawyer with little interest in the study of the subject elsewhere in Europe, despite his love of France!

Ben Atkinson Wortley CMG OBE QC (b 1907; d 1989); elected 1956 (Associate); 1967 (Member)

Educated at the University of Leeds, after leaving university he was Called to the Bar and practised as a barrister until 1931. He then took up an academic career, teaching first at the London School of Economics and then at the University of Birmingham. In 1936, he joined the University of Manchester where he remained, apart from the war years, for the rest of his academic career. During the Second World War, he served in the Ministry of Home Security, followed by three years as a Royal Navy instructor. In 1946, he returned to Manchester as Professor of Jurisprudence and International Law until his retirement in 1975. He served on the Council of Unidroit from 1950 to 1975. His publications included *Public International law* (1959) and *Jurisprudence* (1967), and he was one of the editors of the 1949 edition of Dicey's *Conflict of Laws*.

Sir Robert Yewdall Jennings QC (b 1913; d 2004); elected 1957 (Associate); 1969 (Member); 1985 (Honorary Member); 1981–83 (President); presided over the meeting in Cambridge in 1983

Educated at Cambridge University, after a year spent at Harvard University he joined the London School of Economics as a lecturer in law, returning to the Cambridge Law Faculty in 1939. During the Second World War, he served in the Intelligence Corps, with a short period of military service overseas at the end of the war. He then returned to academic life in Cambridge and was appointed Whewell Professor of International Law in 1955. It is said that, in that role, 'he will be remembered as much for his teaching as for his writings', but the latter were not negligible as exemplified by his editorship of the 9th edition of Oppenheim's *International Law* and his *The Acquisition of Territory in International Law* (1963). During his time as Whewell Professor, he also developed a significant international law practice, not least in relation to international oil disputes, and also for example acted in the Beagle Channel dispute. In 1982, he was appointed as a Judge of the International Court of Justice, serving until 1995, having been President of the Court from 1991 to 1994. He also served as a member of the Permanent Court of Arbitration from 1982.

Sir James Edmund Sandford Fawcett DSC QC (b 1913; d 1991); elected 1961 (Associate); 1973 (Member); he had resigned by 1983

Educated at Oxford University, he was Called to the Bar in 1938, but, on the outbreak of the Second World War, he joined the Royal Navy Volunteer Reserve and was awarded the DSC in 1942 while serving on a destroyer. After the war, he joined the Foreign Office as a legal advisor, being involved in the drafting of the Universal Declaration of Human Rights. After five years, in 1950, he returned to practice as a barrister, appearing on occasions before the International Court of Justice. From 1955 to 1960, he was general counsel to the International Monetary Fund. In conjunction from time to time with an academic career, as for example being Professor of International Law at King's College London for four years, he then served as a member of the European Commission on Human Rights for over twenty years, being the President from 1972 to 1982. His various publications included: *International Law and the Uses of Outer Space* (1968); *The Law of Nations* (1968); and *The Application of the European Convention on Human Rights* (1969). He never attended a meeting of the Institut because he said that he was 'not a conference man'.

Sir Otto Kahn-Freund QC FBA (b 1900; d 1979); elected 1963 (Associate); 1975 (Member)

Born in Frankfurt am Main, he was educated at the Universities of Heidelberg, Leipzig, and Frankfurt; and in 1929 he became a judge of the Berlin labour court—the start of a lifelong interest in and commitment to labour law. Being Jewish, he was dismissed by the Nazis and fled to London, where he became a student at the London School of Economics, joining the Law Faculty as a lecturer in 1936, the year when he was Called to the Bar. Having become a British citizen in 1940, he remained at the LSE for nearly thirty years, being appointed a professor in 1951. Almost singlehandedly, he established labour law as a particular area of legal study, playing an important role in its legal development through service from 1965 to 1968 on the Donovan Commission concerned with reform of trade unions and employer associations. In 1964, he moved to Oxford as Professor of Comparative Law. It is fair to say that, of his varied legal interests beyond labour law, the two most significant were family law and private international law. As for the former, he not only lectured on the subject, but was a considerable influence on the reforms of the late twentieth century. In the case of private international law, not only was he one of the editors of Dicey's *Conflict of Laws* for three editions, but his *General*

Problems of Private International Law (1974), being the General Course of lectures that he delivered at The Hague Academy, were of particular significance. One of the major contributions that he made to the study of the subject in England was to bring to it a more broadly based, comparative, and international approach.

Sir Francis Aime Vallatt GBE KCMG QC (b 1912; d 2008); elected 1965 (Associate); 1977 (Member); 1995 (Emeritus)

Born in France, he was educated at the Universities of Toronto and Cambridge. He was Called to the Bar in 1935 and, after a year teaching at the University of Bristol, practised as a barrister until the outbreak of the Second World War. During the war, he served in the Royal Airforce Volunteer Reserve as a signals expert. At the end of the war, he joined the Foreign Office as an assistant legal advisor, ultimately being promoted in 1960 to the position of Legal Advisor, where he served until 1968. During this period, he appeared for the UK Government in a number of cases before the International Court of Justice. Having taken early retirement from the Foreign Office, he then moved to become a professor at King's College, London until retirement again in 1976, having resumed his legal practice in 1968, again appearing quite often before the International Court of Justice, particularly in boundary disputes. He was a member of the Permanent Court of Arbitration and served on the International Law Commission from 1973 to 1981. Though he did not write a great deal, he published *International Law and the Practitioner* in 1966.

Ronald Harry Graveson CBE QC (b 1911; d 1991); elected 1967 (Associate); 1979 (Member)

Educated at the University of Sheffield and Harvard University, he started his teaching career in 1938 at King's College, London; but this was interrupted by six years' war service in the Royal Army Service Corps. After the war, he was Called to the Bar in 1945, but also returned to a teaching career almost all of which was spent at King's College, ultimately as Professor of Private International Law, his major field of interest. He also served as Dean of the Faculty of Laws of King's College and of the University of London. Among his extensive list of publications were *The Conflict of Laws* (1948) which ran for seven editions; *Problems of Private International Law in Non-Unified Legal Systems* (1975); and *Comparative Conflict of Laws* (1977).

Clive Parry (b 1917; d 1982); elected 1969 (Associate)

Educated at Birmingham and Cambridge Universities and at the Kaiser Wilhelm Institute in Berlin, he was later Called to the Bar. After service in the army in the Near East in the Second World War, he taught first at the University of Ankara and then for a year at the London School of Economics. In 1946, he returned to Cambridge where he taught until his death in 1982. In 1969, he was appointed Professor of International Law. Although devoted to teaching, his published contributions to international law were substantial. He has been described as having a 'flair for assembling, organising and inspiring teams of eager young helpers'; and there are many instances where his scholarly team leadership has made accessible a huge quantity of legal material. This work can be exemplified by such publications as *Nationality and Citizenship Law of the Commonwealth and the Republic of Ireland* (1957–60); *The Sources and Evidence of International Law* (ed) (1965); *British Digest of International Law* (ed) 1965–; *British International Law Cases* (ed) 1964–; and *The Consolidated Treaty Series* (ed) (1969–80).

Frederick Alexander Mann CBE FBA QC (b 1907; d 1991); elected 1973 (Associate); 1979 (Member)

Known to most people either as Francis Mann or FA Mann, he was born in Frankenthal in Germany, and educated at the Universities of Geneva, Munich, and Berlin. When the Nazis came to power in 1933, he and his wife moved to England, and he studied at the London School of Economics. During the Second World War, though an enemy alien, the local police in Sussex chose not to arrest him and he became a British subject in 1946, the year that he qualified as a solicitor, his firm merging with the major London firm of Herbert Smith in 1956. He managed to combine an extremely busy and high-level practice as a solicitor, having a wide range of international clients, with the ability to make a major contribution to the world of scholarship—relating to both public and private international law. His first book, written soon after his arrival in England, *The Legal Aspect of Money* (1938), has remained authoritative ever since. This was followed, after the war, by a steady flow of contributions to the study of international law, not least *Studies in International Law* (1973 and 1990) and *Foreign Affairs in English Courts* (1986).

Sir Ian Brownlie CBE QC FBA (b 1932; d 2010); elected 1977 (Associate); 1983 (Member)

Educated at Oxford University, he was Called to the Bar in 1958. He began his teaching career in 1957 at the University of Nottingham and from there moved back to Oxford in 1963. In 1976, he was appointed Professor of Public International Law at the London School of Economics, but, after four years, he returned to Oxford as Chichele Professor of Public International Law, a position he held for nearly twenty years until his retirement in 1999. Both before and after retirement he was much in demand as a barrister, appearing before the International Court of Justice in over forty cases amounting to well over half the cases before the court in a twenty-five-year period, cases which were wide ranging in subject matter, including *Nicaragua v USA* (1986), *Denmark v Norway* (1993), and *Malaysia v Singapore* (2008). He also appeared quite frequently before the European Court of Human Rights, as well as in the Augusto Pinochet proceedings before the House of Lords in 1999. He served as a member of the International Law Commission from 1997 to 2008, including serving as President in 2007. His publications on public international law were extensive and included: *Principles of Public International Law*, which by the time of his death had gone into seven editions; *International Law and the Use of Force by States* (1963); *Basic Documents on International Law* (6th edn, 2008); and *Basic Documents on Human Rights* (5th edn, 2006). He died in a car accident in Cairo in 2010, his death leading to extensive litigation right up to the UK Supreme Court.

Sir Elihu Lauterpacht CBE QC (b 1928; d 2017); elected 1979 (Associate); 1983 (Member); 2017 (Honorary Member) (posthumously elected)

Educated at Cambridge University, he joined the Law Faculty there in 1953, teaching in Cambridge, ultimately as an honorary professor, until his retirement in 1994. Having been Called to the Bar in 1950, he combined a distinguished academic career as an international lawyer with an equally distinguished career as a practitioner. He appeared before the International Court of Justice on many occasions, in such notable cases as the *Nottebohm Case* (1955), the *Barcelona Traction Case* (1962), and the *Nuclear Tests Case* (1973). He acted as legal advisor to the Australian Foreign Ministry and served as an ad hoc judge of the International Court of Justice in the *Bosnia Genocide Convention Case* (1996). He has been described as 'for many years the undisputed doyen of British public international lawyers'. His name lives on in the Cambridge Research Centre for International Law, established in 1983 and renamed the Lauterpacht Centre in honour of him and his distinguished father, Sir Hersch Lauterpacht—a second British instance of father and son being Members of the Institut.

Sir Derek William Bowett CBE QC FBA (b 1927; d 2009); elected 1981 (Associate); 1987 (Member); 1997 (Emeritus)

After a short period of war service in the Royal Navy on mine clearance, he was educated at Cambridge University, after which he embarked on an academic career at the University of Manchester, also being Called to the Bar in 1953. In 1957, he moved to New York to work for the UN and shortly after his return moved back to Cambridge to join the Law Faculty as a Fellow of Queens' College. During this period, he also advised the Government of Somalia on its territorial disputes and also acted as Legal Advisor to UNRWA in Beirut. In 1969, he was elected as President of Queens' College and in 1981 he was appointed Whewell Professor of International Law, serving until early retirement in 1991. He combined this academic work with a substantial international law practice appearing for a variety of States before the International Court of Justice in such cases as the *Tunisia–Libya Case* (1982), the *Gulf of Maine Case* (1984), and the *Nuclear Weapons Case* (1996). He served as a member of the International Law Commission from 1991 to 1996. His major published works include *Self-Defence in International Law* (1958), *The Law of International Institutions* (1963), *United Nations Forces* (1964), and *The Legal Regime of Islands in International Law* (1979).

Sir Ian McTaggart Sinclair KCMG QC (b 1926; d 2013); elected 1983 (Associate); 1987 (Member); 2007 (Emeritus)

Educated at Cambridge University, starting his law studies in 1942 but which were then interrupted by war service in the Intelligence Corps, serving in Malaya. He completed his degree in 1948, and in 1950 he joined the Foreign Office as an assistant legal advisor, having been Called to the Bar. He served in the Foreign Office for over thirty years and was Legal Advisor from 1976 to 1984. During his time there, he played a major advisory role in the negotiation of Britain's accession to the European Economic Community (now the EU) and during the Falklands conflict in 1982. Unhappy with the government's position over Europe, he took early retirement in 1984. In retirement, he had a very successful career as a barrister, appearing at times before the International Court of Justice, mainly in relation to territorial and sovereignty disputes. He also served on the International Law Commission from 1981 to 1986, and on the Permanent Court of Arbitration from 1992 to 2003. He also found time to write—publishing, for example, *The Vienna Convention on the Law of Treaties* (2nd edn, 1984) and *The International Law Commission* (1987).

Sir Peter Machin North CBE QC FBA (b 1936); elected 1985 (Associate); 1993 (Member)

After two years' service in the army, mainly in Cyprus, he was educated at Oxford University. His first academic appointment, in 1960, was at Northwestern University, Chicago, followed by short periods at the University College of Wales, Aberystwyth and the University of Nottingham. In 1965, he returned to Oxford, where he taught for a decade. In 1976, he left academic life on appointment as one of the five Law Commissioners for England and Wales, charged with making proposals to the government on areas of law reform, not least in the field of private international law, involving negotiations within the EEC on the UK accession to what were originally conventions on jurisdiction, recognition, and choice of law in contract. Legislative reform of UK rules of private international law extended to the whole range of family law, as well as choice of law in tort. After a decade or so of law reform activity, in 1984, he returned to Oxford as Principal of Jesus College, Oxford, a position he held for over twenty years, also serving during this period as the Vice Chancellor of Oxford University. While maintaining a continuing interest in teaching and researching private international law as well as chairing the UK Government's main private international law advisory committee from 1998 to 2009, he also chaired a number of public enquiries into quite different areas of reform—on road traffic law and enforcement, on drink and drug driving, and on the vexatious issue of parades and marches in Northern Ireland, as well as on the whole governance and operation of Oxford University. Called to the Bar in 1992, rather late in his career, he practised as a barrister for a number of years, essentially in the private international law field. Although he has published works on the law of torts, most of his writing has been on private international law, including for some forty years editing what became Cheshire, North and Fawcett, *Private International Law.* His authored works include *Private International Law of Matrimonial Causes* (1977); with Morris *Cases and Materials on Private International Law* (1984); *Private International Law Problems in Common Law Jurisdictions* (1993); and *Essays in Private International Law* (1993); and also edited *Contract Conflicts* (1982).

Dame Rosalyn Higgins GBE QC FBA (b 1937); elected 1987 (Associate); 1993 (Member); 2019 (Honorary Member)

Educated at Cambridge and Yale Universities, she has described 'the former as where she learned her black letter law and the latter where she learned what the law was for'. On her return to England her academic career started at the London School of Economics in 1961, but was soon followed, in 1963, by appointment as the staff lawyer at the Royal Institute of International Affairs, working extensively on UN peacekeeping. After serving in that role for more than a decade, she returned to academic life in 1978 as Professor of International Law at the University of Kent, moving three years later to a similar position at the London School of Economics, where she remained until 1995. During this period, she developed a particular interest in Human Rights, serving for ten years on the Committee on Human Rights, monitoring State compliance with the International Covenant on Civil and Political Rights. Having been Called to the Bar, over the years she developed an extensive international law practice, concentrating on petroleum and State immunity issues in cases before the UK courts, and acting for the UK and a number of other States before the International Court of Justice. In 1995, she was appointed a Judge of the International Court of Justice, serving there until 2009, and presiding over the Court from 2006 to 2009, this being a period of increased judicial activity. Her publications include: *The Development of International Law through the Political Organs of the United Nations* (1963); *Conflict of Interests: International Law in a Divided World* (1965); *UN Peacekeeping: Documents and Commentary*, 4 Volumes (1969–81); *Problems and Process* (1994); and *Oppenheim's International Law: The United Nations* (2017).

Lawrence Antony, Lord Collins of Mapesbury FBA (b 1941); elected 1989 (Associate); 1993 (Member)

Educated at Cambridge and Columbia Universities, he became a solicitor in 1968, and subsequently a partner in Herbert Smith in London from 1973 to 2000, specializing in international law; and he was one of the first two solicitors to be appointed QC. In 2000, he became the first solicitor to be appointed directly as a High Court judge. Promoted rapidly through the judicial structure, he served as a Justice of the Supreme Court from 2009 until he reached the compulsory retirement age in 2011. Since then, he has practised as an international arbitrator. During his time as a solicitor, he was extensively involved in aspects of international law litigation and has, over a forty-year period, served as a member of a range of British advisory bodies concerned with the reform and development of private international law, both within the UK and more widely in what is now the EU. After his retirement from British judicial office in 2011, he was appointed to a law professorship at University College, London. Although working as a full-time practitioner and then senior judge, he has pursued academic interests in both public and private international law. Since 1987, he has been the General Editor of what is now known as *Dicey, Morris & Collins on the Conflict of Laws*. Other publications include *European Community Law in the United Kingdom* (4th edn, 1990), *Civil Jurisdiction and Judgments Act 1982* (1983), and *Essays in International Litigation and the Conflict of Laws* (1994).

Sir Arthur Desmond Watts KCMG QC (b 1931; d 2007); elected 1991 (Associate); 1997 (Member)

Educated at Cambridge University, he joined the Foreign Office as a junior legal advisor and was Called to the Bar in 1957. He spent thirty-five years at the Foreign Office, rising to the most senior position of Legal Advisor for his last five years from 1987 to 1991. Over the years, his responsibilities ranged from dealing with the consequences of the nationalization by the Egyptian Government of British properties there in the late 1950s to addressing the legal issues arising from the UK accession to the EEC in the 1970s. Retirement from the Foreign Office at the age of 60 allowed him as a barrister to develop a much wider international law career—appearing before the International Court of Justice on behalf of a range of countries, as well as acting as an arbitrator or mediator in a variety of international disputes. He managed to combine both his Foreign Office responsibilities and his later busy practice with extensive writing on international law matters as exemplified by his 4th edition of *Legal Effects of War* (1966), the 9th edition of Oppenheim's *International Law* (1992), *International Law and the Antarctic Treaty System* (1992), and the three-volume *The International Law Commission 1949–1998* (1999–2000).

Kurt Lipstein QC (b 1909; d 2006); elected 1993 (Associate); 1999 (Member)

Born in Frankfurt am Main, he was educated at the Universities of Grenoble and Berlin. He emigrated to England in 1934 after the Nazis came to power, studying further at Cambridge University. As an enemy alien, he spent some time in an internment camp during the Second World War, but returned to Cambridge on his release where, having become a British subject, he remained for the rest of his life. Called to the Bar in 1950, his practice was not extensive, though he did appear before the International Court of Justice in the *Nottebohm Case* (1955). Expert also in the study of Roman law, he wrote extensively on private international law and on the law of the EEC, much of his writing having a comparative dimension. He was appointed to a Cambridge professorship of Comparative Law in 1973, just three years before his official retirement, though he never stopped teaching and writing. He had a particular interest in the application of private international law rules before international tribunals. His publications were wide ranging; he was one of the editors of Dicey and Morris, *Conflict of Laws*, for three editions, from 1949 to 1967; and wrote *General Principles of Private International Law* (1976) and *The Law of the European Economic Community* (1974), one of the first English books on this then new organization.

Hazel Mary, Lady Fox CMG QC (b 1928); elected 1997 (Associate); 2001 (Member); 2017 (Honorary Member)

Educated at Oxford University, she was Called to the Bar in 1950 and practised as a barrister for a short period. She later taught law at Oxford University and then chaired a number of legal tribunals. She returned to practice at the Bar for some fifteen years from 1994. Her activities within the international law field include the Directorship of the British Institute of International and Comparative Law in the 1980s and serving as the General Editor of the *International and Comparative Law Quarterly* for over a decade. Her publications include: *International Arbitration* (1959); editing *International Economic Law and Developing States*, Vols I and II (1988, 1992); and *The Law of State Immunity* (2002; 3rd edn, 2015).

John David McClean CBE QC FBA (b 1939); elected 2001 (Associate); 2009 (Member)

Educated at Oxford University, he was Called to the Bar in 1963, but then embarked on an academic career which, apart from visiting positions in Australia, he spent entirely at the University of Sheffield, where he served for over forty years until retirement in 2004, including thirty years as Professor of Law; he also served for five years as Pro Vice Chancellor of the University. He is a private international lawyer, but also one with wider interests. He has been General Editor of *Shawcross and Beaumont on Air Law* for many years, has written on conventions dealing with drug trafficking and international organized crime, and on international cooperation in both civil and criminal matters. Outside the academic world, he has been active in the field of ecclesiastical law both as a legislator in the Church of England General Synod and as a judge. Although his academic interests are broad, private international law has been a central area of his research. Not only has he served on a variety of advisory bodies within the UK, he has also done much work for the Commonwealth Secretariat, including drafting model laws on the enforcement of foreign judgments and maintenance and representing the Secretariat in the work of the Hague Conference on Private International Law. His publications in this field include: *Recognition of Family Judgments in the Commonwealth* (1983); the editorship of six editions of Morris, *The Conflict of Laws* (the 9th edition being in 2016); and acting as an editor of what is now *Dicey, Morris & Collins on the Conflict of Laws* since 1980.

Alan Vaughan Lowe QC (b 1957); elected 2005 (Associate); 2013 (Member)

Educated at the University of Wales Institute of Science and Technology, his academic career started in the Cardiff Law School in 1973, moving from there first to the University of Manchester and then, in 1988, to the University of Cambridge, where he stayed until his appointment in 1999 as Chichele Professor of Public International Law at Oxford. He had been Called to the Bar in 1993 and rapidly developed an international law practice, resigning his Oxford Chair in 2012 to concentrate on his practice as a barrister, appearing before a range of courts, including the International Court of Justice and the International Tribunal for the Law of the Sea. He was appointed as a Judge of the European Nuclear Energy Tribunal and has served as President or a Member of a number of arbitral tribunals. His major publications include: *Extraterritorial Jurisdiction* (1983); *The Law of the Sea* (3rd edn, 1999); *Fifty Years of the International Court of Justice* (1996); and *International Law* (2007).

John Graham Merrills (b 1942; d 2018); elected 2007 (Associate)

Educated at Oxford University, he spent the whole of his teaching career at the University of Sheffield, beginning in 1964 and culminating in his appointment as Professor of Public International law in 1985, in which role he served until retirement in 2007. Away from the University of Sheffield to which he was devoted, he served as an Alternate Member of the UN Sub-Committee on Prevention of Discrimination and Protection of Minorities. His interest in, and commitment to, human rights can be seen from his major work *The Development of International Law by the European Court of Human Rights* (2nd edn, 1993) and also *Human Rights in Europe* (4th edn, 2001) and *Human Rights in the World* (4th edn, 1996). Perhaps the work by which he is best known is *International Dispute Settlement*, the 6th edition of which was published not long before his death in 2018. Sadly, continuing ill health prevented him from ever attending meetings of the Institut.

Malcolm Shaw QC (b 1947); elected 2013 (Associate)

Educated at Liverpool University, the Hebrew University of Jerusalem, and Keele University, his academic teaching career started in 1972 at Liverpool Polytechnic, followed by a period at the University of Essex. Ultimately, he moved to a chair at the University of Leicester, where he was Sir Robert Jennings Professor of International Law from 1994 to 2011. He has been a Senior Fellow at the Lauterpacht Centre for International Law in Cambridge since 2010. Called to the Bar in 1988, he has appeared widely in British courts, the International Court of Justice, and the European Court of Human Rights. His publications include: *International Law*, the 8th edition of which was published in 2017; *Title to Territory in Africa* (1986); *The International Law of Territory* (2008); and the 5th edition of Rosenne's *Law and Practice of the International Court of Justice* (2015).

Sir Christopher Greenwood GBE CMG QC (b 1955); elected 2015 (Associate); 2019 (Member)

Educated at Cambridge University (and President of the Cambridge Union), he was Called to the Bar in 1978, the same year as he took up an academic legal appointment in Cambridge, which he held until 1996 when he was appointed Professor of International Law at the London School of Economics. Serving in that position until 2009, he was also active as a barrister before British courts and as counsel before the International Court of Justice and the European Court of Human Rights, and has acted as an international arbitrator on the Law of the Sea Convention and the International Centre for the Settlement of Investment Disputes. In 2009, he was appointed as a Judge of the International Court of Justice, serving in that capacity until 2019. He is a UK member of the Permanent Court of Arbitration and a judge of the Iran–US Claims Tribunal. He has been Master of Magdalene College Cambridge since autumn 2020. His publications include *The Kuwait Crisis: Basic Documents* (1991) and *Essays on War in International Law* (2006); and he has been the joint editor of the International Law Reports since 1990.

Malgosia Fitzmaurice (b 1955); elected 2019 (Associate)

Born in Poland, she later also acquired British nationality. She was educated at the University of Warsaw and, after postgraduate research, she worked as a legal assistant on the Iran–US Claims Tribunal. She then embarked on an academic career in the field of public international law, first at the University of Amsterdam and then at King's College, London. In 1995, she was appointed Professor of International Law at Queen Mary University of London, having a particular interest in international environmental law. Her major publications include: *International Protection of the Environment* (2002); *Contemporary Issues in the Law of Treaties* (2005); and *Whaling and International Law* (2015). She provides a further example of family links within the Institut, being the daughter of the late Judge Manfred Lachs, a Polish Member.

Selected List of Lord Collins's Publications

Books

The Civil Jurisdiction and Judgments Act 1982 (Butterworths 1983)
Specialist Editor, *Dicey & Morris on the Conflict of Laws* (Stevens & Sons, from 3rd Cumulative Supplement to 9th edn 1976, 10th edn 1980)
General Editor, *Dicey & Morris* (now *Dicey, Morris & Collins*) *on the Conflict of Laws* (Sweet & Maxwell, 11th edn 1987, 12th edn 1993, 13th edn 2000, 14th edn 2006, 15th edn 2012, 16th edn [with Jonathan Harris] 2022)
European Community Law in the United Kingdom (Butterworths, 1st edn 1975, 2nd edn 1980, 3rd edn 1984, 4th edn 1990)
Essays in International Litigation and the Conflict of Laws (OUP 1994)

Book chapters and articles

'The Effectiveness of the Restrictive Theory of Sovereign Immunity' (1965) Colum J Transnatl L 119
(with Aaron Etra), 'Policy, Politics, International Law and the United States Investment Guaranty Program' (1966) 4 Colum J Transnatl L 240
'Interaction between Contract and Tort in the Conflict of Laws' (1967) 16 ICLQ 103
(with Wolfgang Friedmann), 'The Suez Canal Crisis of 1956' in Lawrence Scheinman and David Wilkinson (eds), *International Law and Political Crisis: An Analytic Case-book* (Little Brown 1968)
'Arbitration Clauses and Forum Selecting Clauses in the Conflict of Laws: Some Recent Developments in England' (1971) 2 J Mar L & Com 363
'Forum Selection and an Anglo-American Conflict – The Sad Case of *The Chaparral*' (1971) 20 ICLQ 550
'Exemption Clauses, Employment Contracts and the Conflict of Laws' (1972) 21 ICLQ 320
'Some Aspects of Service out of the Jurisdiction in English Law' (1972) 21 ICLQ 656
'Choice of Forum and the Exercise of Judicial Discretion – The Resolution of an Anglo-American Conflict' (1973) 22 ICLQ 332
'Treaties and/or Statutes' (1974) 33 CLJ 181
'Art. 177 of the EEC Treaty and English Interlocutory Proceedings' (1974) 23 ICLQ 840
'Where is the Locus Delicti? (Based on *Moran v Pyle National (Canada) Ltd*)' (1975) 24 ICLQ 325
'*Harris v Taylor* Revived' (1976) 92 LQR 268
'Contractual Obligations – The EEC Preliminary Draft Convention on Private International Law' (1976) 25 ICLQ 35
'Some Thoughts on the Control of Abuse of Executive Discretion in International Law' in Werner Flume and others (eds), *Internationales Recht und Wirtschaftsordnung: Festschrift für FA Mann zum 70 Geburtstag am 11 August 1977* (CH Beck 1977)

'Vicarious Liability and the Conflict of Laws' (1977) 26 ICLQ 480
'Floating Charges, Receivers and Managers and the Conflict of Laws' (1978) 27 ICLQ 691
'Opportunities for and Obstacles to Obtaining Evidence in England for Use in Litigation in the United States' (1979) 13 Intl Law 27
'Personal Jurisdiction of the European Community – Some Comments on the Application of Civil and Penal Jurisdiction' (1980) 17 CML Rev 487
'Arbitration and the Law Governing Contractual Relations' in Frédéric-Edouard Klein and Frank Vischer (eds), *Basle Symposium on the Law Governing Contractual Obligations, 30–31 October 1980: Reports and Proceedings* (Helbing and Lichtenhahn 1983)
'Blocking and Clawback Statutes – The United Kingdom Approach: Part 1' [1986] JBL 372
'Blocking and Clawback Statutes – The United Kingdom Approach: Part 2' [1986] JBL 452
'The Law Governing the Agreement and Procedure in International Arbitration in England' in Julian DM Lew (ed), *Contemporary Problems in International Arbitration* (Springer 1987)
'The Hague Evidence Convention and Discovery: A Serious Misunderstanding?' (1986) 35 ICLQ 765
'Problems of Enforcement in the Multinational Securities Market: A United Kingdom Perspective' (1987) 9 U Pa J Intl Bus L 487
'The Territorial Reach of Mareva Injunctions' (1989) 105 LQR 262
'The High Court of Australia and Forum Non Conveniens: A Further Comment' (1989) 105 LQR 364
'Fraudulent Conduct in International Law' [1989] CLP 255
'Anton Piller Orders and Fundamental Rights' (1990) 106 LQR 173
'Forum Non Conveniens and the Brussels Convention' (1990) 106 LQR 535
'Temporary Presence, Exorbitant Jurisdiction and the US Supreme Court' (1991) 107 LQR 10
'The High Court of Australia and Forum Non Conveniens: The Last Word?' (1991) 107 LQR 102
'The Prospects for Transnational Litigation' (1992) 8 Intl Fin L Rev 3
'The Legacy of *The Siskina*' (1992) 108 LQR 175
'Illogical Survivals and Astonishing Results' (1992) 108 LQR 393
'Negative Declarations and the Brussels Convention' (1992) 108 LQR 545
'Provisional and Protective Measures in International Litigation' (1992) 234 RdC 9
(with Campbell McLachlan) 'Export Control: United Kingdom Report' in Karl Meessen (ed) *The International Law of Export Control* (Nijhoff 1992) 147
'Dr FA Mann: His Work and Influence' (1993) 64 Br YB Intl L 55
'Francis Alexander Mann, 1907–1991' (1993) 84 Proceedings of the British Academy 393
'Costs and Court Time' (1993) 109 LQR 172
'The End of *The Siskina*?' (1993) 109 LQR 342
(with Brian Davenport) 'Forum Conveniens within the United Kingdom' (1994) 110 LQR 325
'The Brussels Convention within the United Kingdom' (1995) 111 LQR 541
'*The Siskina* Again: An Opportunity Missed' (1996) 112 LQR 8
'Foreign Relations and the Conflict of Laws' (1995–1996) 6 KCLJ 20
'International Jurisdiction and Forum-Shopping: An Overview' in National University of Singapore, *Current Legal Issues in International Commercial Litigation* (1997) 3
'United States Supreme Court Rejects Mareva Jurisdiction' (1999) 115 LQR 601
'Provisional and Protective Measures in International Litigation: *Mareva* and *Grupo Mexicano*: Summary of Remarks by Lawrence Collins' (2000) 94 ASIL PROC 60
'Choice of Law and Choice of Jurisdiction in International Securities Transactions' (2001) 5 Sing J Intl & Comp L 618

'Foreign Relations and the Judiciary' (2002) 51 ICLQ 485
'Comity in Modern Private International Law' in James Fawcett (ed), *Reform and Development of Private International Law: Essays in Honour of Sir Peter North* (OUP 2002)
'The United States Supreme Court and the Principles of Comity: Evidence in Transnational Litigation' (2006) 8 Yrbk Priv Intl L 53
'Revolution and Restitution: Foreign States in National Courts' (2007) 326 RdC 9
'Reflections on Holocaust Claims in International Law' (2008) 41 ILR 402
'Aspects of Justiciability in International Law' in Mads Andenas and Duncan Fairgrieve (eds), *Tom Bingham and the Transformation of the Law: A Liber Amicorum* (OUP 2009)
'Professor Lowenfeld and the Enforcement of Foreign Public Law' (2009) 42 NYU J Intl L & Pol 125
'Introductory Essay' (2014) 26 S Ac LJ 789
'Professor FMB Reynolds, QC (Hon), DCL, FBA' (2014) 130 LQR 173
'The Enforcement of Foreign Revenue Laws' (2014) 130 LQR 353
'Sovereignty and Exorbitant Jurisdiction' (2014) 130 LQR 555
(with Siddharth Dhar) 'Remedies—Interim Measures' in Jeffrey Golden and Carolyn Lamm (eds), *International Financial Disputes: Arbitration and Mediation* (OUP 2015)
'In Memoriam: Andreas F (Andy) Lowenfeld' (2015) 59 AJIL 58
(with Tom Cross) 'Law of International Custom in the Case Law of the House of Lords and the United Kingdom Supreme Court' in Liesbeth Lijnzaad and Council of Europe (eds), *The Judge and International Custom / Le juge et la coutume internationale* (Brill 2016)
'Dicey, Albert Venn' in Jürgen Basedow, Giesela Rühl, Franco Ferrari, and Pedro de Miguel Asensio (eds), *Encyclopedia of Private International Law* (Edward Elgar 2017)
'Captain Duff, the Sultan of Kelantan and Their Legacy in the Law of State Immunity and International Arbitration' (2021) 37 Arb Intl 463
'Nullity, Invalidity, the Conflict of Laws and Articles II(3) and V(1)(A) of the New York Convention' in Franco Ferrari and Friedrich Rosenfeld (eds), *Autonomous Versus Domestic Concepts under the New York Convention* (Kluwer Law 2021)

Reports

(with Georges Droz) 'Preliminary Exposition and Questionnaire (November 2000)' (2002–03) 70(1) Ann IDI 14; Resolution 'The Principles for Determining When the Use of the Doctrine of Forum Non Conveniens and Anti-Suit Injunctions Is Appropriate' (2004) 70(2) Ann IDI 251
'Provisional Measures: Final Report' (2017) 77 Ann IDI 259; Resolution (2017) 78 Ann IDI 129

Index